# THE W. R. BION TRADITION

**LINES OF DEVELOPMENT**
**Evolution of Theory and Practice over the Decades**

*Series Editors: Norka T. Malberg and Joan Raphael-Leff*

Other titles in the series:

*The Anna Freud Tradition: Lines of Development—Evolution of Theory and Practice over the Decades*
    edited by Norka T. Malberg and Joan Raphael-Leff

*Fairbairn and the Object Relations Tradition*
    edited by Graham S. Clarke and David E. Scharff

*The Winnicott Tradition: Lines of Development—Evolution of Theory and Practice over the Decades*
    edited by Margaret Boyle Spelman and Frances Thomson-Salo

# THE W. R. BION TRADITION
## Lines of Development—Evolution of Theory and Practice over the Decades

*Edited by*
*Howard B. Levine and*
*Giuseppe Civitarese*

LONDON AND NEW YORK

First published 2016 by Karnac Books Ltd

Published 2018 by Routledge
2 Park Square, Milton Park, Abingdon, Oxon OX14 4RN
52 Vanderbilt Avenue, New York, NY 10017, USA

*Routledge is an imprint of the Taylor & Francis Group, an informa business*

Copyright © 2016 to Howard B. Levine and Giuseppe Civitarese for the edited collection, and to the individual authors for their contributions.

The rights of the contributors to be identified as the authors of this work have been asserted in accordance with §§ 77 and 78 of the Copyright Design and Patents Act 1988.

All rights reserved. No part of this book may be reprinted or reproduced or utilised in any form or by any electronic, mechanical, or other means, now known or hereafter invented, including photocopying and recording, or in any information storage or retrieval system, without permission in writing from the publishers.

Notice:
Product or corporate names may be trademarks or registered trademarks, and are used only for identification and explanation without intent to infringe.

British Library Cataloguing in Publication Data

A C.I.P. for this book is available from the British Library

ISBN-13: 9781782200369 (pbk)

Typeset by V Publishing Solutions Pvt Ltd., Chennai, India

# CONTENTS

ABOUT THE EDITORS AND CONTRIBUTORS     xi

SERIES EDITORS' FOREWORD     xix

EDITORS' PREFACE     xxi

## PART I: PERSONAL, HISTORICAL

Editors' introduction     3

**CHAPTER ONE**
Impressions of my analysis with Dr. Bion     5
*José Américo Junqueira de Mattos*

**CHAPTER TWO**
A long meeting with Bion     23
*Claudio Neri*

**CHAPTER THREE**
Non-analytic influences on the psychoanalytic theorizing of Wilfred Bion     29
*Ronald Britton*

**CHAPTER FOUR**
W. R. Bion: his cultural, national, and historical background, and its impact on his thinking     39
*Robert Snell*

## CHAPTER FIVE
"I shall be blown to bits": towards Bion's theory of catastrophic trauma  47
*Carole Beebe Tarantelli*

### PART II: PREVIOUSLY UNPUBLISHED SUPERVISIONS
Editors' introduction  67

## CHAPTER SIX
Supervision A34  69
Commentary on supervision A34  73
*Roosevelt M. S. Cassorla*

## CHAPTER SEVEN
Supervision D14  79
Commentary on supervision D14: a language for the job  89
*Giuiseppe Civitarese*

## CHAPTER EIGHT
Supervision A42  93
Commentary on supervision A42  99
*Howard B. Levine*

### PART III: CLINICAL/THEORETICAL: ONE
Editors' introduction  105

## CHAPTER NINE
Turbulence and growth: an encounter between Ismalia and Isaura  107
*Gisèle de Mattos Brito*

## CHAPTER TEN
Mental states and emotional relations in the analytic setting: implications for therapeutic work  121
*Raul Hartke*

## CHAPTER ELEVEN
The function of evocation in the working-through of the countertransference: projective identification, reverie, and the expressive function of the mind—Reflections inspired by Bion's work  141
*Elias M. da Rocha Barros and Elizabeth L. da Rocha Barros*

## CHAPTER TWELVE
The truth object: growing the god within  155
*Annie Reiner*

CHAPTER THIRTEEN
Making contact with psychotic and autistic phenomena: container/contained
   and autistic transformations   171
Celia Fix Korbivcher

## PART IV: CLINICAL/THEORETICAL: TWO
Editors' introduction   185

CHAPTER FOURTEEN
Changes in technique and in the theory of technique in a post-Bion
   field model   189
Antonino Ferro

CHAPTER FIFTEEN
Containing systems in the analytic field   201
Duncan Cartwright

CHAPTER SIXTEEN
The hat on top of the volcano: Bion's 'O' and the body-mind relationship   223
Riccardo Lombardi

CHAPTER SEVENTEEN
Bridging the gap: from soma-psychosis to psychosomatics   239
Catalina Bronstein

CHAPTER EIGHTEEN
A Note and a Short Story   251
Nicola Abel-Hirsch

CHAPTER NINETEEN
Flying thoughts in search of a nest: a tribute to W. R. Bion   259
Salomon Resnik

## PART V: A CLINICAL EXCHANGE
Editors' introduction   273

CHAPTER TWENTY
A silent war: dreading recovery   275
Antoine Nastasi

Dreaming into being   285
Howard B. Levine

St. Sulpice 291
*Antoine Nastasi*

## PART VI: SENSE, MYTH, AND PASSION

Editors' introduction 295

### CHAPTER TWENTY-ONE
Sense, sensible, sense-able: the bodily but immaterial dimension of psychoanalytic elements 297
*Giuseppe Civitarese*

### CHAPTER TWENTY-TWO
Myth, dream, and meaning: reflections on a comment by Bion 307
*Howard B. Levine*

### CHAPTER TWENTY-THREE
Passion 315
*Anna Migliozzi*

## PART VII: LATE PAPERS AND BASIC CONCEPTS

Editors' introduction 329

### CHAPTER TWENTY-FOUR
"Notes on memory and desire": implications for working through 333
*Lawrence J. Brown*

### CHAPTER TWENTY-FIVE
On Bion's text "Emotional turbulence": a focus on experience and the unknown 345
*Rudi Vermote*

### CHAPTER TWENTY-SIX
On "Making the best of a bad job" 353
*Irene Cairo*

### CHAPTER TWENTY-SEVEN
Reflections on "Caesura" (1977) 361
*Rogelio Sosnik*

### CHAPTER TWENTY-EIGHT
Evidence 369
*Arnaldo Chuster*

### CHAPTER TWENTY-NINE
Is the concept of O necessary for psychoanalysis? 377
*Howard B. Levine*

## PART VIII: GROUPS

Editors' introduction ... 387

### CHAPTER THIRTY
Affect, reverie, mourning, and Bion's theory of groups in our time ... 389
*Walker Shields*

### CHAPTER THIRTY-ONE
Containing primitive emotional states: approaching Bion's later perspectives on groups ... 407
*R. D. Hinshelwood*

### CHAPTER THIRTY-TWO
Bion and the large group ... 421
*H. Shmuel Erlich*

### CHAPTER THIRTY-THREE
The influence of Bion on my research ... 431
*René Kaës*

## PART IX: AESTHETICS

Editors' introduction ... 447

### CHAPTER THIRTY-FOUR
Using art for the understanding of psychoanalysis and using Bion for the understanding of contemporary art ... 451
*Adela Abella*

### CHAPTER THIRTY-FIVE
The buried harbor of dreaming: psychoanalysis and literature—towards a Bionian, non-archaeological approach ... 467
*Francesco Capello*

### CHAPTER THIRTY-SIX
Communicating pictures: aesthetic aspects as a developmental tool for the container-contained interaction ... 489
*Elena Molinari*

INDEX ... 501

## ABOUT THE EDITORS AND CONTRIBUTORS

**Nicola Abel-Hirsch** is a fellow of the British Psychoanalytical Society, and works in private practice. She is the 2013–2015 visiting professor at the Centre for Psychoanalytic Studies, University of Essex. Her work on Bion includes: on suffering; Freud and Bion on the life instinct; narcissism and socialism; Bion's containing and Winnicott's holding; and currently, on the place of sexuality in Bion's work. She is the editor of Hanna Segal's book *Yesterday, Today and Tomorrow*.

**Adela Abella** is an adult, child, and adolescent psychiatrist and psychoanalyst, a training analyst of the Swiss Psychoanalytical Society (SSPsa-SGPsa), a member of the culture committee of the IPA, a member of the Board of the IJP, and past president of the Centre de Psychoanalyse de la Suisse Romande.

**Gisèle de Mattos Brito** is a member, training analyst, and teacher at the study group of Minas Gervais Center of Belo Horizonte, Brazil. She is also a member and teacher at the Psychoanalytical Society of São Paulo. An earlier version of her chapter was selected as the best paper by a training analyst at the 2009 Brazilian Congress of Psychoanalysis, and given the *Award Durval Marcondes*.

**Ronald Britton** is a fellow of the Royal College of Psychiatrists and distinguished fellow of the British Psychoanalytical Society, and was given the "IPA Award for Outstanding Scientific Contributions" in July 2013 and the Sigourney Award for distinguished contributions to psychoanalysis in January 2014. He was chair of the children and families department of the Tavistock Clinic in the 1980s where he met Bion, and was president of the British Psychoanalytical

Society from 2002 to 2004. His books include *The Oedipus Complex Today*, *Belief and Imagination*, and *Sex, Death and the Super-ego*.

**Catalina Bronstein** is a training and supervising analyst of the British Psychoanalytical Society and visiting professor in the psychoanalysis unit, University College London. She studied medicine and qualified as a psychiatrist in Buenos Aires. She then trained as a child psychotherapist at the Tavistock Clinic in London and as an analyst at the British Institute of Psychoanalysis. She lives in London and works as an analyst in private practice (with adults and adolescents) and at the Brent Centre for Adolescents. She was the former London editor of the International Journal of Psychoanalysis and is currently on the board of IJP. She is the editor of *Kleinian Theory. A Contemporary Perspective* and co-editor of *The New Dialogues Klein-Lacan*.

**Lawrence Brown** is a graduate of the Boston Psychoanalytic Institute in both child and adult psychoanalysis and is a supervising child analyst there. He has served on the editorial boards of the *International Journal of Psychoanalysis* and the *Psychoanalytic Quarterly*. Dr. Brown was co-chair of the Bion in Boston International Conference held in July 2009 and more recently co-chair of the Bion in Marrakech conference held in March 2013. His book, *Intersubjective Processes and the Unconscious: An Integration of Freudian, Kleinian and Bionian Perspectives*, was published by Routledge Press in early 2011 and another book, co-edited with Dr. Howard Levine, *Growth and Turbulence in the Container/Contained*, published by Routledge in 2013. He is currently co-editing a book, *On Freud's "Formulations on the Two Principles of Mental Functioning"*, to be published in the IPA series, Contemporary Freud: Turning Points and Critical Issues. He is also the author of many papers covering such topics as countertransference, trauma, the Oedipus complex, and dreaming.

**Irene Cairo** received her medical degree at the University of Buenos Aires, Argentina. She is a graduate, member, and faculty of the New York Psychoanalytic Institute and a member and Training and Supervising Analyst of the Contemporary Freudian Society. She has co-edited an issue of *Psychoanalytic Inquiry* on the "Ethical texture of psychoanalysis" and written on the social dimension of the building of subjectivity. Since 1996 she has co-chaired a discussion group on the value of Bion's ideas at the biannual meetings of the American Psychoanalytic Association. She is currently the North American co-chair of the committee on ethics of the International Psychoanalytical Association.

**Francesco Capello** is Lecturer in Italian at the School of European Cultures and Languages at the University of Kent. He has studied at the Scuola Normale Superiore di Pisa and at the University of Leeds. His monograph *Città specchio* (2013) investigates the relationship between the trauma of modernity, mourning, and literary subjectivity, taking early twentieth-century urban representations as a vantage point. His more recent research focuses on post-Bionian psychoanalytic aesthetics.

**Duncan Cartwright** is head of the Centre for Applied Psychology, University of KwaZulu-Natal, Durban, South Africa. He is the author of *Murdering Minds: Psychoanalysis, Violence and*

*Rage-Type Murder* (Brunner-Routledge, 2002) and *Containing States of Mind: Exploring Bion's Container Model in Psychoanalytic Psychotherapy* (Routledge, 2010).

**Roosevelt M. S. Cassorla** is a psychoanalyst in private practice in Campinas, Brazil and training analyst of the Brazilian Psychoanalytic Society of São Paulo. He has worked as full professor at the psychological medicine department, State University of Campinas and the postgraduate course in mental health. He is a member of the editorial board of the *International Journal of Psychoanalysis*, has edited three books on suicide and death, and is the author of a number of book chapters and papers on medical psychology and psychoanalysis. His recent papers refer to analytical technique and borderline configurations.

**Arnaldo Chuster** is a member of the Brazilian Psychiatric Association, training and teaching analyst at Rio de Janeiro Psychoanalytic Society (FIPA), full professor at the W. Bion Institute in Porto Alegre and has authored eight books published in Portuguese about Bion's work and written chapters in eight further books in Spanish, Italian, and English.

**Giuseppe Civitarese** is a training and supervising analyst in the Italian Psychoanalytic Society (SPI), and a member of the American Psychoanalytic Association (APsaA) and of the International Psychoanalytic Association (IPA). He lives, and is in private practice, in Pavia, Italy. Currently he is the editor of the *Rivista di Psicoanalisi*, the official journal of the Italian Psychoanalytic Society. He has published several books, which include: *The Intimate Room: Theory and Technique of the Analytic Field*, London, 2010; *The Violence of Emotions: Bion and Post-Bionian Psychoanalysis*, London, 2012; *The Necessary Dream: New Theories and Techniques of Interpretation in Psychoanalysis*, London, 2014; *I sensi e l'inconscio* (Senses and the unconscious), Rome 2014; *Losing Your Head: Abjection, Aesthetic Conflict and Psychoanalytic Criticism*, Lanham, MD 2015. He has also co-edited *L'ipocondria e il dubbio: L'approccio psicoanalitico* (Hypochondria and doubt: the psychoanalytic approach), Milano, 2011.

**H. Shmuel Erlich** is past president of the Israel Psychoanalytic Society; training and supervising analyst and faculty member of the Israel Psychoanalytic Institute; Sigmund Freud Professor of Psychoanalysis (Emeritus) and former director of the Freud Center at The Hebrew University of Jerusalem. He served four terms as European representative on the IPA Board. His psychoanalytic practice is in Jerusalem and Tel Aviv and he is also consultant to organizations. He received the Sigourney Award for outstanding contributions to psychoanalysis. He is a founding member of OFEK, the Israel Association for the Study of Group and Organizational Processes, and PCCA (Partners in Confronting Collective Atrocities). He has published on psychoanalytic and applied subjects, including: adolescent development and treatment; experiential factors influencing object relations; and psychoanalytic-systemic studies of group, organizational, and social processes. His recently published books are: *Fed with Tears—Poisoned with Milk, The "Nazareth" Group-Relations-Conferences: Germans and Israelis—The Past in the Present* (2009, Psychosozial Verlag, Giessen); and *The Couch in the Marketplace: Psychoanalysis and Social Reality* (2013, Karnac).

**Antonino Ferro** is a practicing psychoanalyst, current president of the Italian Psychoanalytic Society (SPI), and holds full membership in the American Psychoanalytic Association and the

International Psychoanalytical Association. He has held supervisions, lectures, and seminars at major psychoanalytic societies in Europe, North America, South America, and Australia and his publications include *Psychoanalysis as Therapy and Storytelling* (2006), *Mind Works* (2009), *Avoiding Emotions, and Living Emotions* (2011), *Torments of the Soul* (2014). In 2007, he received the Mary Sigourney Award.

**Raul Hartke** is a psychiatrist and a training and supervising analyst for the Porto Alegre Psychoanalytic Society, where he was a former scientific director, president, and director of the institute. He is professor and supervisor for psychoanalytical psychotherapy at the Psychiatry Department, Medical School of the Federal University of Rio Grande do Sul.

**R. D. Hinshelwood** is a fellow of the British Psychoanalytical Society, professor in the Centre of Psychoanalytic Studies, University of Essex, and previously clinical director of the Cassel Hospital, London. He is the author of *A Dictionary of Kleinian Thought* (1989, 1991) and *Clinical Klein* (1993). He has written on various topics in social psychodynamics, including (with Marco Chiesa) *Organisations, Anxieties and Defence* (2000), and (with Wilhelm Skogstad) *Observing Organisations* (2001).

**José Américo Junqueira de Mattos**, who was an analysand of Bion's, is a training analyst of the Brazilian Society of São Paulo and Ribeirão Preto. He has published many works in Brazil and the USA, the majority of which are contributions to Bion's thoughts and ideas.

**René Kaës** is a psychoanalyst, psychodramatist, and group analyst and professor emeritus in psychology and psychopathology at the University of Lyon2. He is the author of several works of psychoanalysis on subjects such as the group and the institution, the dream, the subject and intersubjectivity, unconscious alliances, the fraternal complex, the transmission of psychic life between generations, and, most recently, disease in hypermodern society.

**Celia Fix Korbivcher** is a child psychoanalyst and training and supervising analyst of the Brazilian Psychoanalytic Society of Sao Paulo and the author of *Autistic Transformations: Bion's Theory and Autistic Phenomena* (Karnac, 2014). She has a private practice analyzing children, adults, and adolescents and a special interest in the study of autistic phenomena in neurotic patients, publishing widely in local and international journals. She has been awarded the 2004 Parthenope Bion Thalamo International Prize, the 2006 Frances Tustin Memorial Prize, and, in 2001 and 2004, the Fabio Leite Lobo Prize.

**Howard B. Levine** is on the faculty at the Psychoanalytic Institute of New England East (PINE) and in private practice in Brookline, Massachusetts. He is a founding member of the Group for the Study of Psychoanalytic Process (GSPP) and The Boston Group for Psychoanalytic Studies, Inc. (BGPS), has authored numerous articles, book chapters, and reviews on psychoanalytic process and technique, intersubjectivity, the treatment of primitive personality disorders, and the consequences and treatment of early trauma and childhood sexual abuse. He is the editor of *Adult Analysis and Childhood Sexual Abuse* (Analytic Press 1990), co-editor (with Lawrence

Brown) of *Growth and Turbulence in the Container/Contained* (Routledge, 2013), (with Gail Reed and Dominique Scarfone) of *Unrepresented States and the Construction of Meaning* (Karnac, 2013), and (with Gail Reed) *Responses to Freud's Screen Memories Paper* (Karnac, 2014).

**Riccardo Lombardi** is training and supervising analyst of the Italian Psychoanalytic Society (SPI) and the author of several papers on the body-mind relation, time, psychosis, and other severe mental disturbances, which have been published in the leading psychoanalytic journals. He has a full-time private practice in Rome. He is the author of the book *Formless Infinity: Clinical Explorations of Matte Blanco and Bion* (London, Routledge, 2014).

**Anna Migliozzi** is a full member of the Italian Psychoanalytical Society (SPI) and specialist and supervising analyst in child and adolescent psychoanalysis. She has a private practice in Milan, working with severe psychotic and borderline patients. She is, first and foremost, a clinical psychoanalyst who is committed to the use of Bionian theory in the treatment of children and has presented numerous papers at FEP and IPA Congresses.

**Elena Molinari** is a member of the Italian Psychoanalytic Society (SPI). She started her professional life as a paediatrician listening to the experience of ill children and the grief of their parents. Since 2004 she has been teaching child neuropsychiatry for the postgraduate course in art therapy at the Academy of Fine Arts of Brera in Milan.

**Antoine Nastasi** is a training analyst and founding member of the Société Psychanalytique de Recherche et de Formation (Psychoanalytical Society for Research and Training). He was co-chief editor of *Psychanalyse et Psychose* and is currently chief editor of the journal *Esquisse(s)*. He has written numerous articles, many of them focused on transference and working through in psychotic ways of being, and, as a psychoanalyst of the Evelyne et Jean Kestemberg Centre, has conducted psychoanalytic treatments of psychotic patients for the past twenty-eight years.

**Claudio Neri**, professor of techniques of psychological intervention in groups at the postgraduate school in clinical psychology (La Sapienza University of Rome), is a training and supervising analyst of the Italian Psychoanalytic Society (SPI); full member of the International Psychoanalytic Association (IPA), International Association of Group Psychotherapy (IAGP), London Institute of Group Analysis; and honorary member of the board of the Gordon Lawrence Foundation. He is also a member of the scientific committee of many international psychoanalytic journals and author and editor of numerous books. Among them are: *Group* (Jessica Kingsley Publishers, London & Philadelphia, 1998; *Dreams in Group Psychotherapy* (edited with M. Pines and R. Friedman) (Jessica Kingsley Publishers, London & Philadelphia, 2002).

**Annie Reiner**, PhD, PsyD, LCSW, is a member, senior faculty member, and training analyst at The Psychoanalytic Center of California (PCC) in Los Angeles. Her work was profoundly influenced by the ideas of Wilfred Bion, with whom she studied briefly in the 1970s. She has published in various journals and anthologies. Her most recent book is *Bion & Being: Passion and the Creative Mind* (Karnac, 2012). In addition to her psychoanalytic writing, Dr. Reiner is an accomplished poet, playwright, and painter, the author of four books of poems, short stories, and four children's books, which she also illustrated. She maintains a private practice in Beverly Hills, California.

**Salomon Resnik** became a member of the Argentine Psychoanalytical Association in 1955, after specializing in working with autistic children and young schizophrenic patients, and later became a training and supervising analyst. In 1957, he went to Paris for one year and studied with Maurice Merlau-Ponty, Claude Lévi-Strauss, and Roger Bastide. In 1958 he went to London to work with Melanie Klein and underwent analysis with Herbert Rosenfeld, from whom he gained new insights into dream interpretation. In London, he practiced psychoanalysis for twelve years, attended Bion's seminars, and was in supervision with Bion. Since 1972, he has been living and working in Paris and Venice. He has also been a senior lecturer in psychiatry at the University of Lyon, and at the Catholic University in Rome. In 2012 he was given a degree *honoris causa* in philosophy from the University of Cosenza in Calabria, Italy.

**Elias Mallet da Rocha Barros** is training analyst and supervisor of the Brazilian Psychoanalytic Society of São Paulo, fellow of the British Psychoanalytical Society and Institute, recipient of the Sigourney Award 1999, past Latin American editor of the *International Journal of Psychoanalysis*, and Latin American chair of the IPA International encyclopedia and dictionary.

**Elizabeth Lima da Rocha Barros** is training analyst and supervisor of the Brazilian Psychoanalytic Society of São Paulo, fellow of the British Psychoanalytical Society and Institute, child analyst trained by the British Psychoanalytical Society and Tavistock Clinic, and DEA in psychopathology, Sorbonne University.

**Walker Shields** is a member and faculty, Boston Psychoanalytic Society and Institute; member, Boston Group for the Study of Groups and Social Systems; member A. K. Rice Institute; member, Northeastern Society for Group Psychotherapy; fellow, American Group Psychotherapy Association.

**Robert Snell** is an analytic psychotherapist and member of the British Psychotherapy Foundation. He has a doctorate in art history from the Courtauld Institute and is the author of *Uncertainties, Mysteries, Doubts: Romanticism and the Analytic Attitude* (Routledge, 2012).

**Rogelio Sosnik** is training and supervising analyst, Buenos Aires Psychoanalytic Association; training and supervising analyst and faculty, Contemporary Freudian Society; and member of the American Psychoanalytic Association and the IPA. He has published papers in Argentina, Uruguay, Italy, and the US, on the relationship between Ferenczi and Bion, on the British School, and on the work of Bleger. He has written on the ethical texture of psychoanalysis and co-chaired a workshop on the death penalty at the meetings of the American Psychoanalytic Association. For many years he has chaired a discussion group on the clinical value of Bion's ideas at the meetings of the American Psychoanalytic Association. He is in private practice in New York City.

**Carole Beebe Tarantelli** is a psychoanalyst in private practice in Rome, Italy and until her retirement was an associate professor of literature and psychoanalysis at the University of Rome. She is a full member of the Centro Italiano di Psicologia Analitica and IAAP. She was elected three times to the chamber of deputies of the Italian Parliament, where she principally worked on the reform of psychiatric services, prison reform, and the reform of the antiquated law punishing the crime of rape. She was instrumental in founding an association, Differenza Donna, which runs shelters for battered and trafficked women, where she conducts groups for incest survivors and for trafficked women. She has studied catastrophic trauma, violence, and terrorism for many years.

**Rudi Vermote** is a full member of the International Psychoanalytic Association, past president of the Belgian Society of Psychoanalysis, and member of the editorial board of the *International Journal of Psychoanalysis*. He is head of the psychoanalytic psychotherapy unit for personality disorders (KLIPP) at the University Psychiatric Centre of the University of Leuven, Campus Kortenberg, aassociate professor at the faculty of medicine and the faculty of psychology at the University of Leuven, and head of the postgraduate training in psychoanalytic psychotherapy at the University of Leuven. He has published and presented papers on Bion's work in major psychoanalytic journals and at several congresses and wrote *Reading Bion* in the teaching series of Routledge (series editor, Dana Birksted-Breen), which is in publication.

# SERIES EDITORS' FOREWORD

## "Lines of Development": evolution of tradition, theory, and practice over the decades

*Norka T. Malberg & Joan Raphael-Leff*

It is rare that a book breaks through existing theoretical frontiers. This one certainly does.

The exciting ride provides the reader with a catalyst to new understanding, as the 34 authors reformulate, interrogate, and expand on Bion's thinking.

The co-editors commissioned these chapters, confident in their contributors' erudition and capacity to explore the fringes of the unknowable and ineffable. Giuseppe Civitarese and Howard Levine's faith paid off, and through their editorial efforts they have produced an extraordinary book, rich in innovation yet rigorously rooted in theory.

You, the reader, are very much present in this book. You are invited not merely to read, but to *feel* as you do so, "what it might be like to participate in and experience the process of psychic transformation from sense impressions to images and thought" (p. 185). In this sense, the text is "performative as well as communicative", since the act of reading "has to produce emotional turbulence if something valuable is to be achieved from it" (as the co-editors say in their introduction to the late papers).

So, this is not a book for the fainthearted: it requires "negative capability" from the reader; a readiness to "give him or her self entirely to the text and to renounce what is already known" (p. 330). For those who can, the pay-off is manifold!

Throughout its many chapters this volume provides a clear, comprehensive, and sequential account of Bion's thinking, his life experience and technical innovations, saturated with quotes from his diaries and theoretical papers, as well as offering clinical vignettes to illuminate salient aspects of the therapeutic encounter. By positioning Bion's imaginative leaps within a coherent psychic construction across his lifeline of childhood, school, army, marriages, psychoanalytic and group experiences, this book provides conceptual answers, albeit tentative ones, to some of the many puzzles that preoccupied Bion and ourselves, in enigmatic moments in the consulting room and in our own daily lives.

As series co-editors, we are delighted to welcome this, the fourth volume in our series, and trust that, like our previous books on Anna Freud, Fairbairn, and Winnicott, this fine collection of essays on Bion's legacy will prove a rich resource for practitioners and candidates, students, and interested lay readers.

# EDITORS' PREFACE

Why Bion? Why "The Bion *tradition*"? The contributions of Wilfred Bion are among the most cited in the analytic literature. Their appeal lies not only in their content and explanatory value, but in their generative potential. Although Bion's training and many of his clinical instincts were deeply rooted in the classical tradition of Melanie Klein, his ideas have a potentially universal appeal. Rather than emphasizing a particular psychic content (e.g., Oedipal conflicts in need of resolution; splits that needed to be healed; preconceived transferences that must be allowed to form and flourish, etc.), he tried to help open and prepare the mind of the analyst (without memory, desire, or theoretical preconception) for the encounter with the patient.

Bion's formulations of group mentality and the psychotic and non-psychotic portions of the mind, his theory of thinking and emphasis on facing and articulating the truth of one's existence so that one might truly learn first hand from one's own experience, his description of psychic development (alpha function and container/contained), and his exploration of O are "non-denominational" concepts that defy relegation to a particular school or orientation of psychoanalysis. Consequently, his ideas have taken root in many places—not only London, Los Angeles, Sao Paolo, and Rome, where he lived and taught, but in an ever widening circle to now include Pavia, Boston, Rio, Porto Alegre, Buenos Aires, San Francisco, New York, Seattle, etc.—and those ideas continue to inform many different branches of psychoanalytic inquiry and interest. At present, post-Bionian psychoanalytic models and developments may even be moving towards a long-awaited, shared new paradigm that holds out the promise of preserving the best of Freud's legacy, while being free to go beyond its limits.

Looked at in retrospect, many developments from the 1970s onward—for example, self psychology, relational psychoanalysis, intersubjectivity, attachment theory, and various branches of object relational theory—can be recognized as symptoms of the need for something new. The epistemological framework of the first Freudianism was changing. It was Lyotard (1981) who introduced into philosophy the term *postmodern*, the most successful designation for this deep change. However, many of the attempted new models were constructed at the expense of maintaining the centrality of the concept of the unconscious, something that, following Freud, we feel should be an invariant in any *psychoanalytic* model worthy of the name.

In contrast, many post-Bionians' models tend to be rigorous and coherent in regard to the unconscious, even as some have expanded the meaning of the term to more fully encompass the unstructured unconscious in addition to the dynamic or repressed unconscious. In so doing, these models offer a continuation of many of the theoretical fundamentals enunciated by Freud, Klein, and other authors, while introducing new innovations, expanding upon what had previously appeared only in outline or inference and containing elements of discontinuity. This state of affairs is one that Bion himself, no doubt, would have approved of. He insisted that the relationship that must obtain between the creative individual, whom he often referred to in shorthand as the "genius" or the "mystic", and the Establishment should be a dialectical one that allowed for both stability and continuity on the one hand and the destabilization and turmoil that is an inevitable accompaniment to creativity and growth on the other.

Thus, in his own work, Bion did not restrict himself to trying to answer old questions at all costs, but raised new ones and allowed his thought the latitude of setting off to explore new directions. For example, he conceptualized the unconscious not simply as a structure and place of hidden contents, but as an ever expanding, inexhaustible domain and a psychoanalytic function of the personality. He postulated that dreaming was a continual process of psychic construction and elaboration that went on not only at night but also during the day (waking dream thoughts) and strenuously insisted that analysis concerned not just the patient or the analyst, but the relationship, the *something-between* them. In so doing, he created a Copernican revolution in our field. Looking at the trajectory of his own life, we may even conjecture that in order to do so, to free himself from the inevitable constriction that widespread acceptance and becoming part of the "establishment" can produce—he had been president of the British Psycho-Analytic Society and a leading figure among the London Kleinians—he had to leave London and come to California to better and more freely expand the scope of his thinking and explore new frontiers.

In regard to therapeutics, what matters most is that the innovations introduced by Bion do not remain at an abstract theoretical level but can be translated into precise conceptual devices or tools that may allow analysts to perform with humility and humanity the task of caring for patients and addressing mental suffering. We think here of transformations in dreaming, in hallucinosis, in play, and of autistic transformations; capacity for reverie, alpha function; alpha, beta, and "balpha" elements; container-contained, negative capability, and so on. As Grotstein (2014) has noted, there is a strong sense in which Bion, despite his enormous intellect, scholarship, and erudition, was a very practical man, who, as analyst, spoke about issues that were very practical issues in and for the life of his patients.

Bion's respect and support for the subjectivity and unique creative potential of each individual is reflected in his encouraging "wild thoughts" and shifting vertices for the new perspectives that they might bring and in his often prefacing his seminars and supervisions with the caveat that he would be telling his audience something about how he believed that he did analysis not so that they would do analysis as he did, but so that they might better understand something about how they believed that *they* did analysis. He did not want to create a cadre of "Bionians." For patients, students, and colleagues alike, Bion aimed to help them become more and more themselves by virtue of engaging more deeply in the dialectic between subjectivity and alterity that can lead to psychic transformation and recognition, acceptance and tolerance of the emotional turbulence and threat of change that inevitably accompanies the emergence of truth.

We see still another side of Bion as man and as analyst in a story told by Grotstein (2014) concerning the first hour of his analysis with Bion. As Grotstein entered Bion's Los Angeles office, he noticed an English magazine on the back of which was an advertisement for a then famous London restaurant called The White House. He began the hour by casually telling Bion that he had been there with his wife and they had enjoyed a lovely evening and meal. He went on with some associations and Bion commented that Grotstein seemed to be hoping that their two White Houses—the English and the American—might come together in the future in the analysis and produce something that would be of value and pleasure. This comment, like many of those described by Junqueira de Mattos (Chapter One) in his analysis with Bion, reflects Bion's sensitivity towards and emphasis upon the positive, wishful hopes and needs of the analysand and his readiness to interpret and explore them.

This is a far cry from the caricature of the Kleinian analyst who only focuses upon envy, destructive impulses, and the negative. Here, we see Bion operationalizing the communicative aspect of projective identification and the view that the patient comes to analysis seeking an object who can receive, hold, and help transform the primitive distress that is overwhelming him and being projected into the analyst; that there is an urge in each of us to communicate emotional experience as a driving force in psychic growth and development. Such views and the sensitivity that they embody easily lend themselves to the adoption and use of Bion's ideas in ways that may fit comfortably within each analyst's own personal idiom, theory, and tradition.

Although perhaps less well appreciated, Bion's innovations and new conception of the unconscious as an apparatus for symbolization also implies fruitful consequences in the interdisciplinary area. It may even prove possible to revitalize and renew the stale relationship between psychoanalysis and the arts and rebuild psychoanalytical criticism on a new foundation.

Readers will catch the reflections of all of these aspects in the many chapters of this book, which brings together a distinguished group of scholars of Bion's thought and its subsequent developments. Marked by variety, abundance, authority, liveliness, and vitality, this collection of essays offers continuing evidence of the growing support that the Bionian tradition now commands at the international level, a support that is also evidenced by the proliferation of conferences, editorial initiatives, works published in leading psychoanalytic journals, and statistics about the most cited authors in the databases of the psychoanalytic literature. It is fitting that this statement of where we are now comes on the heels of the publication of the complete works of Bion by Karnac in 2014. We offer this volume to our readers as Bion himself might have: as a way station to and preparation for new and individually meaningful further developments in an ongoing and hopefully inexhaustible process of development and change.

## *References*

Grotstein, J. (2014). Personal Communication.
Lyotard, J. -F. (1981). *The Postmodern Condition: A Report on Knowledge*. Minneapolis: University of Minnesota Press.

# PART I

PERSONAL, HISTORICAL

*Editors' introduction*

Those who have read or studied Bion know something of his theories and ideas, but as time wears on, there remain fewer and fewer colleagues who have had first hand experience of the man and his *presence*. A fortunate exception is Junqueira de Mattos, who, after being exposed to Bion and his teaching in his native Brazil, travelled to Europe and the US to seek him out for periods of analysis. Junqueira's poetic and elegiac memoir of his experience brings Bion's voice as analyst to life for readers, as it illustrates Bion's view that "Our feelings are among the few things we can be sure of. The problem is that we do not always pay attention to, or respect, what we feel" (Junquiera de Mattos, Chapter One). Junqueira's essay also illustrates one man's first hand experience of the fact that the heart and value of analysis lies in the struggle to pay attention to the truth of one's feelings, so that the frightening unknown may become liberating knowledge and pave the way towards new expansions and still further encounters with the as yet, undiscovered, unknown.

Neri, who was influenced early in his career as group analyst by attendance at Bion's Italian seminars, follows by describing Bion's importance for developments of group therapy and field theory in the Italian Psychoanalytic Society (SPI).

The essays by Britton, Snell, and Tarantelli help locate Bion in his cultural and historical context. While including his early years in India as a child of the colonial ruling class, the loneliness and cruelty of the English class system and his public school education, his time at Oxford with the philosopher, H. J. Paton, and the influence of Wilfred Trotter, John Rickman, Wittgenstein, and the Cambridge Philosophers, etc., they inevitably center on his traumatic experiences as tank commander in the First World War and the ongoing influence of those experiences on his personal life and theory.

Looking back over Bion's life, Snell notes that "Bion's passage from India left him with a lifelong, Forster-like sense of an irreconcilable tension, between dark, atavistic forces, and the equally insistent claims of gentility" (Chapter Four). Britton adds that "His time in the First World War not only left him emotionally battered it also gave him an awareness of the crucial difference between learning from experience and fanciful theorizing, and that entered into all his thinking" (Chapter Three). And Tarantelli (Chapter Five) concludes that "If we view the body of the theory Bion began to publish nearly forty years after the end of the war against the backdrop provided by his literary representations of his war experience, his paradoxical feeling of being dead but also alive can be retrospectively interpreted as one of the points of origin of his thought: his theory was obligated by the necessity of understanding the simultaneous destruction and continuing in being of his psyche/soma."

# CHAPTER ONE

# Impressions of my analysis with Dr. Bion*

*José Américo Junqueira de Mattos*

> "These ideas that we hear in the course of analysis have at some time been interpretations though now free associations. We are dealing with a series of skins which have been epidermis or conscious, but are now 'free associations'."
>
> —*Bion*, Two Papers: "The Grid" and "Caesura"

## Introduction

One day, walking in Kenwood Park, London, a week before the end my analysis, I was thinking about interpretation in psychoanalysis, when suddenly I came across, in a hollow, an enormous leafy and welcoming tree, its thick branches—strong arms greeting and toying with the cold autumn breeze—inviting lingering memories both dear and painful. I was surprised with the singular similarity between this tree and those of my early youth. And this wind? Did it not remind me of those cold July winds at the ranch, bringing the sad lowing of cattle that thirsty, mute, followed the trail ahead, in search of grass or water?

During analysis, I told Dr. Bion of the provoked emotions and evoked reminiscences brought back to me by the walking in the park and stressed the similarities and differences between the vegetation of Britain and Brazil. Then, I spoke of my wish to write a paper on interpretation in psychoanalysis. Yet, how could I write such a paper since, in fact, I would merely be

---

*Paper presented at the "First Scientific Seminar on W. R. Bion", held by the Brazilian Society of Psychoanalysis of São Paulo, October 17 and 18, 1980, on analysis that Dr. José Américo Junqueira de Mattos, member and training analyst of the Brazilian Society of Psychoanalysis of São Paulo, had with Wilfred R. Bion. The works, originally written in Portuguese, were translated into English by the author with the assistance of Paula di Mattei.

repeating what I had learnt with him? This would not be an original but simply a copy. Dr. Bion interpreted thus: "As the tree reminded you of those of your childhood, although it is not the same, what you are going to write also is not going to be the same."

Remembering these words encouraged me to accept the invitation extended by Dr. Cecil Rezze, President of the Brazilian Society of Psychoanalysis of São Paulo, to write on his suggested subject, that is, my experience of analysis with Dr. Bion.

Among my recollections I have chosen not only those which were important for me, personally, but, mainly, those which I feel may be useful or even important for others.

I have not limited myself to a single subject. Each matter has its own title and has been developed as such, although in an abbreviated form. Proper understanding of some passages, especially those concerned with Bion's theories on memory and desire, preconception, thoughts without a thinker, the theory of transformations and invariants, thus requires some familiarity with his ideas.

An attempt has been made to include parts of sessions. I try to show how the subject was grasped by me in the course of the work with Dr. Bion. I feel that this may be the most vivid way to transmit, today, something of my experience during analysis.

I was in analysis with Dr. Bion from September 2 to November 10, 1977, a further week in May, 1978 during his last stay in Brazil and from September 4 1978 to October 5 1979, one month before his death. During this period, no break occurred in analysis, and, at my request, analysis was continued during Dr. Bion's vacation in March and April 1979 in London and Saint Cyprien, France, and then after his return to Britain, in September, 1979. Until October 1978, five weekly sessions were held. At my request, Dr. Bion then added a sixth session, including a double, 100 minutes session, on Mondays. The entire analysis was conducted in English.

## *On preconception—a content in search of a container*

When I went to Los Angeles for the first time, I was worried. I feared that my long-standing wish for analysis with Dr. Bion could have been a product of my greed, maybe idealization of this person ... Had I not, I asked myself, tried all possibilities of development during previous analyses? On the other hand, how to undergo analysis in English, a language I was not yet familiar with? Would Dr. Bion understand my Brazilian accent? However, these doubts were much weaker than a strong intimate feeling that he was the person who would be able to help me. Well, full of anguishing uncertainties *contained* by the certainty born from I do not know where ... maybe from hope ... One day, it was the beginning of spring. I left.

When I lay on the couch at the first session, I told Dr. Bion that, without really knowing why, I felt that he could understand me and help me. He said: "If you knew why, you would have not bothered to come here and would not have wasted your time to see me. You came exactly because you don't know why." I then told Dr. Bion that my wish for analysis with him arose when, during his first visit to Brazil, he spoke about Milton's *Paradise Lost*, at a lecture. I further told him that my father had an edition of *Paradise Lost*, (illustrated by Doré), which I remembered having leafed through when still a child. This Dr. Bion interpreted almost as follows: "You feel that you speak a language I understand. However, what is this language? English, Portuguese or the language of Milton?" I said I felt he could help me and that this feeling was so irresistible that I could not avoid coming to him. He answered: "Our feelings are among the few things we can be sure of. The problem is that we do not always pay attention to, or respect, what we feel."

During that week, while driving to Dr. Bion's office, I was listening to the news about the drought in California. They were stressing the possibility of future water rationing if it did not rain. When I laid down on the couch, I mentioned this news bulletin. Then, I remembered our rustic cashew tree, a shrub, I told him, that grows on the barren plains of Central Brazil. Its main root has the peculiarity of penetrating several meters into the ground in search of water in deeper layers. Dr. Bion commented: "As this tree knows, by a singular hydrotropism, how to find water so important for its survival, you also, by a quality that you are unable to explain, felt that you knew how to look for me and find me."

During one of these sessions, I was reminded of a poem by Castro Alves, which I had learnt by heart when I was about thirteen. It had always moved me, although up to that moment I had not known why. It is at the beginning of "Floating Foams". When this poem came up in my associations, I attempted to translate it into English. Dr. Bion asked me to first quote it in Portuguese and then to translate it as best I could. Here it is:

*Dedication*

The dove of alliance the flight extends
Above the endless blue sea.
Close … close to the foam it almost falters
Measuring the curve of the vast horizon …
But far away a stretch is seen … the beach
Clearly tears the dense fog! …
Oh! resting place! Oh! mountain! Oh! olive branch!
Friendly nest of the alien dove!

Thus my poor book its wings spread
On this ocean, dark, endless, eternal …
The sea casts its bitter spittle,
The heavens casts their winter storm …
The sad bow under this heavy load!
Who opens to the sad a fatherly heart? …
How good it is to have as tree—some love! …
How good it is in some affects—to make nests! …

Upon which, Dr. Bion said something like: "As the poet looked for a reader who was able to read his book, you hope that I may also be able to 'read' you and show you what you can't read and know by yourself". And, further: "Like the dove, you took flight and crossed the ocean, looking for a branch, the branch of Hope, hoping that there would be someone to correspond to your [longing] yearning to be understood, for understanding yourself. This hope has always existed … Before, it hadn't been named but now and here, you can call it psychoanalysis with me." Deeply moved, I recalled an engraving by Caulas, "The Desert", which I had bought at an art auction. It shows a bird flying over a destroyed forest and thinking about a tree upon which to rest. The artist shows this in the manner of a cartoon with dialogue—in this instance an undamaged tree—put in squares. At the auction, this engraving immediately attracted me and I bought it on the spot.

Today it hangs in my living room and whenever I look at it, I sorely and tenderly miss Dr. Bion. This wise and generous man to whom I am so greatly indebted.

## On interpretation

> "Which, of all the right interpretations, are we to choose to formulate? The analyst's freedom, though great, can be seen to be limited, at any rate on one boundary, by the need to be truthful, to give an interpretation which is the true one. If the analysand is sincere in his wish for treatment he likewise is limited; his free association should be as near to what he considers to be the truth as he can get."
>
> Bion, *Two Papers: "The Grid" and "Caesura"*

Interpretation is an essential factor, which, on the one hand, emerges from the patient's associations in search of a deep, revealing meaning, while on the other hand, it finds in the analyst's "floating attention" the proper state of mind to grasp their understanding, to reveal them. Out of this dynamic binary, interpretation catalyzes ideas and emotions, giving coherence to what was formerly vague and dispersed … (H. Poincaré, quoted by Bion, 1977a). Thus, the unconscious becoming conscious, the frightening unknown becoming liberating knowledge, paving the way towards new expansions, towards the unknown. New associations spring, vague, anguishing. Intuition, if freed from the opacity of memory and desire, captures the idea. Another interpretation is glimpsed, communicated. Once more, everything is transformed into the dynamic container-contained forge. So, from question to question, in this creative turbulence, two minds, analyst-analysand, agitate, moving and preparing to form a new search, new discoveries and new unknown. This is the ceaseless labor of analysis looking for the unifying synthesis.

Since interpretation is so essential an element, how to evaluate it? How to prove its correctness or incorrectness, its accuracy or inaccuracy? In analysis, it is through what may emerge from this movement of container-contained that we may find an answer.

What struck me from the very beginning of my analysis was the extent to which Dr. Bion was attentive to all I said and how seriously he took it all. (This observation may seem obvious, but I did learn from him that the obvious is not always easily seen. I even think that sometimes the obvious may be the most difficult. I might say without exaggeration that, to a great extent, my analysis with Dr. Bion was the "discovery" and recognition of the obvious).

One day, after stating several associations, I feel silent. Then, Dr. Bion told me that he saw no sense in what I had said and asked me what I thought about it. After reflecting on this, I told him that I thought nothing at all. No doubt, what I had said was unimportant. After this, Dr. Bion told me something I was never to forget: "If you think that what you said is unimportant, why did you say it at all? Do you think that you are so rich that you can afford to waste time and money to come here and say futile, unimportant things?"

I realized that my association contained some things I knew and others I ignored. His function was to show me the underlying meaning that I ignored. Thus I clearly perceived—once again, the obvious—that I only took from analysis what I put into it. I started to feel responsible for everything I put into words and to follow the simple rule, telling everything that would come in my associations. With the expansion of analysis, my link with Dr. Bion strengthened.

He always and entirely interpreted any of my protracted silences as a difficulty I found in being frank, spontaneous, and in saying what I thought.

In Dr. Bion, I met an unwavering integrity, rectitude, and honesty and he had no scruples whatsoever in interpreting what he felt to be the right interpretation or on the right track, without fear of making a mistake. I soon learnt—obvious once more—that he wanted to say exactly what he did say. "I mean what I say and I say what I mean," he told me once, probably paraphrasing Shakespeare.

I remember that in my view some of his observations and interpretations appeared wrong. Sometimes I told him that I felt that what he had said was not true for me, or did not correspond to what I felt at that moment. He either remained silent or used to say something like: "I think that my interpretation is right. You say it is not. I respect your opinion. Maybe we can clarify this matter in the future." I perceived that Dr. Bion had not the slightest wish to engage in polemics with me and, if he respected my opinion, I also felt that he had not made an interpretation without basing it on something he had grasped during the session. Soon, I learnt to greatly prize and respect what he interpreted. Indeed, the future frequently confirmed that interpretations I had questioned were perfectly true.

I remember that several times, after I had not agreed with one of his interpretations, I associated some ideas that were interpreted by him along the following lines: "Apparently you don't agree with what I have just told you. Pay attention to what you have just said. It seems to me that this confirms my previous interpretation." This gave me the opportunity to confront what I thought I was feeling or thinking with what this association actually showed me I felt or thought. I was thus enabled to compare both sets of ideas. This was a "bi-ocular"[1] view between my conscious and unconscious.

A few times, after I had expressed that I found such an interpretation wrong and not in accordance with what I felt, he told me something extremely wise and curious: "You will now be able to make good account of a poor interpretation, you can now compare what I say you are, feel or think with that you really think you are, feel or think. Then, this interpretation will not actually clarify who you are, feel, or think. However, you may be in the position to know that what I say you are, feel or think is not what you are, feel or think. Thus, by a tortuous and circuitous route, you may approach what you truly are, feel or think."

After certain interpretations, I came across an association, interpreted as follows: "What you have just said confirms my previous interpretation. You therefore show me that I am on the right track." I realized that my reactions to his interpretations, verbal or otherwise, were fundamentally important to confirm or deny their truth, thus guiding me, whether or not he was following the right way; or, as Dr. Bion frequently said, they were useful "to keep me on the right track".

If we associate Dr. Bion's quotation of Kant: "Intuition without a Concept is blind. Concept without Intuition is empty" with his reference to verses 51 to 55 in Milton's Introduction to the Third Book of *Paradise Lost*:

> So much the rather thou celestial light
> Shine inward, and the mind through all her powers
> Irradiate, there plant eyes, all mist from thence
> Purge and disperse, that I may see and tell
> Of things invisible to mortal sight

we may understand that the genial poet, feeling that he was the container for this light-intuition, put himself into the right mental frame to *see* the contained and to reveal it to those unable to *see* for themselves.

The analyst's function would be—eschewing himself of memory and desire, and attempting to "blind himself artificially" (Freud, Letter to Lou Andreas Salomé, quoted by Bion, 1977c, p. 58)—to look inside himself, thus being able to be in the proper frame of mind to "transform" into a concept what is presented by the patient's intuition.

## On the human being's feeling of dependency and solitude

The first time I went to Los Angeles, I went alone. During the first days, everything seemed strange: the language, food, physical environment, culture, etc. One day, when I felt particularly sad, I started to cry during the session, whilst talking about how strange everything, and particularly the language, seemed to me, and how difficult it was for me to express myself in English. When I spoke to people, they asked me to repeat what I had just said. It surprised me, I told Dr. Bion, that here everything was different, that there was no difficulty in communication and that he understood me. He interpreted as follows: "You feel that you are in a strange, incomprehensible world and since you don't know how to express yourself, you cry. Crying is the language you know right now for communicating. On the other hand, in this strange, incomprehensible world you feel that someone understands you, understands your crying, and at this time I am this someone. However, there must have been a time, when you were born, when you met this strange, incomprehensible world for the first time, and depended on someone—your mother, at that time—to understand the meaning of your language or your crying." And further: "You seem to have had the experience of meeting someone who understood you and, at the same time, on whom you depended. Today, you are no longer a child, but the feeling that you are dependent and all alone continues."

I cannot recall whether at this or a following session I remembered, after an interpretation of my being dependent and all alone, one of Picasso's paintings, "Family of Saltimbanques", painted in 1905, between the Blue and the Rose periods, and now at the Washington National Gallery. In the context of Dr. Bion's interpretation of my being dependent and all alone, I spoke of the feelings this painting awoke in me. I said that these figures did not only impress me by their solitude and by the deeply tender sadness that emanated from them, but also, and mainly, by the fact that they did not communicate.

Dr. Bion replied: "A great artist like Picasso is able to paint something which does not only show his own feelings, yours at this moment, but also feelings that belong to humanity in general."

## Use of the model in "construction" and interpretation

"What are the rules which have to be obeyed if the analysand can reasonably be expected to understand the analyst and vice versa?"

Bion, The Grid

Ever since the start of my analysis with Dr. Bion I was impressed with his way of interpreting. Besides using the right word at the right time, he spoke like a great painter whose brush strokes showed me what he was *seeing* so that I could *see* in my turn. At any time, he used a model in which his interpretations were transformed into constructions highlighting the relationship, by analogy, between psychoanalytical theories and my own theories, myths, and experiences. (See Bion, 1977c, p. 36, and also 1977b, Chapter Three).

About a fortnight before the end of my first stay in Los Angeles I was particularly moved and surprised, both pleasantly and painfully, to realize why Milton's *Paradise Lost* had always held a particular attraction for me. I spoke to Dr. Bion of the figure of Satan, his uncommonly human qualities, his noble vanity, his unbending pride, which, permeated by vindictive envy, compelled him to rebel and challenge the Almighty and brought about his expulsion from Paradise. Dr. Bion told me that, according to Blake, Milton had unconsciously put himself at Satan's side in his insubordination and rebellion against God.

At the end of that week, I visited Yosemite National Park and its sequoias: there, between winding valleys, brooks of limpid and chanting waters, birds, all kinds the animals, in a profusion of colour and song, they reign. These majestic, wise and noble trees congregate to form enormous vaults, into which light, found I do not know where, forms invisible prisms that decompose into multi-formed luminescence. Natural scenery worthy of Beethoven's Pastoral Symphony. Well, walking in this paradisiac corner, I came across an enormous fallen sequoia, known as The Fallen Monarch. A number of reflections came to my mind. Attributing to the tree anthropomorphic qualities, I reflected that even the oldest and most powerful one day fall, die, or are dethroned. At the park gate, I saw a postcard of this sequoia. I bought several of them. On the following Monday, before lying down on the couch, I handed Dr. Bion the postcard. An inner pressure, which was so strong that I could not resist the impulse, had made me give one to him. He took it and read it. I lay on the couch and my first associations took me to the ranch where I spent my early childhood. In the screen of my imagination, I once more saw the large, welcoming colonial house: the living room with its enormous table, where my brothers and I would play without cares; the water-wheel next to the powerhouse; the sawmill, designed by my great-great-grandfather, powered by the water-wheel, its beams carved by the arms of slaves; the doleful chant of the monjolo.[2] My associations lingered on a photograph taken there years ago, with me sitting under a mango tree, avidly biting into a juicy mango. At this point, Dr. Bion intervened and said: "You suffer from the loss of your childhood. However, there is still another meaning. You suffer from the loss of your mother, the loss of her breast (these delicious mangoes) which, as you felt even at that time, did not belong to you alone, but to your father and to the brother that came before you and those that would come after you. One day, you had to renounce this breast, this paradises, this welcoming ranch, as one day you also were expelled from your mother's body. There is, however, an updated version. Here and now the same happens with me. In your view, you have found in me this ranch, this mother, this breast, which you are now going to lose. As a fallen monarch, you once again lose your paradise. In handing me this postcard, you show that you feel like this Fallen Monarch who sadly returns to Brazil." Indeed, at the time I greatly feared losing Dr. Bion, since I had not yet succeeded in selling my house, transforming the money into dollars and covering the cost of analysis and my stay in Los Angeles.

Another time, I told Dr. Bion about my admiration for Milton's *Paradise Lost*, which, in my view, implicitly contains Klein's theory as well as Freud's theory of dreams as the realization of desires. Dr. Bion told me that if such a work, written over three centuries ago, is still finding someone to read it, it is not only due to its outstanding beauty, but also to the fact that it contains a message, expressing in mythical form a truth and thinking process inherent to man.

This construction implies the theories of the Oedipus complex, genital and pre-genital, the theory of transference, Melanie Klein's theories of envy, of the breast as repository of all kindness, power, and satisfaction, and Bion's ideas on caesura (see Bion, 1977c).

Besides the frequent use of a model, as in the example just given, Dr. Bion's comments and interpretations had the peculiar quality of never being *saturated*. In each of his constructions, the universe of discussion expanded and pointed towards the unknown beyond. His answers, when clarifying a matter, always brought in its wake new questions, new inquiries. With him I learnt how important it is to know what one ignores and where one ignores, or, as he put it "to be better prepared to show ignorance".

## On the self

Once, when speaking about my maternal grandfather, I remembered a photograph showing him holding my older brother on his knees. I told Dr. Bion how much I had loved my grandfather and about my family's traditions, as well as the main building on the ranch, built by my great-great-grandfather's slaves. There is a very large drawing-room with grandfather's hunting trophies and my ancestors' portraits. I told him how much I had liked to look at these portraits when I was a child and to listen to my mother's tales about my grandparents, the building of the ranch, etc. To this, Dr. Bion replied: "You feel that as an integrant part of yourself, there is not only you, but also your parents, grandparents and grandparents' parents, as well as your wife, your children and your children's children. The same may be said as regards to your analytical personality, which includes your analyst, your analyst's analyst, as well as your analysands and yours analysands' analysands".

After this session I brought Dr. Bion several photographs of this ranch. He examined them carefully and asked a number of questions.

On another occasion, in reply to one of Dr. Bion's observations, I remembered a painting by Manet "The Execution of the Emperor Maximilian" (Staedtische Kunsthalle, Mannheim,

Germany). This painting shows an execution by firing squad. A few boys sitting on a wall observe the firing squad performing its macabre duty. Dr. Bion commented: "You identify yourself at the same time with the victim, the executioners and the witnesses."

He more than once stressed that one might say that three persons are present during analysis: "You who speak, I who listen and you who hear what you say and what I say."

When Dr. Bion visited São Paulo for the last time, in May 1978, I took another week of analysis. Since I wished to take part in his supervisions, I asked whether he had any objection. Dr. Bion asked me what I thought about this. I replied that I did not see any problem, but that, without knowing why, I feared that he might not like the idea and that this might interfere with my analysis. He interpreted as follows: "You feel that analysis with me helps you. You also feel that taking part in supervisions may be useful. Your thought that I might not like you to take part shows your own fear of progress and development. I think that there is a part of yourself that does not want progress and development. That part envies the other which progresses and develops."

One day in Los Angeles, our landlord offended my wife whilst I was away. I became very angry and quarreled with him before settling the matter. Next day I reported what had happened to Dr. Bion, who said: "You are angry because you feel that he who offends your wife, also offends you. Your wife is part of yourself and vice-versa. What you do affects her and what she does likewise affects you."

These notions of a multi-faceted, familiar self, and the dynamics of its relationship with myself, the family, and society helped me to understand my complex relationship with myself and my family and highlighted the importance of my ancestors in forming my personality. I feel that, at present, I face death with greater peace of mind. Something will remain, will continue, will perpetuate. There remain roots, new trees, new fruits for new transformations.

## Present, past and future

One of the most impressive aspects of analysis with Dr. Bion was the sense of continuity, resemblance, and coherence he showed me that exists in the human being, even when divided by such barriers as culture, language, time, etc. On the other hand he viewed man in a historical and evolving, evolutionary sense.

Once, I told him about a fishing trip to the Bananal Island. At the time I wanted to kill a few crocodiles in order to, as I rationalized, tan their skin and eat their meat. With a friend, I went to a lagoon a few kilometers from our camp, where we found hundreds of crocodiles. After choosing the best specimens, we killed five. I felt depressed since I perceived within myself the pleasure of killing them. How, my conscience demurred, can you, a purportedly civilized being, kill for pleasure? Dr. Bion commented: "Crocodiles are the remnants of the enormous prehistorical saurias and at present are the descendants of the first inhabitants of this planet. This impulse to kill you felt also has its roots in the primitive man, whose remnants you still have within yourself when you feel pleasure in killing."

Another time, Dr. Bion mentioned the well-known fact that the human being makes good use of only one eighth of his brain, and continued: "It would seem that our brain is waiting for the time when we will have expanded our capacity for thought to use it fully."

At Saint Cyprien, on the banks of the Dordogne river, which quietly wanders through fertile valleys, we find medieval castles perched on high mountaintops, which in their day protected their dwellers from wars and hostile neighbours. Now looking not to the sky to protect them but to the deep underground, we find prehistoric caverns, the home of our troglodyte ancestors. One such cavern at Font-de-Gaume is covered with remarkably preserved paintings, 12,000 years old. These paintings are well-known and reproduced in books on art history. Some, showing enormous bison and unworried does at pasture are particularly beautiful. When we spoke about them one day, Dr. Bion told me that they might represent man's first effort to restrain the beast within us. Thus, one of art's functions would be to pacify this beast. While writing I am reminded of Picasso's "Guernica", where this subject returns. In this masterpiece of human spirit, Picasso's extraordinary genius traces a lampoon against war. Among torn bodies and crying mothers holding shattered infants, reigns a Beast that, uncontained, freely feasts on flesh and blood that gushes from its enormous mouth in a macabre banquet.

One day, I spoke to Dr. Bion about Renoir's paintings, which I had just seen at the Jeu de Palme in Paris, and the deep impression they had made on me. They were so beautiful, but so beautiful that I wasn't able to describe them. He answered: "Obviously you can't describe them. If you were able to reproduce them, you would be Renoir." Later, I don't recall how, I related Renoir's paintings to those at Font-de-Gaume. Dr. Bion commented: "Could it not be that Renoir's origins are at Font-de-Gaume? What is the relationship between Renoir and the painter of Font-de-Gaume which you see here and now?"

Les Eyzies-de Tayac, called the capital of prehistory, is located six kilometers from Saint Cyprien. The Neanderthal and Cro-Magnon man lived in this region. The local paleontology museum is built on a hillside, overlooking the valley of the Dordogne. On a terrace on top of the building stands a statue of Neanderthal man, about three meters high, gazing towards the valley. What I found most impressive about this sculpture was the fact that the artist had managed to convey an inner force which seems to compel this ape-man to overcome his animal bestiality. Well, 150,000 years have gone by and suddenly here I stood, looking at the same scenery, the same valley, meditating.

When I raised this matter during a session, Dr. Bion told me: "The important point is to know, as far as possible, what kind of force is this and if it exists, whether it still operates within you and, assuming it does, in which direction it is thrusting now and will thrust in the future …" Replying to my remark that the sculpture's subject appeared to meditate, Dr. Bion said: "What do you think he would feel if today, in the twentieth century, he could return to this valley, to this same spot and contemplate what he had become?" I had to confess that I lacked an answer.

Dr. Bion's every comment always showed a deep understanding of the human being, his greatness and his villainies. One day I mentioned an acquaintance who, possibly through ignorance, had come close to doing me great harm. Dr. Bion, quoting Shakespeare, said: "If justice were to be done, who would not deserve to be hanged?" In such instances he showed a deep kindness, molded by the wisdom that emanates from his outstanding mind. Without any doubt, those were the qualities that I most admired in him. It seems to me that they made it easier for me to speak freely about myself, my conflicts, and my concerns. His interpretations never were critical or moralizing, they were not products of desire. Although I am unable to explain, since objectively he did nothing to please me, but only (?) interpreted, I did feel in him a loving container, wise and generous.

Although Dr. Bion's interpretations were almost always directed towards the here and now of the transferential relationship, they were, at times, a prelude for *constructions* of truly cosmological scope. Highlighting the matter at hand, they placed me in time, in the universe, in the history of the race, and made me feel the relationship between the innumerable generations and cultures which preceded us and those that will come.

Earth, a small spaceship, navigating incognito in a boundless, infinite, sideral space.

Man (who calls himself *Homo sapiens*) viewed with all his limitations and in his dependency on a nature utterly indifferent towards the beings living in it.

The individual, this singular, peculiar, and unique cell of a complex social organism, is essential and therefore deserves from the analyst his unrestrained attention, time, and effort. Psychoanalysis, as Dr. Bion put it "has a prejudice in [favor] of the individual".

Psychoanalysis—this tender, incipient plant still in its infancy, needs the proper climate and mental space to grow. And it will be in the future what today's psychoanalysts make of it.

### Thought without a thinker

During my first stay in Los Angeles, there were days when I felt very, very sad. A feeling of nostalgia from what I did not know. The night before, I had two or three whiskies, to no avail. They did not provide any relief but, rather, further depressed my state of mind, and the next morning I felt still worse. I did not know the reason for this sadness. Dr. Bion told me: "You are not feeling comfortable in feeling what you feel. You tried to drown this feeling in whisky, to no avail. Since you do not know the reason for this feeling, you are talking about it, in order to understand it and to feel better." I then remembered one of Picasso's Blue Period pictures, "La Pobre Acurrucada", painted in Barcelona in 1902, now at the museum of Toronto, Canada. I spoke about the feelings generated by this lonesome, sad woman, trying to protect herself from the cold. At this point my associations dwelled on the fifth movement of Beethoven's Quartet, Opus 130, The "Cavatina", in my view the most beautiful, sublime, and pungently nostalgic piece of the composer's works. Well, at this point I was crying. After a protracted silence, I recalled a sonnet by Raimundo Corrêa, "Secret Evil" and quoted:

*Secret Evil*

> How many who laugh, maybe inside
> Keep an atrocious recondite enemy,
> Like an invisible cancerous sore!

> How many who laugh maybe exist,
> Whose only happiness consists
> In showing happiness to others!

Dr. Bion waited for some time, possibly for my tears to stop, and then said: "Since you don't know how to express your sadness, you borrow from Picasso, Beethoven, and Correa, who knew, in a way you don't know, how to express sadness, putting it into paintings, music, or poetry. However, not even Picasso, Beethoven, or Correa were able express in painting, music, or poetry, everything they felt, saw, or observed. What they were able to express was only a small part of what they felt, saw, or observed."

Compare what Dr. Bion said with that remarkable sonnet by Augusto dos Anjos, where his muse in a moment of genial inspiration touches on the same subject.

*The Idea*

Whence does she come? From what brute matter
Springs this light that above the nebula
Falls from incognito mysterious crypts
Like stalactites of a cave?!

She comes from the psychogenetic fight
Of the bundles of nerve molecules,
Which, in marvelous disintegrations,
Deliberates, then wants and executes!

She comes from the opaque encephalon, that constricts her
Then reaches the larynx chords,
Phthisic, tenuous, minimal, rachitic …
Breaks the centripetal force that ties her,
But suddenly, almost dead, stumbles
On the babble of a paralytic tongue!

## On truth

Once, after we had spoken about the importance of truth even when, as Dr. Bion put it, we do not know what it is, I remembered that the Indians of the Bananal Island harpoon the *pirarucu* when it comes to the surface to breathe and exposes its head or part of the body. At that precise moment, they hurl the rapid, treacherous harpoon. Dr. Bion remarked: "As oxygen is essential for the life of the body, truth is the same for the mind; but as the *pirarucu* in search of oxygen essential for its survival, exposes itself and risks death, the same happens to those who search for truth. They also become exposed and vulnerable. So the fear that the truth provokes in you and in all those searching for it."

Another time I spoke about an airplane crash that had recently occurred. On a flight from Chicago to Los Angeles, a DC-10 had lost an engine, crashed, and exploded. Two hundred and forty-seven died. I followed the investigation of the cause of the accident in the *Los Angeles Times* and I was impressed to find that the probable cause of this tragedy was the failure of a small bolt. This bolt had broken, and as a result the fastening system between pillar and wing was displaced and in a chain reaction other parts of the structure failed until the engine came off. Well, 250 tons of aircraft disintegrated because of the failure of a small bolt, weighing just a few grams. During analysis, I told Dr. Bion that it was suspected that this bolt had broken, because, in the course of periodic overhauls, procedures recommended by the manufacturer had not been followed. According to these, the engine should first be removed from the pillar, and then the pillar from the wing. However, engine and pillar had been removed as a unit and this was said to have led to the breakage of that bolt. Dr. Bion remarked: "This shows the consequences of negligence and contempt for truth."

One day, when cashing a five-hundred-dollar check, I asked the cashier for fifty dollar bills. Since she did not have them to hand, she went to get them from the treasurer in another part of the bank. When paying, she put the bills on the counter. When I counted the money, I noticed that one fifty dollar bill was missing; there were only nine bills instead of ten. The cashier checked and, to her surprise, found that there were indeed only nine bills! She told me that she had counted the bills when taking them from the treasurer and that everything was correct at the time. She went back to the treasurer who confirmed that the correct amount had been paid. When searching the floor and desk, nothing was found … What on earth had happened to that bill? The treasurer confirmed that the right amount had been paid. The cashier said she had counted correctly. As far as I was concerned, I was sure that I had not pocketed the bill. Where was it, then? This was so intriguing, since everybody seemed to be telling the truth. At the session, I mentioned this to Dr. Bion, who commented: "See, in a simple matter like this, you can notice how difficult it is to find out the truth. Even here, it may happen that you are truthful, I may be truthful but the ultimate truth may not come up …"

## *The responsible being*

When Dr. Bion told me that he was going to take his vacation in March and April, 1979, I asked him whether he thought it would be possible to continue seeing me during his vacation. He told me he would be going to Europe and asked whether I could go there. I said yes. When, some time later, he told me that he would be able to see me, I became worried. On the one hand, I did not want to lose time and was keen to continue my analysis; but on the other hand, I reasoned, how would my wife and five children fare in this alien land, where they still experienced difficulties in communicating and were practically alone, except for a couple of recent friends, if an emergency were to arise? When I consulted my wife, I felt that in spite of her courage and determination she was somewhat anxious and certainly worried. However, she told me: "If you think that it's essential to go, go. We'll manage to get through." Anguished, I brought this matter to Dr. Bion's attention, who told me: "You would like me to tell you what to do, to go or stay, to take a decision for you. You may not know which is the best decision, but only you know what it is to feel what you are feeling, not I or your wife. Even if you do not know what the best decision is, you are the one who knows best although you are reluctant to accept this fact. Neither your wife nor I can tell you what you should do. At present you are the father and don't have your father or mother to tell you what you should do. At present, whether you like it or not, you are a responsible adult. To be responsible is to choose when one does not know which is the right answer. For example, if you knew that everything would be well for you when going to London or Saint Cyprien and that your family would be well in Los Angeles, without the prospect of difficulties or emergencies, there would be no doubts, you would not have to choose. Since you do not know, you have to choose. To be responsible is to decide when one does not have an answer."

On another occasion, he told me: "When you choose something, you also choose not to choose what was not chosen; at this moment you are alone, utterly alone, to take this decision or to make this choice."

This also applied when, in September, 1979, I decided to end my analysis. When I arrived in London in early September, I told Dr. Bion that I intended to stop in October. He answered: "Only you know when to stop your analysis and only you can decide whether you have had enough."

## On transformations and invariants

> "The practising psychoanalyst, the portrait painter, the musician, the sculptor, all have to 'see' and demonstrate, so that others may see, the truth which is usually ugly and frightening to the person to whom the truth is displayed.
>
> In the same way the ugly and frightening are usually [believed] identical with the truth to the person to whom they are displayed."
>
> Bion, *Two Papers: "The Grid" and "Caesura"*

Once—I do not recall in what context—I told Dr. Bion that Picasso, after finishing the portrait of Gertrude Stein (around 1905, now at the Metropolitan Museum, New York) was told that she did not like it and that it did not look like her. Picasso replied: "It will one day." Dr. Bion interpreted this as follows: "An artist like Picasso is able to grasp characteristics of the human personality which are hidden to most. Here and now you expect me to see traits of your personality which are present today and here but which were also present when you were a child and will still be present in your old age, if you reach it."

Another time, while we were speaking about music, which I love dearly, I repeated to Dr. Bion a story my mother had told often, especially when she watched me listen to music. She used to say that, during the last months of pregnancy, whenever she came to a place where music was being played, I started to move inside her. This became so frequent and strange that she imagined I would become a musician. Dr. Bion said: "If we were to trust your mother's feelings, your capacity to enjoy music was born before you were."

In this context, I am reminded of Graham Sutherland, the famous British surrealist painter. In the Fifties, he painted a portrait of Sir Winston Churchill, to be placed in the British Parliament. Churchill hated this portrait to the extent that, after his death, his wife did what the great statesman might have wished to do: she burnt it. What were the "invariants", that, captured by Graham Sutherland put on canvas, and displayed to Churchill, made him face a truth that annoyed him so much? I don't know.

## On the capacity to love

One day, when I was at Saint Cyprien, my wife wrote to me from Los Angeles to convey unpleasant news about one of our relatives in Brazil. I did not particularly care. During analysis, I told

Dr. Bion that I had been shocked by my indifference to this news and surprised not to be moved by it. Dr. Bion remarked: "You think that I am not greatly concerned about you. You yourself think that you are not greatly concerned with your relatives. You feel either there is something wrong with the human being, or the capacity for what we call love is still small, incipient."

## On conscience

At times, in the course of my analysis, Dr. Bion stressed a peculiarity of conscience, in so far as it is always ready to tell us what we should not do or think, but never what we should.

## On freedom

"Better to be Lord in hell than slave in paradise."

Milton, *Paradise Lost, Book I* (Satan)

Once, at Saint Cyprien, during a session, I remembered a dream I had had during my first analysis over ten years before. In that dream I saw my maternal grandmother, at our ranch house, singing the Marseillaise. Whilst she was singing, the house came tumbling down. Grandmother, I told Dr. Bion, spoke French well, had a beautiful voice and loved to sing, among other songs, the Marseillaise. I always found it moving to listen to her. Then, I recalled the "Victory of Samothrace" I had seen at the Louvre, the week before. Dr. Bion asked whether I meant "Winged Victory". I replied that I did not know it under this name and attempted to describe the painting to Dr. Bion; it shows an extraordinarily beautiful, bare-breasted girl, armed with a rifle, marching at the head of a crowd to take the Bastille. At this point, Dr. Bion remarked that when the people took the Bastille, they only found six prisoners there. My associations then led to Beethoven's Fifth Symphony. His words about that symphony: "Destiny knocks at the door" (alluding to the first chords of this masterpiece of music). "I will take Destiny by the throat". Then I lingered on the Fourth Movement, its passage from C minor to C major in an extraordinary crescendo of sound, an explosion of notes transfusing hope. Dr. Bion waited until I had stopped crying and then told me: "You speak about your search for freedom. This search started when you were a child listening to your grandmother, or it was probably present even before. You also notice that they are not only personal feelings, they belong to humanity since time immemorial and are expressed in sculpture, paintings, and music. The question is: from what do you wish to free yourself, or to put it differently, what is tying you down? If these questions could be answered, the next would be: why do you want to free yourself from this? Can analysis with me help you to do so?"

One day, in Los Angeles, I saw the film version of *Papillon* on television. During the session I told Dr. Bion how impressed I was with this personage who, a prisoner in French Guyana for thirty years, had never abandoned the idea to escape, to be free. Punishment, solitude, hunger, sickness, or humiliation were all unable to bend his untamable fiber. In the end, he devised a raft with bags of dried coconuts as a guise of a primitive vessel and, helped by the balmy winds and waves, achieved his freedom. Dr. Bion commented: "You feel that your Body is like a prison from which your mind wishes to escape."

## On psychoanalysis in general

One of the advantages of analysis, said Dr. Bion, "is that here we have time and means to discuss matters and situations which do not only happen here. They also happen out there. Out there, however, there is not always time or possibility to discuss them."

Another advantage "is that analysis allows us to discuss and think in advance, so that when things occur, you are already prepared. Indeed, at times, things happen so fast that there is no time to think."

Once we discussed the cost of analysis, Dr. Bion stressed a cost which could not be measured in dollars or cents. For instance, he said: "How much does it cost you to be far from your country, from your work? Or, what would have been the cost if you had never taken analysis? How much would you have 'paid' for that?" I then referred to the actual economic cost of analysis, and he replied: "Who should pay for analysis? The government, the family, or the patient? If the patient is unable to pay, who will bear the consequences? Only the patient, or his family and society as well? What, for instance, will be the future of psychoanalysis if it were only available to the unemployed rich?"

## On caesura

"There is much more continuity between intra-uterine life and earliest infancy than the impressive caesura of the act of birth allows us to believe."

Freud, *Inhibitions, Symptoms and Anxiety*, quoted by Bion in *Caesura*

During my first stay in Los Angeles, the more inexpensive dishes in the hotel restaurant where I stayed were numbered from one to three. One morning, when ordering breakfast, I said: "I want the second." Since the waitress did not understand, I took the menu and pointed to the dish I wanted. With a gesture of surprise, she exclaimed: "Ah, number two?" I replied: "Yes, the second."

This was one of the many unpleasant pitfalls of American English of which my first period in Los Angeles was full.

Afterwards, on my way to analysis, I reflected on the difficulty I was having in communicating. How, I wondered, would I be able to command this mad language? Would I have to speak it in just one manner—their manner—to be understood?

When I laid down on the couch, still anguished and depressed, I told Dr. Bion about what had happened and said that I felt as if I had been put in a Procrustean bed to meet the demands of a language and a culture that constricted me. When I had to express myself in English, I felt like a cripple, deprived of my capacity to communicate. I felt as if I had to learn everything all over again. Dr. Bion interpreted this in approximately the following manner: "You feel that it is not easy to adapt to America. You came from Brazil and there you left your family, your work, your friends. You also left your language, your food, your habits. This change, this sudden rupture makes you feel crippled and deprived, as if you had to learn everything once again. Look at the price you are paying to learn. However, can there be knowledge and learning without pain?" And further: "There was a time when you also did not know how to talk and pointed to what you wanted. You had the desire and did not know how to put it into words. We might say that you are now being born into a new world. I think that this experience has a long history. It did not start now. For you, this revives your birth, at which you might, as now, have felt crippled and deprived, or mutilated and castrated. The first Procrustean bed you experienced was at birth."

## Conclusion

Whoever today listens to Moussorgsky's "Pictures at an Exhibition" does not have before his eyes the ten paintings by the composer's friend Hartmann, which Moussorgsky saw, felt, and transformed into this outstanding work of music. Thus, the listener will be unable to compare the paintings with the "transformations" that occurred in Moussorgsky's mind and which resulted in this incomparable music.

So, Dr. Bion is not here among us to say what he said, and how he said it. I hope, however, that the impressions gathered here may not have undergone too many "transformations", that the "invariants" contained herein, in portraying the experience described, may be consistent with the lived experience.

## Notes

1. "Bi-ocular," meaning two separate and different images that alternate rather than unite, rather than "binocular," which melds two images into one unified whole.
2. A simple water-driven Brazilian engine used to pound corn, peel coffee, rice, etc.

## References

Bion, W. R. (1977a). Learning from Experience. In: *Seven Servants*. New York: Jason Aronson.
Bion, W. R. (1977b). Elements of Psycho-Analysis. In: *Seven Servants*. New York: Jason Aronson.
Bion, W. R. (1977c). *Two Papers: "The Grid" and "Caesura"*. Rio de Janeiro: Imago Editora. Milton, J. (1894). *Paradise Lost*. London: Cassel.

# CHAPTER TWO

# A long meeting with Bion*

*Claudio Neri*

I came to know Bion as a consequence of meetings I had with two other people—namely, Francesco Corrao and Parthenope Bion Talamo.

Francesco Corrao was the most brilliant and creative of the Italian psychoanalysts. It was he who introduced Bion's ideas to Italy and arranged for his books to be translated. I remember a remark of his: "It is possible to love someone's mind; well, I loved Bion's." At the time of my meeting with Bion, Corrao was president of the Italian Psychoanalytic Society (SPI); he was living in Palermo but came to Rome every week for two days. There was something heroic about the man: I never heard him complain about being tired, about airport delays, or indeed about anything else.

Parthenope—Bion's daughter—had studied philosophy in Florence; she had then moved to Rome, where she was living with her cellist husband. She was in personal analysis with Adda Corti and was waiting to be accepted by the SPI as a candidate. At university Parthenope had been a contemporary of two of my friends, the philosopher Francesco Marramao, and Nando Riolo, who, many years later, was also to become president of the SPI.

## The Italian school of group psychotherapy

At that time—around 1968/9—I was engaged in specialist training as a psychiatrist and was very much involved in the student movement. I was a member of the group that had "occupied" the psychiatry congress in Milan. I had been working for a while in Gorizia with

---

*Translated by Philip Slotkin, MA Cantab. MITI.

Franco Basaglia. I was also a candidate at the SPI and in training analysis with Giulio Cesare Soavi.

I had been running therapy groups at the external unit of the Institute of Psychiatry for some months when Soavi suggested that I should talk about my work to Corrao and perhaps ask him to be my supervisor. I went along to Corrao and acted out a "scene" that, while at variance with my position as a candidate of the SPI, was consistent with the prevailing attitude within the student movement: "You people in the psychoanalytic society—there is no way you will accept me!"; "We are against official psychiatry; we are against all institutions!"; and "The only person who has said anything interesting about group psychotherapy is Bion!" Far from shunning the challenge, Corrao in fact appreciated it, for he was a Bion enthusiast. On that there was a meeting of minds.

The next move in our supervision work was somewhat disconcerting. During the supervisions (which lasted two hours) I often talked about my group of aspiring-specialist friends. Corrao told me: "Now our supervision work involves a mixture of the real and symbolic levels. Your friends in the aspiring-specialist group belong to everyday reality and interfere with the therapy group, which should instead be operating on the symbolic level. I think it would be best for us to try to get the "aspiring-specialist group" to enter fully into everyday reality so as to make it easier for you to accommodate the "patient group" on the symbolic level. Would you have anything against letting me meet these friends and colleagues of yours?" A few weeks later I organized a meeting between Corrao and my colleagues in my office. That meeting led to the formation of a research group called *Il Pollaiolo*, which played an important part in establishing the theoretical foundations of group psychotherapy in this country.

## Psychoanalysis and group psychotherapy

The relationship between the Italian Psychoanalytic Society and the protagonists of group psychotherapy in Italy was very different from that which had arisen in other countries, such as France: my "group-oriented" colleagues and I did not meet with any opposition. Corrao and Eugenio Gaddini, his successor as president of the SPI, gave us their full support. So did Franco Fornari, who was SPI president before Corrao. Fornari was the author of an important book on the subject of social psychoanalysis entitled *The Psychoanalysis of War*.

From the beginning a clear theoretical and methodological basis was laid down and played a fundamental part both in the development of the "Italian model" and in the evolution of relations with the SPI. Francesco Corrao and I were convinced that there was no point in extrapolating concepts such as the transference from the sphere of classical (couple-based) psychoanalysis to the group situation. It was instead preferable to espouse only certain very general ideas and values from psychoanalysis, and to evolve the operational concepts of group psychotherapy on the foundation of experience.

## The concept of the field

The first concept to be developed was that of the field. Its Italian version, while sharing certain elements with Kurt Lewin's hypothesis, differed from it in some significant respects. It is also very different from the idea of the field in the work of Madeleine and Willi Baranger.

During those years I presented a paper at the Salpêtrière in Paris in which I maintained that the concept of the field was not analogous to, but homologous with, that of the transference in psychoanalysis. In other words, the field played as important a part in group theory as the concept of the transference in psychoanalysis.

I was very moved to be presenting this paper. The Salpêtrière, after all, is the hospital where Charcot and Freud had worked. The congress theme was "The transference in group psychoanalysis". The hall was packed.

This was the first international presentation by the Italian group psychotherapy school. When I finished speaking there was a pregnant pause, following which Didier Anzieu got to his feet and applauded warmly. The entire hall then joined in the ovation, which went on for several minutes.

## The first major SPI congress on the work of Bion

At about the same time something happened that would be hard to imagine today. Francesco Corrao asked me and Parthenope Bion Talamo to organize a congress on the Italian psychoanalysts' reading and reception of the ideas of Bion. I was then a mere candidate at the SPI and Parthenope was in the middle of her personal analysis, but had not yet been admitted as a candidate.

The congress featured twenty presentations from all the leading psychoanalysts currently working in Italy, including Corrao, Gaddini, Fornari, Matte Blanco, Luciana Nissim Momigliano, Adda Corti, Di Chiara, Anna Baruzzi, and Riolo. The intention was that each should contribute a personal view. The guiding idea was that "we cannot be Bionians": Bion himself taught that one can "only be oneself" and must accept all the associated risks.

Parthenope and I later edited a special issue of the *Rivista di psicoanalisi* in which all these contributions were reproduced. This was also the first issue of our journal that was published in English as well as Italian.

## Personal acquaintance with Bion

Shortly after this congress, Corrao, Parthenope, and I decided to issue a joint invitation to Bion from the SPI and *Il Pollaiolo* to hold a series of seminars in Rome. I wrote to Bion, who politely accepted.

There was a huge sense of expectation, and additional space was created in a room at *Il Pollaiolo* to accommodate more people. Fachinelli and Fornari came from Milan and Hautmann from Florence.

We also arranged three larger-scale seminars to be held at the French school of Trinità dei monti, where Parthenope was teaching.

In this way I was able to make closer acquaintance with Bion. Parthenope invited me to the Hotel Hassler, where Bion was staying, and then several times to her home with her family.

Throughout Bion's time in Rome, I also acted as his guide and chauffeur, picking him up and taking him back to his quarters.

My first impression of him was as a grandfather. Parthenope had a little girl, one or two years old, towards whom Bion's attitude was absolutely that of an equal. He told me he was trying to learn Italian from his granddaughter.

I was also impressed by his great physical vigor: Bion was a real athlete despite his eighty years.

I remember, too, his enormous aptitude as a psychoanalyst and teacher. As stated, after the seminars I would drive him back to his hotel. In the car, I spontaneously made some remarks about the seminar that had just ended. Bion did not respond; he did not comment, but remained silent. He felt that there was nothing to add. He had an extremely strong view of the setting.

Another memory that occurs to me is of Bion in my little car weaving its way through the traffic in Rome. As we reached the intersection outside the Navy Ministry where dozens of vehicles were crossing in all directions and changing lanes at high speed, he experienced moments of sheer terror.

## The Roman seminars

Bion always stood while conducting his seminars; his presentation was rich in biblical metaphors and quotations from the poets.

During the seminars certain ideas that have remained the cornerstone of my activity ever since crystallized in my mind. The first is that Bion should be read in literal terms. He says and writes exactly what he thinks. He says and writes what he thinks as directly and clearly as he can express it. Bion also does his best to see that the emotions connected with the content of a communication are incorporated in that communication. The second idea concerns the way he induced oscillations between D and PS in his audience.

One understood little of what he said. The impression was gained that Bion had an outline in his mind from which he presented various extracts. It was more a matter of seizing hold of fragments of images and thoughts.

Everyone—including myself—joined in the debate, seeking Bion's approval. His bearing was so powerful, the level of fascination he inspired so high, and his delivery so *ad hominem* that he, at least in part, generated the kind of dependence that he later interpreted as a mass phenomenon. Although there was much anxiety, enthusiasm was predominant. There was no doubt about it. Fornari was bewildered, Corrao fascinated.

At a certain point I asked him whether basic assumptions could evolve. In his idiosyncratic style, he replied: "If one day the adrenal glands [i.e., the basic assumption of *fight-flight*] were to take over, that would be the end of mankind. But that would not be a disaster: the task of living would then be carried on by the ants." At a subsequent seminar, when I asked him a question framed in rather complicated terms, he answered: "The *Titanic* was the greatest construction ever devised by the wit of man [an allusion to the complex, involved style of my question], but it ran up against a fact and sank."

Not only myself but all those attending the seminars found it hard to absorb these blows and then to resume contact with him—but we learnt tolerance.

Bion had two outstanding qualities: first, he made these pronouncements (however terrible) without a trace of arrogance; and, second, he never did so in order to show off or to put others down. Bion felt himself to be a psychoanalyst and teacher in the service of truth. He was simply telling the truth, whether we liked it or not. In the battle for truth, you have to take sides. Alluding to Shakespeare, he said: "My dear Macduff, the battle of … is over and you were not there. Go and hang yourself from the nearest tree!!" In other words, if you can keep going and fight for the truth, it will be better for you. If you can't hold out, you should preferably get in training until you succeed.

### *Letture Bioniane* (Reading Bion)

I realized that my own and my colleagues' idea of a "Bion of the generation of '68", an anarchic Bion, needed to be reconciled with the reality we had experienced of a "Colonel Bion", a "soldier Bion", and a "Bion who demands discipline".

Bion's roots lay in Imperial Britain and India. He had a powerful sense of the establishment and of belonging. However, this also enabled him to be very original.

These were the foundations of the book *Letture bioniane* (Reading Bion) (Neri, Correale, & Fadda, 1987), which was later translated into French as *Lire Bion*. This volume has a particular history. Following a number of seminars and study groups, a second congress devoted to the work of Bion was held. The young people attending the congress (students or candidates) presented papers and their elders (established analysts such as Matte Blanco, Gaddini, Fornari, and Corrao) acted as discussants.

This choice at first aroused Franco Fornari's ire: "You summoned me here to Rome to talk to these incarnations of the Infant Jesus [the young boys with their contributions]!" But we held firm.

### *The final personal meeting*

The occasion of my third "personal" contact with Bion was the first international congress on Bion's thought held in Turin to commemorate the centenary of his birth.

The first day of the congress coincided with Bion's birthday. Parthenope (who had meanwhile moved from Rome to Turin) prepared a small supper at her home. The guests were Francesca (Bion's widow), Parthenope's brothers, and some close friends. I well recall the comic side with its black humor: a kind of performance, a candlelit ceremony, and the birthday cake for the dead Bion.

### *Bion and my own work*

If I am faced with a problem—for instance, if I am asked to write a paper on regression—I spontaneously find myself asking: "Now what would Bion have said? What would his approach have been?"

A sentence or formulation of his would often occur to me. However, I had also learnt to be aware of his way of using aphorisms. Unless Bion's ideas and phrases are "reopened", they may well obstruct the process of thought, if used as a formula to be resorted to at every opportunity rather than a basis for dialogue and reasoning.

Furthermore, I gradually noticed, too, that certain of Bion's ideas (as specifically formulated by him) were embodied less and less frequently in my clinical practice. In other words, a kind of split had arisen, which I can illustrate by the image of two horses. There are two types of horses: parade horses (where the aim is for horse and rider to be seen) and draught horses (which are there to help us in our day-to-day lives). The risk as I saw it was that taking Bion as my reference might become a parade horse.

Let me give you an example. Bion makes a sharp distinction between the "work group" and "basic assumption" mentalities. In his view, the therapist should be the leader of a work group. Basic assumptions are what prevent us from making contact with truth. I noticed that this was not my approach. For me there was an intermediate area: that of conviviality, which perhaps corresponds in part to Bleger's (2013) "syncretic sociality".

For me, another bone of contention in Bion's texts concerns beta elements. In my view, these can be used only for projective identification and cannot on any account be digested by the alpha function. It would be wonderful if they were digestible by the alpha function as Nino Ferro maintains. But this is the locus of the rift between psychotic and non-psychotic thought. Here irreducibility is the order of the day.

Yet another crucial point to which I have devoted a great deal of attention is Bion's concept of truth and lies. I eventually came to realize that it did not work for me in the clinical situation. The foundation of my activity which I was able to espouse was instead an aspiration of authenticity to be attained by the patient in the course of analysis, coupled with a position of sincerity in myself as analyst.

That is why I chose as my title "A long meeting with Bion"—for a meeting involves not only a coming together, but also a separation. If the meeting has been fruitful, however, separation does not mean that one is left all by oneself.

## References

Bleger, J. (2013). *Symbiosis and Ambiguity*. London: Routledge.
Neri, C., Correale, A., & Fadda, P. (Eds.) (1987). *Letture bioniane*. Roma: Borla.

CHAPTER THREE

# Non-analytic influences on the psychoanalytic theorizing of Wilfred Bion

*Ronald Britton*

This is an attempt to discuss influences from outside psychoanalysis on Bion's analytic theories. His theories were essentially based on his clinical experience but like everyone else he brought to it ideas he had about the world in general. He also experimented with how analytic findings could be formulated and communicated using models analogous to those in mathematics, such as his construction of "the grid" as a means of locating events occurring in analytic sessions. This is an application of a mathematical structure onto his analytic findings, not as a means of making them, but of recording them. However the grid exemplifies, and to some extent illustrates, his metapsychology. One could say that the move to producing a mathematical expression of psychoanalytic findings became for Bion an aspiration rather than an influence. There was, however, one mathematical theory that profoundly influenced his analytic approach in practice. This was Poincaré's theory of the nature of scientific discovery, namely his concept of "the selected fact", which became a cornerstone of Bion's psychoanalytic approach and advice for analytic technique.

Bion also used religious descriptions, as he did other myths, to illustrate his ideas on internal object relations and external group relations but I regard these as analogies rather than influences. The more subtle unspoken influence of his lifelong ambivalent relationship to the Protestant Christianity of his childhood is evident in his thinking about the superego. He used words from remembered hymns, the Bible, and the Anglican Book of Common Prayer in his discourse as he did with poetry such that of Milton. One could say that the language of these very familiar sources entered into his imagery and therefore influenced the shape of his concepts.

Also remembered as sardonic commentaries on facile devotionalism and the hypocrisy of any establishment are the skeptical, satirical words the troops of the First World War substituted for those of familiar hymns or traditional ballads. "Onward Christian Soldiers", for example, was transformed and the following words sung to the familiar hymn tune:

> Forward Joe Soap's army, marching without fear
> with our old Commander safely in the rear.
> He boasts and skites from morn till night
> And thinks he's very brave
> But the men who really did the job are dead and in their grave. (Chilton, 1963)

Bion acquired a belief that it was only those in the trenches who knew what war was like while those at HQ invented an imaginary version it. He applied this to psychoanalysis. As he says in the introduction to *Attention and Interpretation*, "I doubt if anyone but a practicing psychoanalyst can understand this book ... because he ... has the opportunity to experience ... what I in this book can only represent by words ... designed for a different task" (Bion, 1970, p. 1). His time in the army in the Second World War seems to have confirmed his scepticism about the amateurism of high command in contrast to the professionalism of veteran soldiers. His time in the First World War not only left him emotionally battered, it also gave him an awareness of the crucial difference between learning from experience and fanciful theorizing, and that entered into all his thinking.

### The experience of the First World War (1914–1919)

In January 1916, at the age of eighteen, Wilfred Bion joined the "Inns of Court Officer Training Corps" as a volunteer; from there he became a newly fledged officer in the 5th Tank Battalion (subsequently known as 5th Royal Tank Regiment). This is his description of his officer training: "Schoolboys of all ages playing soldiers rehearsing for the real thing, but never learning that war and yet more terrible war is normal, not an aberrant disaster" (Bion, 1986, p. 113). He begins here the thread he follows of the distinction between amateurism and professionalism throughout his service in two wars and on into his ideas on the profession of psychoanalysis. The contrast between the expectant idea of something and the reality of its experience is the theme of the part of his autobiography, *The Long Weekend 1897–1919*, devoted to his account of that most brutal of wars. Sir Arthur Bryant said of this: "The part about the war is amongst the greatest and most terrifying I have read about the 1914–1918 war. It is a very great piece of literature" (Bion, 1986). I agree with this; reading and re-reading it compels one to share the emotions that accompanied the events. He wrote this between 1968 and 1970 after he had moved to California; he had available to him the "diary" (later published as *War Memoirs 1917–1919*) that he wrote in the immediate aftermath of the war, plus a piece he wrote in 1958 prompted by travelling through Amiens on holiday, which remained unfinished. I find the autobiographical version written in 1968 the most useful, as he wrote it with hindsight after years of practicing analysis, and though he follows the earlier detailed account from the contemporaneous diary the later version is interlaced with commentary. In this sense it is rather like his book *Second Thoughts* in which he publishes his germinal clinical papers and his commentary on them.

He prefaces his autobiography with a characteristic statement. "In this book my intention is to be truthful ... the most I can claim is to be relatively truthful ... I leave it to be understood that by truth I mean aesthetic truth and psychoanalytic truth: This last I consider to be a grade of scientific truth. In other terms, I hope to achieve in part and as a whole the formulation of phenomena as close as possible to noumena" (Bion, 1986, p. 8). The idea that aesthetic truth is the basis of scientific theorizing he has taken from Poincaré: "The most useful combinations are precisely the most beautiful, I mean those that can most charm that special sensibility that all mathematicians know …" (Poincaré, 1952, p. 59).

Bion includes multifaceted psychic reality in this, including dreams. He wrote, "So I slept and I had a dream. I woke just as [in the dream] I was about to go into battle; it was unnerving to find that I was … The dream was grey, shapeless; horror and dread gripped me. I could not cry out, just as now, many years later, I can find no words. Then I had no words to find: I was awake to the relatively benign terrors of real war. Yet for a moment I wished it was only a dream. In the dream I must have wished it was only a war" (Bion, 1986, p. 237). Here I think we have the genesis of his notion of nameless dread, and it is the namelessness of the terror in the dream that makes the identifiable terror of the battle field seem "relatively benign". Somewhat similarly he compares the nightmare that follows him for years after the battle of Ypres—Wipers as the soldiers called it—with his daytime memory of it. Ypres was a morass of mud in which soldiers literally sank and perished and tanks were hopelessly bogged down. At the heart of it was a stream, the Steinbeck, across which Bion and other tank commanders were supposed to facilitate a crossing. "Where was the Steinbeck", he asked a soldier who, grinning, "pointed down to the quagmire where we stood, so that was the Steinbeck" (ibid., p. 126). Later in Oxford when the war was over "night after night I found myself on my belly clinging by my toes and fingers to a glistening slope at the bottom of which was a raging torrent—the dirty trickle of the Steinbeck" (ibid., p. 211). The tanks did indeed get stuck and were obliterated by shellfire. Ypres remained for Bion an exemplar of unrealistic planning and collusive denial by all involved, where a clear blue line on a map represented an evident, bottomless, muddy reality. The psychic elaboration of this disastrous attempt to cross the Steinbeck then became an internal trauma invading his dreams and shaping his expectations. He continued to fear meeting yet another Steinbeck again, in another place, under another name, even when dry terrain and good tank conditions existed, right through to the end of the war.

The battle of Ypres exemplified what he called amateurism, a quality he despised in military situations where professionalism was needed. He saw himself, and even more he saw the staff officers who planned but did not engage at the front, as schoolboy amateurs in uniform facing a professional enemy. "I was impelled to prove my courage—the lack of it being as I thought my main defect. This erroneous idea was and still is generally held" (ibid., p. 201). He contrasted the famously gallant Rupert who commanded the Royalist cavalry in the English Civil war with his opponent Cromwell who was, Bion said, "temperamentally a professional … a farmer he had learned in his contact with the real forces of nature that there is no substitute for discipline" (ibid., p. 200). Bion had been recommended for the highest award of VC and was actually given the DSO and the Légion d'Honneur for bravery in those battles, but he felt they created a burden of unrealistic expectation based on a phantasy about his courage that he did not share.

Of his actual courage as judged by others there is an objective account in *The History of the Royal Tank Regiment*. "Some of the tank men fought on when dismounted. A striking example was that of Lt. W. R. Bion who, when his tank was knocked out, established an advanced position at an Agerman trench with his crew and some stray infantry, and then climbed back on the roof of his tank with a Lewis gun to get better aim at an opposing machine-gun. When the

Germans counter-attacked in strength he kept them at bay until his ammunition ran out and then continued to fight with the use of an abandoned German machine-gun, until a company of Seaforths (infantry) came up. Its commander was soon shot through the head, whereupon Bion temporarily took over the company. He was put in for the VC and received the DSO."

Implicit in this account are several factors that Bion believed in and which remained basic beliefs in other spheres of his activity such as medicine and psychoanalysis. They would include duty as something transcending pleasure and disregarding fear; the role of leader being an unchosen responsibility; the need to apply pre-existing principles to new situations in concert with the necessity for improvisation. These he would include in his formula for the professionalism of a psychoanalyst, learnt, as Trotter would say, as an "apprentice" in a "Practical Art".

In speaking of these things in his "autobiography" it is clear he is referring to practicing psychoanalysis as much as practicing war. In battle he says, "How does one decide what is a good idea and what is a daft idea? The answer is that one does not decide if one can help it these things in war. They are decided in peace, formulated in training manuals, enforced by orders. Such is the perversity of the human animal that these prudent dispositions … are [sometimes] erected into rigid barriers as a defence against thought" (ibid., p. 204).

Here we see the idea reproduced in his teaching and in the grid, that a concept can be used for purposeful, appropriate action (E6) or a concept can be used to stifle thought and prevent realization (F2).

His experience of that war informed his later judgment about analysis. One needs discipline, one needs theories, one needs to learn procedure, but they must not be a substitute for experience. His scorn for the staff officers who pontificated about action whilst playing no part in it and having no experience of its reality has its counterpart in his insistence on analytic practice being the only way to theory. In the military world the ultimate test of theory is action in battle, and the only place where that is real is at the front and not in Command HQ. Later he was to write in his notebook … "the conviction has been borne in on me by the analysis of psychotic or borderline patients. I do not think such a patient will ever accept an interpretation, however correct, unless he feels that the analyst has passed through this emotional crisis as a part of the act of giving the interpretation" (Bion, 2014, p. 279). It suggests that it is not just learning from experience that is necessary but also that suffering experience is necessary to validate witness.

He would later use another finding about leadership to understand transference in analysis. Two junior officers sought acceptance from their tank crews by a familiarity that seemingly abolished rank difference. "Osprey and Cokran had been alike in this; they did not seem able to feel with their men and yet retain their awareness that although they were men … they were paid to be gods, very minor gods perhaps but gods" (Bion, 1986, p. 236). In other words, the officers, like the analyst, failed to accept the reality of the transference. He realized in the war that how one is regarded does not depend on how one feels about oneself. He makes clear that though he was an officer he felt far from being superior in knowledge, or in fearless confidence, but that his men necessarily did see him that way, and *needed* to be able to project on to him the qualities of the figure they were disposed to believe he was. Failing the acceptance of that projection they would be unbounded and anticipate the intoxication of anarchic freedom but also be deprived of the totem that offered security in the face of danger. Bion well understood as an officer and later as an analyst the need to accept the imputed identity projected, however discordant it might be with one's subjective reality. However, when this is in a positive transference, it is important that the analyst should not see the proffered divine status as merited or realistic. Analysts find it easy to realize this in the case of negative transference; less easy in the case of positive transference. Once he had been decorated with the DSO, Bion realized that the Army's need to believe in heroes meant that the perception of him by others would be completely out of step with his self-perception and that there was nothing he could do about that. His fear was that he might be driven to act out their phantasies of his courage by doing something stupidly brave.

### The profound influence of Wilfred Trotter

When he was at Oxford after the First World War Bion was influenced by his tutor, the philosopher H. J. Paton. Paton was a particular authority on and enthusiastic follower of Kant, and Bion's acceptance of a distinction between the perceived object and the noumenon, "thing in itself", would have come readily to him when he needed it for his metapsychology later. However, I think the most influential figure in his intellectual development was somone he met when, in order to become a psychoanalyst, he did his medical training at University College Hospital. Wilfred Trotter by this time, around 1930, was celebrated as a surgeon and pioneer in neurosurgery. As a young man in 1908 and 1909 he had written two of the earliest papers on group psychology that were later included and expanded in a book *Instincts of the Herd in Peace and War* (1915). The clear influence of these on Bion's ideas on groups is evident. Bion writes in his notebook that there must be an additional component to establish the identity of things that seem constantly conjoined; this was previously called God by Descartes or Berkeley, but Bion says, "[it] is none other than a social component, *Vox populi, vox dei*, of the instinctual equipment" (Bion, 1992). When he writes this he is simply reproducing Trotter; the voice of the herd is the voice of God or at least the Church. He writes this without acknowledgement. The lack of acknowledgement of Trotter's ideas in his writings is puzzling when one reads Bion's autobiography where Trotter figures as a hero. Even the celebrated phrase "learning from experience"', which becomes one of his book titles, is borrowed from Trotter, and there are many others. Nuno Torres also comments on this surprising omission of references to Trotter in his bibliography of Bion's sources (Torres & Hinshelwood, 2013, p. 8). Bion's acquaintance with Trotter was a personal one and he may have heard various fundamental comments on the influence of group consensus, the relationship between attention and retention, the misuse of reason to resist new ideas, the nature of intuition in clinical practice, and so on in Trotter's addresses to students as well as perhaps personal conversation. It is as if he prioritized Trotter's teachings as a primer of his own personal apprenticeship, as a private influence in his own development, not one gleaned from publications shared with other readers.

It is not only Bion who adopted one of Trotter's original ideas and made it his own in the realm of psychoanalysis. The concept of rationalization was credited by Freud to Ernest Jones as his one original contribution, but it was a particularly strong idea of Trotter's in his discussion of reason as a defense against any new discovery. This, Jones acknowledged in the obituary he wrote on Trotter. He also wrote that he was introduced to the importance of Freud's writings by

Trotter, who was his medical mentor, in the first years of the twentieth century, when hardly a soul in England knew of their existence.

There are two particular human propensities, to which Trotter drew attention, that result from "herd instinct". One is that, "impulses derived from herd feeling will enter the mind with the value of instincts … they may give to any opinion whatever the characters of instinctive belief" (Trotter, 1915, p. 30). The other is the instinctual nature of altruism: whether it can be called noble or compulsive, it is at root instinctive.

Whenever new observations, experiences, or ideas contradict herd-shared beliefs they are resisted and the old group-based assumptions are rationalized by more or less elaborate intellectual justifications. Bion's description of basic assumptions in groups was clearly influenced by Trotter who also insisted that altruism is instinctual in man as a herd animal and is not as other psychologists, such as Lester Ward (1903), had suggested derived from enlightened self-interest. Trotter's view chimes perfectly with the centrality of depressive anxiety, guilt, and reparation in Klein's theorizing whereas in Freud it is—as it was for the American psychologists of the time—secondary to self-regard. Freud was incredulous at the Christian doctrine of "love thy neighbor as thyself", whereas Trotter, Klein, and Bion saw it as natural, like Auden, who used the term Agape for this as opposed to Eros. Bion described there being a conflict between "socialism" and "narcissism", meaning altruism versus self-regard. In the realm of knowledge, Trotter saw the conflict as being between the conservative, herd instinct and individual radicalism, in the search for new discoveries. Bion later described this under the rubric of "the Mystic and the Group".

Bion's conviction of the need for "professional" competence above all was derived from his war experiences, although it would have found new justification when he encountered Trotter's views on the nature of medical education. Trotter advanced the view that medicine in the twentieth century had two essential identities; one was as an applied science derived from experimental work, and the other as a practical art learnt at the bedside. Medicine, he said, "Must be classed with what we may call the practical arts, like those of the farmer, the builder, the blacksmith, the joiner, or the sailor" (Trotter, 1941, p. 93). He went on: "An applied science carries on its tasks by the application of ascertained principles to particular cases … a practical art has no complete and sure foundation of ascertained principles. Its possessions are made up of separate and fragmentary conquests from the unknown … in a practical art satisfactory action is judged not wholly by its object being attained, but by whether the artist followed the established rules … In a true applied science failure can be due only to ignorance, in a practical art … success as a sole test for correct action is obviously impracticable. To adopt for a practical art the standard of attainment applicable to an applied science is not to improve its status, it is only to convert it into quackery" (ibid., pp. 94–95). In the current field of medicine in the twenty-first century there is a crisis between doctors and patients about patients being treated as if they were only the singular representatives of general, known diseases. One could say that applied science is flourishing but the practical art of medicine is languishing. Trotter's distinction clearly applies even more to psychoanalysis than to medicine, as the proportion of practical art to applied science is even greater. One can see that Bion was keen to increase the proportion of applied science to practical art in psychoanalysis whilst adhering to the methods of the latter gained through apprenticeship and experience.

## Philosophy and science

Bion was impressed by philosophical writers such as Russell and Whitehead who turned to mathematics for logical reasoning, and particularly Braithwaite whose particular subject was the philosophy of science. He was reading Braithwaite's *Scientific Explanation: A Study of the Function of Theory, Probability and Law in Science* in 1958 at the time he was writing "Attacks on linking" but it is in his subsequent books, starting with *Learning from Experience* in 1962, that Braithwaite's influence is most evident. Bion's comment on reading Braithwaite says a great deal about his developing rigor in accounts of analytic experience: "I cannot help thinking as I read this book ... what a terrible lot of bilge I have read in my time. There has always been a certain amount, too much I think, of gullibility about me, and it makes me swallow a lot of nonsense ... I wish I could feel more confident that I wouldn't add to the flood of rot but of course if I did I would probably lack the necessary self-criticism" (Bion, 1985, pp. 123–124).

What Bion took from Briathwaite was his idea that a scientific theory is a general deductive system, which has particular observable consequences, which can only be seen in practice. The SDS (Scientific Deductive System) itself should be in the form of a mathematical calculus. The measurable consequences of the generality can be verified only in particular examples; they can negate the SDS by being contrary to expectation but they can never prove it. The SDS provides a means of working with these abstractions as formulae without needing particulars to illustrate them, as in the mathematics of theoretical physics.

One can see how Bion, constantly thinking about how to relate particular experience to general hypotheses, is drawn to Braithwaite. It inspired his creation of the "grid". In this he ingeniously turns this idea upside down so that the basic data comes first, to be followed by its organization into a model which in turn, in some unrealizable time, would become a Scientific Deductive System.

This is the heart of Braithwaites exposition of scientific conceptualisation. "As the hypotheses of increasing generality rises, the concepts with which the hypotheses are concerned cease to be the properties of hints which are directly observable and instead become 'theoretical' concepts—atoms, electron, fields of force, genes, unconscious mental processes—which are connected to the observable facts by complicated logical relationships" (Braithwaite, 1946). His reading of Braithwaite in 1958 crystallized Bion's attempt to encourage psychoanalysts to move their theorizing upwards from their observation of empirical events through a classifiable phenomenology to a definatory scientific hypothesis (SDS), which is a general proposition that converges all the things of a certain sort. Readers of Bion will recognize this process in his discussion of what he called "psychoanalytic objects"; these are not what are meant by internal objects in Kleinian clinical descriptions of internal processes. Bion meant the abstractions to which psychoanalysts attribute general or even universal identity based on the familiar phenomena of psychoanalytic practice, such as "transference", for example, or the Oedipus complex. This took further something I think he learnt from Trotter, that "number is the only quality that can be completely abstracted from objects, so that the experience of number within the mind is just as valid as the experience of number attached to external objects" (Trotter, 1941, p. 145). For Bion, this is a validation of psychoanalytic thinking if it can be achieved, and it illuminates the reasons for his search for a system of notation that would be a true abstraction of actual experience in analysis. An example of this is his use of the terms "factors" and "functions" in their mathematical senses, meaning that one is linked to the other permanently by a mathematical formula, such as $x = y-1$. This is easily confused with the biological sense of the term, as in "the function of the heart is to pump blood". His conflation of these meanings by his use of the same word deliberately seems to satisfy a wish he has to find a joining point for two different systems of thought, one mathematical, the other physiological/psychological. It is as if he is answering an imaginary challenge from his former mentor to find a way of producing abstractions from primary data—in his case the primary data of psychoanalytic practice that is as undistorted as mathematics. As a system of notation, Bion's formulas and numerical analogies are useful models but they are not mathematical and they do not meet Trotter's claim that only numbers can make representation correspond exactly with reality. This means that psychoanalysis remains, as yet, in large part a practical art from which science can gain a great deal, as did physiological science from medical practice, but only when observation is accurate, learning is from experience, and some method of record is devised that does not distort the primary data. This is what most concerned Bion in his later period.

Bion made the point that some of the theoretical issues in philosophy are actually practical matters for psychoanalysts. In particular, the relationship between the models of the world constructed by, first the brain, and then the mind, and the unknowable "thing itself", which is only graspable by the senses and represented by the model they create. His thoughts about this were intensified by his analyses of psychotic thinking and fortified by his reading of such books as Heisenberg's *Physics and Philosophy* (1958) and Braithwaite's *Scientific Explanation* (1946). These, together with Henri Poincaré's much earlier book *Science and Method*, influenced his thinking in the late 1950s. Poincaré's writings on "The selection of facts" (1952, Ch.r 1) led Bion to formulate its application to psychoanalytic practice as "the selected fact", which, intuitively chosen, made sense of multiple connections, including facts previously known but not integrated.

The analogy with probability and hypothesis, now at the heart of quantum physics, heartened him by telling him that psychoanalysts are not alone in dealing with "hypotheses about hypotheses about hypotheses", which was his own description of psychoanalytic theorizing. The "uncertainty principle" was fairly new when he read about it and it generated excitement outside physics, particularly amongst those longing for scientific uncertainty in order to reinstate their all too certain hypotheses about the world. If it had been named more accurately as the "indeterminacy principle" it may not have been so exciting. Now that we have become accustomed to its exact mathematical formulation relating the degree of uncertainty in measuring velocity when accurately measuring momentum and vice versa, it does not cast such a wide shadow of obscurity as it seemed to then. As Heisenberg wrote, "The structure of space and time which had been defined by Newton as the basis of his mathematical description of nature ... corresponded very closely to the use of the concepts space and time in daily life ..." We know now that this impression is created in daily life by the fact that the velocity of light is so very much higher than any other velocity occurring in practical experience; but this restriction was not realized at that time. And even if we know the restriction now we can scarcely imagine that the time order of events would depend on their location.

The philosophy of Kant, later than Newton, drew attention to the fact that the concepts of space and time belong to our relation to nature, not to nature itself; that we could not describe nature without using these concepts; they are "'a priori' ... and not derived from experience" (Heisenberg, 1958, p. 80). The theory of relativity and the quantum revolution in physics broke the barrier and enabled us mathematically, but only mathematically, to transcend these natural *a priori* concepts of space, time, and cause and effect. But when it did so it enlarged the gap between the world of daily life and the more accurate description of the physical phenomena that underlie the tangible experience created by our senses, which have been adapted, by evolution, to the world we live in, on a particular, small, planet.

Once one accepts that belief, not factual knowledge, is the bed-rock of psychic reality; once one accepts that probability is all we can expect, and that we habitually treat probability as certainty; when we realize that we live in a universe where random facts nevertheless produce a regular pattern, as described in chaos theory; when all this is understood, the world, as described, is changed. Even so, everyday analysis seems much the same as before. Hume was the first to draw attention to the fact that these *a priori* suppositions, such as cause and effect, were not logically justifiable. But Hume also spoke about the resumption of the "natural beliefs" he shared with everybody else once he was outside his philosophical study and he made clear that ordinary sanity depended on being able to do so. The psychotic patient may not be able to do this and may lack natural beliefs, which means he lives in a precarious or bizarre world. Bion was much influenced by Hume and adopted his notion of "constantly conjoined" (Hume, 2007) to describe phenomena always found together, without commitment to the notion that one is the cause of the other. There is a thread running through Bion's writings that suggests the analyst should eschew causality and address "what it is" and not "why it is" when interpreting the patient's psychic reality.

I think Bion's advocacy of the analyst living with uncertainty in analytic sessions has been rightly and virtuously influential; however, it should not be confused with the advocacy of uncertainty in all things as if it is a superior sort of wisdom. Bion's emphasis on the recognition of unashamed ignorance when it is appropriate is not an idealization of not knowing, but a first step towards knowledge.

## *References*

Bion, W. R. (1970). *Attention and Interpretation*. London: Tavistock.
Bion, W. R. (1985). *All My Sins Remembered: Another Part of a Life* (Ed. F. Bion). Abingdon: Fleetwood Press.
Bion, W. R. (1986). *The Long Week-End 1897–1919* (Ed. F. Bion). London: Free Association.
Bion, W. R. (2014). *Cogitations*. In: C. Mawson (Ed.), *The Complete Works of W. R. Bion, Vol XI*. London: Karnac.
Braithwaite, R. B. (1946). *Scientific Explanation*. Cambridge: CUP.
Chilton, C. (1963). *Oh, What a Lovely War*. Musical play. Stratford East Theatre, London.
Heisenberg, W. (1958). *Physics and Philosophy*. London: Penguin, 1989.
Hume, D. (2007). *An Enquiry Concerning Human Understanding* (Ed. P. Millican). Oxford: OUP.
Poincaré, H. (1952). *Science and Method* (Trans. F. Maitland). New York: Dover.

Torres, N., & Hinshelwood, R. D. (Eds.) (2013). *Bion's Sources: The Shaping of His Paradigms*. Hove: Routledge.
*The History of the Royal Tank Regiment.* www. Forces War Records .co.uk
Trotter, W. (1915). *Instincts of the Herd in Peace and War*. London: The Scientific Book Club.
Trotter, W. (1941). *The Collected Papers of Wilfred Trotter*. Oxford: OUP.
Ward, F. L. (1903). *Pure Sociology: A Treatise on the Origins and Spontaneous Development of Society.* New York: Macmillan.

CHAPTER FOUR

# W. R. Bion: his cultural, national, and historical background, and its impact on his thinking

*Robert Snell*

For a British person of a certain class and generation living in 2015, the social and cultural world into which Bion was born can feel both archaic and strangely familiar. It invites satire and post-colonial unease, alongside a lingering, respectful fascination. Bion came into being and consciousness in India while the Raj was at its height. His vivid accounts of his childhood in the Punjab are, however, anything but nostalgic imperial celebration. They tend rather towards witty, pained satire, of himself and the unfathomable world of grown-ups around him.

Childhood, he wrote, was a "horrible, bogey-ridden demon-haunted time" (Bion, 1985, p. 76). His memoirs evoke awesome unknowns: "Arf Arfer", for example, a terrible figure associated with the sound of grown-up laughter and the first words of the Lord's Prayer; a live goat kid in a tiger trap; the roars of a tiger, whose mate had been shot in a big-game hunt, reverberating through the earth over the course of two long nights. Bion's passage from India left him with a lifelong, Forster-like sense of an irreconcilable tension, between dark, atavistic forces, and the equally insistent claims of gentility. Over fifty years after the event he still recalled the question discreetly put to him by a lady in genteel Cheltenham, where he was on leave from the trenches in 1918: "What was it like … when you drove your tank over people?" (Bion, 1986, p. 266). Whether it was Kleinian hindsight that led him to such memories or such experiences that later drew him to Klein, innate sadism, necessary mourning, and inevitable incomprehension are in the foreground of his accounts of his world.

The consciously held values of his family and national culture undoubtedly also left their marks. As well as an excellent shot, Bion's father was a civil engineer in Indian Public Works, in irrigation, a vital profession, particularly for the agricultural Punjab, and one held in high esteem by Rudyard Kipling (Bion, 1991, p. 227). Bion's father also served as part-time secretary to the Indian Congress; he was "a trusted administrator deeply identified with the Indian scene" (Bléandonu, 1994, p. 10; Lyth, 1980, p. 269), and this spirit of public service and responsibility is evident, albeit tinged with ambivalence, in Bion's later life, in, for example, his presidency of the British Psycho-Analytic Society in the early 1960s. It is the wider background to his conviction that functioning, work-based groups are possible.

Bion's paternal grandfather had been "some sort of missionary in India" (Bléandonu, 1994, p. 8); a premium on truthfulness and an intolerance of lies and deception crucially fed into his psychoanalytic theory of mind and its development. The Bion family's Huguenot ancestry (Bion, 1991, p. 219; Bléandonu, 1994, p. 7 & note 1) might certainly have predisposed him to the independence of thought, against the odds, which was characteristic of him. The motto on the family crest, *Nisi dominus frustra*, is echoed in Psalm 127, "Except the Lord build the house, they labour in vain that build it: except the Lord keep the city, the watchman waketh but in vain", which might loosely translate or paraphrase as Freud's "the ego … is not even master in its own house, but must content itself with scanty information of what is going on unconsciously in its mind" (Freud, 1916, p. 285). Truly independent thought of the kind Bion manifested must have humble regard to the mysteries of thought's own limitations.

The mores and customs of his era and class required him to be sent, at the age of eight, 9000 kilometers away to England and boarding school, an experience which must have been traumatizing. As if to mark a caesura that was historical as well as personal, Bion recalled in his seventies his mother's elaborate Edwardian hat, "like some curiously wrought millinery cake", disappearing beyond a high hedge as she left him on his first day (Bion, 1986, p. 33). A multicultural boy Wilfred Ruprecht Bion would have been, in the eyes of his peers: Anglo-Indian with a French surname and German middle name, a heterogeneous group in one small person. Like his near contemporary the German-Jewish exile S. H. Foulkes, Bion's social identity was established with the help of a public school and sporting convention: surname preceded by initials, W. R. (see too, Winnicott, D. W., etc.). Sporting prowess, in swimming and rugby (he was a champion swimmer, a "half-blue", at Oxford, and played for the famous Harlequins rugby team in the early 1920s), helped Bion sustain a sense of identity externally, at times when internally he had little access to a feeling of coherence or stability: exo-skeleton as emergency sense of self. At the same time he discovered that games were enjoyable in themselves and could be played merely "for the sake of the game" (Bion, 1986, p. 93); that it was possible, in other words, in spite of surrounding taboos and constraints, simply to *like* something.

Bion was a boarder at Bishops Stortford School in Hertfordshire, north east of London, for nine years, from 1906 to 1915; the school had been founded in 1868 and it still exists. Its social purpose, like that of other British public schools, was to prepare the sons of upper-middle-class families for life in the professions (church, law, armed services, finance, business, or the domestic or colonial civil service); the public school system aimed to foster future leaders. Bishops Stortford was a non-denominational Christian establishment, and as such reinforced the rather unspecific and undogmatic Christianity that Bion brought with him from his parents and which in a certain sense he never lost; he was certainly aware of being seen as one of the Christian or "Pi" set by fellow officers in World War One. Religion provided one form of social cohesion within the closed, all-male school community; it was a bulwark against sex. For school was "a kind of gigantic sexual pressure cooker" (Bion, 1986, p. 77). If Bion eventually and painfully overcame his guilt about "wiggling", "the only redeeming thing in our lives" (Bion, 1986, p. 47), and his anxiety around women, a respect for sex's profound power and mystery remained deeply inscribed in his analytic thinking.

Later he *almost* seemed to attribute some of his independence to the experience of being sent away to school. He wrote in a letter to one of his children (probably his son Julian): "All my memories of homesickness are of it as the most ghastly feeling I ever knew—a sort of horrible sense of impending disaster without any idea what it was or even any words in which to express it ... But I believe it is from one's ability to stand having such feelings and ideas that mental growth eventually comes" (Bion, 1991, p. 173). Through his friendships, with the family of one friend in particular, he was confronted with the cold rigidities of social class, although he could not yet really make sense of this: "What I might have learned ... but did not, was that breeding is ruthless. The graces and civilities play like a beautiful iridescence on the surface when feelings are absent or in abeyance" (Bion, 1986, p. 75).

Cruelty was "embedded in the school system ... Masters and boys alike were caught in a web which we did not see even as we struggled to free ourselves". Who, he later wrote, could recognize danger in piety or patriotism, which could work to "bury the growth of personality", like a "disastrous cancer" affecting the morale of the whole school community (Bion, 1986, pp. 92–93, 85)? Bion came to understand the tragedy of his prep-school headmaster, whose wife had been sent away to a lunatic asylum, as paradigmatic of wider attitudes. "What was done to him by the laws of his time seems to me to be the outcome of the unspeakable cruelty of a nation dominated by a prep-school mentality" (Bion, 1986, p. 85). The idea must have been embryonic in him at the time, a thought waiting for a thinker: a dominant mentality can catch everyone in its web, a whole nation even, with insidiously destructive effects. It was an idea that became central to Bion's work, first with traumatized and demoralized officers at Northfield Hospital in World War Two, and subsequently to all his work with groups.

School did, however, also expose him to literature and its "unforgettable impact": to Ruskin, Milton, Virgil, Shakespeare, Keats, Shelley. Bion would not have been unusual among young British officers in having a copy of Palgrave's *Golden Treasury of English Songs and Lyrics* in his pocket in the First World War (Bion, 1991, p. 240); his love of poetry flourished at Oxford after the war. His psychoanalytic writing is rich in literary allusions and quotations, perhaps most famously from Keats, whose notion of "Negative Capability" was for Bion the most profound and succinct statement of the quality of attention necessary for the psychoanalyst. He met W. B. Yeats before the war, and throughout his life was moved by nature poets from Gerard Manley Hopkins to James Elroy Flecker (Bion, 1991, pp. 226, 230, 240); he enjoyed painting the Norfolk landscape. Late in his life—he was planning to revisit India but never did so—he was reading or rereading the *Mahābhārata* (Bion, 1991, p. 236).

The work of groping towards "words in which to express it", towards meanings which must ultimately remain only ever partially communicable, became central to his life, and not just his professional life (with Bion the distinction between private and professional can come to seem meaningless). Perhaps his early and most famous patient, Samuel Beckett, with whom he worked between 1933 and 1935, indirectly helped him find forms and courage for this (*Murphy*, Beckett's first, remarkable, novel, was started during the analysis and completed shortly after). Superficially, there are Beckettian echoes in Bion's prose, as here, for example, from one of his great papers of the 1950s, "Differentiation of the psychotic from the non-psychotic personalities" of 1957:

> "Nothing but filthy things and smells", he said. "I think I've lost my sight." … A handkerchief was disposed near his right pocket; he arched his back … A lighter fell out of his pocket. Should he pick it up? Yes. No, perhaps not. Well, yes. It was retrieved from the floor and placed by the handkerchief. Immediately a shower of coins spilled over the couch on to the floor. The patient lay still and waited. Perhaps, his gestures seemed to suggest, he had been unwise to bring back the lighter. It had seemed to lead to the shower of coins … (Bion, 1984, p. 53)

Are the echoes here perhaps of *Endgame*, which was first performed in London in 1957? In the end, the source of these echoes is not so much conscious or unconscious mimicry as a commitment shared by both writers to attend to the unknowable and ineffable, as it makes itself felt even, or especially, in mundane actions and gestures. It is what Bion termed O, which "cannot fall into the domain of knowledge or learning save incidentally", and then only "when it has evolved to a point where it can be known, through knowledge gained by experience, and formulated in terms derived from sensuous experience …" (Bion, 1984, p. 26).

Bion's insistence on finding "terms derived from sensuous experience" goes some way to accounting for the sheer evocative and metaphorical force of his memoirs. He never ceased needing to register in words the utterly lifelike strangeness of the world in which he had found and continued to find himself. In 1916, as a newly trained army officer, he encountered his first sinister, "immobilising" tank, from inside which came a "metallic hammering". Then a soldier emerged, "and the day sprang into life again". A single incident seems to open the doors to the preoccupations of a whole career: the frightening pull between inside and outside, human and mechanical, between a desire to "penetrate the secrecy" and an impulse to "get away"; finally an unbidden drive to celebrate signs of life (Bion, 1986, p. 115).

In many respects the teenage Bion had been well prepared for the very large group of the British army by his experiences to date, at least in so far as they had maintained him, as he was to put it himself, in a state of ignorance. If we were for a moment to adopt his mature analytic practice of switching vertices, shifting our point of view, we might want to consider the tanks the nineteen-year-old Bion commanded in north-eastern France in 1917 from the other side's perspective, for example that of a young army telephonist such as Siegfried Heinrich Fuchs from Karlsruhe, who was at the French front at the same time. Interestingly, alongside the memoir of his army experiences that Bion produced for his parents shortly after the war, there was a collection of his photographs, including a picture of a tank crossing a trench, terrifyingly seen from underneath, as the defenders of the trench might have seen it (Bion, 1997, fig. 36, facing p. 119); his ability to shift viewpoints and "see the reverse as well as the obverse of every situation" (Bion, 1989, p. 86 *et seq.*), which he came to regard as mandatory for analytic practice and emotional growth, was starting to develop, in spite or perhaps because of his traumas.

He had been awarded a DSO, a Distinguished Service Order, in 1917 after the battle of Cambrai, the first-ever battle in which tanks were successfully deployed in large numbers; a Victoria Cross, the highest British military decoration, had been mooted. An extract from

Bion's immediately post-war account of his action in this battle gives a flavor of the constricted emotional and literary range of the war-ravaged ex-public-schoolboy:

> Richardson took a Lewis gun, loaded it and then flinging the door open tumbled out. He was hit through both legs doing it but opened fire and shut their gun up ... the enemy seemed to be opening fire on us from all sides, and we didn't quite know where they were. I was very excited at this time ... I decided the chief fire was coming from the wood in front from behind the wall. So I took my Lewis gun with two drums of ammunition ... and got on top of the tank behind the facine [sic]. From here I could see over the wall ... I fired into the wood over the fascine and saw the enemy begin to run about and clear out ... (Bion, 1997, p. 50) [A fascine was a large bundle of faggots carried on top of the tank for use in crossing trenches.]

This is matter-of-fact, muted, stunned, and in places touchingly school-boy- or child-like: Richardson "shut their gun up"; "I was very excited"; the enemy began "to run about and clear out". Another post-war account, by a former tank commander named Frank Mitchell, gives an idea of the way war experiences, then as now, tended to be framed for ease of public consumption, and thus of a cultural mindset within which Bion might have been expected to locate his experiences:

> Private Richardson ... did not hesitate. Seizing his Lewis gun, he courageously jumped out of the door, and, flopping to the ground amid a hailstorm of bullets, got his gun into action ... Lieutenant Bion then re-opened fire with his Lewis gun ... One enemy machine-gun, in a hidden position, annoyed him so persistently that Bion crawled out of the trench ... climbed up to the top of the tank, and sheltering behind the huge fascine, blazed away until the nuisance had abated. (Mitchell, 1936, p. 48)

This more "gung-ho", *Boy's Own Paper* narrative (Ha! That showed 'em!) appeared in a chunky volume of 1936 called *Fifty Amazing Stories of the Great War*, with stirring line illustrations; this, as far as I know, is the first time it has been noted in the context of a study of Bion. Bion was never to lose a sense that he was a fraud, expected to be and to have been brave when brave was the last thing he felt he was. Here is his own mature account, from the autobiographical *The Long Week-End*, which is informed by an ever-present awareness of this predicament and of his mental state at the time, as well as of the real squalor of war:

> Richardson tumbled out with only one bullet through his thigh ... My utter ignorance of fighting, as contrasted with the professional soldier's knowledge, was mercifully hidden from me. I could feel it, but I did not know it ... We were under fire, but I had not the slightest idea where the bullets were coming from ... Taking four drums of Lewis gun ammunition attached to my waist and a Lewis gun, I clambered clumsily onto the top of the tank and set up my gun under cover, as I thought, of the fascine ... I ... experienced none of the fear which might have served as a substitute for my common sense which was wholly lacking. I commanded a good view of the little copse ... this I proceeded methodically to spray. (Bion, 1986, pp. 163–164)

Bion finds a way of marrying painful self-awareness with the matter-of-factness of his original account, and the stiff-upper-lip irony, the phoney, suave understatement, of the 1930s Mitchell version. This he deftly subverts: instead of "blazing away" at an enemy who "annoyed him so persistently … until the nuisance had abated", he banally proceeds "methodically to spray" a little wood.

A whole speculative essay, not entirely sympathetic to Kleinian practice, might be written about Bion's tanks and the extent to which they may have shaped his clinical thinking. These very early Vickers machines, bizarre objects indeed, were designated "male" or "female" depending on their armaments; although Bion did not recall driving over anyone, it was a standard tactic for the tank commander to direct his driver to steer, like a good Kleinian analyst, as straight as possible (and at agonisingly low speed) towards the source of aggression. As a metaphor for the risks of working blindly in the countertransference, and the courage or bloody-mindedness required for this, World War One British tank tactics could hardly be bettered. The bullets hitting the front of the tank told the occupants (the analyst's internal objects?) they were heading in the right direction; the idea was to keep going until the bullets stopped. While they could not penetrate, except through an inadvertently open observation flap, the enemy's bullets produced "splash"—little fragments of hot metal which flew about among the crew, who wore chain-mail masks, like medieval knights, for protection; inside the tank it was already stiflingly hot, from the huge engines, and full of fumes; tanks also tended to turn into balls of fire if directly hit by artillery shells.

The war exposed Bion for the first time to other social classes, to the Private Richardsons and Gunner Allens who figure in his memoirs; he also saw some more of the worst of the British upper class, and was witness to deteriorations of mind which were underway quite independently of the conditions of war. Among the military tasks that most taxed him emotionally, for many lives and the outcome of a battle might depend on it, was the work of triangulation: finding bearings in the dark, in fog or under bombardment, and laying directional tapes on the ground prior to tanks going into action, with all the mathematics required for this. Perhaps this worked its way through both to the tripartite structure of the basic assumptions, means by which the conductor seeks to orient himself in the fog and heat of the group, and to the algebra of the grid, with its similar bearings-finding function.

At Oxford Bion joined "… a pretty battered crowd of psychological wrecks just out of the war". The dons (professors) felt "'they [us] couldn't be expected to do very well after the strain of war'. Now I realise of course they were quite right … I have since only very slowly come to realise what a *very* long time it took me to recover". Thus he wrote in a family letter in 1973 (Bion, 1991, pp. 216–217). In all the scientific and emotional education that followed in the 1920s and 1930s, from Oxford, to medical school, to the Tavistock, to marriage and fatherhood, to the Institute of Psycho-Analysis, there is a sense of Bion feeling his way, blinking, sometimes stumbling very painfully. No doubt he shared with many of his contemporaries a need to find meaning in and somehow come to terms with the madness and trauma of unprecedented, mechanized slaughter, as well as the incomprehension of those who had not been part of it. How could anyone claim to know and understand? His insistence on the necessary modesty of psychoanalytic claims to "knowledge" paralleled a profound personal lack of self-confidence or self-importance, which he repeatedly asserted in his autobiographical writings. The experience of the First World War cannot but have pushed him towards a Kleinian conviction that we all float precariously on a sea of psychotic phantasy. As a student of the group, he could be left in no doubt that there are times when, as he is alleged to have said, "the circumstances [are not] right for thought" (cited in Symington, 1986, p. 278).

His culture and experiences certainly also left him hungry for thought, and open to a great range of intellectual stimuli. The philosopher H. J. Paton at Queen's College, Oxford got him interested in Kant; at University College Hospital, London, he worked closely with Wilfred Trotter, the author of *Instincts of the Herd in Peace and War*, and if Bion did not directly acknowledge the book's influence on him, Trotter's intellectual and personal example—Bion admired his ability to listen to his patients—certainly "took", just like Trotter's surgical skin grafts (Bion, 1991, p. 38). On the one hand, for Bion, was the ineffable and unknowable, Kant and of course Plato, whose philosophy was the essential ingredient for the evolution of the idea of O; on the other, pragmatism and robust, critical common sense. He was later to draw on Wittgenstein and precursors of the Vienna Circle such as Henri Poincaré and Gottlob Frege for the development of his own epistemology (Bléandonu, 1994, pp. 116–117; 187–192).

But we are, perhaps inevitably as Bion grows into maturity, straying into the territory of his intellectual rather than deeper cultural debts. The social composition of the psychoanalytic world he found in London in the 1930s and how this may have impacted on him would be a rewarding area of future study. How much might the Quakerism of John Rickman, his analyst between 1937 and 1939, have confirmed or reawoken in him some of the values of responsibility and truthfulness enshrined in his own religious background (another Quaker, Quainton, had been a close comrade and friend in the war)? Bion's French biographer, Gérard Bléandonu, is surely right to hint that Melanie Klein, with whom Bion entered analysis in 1945, would, through her own cultural upheaval and worked-through experiences, have appreciated the sufferings of his infantile self and been "unlikely to be hampered by his narcissistic and schizoid defences" (Bléandonu, 1994, p. 95).

Two final thoughts. When Bion returned to the army in the Second World War, his military superiors were generally (although not universally) uncomprehending or unsympathetic about what he was doing at Northfield. It seems possible that his laconic writing style may also have evolved as a response to this, as a means of protecting himself and his work from easy dismissal and malign projection. How might his late removal to California and his visits to South America further have shaped him? Or rather, to put the question another way, might they have offered a new kind of container within which he might take new shape? Perhaps this late change of air further allowed him to speak, with unsettling precision, as in *A Memoir of the Future* (Bion, 1991), of mystery and conflictual, creative multiplicity, above all his own.

## References

Bion, W. R. (1984). Differentiation of the psychotic from the non-psychotic personalities. In: *Second Thoughts: Selected Papers on Psycho-Analysis*. London: Karnac.
Bion, W. R. (1986). *The Long-Week-End 1897–1919: Part of a Life* (Ed. F. Bion). London: Free Association.
Bion, W. R. (1989). *Experiences in Groups and Other Papers*. London: Tavistock.
Bion, W. R. (1991). *A Memoir of the Future*. London: Karnac.

Bion, W. R. (1991). *All My Sins Remembered: Another Part of a Life & The Other Side of Genius: Family Letters* (Ed. F. Bion). London: Karnac.

Bion, W. R. (1997). *War Memoirs 1917–19* (Ed. F. Bion). London: Karnac.

Bléandonu, G. (1940). *Wilfred Bion: His Life and Works 1897–1979* (Trans. C. Pajaczkowska). London: Free Association.

Freud, S. (1916). *Introductory Lectures on Psychoanalysis. S. E., 16*: 243–463. London: Hogarth.

Lyth, O. (1980). Wilfred Ruprecht Bion (1897–1979). *International Journal of Psychoanalysis, 61*: 296–273.

Mitchell, F. (1936). The only way at Cambrai. In: *Fifty Amazing Stories of the Great War*. London: Odhams Press. First published in Mitchell, F. (1933). *Tank Warfare: The Story of the Tanks in the Great War*. London and Edinburgh: Thomas Nelson and Sons.

Symington, N. (1986). *The Analytic Experience: Lectures from the Tavistock*. London: Free Association.

CHAPTER FIVE

# "I shall be blown to bits": towards Bion's theory of catastrophic trauma

*Carole Beebe Tarantelli*

> "… life had now reached such a pitch that horrible mutilations or death could not conceivably be worse. I found myself looking forward to getting killed."
>
> —Bion, Diary, 1997a, p. 94

> "Heart ache, belly ache, shell-shock, death,
> Head wound, leg off, blinded, death,
> Rich man, beggar-man, hero, thief … OK?"
>
> —Bion, *The Long Week-End*, 1982, p. 224

While Bion almost never explicitly refers to trauma in the body of his theoretical work, the narration in his autobiographies of his experiences as a tank commander in World War One are accounts of a psychic catastrophe. The war was an experience of utter extremity, of continuous engulfment in what in *A Memoir of the Future* (1991) is called "subthalamic fear", a terror "so intense that verbal formulations are inadequate to do it justice" (p. 648). In one of his narrations of the battle of Amiens, referring to himself in the third person, he says that during that battle "even the very grasses seemed to scare the life out of him" (1997c, p. 290).

In the course of the years, Bion repeatedly narrated the catastrophe he underwent in the war. Almost immediately after his demobilization in 1918 he wrote a Diary (1997a), which was a detailed account of the war in the form of a letter to his parents. In 1958, after a silence of forty years, he wrote an unfinished narrative, "Amiens", after the train carrying him and his wife on vacation passed near the battlefield where he had fought in 1918. In 1972, after Francesca Bion had made a typescript of his youthful Diary, he wrote a "Commentary" in the form of a dialogue between "Bion" and "Myself".¹ He wrote an account of his life up through to the end of the war with a ferociously ironic title, *The Long Week-End* (1982), and a pitilessly self-critical account of the psychological aftermath of the war entitled *All My Sins Remembered* (1985). And he returned to the experience again and again throughout his last major work, *A Memoir of the Future* (1991).² The first book of the trilogy, *The Dream*, is set in the midst of a war in a future in which England has been invaded, defeated, and occupied. In this and the other two volumes, the accounts of the war inserted throughout the text are often drawn verbatim from the earlier autobiographies. And, as if to underline the extreme nature of his vision of experience, Bion ends the book with the words "Q. I must rush; I have a date to meet Fate. A. Bye-bye—happy holocaust" (p. 577).

In *The Long Week-end*, Bion recounts a terrible episode, which is an illustration of the fact that his war experience continued to necessitate narration. Before a battle, he unexpectedly encounters an old school friend, Bonsey, and as they are walking together towards the front, they hear "a groan from the mud in the distance; followed by a cry further off ... like marsh birds" (1982, p. 142), a rather pleasing sound. This "gentle chorus", however, was coming from wounded companions, who were lying abandoned in "the mud in the distance" (p. 142), unrescued and dying alone. "Shut up! Shut up! You noisy sods, you bleeding pieces of Earth", Bion apostrophizes them. "But they didn't; and they don't" (p. 143). In the autobiographies and *A Memoir of the Future*, Bion attempted to dream his war experience, but we might speculate with Bion Talamo (1997) that many episodes remained, not memories, but facts which it was nearly impossible for him to digest.³

From these accounts of his exposure to battle, it is evident that the effect on Bion[4] was catastrophic. In his 1919 Diary (1997a) he writes, "I found myself looking forward to getting killed" (p. 93). In the 1972 "Commentary" (1997b) on the battle of Amiens he wrote, "I never recovered from the survival of the battle of Amiens" (p. 209) and "I can still feel my skin drawn over the bones of my face as if it were the mask of a cadaver" (p. 204), a sensation he returned to twenty years later in *A Memoir of the Future* (1991, p. 281). In the chapter immediately following a horrific memory of falling into a shell-hole full of decomposed corpses, MYSELF comments, "He says the consistency of his mind never recovered" (p. 55). And towards the end of the book, P.A.[5] affirms that "nobody told me ... that war service would change utterly my capacity to enjoy life" (p. 508).

In fact, Bion makes the terrible and paradoxical affirmation that this immersion in death killed him. In *The Long Week-end* (1982), he writes, "they have a way of making people look so life-like, but really we are dead. I? Oh yes, I died—on August 8th 1918" (p. 265). In *A Memoir of the Future* (1991) one of the avatars of the author affirms, "I get shot at; I get killed; only I don't die" (p. 59), and another "I would not go near the Amiens-Roye road for fear I should meet my ghost—I died there" (p. 257). How are we to understand these affirmations? Of course, we can take Bion's assertion that he had died as a metaphor: it was as if he had died but he hadn't. This is the literal truth, but Bion used language with utter precision, and he does not say that he almost died, or that he felt as if he had died. He states that he died.

In *The Writing of the Disaster*, Blanchot (1986) provides a metaphor that expresses the paradox of the effect on the mind of catastrophic experience: it is experience which "ruins everything, all the while leaving everything intact" (p. 1), experience where "I disappear without dying (or die without disappearing)" (p. 119). Evidently, as Bion affirms in *Transformations* (1965), "The rule that a thing cannot both be and not be is inadequate" (p. 102).

If we view the body of the theory Bion began to publish nearly forty years after the end of the war against the backdrop provided by his literary representations of his war experience, his paradoxical feeling of being dead but also alive can be retrospectively interpreted as one of the points of origin of his thought: his theory was obligated by the necessity of understanding the simultaneous destruction and continuing in being of his psyche/soma. He states the question in *The Long Week-end* (1982): "there must have been few who did not, like me, wonder how anyone survived exposure to such hell" (p. 121). But he did survive, and, as he writes in *A Memoir of the Future* (1991), he was faced with the task of understanding how "those same dead bones gave birth to a mind" (p. 60).

As we know, Bion's theory began as an investigation of the psychotic part of the personality. In 1956 he explicitly states that, although psychosis "springs from an interaction between (i) the environment, and (ii) the personality" (1967, p. 37), he intends to ignore the environment. In this paper I will nevertheless argue that, read against the template of his literary representation of his experiences in the war, his theoretical discoveries can in part also be used to illuminate the intrapsychic mechanisms which come into existence following catastrophic psychic trauma.[6] And, we might suppose, this was part of a lifelong effort to work through his traumatic experiences.

In the first section of this paper, I will attempt to describe Bion's representation of catastrophic trauma as it is illustrated in his literary works. In the second, I will argue that Bion's analysis of the state of the mind during the explosion of psychosis in *Attention and Interpretation* (1970) can also be usefully seen as a metapsychology of catastrophic trauma. In the third, I will attempt to illustrate how the intrapsychic mechanisms he conceptualized in his theoretical works are relevant to his representation of extreme experience in his literary works.

### The phenomenology of catastrophic trauma: the autobiographies

> "How does a person know of ... pain so impalpable that its intensity, pure intensity, is so intense that it cannot be tolerated but must be destroyed even if it involves the murder of the 'anatomical' individual?"
>
> Bion, *A Memoir of the Future*, 1991, pp. 51–52

Bion's autobiographical narrations are tales of what Freud (1920) called "external trauma", the disastrous affirmation of the outside.[7] He climbs out of one of his tanks during a battle, and seconds later "its sides seemed to open like a flower, a sheet of flame shot above it, and there lay the tank with its sides bulged open and its roof gone ... It looked like the guts of some fantastic animal hanging out of a vast gaping wound" (1997c, pp. 253–254). All the men he had left inside were dead. The instantaneous destruction of the "protective shield" of forty tons of steel is a concrete illustration of the fact that "no protection [exists which is] more solid than a figment of the imagination" (1982, p. 130), and that safety is a "delusion" (1982, p. 131). As P.A.

says in *A Memoir of the Future* (1991), "we hoped that the ugly reality would not penetrate the joke armour-plate" (p. 396). "Imaginary security; imaginary aggression? Yet men died" (1982, p. 131).[8]

Bion's portrayal of his war experience in the autobiographies is a narration of an immersion in death, of life within death. In *The Long Week-end* (1982), a soldier called Broome, "pink, baby-faced and foul-mouthed", tells his companions that he had tripped over a bit of barbed wire and slithered into a shell-hole, "huge, filled with water. I didn't stop till I was up to my waist. It stank—full of arms and legs and blown-up bellies. I tell you, it was a kind of human soup" (p. 139). In *A Memoir of the Future,* Bion replays the memory, but here he attributes it to Captain Bion: "Boo-ootiful soup; in a shell-hole in Flanders Fields. Legs and guts … must 'ave been twenty [dead] men in there" (p. 53). By the war's end, he tells us, "not a single one of my personal friends was in existence" (1997b, p. 211), and many of these deaths happened before his eyes. He recounts giving instructions to a soldier "with a sturdy, cheerful demeanor" whose name was Smith: "while I was facing him he seemed to stop paying attention; his face became flabby and lifeless. It was peculiar to discover that the lifelessness of his expression was due to his being lifeless; he toppled forward onto me and slithered into the trench" (1982, p. 220). Later Bion and his companions attempted to give Smith a proper burial, but *rigor mortis* had set in, and "he seemed to have arms everywhere" (p. 221) so that his limbs kept popping out of his grave—a dead/alive soldier. Bion asks himself if Smith is "now qualified to be called only It?" (p. 221), but whatever he is now, he is clearly "an infernal nuisance" (p. 221). Smith has become a bizarre object.

The chance of survival, the experience of having missed death by seconds or by inches is a constant in the narrative: "a bullet had splattered, missing my head. I had not heard it or been aware" (1982, p. 132). After an intolerable number of days at the front, his company is relieved right before the attack at Mount Kemmel: "of the 84 men that relieved our 56, there escaped only one man" (1997a, p. 99). In the battle of Cambrai, "our company had lost almost two thirds of our officers and men, killed, in the one and a half hours from zero" (1982, p. 182). That Bion was not dead along with his companions was completely fortuitous. There was no reason why they died, and he did not.

The autobiographies depict subjection to the most primitive possible experience, that of utter helplessness, of the absolute inability to act to modify reality, of being trapped with nowhere to go except the grave. In his second reworking of his memory of the battle of Amiens (1997c), Bion recounts how he and his runner, a boy he calls Sweeting, are due at their rendezvous at Berle au Bois at 10.15, but they are under fire and take refuge in a shell hole near what seemed to be a metal track. Bion tries to think against the overwhelming sensorial stimuli of the enemy barrage, "the battering of thundering pressure of the wind of the explosions against his body" (p. 254). The self-deprecating thought which assaults his mind indicates that he has, as usual, judged the situation inadequately and has taken refuge in the most exposed position possible. "Surely you ought to know better than this. Have you not been told *never* to wait by a landmark" (p. 254, emphasis in original). He must move. "What are you waiting for?" But he is helpless. "The shell-fire is too heavy, I can't move … If I try to go forward out of the shelter of this hole, then I shall be blown to bits. I can't move" (p. 254). In *The Long Week-end* (1982), he recounts how, under fire in his first battle and trapped in his tank, he realizes that "we were very near the bursting point of a heavy shell" and hence instant death. But, again, he was helpless, immobilized: "I felt we should move; there was nowhere to go" (p. 130). Advancing meant death; retreating meant death; staying where they were meant death; leaving the tank meant death. Being trapped is an experience which is repeatedly present in the texts. The ability to modify frustration is an illusion.

Bion was also helpless to avoid disastrous orders from incompetent and arrogant commanders who sent their men to certain death, ordering the tanks to the front, not under the cover of darkness but in full daylight, where their inevitable destiny was destruction by enemy fire: "They were not orders; they were sentences of death" (1982, p. 253). In an hour, all the tanks were destroyed, and all the men who had been in them were dead.

What is more, the experience of battle is an assault on the mind by internal and external events with which it is *intrinsically* unable to deal. Beside the constant onslaught of "subthalamic fear" from within and the assault of the barrage from without, sensory experience in battle is an agglomeration of uninterpretable sensory impressions which cohere without the possibility of being decoded—like the terrifying "human soup" in the shell-hole "full of arms and legs and blown-up bellies" in Flanders Field (1982, p. 139). The terrain of the battle of Ypres was transformed by days of rain into an "ochreous slime, glistening, featureless, stretching for mile after pock-marked mile" (1982, p. 126), a devastated landscape made more terrifying by the fact that it had no discernable landmarks. Similarly the battlefield of Amiens was covered with a "great wall of fog" (1982, p. 247) so impenetrable that one of Bion's runners was swallowed up by it and disappeared. It was impossible for Bion to rely on the evidence of his senses; it was impossible for him to know where he was; everything was unrecognizable. The battlefield was a bizarre object; it was perceived as a thing in itself, leaving the soldier suspended in a timeless, formless, incomprehensible world. In other words, it was impossible to convert sense impressions of both internal and external events to alpha-elements. Verbal thought (and thus sanity, contact with reality, and the ability to learn from experience) depends on the ability of the alpha-function to transform raw emotional experiences into manageable psychic events. But these were experiences on which the mind could impose no truthful explanation, experiences which could not be stored and used in the future, experiences from which nothing could be learned.

Moreover, aspects of the physical world which had heretofore been ordered, solid, and structured are disarticulated in battle, and this betrayal of basic expectations for the physical world further undermines faith in the mind's ability to order the elements of sensory experience. For example, the battery of gunfire caused the forty-ton tank with which Bion "was familiar as a solid mass of steel" to shake continuously "like a wobbling jelly" (1982, p. 130). In the battle of Ypres, he has been ordered to take and hold Hill 40, and he needs to check his direction in order to orient his tank. Leaving the tank meant death, but it was impossible to orient his course from inside the tank: "each time I opened the flap at all widely, I found it difficult to make my fleeting glances cohere" (1982, p. 131).

Furthermore, descriptions of the battle presented by those who have not undergone it are completely irrelevant to the man who has. Before Bion's first battle, the section commander provides him with a map of the terrain they are to conquer and instructions as to his place in the battle plan. But the map's ostensible purpose, which was to orient tank commanders on the battlefield, was a purpose for which it was useless: Bion could find no discernable link between the signs on the map and the reality of the battlefield. "What the devil had [the map] to do with the mud in which we wallowed?" (1982, p. 132). Rather, if map-reading had a purpose, its use was "to meet the requirements of the fiction that we were going somewhere" (1982, p. 224). Furthermore, experience in battle was so intrinsically uninterpretable that "facts" and "experience" are unrelated: the official description of the battle for which Bion was awarded the Legion of Honour communicated a pseudo-meaning to everyone else which was irrelevant to the soldier who was receiving the award: "the citation had a curiously plausible resemblance to the 'facts', yet I could not believe that the battle I had experienced and the one cited were the same" (1982, p. 273). In other words, the map and the citation were a parody of the alpha-function; they served to impose a useless fictitious order on what remained an undecipherable agglomeration of elements.

The episode which Bion says killed him occurred during the battle of Amiens, and he recounted it in all of the war autobiographies and returned to it several times in *A Memoir of the Future*. In the account in *The Long Week-end* (1982), panic-stricken and unable to find his way to his position in the intense fog which covered the battlefield, assaulted by "the shrill, demented screaming air above and the roar of the barrage" (p. 247), Bion and his runners, the Sweeting brothers, hurry "as if we were going somewhere". All of a sudden, one of the brothers disappears. "What the hell had happened to him? Lost in the fog? Stopped to do up his bootlaces? His disappearance was complete". Bion impatiently orders the other brother to ignore the disappearance and to "come on" (p. 247), but the barrage is too intense, and they take shelter in a shell-hole. Sweeting suddenly asks his commander, who is frantically trying to get his bearings in the fog, "Sir! Sir, why can't I cough?" Bion is amazed at the question. "What a question! What a time … I looked at his chest … the left side of his chest was missing" (p. 248). In the 1958 account (1997c), when he saw the "gusts of steam coming from where his left side should be … Bion began to vomit unrestrainedly, helplessly" (p. 255), an explosive evacuation of the horror provoked by his identification with Sweeting: it could just have easily have been his chest which got blown away in the shell-hole.⁹ The vacuum created by the expulsion of his terror of Sweeting's wound is instantaneously filled with abhorrence, hatred, and revulsion, and he becomes enraged with the boy: "Oh, for Christ's sake, shut up" (p. 255). In the account in *The Long Week-end* (1982), Sweeting tries to sit up, and, again, Bion is enraged: "Lie down blast you!". The dying boy's thoughts then shift to his childhood. He calls out, "Mother, Mother, Mother", and Bion jumps at the chance to be distracted from Sweeting's wound: the barrage is less deadly than the dying boy. "Well, thank God for his damned mother. Now at least I could have some peace and pay attention to the shell-fire" (p. 248). But when the boy turns his attention back to his commander, pleading: "Sir! You will write to my mother? Won't you?" (p. 249), Bion's reaction is terrible. In "Amiens" (1997c) he tells us "I wish he would shut up. I wish he would die. Why can't he die?" (p. 256). In *The Long Week-end* (1982) he apostrophizes the boy, "Sweeting, *please* Sweeting … please, please s*hut up*." But the end does come. "'You *will* write, sir?' … And then I think he died. Or perhaps it was only me" (p. 249, emphasis in original). "Sweeting. Gunner. Tank Corps. Died of wounds. That, for him, was the end" (p. 250).

Who was wounded? Who died? Bion had frantically attempted to preserve the integrity of his mind—the distinction between the dying Sweeting and himself—by expulsive vomiting and by his rage at the boy's attempt to distract his commander's attention from his frantic attempt to find his bearings in the fog. That is, his description of his reaction to Sweeting's wound is a dramatic representation of the mechanism which is one of the cornerstones of Bion's theory of the psychotic mind (1962), in which the emotions which flood the mind are "so feared that steps are taken to destroy awareness of all feelings, although that is indistinguishable from taking life itself" (p. 10). As is evident here, this is a survival mechanism.

Bion's death shows us that the denudation of his mind was only partially successful. On the one hand, the explosion of uncontainable emotion was instantaneously expelled thus ensuring survival. On the other hand, the destruction of the awareness of emotion failed, and he was killed by the experience. We might speculate that the explosive terror provoked by Sweeting's wound annihilated the contact barrier which separates conscious and unconscious thoughts, thus dissolving the separation between life and death, between him and me, between aliveness and deadness. This left Bion to die "unphenomenally … wordlessly, without leaving any trace and thus without dying" (Blanchot, p. 32).

### Catastrophic trauma from a theoretical vertex

> "Suppose the patient to be, or to have been, capable of normality: the conglomerate of fragments of personality which serves the patient for a personality can only be regarded as evidence of a disaster. The discussion of such a case is difficult because we are concerned not with the ordinary structures of the human personality …, but with the shattered fragments … which have now been reassembled but not rearticulated".
>
> Bion, 1992, pp. 74–75

The devastated psychic mechanisms succeeding the catastrophe are amply illustrated in the autobiographies. That a disaster has occurred can be inferred from its product, "the conglomerate of fragments of personality which serves the patient for a personality", which is the self-representation in the autobiographies of the Bion who survived the catastrophe. In all of the literary works the tone is one of painful and intense disapproval of his own inadequacy. In *All My Sins Remembered* (1985), for example, Bion portrays himself as an "unprepossessing mass of ineptitude" (p. 19); when his abilities are recognized at Oxford, he is nevertheless "completely unworthy of the confidence" his teachers had in him (p. 26); and the "passport" which had gained him acceptance to medical school was "fraudulent" (p. 26). And in *A Memoir of the Future* (1991), Captain Bion is, among other things, a "consequential idiot" (p. 156).

It is evident, though, that while the psyche, however devastated, can be represented, death, or absolute absence, cannot: it is the forms which can be wrested from "the void and formless infinite" (Milton, *Paradise Lost*, Bk. III, 12) which can be inserted in the temporal succession of narration, not the "vast infinitude" (Milton, *Paradise Lost*, Bk. III, 711) itself. There is no narrative for the instant of death or the state of being dead. The dead Bion is not present and cannot be described.

But there are several extraordinary pages in *Attention and Interpretation* (1970) in which Bion describes the psychotic reaction to unbearable frustration, and I would suggest that this analysis can also be taken to describe the reaction to psychic catastrophe at the instant of its occurrence, or, to "pain so ... intense that it cannot be tolerated but must be destroyed even if it involves the murder of the 'anatomical' individual" (1991, pp. 51–52). Bion (1970) represents the psychotic reaction with a metaphor: it is an intense catastrophic emotional explosion which is "violent and is accompanied by ... immense fear" (p. 12). In the pages which follow, he analyzes the effect on the mind of the catastrophic explosion, whose most extreme consequence is felt to be death.

He describes the state of the mind at the instant of the explosion as absolute absence, depicting this by using the concept of the realization of mental space when the equipment to map it, or to delimit it so it can be perceived, is lacking. "The explosive projection is therefore felt to take place in ... the *realization* of mental space: a mental space that has no visual images to fulfill the functions of a co-ordinate system ... The mental realization of space is therefore felt as an immensity so great that it cannot be represented even by astronomical space because it cannot be represented at all" (p. 12, emphasis in original). That is, the explosion is felt to produce an infinite (or what is the same thing, a null) space in the mind, a space which is empty of visual images and thoughts and thus of all subjective existence. Bion is portraying a mind with no content, or *a mind which has died*. He uses a medical metaphor, the model of surgical shock, to portray this state: "the dilatation of the capillaries throughout the body so increases the space in which blood can circulate that the patient may bleed to death in his own tissues" (p. 12).

This is a representation of an emotional experience that the alpha-function cannot transform: the absence of visual images is the sign that it has failed.[10] The corollary of the failure of the alpha-function is the destruction of the mind as a container of thoughts and emotions. As a consequence, projective identification of emotions or parts of the personality, which would be the response in less extreme conditions, is precluded because there is no conception of containers into which projection could take place (p. 12). A further corollary is that the violence of the explosion is felt to destroy the contact barrier separating the conscious from the unconscious mind, so that the unconscious overwhelms the conscious mind, inundating it with infinite stimuli which it cannot contain or transform. The mind thus regresses to a state of primary meaninglessness and is reduced to the state of absolute helplessness.

In this state, emotions are felt to drain away and be dispersed in the immensity: "the realization of mental space, being unbounded, permits of a continuous and continuing expansion and separation of beta-elements" (p. 14). In several of his works, Primo Levi (1979, 1988) describes a sensation which might be taken as a representation of this concept: in Auschwitz, he felt that he was hovering on the edge of "the dark and cold of sidereal space" (1979, p. 62), "a deserted and empty universe ... from which the spirit of man is absent: not yet born or already extinguished" (1988, p. 65). The dispersion of emotion in infinite space also implies the annihilation of time, whose existence is predicated on the possibility that sensory data and emotions can be transformed into visual images and thoughts that are arranged in a sequential narration.

The ultimate effect of the evacuation of emotion from the mind is, in Bion's words (1970), the creation of "a domain of the non-existent" or a state of "non-existence". The closest realization of this state that he can imagine is an intense stupor (p. 20). He describes an experience which might be taken to represent it in *The Long Weekend* (1982): looking into No Man's Land for possible enemy attacks produced an extraordinary state which was "not nightmare, not waking, not sleep ... One did not think; one did not look; one stared" (p. 210). But perhaps it is the authors who recount their experience in the Nazi death camps who give the fullest representation of the state Bion is describing; there it was always terminal. The inmates who were psychologically annihilated before they died physically were called the Muselmänner. Levi (1979) describes them as "an anonymous mass of non-men ... faceless presences ... emaciated [men] ... on whose face and in whose eyes there is not a trace of thought" (p. 96, translation modified). They no longer engaged in life-preserving activity, no longer conserved their energy or tried to find food (a necessary activity for persons who were performing exhausting physical labor on a few hundred calories a day); they no longer avoided blows; and they no longer looked at the other prisoners or their surroundings (Krystal, 1968, pp. 34–35; Niederland, 1968, pp. 64–66). In Bettleheim's words (1960), they were "walking corpses" (p. 151), whose mental activity and hence individuality, subjectivity, or personal being had been destroyed before the demise of their bodies, which inevitably followed shortly thereafter.

The state of non-existence is incompatible with the continuing in being of the mind, and Bion (1970) affirms that the realization of it can last for a few moments at most before it is evacuated (p. 20). But the mind starts back into existence only to find itself immersed in a world of horrifyingly objects of murderous ferocity: the projected "non-existence" immediately becomes "an object that is immensely hostile and filled with murderous envy towards the quality or function of existence wherever it is to be found" (p. 20). This sets into motion the intrapsychic reaction to annihilation which follows catastrophe and which the autobiographies amply illustrate.

In his theoretical works, Bion analyzes mechanisms which are intrapsychic. But we should also remember that in the autobiographies the hostile and murderous object projected and reintrojected after psychic catastrophe is not only an externalized inner object; it is also real. Bion undergoes murderous attacks from without and within, and inner reality becomes a nightmarish reflection of outer reality.

## *The theory and the representation of catastrophe*

"... but I felt things now could get no worse and that actually a gleam of hope had appeared—it was always possible to get badly wounded or perhaps even killed".

Bion, Diary, 1997a, p. 94

"I am sure that a grateful establishment would have inflicted [a Victory Medal] on my completion of so many years of undetected nothingness, the ribbon designed in lavish colours of a nightmare".

Bion, 1985, p. 62

Bion's narration of his reaction to the disaster he underwent in the war is a literary representation of a man whose "normal" personality has been shattered and the "fragments ... reassembled but not rearticulated" (1992, p. 75): his portrait of himself is that of a personality often overwhelmed by psychotic mechanisms. The temptation to speculate that Bion's insight into the psychotic mind was also enabled by his own experience of madness is inevitable. However, I am proceeding on the assumption that, while what motivated the *historical* Bion is unknowable, the theoretician's insights into the functioning of the psychotic (or traumatized) mind can illuminate the *character* Bion's reactions to war. In other words, I will argue that Bion conceptualized states of mind in his theoretical works for which he created a literary representation in the autobiographies.

To take one example, the episode of Sweeting's death is an exemplification of Bion's affirmation in *Transformations* (1965) that when the mind is reduced to utter helplessness (or when it is exposed to frustration it cannot tolerate), it automatically resorts to omnipotent phantasy as a flight from reality and in particular from feelings of helplessness and terror (p. 53).[11] Faced with the threat constituted by the boy's persistence in being despite his terrifying wound (his sitting up and calling for his mother), Bion omnipotently wills the qualities of death (immobility and silence) onto Sweeting in his frantic need to be rid of the horror of the boy's dying by instantaneously transforming him into an inanimate, rather than a dying object.[12] But, of course, he is helpless to make Sweeting "shut up". His state of mind in this and other episodes is that of "an adult who maintains an exclusively primitive omnipotent ↔ helpless state" (1965, p. 53) which is intrinsically violent: internal and external objects which are alive and consequently not subject to omnipotent control are a source of terror, and the mind is therefore denuded of the sense of their aliveness. In other words, the autonomy of objects is equated with a threat to life; they are tolerable only insofar as they are automatons.

Bion's attempt to reduce Sweeting to immobility shows that he has attacked and expelled the link between them. Another example of an attack on a link between Bion and a live object occurs in *The Long Week-end* (1982) in the narration of the encounter at the front with his old school friend, Bonsey. They recognize each other ("Good God! It's you Bion isn't it?", p. 142) and begin to walk towards the front while Bonsey gives Bion some advice. After the battle, Bion thought that he would continue the conversation and "have a last word with Bonsey on the way back, but he had been killed … I was shocked; I was shocked to find I did not care" (p. 144). Upon hearing of his schoolmate's death, Bion avoids the awareness of any emotion regarding Bonsey, and the link between them is instantaneously attacked, destroyed, and evacuated from his mind. Thus his classmate is left twice dead, once literally, of course, and another as an inanimate internal object about whom there is no possibility of caring.

There is no doubt that Bion's attempt to destroy the links to the dead and dying Bonsey and Sweeting is not a defensive but a survival mechanism: psychic survival involves denuding the representation of the catastrophic event of its meaning for the subject. But we can speculate that the soldier's immersion in death *also* created an unconscious identification with the wounded, dying, and dead, an interpretation suggested by an image which appears several times in the autobiographies and *A Memoir of the Future*, the image of a desiccated corpse whose "green skin was stretched tight like parchment over the bones of the face" (1982, p. 138). In the 1972 "Commentary" (1997b), Bion presents this image as a memory of his own past and present state: "I can still feel my skin drawn over the bones of my face as if it were the mask of a cadaver" (p. 204). In *The Long Week-End* (1982), on the other hand, the description is of a corpse with which (whom?) Bion had shared a shell-hole at the battle of Ypres (p. 138). Whereas in the account in which *he* is the corpse, Bion remembers the absolute incommunicability of his emotions and therefore of his intense loneliness, in *The Long Week-end* (1982) his bitterly ironic observation is that at any rate the corpse with which he shared the shell-hole—the corpse had not been blown-up and therefore it "didn't stink, for which I was thankful" (p. 138)—was at least company: "anyhow I was not alone" (p. 138). Here corpses have the qualities of life, and the living have the qualities of death; death in life and life in death. The image occurs a final time in a dialogue in *A Memoir of the Future* (1991) where it is narrated in a compressed re-evocation of several of the most horrific memories recorded in the earlier autobiographies; they are attributed to Roland, the character who here is the repository of Bion's war memories, and the fear they engender. Roland synthetically alludes to these immersions in death: "My cheeks are cold; the skin is tight over my skull. It is hideous, this eye-wearied search at those corpse-stenching huts. I have stared and stared and stared at them. Nothing" (p. 281). Huts filled with stenching corpses: immersion in death; shock: unconscious identification with the dead and dying; cold: staring, staring until the stenching corpses are evacuated and a state of non-existence is produced in the mind.

The immersion in death and the resulting dialectic between the identification with the dead and the defense of survival through the minute splitting and evacuation of the hatred and terror engendered by the fear of dying constitute one of the principal effects of psychic catastrophe as it is portrayed in the autobiographies.

In *The Long Week-end* (1982), Bion paints a verbal portrait of the state of the mind produced by terror: his company's first march to the front exposed him to "hell", but his reaction was that it "was just a bore spoiled by hideous mis-shapen blobs of fear" (p. 121). Obviously he is describing a state of dissociation, or what he also calls the "shelter [of] mindlessness" (p. 130). As Brown observes, in this state of mind, the alpha-function fails and the capacity for thinking becomes disordered (2005). In one passage, he describes a close call with death: a bullet just misses his head, and "I had not heard it or been aware" (Bion, 1982, p. 132). His reaction is immediate "dis-association, de-personalization":[13] "as I looked at my map and hands in the tank I felt I was floating about four feet above my self" (p. 132).

On the one hand, disassociation is a blessing: when he is not aware of any danger Bion is free of fear (p. 164). But, on the other hand, as he writes in another passage, fear "served as a substitute for my common sense which was totally lacking" (p. 164). That is, spontaneous dis-association is an escape into delusional self-preservation, but illusory safety can also be potentially costly, for the consequence of the expulsion of the perception of the lethal nature of reality is that the residual capacity to make realistic judgments about life-preserving action is undermined, as Bion's actions in combat demonstrate again and again. In fact, Bion repeatedly describes how the heroic actions for which he was so highly decorated were the result of his entering into an altered state of mind in which judgments based on a realistic evaluation of danger were impossible. As P.A. says in *A Memoir of the Future*, "I was not scared—I was nothing" (1991, p. 475).

One of the episodes which most strikingly illustrates the effect of the lack of common sense, or what Bion calls his "sheer, unadulterated lunacy" (1997a, p. 106), is described in detail in *The Long Week-end* (1982) and then again in *A Memoir of the Future* (1991). Bion's tank is under heavy fire, and, in *The Long Week-end* (1982), he orders his men to evacuate the tank for fear that they will be hit, while he remains inside, driving at full throttle toward enemy lines. Then, he writes in *The Long Week-end*, "before I knew what I was doing I had left the driver's seat and joined the crew behind" (p. 262). It was "then, only then", that is only *after* he had saved himself from certain death, that "panic overwhelmed [me]" (p. 262). But Bion's terror is not panic at the thought that he could have been blown to bits. Rather, he is terrorized by the thought of his lack of "bravery" and at the potential consequences of the "cowardice" which he considers to be his most distinctive trait: he had abandoned his fully functioning tank and left it heading straight towards enemy lines where it would be captured. *This propelled him to run after the tank in the attempt to get back into it*, but it was hit just before he reached it and blew up, "flames spurting everywhere" (p. 262).

In this and other episodes, Bion's state of mind is one in which contact with reality is lost and the non-psychotic part of the personality is submerged, so that the ability to distinguish between internal states and the perception of an actual event—one which is subject to the laws of nature—is obscured. What is important in determining his actions in this episode is not the *reality* of the enemy's possession of weapons which will destroy his tank and kill him; rather they are dictated by the internal dialogue between his superegoical self-reproaches (re-projected onto his comrades-in-arms and their commanders who would finally see him for the "coward" he was) and his impulse to get out of the tank and so to avoid being killed.

This episode also illustrates the consequences of denuding the mind of feared and hated emotion, for in addition to the reality principle, pieces of the personality and the fear of dying are expelled along with emotion. If the process of denudation is extensive, as it is here, the will to live, which is necessary for the fear of dying to be felt, is also expelled (see Bion, 1962, p. 97). In fact, beginning with his youthful Diary (1997a), Bion affirms that when hope did appear during the war, it was hope of being killed (p. 94).

In *The Long Week-end* (1982) the description of the state of one of his tank commanders illustrates the seemingly extravagant affirmation Bion made in *Learning from Experience* that projection can be so excessive that it is as if virtually the whole personality has been evacuated (1962, p. 97). The soldier, who had been a spirited and ardently religious man named Cohen, had been killed without dying. Wounded in the battle of Cambrai, he had lost both eyes, his right arm, and both legs. After the war, he lived in an institution, unable to recognize anyone; he "just has a silly grin" or "every now and then he becomes terrified, cowers down in a corner of the room and sucks his thumb" (p. 186). Cohen's personality has been definitively extinguished without extinguishing his physical being: "God knows what had hit Cohen; somehow it managed not to kill his body, but killed *him*" (p. 220, emphasis in original).

The autobiographies describe many other instances in which the distinction between inner and outer reality is blurred: among them are nightmares in which the terror generated by the dream threatens to submerge Bion's conscious mind. From as early as the 1919 Diary (1997a) he records nightmares in which "it was almost impossible to distinguish dream from reality" (p. 94). Over forty years later, in *The Long Week-end* (1982), he describes his utter confusion upon waking from a nightmare before the battle of Amiens:

> the dream was grey, shapeless; horror and dread gripped me. I could not cry out, just as now, many years later, I can find no words. Then I had no words to find; I was awake to the relatively benign terrors of real war. Yet for a moment I wished it was only a dream. In the dream I must have wished it was only a war. (p. 237)

The experience in the dream was so extreme that at the time he dreamt it there was no possibility of containing the emotion it generated in a cry, just as many years later the emotion could not be contained by words. The nightmares continued after the war, and in *All My Sins Remembered*

(1985) Bion recounts that the terror he is able to contain while waking "burst out" in a recurrent nightmare in which he is frantically trying to avoid plunging to certain death by maintaining his hold on the slippery walls that fall sheer into the raging foaming river Steenbeck. The river, which in reality had been a mere trickle in the immense expanse of mud which was the battlefield at Ypres, is a bizarre object swollen with projected terror in the dream, and his fear is that the emotions it generated will overwhelm his awareness of reality when he is awake: "suppose broad daylight was not thick enough to keep out the terror" (p. 16).

But the terrible paradox is that when survival mechanisms—the splitting and evacuation of fear, the illusory assurance of safety—fail, and the soldier perceives the *reality* of war, the fact of "no protection" causes the hideous blobs of fear to coagulate, and then the contained explodes the container. For the fact of helplessness cannot be borne, and the perception of "the truth" means intolerable pain, shell-shock, and disintegration. This is the case of Gates, who "went sane long before the war was over; he couldn't bear the truth ... It was pitiful—lying there in a ditch blubbering. He took to drink; even that couldn't save him from reality" (1991, p. 423). While the soldier is immersed in the violence and death of the war, remaining "sane" is impossible.

As Bion indicated in *Learning from Experience* (1962), when objects are stripped of meaning, split into pieces, and projected, the mind feels surrounded by agglomerates of undigestible beta-elements, sadistic persecutory bizarre objects, which, when reintrojected, are "returned to an object that covers them with little more than the semblance of a psyche" (p. 97). In the episode of the tank referred to above, these beta-elements have cohered to form an exo-skeleton which provides Bion's personality with an illusion of coherence, and it is this semblance of a personality which he has reintrojected: in his case the spurious personality is made up of unthinking adherence to collective values—the terror of being a coward, the fear of making wrong decisions, the aim to "deserve" the medal for bravery he had been awarded, which meant holding bravery above life. It is this personality which orients Bion's actions in the war. But, as he states in *Second Thoughts* (1967), while the links between the elements which compose his character appear to be logical, they are not emotionally reasonable (p. 109), for they have been divested of the will to live and hence of all subjectivity.

In both of the autobiographies the tone is one of painful and intense disapproval of his own inadequacy; they are a record of his "completion of so many years of undetected nothingness" (1985, p. 62). As Bion argues in *Attention and Interpretation* (1970), when feared and hated emotions are projected and reintrojected, they become an immensely aggressive object which implants itself in the mind as a hostile and destructive superego (p. 21). Perhaps the most terrible example of Bion's unforgiving judgment of himself is his phantasized answer to the question about the death of his first wife, who died in childbirth while he was absent in France during World War Two. Having asked himself, "What killed Betty and nearly killed her baby?" he answers the question by comparing her to a sensitive conductor who discovers that she has been "condemned ... to an eternity of eliciting a harmonious response from a tone-deaf, malicious, instrumentally armed orchestra" (1985, p. 62), by extension, his "chitinous semblance" of a self (1982, p. 104). The two autobiographies are the portrait of a man who is engaged in an incessant struggle with his internal objects (1967, p. 27), a man who has improvised a personality out of elements which he feels to be worthless (1962, p. 20), a man in the grip of a persecutory, primitive superego (1967, p. 101) that ferociously indicates where Bion "ought" to be but never is (1965, p. 53). The autobiographies leave us, in Francesca Bion's words (1985), with "an abiding impression of unrelieved gloom and profound dislike of himself" (p. 6).[14]

## By way of a conclusion

"Before I knew what I was doing I had left the driver's seat and joined the crew behind".

Bion, 1982, p. 262

It is assuredly true that Bion could have done nothing to avoid death from the stray bullet or the direct hit in the trench or the tank. The fact that he was the only one of his friends to survive the war was purely fortuitous. But while his accounts of the war did portray a personality in the grip of a hatred of life and other psychotic states of mind, it is also true that in the episode of the tank he acted to save his life: he jumped out before it was hit and exploded. What started into action to save him before "I knew what I was doing", that is beneath, behind, and beyond the death he had undergone, and before and without thought? At one point in *A Memoir of the Future* (1991), Bion represents this level of the personality as a character, DU, whose function was to keep Bion alive despite his "bloody heroism and conceptual rubbish" (p. 279). When asked what he was doing during the war, DU says that he was "keeping quiet, lying as close to your CNS as I could get and trying to make you have the sense to lie flat on the ground" (p. 279).

A full treatment of the question of what got Bion out of the tank is beyond the scope of this paper, but his life-saving action deserves to be discussed, however briefly. In this episode, Bion is pointing to an action originating before mind, prior to purpose, thought, or choice, an action which is automatic and involuntary.[15] In *Cogitations* (1992), he uses the analogy of tropism in plants to indicate an innate behavior where the organism turns towards or away from a stimulus, which in humans is an automatic seeking for an object which can contain the seeker's projective identification (p. 35) and so permit the structuring of his mind: the action of seeking and finding the object is the primitive matrix from which mental life springs (p. 35).[16] In *Transformations* (1965) he further develops the psychological relevance of the concept, inventing the sign, $\pm \leftarrow \uparrow$, or "in search of existence" (p. 107), which indicates both the negative/positive tropisms.

Bion's war experience is a portrayal of the negative tropism, which is personified by seeking that has failed to find the object which can contain deathly terror: it is a portrait of an individual who has therefore ceased to exist, a "non-existent 'person'", an "it" whose failure to find results in a hatred of life (1965, p. 111). In fact, Bion's autobiographies are demonstrations of the irreducible impossibility that an object capable of containing his explosive emotions is or can be in existence. The result is the rejection of the positive tropism, a turning away from the search for existence, a disavowal of the movement towards life and its replacement by a turning toward death. When under the sway of the negative tropism, what is sought is an object to murder or be murdered by (1992, p. 35). This is a description of Bion's state in his accounts of the war.

The positive tropisms, +←↑, on the other hand, indicate an expectation of existence, an innate and involuntary turning toward the life-giving stimulus, "an awareness of a lack of existence that demands an existence, a thought in search of a meaning, a definitory hypothesis in search of a realization approximating to it, a psyche seeking for a physical habitation to give it existence, ♀ seeking ♂" (1965, p. 109). In the instant in which Bion leapt out of the doomed tank, the positive tropism held sway, and he unthinkingly and involuntarily sought life, not death. His frantic attempt to catch up with the tank so he could get back in it was subsequent to the automatic, life-seeking tropism; it was the product of thought.

It is evident that the necessity of understanding "how those same dead bones gave birth to a mind" (1991, p. 60) led Bion nd his attempt to understand the functioning of the psychotic and the traumatized minds. The body of his work is also and perhaps principally a theory of the functioning of the the theoretician far beyond his attempt to understand the functioning of the psychotic and the traumatized minds. The body of his work is also, and perhaps principally, a theory of the functioning of the non-psychotic mind. On the one hand, the Bion of the autobiographies was the man who went mad during the war, the man who died at Amiens, the man who towards the end of his life wrote that "nobody told me … that war service would change utterly my capacity to enjoy life" (1991, p. 508). On the other hand, the historical Bion was the man who against all odds survived the war and, not withstanding his experience of atrocity, sought and found thoughts that, while they are an attempt to understand the effect of catastrophe on the mind, are also an attempt to fathom the stupefying fact of aliveness, of the mind's coming into being out of mindlessness and continuing in its existence.

## Notes

1. All of these texts are included in the volume *War Memoirs* (1997).
2. He published *A Memoir of the Future* in his lifetime, but we owe the other volumes to Francesca Bion, who edited them.
3. In "Aftermath", her afterward to *War Memoirs*, Bion Talamo (1997) speculates that where episodes are carried over almost verbatim from the earlier autobiographical works to *A Memoir of the Future*, this is a sign that "no further working-through [was] possible" (p. 309). Another indication of Bion's difficulty after the war is that, as Francesca Bion (1985) noted, most of his creative work was done after his marriage, or nearly forty-five years after he was demobilized. (p. 6).
4. I would like to make it clear that my intention in this paper is not to attempt to add to Bion's biography—or, to use a word of his, to "conjecture" about his subjective reaction to his war experience, an endeavor which he would certainly think was "wasting time" (1991, p. 213). When I speak of "Bion", I am speaking of the narrator of these imaginative works, of the representation in these narrations of the person who underwent those experiences, or of the author of his theoretical works. This is the "Bion" which is accessible to us.
5. P.A. is a psychoanalyst.
6. See Meltzer (1981), Symington and Symington (1996), Sandler (2003), Souter (2009), Williams (2010), Szykierski (2010), and Brown (2012), who have written persuasively of the importance of Bion's experiences in the war for his understanding of the mind.
7. See Tarantelli, C. B. (2003). Life within death: Towards a metapsychology of catastrophic psychic trauma. *International Journal of Psychoanalysis*, 84: 915–928.

8. I would take this as a subtle criticism of Melanie Klein and her school with their emphasis on the primacy of phantasy.
9. In addition, see Tarantelli (2003) for an analysis of nausea as the most primitive possibile defense against the disintegration of the mind: it registers a physical sensation, which "attracts attention, impels attention, necessitates attention". The ability to register sensation is "a sign that the body is still alive and that the mind perceives it" (p. 924).
10. We should keep in mind that, in order to be discussed, the effects which accompany the explosion must be recounted in a sequential fashion, but also that these effects are not sequential or subsequent to the explosion or caused by it. They are not effects at all: they are but simultaneous to the explosion, synchronous with it or the same thing as it. See Tarantelli, 2003, p. 919.
11. Grotstein (2007) reports that in his analysis with him, Bion often made reference to this concept: "whenever I may have appeared 'omnipotent' to him, he would interpret to me that I was *reduced* to becoming omnipotent' because of my feelings of helplessness in a situation" (p. 29, emphasis in original).
12. In one of his several narrations of Sweeting's death in *A Memoir of the Future* (1991), Bion recalls with infinite regret his treatment of the boy, for, in his intentions, he has robbed Sweeting of his own dying. P.A. says, "if I could believe in God I would ask him to forgive me … I use the saddest words in the language—'I didn't mean it to happen'" (p. 256).
13. To my knowledge, this is the only time he uses a technical term in the autobiographies.
14. She could not accept that this was a complete portrait of her husband, because, as she affirms, he also "came to derive great happiness from his … marriage, family and work" (1985, p. 6). As a correction to the portrait in the autobiographies, she includes a selection of Bion's letters to herself and their children in *All My Sins Remembered* (1985). The letters written during the period of their courtship are a moving and beautiful portrait of the creative power of love: the beloved's presence "pours a soft radiance of joy over my life" (p. 77), causing "the dull numb mechanical routine into which I have fallen [to burst] wide open" (p. 84). Now the inadequacy of words to represent experience is due to the fact that the expression of feeling "needs a full choir, orchestra and organ" (p. 97). It is certainly relevant, as Francesca Bion noted (1985, p. 6), that almost all of Bion's major works were written after his marriage.
15. In his last evocation of this episode in *A Memoir of the Future* (1991), Bion does realize his intention to get back in the tank but here, too, something involuntarily expels him from the tank just before it explodes: "without thought I shot out of the hatch as the flames of petrol swathed the steel carcass … [and] fell on my arse" (p. 476).
16. Elsewhere, for example in *Elements of psychoanalysis* (1963), Bion also affirmed that beta-elements were the matrix of the mind (p. 22).

## References

Bettleheim, B. (1960). *The Informed Heart: Autonomy in a Mass Age*. New York: The Free Press, 1971.
Bion, F. (1985). Foreword. In: F. Bion (Ed.), *All My Sins Remembered*. London: Karnac.
Bion Talamo, P. (1997). Aftermath. In: F. Bion (Ed.), *War Memoirs: 1917–1919*. London: Karnac.
Bion, W. R. (1962). *Learning from Experience*. London: Karnac.
Bion, W. R. (1963). *Elements of Psychoanalysis*. London: Karnac.
Bion, W. R. (1965). *Transformations*. London: Karnac.
Bion, W. R. (1967). *Second Thoughts*. London: Karnac
Bion, W. R. (1970). *Attention and Interpretation*. London: Karnac.

Bion, W. R. (1982). *The Long Week-End* (Ed. F. Bion). London: Karnac.
Bion, W. R. (1985). *All My Sins Remembered* (Ed. F. Bion). London: Karnac.
Bion, W. R. (1991). *A Memoir of the Future*. London: Karnac.
Bion, W. R. (1992). *Cogitations* (Ed. F. Bion). London: Karnac.
Bion, W. R. (1997). *War Memoirs: 1917–1919* (Ed. F. Bion). London: Karnac.
Bion, W. R. (1997a). Diary. In: *War Memoirs: 1917–1919*. (Ed. F. Bion). London: Karnac.
Bion, W. R. (1997b). Commentary. In: *War Memoirs* (Ed. F. Bion). London: Karnac.
Bion, W. R. (1997c). Amiens. In: *War Memoirs* (Ed. F. Bion). London: Karnac.
Blanchot, M. (1986). *The Writing of the Disaster* (Trans. A. Smock). Lincoln: The University of Nebraska Press.
Brown, L. J. (2005). The cognitive effects of trauma: reversal of alpha function and the formation of a beta screen. *Psychoanalytic Quarterly, 74*: 397–420.
Brown, L. J. (2012). Bion's discovery of alpha function: thinking under fire on the battlefield and in the consulting room. *International Journal of Psychoanalysis, 93*: 1191–1214.
Freud, S. (1920). Beyond the pleasure principle. *S. E. 18*. London: Hogarth.
Grotstein, J. G. (2007). *A Beam of Intense Darkness: Wilfred Bion's legacy to Psychoanalysis*. London: Karnac.
Krystal, H. (Ed.) (1968). *Massive Psychic Trauma*. New York: International Universities Press.
Levi, P. (1979). *If This Is a Man*. London: Abacus, 1987.
Levi, P. (1988). *The Drowned and the Saved*. London: Abacus, 1989.
Meltzer, D. (1981). Memorial meeting for Dr. Wilfred Bion. *International Review of Psycho-Analysis, 8*: 3–14.
Milton, J. (1933). Paradise Lost. In: F. A. Patterson (Ed.), Milton's Complete Poems. New York: Appleton-Century-Crofts. Poem first published 1667.
Niederland, W. (1968). An interpretation of the psychological stresses and defenses in concentration camp life and the late aftereffects. In: H. Krystal (Ed.), *Massive Psychic Trauma*. New York: International Universities Press.
Sandler, P. C. (2003). Bion's war memoirs: a psychoanalytical commentary—living experiences and learning from them: some early roots of Bion's contributions to psychoanalysis. In: R. M. Lipgar & M. Pines (Eds.), *Building on Bion: Roots, Origins and Context of Bion's Contributions to Theory and Practice* (pp. 59–84). London: Jessica Kingsley.
Souter, K. (2009). *The War Memoirs*: Some origins of the thought of W. R. Bion. *International Journal of Psychoanalysis, 90*: 795–808.
Symington, J., & Symington, N. (1996). *The Clinical Thinking of Wilfred Bion*. New York, NY: Routledge.
Szykierski, D. (2010). The traumatic roots of containment: The evolution of Bion's metapsychology. *Psychoanalytic Quarterly, 79*: 935–968.
Tarantelli, C. B. (2003). Life within death: towards a metapsychology of catastrophic psychic trauma. *International Journal of Psychoanalysis, 84*: 915–928.
Williams, M. H. (2010). *Bion's Dream: A Reading of the Autobiographies*. London: Karnac.

# PART II

## PREVIOUSLY UNPUBLISHED SUPERVISIONS

*Editors' introduction*

We are indebted to José Américo Junqueira de Mattos and Gisela Brito for having made available for this book three previously unpublished supervisions by Bion. It is a precious gift. Many of those who find Bion's books impossible to read, desperately inaccessible, full of strange and unfamiliar jargon, abstract or mystical, respond more positively to the seminars and supervisions, which revolve around the presence of clinical material. These are apt to be much more friendly to the reader and contain true gems of understanding, suggestions, evocations, and sound clinical wisdom. Furthermore, they give us the opportunity to experience something of Bion's voice and style of talking. Perhaps that is why in his comment to supervision A34 Cassorla felt impelled or empowered to adopt the rhetorical form of an imaginary conversation with Bion. Of course, this gesture echoes Bion's own decision to write his last book, *Memoir of the Future*, as a kind of theatrical piece or Joycian "wake", the aim of which is to disturb and de-center his readers, forcing them to think and re-think; and here also it is a kind of a-wake-ning!

In Cassorla's imaginary encounter, Bion complains of being dead (!) and not having the possibility to envisage the exciting developments of his attempts to rewrite and reanimate psychoanalysis. As we go through this intriguing *nekya*[1], accompanied by our Cassorla-as-Virgil, we are not informed in which Dantesque regions the great man is hosted, but exactly as in the *Divine Comedy*, his shade does not escape from the worries that tormented him most during his life: how not to become/be "Bionian", how not to present oneself as the priest of a new religion, how to gently practice skepticism and curiosity, how to avoid imitation and critical acceptance. And like the characters in the *Comedy*, he can see the past but not the future and so is curious, and expresses a wish saying that he hopes that by 2009 we have advanced further than he had in our capacity to observe. We hope that this collective book may sound as answer to "his" question.

Somehow in his comment on supervision A42 Civitarese follows Cassorla's path, because he emphasizes some other elements of style: a certain play of metaphors, which render it very animated and alive: dogs that hunt and kill snakes, fights, etc. This imagery is employed in order to try and give a glimpse of what Bion means by the term "intuition", when used as a tool in clinical practice. A second element of style that can be assumed is the organization of the text itself, featuring voids, missing lines, and empty paragraphs, so suggesting the void of memory, desire, and understanding that Bion recommended to us. A third set of images, then, is the recruitment of the discourse on art to illustrate the place of creativity and emotions in analysis. The analyst is like a poet or a painter; playing the music of his or her words or silences, he does something very close to performing artistic "transformations".

Finally, Levine underlines the work of intuitive thinking that Bion demonstrates and allows the reader to experience in supervision A42; wave after wave, the continuous play of questions, "wild" thoughts and educated conjectures. So we are once again back to the issue of what kind of "evidence" the analyst has at his or her disposal, and this seems to be not just one issue among others, but *the* issue. In fact, Bion started his theoretical journey having in mind that it was necessary to develop better instruments for observation—as Cassorla also recalls putting the aforementioned wish of progress in his mouth. Levine suggests that Bion accepts a radical asymmetry in the relationship, a view that is far different from the Relationals' insistence on symmetry and Lacan's concept of the "subject supposed to know"—even if, seen from the outside, it seems that the Lacanian analysts never really dismisses an authoritative stance when deciding the *coupure* of the session. The point here, and one of the utmost theoretical and ethical importance in Bion, is that the analyst's taking responsibility for his or her actions and beliefs is not the same as presuming always to know and to be right. The latter view is perhaps a residue of a more or less one-person psychoanalytic model based on the analysis of a transference neurosis that is saturated by past phantasy and experience, instead of the alive "something between" patient and analyst that, for Bion, is the intermediate area where analysis should take place.

## Note

1. A *nekya* is a journey to the underworld.

CHAPTER SIX

# Supervision A34

A = Analyst:   This patient is thirty-one years old; he's a doctor, a psychiatrist. He consulted me at the end of last year and started analysis in February this year, with four sessions each week, Monday to Thursday. I have a [Wednesday] session, from the 23rd of February, in which the patient brings two dreams.

The patient says: "I have brought a dream I had—I think it's the best material for analysis! I was going to tell you yesterday, but the ending of the session didn't allow me to. I dreamt: I was with my father and he was in front of me. He was with my mother in bed, in a position of having sexual relationship, I was with my wife in another bed."

I asked the patient: "What do you mean in front of?" because he had said he was in front of his father. He explains the position of the beds (but unfortunately the tape is unclear here and we are unable to describe for readers what Bion was told or shown with gestures).

BION:   I'd like you all to consider what you'd feel if the patient came to see you. Would you want to go on seeing him or wouldn't you? Would anybody like to offer a suggestion of what his or her reaction would be to hearing this story for the first time? Would you want to see the patient, again or wouldn't you? See, it's an ongoing question. It's a question, which you could ask yourself many, many times throughout the analysis.

A:   When I listened to this case I felt a certain disgust—first impression—as if the patient were playing a game with me. But then the image of *The Creation of Man* by Michelangelo[1] came to my mind. In it man and God's fingers are almost—very near—but not in physical contact.

BION:   Not in contact!
Not in contact but very near. When he asks to be helped to grow, I felt that—more or less

that. Why would you think the patient would come to see you? Why should he come to see you at all? What would he want? I'm not asking easy questions or they're easy questions, but they are not easy answers.

A: I think the patient … came to analysis on account of fears that he has, but that covered other kind of problems.

BION: Hum … what did he expect the analyst to do?

A: Perhaps the patient expected to be reinforced about his character structure. With the progress of his analysis, the apparent phobic mechanism gave way to an understanding of other aspects which were related to dangers to the ego and fear of not being able to keep the ego integrated.

BION: You see, if he had a physical injury then he might go to a surgeon and he'd expect the surgeon to repair it, if it was a cut, put in stitch and so forth. What does a patient expect an analyst to do? If he wanted shoes, he'd go to a shoe shop. Why does he go to an analyst? What for? This question crops up all the time. Why does the patient come to me today? Tomorrow the same question: why does the patient come here today? As far as the past is concerned nothing can be done about it, because the past is past. It's quite useful for the analyst to know something about the past, but you can't do anything about it. The analyst can't undo the past. So, why does he tell you this story? If he, as I say, if he wanted a pair of shoes, he would say to the shop assistant what he wanted. What sort of shoes, what his measurements were and so on. Now why is he seeing an analyst?

A: The patient has tried to solve his problems through different ways: religion, forming a couple with someone, and now, after not meeting with success, he has turned to analysis. And another way the patient tried to solve his problems was to become a physician. He believed being a physician would make him a man. Now, he has turned to analysis, but also is very afraid of the analyst, because he is afraid of every person who he considers is able to see what he is hiding.

BION: Did he give any explanation of how he'd come to hear of analysis or when he felt that analysis was what he wanted?

P1: From a certain time before the consultation, the patient wished to be analyzed, because he felt very badly about his life in a general sense and he was afraid that he could become … his behavior was becoming disorganized and he was not satisfied with the course of his life. He felt very bad.

BION: Hum … in other words the patient has had a lot of experience. The patient … If it was physical he could say: "My arm hurts, it hurts. I've been to a physiotherapist and so on, it's no good. Would you tell me what's the matter with my arm?" This patient has been to the priest, to the church and so on, but about a mental pain. One thing that he has concluded was that this mental pain would be cured if he were a good boy. So he tries being a good boy. He is good, he's a good student, he didn't have sexual relationships, but he still isn't cured. So, being good doesn't cure this pain. One of the questions would be: what sort of pain is this? I said mental pain, but that doesn't mean anything.

A: He had fears and pains. His fears could be related to establishing relationships with other people, or people, like psychiatrists or psychoanalysts, who could know things that he was trying to hide from himself or keep hidden, fears of old women … Beautiful women. Fears of rich people. And the pains could be related to his feeling unsuccessful, in certain situations, in which he had aspired to be successful and failed.

BION: Yes, but what is frightening about being unsuccessful? What does that matter? All human beings aren't successful. The earliest years of our life, when we learn most readily, the one lesson that we all learn is that we are unsuccessful. If, as a baby, I want to go from here to there, I can't do it, I'm unsuccessful and that happens all the time. As soon as you can crawl, you want to walk. If you try to walk, you're unsuccessful. If you learn to walk you want to run. If you try to run, you fall down and hurt yourself. It's all failure and the successes you don't notice because everybody is successful, except you. But now failure has a great meaning for him. He thinks that this failure means something and he would like to ask the analyst: "Why am I a failure?" But he dare not because he doesn't want to know; he's afraid of hearing why he's a failure.

A: Because the patient [is] … trying to maintain the idea that it's possible not … to be [a] failure—to not fail.

BION: Yes, but all this means is that the failure is really felt to have great significance and importance. He's got to be successful and he can't be successful. Anybody, any ordinary human being knows what it is to fail. Now, why does he think that being a failure is so important? What's he afraid that you would tell him, if you were honest and really told him the truth, what is he afraid that you would tell him? Umm … Let me put it this way: if I've got a pain in my arm and nobody had cured it, then I might go to a very good physician and I might be afraid that he would tell me that it was some terrible disease. So, I'd want him to tell me what's the matter, but I wouldn't want him to tell me that it was a terrible disease. Now, what is the terrible disease that this patient is afraid of hearing? Noting, religion has failed, it's all failed. So, what is the terrible disease that he expects to hear about?

A: Perhaps it is anger. Or his madness; his psychotic nuclei; his fear that he would not be able to have a sufficiently strong and integrated ego to bear it …

BION: I think quite simply he's afraid that he's going mad and that you'd tell him so. I think you're right. But if you don't tell him that he's going mad then, in a little while, he's satisfied but then he'll begin to doubt it again. He'll begin to think: "Ah … well, perhaps you don't really know." Or perhaps he didn't tell you the whole story. So, he'll feel better for a short while, for a day or two, or a week or two, a month or two, but not more. And then, again, he'll have doubts. Again, he'll be afraid that he's going mad. Again, he'll be afraid that the reason why he failed at … games that he played, at sexual games—at anything—because there's something wrong with his mind, some fatal, mental complaint. Now, the trouble is that he has been to lots of people, socially, medically, religiously, he's been to lots of people, but you know, people don't believe there is such a thing as mental pain, they don't believe it and so they are likely to say: "Oh, well, we're all like that, it's quite alright, you don't have to worry about that." They say it about masturbation, they say it about sin, they say it about drinking, and they say it about eating: "Ah, we're all like that. There's nothing to worry about." So, he's tired of being told that there's nothing the matter, because he knows there's something the matter, he knows what it's like to feel mental pain. So, in this respect, he is quite used to being told, perhaps, that he has a neurosis or something of that kind, but you know, people nearly always mean when they say that a person's got a neurosis that he is hypochondriac, but therefore there's nothing the matter with him. It's only a long word for saying: "Nothing is the matter with you." So, they can never get seriously treated, they can never find anybody who treats their trouble seriously. Now, when you come across an analyst, who listens to what you say, then you feel a bit better, but, then you get frightened that the analyst thinks there's something terrible the matter with you. And people can say: "Ah … don't bother about that, I'll give you a nice car, motorcar, and then you can drive about and have a fine time." But that doesn't work. For a short time he is glad to have a motorcar, he's glad to be able to get about, but once again it doesn't work. So, there's always this anxiety about getting the wrong treatment. People can give him a car, they can give him holidays and his wife even gives him herself. But it all means that if all these cures are no good, then what is this serious state of affairs? That's when the patient comes to see an analyst. When everything else hasn't worked, then they come to see you. So, naturally they believe that psychoanalysis is the same as all the rest, that won't work either. But, as a matter of fact, the patient does get some relief because you'll listen to him because you don't say: "Oh, you're alright and goodbye." You don't do that and he gets a certain degree of relief because you listen to him. However, taking it to that point, one would say: now, what is the analyst to say to the patient, when the patient comes to see him tomorrow? In analysis, the past is quite interesting, but you can't do anything about it. It's quite useful to know the story, but what the analyst is concerned with is the present and what's going to happen next. Now, again, if the patient thinks it's a matter of sin, then he can confess his sins. He can spend his life undergoing penitential exercises and going to the priest and confessing his sins. So, he may want to do the same with the analyst. He can produce sin after sin and confess them to the analyst, but that is a very old method of treatment, and it's only to do with sin anyway. His troubles are all sorts of things besides sins. Now, the process is rather like the archaeologist's because you listen and you hear something more and another little bit there and gradually you can see the more of who or what that person is. And in this way you can gradually get him to discover; help him to discover himself. So, after a time, he gets more used to who he is and not so terrified about his being the person, who fails, or his being the person who masturbates or his being the person who … well, all the various things. He gets more used to it because you're more able to introduce him to himself. It's like archaeology. It's like revealing the person who's hidden behind what you can see.

# Commentary on supervision A34*

*Roosevelt M. S. Cassorla*#

**Cassorla (hereinafter indicated as C):** The reading of supervision A34, especially the beginning, reminded me of the film *Lost in Translation*. In it a man and a woman, in Tokyo, are lost in terms of language, and they realize that, in fact, they are lost in terms of communication with themselves. As happens in psychoanalysis, their encounter gives them a certain perception of this fact. We will see that the main theme of Bion's words here has to do with the difficulty patients have in coming into contact with themselves, but his comments are especially related to the role of the analyst.

**Bion's Ghost (BG):** That's what you think, but I can't say anything about what you think, and what I think would be of no help to you. I didn't see the film—I was dead at the time—but many encounters are really disagreements, and vice-versa. I have trouble with supposed encounters between the living and the dead, like what you are trying to do. I'm afraid it's so daring that it borders on the arrogant. Look at Freud in his *Mourning and Melancholia*. I'm not responsible for the words you're putting into my mouth. In any case, I'm amazed at the way some people would rather ignore the facts and, for this reason, fail to develop their own opinions. Sometimes they would rather repeat what the dead might have said. One of the irritating things about being dead is to have to watch all this without being able to do anything at all about it.

**c:** Three languages are spoken in this supervision—Spanish, Portuguese, and English. There is a translator who does not understand Spanish and has trouble expressing himself in

---

*Supervision and comments discussed in October 2009 by the study group on Bion's supervisions, at the São Paulo Psychoanalytic Society (co-ordinated by Gisèle Matos Brito).
#Member of the São Paulo Psychoanalytic Society and the psychoanalytic study group of Campinas.

English, a second translator, we might say, and a psychoanalyst who corrects the translator and talks quite a bit. I was unable to identify any of the other participants in the discussion, but I might be wrong.

BG: I'd be worried if you thought you were right. Speech, or language, which includes concepts like linguistics and semantics, consists of words that, in their attempt to communicate, can kill curiosity. I see curiosity as the willingness to be guided by the unknown. It might be an attempt to grasp things that, I suppose, are primordial aspects of the self. They are not yet born, and they "speak" in ways other than common speech.

C: Bion starts off by asking some of those present about their reaction when they hear a patient's story for the first time. Through the reading here we know only the account of a dream of a patient described as a thirty-one-year-old male psychiatrist. The account begins with self-praise, together with a criticism of the analyst, when he says: "I think it's the best material for analysis! I was going to tell you yesterday, but the ending of the session didn't allow me to". But the end of the account of the dream is not clear ("empty pages to be filled in"). I speculate on the distance between generations, between patient and analyst, but these are hypotheses that cannot be validated. It also seems that part of the tape (the story) was lost, with blank pages and maybe interrupted communication.

BG: I wouldn't worry about things that are lost. Patient and analyst always have blank and lost pages. If this didn't happen would there be analysis? You could ask yourself whether you couldn't put up with the "blank pages", and that's why you're in such a hurry to make hypotheses, like the one about the "distance between generations, between patient and analyst." *La réponse est le malheur de la question.* If I weren't dead I would come up with some hypotheses about what might have led you to make your hypotheses. But if I did that, I wouldn't tell you about it unless I were a little disturbed.

C: Bion starts off the supervision by asking, "What [would you] feel if the patient came to see you?" He wonders if you'd like to treat this patient, or not, whether you'd like to see him again. He says, "It's an on-going question […] which you could ask yourself many, many times throughout the analysis." I think that here Bion encourages thinking about theory and technique of observation.

BG: You can think whatever you want. What matters is to watch what happens when you talk about it, if you can. You could observe what you're feeling now, as you write. Do you like what you're doing or not? Do you want to go on?

C: Bion encourages analysts to observe themselves, to perceive what they feel, what they like, what they don't like. I feel that his presupposition is that the patient stirs up feelings in the analyst and that the feelings should be paid attention to. What might have been the impact of this position at that time? What about today? Grotstein once said that Bion was the first intersubjectivist. The second translator confesses that he felt a certain disgust, as if the patient were playing a game with him, and he remembered the image of the *Creation of Man* by Michelangelo. Bion says that he too "felt more or less that". This "feeling" of Bion's might be referring to some repugnance, a "not in contact", and to the patient's wish to be helped. Then Bion wants the group to wonder why "The patient would come to see you. Why should he come to see you at all? What would he want?"

I propose that, after Bion encourages the analyst to think about what he feels, he suggests that the analyst puts himself in the patient's place and tries to feel what he (the patient) feels. The suggestion to observe (from an intersubjective perspective) would be something like: "Perceive what you, the analyst, feel, and then, based on what you observed in yourself, try to realize what the patient feels."

BG: I didn't know that Grotstein said that about me. It's his opinion and I can't do anything about it. Reverential awe encourages acritical acceptance of what others say. Another advantage to this is that we don't have to create our own ideas—we won't have any aches or pain from pregnancy and childbirth. You said that, in the text, I stressed the importance of observing the analyst's feelings and that I suggest intersubjective observation. I would like to be alive to see where this will go. I hope that by 2009 you have advanced farther than me in your capacity to observe. I notice that, by showing hope, I might be influenced by you. After all, you're the ones who are putting words into my mouth … and there's nothing I can do … Perceiving that the patient does something to us, something that we aren't always aware of, shakes up the belief some analysts have that they are "better" (or sharper) than their patients.

C: The analyst should pay attention to his "dream", knowing that it is his own dream, but that this "dream" was elicited by the patient's "dream". By shifting the focus from himself to the patient and back again, he can grasp what is going on in the intersubjective space, that is, between the two. This could be the space between God and man, or that of blank pages that seek to be filled in, or of close interaction (but that allows for some space for the dream). If this space does not exist, we will have no dreams. Other authors, based on Bion, have elaborated on this topic, Meltzer, Grotstein, Ogden, and Ferro being the most widely known. And there are our local Brazilian masters, many of whom, unfortunately, are less well-known due to their being "lost in the translation". In this text I underscore the consideration that Bion has for the person of the analyst, another topic that is a major concern these days.

BG: Thank you, but these opinions were expressed by the colleagues you mentioned. I'd like to know their opinions better so I can compare them to my own experience. You mentioned my consideration for the person of the analyst, literally calling it "another topic that is a major concern these days". But I'm afraid I didn't understand, especially the part where you say "these days". Ever since the beginning, without the person of the analyst there has been no analysis! I presume that my failure to understand has something to do with my being dead.

C: After another confusion of languages the analyst talks about the need for the patient to be reassured—the patient is afraid of going mad. Bion brings up some models of reassurance, that of the surgeon and that of the shoe shop. And he rouses up the audience again: "What does the patient expect from the analyst?" He says that nothing can be done about the past, that the analyst might know something about the past but he can't undo it. Bion insists by asking why the patient tells this story.

I think that Bion is insisting on the topic of observation. Concerning the past (which has already passed) he is emphatic and repeats this warning several times. Maybe he intuitively realizes the listeners' difficulty in coping with this fact at that moment.

BG: What do you want with this supervision? What's gotten into you, reading and discussing something that happened over thirty years ago? If you think you'll learn something from it, I suggest you think otherwise. There is the risk of imitating me, of wanting to be like me, or even being just like me, and this will take you even farther away from yourself. This might be an advantage, if you're very afraid of going mad, but don't throw the responsibility on me.

C: The patient wants to be analyzed because of his fears, but they cover up other kinds of problems. Bion insists: What did the patient expect the analyst to do? This implies: What does the analyst hope to do? Bion seems to be trying to get the analyst to declare his desire. Other kinds of reassurance come up: religion, becoming a doctor, being a good student, doing without sexual intercourse, getting over his mental pain. He asks: What kind of pain is this? "Mental pain" means nothing.

BG: The joining of authors (living or dead) plus reverential awe reassures the psychoanalyst that he has no fears, or that he knows how to cope with those he has. The author would give some tips about what to do, to say, or even to feel! Gods and psychoanalytic religions emerge. Instantaneously, priests appear. The ideal is that they be enigmatic—they will always be "explaining", enjoying themselves with their falsifications. I have noticed that some analysts copy me. They write the way they imagine I write, and they call themselves "Bionians". If you recognize yourself here, that's your problem!

C: The analyst and the translator move ahead in relation to "pains and fears", but fears are mentioned more often. They talk about establishing relationships with other people, such as professionals, who might know things that are hidden from one's own view. Old women (the analyst makes a correction here: *beautiful women*) are also talked about, rich and beautiful women. There is a description of the pains related to feeling unsuccessful, when the patient was in certain situations where he had hoped to be successful, but wasn't.

BG: Words try to describe something indescribable. You will only know what mental pain is when you can feel it. You won't find out by reading about it. I hope that what I said earlier, if you haven't run away from contact with it, has brought you closer to it.

C: Bion asks "What is frightening about being unsuccessful?" This question and the comments before it (about reassurance) make me think that Bion may have grasped in the general atmosphere of the meeting (or meetings) the belief (desire) that adaptation and success were prerequisites for "good mental health". And not only of the patient, but of the analysts as well. He recalls that limitations are a part of life and he shows how one learns from experience. He ends up talking about the fear patients have of perceiving their insanity and the various ways of running away from this contact (by becoming a doctor, having a nice car, turning to religion, etc.). What terrible illness is this that he is so afraid of hearing about?

Finally Bion says, "I think quite simply he's afraid that he's going mad and that you'd tell him so." He shows how reassurance and everything else that is not psychoanalysis will work only for a short time and that the fear of madness will come back. Material goods, confessing one's sins, getting a diagnosis, taking a vacation, and other such social or cultural solutions will mean that he is never treated. The patient thinks that the analyst is going to do something like that and Bion warns the analyst that he will be frustrated if he does.

BG: I hope you have realized that studying this supervision is not going to free you from the fear of going mad, that is, if you can face the fear. The question is to know whether you are running away from it or not by reassuring yourself, by theorizing about other people's experiences.

C: At this point Bion asks: "What should the analyst say to the patient?" And then he answers: "Now, the process is rather like the archaeologist's because you listen and you hear something more and another little bit there and gradually you can see more of who or what that person is. And in this way you can gradually get him to discover, help him to discover himself. So, after a time he gets more used to who he is and not so terrified about his being the person who fails or his being the person who masturbates or his being the person who ... well, all the various things. He gets more used to it because you're more able to introduce him to himself. It's like archaeology. It's like revealing the person who's hidden behind what you can see."

BG: I heard you are going to take this text and discuss it with your colleagues. Since they will be alive they will be more likely to learn from the emotional experience by "listening and hearing something more and another little bit." If you are successful there will be a side effect that is not at all negligible. You will greatly broaden the area of the unknown, but I doubt whether you will be able to put up with this extension without complaining. It's too bad that I will have no way of finding out about it. Being dead means having to put up with not knowing. You, the living, should do the same thing. But you have the advantage of being aware of this and can expand on it. On the other hand, mankind has had a great deal of experience with very successful strategies for avoiding such expansion. I know, I'm talking too much and you don't have the time. Too bad I can't go into this other subject of time ... So, goodbye.

## Note

1. *The Creation of Adam* in the Sistine Chapel in Rome.

CHAPTER SEVEN

# Supervision D14*

A = Analyst: We thought it would be very interesting to see how you evolved as a person and how your ideas developed. For example, do you remember the motives and the reasons …
[Here the tape is incomprehensible]
[you developed the practice,] the discipline of [attempting to be without] memory and desire? This was the subject of your first paper, notes on memory and desire.

BION: The point about this is that … it is very difficult, if you want to understand what is happening while you are observing. Now, this point is mentioned by somebody who wasn't a psychoanalyst at all, namely Darwin … who said: "It's impossible to observe and judge what you are observing at the same time." In other words, he certainly found the difficulty in making observations and understanding the observations that he made. So, there's nothing new about it. It's really well-known as being a very difficult thing and is sure to interfere with the observation if you're trying to know what it is, or understand what it is that you're seeing while you are seeing it. Yet, in psychoanalysis, it's exactly what we think, or say, that analysts have to do.

I think, actually, psychoanalysts should have to develop a fresh capacity because, … there is quite a lot of evidence which suggests that people find it *very* difficult, while they are observing what is going on, to understand what is going on. So, in a sense,

---

*For purposes of reading comprehension, many of the "spaces" and "gaps" in the recording have been eliminated in this typescript of the chapter. However, some are retained to give the reader the flavor of the original typescript, as described in the editors' introduction.

one could say: if you are having a session, being the analyst, it becomes hopeless to try to do that work while you are wondering about your next vacation or going home or something of that kind, or while you are remembering about some past holiday, because that interferes with the analytic work. It gets very complicated if you say that. It also becomes very difficult to do analysis, if you are trying to understand what is happening, while you are also trying to observe what is going on. Now, if it is true that it is very difficult that analysts have got to solve this problem, this is exactly what, it seems, at any rate, what we're supposed to do!

A: But you arrived at that conclusion after some experience?

BION: Yes, and there's a great deal of truth there and experience, not only of being an analyst, but also of being analyzed. I have never really been convinced that the analyst, who is doing the analysis, is really able to judge or understand what is taking place at the same time. I could go further—I don't know what the importance is—but, it seems to me, very often, that analysts are incredibly bad judges of character. So much so that one could almost say that if analysts regard somebody as being a good or reliable character, that they are almost certainly wrong and if they regard somebody as being a bad character, they are almost certainly wrong. Now, I don't call that a desirable situation but it seems to me that it's a true situation. I think analysts may be very good psychoanalysts, whatever that is, whatever you have to be, but certainly not good judges of character. After all, there's nothing—this is something which happens quite frequently—you can say, some important person … chooses his employees, his firm, his officers, very badly. That's a quite common thing to say. It's not quite common to say that analysts choose their colleagues very, very badly.

A: Why? What do you think that the reason is for the bad choice?

BION: I don't know. Except what I'm suggesting, at the moment, that maybe because you can't judge a character while you are analyzing him.

A: Don't you think that's a quality, that it's important for the analyst to be able to avoid judging the patient?

BION: I think that probably the analyst should avoid doing so, yes. In that way, I could say, I could include understanding the person, while doing analysis, as something, which interferes with analysis, or doing the analysis interferes with the judgement of the character. It may be that at some time or another we should get better at it. One could get to a point where one might be able to do both: to judge character and be analyzing it, at the time that one's doing it. But, certainly one doesn't seem to be able to do both and analysts don't seem to be very good at doing that, at present; [they] might become better at it later on. But, I don't think it is a sort of peculiarity of analysts, because as I say, if you can hear something about a man like Darwin—he himself is doing just that—and I think that there are other people likewise, who have been notoriously bad judges of character and you wouldn't expect them to be. Even in modern days, there are people in positions of authority and power and so forth … who seem to pick their colleagues very badly.

A: I'd like to ask another question maybe in agreement with that … about the meaning of the senses.

BION: Yes, yes.

A: ... [About] intuition ... [Can] you ... explain some steps of these changes?

BION: I think it became obvious to me, I might say it had always been obvious. Take something simple like anxiety: I can't smell it, I can't tell you what its shape is, but I have no doubt at all about anxiety!! So, anyhow, although I have got no sensuous awareness—I can't take a photograph of it, I can't take an X-Ray of it—nevertheless, I'm sure that there's anxiety. Now, this is something which most people would agree about. This is hardly worth talking about, because it is clear that you can't see it, or feel it, or touch it, or say what its shape is, or what its smell is. But it exists and you could go through all the senses, all these emotional experiences, that there is no—as far as we know—sensuous evidence of it. People are angry, people are in love, people are hating, people are ... having all these different feelings, but there's no sensuous experience of it. There's no sensible experience, no experience which is available to the senses of touch, sight, hearing, smell ... as far as we know; or if there is, we still haven't found any words for it.

A: Don't you think that there are some physical signs of anxiety, facial expressions, an activity of glands and so on ... that somehow there are some senses that can capture this feeling of anxiety or other feelings like anger, pain.

BION: ... By the time these feelings betray themselves in senses, it's very late in the story. For example, somebody can be very hostile, you would certainly know that if they came with some weapon which they flourished and threatened you with—one needs to know that long before they do anything of that sort.

A: My question is: wouldn't there be other signs that were not prominent, like a weapon, but still perceptible by the senses?

BION: I think that there probably are. That is why I think it would be helpful if one could develop the *intuition,* when somebody who's very angry, before that somebody attacks you with an axe or a knife.

A: Perhaps some perception that would not achieve the conscious level—taking for instance the model of the seventh chapter of Freud's Dream book—that some perceptions are like the negative of a photograph, but nevertheless, would be perceived somehow.

BION: It's possible, but until we perceive it, it's no good talking about being analysts, or at least, it may be all right talking about it. But it's quite a strong claim to make to say that we can do this; for example: I've known of a man who says: "I can smell that there's a rattle snake here and I can smell that *that* rattle snake is angry." It is possible that so can a dog. Now, I've known—in childhood—a situation where—which is quite common and everybody knows about it—two dogs, quite ordinary dogs, quite ordinary terrier dogs, will go to the hole of a cobra. Now, the cobra is a very dangerous, very toxic snake and it is very fast, indeed, if it's traveling in a straight line! That, it can't do that fast!

[Dr. Bion is, at this point, making a swerving movement with his arm]

Now, two dogs will get together and one of them will dig down the snake's hole and the other one stands at the side. It goes on ... the digging goes on until the cobra is nearly reached, when the cobra will suddenly shoot straight out like that.

[Another gesture is made with the arm]

> Now, the other dog, which is watching stands there. The moment the snake does that, gets it behind the neck and shakes like that.

[Another gesture]

> The first dog that has been doing the digging lies down and gets his breath back. Then, at a sudden moment, the dog which has got the snake and is doing that, drops it and the second dog pounces on it, picks it up and goes on doing it. In this way, as I say, two terriers will go snake hunting—cobra hunting to be exact—and will carry it out in that successful way, for a very long time and kill snake after snake by going on shaking it, until it can't really do anything about it. Now a mongoose, although, mind you, there's a very, very good story, by Kipling—it's a very good story, which he makes a lot out of the mongoose's fight with a cobra. In actual fact, the story is a good story, but it is quite inaccurate because the cobra hasn't got a chance. … Because the cobra can go faster than a horse in a straight line; but, it can't do that.

[Another gesture is made]

> So, the mongoose will just jump from one side to another and the other and will be quickly safe, will then, grab the cobra from the back of the neck and kill it. So, there's no such thing as a fight between a cobra and a mongoose. I've seen one. The cobra hasn't a chance, although it's incredibly fast, on that straight line. … But the point about all this is: how does the second dog know that the first dog is going to drop the snake? How do these animals know that the cobra is nearly, nearly, going to strike out, as a snake, out of the hole? But they *do* know. Now, are you going to talk about the dogs' *intuition?* What is one to call it?
>
> In this work, there simply isn't the language for the job. All our language is really suitable for something much grosser like … and even when it comes to psychology, it's like we talk about fear, sex, hostility, love and so on … but those are very, very gross. All this multitude, sub-divisions aren't expressed, at all. You can't say: "I'm talking about anger one hundred and one, or anger ninety-nine, or anger one, or anger two." But, that is what you have to do. Now, if you changed, if you changed the whole approach: didn't use language at all, then you might be able to *paint* it, because you can get very, very considerable sub-divisions, which *can't* be expressed in language, but can be expressed in paint or color.
>
> Now, I've known a patient whose color sense was so acute that they could not bear ordinary clothes. They had to stick to one particular shade of blue, in one particular material, because the rest were too painful. I've known a patient who couldn't even listen to a performance by the Philharmonic Orchestra in London—when it was the leading orchestra in the world—because he said the clarinet player was sharp and it

wrecked the whole performance, so completely, that he couldn't listen to it. Now, that same patient couldn't learn how to play actually, it was the French horn, because he couldn't stand the noise he made. He could not play, perfectly enough, to be able to put up with it. Yet, there are people who can play it and can be sensitive enough to play it very well, indeed! A man likes Dennis Brain, for example, who's able to play the French horn. He's one of the few players who, you could be certain, would never make a false note.

So, [my patient] had a very sensitive ear and, yet, he was able to put up with the agony of playing it, so to speak—if he was good enough to play it so well. But, there are many people who have to give up playing the musical instrument, whatever it is, because they can't stand being the novice when they are learning it. Whether there's a painter whose eye is so exquisite, that they would have to give up painting, I don't know. If it is true, then, one of the miracles about a man like Picasso is that: he can be so sensitive to color and appearance and yet survive to be a painter.

[While changing sides some words were lost]

… is that a woman's face? Well, the point is: if you can bear to look at it, it may show you something that you are not able to notice until it is shown. A person like Meyer may show you a wall, a brick wall, in such a way, that you feel that you've never looked at a brick wall before and you will never be able to see a brick wall in the way that you used to see it once. It *does* something to *you*. Now, if you take all this you can get some idea of the *scale* of setting up as a psychoanalyst, … that one is sensitive enough to be able to tell something about people's character, personalities and so on …

Most of it is sheer nonsense, because it's difficult to believe that people really get anywhere near it. That's why you get a situation where a mother will say to an analyst: "There's never been anything wrong with this patient until they came to analysis." It's just not true! It's complete fallacy! The analyst can't make a person ill like that. The analyst can only know that a person is ill, or in trouble, or hostile, or dangerous and so forth …

I think it's difficult to believe that you can say: can smell that somebody is angry, or hostile or dangerous. Yet, if it is true, an experienced hunter can smell that there's a rattlesnake about and that it is angry, then, surely, it should be possible for psychoanalysts to become, or to be sufficiently *intuitive* to—well, we call it, falling back on this very clumsy language—"smell" that the person is angry. But the vocabulary doesn't exist. There's no way which the person can write the language of his birth and so forth … with sufficient accuracy to describe it. Somebody like Proust or Strindberg or James Joyce or Shakespeare … they may be able to use words with such a skill.

A: They may convey the meaning of thousands of angers and pains in combinations of words that make you feel …

BION: Something of that sort.

A: The poetic language is much richer than …

BION: Well, the poet is like the painter. He may be able to do something, if he's a great enough poet, to be able to do it. Strachey, a well-known English writer used to say that the words "Nymphs and shepherds dance no more"[1] would always bring tears to his eyes. All those words are perfectly simple. There's nothing obtrusive about them, but put together in that particular shape, they have the most profound affect.

A: The other day when you were speaking about the need for respecting mystery …

[Some words are incomprehensible]

[it] reminded me of the words of a Welsh poet that I like very much—Dylan Thomas. There's a poem by him where he says: "And the mystery staying alive, still in the water and singing birds",[2] and I think it's a very beautiful image of this region of mystery.

BION: Yes. Of course, mind you, that is putting words together in a way, which does not evade the laws of grammar.

A: "Psychoanalytic addiction" is the psychoanalytic process without this mystery. You have spoken about psychoanalytic addiction.

BION: Well, most of us are just not good enough. It would be a very rash or foolish man who said he is a good analyst; because, there's one thing that an analyst ought to be able to learn—if he lives long enough: is that he knows very little about [psychoanalysis]. He may even know something. The trouble there is that if the analyst says: "I know very little about it", somebody else is sure to rush and say: "Oh, I know", but they don't, they're worse.

A: They give place to psychoanalytic addiction. That's what you mean?

BION: Well, the difficulty is: if the psychoanalyst doesn't indicate that he's prepared to be a psychoanalyst, somebody else will, who's even less qualified! So, you're in this dilemma in which you have to make it clear that you're prepared to be a psychoanalyst and, at the same time, not to lose your awareness that it's probably a very exaggerated saying …

A: Dr. Bion, the psychoanalyst has to compromise with himself to profit from all the experience that he participates in …

BION: Well, intuition and judgement and even thinking, are processes which are very easily tired. After all, even in genetics, a person who is a good athlete, might be able to run a mile very fast, but the person who runs a hundred yards very fast has really got to be a person who is able to, in a hundred yards, to finish absolutely exhausted—having used everything, he's got in that short space of time. The person who is able to run a mile is much the same thing. The person who is able to run a marathon, that's different, in a way. There, he's got to be able to be running, at the end, as at the beginning. So is the two hundred yards person too. But … the rate at which they have to be able to spend their energy it differs.

Now, when it comes to a question of *intuition*, it is a matter of judging, as near as you can, the kind of job you have to do with such equipment as you've got to do it with. In a critical situation, an analyst might have to work very fast indeed! If a patient comes into your room and has got a loaded revolver or pistol in his pocket, you may have to think very fast indeed.

A: It already happened to my husband!

BION: Yes.

A: But, we cannot have too much pain in our senses, because that falsifies our perceptions. And how could we proceed in our contact with the patient with such a lack of confidence in our senses?

BION: It's very difficult to find a language that you can say about it, that you have to be tough as well. You have to be very robust. You have to be ruthless, even with yourself. It's no good somebody being so sensitive to music that they can't play the violin or can't play the horn or whatever else it is. They have *got* to be able to both know how badly they are playing and to be able to go on playing badly and listen to the beastly noise they are making. They've got to be sensitive, but they've also got to be tough.

A: Do you mean that we should wait for the convenient [moment] … that we'll reserve for that subject of incomprehensible or unbearable light? Or unbearable or incomprehensible communications?

BION: … The psychoanalyst who can practice psychoanalysis has got to be able, as far as possible, to stand whatever the dangers are and is only competent when he goes on working. A writer has got to be able to know how badly he's writing and yet, go on writing, trying to get it better perhaps. But even then, feeling that the only thing he really learns is how badly he writes; that he can be quite sure of that's why some people are highly regarded. That's why one can say: Shakespeare—whoever that was—or Homer, were great people. They were quite ordinary people, like everybody else, but they were able to stand it. Shakespeare didn't know he was Shakespeare, when he said he was Shakespeare—not what *we* think of Shakespeare. He was simply a man who got into all sorts of difficulties and so forth … and finally he was successful and managed to get a house in Stratford-upon-Avon …

[In these sections words are incomprehensible]

[In the end] he appears to have been fairly satisfied. If you read the sonnets, though, you can see for yourself that he was not really describing a situation in which he was being very successful.

A: But using your contact between [you and] the patient for the success of the psychoanalysis, we hope to be able to work, to trace what we have.

BION: Yes, of course. Mind you, this is more difficult still, because, actually, we have to talk a language, which is understood by the patient. So, it is both saying something which is very difficult to express or formulate at all. But, in addition to all that, it has to be formulated so simply that it can be understood by the patient, who does not know anything about analysis and may not even be a person who likes, or can stand words; for example, I've had a patient who was a very considerable musician. He hated the language. He said: "If you could bring a piano into this room and let me play to you, I would do something, but this ridiculous talking is no good to me."

A: Do you play the piano? Do you play the piano?

BION: No.

A: How could you interpret it?

BION: I couldn't! I had to use the language and he had to learn the language. He had to put up with it, but throughout the analysis, throughout the experience—it was a painful experience to him—he didn't just hate the interpretation and the meanings of the interpretations, he hated the language that was used. In a situation like that you can miss the fact that the person is, *in fact*, feeling hostile and is suffering a lot of pain; but it is not because of the meaning of the words, it is not because you have drawn attention to the fact that he is a coward, or cruel or something of that kind. It sounds as if it is, but it is much more than that. It is not only what you say but also the way that you say it. On the other hand, you can get another patient who'll say: "Alright, I'll draw it for you." But, then, they wouldn't be able to understand the drawing that looks like a person. In short, what I'd say about it is: psychoanalysis is in its infancy. This sort of job has never been done before and it's very doubtful as to how much, if at all, is being done today.

A: We have to be able to give up success, isn't that so? Try to go into an adventure.

BION: As usual, somebody who isn't a psychoanalyst, at all, has said it: "It is not in mortals to command success, but we'll do more to deserve it".[3] The best that a psychoanalyst can hope for is that he deserves, in a sense of doing his best; but being successful, no.

A: Dr. Bion, you said that—another evening—that you did not consider yourself an original painter.

BION: Yes.

A: And, of course, you are not …

[Some words are incomprehensible]

… you have known yourself for such a long time and so on … we have to believe you. Nevertheless, we all that listen to you have the impression and … that have read your book, that you are original … Do you consider anything that you have written, so far, or done, as an original contribution to psychoanalysis?

BION: I don't know a single one, not one!

P2: Not even your … what seems to me, at least, the most original of all your written books, *The Theory of Transformation*.[4] Don't you consider that an original contribution? …

BION: Not at all.

A: No?

BION: No! In fact, I've said over and over again, if you read this book, you'll only understand it when you realize that you're perfectly familiar with the experience.

A: Yes, but that's the puzzling thing that all these evenings we have been listening to you and we have these contradictory feelings of listening to something that is at the same time very, very familiar and very, very unexpected … very familiar but is obvious, familiar, just like ourselves. We are very familiar with ourselves, but very unknown to ourselves. That's the experience that we've been having listening to you. The only thing that I can remember that would be like, would be listening to Scheherazade every night: you never know what will come next.

BION: Yes.

A: And we are all sort of spellbound, it's a pity it won't last a thousand and one nights. But … you have, in our opinion, a very different way of expressing your thoughts.

BION: There's rather an amusing illustration of it, in Conan Doyle's Sherlock Holmes stories …

[Lots of laughter]

… in which Sherlock Holmes carries out a piece of deduction and then … I think it is Watson who says: "Oh, well, that's quite simple." Sherlock Holmes says: "The worst of this is that: when I make a piece of deduction and make it clear, everybody thinks there's nothing in it." And, the fate of the analyst is to make his existence unnecessary. In a way, one says it's the fate of the parents that if you bring up your children properly, they don't need parents.

A: What is "bring up properly"?
BION: Everybody knows how to do that, it is so simple …

[A loud burst of laughter]

A: How many children have you had?
BION: Three.
A: Three children.
BION: Three children have had to put up with me as a parent!

[Laughter again]

A: Mustn't have been easy!

[This was said in a joking tone of voice]

BION: Well, it's a severe problem as to how children are able to stand having an analyst as a parent, as a father or mother; luckily, some of them survive!
A: I have had to put up with two, a husband and a father!
A: Do you see any difference between bringing up a child and educating a child, because, I think, you told us that sometimes education, or at least substitute education, inhibits certain points of perception.
BION: Yes. Well, it is so because, in fact, do you actually give the child a chance to discover things for itself? You can try, but suppose a baby starts crawling towards the fire and wanting to pick out one of the pretty, red coals. You can't let it do that, you've got to stop it.
A: This is education?
BION: Well, it is a part of education and it is, as far as we know, there's no way of knowing—how to let the child learn that fire burns, without its killing itself. This applies to even to the metaphorical use as to how to teach a child that it's living in a dangerous world, without making it so frightened that it's afraid to live in it, at all. Indeed, one can get a situation where the mother or father are so fussy—"Don't do that, don't do that, don't ride a bicycle, don't go in the street", and so on—that in the end, they are so terribly frightened.

## Notes

1. This phrase is from Milton's *Arcades*.
2. The poem is "Poem in October" and the correct lines are: "And the mystery/Sang alive/Still in the water and singing birds".
3. *Cato, a Tragedy*, from Joseph Addison, English poet and essayist (1672–1719). The original text to which Bion refers to is: "'Tis not in mortals to command success; but we'll do more, Sempronius, we'll deserve it."
4. The original name is: *Transformations*.

# Commentary on supervision D14: a language for the job

*Giuseppe Civitarese*

At the very start of this supervision Bion is asked to tell how he came to formulate his idea that the analyst has to listen to the patient "without memory and desire". His answer is that the analyst has to deal with elements that are very subtle. He cannot smell, touch, see, or hear them. How then can he do his job if he lacks even a language for it? But this is exactly, we might say in hindsight, what Bion dedicated his life as a psychoanalytic theoretician to accomplish: to forge a new and effective language for this job, for what he calls elsewhere (in supervision A42) "the game of psychoanalysis".

The word "intuition" is the one that seems capable of "doing the job". It gives a nice definition to the task of the analyst and, for Bion, possessing a nice definition is of essential importance, because the game of psychoanalysis, as it is presented here, looks quite dangerous. We only need to pay attention to the metaphors Bion chooses: "a fight"; two terrier dogs that instinctively hunt and "kill snake after snake"; the leap of the mongoose at the cobra's neck; and so on. Another quite striking image is that of being surprised and attacked by someone "with an axe or knife" (!).

The other key factor that makes the game dangerous is time. The analyst's thoughts and interventions, as in war, have to be quick, because there is no time to think, at least in the usual reflective and logical ways. The analyst cannot "do analysis" and at the same time "judge characters". Now, why is Bion using this verb, "to judge"? In fact, somebody asks him if it is not more a matter of understanding than of judging. He concedes that, but uses again the same verb soon after. It is because—we might speculate—he wants to choose a term that emphasizes the rational pondering of things even more. But, again, he repeats that it is impossible to judge or understand what really is going on at the same time that one is conducting an analysis. So, that is why, as in a fight, that the analyst within the inevitable turmoil of the session needs to be quick and instinctive (or intuitive).

> "Now, when it comes to a question of *intuition*, it is a matter of judging, as near as you can, the kind of job you have to do with such equipment as you've got to do it with. In a critical situation, an analyst might have to work very fast, indeed! If a patient comes into your room and has got a loaded revolver or pistol in his pocket, you may have to think very fast indeed."

By the way, in these passages it's very interesting how Bion's discourse may be listened to as if referring to what in contemporary Bionian field theory is meant by the expression "casting of characters" in the psychoanalytic narrative in order to transform unthought emotions into thoughts. It is equally true that even when "judging" the field function of narrative characters, it is necessary that the analyst be quick and intuititive.

Another evocative après coup effect is the arrangement of the original text of the supervision D14. Due to the imperfections in the recording process, there is an alternation of regular paragraphs with missing lines and empty paragraphs.[1] This physical pattern on the original page, unwittingly suggests the void of memory and desire that Bion advocates as essential to the listening stance of the analyst. It indicates a space awaiting saturation or completion and produces a moment of vertiginous uncertainty for the reader, who is called upon to intuit what the lost parts of the text might have said. It is as if the reader, like the analyst in the session, must put himself on the line, body and soul, to intuit a more complete meaning of what the content might have been, thanks to the work of an unconscious understanding.

[Anothere gesture is made], [Here the tape is incomprehensible], [While changing sides some words were lost], [Some words are incomprehensible], [In these section words are incomprehensible]. We might call these gaps and omissions unsaturated spaces, or invitations addressed to the reader to try some "cobra hunting" of meaning.

Then another set of images is recruited, much less menacing. Bion evokes the art of the painter, of someone who perhaps cannot tell something, but is able to paint it, or of a musician, who can play it and thereby express it musically. As Bion continues speaking of people who are naturally very sensitive to colors or sounds, the names of Darwin, Freud, Picasso, Meyer, Proust, Strindberg, Joyce, Shakespeare, Milton, Dylan Thomas, and Homer are cited as examples of men of achievement, of possessors of these exquisite or special sensitive capacities. Bion's point is that you don't need to be a Meyer, etc. It may suffice that somebody like him shows you "a brick wall, in such a way, that you feel that you've never looked at a brick wall before and you will never be able to see a brick wall in the way that you used to see it once. It does something to you". In the same way an analyst should be able to speak to a patient, affect him and help him expand his capacity for sensing the real.

At a certain point somebody from the audience comments on the richness of the poetic language. Bion picks it up immediately: "Well, the poet is like the painter."

By the end of the text it should be clearer what the link between judging—and why Bion insists on this verb—and intuition is. Intuition is not in opposition to rationality but, if disciplined, it may be a more sophisticated version of it; one which is suited for this impossible, not based on sensuous awareness, job. So "impossible" that the analyst has to be "tough", "robust", and "ruthless", even with himself. He has to develop the sensitivity that the analytic task requires. At the same time, he has to speak to the patient in the simplest possible way.

Here Bion gives the reader one of his typical illuminating sketches, which is worth more than innumerable words of commentary:

> I've had a patient who was a very considerable musician. He hated the language. He said: "If you could bring a piano into this room and let me play to you, I would do something, but this ridiculous talking is no good to me."

One might say that with every patient the *music of words* is what is most meaningful. That is, it is affect that lies at the very centre of psychoanalysis, a point that Bion alludes to when, finally, he comments that the fate of analysts, like that of parents, is to "bring up" patients and then to disappear and make their own "existence unnecessary". In this way a patient will not need an analyst anymore, or a child a parent. But here the difference between education and "properly" bringing up a child (or a patient) is of great theoretical value. The analyst needs to seek a difficult balance between protecting the patient while letting him discover things on his own; he has to learn "how to teach a child [a patient] that it's living in a dangerous world, without making it so frightened that it's afraid to live in it, at all".

## Note

1. In order to facilitate reader comprehension, many of these gaps and spaces have been eliminated in the printed version. However, several have been retained to give the reader a sense of the flavor of the original typescript.

CHAPTER EIGHT

# Supervision A42*

T = Translator: ... [The patient began analysis] three years ago. He was twenty years old, he was of Jewish origin and he came [referred] by the Institute of Psychoanalysis. He is a medical student, in the second year and he did not pass the examination in his course of anatomy ... [and] brought a complaint of feeling tense, anxious.

BION: Who said he was Jewish?

T: On his first interview, he didn't tell [his analyst]; but later on ... he brought up the subject. He said that his father and mother were Jewish, but he didn't feel like a Jew; or better, that he was and he was not a Jew. He was a Jew, because people told him he was a Jew. So, he accepted it in a way; but he was not a Jew, because he didn't follow their religion. He didn't feel as if he were a Jew ...

BION: One question is: how does he know he doesn't feel like a Jew? Because what does a Jew feel like? If you say: "I don't feel like a well person." A statement like that means that you *must know* what it feels like to be a *well* person.

T: ... He told her that he didn't know what a Jew was, he heard people say that he was a Jew; therefore, he didn't know and he didn't feel as if he was a Jew.

BION: Yes. But what I'm saying is: that is a wrong statement. If I say: "I don't feel like a Jew", how do I know what a Jew feels like? Either: I don't know what I'm talking about, or I must think that I know what it feels like to feel like a Jew; therefore, what I feel is different from what it feels like to feel like a Jew.

---

*Supervision given by Wilfred Bion in São Paulo, Brazil, in 1978. Transcribed from the tape by Dr. Jose Américo Junqueira de Mattos, training analyst of the Brazilian Psychoanalytic Society of São Paulo.

If I was told that, I should feel suspicious about this, even if I heard myself saying it. I could say that: I must feel that I'm just like one of these Jews that I'm not like. I must be doing something to say that I'm not one of these Jews; but, it must, in fact, be that I am a Jew who does not want anyone to know I'm a Jew. Therefore, in a sense, it's like saying: "I don't feel like a Jew. I feel superior to a Jew. I'm better than Jews." I don't know what sort of better, but one of them.

In short, in any choice, any choice whatever, you are also bound to choose what you're not choosing. To quote an Arab verse: "Lord, thou make me free of all thy flowers, but I chose the world's sad roses and that is why my feet are torn and my eyes are blind with sweat." Now, I quote that verse, because it's a typical English translation of an Arabian poet. The Arabian style of poetry, and the Arabian discipline, gets nearer to what I'm wanting to draw attention to here, namely: that at some point or another, these various choices are made. Instead of "all thy flowers" I could say "all the options" and you can cut down the number of options to the number of things that you choose. So you choose, say, three things, but you also choose not to choose all the rest. Now, amongst the options of this particular patient, is that he could be a Jew, or a Russian, or a Brazilian, or an English and so on … but, he chooses to be—whatever he chooses—and he chooses not to be a Jew.

Now, how did he know what a Jew was, so as not to choose it? It becomes a matter of some importance, if it means that he chooses not to be one of the children of his parents. If he wants to say: "My father and mother, no, I don't want to be like that." It becomes more serious still if it means: "I don't want to be like my father or my father's father" or even before that; because, that is a repudiation of your ancestry. So, that is apparently a simple statement, probably made at a time when the patient didn't really know very much. He mightn't even know that Jews have a very ancient culture, or history. Anyway, he chooses *not to be* one of these inferior creatures. Now, if that is really effective, he's wiped out hundreds and even thousands of years of history and the history of his race. Now, one can begin to have an idea of what he has chosen through knowing what he has chosen not to choose.

However, all that I have just been saying is very conjectural. This is what I mean by *imaginative conjecture*. This is what I want to include as a part of scientific thought; but, that doesn't mean that one doesn't want to know some more as well. It seems to me to help to map out a kind of area, which one would like to inhabit with ideas or knowledge.

To come back to the point of this patient, we can hear what he has chosen; but, we want to fill in this area of what he has chosen not to know, not to learn. To put it more precisely: has one got any idea of what he wants to know, instead of himself? What areas of himself does he want *to know nothing about?* Well, we may get a clue from hearing a bit more about what he has chosen to know. So, as we listen to this story, we can get a chance of learning something about what he has chosen to know and from that, some idea of what he has chosen *not to know:* the self that he doesn't want to know!

Now, falling back here—not so much on imaginative conjecture—but, what one could call *rational conjecture*, one could say … well … a rational theory, a rational psychoanalytic theory, could it be said to be: not wanting anything about sex at all? Because, genetically, he must have both: a father and mother and they may be Jewish fathers and mothers. It doesn't tell us very much, because we don't know what Jewish fathers and mothers are; and it's no good going to the dictionary and looking up Jewish, and looking up father and looking up mother. There's no way of answering this question except: looking at, observing this personality that's coming into the room. This is one reason why I'd like to stress *so much* the importance of *observation:* not the importance of what you read in books, or hear, or hearsay, but what your own observations tell you. [*Nota sobre* Charcot]

So, shall we go on a bit more, with this particular instance and hear a bit more about this person. … We can now listen to what our senses, in the shape of what the analyst can tell us.

T: You mentioned as a conjecture, that his repudiation of not being a Jew could be a refusal to accept his parents. [The analyst] can observe that he is very hostile to his parents and that sometimes he makes comments, like his mother is a real crazy woman; the only thing she can do is to interfere in his life and that his father is weak and absent …

When he came for treatment, it was at the same period in which he had failed his examination. Formerly, he was a good student, he always had very good grades and after that he started having difficulties in his relationships with his fellow students and with people in general. This feeling of inferiority was also associated to what he felt as poverty in his parents; poverty in money and also poverty in culture, as people.

BION: What effect does that create on you? What's the impression you get from what the analyst has told us?

T: [The analyst] has the impression that after he failed his exams, he became [in his mind] "a Jew".

BION: Any other suggestion? I'm quite glad to give you my impression, the only thing is: that there's always the danger of thinking my impressions matter—they don't. But, I can imagine a situation in which when you decided not to feel like a Jew, at the same time, you lose your ability to be tolerant and achieve an ability to be bigoted and selective. So, you achieve a whole area of *not to be*. So, we could say: there's only a half of you or a quarter of you, or some still smaller fraction of yourself left and there's a vast area which you can't learn, because it's wrong, it's inferior. And now, you're supposed to pass an examination. So, the problem is: how to be a person who knows nothing about a culture, who knows nothing about the boundaries of that culture, especially if it's the culture of what I could call your *breed*. In fact, how is it possible for him to know himself, because to know himself, involves …

[Side one ends here and some words are lost while changing sides of the tape. Nevertheless, from what the translator translated from English to Portuguese to the group, I could reconstruct what Dr. Bion probably said: "… because to know himself involves knowing himself and his breed and the exclusion of breed involves a repudiation of breeding."]

I have to use that word [breed] because I don't know any other. I could try to tell you what I mean by suggesting: not to know your breed involves a repudiation of breeding—it's very difficult to describe. But, in real life, I think that you'd be able to feel the difference between a person of breeding and a person who had no breeding. If you consider the animal world, we're always engaged in matters like the breeding of animals, the breeding of plants. I've even known people who had no long schooling or education who, nevertheless, have learnt how to achieve cross-fertilization, for example: of plants, vegetables and so on … So, it's hardly surprising that this patient now begins to fail at examinations, it might have been much easier for him to pass examinations if he wasn't engaged in having to say: "I don't know this, I don't know that, I don't know the other: it's inferior."

Now, a great number of people that I see coming to me for help have learnt very thoroughly that many nice girls and really nice boys don't know anything about sex. Well, when a nice girl and a nice boy meet and decide to become husband and wife, what are they going to do if they've learnt to go on being nice? What are they going to do, or be, if they mustn't know or learn anything to do with sex? Supposing they decide to go to bed together, in a way that married people do, are they going to continue to learn nothing about sex? Are you going to be producing children and your children's children, without knowing anything about your fathers and your father's fathers? One could say here, to make it more general, is there any future for the Brazilian culture if Brazilians don't want to know who their fathers were, or their father's fathers? Are there going to be any children and any children's children? That is taking the wide view. Now, let's narrow it right down, like that and look at this patient and his girl and boyfriends: just one little bit of human culture, as it were, one little bit of the human family. We needn't bother about looking at the human race, or human family, because we can't do anything about it, but we can, perhaps, do something about discussing, at any rate, this little bit of the human family, who's met with this analyst.

T: Your words, Dr. Bion, reminded [the analyst] of the patient's sexual problems that started almost at the same time when he came for treatment. Oh! It's a bit before that, that he started with sexual problems, although some time ago he had a girlfriend with whom he had sexual relationships.

BION: Yes. May I interrupt? The trouble is: you can't do analysis unless you *observe* the patient, but if you observe the patient, the patient can't help knowing that he's being observed. Now, it becomes very difficult to be, whoever he is, while he is being observed. So, the very act of analysis, when one … is observing the other; it's not surprising if this difficulty crops up in analysis and if it doesn't crop up in the bedroom, when the nice girl and the nice boy lie together and the nice boy might see what the nice girl was doing, the nice girl might see what the nice boy was doing. Something is bound to happen: either they'll have to stop being nice, or they'll have to stop lying in the same bed and that would very rapidly turn into divorce. But, the same thing applies in analysis; it doesn't matter very much, because analysis is only a temporary affair, anyway. But, it is possible to try to be frank, or sincere, or honest in the analysis, whether you are the analyst, or the analysand, or both.

It's not quite so serious, as what happens if you're married, because that is not a game, it's not even a psychoanalytic game, it's life itself. That is why the analysis is, in fact, a serious game. It's a game in the sense of being fun, or could be, but it is also serious, in the sense that it matters what we do, besides having fun. It's a curious situation, because I think it leads to the feeling that analysts shouldn't play sexual games, or have sexual intercourse with their man or girl patient; at the same time, neither of these two people should be so *carefree* that they are really *careless*; that is why, the practice of analysis is so difficult. It's much easier for me here to talk about psychoanalysis than it is for me to practice psychoanalysis and that applies to everyone of us. But, both of these things are similar to the fact that it's easier to play games, like fathers and mothers, than to be a father or a mother. This game of fathers and mothers has in it, implicit, the people who will one day be a father and mother. That is why, when you see children playing—they seem to be enjoying themselves and they also get angry and cross and won't play anymore. They'll go off to their father and mother and say: "What can I do now, please?" And whatever the father or the mother says is not the right thing! But, this becomes serious when they *are* father and mother. In analysis, therefore, it is that you're dealing with a doubly serious situation. One of them is the actual analysis, itself. It is so important how that psychoanalytic game is to be played. But, at the same time, there's something which *isn't* the rehearsal, but *the-thing-in-itself*. To get back to this actual analysis, the one that the analyst is having, the one that we are hearing about. I would like to suggest that the analyst is like a person who is turning the pages of a book, like rather idly and the analysand can say: "Oh, page forty-six" or, to put it in different words, "I'm the forty-six or forty or thirty" or whatever and the analyst is then listening to the story of the book, which is opened at page thirty, forty, or whatever.

Now, as the patient reads the story of his life, starting at page thirty, can you imagine what happened on pages one to twenty-nine? Can you imagine what will happen on pages thirty to forty? As a matter of fact, we don't even know if he gets to page thirty or forty; when the analyst or the patient walks out into the street, they may get run down and killed then and there. So the story could end on page thirty-one.

These things that we call interpretations are really *imaginative conjectures* about the missing pages. Now, this patient has already torn out a whole number of pages, all the Jewish pages have been torn out. How are we to read this story? How is he to pass the analytic examination? Is it surprising that he can't get through the analytic examination? Because, it's like saying to the analyst something which is analogues to saying to a doctor: "Doctor, I've got a pain!" or "No, I don' want to take my clothes off! No, I don't want to have an X-ray! You want a blood sample? No, I don't want my blood examined, in the path lab!" The funniest thing that you can say is: "It's no use coming to me, I'm only a doctor. You'll have to find somebody else!" Or alternatively: "You will have to take off these layers of clothes, you'll have to lie on the examination couch!" That is why the practice of analysis is so difficult, because we try to make these things as easy as possible for the patient, but also, for ourselves as the analysts. So, the analyst could feel—I don't say the analyst could say—but the analyst could feel: "I'll have to know more about this patient, I'll have to arrange to see this patient tomorrow and tomorrow and tomorrow."

[There is a long silence, as Dr. Bion was thinking and he continues.]

As Shakespeare puts it:

> "Tomorrow and tomorrow and tomorrow,
> Creeps in this petty pace, from day to day

> To the last syllable of recorded time,
> And all our yesterdays have lighted fools
> Way to dusty death."[1]

This patient's yesterdays, the patient's tomorrows, which creep in a petty pace, but, in fact, they are all over very quickly! The time between nought and the day of the patient's death, we simply don't know. We don't know how many pages there are to the book. So, the patient is in a situation and the analyst is in a situation, in which one doesn't really know quite what the metronome time is—I'm borrowing from the analogy of music—at which the analysis should be conducted.

All this is involved in what we call psychoanalysis!

Well, I'm afraid we have to stop again.

## Note

1. The original is:

   *"To-morrow, and to-morrow, and to-morrow,*
   *Creeps in this petty pace from day*
   *To day to the last syllable of recorded time.*
   *And all our yesterdays have lighted fools*
   *The way to dusty death."*
   (Macbeth V, 5)

What follows is, perhaps, even more meaningful to the theme of this supervision:

   *"Out, out, brief candle!*
   *Life's but a walking shadow, a poor player*
   *That struts and frets his hour upon the stage*
   *And then is heard no more."*

As we can see, Dr. Bion recited by heart, perfectly identical with the original ... he had only missed the article, *"The"*, in the last phrase ...

# Commentary on supervision A42

*Howard B. Levine*

In this brief fragment of a supervision, we not only get to see Bion put into practice many of the clinical injunctions and attitudes that he described conceptually, especially in *Attention and Interpretation* (Bion, 1970), but to feel and experience more directly the sense of his presence and the provocative/evocative acuity of his mind, his listening stance, and the impact of his interventions. The presenter has hardly begun the presentation by noting, seemingly parenthetically or in passing, that the patient is Jewish but does not feel like a Jew, when Bion interrupts and asks, "How does he know he doesn't feel like a Jew? Because what does a Jew feel like?"

The effect on the reader is startling and abrupt. Having followed the freedom, play, and intuition of his own fertile imagination, Bion radically shifts the vertex of our attention. We can surmise that he has "made room for wild thoughts", noticed an often overlooked truism about the nature of repression—that in order to "forget" something, you must constantly remember what you wish to forget!—and shaped it into an "imaginative conjecture": namely, that in order to know that he did not feel like a Jew, then the patient must first be very clear about what it is that a Jew feels like.

In fact, Bion asserts that:

> In any choice, any choice whatever, you are also bound to choose what you're not choosing.

Thus we both see and dramatically experience the result of Bion's *intuition*, which is something that he urges us to include in the domain of scientific thought, because the conjectures that intuition can lead to "help to map out a kind of [unsaturated] area, which one would like to inhabit with ideas or knowledge."

Bion further conjectures that for this patient, it is heritage, lineage, and filiation that he is constantly in mind of so as to repudiate. But if so, then why is this felt to be necessary? Working out the answer to this question may turn out to be an important part of the analysis. In fact, the structure or shape of inquiry that this line of thinking leads to offers a potentially powerful heuristic of analytic investigation that may be applicable to any patient or situation in which repression and related defenses are operating. It may be very useful for the analyst to ask him or herself in relation to every patient:

> What areas of himself does he want *to know nothing about?* … As we listen to this story, we can get a chance of learning something about what he has chosen to know and from that, some idea of what he has chosen *not to know:* the self that he doesn't want to know!

"The self that we do not wish to know"! Doesn't that lie at heart of every encounter with the unconscious?

Later on in the presentation, by virtue of the assumed association between lineage, affiliation, procreation, and the sexual activity required to produce offspring, Bion will speculatively—and as it turns out, correctly—anticipate an associated symptom that accompanied the patient's failure of his anatomy [!] exam, a failure that for the patient seems to also reflect a fall from grace into a castrated state (the loss of sexual desire), which the patient may unconsciously equate with being Jewish.

At one point in the discussion, after some additional, new material has been added, Bion turns to the audience and asks:

> What effect does that create on you? What's the impression you get from what the analyst has told us?

And after the audience has had its brief say and there is presumably a space of silence, he says:

> I'm quite glad to give you my impression, the only thing is: that there's always the danger of thinking my impressions matter—they don't.

He thus illustrates his beliefs that:

1. The only relevant *evidence* is the first hand experience gained in the here-and-now—the analyst's noticing the impact that the patient and the patient's story have had on him—all the rest being "hearsay".
2. The analyst cannot tell you what *is* so, he or she can only tell you what they *believe* is so.

There is a radical decentering of authority in this stance that is consistent with what others—for example, Lacan and *le sujet supposé savoir*[1] or the American Relational insistence on the epistemological symmetry that exists between patient and analyst—have also advocated and observed.

As Bion goes further, a picture develops in the mind of the reader of the picture of the patient in Bion's mind: that of a man who has torn so many "pages"—the Jewish pages, the filial pages, etc.—out of the "book" of knowing his life, that he cannot but fail his *analytical* examination. In this "crossover word", this use of metaphor, we see an anticipation of Ferro's field theory, in which the derivative discourse of "failed anatomy exams" is a signal from the field and stand-in for the unsayable, which repeats itself in the total situation transference.

Here, Bion's remarks condense and convey a description of the consequences of what happens when one throws away too much of one's life history, too many parts of oneself, so that there is a seeming blank (repression) where the foundations of identity and values, those signposts and guides, what in this context Bion might call "breeding", might otherwise be. Without them, we are apt to be lost, as I believe this patient was when he first appeared for analysis.

*Note*

1. It may be argued that in the practice of the truncated session, the Lacanian analyst nevertheless retains some actual role as arbiter of reality, (i.e., the one who actually *does* know) by virtue of having to decide when the patient is or is not expressing the full meaningfulness of the words that are being used.

*Reference*

Bion, W. R. (1970). *Attention and Interpretation.* New York: Basic Books.

# PART III

CLINICAL/THEORETICAL: ONE

*Editors' introduction*

Contemporary thinking about analytic goals and curative factors has engendered a shift in therapeutic aims away from an almost exclusive emphasis on the recovery of hidden or split off *contents*—for example, phantasies, memories, conflicts, desires—towards the development and/or strengthening of the capacities for mentalization, containment, and thought itself. Although Bion's work is not necessarily solely responsible for these changes, his descriptions of alpha function, reverie, transformations, and container/contained have been major influences in helping to bring them about. Concomitantly, analytic technique has broadened in response to this shift in aims to help analyst and patient better achieve the expansion of the analysands' capacities to face the emotional truth of their existence, contain thoughts and emotions, and process the sensorial disturbances that are part of psychic growth and change and being-in-the-world.

In a moving account of the inevitable turbulence that must be encountered if an analytic process is to foster psychic growth, Brito illustrates how mind is created through reflective communication with another. Her sensitive and poetic interventions emphasize the value of the analyst's acknowledgment and naming of the patient's progress, as she encourages and enables the patient to face and suffer the painful truth of her existence. Hartke, too, references the contemporary emphasis on the capacity to think thoughts (the mind as *container*) rather than on contents (e.g., expansion of mind via the recovery of repressed or split-off contents), as he demonstrates how he takes into account and prioritizes the level of the patient's mentalization, as well as the use that is being made of the products of the patient's mind.

The Rocha Barroses deepen this theme, as they trace the evolution of the concept of reverie in analytic thinking from its origins in countertransference, noting that reverie is the basic, intersubjective tool for building an interpretation of emotional meaning between the pair, be that mother/infant or analyst/patient. Assigning a central role to words and language in the organization, structure, and development of the psyche echoes and expands Freud's (1915) view of the importance of "word presentations" in the creation of mind and the structuring of consciousness. It also reaffirms the centrality of verbalizable interpretation as a therapeutic agent in the analytic process. Their essay examines how the addition of *meaning* to an understanding of an experience changes the function of that emotional experience in our lives. "Language, in this context, is not a copy of an experience, but that which gives it meaning stemming from a resonance" (Rocha Barros & Rocha Barros, Chapter Eleven).

Reiner continues these explorations with her study of O and the question of whether and to what extent any of us can know or stand to know the truth of our existence. Many readers will be familiar with Bion's (e.g., 1962, 1970, 1992) assertions that the mind needs truth to grow, as the body needs alimentation. Faced with the inevitable limits and frustrations of life, the patient—indeed, any of us—must decide between two broad courses of action: to allow and learn from (to "suffer") our emotional experience or to evade, falsify, or otherwise avoid it. Reiner argues persuasively that however we may conceive of the therapeutic action of psychoanalysis, curative factors and psychic development will rest upon the patient's "relationship to truth, to O, for which the analyst serves as ambassador. This relationship is the basis of the development of a self in a constant process of becoming. It is how the mind grows" (Reiner, Chapter Twelve). From this perspective, "obstructions to mental growth represent a dysfunction in one's relationship to O" (Reiner, Chapter Twelve).

Korbivcher follows with an essay on autistic nuclei, their clinical presentation and analytic transformation, which similarly deals with the problems and potentials of the patients' capacities to make deep and truthful contact with themselves and their objects (analysts), so that processes of transformation and working through can occur.

The transformational processes that all of these authors describe are of course complex and slow to accomplish. True analytic work at this level requires patience and the capacity to bear ignorance and live with uncertainty and doubt (Bion's *negative capability*). At odds with these requirements is the universal human propensity to cling to the familiar—past knowledge and other forms of pseudo-certainty—in ways that close down curiosity and hamper creativity and discovery. As Reiner (Chapter Twelve) notes, "The illusion of certainty simplifies reality in the hope of making it manageable. Instead it deadens reality and the mind capable of contact with truth. The lies which shrink the truth also shrink the mind." Where that leaves us is with the need to accept that the minds of analysand and analyst, and what happens between them, must ultimately remain a mystery, about which we can only formulate partial and temporary conjectures.

## References

Bion, W. R. (1962). *Learning From Experience.* London: Heinemann.
Bion, W. R. (1970). *Attention and Interpretation.* New York: Basic Books.
Bion, W. R. (1992). *Cogitations.* London: Karnac.
Freud, S. (1915). The unconscious. *S. E., 12.* London: Hogarth.

CHAPTER NINE

# Turbulence and growth: an encounter between Ismalia and Isaura*

*Gisèle de Mattos Brito*

This article is a clinical text about an intense encounter between "madness" and "sanity" or, we might say, between the psychotic and the non-psychotic part of our personalities (Bion, 1967). Between the search to know (K) and not know (–K) as described by Bion (1962, 1963). A variety of fragments of different moments of the analysis are presented, making it possible to see how patient and analyst weave a container to contain the analytical object.

The patient we will call Isaura is married, a devoted mother and a competent professional. She had a very unfortunate family history and she thus felt she had lost a great deal of time in life. The patient had been sexually harassed by her father. She was locked into an oedipal situation and was unable to organize her life.[1] That is, she seemed unable to apply her knowledge to her work and to finish what she had begun. She blamed herself for having cheated on her husband, for her madness. Her feeling was one of being lost without knowing how to make use of her time and her creativity, even though she wrote with ease and was familiar with literature and art.

This pungent feeling of frustration eventually led her to invest in herself. The question that would not stop clamoring was "Why am I paralyzed? Other people grow but I don't."

I felt deeply touched by her suffering and saw her as being willing to work together with me. We started with three sessions per week, but there were often four or even five.

We worked intensely. Her suffering was touching and at every session I came into contact with her complete confusion. She had a deep feeling of helplessness about her marriage and felt

---

*An earlier version of this chapter was selected as the best paper by a training analyst at the 2009 Brazilian Congress of Psychoanalysis, and given the *Award Durval Marcondes,* presented at the International Congress of the IPA in Chicago, USA, in 2009.

very lonely in raising her children. She was becoming more aware of the hallucinatory world she had created. *The Bridges of Madison County*,[2] the endless, unfulfillable search for an impossible, idealized love …

## The weaver girl

As I open the door to my office for one of our sessions the patient is sitting in the waiting room, ready to be called in. She looks at me with a glance of satisfaction and interest, and says: "It's not so rainy today."

During the previous session I had commented on the heavy rain that was falling. I note how intensely she looks at me, and agrees about the weather. She lies down but says nothing. I also remain silent for a few minutes, involved in the feelings that her glance and the way she greeted me had affected me.

I say: "I think you pay close attention to the way I talk to you, the way I receive you. And I have the impression that this waiting and being with me have been very important for you, especially because this gives you the chance to encounter yourself." After a long silence she says: "I feel I'm taking strides toward self-knowledge. And, especially, I'm moving towards interior organization."

She comments on how she is remodeling her house and how much she is also remodeling her internal house. She talks about the comment I had made the previous session when I noted that "there was a lucid part in her that keeps her from tearing everything apart."[3] I say she has been clear-minded and it was very good for her to have realized this. She talks about her hopes to free herself from the scorpion's poison[4] and about how important her analysis has been for her. Every day she keeps waiting and looking at the clock, thinking about the time to come.

Then she remembers a short story by Marina Colasanti entitled "The Weaver Girl". She tells me that this story is about a girl who wove things, and what she wove appeared to her. In other words, if she was hungry and wove food, the food would appear. When she was sleepy she would weave the moon in the evening and the moon would rise and she would fall asleep. She made it clear that the girl was happy. The story says that all the girl did was weave; that was all she wanted to do. But the girl began to feel lonely, and one day she wove a man to be her companion, and when she was finished, a man appeared in her house. But when he discovered that whatever she wove became reality, he had her weave him a castle to live in. Then he wanted silver and horses and other things and she had to keep weaving all the time for him.

Gradually she got tired of weaving. She became very sad, very gloomy. Then one day she decided to start pulling the yarn out of what she had woven and pulled and pulled until she had unraveled the entire man and everything else she had woven for him.

We smiled. She said this was the story of her life. Then I asked what associations she had to this story. She said that she liked it because it was like the story of herself and her lover. She said that she had created this madness, this man and everything she had experienced with him. She also said that unraveling the thread was like what she was doing in analysis, in the sense of becoming aware of her madness and freeing herself from it. She wanted to weave, and weaving was what she liked doing. She repeated this sentence with great emotion, and started crying.

As she spoke I felt touched by her associations. I saw how sensitive she was and how much insight she had gained. I said something to the effect that she was coming into contact not only with her madness but, especially, with the possibility of containing it there with me, unlike the weaver girl in the story, who was all alone. I also commented that she now realized that she had created many different stories in her life that did not really exist. Then I reminded her of the story about the flowered print skirt.[5] She wove illusions that disillusioned her. Like Sinhá Victoria in *Barren Lives*, she felt as if she was wearing a flowered print skirt, but she imagined that she did not have one and would have to seek one in a relationship with some man who was not her husband.

She recalled something that happened with the psychologist who had worked with her in the past. The psychologist became involved with her story with the lover and saw it as a story of love, and the psychologist had encouraged her. She realizes that it had been very important when I said I didn't see it as a love story but as a great adventure in madness. She said that this had helped her a great deal.

Then she remembers a dream. In it she was at home. She explains that she still has some dogs at home and that she and her husband are very attached to them. In the dream, the doghouse was a coffin. She then laughs and says: "It was a big transparent red box made of acrylic." She saw herself lying in the coffin with her husband but it also looked like the couch. She says she woke up with the feeling that it was a coffin, in the form of a coffin but, later on, she didn't think it was a coffin, but a big red box. She says she felt confused. She talks about her relationship with her husband and that sometimes she feels that he leaves too many things for her to take care of for him. She mentions the remodeling of the house, since she has to keep in contact with the stone masons and handle other matters.

She says: "You have to keep blowing if you want the fire to stay lit."[6] Then she comments that her husband has fire, but she has to blow on it, and we laugh together. I say that she is becoming aware of something that confused her, something ambivalent in her feelings about the relationship between her and her husband. She didn't know whether their marriage was a coffin or a living transparent and permeable red box that let her see and live with him. But for there to be fire, heat, and red flames, they both have to be involved.

She thus showed me that she was paying attention to what I said and to the way I deal with her. In this way, she might be able to decide what we were weaving, a coffin, another mad illusion, a big box, or a living container of her encounter with herself. I also say that it was very important that she is taking care of herself. Attention and dedication were needed to build real knowledge and not just something illusory, and that this was a job we were weaving together.

She nods in agreement.

### Madness

When Ismalia went mad,
She went to the tower to dream ...
She saw one moon in the sky and another in the sea.

In the dream she was lost
As she bathed in the moonlight ...
She wished to float up to the sky,
And she wished to plunge into the sea ...

And in her lunacy
in the tower she began to sing …
She was so close to the sky,
And also so close to the sea …

Like an angel she lifted her wings,
She felt the desire to fly …
She wanted the moon in the sky,
and she wanted the moon in the sea …

She lifted the wings that God gave her
She set out to flutter away …
Her soul wafted up to the sky,
And her body plummeted down to the sea … (Alphonsus de Guimaraens, 2001)

The patient comes to a session in tears.[7] As she lies down on the couch she cries even more. She tells of her suffering, her embarrassment before her children, her sadness at having caused them so much suffering.

She remembers a conversation with her son about an anonymous letter he received containing details about the affair his mother was having with another man. She was moved by her son's understanding. "Mom," he said, "this can happen to anybody. Nobody's free from this kind of thing." She cries and tells me how she felt with her son's warm understanding.

She is deeply remorseful about her madness. She tells me a dream she had and that we had already discussed at length in analysis. A couple was having wild sexual intercourse on one side of a curtain. From the other side she sees herself lying down, watching the couple. She was raising her fingers stiffly and saying that she needed two, she wanted two penises. Then the man comes over to her and positions his anus near her face. She says, "This is madness, Gisèle, lunacy."

Then she remembers the poem about Ismalia. When she finishes declaiming the poem, she says, "Gisèle, why did I remember this poem just now? My Lord!"

I feel deeply touched. I tell her about her identification with Ismalia's derangement,[8] her madness, and I say that she was feeling involved and mixed in with the frenzied couple in the dream. She too wanted everything, the moon in the sky and the moon in the sea. She wanted her own husband and the other woman's husband at the same time. She wanted to be the queen of all kingdoms.

She says, "You mean I want to be part of the Holy Trinity?"[9] I tell her that's probably right. She might also want to be mixed in with her parents. At this point I remember the words of the character Riobaldo in *The Devil to Pay in the Backlands*,[10] by Guimarães Rosa (2006). I relate all this confusion about the letter to her children with the confusion with her parents, being mixed into their marriage. And I say: "Like Riobaldo said: 'We really live, I guess, to get dis-illusioned and un-mixed.'"

She sobs and declaims part of the Ismalia poem:

> Like an angel she lifted her wings
> She felt the desire to fly …
> She wanted the moon in the sky,
> And she wanted the moon in the sea.
>
> She lifted the wings that God gave her
> She set out to flutter away …
> Her soul wafted up to the sky,
> And her body plummeted down to the sea.

"Oh, Gisèle, how can I stand it? What pain, what pain … How am I going to get un-mixed?" Then she asks what it would be like to live as a whole. She says that for her entire life she had experienced this madness: she wanted the moon in the sky and she wanted the moon in the sea.

And I say, "You wanted, you wanted …." She says, "So, Gisèle, now you're the one who's going to be warm and understanding with me," and repeats, "I wanted, I wanted …"

I comment that she partially knows what it means to live as a whole, since she had lived wholly as a mother and has been very devoted to her children. Today she can be understood and accepted, by them and by me.

In the next session she says that she had a dream and she feels it is closely related to our conversation of the day before. She dreamed she was a midget and was facing a steep flight of wooden stairs. She thinks that this has something to do with her analysis because she imagined that she would grow with each step she took up the stairs.

She mentions that it also has to do with my comment that she partially knew what it is like to live wholly, because she experienced this wholeness in her relationship with her children. She says that she had a productive day at work and that she managed to co-ordinate a meeting very well, finished a task, and other things.

As she tells me the dream I remember Ismalia's tower. I thought that the stairway might also lead to the tower, but I keep quiet because her associations were in a different vein. So I wait. We start talking about her associations with the dream, about the feeling of strength, a strength that she hoped her analysis would help her acquire. We talk about her desire to develop and to grow professionally. My comment is that "This is one path."

She says, "It's one path. But there might be another, don't you think?" I agree. And I mention that Ismalia went up in the tower and began to dream. She wanted the moon in the sky and she wanted the moon in the sea.

She says, "That's true. I didn't think about that. Ismalia went up in the tower and began to dream … That's right … It might be a mad dream too." Then she remembers the weaver girl. She comments that, like the girl, she also wove a mad dream and that it hurts too much to pull out the threads in analysis. She says, "Oh, Gisèle. How it hurts …"

She says that yesterday she was talking to her supervisor, who is a very understanding woman. Isaura had told the woman about remembering Ismalia in analysis, and the supervisor said, "Oh! Ismalia!" "We hugged each other," she says. "It was a very strong hug. I can't explain it to you."

I say, "Yes, maybe, like you, like her or me, any of us can embrace the Ismalia that is inside us. This is a poignant encounter that analysis gives us, the encounter with our madness."

According to Bion (1962, p. 42):

> A central part is played by alpha function in transforming an emotional experience into alpha-elements *because a sense of reality matters to the individual* in the way that food, drink, air and excretion of waste products matter ... Failure to use the emotional experience produces a comparable disaster in the development of the personality. (My emphasis)

Farther down, on the same page, he says: "An emotional experience cannot be conceived of in isolation from the relationship."

Also regarding emotional experience, he says, in *Transformations* (1965, p. 81), that:

> The infant's experience of the breast as the source of emotional experiences (later represented by terms such as love, understanding, meaning) means that disturbance in relationship with the breast involve disturbance over a wide range of adult relationships. The function of the breast in supplying meaning is important for the development of a capacity to learn. In an extreme instance, namely, the fear of the total destruction of the breast, not only does this involve fears that he has ceased to exist (since without the breast he is not viable), but fears that meaning itself, as if it were matter, had ceased to exist.

Bion explains that, for the mind to develop the capacity to think thoughts, it must be contained. Through the concept of containing he develops the idea that the mother, with her alpha function operating, metabolizes the child's emotional and sensory experiences and turns them into alpha elements. That is, the mother with reverie digests, transforms before naming, in order to offer meaning. The infant has to find this function of digestion and transformation of emotional experiences in its mother and, if it does not, later, in an analyst, in order to identify with him and create an internal container to contain the emotional contents.

According to Bion, transformations in hallucinosis are related to primal disasters and to catastrophes in this relationship with the breast and with the parents. They are changes in the psychotic area of the personality. Envy and voracity are elements present in this area.

Braga (2003) remarks the important presence of the hallucinatory processes, within the vision of a multidimensional mind, in which the hallucination and hallucinoses co-exist with the dimensions of sensoriality, of thought, of being reality, and of thought without thinker.

Using the transformations in hallucinosis as a way to manage and manipulate emotional experiences, the person "believes" that she generates a reality that is convenient to her. The person can weave and unravel at will. But this created reality is unsustainable. Sooner or later the individual must face the facts about unadorned internal and external reality.

Ferro (2000) says that delusions are similar to transformations in hallucinosis, and emphasizes that what is projected into the outside is confused with reality because it is recognized by the subject as real.

Madness/Ismalia, that is, the acts derived from an attempt to escape from mental pain and feelings of responsibility, as well as the creation of a hallucinatory world, gain verbal expression in the analytical relationship. On the other hand, sanity/Isaura, understood as the lucid contact with self and object, is also revealed and expressed.

Isaura seeks a sense of reality. She tries to face her psychotic part and its responsibility in her having gone mad. She struggles against accepting this perception and insists on thinking that she has the power to weave and unravel reality. She is reluctant to cope with the consequences of her acts and to relinquish her feeling of unlimited power.

### *Hell*

"They leave heaven because it is dark, and go to hell in search of light."

Lupicínio Rodrigues[11]

We continue working intensely on her madness, her insanity. During one session from this period she brings me the lyrics of a Brazilian song by Lupicínio Rodrigues entitled *These Young Men, These Poor Young Men*. She says: "Oh my gosh, Gisèle. That was what I was doing, but I didn't realize it! Those young people in search of love ... end up in hell."

We then talk about her pain, about the fact that we cannot always find the light we need to bear the darkness, the bad weather, the rough going, as we struggle to find the light again. She says, "The sky is dark, too, isn't it? Like the verse in the song: '*Because it's dark.*' It's dark too. It's not just light. There is thunder and lightning."

The thunder and lightning appeared in her sky. The sky of her life became terribly dark. The consequences of her derangement, her lunacy, overflowed into her life and family with the fury of a tornado.

The person who had sent the letter to her children attacks again, more bitterly this time. The person sends other, more daring letters by giving the patient's home address, telephone numbers, and all sorts of information about her husband. She is forced to tell her husband everything. Some of her children turn against her. They accuse her of being false, of living a sham. Her house, the family, everything is make-believe.

Isaura becomes desperate. There is no way to escape the consequences. She suffers terribly. She cannot bear to see her children suffering like this. She goes into a period of intense guilt and is repentant for what she did. She is ashamed of herself, and her husband suffers as well. She tries to prove to him that she chose him and she tells him she wants them to face old age together.

She wants her husband to forgive her, without her having to go through all the suffering involved in the process of forgiving. She argues with me when I show her the moments when she tries to magically unravel the thread. She says, "You and Rodolfo want me to stay in this hell. I already told you I'm getting out of hell. If he likes he can come with me."

Her guilt is greater with each passing day. She feels remorseful. At the same time, she is also able to see how lonely and defenseless her husband had left her. He worked away from home and she had to take care of the children alone. When he was home they had a very intense social life. There was no time left for the couple to be alone together.

The sessions during this period involved extreme suffering. I accompany her and help her clear certain things up. She is terrified when she realizes she identified with her father in his disordered character. I show her that hers was a disorder of conduct, but not of character.

On a number of occasions she says: "Hell is right here … and how it pains me …" The guilt and persecution advance. She becomes depressed and we work hard. Little by little she recuperates. She becomes more involved in her work, she studies, she struggles to get over the depression and the moments of despair and desperation.

"Life is ungrateful in its very mildness, but it transbrings[12] hope even in the midst of bitter despair" (Guimarães Rosa).

Riolo (2007, p. 1376) says that, in Bion's terms, and at this moment, analysis "is in turn conceived not only as a process of deciphering symbols, of revealing already existing unconscious meanings, but also of symbol production—of a process for generating thoughts and conferring meaning on experiences that have never been conscious and never been repressed because they have never been 'thought'."

And so we move on. Isaura remembers many moments in her lifetime and is surprised at some of the things she has done. In fact, she feels afraid of herself. She says: "Today I am convinced that I am a sick person, and all this sickness has been very bad for my life."

### The rebirth of Isaura

The patient arrives from an event where she represented the company she works for. She is visibly excited and says: "Gisèle. I had a wonderful experience." She tells me that the event took place in a town we will call Rosário, in one of the poorest regions in the state. A singer from the town gave a beautiful recital that moved the entire audience. At the end of her presentation the singer was applauded when she said that there was more than poverty and crime in their town. There was also culture and poetry.

One woman shouted: "Rosário exists!"

Later Isaura went up to the woman and asked her why she had shouted that and what she meant by it, and the woman explained. One of the people present asked if Rosário was on the map and another said it surely was, and there were lots of voters there. The woman looked astonished and said "I think I see myself for the first time." And Isaura looked on.

She is greatly moved when she tells me this, and says: "Gisèle, that woman said what I have noticed in my work. People need to be a part of culture, of a group, if they want to belong to the community. It's in the constitution. Everyone has the right to culture and leisure." She cries, and says she doesn't know why this moved her so much.

I tell her that, in her conversations with me, she has the opportunity to come into very close contact with herself. On the one hand, there was this wonderful experience. But on the other, there was pain. Now she has to realize that to exist is to have to cope with the perception that, for a long time, it had not been possible to feel this.

She cries bitterly and tells me that she had taken out her identification card at a relatively advanced age, and at the event in Rosário she was able to realize her identification with the woman who spoke.

She says, "All this is so amazing …" She describes the whole scene to me again and talks about the population that is so poor that they have nothing. They only work. And she ends up by telling me that the woman could identify herself with the value she saw and heard in the singer.

I feel moved. We talk about her discovery of a creative and sensitive Isaura who has an identity, a history. An Isaura who exists!

That night she phoned me at home. She said she couldn't stop crying and asked for an extra session the next day. She comes into that session seeming more relaxed and tells me she had called a friend of hers, a man, who was also my analysand and who had suggested she come to me in the first place. He had told her that the pain she felt was a positive pain and that all her flood of emotion was related to the process of analysis. She agrees with him.

I say: "Yes, it's a positive pain, a pain of integration and growth." And I tell her how important it was for her to be able to think, to work, and to feel that she has a positive identity and that she exists. She tells me she is going to carry out a project by herself. I mention that she wants to exist, and she cries. She tells me how her father had taken advantage of her for years by taking away her salary. She could not even keep one third of what she earned. She says that her father emancipated her and her brother in order to take out a loan at a bank, and never paid it back. So her name was on the credit blacklist for years.

We talk about her recollections and her anguish at having been sexually harassed and abused by her father. There was a pain of not existing, of being abandoned and excluded, when she couldn't feel like part of the Holy Trinity.

One day during this period she comes into a session and gives me a copy of her article. Then she goes over and lies on the couch and, in tears, says: "This article is yours." I say that it definitely was not mine and firmly insist that it is hers. "I understand you are grateful that I'm able to help you, but it's yours." We talk about how important it is to recognize her own merit. It is essential if she is to exist.

Her production increases daily. She is enthusiastic about her work and, more than anything else, she is enthusiastic about herself.

Symington (2007, p. 1410) develops a number of ideas. At one point he says:

> That a mind has to be created. We are not born with a mind but with the potential for creating a mind; that envy, jealousy, greed, paranoia, infantile dependence and omnipotence are the products of an undeveloped mind; that mind is created through reflective communication with another; and that psychoanalysis, as communication between two people, needs to occur according to certain principles if creation of mind is to happen.

He stresses how important it is for the analyst to recognize indications of growth in the patient. This recognition makes expansion possible and establishes further growth. As Symington says, "What was fragile becomes more secure and solid." This is the road to the development of a person's own mind (Caper, 2002).

### *Isaura reborn*

"A flower peeks out in the street!
Streetcars, buses and rivers of steel traffic pass at a distance.
It's still a colorless flower.
It hides from the police but breaks through the pavement.
Everyone be quiet! Stop running about!

> I'm sure there's a flower in the street …
>
> … It's ugly, but it's a flower. It broke through the pavement, the boredom, the disgust and the hatred."
>
> Carlos Drummond de Andrade, 2001

When I open the door of my consulting room the patient comes in and greets me with a broad smile and says that something very important happened in her professional life (which I will decline to describe here for reasons of discretion). We embrace. Her feeling of joy is immense and I congratulate her. She comments on this achievement, about her feeling of self-confidence. And I say: "The time and moment of Isaura."[13]

We laugh together and she repeats: "The time and moment of Isaura." She goes on to tell me about a talk she had given and the receptivity she felt from her audience. She comments that, in her talk, she made a reference to something mentioned by the person who had spoken before her, about elections and votes. She hitched onto the topic and said that, for democracy, votes were like the block of marble out of which Michelangelo sculpted the *Pietà*. There is need for people who think and who become involved, if changes are to be made in issues related to the theme of labor.

I remembered a metaphor by Dr. Bion, quoted by Junqueira Mattos (1998). Bion compares the analyst's work to the work of a sculptor, and he called special attention to Michelangelo's unfinished statues in Florence, *The Slaves*. "They appear stuck into the stone, as if they had always lived there, … awaiting the work of the sculptor who, with his chisel, could give life to what had only pre-existed."

She also tells me excitedly about the metaphor she used of the lonely navigator and of a canoe with people rowing together. The lonely navigator was like a single city or town, living alone, waiting for help from numerous institutions or even from the Holy Spirit. People who row together have a common objective and they join hands to attain it.

She tells me about the end of an article she wrote concerning a certain region in the state, and remembered that it is one of the poorest regions and has high crime rates. The neighborhood she had visited there was named after a flower, and she recalled Drummond de Andrade's poem "The Flower and the Nausea". She says: "The flower peeked through the pavement. It was born under impossible conditions but it fooled everyone. A pallid flower breaks through the pavement."

I say, "Yes, Isaura. But what I see is that you're now able to use all your resources, your life-long reading and your professional experience." And I mention her professions. "You're bringing all this together inside yourself, into the same boat, working together. And a vibrant living flower is blooming. This flower that is born here in our work together has been planted and has been painstakingly cared for. It doesn't have to hide to grow. It was born because you gave it space and the possibility of blossoming and flourishing. It is Isaura's time and moment." Isaura cries and thanks me.

But we do not forget the nausea, the disgust, the hatred. They are also present. We work on this duality in many subsequent sessions. She is sad because she has not gotten out of hell and does not live in paradise. She recently dreamed that she had sent her father a photograph in which she is naked and on all fours. The dream frightens her. She associates it with the story recently described in the press about the girl who was held as her father's sexual slave and prisoner in a cellar for twenty-four years. Ismalia insists on being present.

We talk about the need to tolerate both the flower and the nausea, the love and the hatred, the madness and the sanity. I say something I heard from my first supervisor:[14] "There is no sea without swamps." Then, thinking about the sea and the swamps, I remember the episode of Penelope in the Odyssey.[15] Penelope wove tapestry during the day and unraveled it at night, waiting for her true love ... Isaura is moved by this.

I mention something she had told me earlier about not being able to separate from her husband, and she associated this with Penelope's love and hopes. She asks me to recount this passage in the Odyssey. I tell her part of it and she adds others. Then she remembers that she had thought about separating from her husband, but she couldn't do it. She remembers having said to her lover: "I can't leave Rodolfo, because he is important to me."

I associated the swamps to Ismalia's madness, to the madness of the weaver girl, and to Isaura's own madness. I associated the ocean to the life she was able to establish with her husband, her children, and with me in analysis.

"This construction," I say, "is true and it continues alive. It blossoms and now you can recognize it." Isaura agrees. She says, "I waited for him ... and he waited for me, too. Rodolfo agrees that we are both responsible for what happened, although I realize that my responsibility for all this is greater."

Bion (1987, p. 224) says:

> Breakdown, neurosis, psychosis may, in their turbulence, be difficult to discern, but they may be a birth inseparable from repression and death. In analysis we often have reason to think that we cannot penetrate the impressive caesura of resistance or its varieties.

But Bion (1987, p. 230) also stresses that, despite all the violence and destructiveness in human life: "So far the human being has survived and preserved a capacity for growth."

Isaura says: "One of the most important things I'm learning in analysis, and I told this to Rodolfo, is that the more you want to get out of hell, the more you stay in it. I used to want to be free from this suffering, which I experienced in my whole life. I thought that it was the only way to waft up to the sky. Today I know that I can experience both things together. Sometimes I see myself in Ismalia's tower, and I ask myself: 'What are you doing here, Isaura?'"

We laugh together.

I say: "The flower and the nausea ..." Our work continues. My feeling is that we move on, day by day.

Thank you, Ismalia.

Thank you, Isaura.

## Notes

1. She said he had made her place her hand on his penis, and there were passionate embraces and kisses. Sometimes she escaped. These experiences had deeply influenced her emotional and sexual life, and much of her despair and madness had to do with oedipal fantasies and the seduction she had suffered.

2. The "Casta diva" aria in Bellini's opera *Norma* can be heard at a certain point in this movie. In one of the most beautiful pieces of music ever composed, our patient Isaura identifies herself with the main character, Norma. But, differently from the character, Isaura discovers in analysis that her love is a hallucination.
3. A reference to having succeeded in keeping her family and marriage together.
4. In the preceding session she had told me a dream where she had been stung by a poisonous scorpion. She associates the scorpion to her father and says how embarrassed she was about him. She had told me of a number of episodes of dishonesty and corruption committed by her father and, with great sadness, we talk about her identification with him in her desperate search for partners outside of wedlock.
5. Reference to the protagonist in Graciliano Ramos's book *Vidas Secas* (*Barren Lives*) (1979), which had come up during her first period of analysis. She had been surprised to see that the character wore a print skirt with leaves and flowers. The patient had felt that the character lived a dry, barren life and a marriage without love or flowers.
6. A reference to the same character in *Barren Lives* who wears a flowered print skirt, bending down to blow on the fire to keep it going. In the text, her words are adapted from a Brazilian expression meaning "You have to have a lot of wind to keep going."
7. Someone (she did not know who) had sent anonymous letters to her children describing details of their mother's love affair. She had already cut off this affair when she returned to the city where she lives with her husband.
8. The patient's identification with Ismalia revolves around the question of madness. At no point did she think of committing suicide.
9. A reference to the oedipal triad.
10. A very well-known Brazilian novel (*Grande Sertão, Veredas*) translated into English as *The Devil to Pay in the Backlands*.
11. From a poem entitled: *Esses moços, pobres moços* (These young men, these poor young men).
12. "Transbrings"—transliteration of the Portuguese, *transtraz*.
13. A reference to the short story *A Hora e a Vez de Augusto Matraga* (*The Time and Moment of Augusto Matraga*), by the Brazilian author João Guimarães Rosa (found in the book *Sagarana*, available in English), which expresses the strength and spirit of the backlands in south-central Brazil. It tells the story of the fall of a powerful man in search of redemption. The duality between good and evil characterizes a world of gunmen and ranchers. In this world there is the possibility of conversion when a person's time and moment have come, as they did for Augusto Matraga.
14. Judith Teixeira de Carvalho Andreucci, training analyst with the Brazilian Psychoanalytical Society of São Paulo. Judith, now deceased, was a very important figure in the development of that society.
15. Odysseus went to war and Penelope was expected to marry again. But, since she loved him and wanted no other man as her husband, she said she would marry only after she had finished weaving a tapestry. By day she wove and by night she unraveled the work she had just completed. She never finished, always awaiting Odysseus, who returned ten years after the end of the war.

## References

Andrade, C. D. (2001). *A flor e a náusea*. Rio de Janeiro: Editora Record.
Bion, W. R. (1962). Learning from experience. In: *Seven Servants*. New York: Jason Aronson.

Bion, W. F. (1963). Elements of Psycho-Analysis. In: *Seven Servants*. New York: Jason Aronson.
Bion, W. R. (1965). Transformations. In: *Seven Servants*. New York: Jason Aronson.
Bion, W. R. (1967). Differentiation of the psychotic from the non-psychotic personalities. In *Second Thoughts*. London: Heinemann.
Bion, W. R. (1987). Emotional turbulence. In: *Four Papers*. Abingdon: Fleetwood.
Braga, J. C. (2003). O Alucinatório na Prática Clinica: aproximando algumas questões. Reunião Científica da Sociedade Brasileira de Psicanálise de São Paulo, 22 de maio de 2003.
Caper, R. (2002). *Tendo mente própria*. Rio de Janeiro: Imago Ed.
Colassanti, M. (2000). *A moça tecelã. Em Doze Reis e a Moça no Labirinto do Vento*. Rio de Janeiro: Global Editora.
Ferro, A. (2000). *A Psicanálise como Literatura e Terapia*. Rio de Janeiro: Imago Ed.
Guimaraens, A. (2001). *Os cem melhores poemas brasileiros do século*. Rio de Janeiro: Editora Objetiva.
Junqueira Mattos, J. (1998). Pré concepção e transferência. *Journal of Melanie Klein and Object Relations, 16*: 683–708; *Revista Brasileira de Psicanálise, 29*: 799-824.
Rosa, J. G. (2006). *Grande sertão: veredas*. Rio de Janeiro: Nova Fronteira.
Ramos, G. (1979). *Vidas Secas*. Rio de Janeiro: Editora Record.
Riolo, F. (2007). Psychoanalytic transformations. *International Journal of Psychoanalysis, 88*: 1375–1389.
Rodrigues, L. Disco 1. *Esses Moços Pobres Moços*.
Symington N. (2007). A technique for facilitating the creation of mind. *International Journal of Psychoanalysis, 88*: 1409–1422.

CHAPTER TEN

# Mental states and emotional relations in the analytic setting: implications for therapeutic work

*Raul Hartke*

The extent and depth of clinical phenomena and their motivations that we are able to recognize, conceptualize, and work through analytically have broadened considerably over these more than one hundred years of clinical work and theoretical reflections.

Currently we are able to, and even need to, ask ourselves questions such as these when dealing with different clinical situations:

1. Is their content oedipal or pre-oedipal? Or, for others, genital oedipal or pre-genital oedipal? (Meltzer, 1973).
2. Does basic anxiety belong to the red (castration), black (mourning), or white (empty) series as Green (1983) proposes? Or, from another angle, is it schizo-paranoid, depressive (Klein, 1946), confusional (Rosenfeld, 1987) "nameless terror" (Bion, 1962), "unthinkable anxiety" (Winnicott, 1963), objectless anxiety (Baranger, Baranger, & Mom, 1987)?
3. Are the defense mechanisms basically centered on splitting (Klein, 1946) or repression (Freud, 1926)? Or, as for Lacan (Roulot, 1993), based upon repression, disavowal or foreclosure?
4. What is the underlying drive or motivation? Sexual, aggressive, or even death drive (Freud, 1920)? Links of love, hate, desire to know, or different forms of anti-linking (minus L, minus H and minus K), as Bion proposed (1962)?
5. Is the object relation partial or total (Klein, 1946)? Is it basically narcissistic (Rosenfeld, 1987)? In yet other terms, narcissistic or social-ist (Bion, 1992)?
6. What level of mentalization is present? One-dimensional, two-dimensional, three- or tetra-dimensional (Meltzer, Hoxter, Bremner, & Weddell, 1975)? Or, in the terms proposed by Lecours and Bouchard (1997) at the level of disruptive impulsiveness (acting-out), modulated impulsiveness (catharsis), externalization, appropriation, or association of abstract-reflective

meaning? And, also, according to these same authors, is the drive-affect experience expressed by somatic activity, motor activity, imagination or verbalization?

7. What aspects or parts of the analysand and the analyst predominate and interact at that moment in the analytic space (Hartke, 2007b)? Are we looking at a subjective phenomenon of the analysand or the analyst, or at something that transcends and is greater than the sum of these two subjectivities, as proposed to us by the Barangers, with their theory of the analytic field (1969) or Ogden with the notion of "intersubjective analytic third" (1994)?

Certainly many other questions and possibilities could be added to the list above.

Which among these multiple aspects will be considered as being subject to onset, recognition, and analytic work in the therapeutic relation depends, broadly, on the theoretical conception adopted by the analyst. And as to this aspect, it is also necessary to weigh the distinction between the consciously adopted concept versus those that are mostly unconscious, more fragmentary, less logically articulated, but even so, or also for this reason, more effective. Sandler (1992) calls them "the private face" of analytic technique, as opposed to the "public face" that is explicitly formulated and adopted. The private face, also known as "implicit theory", is based on aspects acquired by the analyst in his own analysis, with his teachers and supervisors, readings, and clinical experience, often presenting both internal contradictions and contradictions with the "official" face. He suggests (Sandler, 1983), that periodically every analyst should try to write out these general ideas, in order to render them slightly more explicit for himself. When there is greater awareness and articulation in a logical form they may even constitute a new theory. I believe that this explication may be attempted, in so far as possible, by the analyst exercising the so called "second look", proposed by Baranger (Baranger, Goldstein, & Goldstein, 1994), that is, a second look at the work with their analysands enabled by a peculiar splitting of the own self. More frequently, however, and probably more accurately, its detection would be in the hands of third party observers, who can then render them explicit to the interested analyst.

In more circumstantial terms, this "selection" will depend on many other unique and momentary factors involving the analyst, the analysand, and the dyad they form.

As for myself (Hartke, 2007a), following a line inspired by Bion, I conceive as the ultimate objective and as a specific curative factor of psychoanalysis the expansion of the analysand's potentials for psychic processing, thus increasing his capacity to contain the emotions (Bion, 1962). In this way the need for more primitive defense mechanisms would be diminished. Consequently, in my opinion, there is a major change in relation to the classically proposed objectives, aiming at remembering psychic representations that have been rendered unconscious by repression (*latu sensu*) to expand the capacities for symbolization (Meltzer, 1983; Ferro, 1995), mentalization (Sugarman, 2006), or representation (Levine, Reed, & Scarfone, 2013) of the emotional experiences undergone. This concept results from Bion's general theory (1962, 1963) of the psychic apparatus as an apparatus to generate thoughts and to think them, that is, to create, develop, and use symbolic formations. Consequently, as well noted by Ferro (1995), the analytic task ultimately turns toward the apparatus to generate and think the thoughts rather than to the contents of thought. In his words, "… work on repression (Freud) or splitting (Klein) will no longer be at stake, but it will be necessary to do work towards the source: that about the "place" to think the thoughts, about the container rather than about the content" (Ferro, 1995, p. 27).

Based on this perspective, it is my priority to take into account, in the analytic session, the current level of mentalization, as well as the use that is being made of its products, in conformity with the columns and rows of the grid proposed by Bion (1963, 1977). And this both in relation to the analysand and to the analyst, or to the dyad that they constitute.

For guidance in this domain, I use an adaptation of that grid, which I employ as a kind of "navigation instrument" for psychoanalytic reflections and exercises outside the sessions (Hartke, 2007a; 2007b). I distribute the different levels and uses of the psychic formations, as well as the possibilities of "facts that have not been psychically digested" (Bion, 1962) in a system of Cartesian coordinates according to a suggestion by Bion himself, but altering the distribution and polarization of the levels and also contemplating the negative phenomena (Figure 1).

Point zero at the intersection of the vertical and horizontal axes would be the facts that have not yet been processed psychically by alpha function (Bion, 1962), which Bion called (1962) the beta elements.

The different levels of abstraction or psychic working through would be allocated along the vertical axis. On the contrary of the Bionian grid, the positive superior extreme would

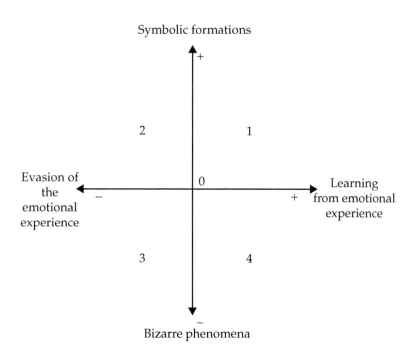

0 = Facts that have not been psychically digested. beta elements
1 = Creative imagination
2 = Neurotic defenses
3 = Psychotic defenses
4 = Psychotic Phenomena used in order to learn from experience.

Figure 1.

host psychic formations with a higher degree of symbolization resulting from an adequate functioning of the alpha function and of the apparatus for thinking (Bion, 1963, 1977). The negative inferior extreme would record what expanding Bion's concept, would be called, more generally, "bizarre" phenomena (Bion, 1962), derived from an inversion of the alpha function.

Along the horizontal axis are the different possible uses of these psychic formations. The closer to the positive right pole, the more their purpose would be to learn from the emotional experience. The closer to the negative left pole, the more they would aim at evading this experience.

These Cartesian axes generate four quadrants. In the superior right one are the psychic productions that constitute the creative imagination in line with the play described by Winnicott (1971). The superior left one receives the classical neurotic defenses and the inferior left the psychotic defenses. The inferior right one contains phenomena resulting from the inversion of the alpha function but used in order to learn from experience.

Actually, besides the two axes mentioned—horizontal and vertical, x and y—I have also included a third one, axis "z", about the type of object relation (Figure 2). In the anterior pole are the essentially narcissistic relations and in the posterior one what Bion (1992) calls "social-ism", as opposed to narcissism. This presentation, however, is a lot more complex, surpassing the objectives present. Thus, I limit myself to mentioning that in the posterior right superior quadrant are included the symbolic constructions used to learn from experience in intimate affective relations (Meltzer 1986). In other words, it represents the "shared playing" described by Winnicott (1971), the essence of creative living and mental health.

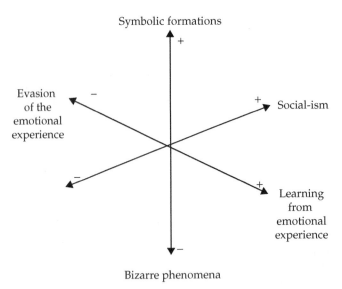

Posterior right superior quadrant = symbolic formations used to learn from emotional experience in intimate relations (shared playing).

Figure 2.

The phenomena belonging to each of these quadrants have different transferential and countertransferential characteristics in the analytic relation, and also require distinct forms of analytic work.

Thus, the phenomena of the left superior quadrant show the clinical and transferential characteristics predominantly described by Freud and are more suited to the analytic work he generally proposed, On the other hand, those very close to the horizontal axis require that the alpha function of the analyst be loaned to the analysand in order to, as Meltzer (1986) proposes, locate and dream for him the emotional experience that he himself does not manage to locate and dream. The analytic space in these cases is a kind of "incubator of symbols" (Hartke, 2005).

The objective of psychoanalysis, according to the diagram, would be to take the mental functioning of the analysand as much as possible towards the posterior right superior quadrant.

I think that these propositions do not exclude analytic work along the general lines classically proposed, for instance, by Freud, Klein, or Winnicott, with certain analysands or at given moments of an analytic process or even of a session. But it is the objectives that become different. Thus, the *a posteriori* removal or modification of defenses, with the consequent recovery of unconscious childhood memories or even the conviction generated by constructions about experiences that are impossible to remember, as proposed by Freud (1937a, 1937b), would no longer constitute a therapeutic factor in itself. They would only represent a means, a way to help the analysand to expand his general capacity to process and symbolize the emotions in such a way that enables him to learn from the experience and grow psychically.

Hence, I feel increasingly liberated from analytic party faithfulnesses. I consider the different general analytic theories that now exist only as partial models that are useful for different clinical situations, instead of totalistic and exclusivist theories. I do not even know whether we will come to a new broad theory that includes these specific models, or whether this constitutes "the end of the road" as the advocates of the Copenhagen School used to say regarding quantum mechanics. Could this be a concept of psychoanalysis that pertains to "liquid modernity", to the "liquid times", as Baumann (2007) says?

Besides everything that has been mentioned above, I consider that the goals of analysis will be achieved only when the patient/analyst dyad manages to establish a relationship that Meltzer (1983, 1986) calls "intimate", differently from the "contractual" and "occasional" ones. At the core of its meaning are the emotions, and it is only they that generate experiences that can promote the desired psychic development. Furthermore, I think that such a relationship implies acceptance of the presence and interaction of two emotionally and mentally whole people in the room where analysis is performed (Hartke, 2007b), with their adult, infantile, neurotic, perverse, psychotic, male, female, and other aspects. This does not mean to ignore the necessary and indispensable "analytic asymmetry" (Baranger & Baranger, 1969) created by the analytic contract, with the preservation and predominance of the analytic attitude in the analyst's mind (Meltzer, 1967), so as to maintain the analytic relationship as a therapeutic process.

In order to try to grasp and formulate the various aspects of this complex situation theoretically, I begin with the assumption that two subjects exist in an effectively analytic space—each of the subjects with their own history and characteristics (subjective domain), that the instituted relationship causes changes in the functioning of both due to mutual influences (intersubjective domain), and that, in addition, phenomena are generated that transcend the sum of the psychic functioning of each of them, in the same way that, as proposed by Bion (1961), group phenomena transcend the sum of the contributions of their participants (trans-subjective domain). The later are conceptualized by the Barangers (1969), based on their theory of the analytic field. Ogden (1994), in turn, understands them within the concept of the intersubjective analytic third, in a constant dialectical tension with the two subjects present in the relationship. For me, the phenomena that occur in the analytic space are, ultimately, always trans-subjective. They constitute what is known as an "emerging property" (Varela, Thompson, & Rosch, 1991), that is, something that appears only beginning from a certain level of an organization (in the analytic dyad, for instance). They will, however, appear as intrapsychic (in the analysand or in the analyst), or, as belonging to the dyad only by virtue of the analyst's (or analysand's) point of view. In other words, only according to the *vertex* (Bion, 1965) adopted by the analyst (or by the analysand), when, thanks to a peculiar cleavage in the ego, it divides into an observing part and another that observes itself, the other, or the dyad they constitute. And further: using the notion of "complementary mode of description" postulated by Bohr (1958, p. 7) based on what he called the "epistemological lesson" (p. 68) favored by quantum physics, I believe that each of these vertexes always generates a different phenomenon. This is the result of the fact that the position of observation will irrevocably modify not only the description, but the very functioning of the phenomenon observed. At the same time, all are important and necessary so that the events present in the setting may be adequately described and worked through.

I will next present two clinical situations. The first of them will mainly illustrate different mental states or levels of symbolization present in the sessions and my way of working them through. Another will predominantly exemplify the presence and alternation of different aspects of the analysand's and analyst's mind in the analytical space and, again, the way I try to use them to fulfill the therapeutic objectives.

I hope that the reader can follow them considering the adaptation of the Bionian grid and the proposition concerning the subjective, intersubjective, and trans-subjective domains, in order to understand the reasons for my interventions. I will make a few brief comments while the cases are reported, reserving other more general remarks for the end.

### Patient "A": from allergies to the red balloon

On a Monday I returned a phone call that A had left on my office answering machine on Saturday requesting an interview for evaluation. But it was her husband who had to talk to me, because she had lost her voice due to what had been diagnosed as severe laryngitis.

During the initial sessions I heard that she wanted to see me because of a severe allergic condition that had appeared, as we later discovered, after a serious professional disappointment. Since these allergic manifestations were recurrent, associated with frequent flus, viruses, etc., her doctor had recommended that she undergo psychotherapy or analysis.

During the sessions she spent most of the time objectively describing facts from her profession and daily life, without connecting them to any affective contexts or showing the pertinent emotions. Her report initially did not have much emotional resonance, giving me the distinct impression that I was only accumulating information, although these "facts" were definitely clear, detailed, and precise. Sometimes she actually told me extremely intimate details about her body and her sex life, but in a completely impersonal way, without any signs of embarrassment or provocation or seduction, and that correspondingly, did not arouse anything different in me. There were no associations, and no indications of phantasies accompanied these and other reports. It was clear to me, although this is difficult to describe briefly, that on these occasions I was not facing an affective distance generated by mechanisms of affective isolation, appropriate to obsessive functioning, generally accompanied by reaction formations and countertransferential feelings of irritation, etc. Instead of this manifest distance, full of intense latent emotional contents, I indeed encountered an "empty presence", and a very "operative" mode of functioning (Marty, 1990).

Throughout this initial period, interpretations addressing emotional contents or resistances, or even attempts to give something that had occurred in her everyday life, or in the sessions an emotional context, were heard by her, but without the expected efficacy. They did not generate a broadening or deepening of her contact with herself or with me. On the contrary, often they gave rise to even more factual material. Much less did my several attempts to relate this functioning to her description of an efficient, cultured, intelligent, elegant, correct, and appropriate but affectively distant mother have any repercussions—a person, according to A, with a propensity to talk too much only about what interested her, without thus managing to tune in with what others were feeling and thinking. This did not prevent her, and on the contrary appears to have triggered and for long years maintained a tendency in A to "stick" to her, always telling her everything that was happening to her. This situation went on until A stopped dating a boy whose parents were friends of her parents, from the same social class—"the son-in-law of their dreams"—to go and live with a man whose origins and way of life were completely distinct from those of her family. For this reason, her parents practically disowned her as their daughter. For some years they did not even know her new home address, and did not accept that she visit them with her companion, and therefore she practically did not see them anymore. The only point of contact with the family was her maternal grandparents, who continued to receive A and her partner and treat them with affection. These grandparents increasingly became her reference and emotional support, which she had felt from very early on. She always saw herself as, and was considered to be, their favorite grandchild, and she was very grateful to them.

There was also the report of a father who she said had completely delegated the task of bringing up the daughters to his wife. A father, who was also correct, well educated, successful, but felt by A as not having much affective sensitivity.

Obviously she began to see the world mostly through the eyes of her companion, which even caused her problems at work.

A often went to the movies and often told me the films that she had seen. Sometimes she even gave the impression that she was using those reports to fill time. I, however, did not take them in this sense. I considered them "borrowed dreams". I tried to broaden and deepen, in so far as possible, a colloquial conversation about scenes that I considered as having more emotional content, conjecturing about possible emotions that were implicated there, or that could be aroused in the spectator. Whenever possible I attempted to select and have a dialogue about scenes that might in some way be related to situations in her life, present or past, without necessarily spelling this out. But, sometimes I did this and on several occasions I noticed that A accepted my proposal and began to tell her own situation more spontaneously. On other occasions, she went back to factuality.

One day, when she told me that her husband had told her a dream, I asked whether she also dreamed; that is, whether at night, while she slept, she "created her own movies". She answered that she dreamed occasionally, but that she never ascribed any importance to her dreams. For whatever reason, from then on she began to tell them to me. But all of them had a common characteristic: they practically repeated something that had happened to her the previous day. Thus, for instance, if she had argued with a colleague at work, at night she dreamed that she had argued with him at work. Or at most, argued with another colleague or with someone unidentified. All of this without any associations, except the memory of the event itself. And further: she brought them in writing and read them to me! They were practically witness statements of events recorded during the daytime. Even so, now we had "films" produced by her, no longer "borrowed dreams", which I considered an important evolution. We talked about what had happened, and A began to manage to locate and express a few emotions, although very general, and without expanding the phantasies much. I also sought to emphasize and talk about any details in the dreams that were different from the real fact, taking them as manifestations of some more symbolic psychic processing.

At this point, her husband presented with a serious organic disease and had to stay in hospital for several days. A was very zealous, taking care of him in hospital and efficiently dealing with all the couple's everyday arrangements. After he was discharged, however, she began to experience something that felt very strange to her: intellectually she still wanted to be with him, sharing the same interests as before. But emotionally, it was as though she had ceased having any affection, as though he were a complete stranger. The situation was such that she no longer managed to remain undressed in front of him, because after all, as she said, "we do not remain naked in front of someone we don't know". The strange thing was that she felt a certain anxiety about this situation. At the same time she began to have an allergy on one of her legs, which her dermatologist ascribed to the soap that she had been using for years. We began to talk about a kind of "leprosy of emotional sensibility", because she had read that this disease destroys nerve endings and generates insensitive areas on the skin. I was then able to point out to her that she seemed to be, in this way, protecting herself *a posteriori* from the fear that she had felt about the risk of losing her husband, and the anxieties that she had suffered when he was in hospital, just as, I told her, we often only experience anxiety after danger is already past! And, then we immediately discovered another metaphor connected to her professional field to express what could be happening to her: she had switched off her emotional "relay". A understood it very well and even managed to extend it to other situations in her life. Immediately after this, she approached her husband affectively again, and then the allergy disappeared, even though she had gone back to using her usual soap. After this episode she never again presented any symptom of allergy.

At the time this improvement began she had a dream in which she and I were dining by candlelight in a good restaurant, and were interrupted by acquaintances, who came there. The aspect that we managed to discuss at this point was that I then represented someone more secure in whom she could deposit her affection and desires, since the husband had become ill and thus left her feeling insecure. I suggested, in addition, that the "emotional leprosy" could also be a protection against these type of feelings about me, but it was not possible to continue along this line of investigation, since A would immediately change the subject to work-related matters, once again reported factually. Then a new phase of her dream productions began. She started to dream—continuing to write them down—about bathrooms and toilet bowls! And there was always some problem that prevented her from urinating or defecating. Sometimes there was no privacy in the bathroom, sometimes the toilet bowl was very dirty. Often it was blocked and overflowing and, at other times, located in a place which was difficult to access or accommodate, such as at the top of a folding ladder, without any support. On some occasions she would defecate and the bowl overflowed when she pressed the flush button. I considered that she was then clearly dreaming about a feeling of not having another mind or her own mind into which she could discharge her emotions. As I understood it, we were dealing with her desire, or rather, her need to find a "toilet breast", as Meltzer (1967) describes it. In other words, an object for which she would already accept and feel a certain dependence, but a dependence only in the sense of being able to use projective identification to discharge her painful emotions to relieve herself from them without needing to take them back, even after they were processed.

But what was generating the repetition of these dreams? And what was my role in this? I consider these questions as key constituents of current psychoanalytic concerns. They imply no longer considering the phenomena that always occur in the analysand only as expressions of their resistance. After some time, I realized that this type of dream occurred more frequently when I intensified my interpretations spelling out psychic contents. I think that in this way, I was too far ahead of her psychic moment. A still needed me above all to help her locate and evacuate her emotions, and I often wanted her to understand them. This would involve, on her part, receiving them and containing them inside herself. But A, at the time, did not have the capacity to do so. Consequently she had also not developed a sufficient introjective disposition. In other words we were, she and I, moving in distinct times: I, sort of walking with a faster step beyond A's capacities. Thus I got ahead of her and generated a distance between us. Bearing this assumption in mind I tried to change my attitude, attempting to improve the "calibration" of my interventions. The frequency of dreams on this theme really diminished, but they did not disappear, nor were they replaced by others except the "operative" ones. Her limits of containment and the correlative insufficiency of psychic processing that existed prior to seeking treatment, were attested to by the multiple psychosomatic manifestations that precisely led her to seek help.

In the course of a situation that left her greatly disappointed at her husband, I had to change two of her appointments in succession so that she would not be left without. And I also had to suspend a third one right after this. At the next session A brought a dream with absolutely unheard of length and content. "I wake up in the morning in the room that I used to share with my sister as a child. I am lying in the bed that was actually hers, I look at the one that would be mine and see that my sister has wet the sheets. So I get up and let my mother know and I think of complaining. But she is with other people gathered in her room, chatting, laughing and organizing my sister's birthday, so she cannot talk to me."

In response to a question that I asked, A answered that the sister was only one year and ten months younger than she was. We already knew this and had talked about it on other occasions, but we had never managed to transform this information into something affectively alive and significant. She then recalled that her mother had told her that she had needed to go back to using diapers at the age of three, with nocturnal enuresis up to around ten years of age. And more: she was very surprised to realize that she had had the dream on the day of her sister's birthday, and that, at the time, during the session, she was wearing pants that her sister had given to her because they no longer fitted.

We then saw that my changes and suspension of appointments had left her feeling neglected and helpless, precisely at that difficult time in her conjugal life. Her feeling was that I had left her alone to go and take care of other personal interests. This had reactivated in her the childhood experiences involving the birth and presence of her younger sister, felt as occupying space in the life and mind of her mother, whom she still needed very much for herself alone. This had also revived, or perhaps, more precisely, led her to feel and experience, more clearly, extensively, and deeply, the painful feelings of neglect, helplessness, and disappointment experienced when her parents practically disowned her as their daughter after she stopped seeing the boy who was to be the family's favorite son-in-law. Until then, A had had very little contact with such emotions. We also had been aware for a long time of her description of her mother as efficient and correct, but with very little affective availability and attunement, as well as of the distant father. But now all of this gained a profoundly affective and present meaning, and was even experienced there in the relationship with me.

It seemed to me, and I told her this, that we could now understand the older meaning of the dreams in which she never managed to defecate or urinate. They expressed the feeling of not finding a mother who was sufficiently available to receive and take charge of her emotions. A participated actively and experienced all these understandings and reconstructions with emotion, and even acknowledged that she had felt that I had placed her in a secondary role. She had heard, through the press, that there was a psychoanalytic event in our city, and she had imagined that I was involved in it.

I think that this is the internal container relationship that she lacked and that left her with an insufficient capacity to process the emotional experiences psychically. This lack is probably also derived from other factors that we did not yet know and maybe would not ever get to know. But at that moment, we were in emotional and cognitive contact with an aspect that appeared fundamental to us. My expectation was that she could internalize the experience of our joint work in an increasingly stable manner. The experience of a relationship in which two people share important emotional experiences, and remain available to try and receive them, support them, and in so far as possible talk about them, thinking about their psychic growth. And this despite all the tensions, difficulties, and temporary disconnects. I insist on this point: what is internalized in a therapeutic relationship—as in childhood—is a *containing* relationship and not only another containing person. Using the concepts proposed by Meltzer (1973; Meltzer & Williams, 1988), I would formulate this expectation theoretically as constituting the introjection of the analytic dyad as an ego ideal with "inspirational" functions (instead of "aspirational").

At that time, we did not discuss the specific meaning of her meeting her mother in the room with other people preparing the sister's birthday, which for me had the connotation of the parents copulating to make a new baby, a topic that became very relevant later on in the treatment.

From this period on her dreams began to refer almost always to situations connected to her childhood with her original family; But now her dreams were generally pregnant with symbolic meanings. Aspects of child sexuality also began to insinuate themselves into the dreams.

A short while ago she lost her grandfather. Her also beloved grandmother, who since childhood had represented a surrogate maternal figure, had died a few years previously. She greatly felt the loss of her grandfather, and this allowed her to come into touch with her pain and suffer it more clearly, intensely, and profoundly than when she lost her grandmother. During the session following the funeral, she told a dream that seemed very significant. Some time previously she had seen a film called *The Red Balloon*. As she told it, a boy is given a red helium balloon, and for this reason all the other children envy him. He is not allowed to take it into the school building. So the boy lets it loose, but the balloon begins to follow him wherever he goes. The other children become even more envious, and they finally throw a stone and pierce it. All the other balloons in town become sympathetic, join together and look for the boy. The movie ends with him holding a heap of balloons, and flying with them until he disappears into space.

In her dream, A was holding the cords of several helium balloons in different colors. She then wishes to separate and hold two of them apart, a red one and a white one. For this, she needs to unravel and cut their cords, at the same time holding onto the two and the others, because she did not want to lose any of them. But, when she cuts the cords, the red and white ones get away and fly off. Soon after this she sees them hit an obstacle and fall empty to the ground, and she is very sad. Very upset, she herself relates this to the death of her two beloved grandparents. The grandfather was an enthusiastic supporter of Sport Club Internacional de Porto Alegre, whose colors are precisely red and white. And A began to cry; it was a silent weeping, with few tears, but expressing a deep inner pain. A crying that also moved me very much. (Translator's note: *comovido* (moved) in Portuguese, leading to a word play "co-movido", co-moved.)

Sometimes she wiped her tears quickly and seemed to be trying to "recompose" herself, talking about some other subject. But, she would return to her grandparents, saying that in these last days she had been catching herself often switching off from the task at hand because she was thinking about them. I remembered the boy rising into space holding tight onto the balloons and told her that sometimes, at times like this, one felt like going with the lost balloons. A agreed, and added again, moved: "But then one might disappear into space together with the balloons!" I agreed and continued: "And even empty and die like them". Yes—she said—but one certainly would like to! ... After a silence that appeared reflexive to me, she added: "But that is not what they would wish for me. They wanted me to be happy in life. They always wanted that for me!" I told her that I understood. Then we did not say anything for a long time, until the end of the session. At that moment, I felt profound empathy with her pain, including recalling personal losses. All the same, at some moments I took the cord of some mental balloon and flew far away from there thinking about a different subject. Who, after all, manages to remain all the time stuck on the ground, when they have such pain!

I am increasingly sure that, in situations like this one, there are moments when we need to simply remain silent, bearing it, and not protecting ourselves with supposedly pertinent and necessary interpretations that are really defensive. In silence, knowing, even if I did not admit it to her, that we were sharing and containing the same emotion, each in their own way, their memories, their history. I would say that such moments constitute the dates marked in red on the calendar of the analytic process. In my opinion, we were at that moment, compatriots and contemporaries of an identical emotional experience. Each in their own mental house, with their families, with their history, but, at the same time compatriots and contemporaries in the same universe of human emotions. A universe of pains and hopes that are part of the life of all of us. Of fears and passions inherent to the process of becoming univocally in tune, *at-one-ment* with the other. Of going from *knowledge of* something to *being in* that moment. I felt that we were there, containing and working through this experience, which was at the same time shared and individualized, without disappearing into space nor emptying and falling to the ground, thanks to this peculiar, mysterious, and fascinating human relationship invented by Sigmund Freud and so prosaically called "psychoanalysis".

## Patient "Z": the secret of the bougainvillea

In the next report—of a recent analysis—I will try to illustrate the onset of the analyst's intrusive curiosity (Meltzer, 1992) in the analytic field, triggered in part by the analysand, but which reactivated in me something that I find compatible with Meltzer's description (1973) of the infantile mental sexual state. In other words, an infantile part of my self temporarily contaminated my analytic self, arousing in me the desire to, secretly, violate the privacy of the patient's sex life. She detects this situation and dreams about it. This allows us to locate and treat it, in a way that, as far as I can perceive, contributed to the psychic growth (of both), and, thus, to the furthering and evolution of the analytic process.

Z is a good-looking single woman, an intelligent and highly successful professional, who sought treatment because she could not maintain deeper, longer-lasting relationships with men, although she intensely desired them. She has good insight and establishes a good emotional contact with the analyst. Her description throughout the treatment suggests a very disturbed mother, who competed openly with the patient, and kept telling her that marriage and children destroy a woman's possibilities of evolving in professional life, without at the same time leading to any greater affective gratification. The father appeared as a loving person who tried to be emotionally present for his daughter, attempting to compensate for his wife's difficulties, but who generally allowed himself to be dominated by her.

Z has two younger brothers who find it difficult to make their way in life.

We held two weekly sessions for a while and then started to have three.

The material I will bring here for illustration refers precisely to this moment when we began to have three sessions.

On the first day of analysis—when she had already lay down on the couch—Z tells the following dream:

> "I go to a fashion show of that friend of mine whose way of dressing I used to admire greatly. My father and I are at a higher level than the room—on a sort of mezzanine, looking down at the place where the models were to walk. But she, who was to show herself, did not appear, and all of a sudden a boy comes running through the room and goes to a patio, and jumps

into the swimming pool that was there. Father runs down to look at him, and I go down after him, a bit later. But, once I get to the patio, I don't even know where my father has gone, because I no longer see him. I then return to the place where the show was, but I know that my friend's participation will be very small and that the event is something simple, almost poor. And I think, at the same time, how this business of beauty is ephemeral, because she, who was at one time even a professional model, was now there playing a simple "bit part". Later, I am again looking at the boy in the swimming pool. Near me, in the patio—there is a tree—a bougainvillea—which I actually think very pretty. But in the dream I see that it is losing its leaves. I look closely at one of the leaves and see that it is sick. It appears that they had even used pesticide."

She then tells me that the bougainvillea has pink flowers, that she really likes this plant very much, and on the weekend before the session she bought one and put it in the garden of her house. The day before the session, however, she was disappointed to see that the plant had already wilted, and that this contrasted with another, which she noticed the same day in a park, flamboyant and pretty.

I perceive that I am feeling a certain amount of curiosity about this plant with pink flowers, which I don't remember knowing, trying to imagine how it is.

Meanwhile the patient changes the subject and begins to talk about going out on the weekend with a man who had left her with good expectations. However, she says that she practically had to "lead him" to greater intimacies, to almost seduce him, because he proved very timid, and possibly insecure. She continued telling this situation in such a way that, gradually, I realized there was a certain invitation, or even instigation, to together try to understand and find explanations for several of her reactions, as well as those of her intended during the meeting. At that moment I saw myself as though I were with her on a mezzanine, looking towards another scene—herself with her partner on the weekend—and as I thought at that time, this gave me a clue to what was happening in the session, that moment in the relationship between the two of us, and that, as I judged it, would be the point of urgency for interpretation. I told her that she wanted the two of us to get together—like she and her father on the mezzanine in the dream—so that, like two companions we could look at something about her, which had occurred outside, on the weekend, and that she might even think would make me curious to a certain extent.

After a slightly longer silence, Z said that indeed the feeling of being with her father on the mezzanine looking at the fashion show was very pleasurable for her in the dream. She then continued, saying that anyway, several things in the dream were still completely incomprehensible to her, such as the fashion show, the boy who throws himself into the swimming pool, and, above all, the bougainvillea She then tried to relate the model to her mother who, as she recalled, in adolescence bought and used identical dresses to those she—the daughter—purchased. She also related the friend to herself, because initially she had greatly admired her for her taste in clothes, but increasingly she was seeing that this was a shallow, and even not very trustworthy, person. Although this is difficult to describe, I want to emphasize that at this point the atmosphere of the session, again and subtly, seemed of two colleagues analyzing a third person. And, deep down, to myself, I felt that I agreed with her understandings. However, for whatever reasons, I didn't offer any intervention. Z then talked again about her date with the man, stating that this was something important to her, since it had to do with her affective life and her difficulties in this sense.

Taken by the feeling that in fact I might be devaluing something that was so important to her, I let her talk this time, extensively and in detail about this topic. I thought to myself that from this material we could understand something more regarding her difficulties in relationships with men, but I must also admit that, at some moments, I was curious about details concerning the meeting. And, furthermore, the bougainvillea with its pink flowers came into my mind, as a curiosity to find out whether I knew it, how it was precisely, all of this without my managing, or actually trying to transform it into an analytic fact, that is, something I could use to understand an unconscious content that was active at that moment in the session.

And so we finished that session.

That evening, in a study group with colleagues, I gave them a summary of the dream, to illustrate a given theoretical point, just as I am now doing more extensively, for this new purpose. During the discussion, the group also had its attention aroused—among other aspects—by the image of the bougainvillea, and the doubt arose as to whether it was a tree or a creeper vine, an issue that remained open.

She brought another dream to the next session, told as follows:

> "I was in a room, at the center of which there was a shower. I was a child and I was naked, taking a shower. An adult, in a corner of the room, was watching me from a distance without saying a word. Then I am already outside the house, dressed and about to cross a street. The adult comes after me, concerned, because I am barefoot, and it is as though he were going to help me cross, and it seemed he was about to give me a pair of slippers. It was as though he were a sort of guardian angel."

I then considered that, at some level or place in her mind, Z had realized that, after a certain point in the previous session, I had allowed myself to be taken by a voyeuristic desire to "spy on her" on her date with the man on the weekend. In the first dream, part of her would like to form a father-daughter union with me, in which, from a higher position we would observe and devalue the friend who, on another level, represented her mother. In this sense, until a short while ago Z only perceived her mother's competition against her. Now, in the dream she revealed *her* competition against the mother, usurping her husband, and using him to "demote her" in the fashion show, besides representing her as a leafless, sick bougainvillea. At the same time, however, another part of her acknowledged her difficulties—the wilted bougainvillea in her own garden—although she still left the impression that she would wish to show me those difficulties dressed as something that would attract me, that is, an instigating bush called *buganvile*, which may be both a tree and a "clinging vine" (the word *trepar* means climbing in Portuguese, but it also means fucking, so *trepadeira*, clinging vine, could have a second intention).

The second dream seemed, as I mentioned, to record her feeling of having managed to attract and catch me in this desire of hers, representing me as an adult-father spying on her naked. In this sense, it was now she who—we might say—showed herself naked, in front of me, replacing the friend/mother of the previous dream. The wish to be helped in her difficulties, in her turn—represented by crossing the street barefoot (analysis)—now is transformed into a desire to be cared for from close up by a father-analyst who offers her slippers and functions as her "guardian angel"—a father, however, at the same time idealized (a "guardian angel") and seduced like a "fallen angel".

It is obvious that there are several other important meanings in these two dreams, but considering the intensity of the incestuous desire at that moment, I interpreted only that she wished and feared that I—seeing her lying before me—would feel erotic desires for her instead of having an interest in treating her. Actually—I continued—she had acquired the feeling that I had let myself be taken by lascivious curiosity about her intimacy.

I had a strong impression that, under such emotional conditions, to continue analyzing her—actually interesting—dreams in detail would be experienced by Z as an enactment of her fantasy of attracting and exciting me with a "disrobing" scene.

Z appeared initially embarrassed by my interpretation, but later told that she had left the session fearing that the fact that she now lay on the couch had wrinkled her clothes and that this might be misinterpreted at her workplace. Besides, right after this she had been to see a clinician, and she had felt very pleased that they had a conversation about traveling. Furthermore, differently from here, she would not have to pay for the visit, because it was paid for by health insurance. At the same time, when she left, she had worried about the possibility that this might have distracted the clinician, making him perform a less accurate examination.

We then continued to examine her desires and fears in her relationship with me, but this no longer matters for my current purposes.

I would only add that in later sessions the bougainvillea, described sometimes as having pink flowers, sometimes red, at other times purplish, revealed itself by several associations as a representation of the female genitals at different degrees of excitement. Besides, some time later, I became aware not only that I knew the bush—without having known its name until then—but also that it grew in the garden of my parents' house, where I had spent my entire childhood. I think that his constituted one of the "hooks" in which Z's transferential proposal got caught inside me, leaving me temporarily dominated by a childish intrusive curiosity.

## Final considerations

Reviewing my everyday analytic work in the light of these and all other patients that I have or had seen, I believe that I can detect the following main tendencies:

1. I try to let myself internally sort of "float" emotionally during the sessions, according to the movement of the prevailing emotional currents, which appears to me different from simply maintaining a uniformly floating attention. My objective is to try and pick up and experience the ongoing emotion. I also intend to grasp what I would call the "implicit relational proposal" of the dyad. I refer to the position or function that we tend to ascribe to each other. To attempt to identify it, I use the "second look" (Baranger, Goldstein, & Goldstein, 1994), as well as the constant returns that the analysand unconsciously offers to the conditions of the relationship and of my mental functioning, according to the propositions of Ferro (1995).

2. As regards the analytic attitude, I try to be able to sustain internally, as well as in my interventions, in so far as I find it possible, a "tolerance to doubt", and a "feeling of infinitude", appropriate, according to Bion (1962) to a K link; that is to the desire to know. In the same sense I also use the distinction proposed by Meltzer (Meltzer & Williams, 1988) between mystery (something unknown and without a definitive answer, permanently stimulating thinking) and secret (for which someone has the definitive solution). The minds of the analysand, the analyst, and also what happens between both, needs to be accepted ultimately as a mystery about which we can only formulate partial and temporary conjectures. However, I consider the intrapsychic defenses, as well as the bulwarks in the analytic field generated by the dyad (Baranger & Baranger, 1969), as attempts to avoid the anxieties generated by the mystery, seeking to transform them into repressed, split secrets, etc. The therapeutic attempt is to help the analysand to increase his capacity as a container (Bion, 1962) and to support the mystery, in the sense given to it by Meltzer (Meltzer & Williams, 1988).
3. On formulating my interventions I am guided by the mental state that I consider to be present at that time, intuitively using the diagram presented previously. From this, and in broad terms, I consider the possibility of the following states:

    a. A state of representational conflict, with alpha function (Bion, 1962), operating but generating "lies" (defenses) due to the anxiety caused by conflicts among representations full of affects. This, in my opinion, is the predominant aspect in the second case reported.
    b. A state of failure due to deficient operation of the alpha function giving rise to little "mentalization". The first analysand I described appears to evidence predominantly this state, especially during the initial part of the therapeutic process.
    c. A state of psychic catastrophe, provoked by the destruction or reversion of the alpha function (Bion, 1962).
    d. A state of creative imagination, as described when the diagram was presented. This appears to be the state achieved by the analytic dyad, for instance, in the session with the dream about analysand A's red balloon, and in the second session with analysand Z.

    I am still seeking to identify whether such mental states are occurring in a basically social-ist or narcissistic relationship (Bion, 1992). In the latter situation I include the state described by Meltzer (1992) as one of intrusive identification into an internal object, with most of the self then living inside a "claustrum". For Meltzer (1992), under these circumstances there would not even be transference, and it would be necessary to carry out own technical procedures to achieve "the rescue of the child" (1992, p. 104) lost inside the claustrum.
4. I perceive myself using at least the following modes of intervention in these different situations:

    a. "Verbal Squiggle Game" (by analogy with Winnicott's Squiggle Game, 1968) aiming, together with the patient, to bring us closer to something still unknown to both. It would have something to do with what Meltzer (1983) calls "exploring dreams", carried out in an environment of "camaraderie" with the patient and distinct from the interpretation proper, directed at the meaning of the dream for transference and/or to the reconstruction of the past. I believe that I did this many times with A, always to the extent possible.

b. Interventions that keep to the manifest content brought by the analysand, but that, as I see it, implicitly contain a comprehension of some latent meaning that I believe I have picked up. I begin with the assumption that those interventions containing a small addition of psychic meaning will be accepted by some part of the patient's mind at that time, obscured by another less receptive one.
c. Interventions that aim at rendering explicit a resistance or an unconscious content. I think that I use them predominantly when there is a state of representational conflict. They correspond to the saturated interpretations described by Ferro (1995) and also probably to the "routine ones" mentioned by Meltzer (1994). There are examples of interventions of this kind, both in the more advanced phase of treatment of the allergy patient and in the sessions with Z.
d. Interventions in which we express to and for the patient the emotion and possible correlated phantasies that he himself does not manage to contact and express. These are formulations in the style of "I was imagining that in a situation like this (the one the patient is describing "operatively'), people may feel …", "I even imagined that one might want (or fear, etc.) to …" I consider that I did this several times, at different moments with A.
e. "Management of the setting", aiming at "holding" as described by Winnicott (1965), probably in the case of the phenomena involving the left inferior quadrant of my diagram.

This listing definitely does not exhaust the technical modalities that can be used in the different clinical situations to be found in the analytic relationship, including those classically described as explanations, confrontations, etc. I like Ferro (2005)'s expansion of the concept of interpretation: "… any linguistic intervention or not, that is able to generate transformation" (p. 110) in the analytic field. Thus, the phenomena prevailing in the analytic space are, as I mentioned previously, always trans-subjective but observed (and modified) in one of the subjects or in the dyad according to the "complementary vertex" used. I conjecture, based on Baranger (Baranger & Baranger, 1969), Ogden (1994), and Ferro (1995), that the analyst's interventions will always be fundamentally performed based on meanings generated by the dyad and referring to the relationship, although directed at the analysand. Even when apparently thought only by the analyst, the significant understandings originate from the collaboration of both. They constitute a construction of the dyad. Otherwise, it will be an ineffectual "autistic" production. Likewise, and this includes the cases in which the manifest content of the interpretations is directed toward external or past situations of the analysand, at the limit they always refer implicitly to dyad. But it would be impossible for the two to bear talking only about the relationship. Besides, it is important to situate the sources of emotions in the past or in the current external relations of the analysand. That is, to use the "analysand subject" vertex, so that the patient can achieve the necessary temporal-spatial discrimination that characterizes him as an individual. Spatial, because it leads him to bring into himself what belongs to him in the phenomena of the dyad, or, more precisely, to take on his new and unique vertex regarding them. Temporal, because it gives him a feeling of personal continuity and historization. But I insist that at root, the emotions present in the analytic space, as well as the meanings ascribed to them, are always generated in the dyad and seek to promote transformations in the analytic field—transformation that can then be introjected, promoting expansions of the mind, and psychic growth also of the analytic dyad.

## References

Baranger, M., Baranger, W. (1969). *Problemas del campo psicoanalítico*. Buenos Aires: Kargieman.
Baranger, W., Baranger, M., & Mom, J. M. (1987). El trauma psíquico infantil, de nosotros a Freud: trauma puro, retroactividad y reconstrucción. *Revista de Psicoanálisis, 44*: 745–774.
Baranger, W., Goldstein, R. Z., & Goldstein, N. (1994). *Artesanías Psicoanalíticas*. Buenos Aires: Kargieman.
Bauman, Z. (2007). *Tempos líquidos*. Rio de Janeiro: Zatar.
Bion, W. R. (1977). The grid. In: *Two Papers: "The Grid" and "Caesura"* (pp. 9–39). Rio de Janeiro: Imago.
Bion, W. R. (1961). *Experiences in Groups*. New York: Basic Books.
Bion, W. R. (1962). Learning from Experience. In: *Seven Servants: Four Works by Wilfred R. Bion*. New York: Jason Aronson, 1977.
Bion, W. R. (1963). Elements of Psychoanalysis. In: *Seven Servants: Four Works by Wilfred R. Bion*. New York: Jason Aronson, 1977.
Bion, W. R. (1965). Transformations. In: *Seven Servants: four works by Wilfred W. Bion*. New York: Jason Aronson.
Bion, W. R. (1992). Narcissism and social-ism. In: *Cogitations* (p. 122). London: Karnac.
Bohr, N. (1958). Essays 1933–1957 on atomic physics and human knowledge. In: *The Philosophical writings of Niels Bohr* (Vol. II). Woodbridge, CT: Ox Bow.
Ferro, A. (1995). *A técnica na Psicanálise Infantil*. Rio de Janeiro: Imago.
Freud, S. (1920). Más allá del principio de placer. *Obras Completas, 18*: 1–62. Buenos Aires: Amorrortu, 1986.
Freud, S. (1926). Inhibición, síntoma y angustia. In: *Obras completas, 20*: 71–164. Buenos Aires: Amorrortu, 1986.
Freud, S. (1937a). Análisis terminable e interminable. *Obras Completas, 23*: 211–254. Buenos Aires: Amorrortu, 1986.
Freud, S. (1937b). Construcciones en el análisis. *Obras Completas, 23*: 255–270. Buenos Aires: Amorrortu, 1986.
Green, A. (1983). A mãe morta. In: *Narcisismo de vida, narcisismo de morte*. São Paulo: Escuta, 1988.
Hartke, R. (2005). A relação terapêutica hoje: para além da transferência, da contratransferência e das representações. *Revista Brasileira de Psicoterapia, 7*: 281–293.
Hartke, R. (2007a). Repetir, simbolizar e recordar. Relatório apresentado no Painel, *El psicoanalisis cura aun mediante la rememoración?* Desenvolvido no 45° congresso da Internacional Psychoanalytical Association, em 25.07.2007, Berlin, Alemanha.
Hartke, R. (2007b). A evolução da teoria e prática psicanalíticas: rumo a uma assintótica situação analítica total. *Revista de psicanálise da SPPA, 14*: 557–576.
Klein, M. (1946). Notes on some schizoid mechanisms. In: *The Writings of Melanie Klein* (Vol. III). London: Hogarth.
Lecours, S., & Bouchard, M. A. (1997). Dimensões da mentalização: delineando níveis de transformação psíquica. *Livro Anual de Psicanálise, 13*: 185–205.
Levine, H. B., Reed, S. G., & Scarfone, D. (Eds.) (2013). *Unrepresented States and the Creation of Meaning: Clinical and Theoretical Contributions*. London: Karnac.
Marty, P. (1990). *La Psicosomática del adulto*. Buenos Aires: Amorrortu, 1992.

Meltzer, D. (1967). *O processo psicanalítico*. Rio de Janeiro: Imago, 1971.
Meltzer, D. (1973). *Estados Sexuais da Mente*. Rio de Janeiro: Imago, 1979.
Meltzer, D. (1983). *Dream-life: A Re-examination of the Psychoanalytical Theory and Technique*. Strathclyde, Perthshire: Clunie.
Meltzer, D. (1986). *Studies in Extended Metapsychology*. Strathclyde, Perthshire: Clunie.
Meltzer, D. (1992). *Claustrum. Una investigación sobre los fenómenos claustrofóbicos*. Buenos Aires: Spatia, 1994.
Meltzer, D. (1994). Interpretación rutinaria e interpretación inspirada: su relación con el proceso de destete em el análisis (1973). In: A. Hahn (Ed.), *Sinceridad y otros trabajos—obras escogidas de Donald Meltzer*. Buenos Aires: Spatia.
Meltzer, D., Hoxter, S., Bremner, J., & Weddell, D. (Eds.) (1975). *Exploración del autismo*. Buenos Aires: Paidos, 1984.
Meltzer, D., & Williams, M. H. (1988). *A apreensão do belo*. Rio de Janeiro: Imago, 1995.
Ogden, T. (1994). *Subjects of Analysis*. Northvale, NJ: Jason Aronson.
Rosenfeld, D. (1987). *Impasse and Interpretation*. London: Tavistock.
Roulot, D. (1993). *Neuroses e psicoses*. In: P. Kaufmann (Ed.), *Dicionário Enciclopédico de Psicanálise*. Rio de Janeiro: Zahar, 1996.
Sandler, J. (1983). Reflections on some relations between psychoanalytic concepts and psychoanalytic practice. *International Journal of Psychoanalysis*, 64: 35–45.
Sandler, J. (1992). Reflections on developments in the history of psychoanalytic technique. *International Journal of Psychoanalysis*, 73: 189–198.
Sugarman, A. (2006). Mentalization, insightfulness, and therapeutic action: the importance of mental organization. *International Journal of Psychoanalysis*, 87: 965–987.
Varela, F., Thompson, E., & Rosch, E. (1991). *The Embodied Mind*. Cambridge, MA: MIT.
Winnicott, D. W. (1963). O medo do colapso. In: C. Winnicott, R. Shepherd & M. Davis (Eds.), *Explorações psicanalíticas* (pp. 70–76). Porto Alegre: Artes Médicas, 1994.
Winnicott, D. W. (1965). The theory of the parent-infant relationship. In: *The Maturational Processes and the Facilitating Environment* (pp. 37–55). London: Hogarth.
Winnicott, D. W. (1968). O jogo do rabisco (Squiggle game). In: C. Winnicott, R. Shepherd, & M. Davis (Eds.), *Explorações psicanalíticas*. Porto Alegre: Artes Médicas, 1994.
Winnicott, D. W. (1971). *O brincar e a realidade*. Rio de Janeiro: Imago, 1975.

CHAPTER ELEVEN

# The function of evocation in the working-through of the countertransference: projective identification, reverie, and the expressive function of the mind—Reflections inspired by Bion's work*

*Elias M. da Rocha Barros and Elizabeth L. da Rocha Barros*

### Intersubjectivity and countertransference

James Grotstein (2011) in his forward to Lawrence J. Brown's (2011) *Intersubjective Processes and the Unconscious* describes the concept of intersubjectivity as "one of the most important, if not the most important, paradigm changes in analytic technique to date."

This new perspective is the result of a shift in focus from the patient's intrapsychic processes to intersubjectivity, that is, to the symbolic exchanges between the analyst/patient pair. This paradigm change reflects a shift from the one-body model psychology to the two-body one. Charles Rycroft (1956), referring to the need to bring about a model change, is one of the first analysts to have insisted on the creation of a metapsychology of interpersonal relations. He writes, "(However) there is I believe, also a need for a related frame of reference arising from the study of the interrelationships between individuals and the means of communication between them. Such a metapsychology of interpersonal relations would prove particularly valuable in clarifying our theories of symbolism, affects, and technique" (p. 63). Brown (2011) also recently did a thorough review of the concept of intersubjectivity.

In this paper we shall concentrate primarily on mapping the metapsychological issues involved in the evolution of the concept of countertransference towards that of reverie. We think the latter is a basic tool for building an interpretation of the meaning of the emotional experience that happens between the analyst-analysand. Bion's contributions to the theme, will be approached, since we regard them as being central to the metapsychological issues we will deal with. These include the study of the process of construction and communication of affects

---

*We would like to thank Dr. Luiz Meyer for his careful reading of this paper and for his very valuable suggestions.

between analyst-analysand and their meanings. We conceive this communication as taking place via evocations generated by representations of emotional experiences or symbolic forms in the mind of the analyst, subsequently transformed through mental work out into a verbal interpretation for the patient. In accordance with our view we will describe a new concept linked to this transformation, that we are calling the expressive function of the mind.

Since we conceive reverie as an outcome of the evolution of the concept of countertransference, we think it is necessary to examine how the latter has evolved. The initial proposals for the redefinition of the meaning and of the clinical use of the concept of countertransference come from Racker (1968) and Paula Heimann (1950). These authors, each on their own, propose the transformation of countertransferential feelings into tools for researching the affective architecture of the patient. This suggestion arises directly from the incorporation of the theory of object relations and makes large use of the concept of project identification (Klein, 1946, p. 8) and containment (Bion, 1962b). These are the kernels for considering intersubjective phenomena, which is the stage on which the process of the construction of meaning for emotional experiences is played out and can be observed. As we see it, during a session we are able to observe in the analyst-patient interaction what we call the living fabric of mental life.

The phenomenon of countertransference has been so much discussed in psychoanalytic literature that to say anything new on the subject is something of a challenge. Paradoxically, however, its being so highly discussed indicates the presence of important gaps yet to be filled towards understanding the process. It is within this article's objectives to delineate some of these gaps we find in the theory of countertransference: for instance, it is not quite known how it is transmitted and how it structures itself in the mind of the analyst, nor how it is worked through, that is, transformed, so as to acquire a meaning upon which a useful interpretation can be worked out (Brown, 2011, pp. 112–124). The notion of reverie, introduced by Bion (1962b) and deepened significantly by Ogden (2004), brings to the concept of countertransference a new dimension, coming at times to be seen as encompassing countertransference and at others as being encompassed by it, but most definitely becoming part of the examination of intersubjectivity.

The way a patient relates to us, beginning by his very presence, has a series of effects on us—be it in the form of feelings that are experienced, thoughts that are evoked, body sensations, desires that surface, states of mind that impose themselves, at times pleasant, others highly disagreeable, all of them suggesting the existence of a peculiar phenomenon underway. It is important to emphasize that this meeting engenders, in both patient and analyst states of mind that can be qualified as emotional-affective. Psychoanalysis as a unique form of relationship cannot keep from asking what to make of these experiences. Shall it ignore them and simply consider them the result of personal idiosyncrasies and/or neurotic manifestations and, as such, discard them? Or shall it try to understand them as forms of communication that tell the analysts something about the patient and that stem from the relational context experienced? How to process them? Shall the analyst become a close observer of what happens in his inner world and try to put in words the feelings wakened in him by the very presence of the patient? If the answer is yes, how does this happen and what is its process?

During the session, as in life, the patient is always in a state of "becoming" and never in a fixed state of being.

How to apprehend this ever emerging person? What is the underlying element that organizes his way of being? Answering these questions will give us clues about the emotional architecture and mental functioning of the patient.

It is worth noting that this concept of man as an ever changing being is put forth by various literary writers, among whom Mia Couto (1994, p. 10) who writes, "A man's story is always badly told. That's because a person never stops being born. Nobody leads one sole life, we are all multiplied into different and ever changeable men."

## Evolution of the concept of countertransference

Let us go over some of the critical moments leading to the construction and reorganization of the concept of countertransference:

1. The introduction of the concept of projective identification: Klein (1946) in suggesting that the patient projects *into* the mind of the analyst and not only *onto* her, introduces the idea that the patient *does* something to the mind of the analyst and in this process prompts feelings frequently associated with an invitation to both act or engage in enacting a certain role associated with specific emotions.
2. The concepts of holding, of transitional, potential, and illusory space, proposed by Winnicott, require of analysts that they once again review the clinical meaning of the term. Bollas (1983, p. 2) later associates these concepts to the notion of the use of the object, which allows the analyst to create internally a "living environment" of "archaic object relations" not worked through.
3. The concept of containment and reverie as introduced by Bion and deepened by Thomas Ogden.[1] Associated with these notions we must also mention the postulation of an alpha function and the proposal of the existence of emotional links L (love), K (knowledge), and H (hate) that structure the psychic dynamics. It should be noted that neither countertransference nor reverie are delimited by clear boundaries separating one from the other, and both from what would be, for instance, a secondary process such as thought.
4. The fourth element, which also leads to a rupture followed by conceptual deepening, does not ensue from a single idea but rather, from a concern in understanding the processes of symbolization and also from that which Green (2002, 2005) calls a *tertiary process*. He defines the latter as a means of intermediation (symbolic) and a link between the primary and secondary processes, delineating the space where these symbols are built. The study of these processes allows us to build hypotheses about the way projective identifications work intersubjectively as part of the countertransference and about their subsequent processing by reverie, which leads afterwards to their being transformed into an interpretation. Under this item we must also include what César and Sara Botella (2001) describe as the work of figurability. That term refers to a vast set of phenomena, above all to a topical regression that manifests itself in dreamwork, which consists in putting into visual images (figurability) emotions experienced during psychic work. Various authors seem to agree that there is permanently in the psyche a pressure to build symbols and/or representations that is linked to an ever present urge of the human spirit to work through

the lived emotional experiences (Brown, 2011; Cassorla, 2009, 2013a, 2013b; Levine, 2013; Rolland, 1998; Roussillon, 2011).
5. Money-Kyrle (1956) writes that the patient's projections can be closely linked with unique internal reactions of the analyst to these (projections) and introduces the idea that feelings wakened in the analyst through psychoanalytic listening interact with his (the analyst's) world of internal objects and, therefore, unconscious phantasies.

Bion (1952, 1958, 1962a, 1962b), rather than using the term countertransference, prefers to underline the impact of projective identifications on the analyst and the use of *reverie*, to deal with them. In this context, intersubjective exchanges become the central focus of the study of the analytic relation. Based on the mechanism of projective identification, Bion proposed the existence of a continual flux of unconscious phantasies taking place as much in waking life as in dreams. In the session, this flux implies a continual invitation for the analyst to abandon his analytical attitude and enact aspects of the patient's internal world. Bion's ideas, according to Ferro (2007), introduce not only the notion that projective identification can have a communicative function but also, and above all, that that which is projected into the mind of the analyst can and must be transformed.

In the history of psychoanalytic concepts it can be said that countertransference at its inception could be viewed as analogous to a photo of a relational moment. Later, with the growing understanding of the analytic relation as a bi-personal, inter-relational process (Ferro, 1995, 1999), countertransference came to be compared analogically with a film, something resulting from the movement of many photos in continual flux in which two characters are playing lead in a relation. From this point on one could no longer speak about countertransference in isolation and it became necessary to associate it with that which Bion named reverie. With its introduction, the mental processes occurring in the mind of the analyst became both the focus of investigation and the field from which the interpretation is built.

*Expressivity*

Pierre Fédida (1986, 1991), reflecting on the appropriation of the concept of countertransference by the French school and concerned with the possibility of the transformation of psychoanalysis into a psychology of communication and/or of interpersonal relations, warns us about the need to build a metapsychology of countertransference. It would have as its model the metapsychology of the dream, namely, the production of representations and the logic which articulates dreamwork. We will deal later with the operational bases of this logic. Fédida's critique addresses the way countertransferential phenomena are described as limited to the ongoing communication processes associated only to hidden latent thoughts. This leaves aside as secondary the emotional experiences that produce them and also the unconscious scenarios being enacted in the transference with the analyst. This is a revolutionary view, because here it is not only countertransference that is at stake, but the whole question of intersubjective relations. The affects involved in countertransference or in reverie are intersubjective constructs and thus require a metapsychology of intersubjective relations that should provide us also with a hypothesis on how affects are apprehended, represented, and modified.[2]

Fédida (1986, 1991) uses, as the basis for a discussion of the processes of transformation lying between what is observed and what is created by the artist, writings left by painters and sculptors, especially Cézanne and Giacometti. These artists describe the relation between their observation of natural landscapes and the processes underlying their creation of the work painted on the canvas. These writings mention, on one hand, how external aspects of reality influenced their paintings by evoking in their subjectivities a specific state of mind, that we are here naming expressive function of the human mind, and, on the other hand, how these states get mentally transformed before being transposed to the canvas.

This expressive function is neither the result of the projection of subjective qualities of affects added to the object of perception nor is it purely and intrinsically subjective. This function gives affective coloring to the inner perception by fusing internal and external qualities. Melshon (2001) suggests that "Expressivity is the unity and fusion of the external with the internal (a notion that corresponds to [the concept of] projective identification) ..." (p. 252).

What is under consideration here is what happens in the mind of the artist between the process of evocation (we will discuss this process in more detail in the following pages) that is fostered by the contemplation of a natural scene and the artistic production underway. The understanding of the dynamics and logic of the process of evocation, which we consider a primordial means of projective identification, differs psychoanalytically from the aesthetic one. While from the latter's stance this evocation of feelings cannot be confused with the elements that produced it and beauty does not depend on interpretation, from the point of view of psychoanalysis we make use of this evocation to interpret what goes on from the emotional standpoint in the relation between two persons in the consulting room.

Linguists, and more especially Roman Jakobson (1963), introduce the notion of an expressive or emotive function of language. This refers to all forms of instilling emotion in linguistic structures through pauses, intonations, reticences, exclamations, etc. People who suffer from what is called expressive aphasia, resulting from a lesion in the brain in Broca's area, become incapable of structuring communication that expresses emotion. They suffer from agrammatism and consequently lose the capacity to communicate affective states through verbalization although their capacity to understand remains intact. As with the brain, we want to postulate that the mind also has this ability to produce expressiveness attached to symbolism. It is following this lead that we allow ourselves to postulate a mental function equivalent to the cerebral which we call the expressive function of the human mind. Interestingly enough, Bion also begins from the same type of pictorial experience when defining the process of mental transformation and referring to the relation between a Van Gogh painting and the field of poppies observed in nature. The painting would be a subjective *transformation* of the poppy field with which it would hold in common an invariant that would guarantee a communality between both. It is important to highlight that the transformation results from the work of an internal structure and not from the gaze addressed to the landscape. The idea of an invariant stems from an analogy with a projection model used in geometry, by means of which a geometric figure can take on diverse "forms" in space when projected from a Cartesian axis and, even so, keep a common essence, that is, an invariance.

Within this perspective it is problematic to conceive the existence of a static moment (invariance, in this case the poppy field) since transformations are continuous and cannot be delimited, and have neither a start nor end point. Among analysts who have taken on this matter we cite H. Levine and A. Ferro.

H. Levine (2013) refers to the unformulated unconscious; as he puts it, the "… formless, not yet organized and not yet articulated subset or 'pre' or 'proto-psychic' elements that we might call the unstructured or unformulated unconscious" (p. 364). With this outlook Levine underscores the existence of unconscious contents that never acquired a form/shape and which need an intersubjective support, in this case the analyst's reverie, to create or co-create a first form or mental representation.

Ferro (1995, 1999) describes a model in which the characters, created in the session's narrated story, are knots of an interpersonal narrative, which emerge as holograms of the here and now emotional inter-relation established between analyst and patient. These holograms, metaphorically speaking, are constituted by the affect in its symbolic representation internalized in the mind of the pair and can for this reason be considered as the third element present in the relation of the pair. They create a type of transitional object, which expresses the unconscious phantasy of the pair at a specific moment.

*Evocation*

We would like to briefly introduce the notion of "evocation" since it plays a crucial role in the way we underline symbolization and expression. Evocation, the media of projective identification, is also a non-discursive form of apprehending complex networks of relations between unconscious affects and ideas permeating the interaction between two subjectivities. It expresses itself most of the time in "imagetic" grasping (body sensations, synaesthetics, expressive gestures, melody, etc, are, in the context of this article, all treated as images) of the feelings that permeate the process of constitution of the mental representations of the patient. It is this production that is the "imagetic" grasping, which later will be the object of successive transformations of a symbolic nature (initially not discursive) until an interpretation is formed (discursive symbolism) that can be verbalized to the patient, which can be considered by us to be reverie. The interpretation is a particular way of thinking (Freud, 1900, p. 506) built from the ongoing process of symbolization, and not something rendered by the mental grasping alone of the analyst.

The evocations produced in the mind of the analyst are forms, as we see it, of organizing the affects (and thus, for example, transforming psychic suffering into something more bearable in being thinkable) through the establishment of certain new and unexpected links between them that are not conscious. These links are not conscious during the ongoing emotional experience no matter how expressive they may be. They are only prone to becoming conscious after the process of working through. What we suggest is that the evocation is already a proto-thought, which among other characteristics has that of grasping diverse contents simultaneously, and not successively as happens in verbal discourse. But in order to be thought these contents must be put into words; that is, in a plastic and abstract discourse.

In our view, a mental content (which in this case can be considered as an unconscious phantasy) is encoded in a projection to be transported into the mind of the analyst. What follows is its transformation into a non-discursive mental representation that can, once again, be transformed into another symbolic form, now of a verbal discursive character. This process needs for its understanding a series of concepts which we will now discuss.

In the process of grasping the emotional experiences, which constitute the unconscious phantasies, we need symbols as their vehicles. The philosopher Suzanne Langer (1942), in her theory of how meanings are formed, proposes a differentiation between presentational symbolism and discursive symbolism. The first is associated with expressive forms of emotion, is non-discursive, and has a nature fundamentally connotative (refers to the subjective meaning and transmits information to evoke other realities through associations and sensorial forms). An example of this is the image of a table. The second is discursive and has a denotative nature (refers to the objective meaning, the word in its dictionary form). An example of this is the word "table". Words are our most powerful symbols, as they provide plasticity to ding thought. Presentational symbolism is intuitive (many times a form of condensed intuition) and feeds on patterns of our emotional life; it is through this form that affects are evoked. Its aim is not the presentation of ideas as propositions or concepts, such as happens in natural language, but to exemplify a *feel like*. This distinction between symbolic forms allows us to grasp, describe, and reflect on evoked representations. These symbolic representations acquire a form that already contains an expressivity.

Langer (1942), commenting on how feelings are grasped and conveyed through symbols, refers to the central role played by presentational symbolism and suggests that it has the property of transmitting what she calls *likeness,* that is, it "exemplifies objectively what feelings seem to be subjectively" (Innis, 2009, p. 47). Other authors (Dewey, 1931; Pierce, 1992) refer to this same property of symbols as a quality of "suchness", that is, of exemplifying a situation or a character through a set of distinctive qualities. By *suchness* these authors understand something very close to *similitude*, or rather, the capacity to suggest types of experience.

Let us look now at the specific qualities of each of these two types of symbolism. Presentational symbolism does not name but exemplifies that about which we are speaking (Innis, 2009). Innis writes:

> Feeling itself, the perceived suchness of things, is a form of meaning-making, and forms of feeling can be expressed in material media [images, for example], which give us true knowledge, although it cannot be put into words. (pp. 47–48)

In this context we are considering symbols apprehended through evocation—as crystallizations of intuitions conveyed through expressive forms. It is interesting on this point, that Paula Heimann (1977), in a work she saw as complimentary to her article of 1950, considered countertransference as synonymous with intuition.

*Expression*

We need now define the role of expression[3] on the non-discursive level to next describe its relation with discursiveness in the internal world in its relations with conscious and unconscious mental life. This term, as we are using it, derives from Collingwood (1938) and Benedeto Croce (1992) and refers to an aspect in art that does not aim only to describe or represent emotions, but centrally to both transmit and produce them in the other or in one's own self through an evocation, a mental representation colored by emotion. Expression precedes the communicative capacity through words. Within our present context we can say that it is a representation directed to someone. This would be the characteristic feature of communicative projective identification. From the psychoanalytic standpoint, expressiveness is one of the essential components of projective identification.

From what has been said, evocation takes shape in a process that generates an affect or a representation that will have to be worked through in the analyst's reverie. At the moment of the initial impact the evocation produces a deconstruction in the mind, a disorganization followed by a new articulation, which allows for the manifestation of unconscious links between affects that interfere in the meaning-making of an emotional experience. These links are not available to the conscience and as such are not felt as a lived experience.

Before building his interpretation it is necessary for the analyst to go through a complex psychic working through, in part conscious, in part not. It is not enough for him to be aware of what feelings are projected into his mind by the patient; he also needs to trace back in what way the experience of these feelings have affected him. This second stage is essential to make efficient usage of reverie and to characterize it conceptually as such. The identification of this experience, in self-analysis, allows the analyst to apprehend the aspect of the patient that is dynamically unavailable. This process bears a certain similarity to what happens in dream production. We think the expression "to dream the patient's dream" (Cassorla, 2013b) is born out from this situation. In this context the word dream does not hold a total identity with the phenomenon which takes place while we are sleeping but rather more directly with the dreamwork similar to that which takes place during sleep. The central characteristic of this "dreaming the patient's dream" is that it happens in an oneiroid state during which the mind is unfocused, and follows the same principle of the evenly suspended attention proposed by Freud as one of the basic analytic rules for listening to the patient. To dream together—patient and analyst—happens upon the transformation of an emotional experience into an expressive phenomenon that makes itself present in the mind of the analyst in the form of an affect. Why does this transmission generate a visual form (as aforementioned not solely, but principally)? We must recall that an imagistic form is highly prone to simultaneously hold within it complex syntheses of experiences and a condensation of links. An example of this is the sketch (think of the satirical political sketches) which many times is more forceful in conveying an idea than 100 written pages. This symbolic visual form, within the process of building an interpretive comment for the patient, must be recaptured in the form of verbal symbols. In this process of symbolic transformation it is necessary that the affect that was transmitted in an encoded manner by the projection keep its expressive qualities, which then acquire the semantic character of a metaphor.

*Meaning*

It is the re-establishment of these links, through the analyst's interpretation, that allows working through the defensive attitude of the patient in denying psychic pain and, as a result, enables him (through the symbolic production) to face it. The interpretation ensuing from this process will not only convey knowledge about the patient but above all afford the chance of transforming his self, thanks to the emotional experience provided by the verbalized interpretation. As such the analyst is generating in the patient this transition from knowing to becoming. We believe also that this is the way to produce what Ahumada (2011, p. 13) called ostensive insight.

It is from countertransference and/or reverie, therefore, that we apprehend representations which allow us to grasp the nature of the transferential relation in the session as it is lived in the inner world of the patient.

This approach is also in line with the ideas of Fédida (1991) when he suggests there is a function of language which is central to the process carried out by countertransference. He writes, creating a neologism to express it, that language gives *réson* to things. The term is made up of the French words *réssonance* and *raison* and suggests that the language of the analyst is the result of a resonance, that is, of a sound which resonates and merges with reason. Reason, here, has the meaning of the individual's capacity to find some sense and a meaning to his emotional experiences. It is through resonance that the emotional character of the experience is maintained and transformed. The incorporation of meaning to an experience changes the function of the emotional experience in our lives. Language, in this context, is not a copy of an experience, but that which gives it meaning stemming from a resonance. Just as the image on the canvas is an apprehension of other links which synthesize the totality of the relations of the subject with the world at that moment, so the evocation of images, sensations, feelings, memories, reveries carries out the same role in the countertransference/reverie of the analyst.

However, this first movement is not sufficient to turn the evocation into an analytical fact. For it to happen it is necessary that the analyst finds, through reflection and self-analysis, the longing for emotional communication and representation implicit in the image. This is not a matter of guessing or simple deciphering, but of building what Fédida calls meaning based on the apprehension of the emotional links present in the evocation but absent from conscious discourse. The next step entails an effort by the analyst to put into words (that is, in discursive symbolic form) that which will be communicated as an interpretation/observation (response to the longing for language, the search for the sayable) addressed to the patient. These are not just casual words, but those aspiring to produce an emotional experience of insight (that creates new links), which generate in the patient a live feeling of "Ah, this makes sense and allows me to understand the meaning of this instance in my life and associate it with *other* moments." What is at stake here is the promotion of knowledge as emotional experience and not a mere process of accumulating information. We know how hard it is to describe the nature of the experience of an insight but every analyst and patient knows when it happens. The whole process happens in instants mediated by a symbolic form which articulates meanings, at a level not necessarily mediated by words. As aforementioned, César and Sara Botella (2001) refer to the first stage of this phenomenon as the work of figurability. Ogden (1997b) refers to the above process as part of what he calls *effects in language* (pp. 224–225). It is these effects which convey the meaning of the live experience that goes beyond naming and describing (also functions of language). He refers to a dimension of language which creates and communicates meanings indirectly, that is, "relatively independent of the content of what is being said." In this article we are trying to associate this dimension of language with expressivity (the experience of emotion as conveyed by the symbol, that is, feeling (or rather, to "being" as verb and not as noun) present in the symbol). Expressiveness gives emphasis to processes in transit, (becoming), and not only to the content of the information transmitted.

Verbal language on the one hand has the function of opening to communication—while the unconscious by definition is a closing—and on the other, the function of symbolization, defined as its ability to enter into more ample, flexible, and open relational sets, which were enclosed in the rigid cycles of unconscious phantasies (Laplanche, 1987).

The analyst's putting into words serves this purpose of an opening of the unconscious by placing the experience in affective nets that are broader and more prone to being thought about, as they come to exist as thinkable symbols that allow for reflection. It is here that "the magical lens of words" (Rolland, 2006) begins working transformations.

Bion believed that the process of containment took place in K (knowledge) and not in L (love) or H (hate). Transformations, changes, and detoxifications do not happen due to being loved or loving, but are the outcome of a desire to know, a curiosity in understanding what is going on emotionally with the other through the experience of knowing these states of mind. James Fisher (2011) in an elucidating chapter shows us that while Bion never literally used the expression "container in K" he indicated that a container can be considered as such only "remaining a container-in-K; wanting to know and understand, not from an emotional distance but by experiencing those emotions and yet retaining a K-state-of-mind" (p. 57).

We suggest that in formulating an interpretation based on the working through of reverie we operate among other processes, a transmutation of the symbolic basis. We believe this concept to be very useful in understanding the function of symbolization in psychoanalysis.

We can here make a synthesis of what has been said up to this point. The patient in the session relates experiences, describes facts, mentions memories or dreams, and through these manifestations evokes feelings and representations in us and/or invites us to act out a certain role. This narrative and its enacted expressions evoke in us metaphors that join discursive and non-discursive articulations which give shape to feelings being projected into us in transference. As we interpret, we place ourselves in these evoked experiences, on another symbolic basis, or better, transmute from a specific symbolic basis, in this case the evocative language of visual symbols of the dream or of the metaphors or yet of the experiences expressive of reverie into verbal language descriptive of meanings (another symbolic basis) and in this way we widen the capacity to think the experience in attributing meaning to our involved feelings. The exchange (mutation) of a symbolic basis for another widens the power of a communication. This amplification is due to a progression in the communicative capacity, stemming from a new symbolic basis. In this context, interpretation is not a causal explanation nor a mere description but becomes a means of widening links between meaningful emotional experiences and promoting new links between affects and affective nets.

In this manner the evoked inner image is analogous (contains in itself a metaphoric virtuality), but not identical, to the feelings of the patient. Interpretation, in its turn, indicates connections between affects and affective nets that did not exist in consciousness. This *presentification* (i.e., making present) of the affective networks of the patient makes visible something which was not present in the discourse or the initial conduct of the patient and can give us access to his unconscious phantasies and beliefs, which give rise to kernels of meaning that organize their feelings and behaviors.

Through the reverie of the analyst and the dream of the patient we have access to the centers of attraction of the unconscious or, putting it in another way, the internal objects around which gravitate the emotional relations, or yet what Meltzer calls the significant kernels of meaning of emotional life. This expression is also adopted by André Green (2002).

Freud used the notion of mental work in various moments of his oeuvre. He meant by this the set of conscious and unconscious operations that transformed raw mental content, most of it unconscious, into a new representation or verbal thought. In this paper, we pointed out the similarity (not equivalence) between the dreamwork and the mental processes operating in the mental work of reverie. We add now, further, that this is also the foundation of the metapsychology needed to understand the processes of transformation involved in producing an interpretation based on the mental work of reverie that results from the interpersonal relations taking place during an analytic session, as put forth in this work.

*Summary*

The authors delineate a history of the evolution of the concepts of countertransference and reverie from their introduction, associating them with new correlate psychoanalytic concepts rising along the way and requiring their redefinition. They then describe the process which permeates the building of reverie and, above all, the role of evocation. Dreams, narratives, and their expressions enacted evoke in us metaphors which combine discursive and non-discursive articulations giving shape to feelings being projected into us in the transference. We, in interpreting, place these evoked experiences on another symbolic basis, that is, we transmute the evocative language of visual symbols of dreams or metaphors or yet expressive experiences of countertransference, into a verbal language descriptive of meanings and in this way amplify the capacity to think the experience on attributing meaning to the involved feelings. These ideas lead the authors to postulate the existence of an expressive function of the mind.

*Notes*

1. We suggest here that the article by Thomas Ogden (2004) should be read, as it very well differentiates the concepts of holding and of containment, often confused.
2. In this article we use the terms "affect", "emotional experience", and "feeling" interchangeably and are aware of a certain loss in precision in so doing.
3. The connection between intuitive knowledge, or expression, and intellectual knowledge, or conceptual, between art and science, poetry and prose, can be expressed in no other way than by talking of a connection between the two levels. The first level is expression, the second, the conceptual: the first can exist without the second, the second cannot exist without the first. There is poetry without prose, but there is no prose without poetry. Expression is, indeed, the first assertion of human activity. Poetry is "the mother tongue of the human species" (Croce, 2002, p. 29).

*References*

Ahumada, J. L. (2011). *Insight Essays on Psychoanalytic Knowing*. London: Routledge.
Bion, W. (1952). Group dynamics: a re-view. *International Journal of Psychoanalysis, 32*: 235–247.

Bion, W. (1958). On hallucination. *International Journal of Psychoanalysis, 39*: 341–349.
Bion, W. (1962a). A theory of thinking. *International Journal of Psychoanalysis, 43*: 306–310.
Bion, W. (1962b). *Learning from Experience*. London: Heineman.
Bollas, C. (1983). Expressive uses of countertransference. Notes to the patient from oneself. *Contemporary Psychoanalysis, 19*: 1–34.
Botella, C., & Botella, S. (2001). *La figurabilité psychique*. Paris: Delachaux et Niestlé.
Brown, L. (2011). *Intersubjective Processes and the Unconscious*. London: Routledge.
Cassorla, R. (2009). Reflections on non-dreams-for two: Enactment and the analyst's implicit alpha function. Paper presented at the Bion in Boston Conference, July 2009.
Cassorla, R. (2013a). When the analyst becomes stupid: An attempt to understand enactment using Bion's theory of thinking. *The Psychoanalytic Quarterly, 82*: 323–360.
Cassorla, R. (2013b). In search of symbolization: the analyst's task of dreaming. In: *Unrepresented States and the Construction of Meaning*. London: Karnac.
Collingwood, R. G. (1938). *The Principle of Art*. Oxford: Clarendon Press.
Couto, M. (1994). *Every Man is a Race*. Cambridge: Heinemann.
Croce, B. (1992). *The Aesthetic as the Science of Expression and of the Linguistic in General, Part 1, Theory*. Cambridge: Cambridge University Press.
Dewey, J. (1931). *Affective Thought*. In: *Philosophy and Civilization*. New York: Putnam.
Ferro, A. (1995). *A Técnica da Psicanálise Infantil*. Rio de Janeiro: Imago.
Ferro, A. (1999). *The Bi-Personal Field: Experiences in Child Analysis*. London: Routledge.
Ferro, A. (2007). Reverie: problemas de teoria e de prática. *Revista de Psicanálise de Fortaleza, 1*: 64–72.
Fédida, P. (1986). *Communication et Répresentation*. Paris: Presses Universitaire de France.
Fédida, P. (1991). *Nome, Figura e Memória*. São Paulo: Editora Escuta.
Fisher, J. (2011). The emotional experience of K. In: C. Mawson (Ed.), *Bion Today*. London: Brunner-Routledge.
Freud, S. (1910). *The Future Prospects of Psycho-Analytic Therapy. S. E., 11*. London: Hogarth.
Green, A. (2002). *La pensée clinique*. Paris: Odile Jacob.
Green, A. (2005). *Key Ideas for a Contemporary Psychoanalysis*. London: Routledge.
Grotstein, J. (2011). Forword. In: L. Brown, *Intersubjective Processes and the Unconscious*. London: Routledge.
Heimann, P. (1950). On countertransference. *International Journal of Psychoanalysis, 31*: 81–84.
Heimann, P. (1977). Further observations on the analyst's cognitive process. *Journal of the American Psychoanalytic Association, 25*: 313–333.
Innis, R. E. (2009). *Susanne Langer in Focus: The Symbolic Mind*. Bloomington & Indianapolis: Indiana University Press.
Jakobson, R. (1963). Linguistique et poétique. In: *Essais de linguistique générale* (pp. 209–248). Paris: Minuit.
Klein, M. (1946). Notes on some schizoid mechanisms. In: *Envy and Gratitude*. London: Hogarth, 1975.
Langer, S. (1942). *Philosophy in a New Key: A Study in the Symbolism of Reason, Rite and Art*. Cambridge: Harvard University Press.
Laplanche, J. (1987). *Le Barquet. La transcendence du Transfert*. Paris: Presses Universitaire de France.
Levine, H. (2013). *Unrepresented States and the Construction of Meaning*. London: Karnac.
Melshon, I. (2001). *Psicanálise em Nova Chave*. São Paulo: Editora Perspectiva.
Money-Kyrle, R. (1956). Normal countertransference and some of its deviations. *International Journal of Psychoanalysis, 37*: 360–366.

Ogden, T. (1994). The analytic third-working with intersubjective clinical facts. *International Journal of Psychoanalysis, 75*: 3–20.

Ogden, T. (1997b). *Reverie and Interpretation*. Northvale, NJ: Jason Aronson.

Ogden, T. (2004). On holding and containing, being and dreaming. *International Journal of Psychoanalysis, 85*: 1349–1364.

Peirce, C. (1992). *The Essential Peirce: Selected Philosophical Writings* (Vol. I) (Eds. N. & C. Kloesel). Bloomington: Indiana University Press.

Racker, H. (1968). *Transference and Countertransference*. New York: Universities Press.

Rolland, J. C. (1998). *Guérir du mal d'aimer*. Paris: Gallimard.

Rolland, J. C. (2006). *Avant d'être celui qui parle*. Paris: Gallimard.

Roussillon, R. (2011). *Primitive Agony and Symbolization*. London: Karnac.

Rycroft, C. (1956). The nature and function of the analyst's communication to the patient. *International Journal of Psychoanalysis, 37*: 114–116.

CHAPTER TWELVE

# The truth object: growing the god within

*Annie Reiner*

Kurt Vonnegut's idiosyncratic writing reflects a unique creative voice. In a speech to graduating students about how best to live one's life, Vonnegut (2011) advised them to, "Practice an art, no matter how badly or well you do it. It will make your soul grow" (p. 137). What was important was not to become rich or famous but to have *the experience of becoming* in order to find out who one is, and that, he added, is as necessary as food or sex. This advice about how to "grow one's soul" has much in common with the psychoanalytic process of becoming oneself inherent in Bion's concept of O. This experience of the truth, the absolute reality of a particular moment, is similarly seen by Bion as equally necessary to mental health as food is to the body. For Vonnegut it occurs through artistic truths, based on emotional truth, but as Bion (1978) pointed out, "… all these various disciplines—music, painting, psycho-analysis and so on ad infinitum—are engaged on the same search for truth" (p. 43). While each moves the soul or mind in different ways, the basis and impetus of growth lies in the experience of truth. As food is essential to maintain and grow the body, the essential need for truth is responsible for growth of the mind, soul, spirit, or self. These terms reflect something for which we have no adequate name and I use them here interchangeably, for Bion (1965, 1970) extended the "boundaries" of mental life into what is really a boundaryless metaphysical self or soul beyond sensual reality. His idea of mental functioning includes an experience at this primal level, and the development of thinking as a container for primitive emotional experience.

I am putting forth the perspective that obstructions to mental growth represent a dysfunction in one's relationship to O. On the surface this is obvious, for if O is reality or absolute truth, few would argue that mental dysfunction reflects a dysfunctional relationship to reality. However, since Bion associates O with the infinite unknown and unknowable, nothing about it is either simple or obvious. O is what is, an impersonal reality, and so the very idea of a relationship to it is enigmatic. However, in becoming one with O, as Grotstein (2013) says, "O becomes the subject." Also described as the Godhead, O reflects a religious perspective as well, but one which differs fundamentally from Freud's (1927) idea of God as a physical being, a representation of an omnipotent parent. Instead it is a metaphysical essence, a distinction which is crucial to an understanding of O, which will be examined here in depth.

Bion (1962) called O the "psychoanalytic object" (p. 68), the aim of psychoanalysis. Related to this is what I am calling a "truth object", a relationship to truth, to O, for which the analyst serves as ambassador. This relationship is the basis of the development of a self in a constant process of becoming. It is how the mind grows. Through this "truth object", the individual becomes an audience for O, for those "thoughts without a thinker" which Bion associated with unknown truths. By becoming one with the emanations of O, one draws back the "curtain of illusion" which separates the individual from an experience of reality (Bion, 1965, p. 147). The relationship to O as the foundation of analytic progress will be illustrated through detailed clinical examples.

## The internal audience

In moments of despair, people frequently call on God for help, but which of these two religious views—God or the Godhead—is the audience for this plea? Will that omnipotent external God answer one's prayers? Or is it like the plea which opens the first of Rilke's *Duino Elegies*?

> If I cried out who would hear me up there among the angelic orders?
> … Beauty is only the first touch of terror we can still bear … (Rilke, 1978, p. 19)

The latter evokes an experience of unknowable truth which pierces one's own ignorance, leaving one curious about that wider unknown. It is a plea to a kind of Muse, to unknowable truth—much the same process required of the analyst who suspends access to physical senses so that the patient's metaphysical unknown can pierce his own.

Patients beginning analysis are generally more interested in relief from pain than in facilitating the kind of creative mental growth to which Bion and Vonnegut allude. However, their assumptions about the analytic process often reflect primitive defenses that unconsciously obstruct a working relationship with the analyst, as well as with their own minds. Early traumas of disappointing objects give rise to twin responses of hatred and idealization of the object, a confused object internalized as a rigid superego that obstructs contact with real objects. By withdrawing from the flawed object in favor of a phantasized object, good and bad aspects of the self and object remain split. The child's potential for an integrated mind is compromised, along with the potential for contact with the transcendent truth or reality—O.

Bion often highlighted the complexity of language as a critical factor in analytic work, in a mental realm for which no adequate language exists. He sometimes asked the enigmatic question, "What language is this patient speaking?" (Bion, 1978). We might also ask, "*To whom* is the patient speaking?" To the analyst? Or is he speaking to that God/parent who is expected to fix whatever is wrong? Who is the patient's audience? The answers reflect the nature of the relationship to one's first audience, generally the mother. If she is unable to listen to her child's internal needs, the child will invent an audience he hopes *can* listen, but in fact this ideal superego God obstructs the capacity to listen to a reality too painful to feel. It is an internal audience petrified and unable to grow. Artists with creative blocks sometimes reflect this kind of internal object, unable to hear whatever artistic truths exist to be told, as if they have lost their audience.

## Psychoanalysis before and after Bion

Bion's ideas ushered in a revolution that the psychoanalytic world is still working at understanding. We might say that before Bion the world of analytic theory was flat, and that afterwards it was round—O. This is not meant to minimize earlier analytic innovations, but to express the idea that without an experience of the infinite reality, O, learning takes place on a more linear, superficial ego level, which Bion denoted as K. Nor does it suggest that no earlier analysts were in touch with this aspect of the mind. In fact, Freud's notion of "free floating attention" and "artificially blinding oneself" in order to perceive whatever bit of light might be gleaned in the darkness, might describe the state of mind of O. However, Freud was quite clear that he had no emotional experience of the "oceanic feeling" of the infant, which his admired acquaintance, Roman Rolland, associated with "religious feeling" (Freud, 1930, p. 65). However, that primal experience represents a fundamentally different mental container that, along with more developed adult ego functions, facilitates a greater depth and breadth of conscious experience (cf. Reiner, 2009).

We are talking about levels of consciousness. The language used to talk about different layers of mental experience sounds the same, but the *experience* is fundamentally different. Bion (1977a) made reference to this, saying that a change in *quantity* may represent a change in quality. A *deeper* experience of a feeling changes the nature of that feeling. Everyday experiences of need, for instance, differ qualitatively from the experience of an analysand who begins to feel the primitive needs of his infant self. O embodies a more vast experience of the unconscious than those described by Freud or Klein, in some ways closer to Jung's collective unconscious, which Bion (1978) associated with "proto-mental" experiences, inherent knowledge we cannot remember or know (p. 4).

Bion's theories are complex in large part because they attempt to represent this infinite mind. It takes time to learn about these theories, but one is then asked to *un*-learn them, to put oneself in that state of mind beyond memory, desire, and understanding which Bion (1965, 1970) describes as mystical. He compares this release of ego functions to a frightening regression of the ego as one suspends one's ego driven knowledge gained through the senses—K. To approach an experience of O requires tolerance of a profound sense of *not* knowing, a shift to an intuitive emotional experience where already known facts obstruct apprehension of new ideas. This requires access to the capacity to dream while awake, to reverie, and alpha function, which form the basis of thinking. The terrifying judgements of the ancient ideal of an all-knowing, hyper-vigilant superego imposes harsh restrictions, and a rigid split from those primal capacities which make growth possible.

## Uncertainty

Bion likened the experience of O to Heisenberg's uncertainty principle, a humbling indictment of scientific determinism inherent in the quantum world. Even Einstein, who contributed to the development of quantum physics, found the lack of certainty disturbing, which was reflected in his famous assertion, "God does not play dice." Hawking (1988) however, pointed out that even "God" is bound by the uncertainty principle, "… a fundamental principle of the universe" (p. 155). The unknowable nature of O remains similarly disturbing to analysts. Britton (2011) writes, "I think Bion was inclined to overstate uncertainty … [which] has tempted some followers to give it the super-natural spin that such terms as ultimate reality develop …" (p. 67). He warns against "embracing too enthusiastically the 'uncertainty', as if it predicated the existence of something eternally, ontologically unknowable; a new kind of certain-uncertainty" (ibid.). However, the notion of unknowable ultimate reality is not hyperbolic; Bion was indeed speaking of an uncertain, unknowable thing-in-itself. In addition, he did seem aware of the dangers of "certain-uncertainty", commenting that Descartes, "… failed completely to doubt doubt. 'Cogito ergo sum' is a failure to doubt doubt" (Bion, 1974, p. 39). Still, despite this unknowable core, Bion does not suggest that thoughts are impotent, that analysts, condemned to ignorance or inaction, are reduced to "playing dice". Rather, they are dealing with a more complex mental universe within which one might get momentary glimpses of understanding more profound than the rational mind can muster. Tolerating the uncertainty which inheres in an infinite mental universe may allow a moment of oneness with a universe we embody but cannot know, finding an answer, perhaps, which is true in that moment. Are these partial truths adequate? Bion's opinion was that analysis, still in its infancy, leaves much we cannot know of its efficacy. Concerning "inadequate" interpretations, he claimed he had "never given any other kind" (Borgogno & Merciai, 2000, p. 75). However, developing sufficient faith in one's capacity to glean or "divine" truths, may prove useful in one's continuing efforts to learn.

Since O cannot be represented, these are realities difficult to imagine or accept, and for some analysts the mystical aspects of O have eroded the positive regard for Bion's work. This was documented in a recent series of articles in the *International Journal of Psychoanalysis*, which described the inclination of many London Kleinians to see Bion's later work as a betrayal of his earlier brilliance (Blass, 2011).

In her "Introduction" to this series of articles entitled, "On the value of 'late Bion' to analytic theory and practice", Blass writes:

> While rarely openly discussed in lectures or publications, it would seem that London Kleinians tend to take an unfavorable view of Bion's later writings … [One] may infer it from passing remarks in the relevant literature, as well as from the almost total neglect of Bion's writings from 1966 onwards. (Blass, 2011, p. 1081)

Bion's later work greatly reflects the concept of O, first described in *Transformations* (1965), as "the absolute facts of the session … [which] cannot ever be known" (p. 17). Those often neglected later works would then also include *Attention and Interpretation*, published in 1970, which elucidated and developed many of Bion's earlier ideas, including O in relation to his ideas about the mystic.

While Bion broached the subject of the mystical, Freud (1933a) largely ignored his own interest in the occult, wary at first of introducing into psychoanalysis something he feared would tarnish its reputation as a science. By now, as we've seen, science has changed, and the predictability of a deterministic universe has given way to a universe in which space itself is not only expanding but accelerating at speeds which could not earlier be observed. Like the un-representable Godhead, our cosmic container is not static and moves ceaselessly further beyond the reckoning of the human mind.

Any attempt to describe O is inherently problematic. While Bion's fictionalized "autobiography", *A Memoir of the Future* (Bion, 1977b), seemed merely nonsensical to some analysts, it can be seen s an effort to convey that which could not be conveyed in linear academic language. In *The Past Presented*, the last of this autobiographical trilogy, Bion expresses what, probably, is the central reason these volumes are written as they are. "… [P]sychoanalytic jargon was being eroded by eruptions of clarity. I was compelled to seek asylum in fiction. Disguised as fiction the truth sometimes slipped through" (Bion, 1977b, p. 302). Since rational language could not communicate unknowable truth of O, the thing-in-itself, Bion felt the need to escape from the rational "eruptions of clarity", which left no room for new or creative thought. In this work, he presented a different means of expression.

## *God* vs. *the Godhead*

O'Shaughnessy writes:

> As O mingles with "ultimate reality, absolute truth, the god-head, the infinite, the thing-in-itself", Bion's earlier work rather than being developed, in my opinion, is confused … Is being in rapport with God and the Godhead to do with O or to do with psychosis? Or both? If both, then, if we follow through the two lines of thought, a contradiction is being embraced—with pleasures and perils for the text. (O'Shaughnessy, 2011, p. 35)

Confusion naturally arises around a concept which is ultimately unknowable. However, God and the Godhead seem here to be equated, despite Bion's careful distinction between the two. O'Shaughnessy further questions whether there is a difference between O and psychosis. Similar questions have historically been asked about those identified as mystics, whose ideas, as Bion (1970) noted, pose a threat to the prevailing power of the group. In addition, while O is not psychosis, capacity for contact with O depends upon an experience of primitive paranoid schizoid mental functions that both Bion and Klein referred to as psychotic mental processes. While the healthy infant is not psychotic, primitive mental functioning contained within higher mental functions throughout adult life forms a necessary component of thinking. Although O'Shaughnessy questions Bion's "embrace" of contradictions, these oscillations referred to by Bion (1970) as PS<->D, while contradictory, are central to his idea of a mind able to bridge the gap between emotion and reason, between linear ego functions and the infinite experience of O. Grotstein (2007) makes the further point that the containment of normal paranoid schizoid anxieties in the adult goes beyond the primitive depressive position, to what he calls the "transcendent position" (O).

Religious rituals, the Holy Eucharist for instance, can devolve into primitive beliefs in incorporation and reification of Christ as an external God, in contrast to the Gnostic view of Christ as a *symbol* for metaphysical truths, a search for one's own essential "godliness" through mental and spiritual growth. The New Testament gospels aim at overcoming sin through identification with Christ, while the aim of the Gnostics is to overcome ignorance through the knowledge of Christ's essence (Pagels, 1989).

In *The Gospel of Judas* (Kassner, Meyer, & Wurst, 2006), another ancient text circa 180 AD, Judas is the only disciple who understands Jesus' teachings on that metaphysical level of the Godhead. Jesus offers to teach him, and only him, the secrets of that infinite, unknowable spirit, which, "… no eye of an angel has ever seen, no thought of the heart has ever comprehended, and … was never called by any name" (p. 33). That is, O, the Godhead, an unnameable spirit, inaccessible to the senses. Bion made clear the risk in introducing religious ideas into analysis, calling any discussion of God as a concrete entity a "digression … [since O] … is not good or evil, it cannot be known, loved or hated" (pp. 139–140).

Since O is a necessary mental state for analytic practice, understanding the distinction Bion made between religious faith in an external God from this *internal* "God" of the Godhead is critical. The Godhead corresponds to Symington's (1994, 2004) distinction between "mature religion", an inner sense of morality, and "primitive religion", an externally derived conscience based on fear of punishment from an external God. Motivated by envy and fear, the latter reflects Freud's (1933b) idea of God as an exalted omnipotent father (or now, mother), a primitive mental functioning. As I have pointed out elsewhere, this may indicate an already pathological development of conscience (cf. Reiner, 2009), as belief in the God/parent derails the natural potential to develop an integrated mind capable of awe, curiosity, truth, and conscience, the experience of the Godhead. Referencing a conversation with Bion, Grotstein (2007) writes, "[M]an needs to worship a god because he is born with a religion instinct, one that matures to become the capacity for awe" (p. 211). Stuck in pre-verbal idealized identifications with the parents, experiences of wonder, reverence, awe, and curiosity which lead to learning in O, are obstructed by the fear, hatred, and envy of that perfect parental superego God opposed to life.

The relationship to the infinite realm of the unknowable "God" within is lost. Kant, among others, referenced the Biblical story of Esau to express this all too common betrayal of the higher mind saying, "We, children of the absolute, sell our birthright for a bowl of pottage" (Applebaum, 1995, p. 25). That pottage, however, is cooked up by the child himself in retreat from a reality in which that mind could not be nourished.

Bion (1965) viewed resistance as resistance to O, to the "fear that reality is imminent" (p. 127). This fearsome reality is represented in *The Bhagavad Gita* by Lord Krishna as an "imperishable" essence, a tumultuous, paradoxical presence of "death that snatches all/and the birth of all yet to be born" (Bolle, 1979, p. 121). This paradoxical, "good" and "bad" metaphysical essence, is seen psychoanalytically in the terrifying psychological births, mental growth experienced by the patient as the death of the self. It is the death, really, of those beloved but obstructive internal objects. Krishna's radiant presence (O) leaves one "enraptured, but bewildered … [before a] …. god of overpowering reality" (Bolle, p. 127), a state of mental wholeness based on a marriage of opposites.

### Container/contained: mindfulness and the god within

The healthy mind is characterized by change, dynamic fluctuations, and patterns of sensations, emotions, and thoughts. Taylor (2011) talks about the direction of this mental movement.

> The motion that we see from the mind involves change in noticing, attending, linking and relating in non-spatial dimensions. These have directions such as towards or against life, towards or against death, toward linking with an object or against. (p. 102)

Healthy mental life moves toward truth and connections, which lead to mental growth. The capacity for attachment reflects the infant's inherent knowledge of the necessity of truth for mental survival. This direction of mental movement underlies the presence of a vital, creative mind. This "mind" is more accurately described as a state of mindfulness, a *process* rather than a fixed entity. One does not *have* a mind, one has experiences of consciousness, transient states of mindfulness and integration. However, this relatively limited capacity, implicit in an experience of O, must be seen as a rare developmental achievement, in which integration requires one to tolerate the disturbing fluctuations of unconsciousness and fragmentation. This dynamic mental existence is in sharp contrast to imprisoning, static superego demands.

Since people often maneuver more or less efficiently through their lives, managing complex tasks and ideas, running businesses and/or households, raising children, etc., we assume the presence of a mind. What may be missing, however, is a capacity to act as a mental container for their primitive experiences. If communication between these two areas of mental functioning is blocked, one cannot feel what one feels or know what one knows.

One patient, a psychiatrist, often said in response to interpretations, "I know, that's what I said," and indeed he had. For instance, feeling anxious about an upcoming vacation, he said, "Maybe I'm going into a manic state so I don't have to miss you." But it was just one among many theories he professed, but lacking access to his own emotional experience, he had no way to know if it was true.

Paradoxically, the capacity *at times* to experience unity or wholeness depends on the capacity *at other times* to experience the fear and wonder of fragmentation/diversity that we finite mortals face in light of an infinite mind that aims but inevitably fails to make sense of the disparate infinite universe in which we live. Feelings of falling or disintegrating are often unearthed in apparently well-functioning individuals as they encounter this inevitable ebb and flow of awareness and ignorance. The intercourse between contradictory male and female mental functions (the "feminine" container and "masculine" contained) is the foundation of a more dependable mindfulness which enables learning, as "male"/"female" mental functions give birth to a sense of existence—an experience of O, the "God" within.

"Regina" (a patient discussed in more depth below), was raised by an emotionally abusive borderline mother. Upset one day after meeting with a "life coach" whom she did not trust, she said, "I realized I don't need another teacher, I have you." Regina's trust in me oscillates wildly between deep need and deep disdain. With my summer vacation looming, I suggested that she didn't trust me either. She paused, and said quietly, "I don't trust anyone!" She then erupted in frustration, "Holy fuck, I'm so confused!"

The issue, I said, was the "holy fuck". Seeing me as her unreliable mother, her need for me terrified and confused her. By splitting the transference with this new teacher, she hoped to avoid the possibility of a "holy fuck" between us, a genuine connection which might cause an internal "holy fuck" between her feelings of neediness and distrust. The primal connection to an object feels "holy" because of its relationship to life, truth, survival. However, needing her mentally ill mother caused pain and confusion, so Regina cannot tell if our analytic intercourse is "holy"—giving birth to something good between us—or just another abusive "fuck". Mental "births" of buried aspects of the self bring uncertainty, a temporary, ever-changing self in the process of becoming. At best, consciousness is a "temporary godliness", mental integration created of the dis-integration of a mind in a process of change.

## The receptive audience—container and contained

The child throws a ball, ties shoelaces, etc., and says, "Look at me!" We need an audience for our external accomplishments, and the infant needs an audience for internal "accomplishments", for mental states. "Look, Mommy, I'm sad," the infant might be presumed to say, or "I'm happy", or "I love", or "I don't know *what* I feel". The mother's capacities for reverie and emotional containment make her an attentive audience, a model for receptive functions in the infant's mind so that the child might eventually see himself. Lacking an attentive audience, the infant develops an inattentive internal object, leaving him with no mental home for his feelings and thoughts, and no means to develop a mind. Content cannot find a form. Grotstein referred to such children as "orphans of O" (Grotstein, 2007) or "orphans of the Real" (Grotstein, 1995), their feelings homeless, locked out of the natural love of truth.

The child creates the necessary mother, who watches over him, but with that chilling feeling in the song by "The Police", "Every breath you take, every move you make, every word you fake, I'll be watching you" (Sumner, 1983). It is a parody of an attentive mother who cannot take her eyes off the child, an idealized hyper-vigilant superego meting out harsh judgements on the angry child. This becomes the child's internal audience.

## Creativity and development of the "God" within

Creative thought requires a receptive audience, not one which judges unreasonably. Each writer speaks to an audience. While he may feel he writes for himself, since the self is a composite of internal objects representing various aspects of the personality, he is often speaking to one of these, or *for* one of these, becoming its voice. He may be trying to express something to an internal parent who was unable to hear, but this newly fashioned internal audience is still an unreceptive faulty container. Fairbairn (1943) viewed internal objects as repressed "bad" objects, an identification with a frustrating or abusive parent. "Impulses become bad," he wrote, "if they are directed toward bad objects" (Fairbairn, 1952, p. 65), as the child seeks to protect the parents' goodness by making himself bad. If "necessity is the mother of invention", the need for a more containing mother provides necessary impetus for the invention of a new improved mother. It is a creative act of psychic survival, protection from the unbearable awareness of having an untrustworthy mother. However, it also creates massive primal confusion between love and hate, good and bad, for the child instinctively "knows" that movement away from reality and truth is destructive, and on that level he too is "bad". Creativity itself, now associated with this early transgression, becomes tainted and dangerous, and constricts imagination.

The degree to which this becomes a rigid defensive structure depends to some extent on the urgency of the need to turn away from reality, the degree of early trauma. One patient, despite years of apparent devotion to analysis, was so devoted to her perfect internal mother that she was unable to change. She idealized me at first but I soon became an annoyance she dismissed like the psychotic mother she had long ago deemed useless. Although now a responsible businesswoman, her ideal internal object was so compelling that on another level there *was* no reality, and no self, so fully was she identified with that perfect mother. This seemingly engaging woman existed in a phantasy with the ideal though tormenting internal parent her constant companion. This was her hidden "audience", watching over everything she did with a jaundiced eye, and everything I said and did, so while her needy infant self often could engage with me, whatever I said was quickly hijacked by a hard supercilious superego (Bion, 1970) determined to destroy our connection.

## The audience

The individual may have lofty ideals, but in the static mind dominated by a rigidly idealized internal parent, no action can be taken to develop them. Development on the level of a self open to anything unknown is blocked. The emotionally receptive parent is the prototype for what Grotstein (2000) called "The Dreamer Who Understands the Dream". "The internalized mother container and her reverie become the Dreamer Who Understands the Dream" (Grotstein, 2000, p. 12). This gives rise to the capacity for reverie and symbol formation, and is the critical factor in whether the internal audience is static or capable of growth and change. This capacity depends upon the mother's ability to experience and integrate her own infant self, allowing for mental transformations in the "transcendent position" (Grotstein, 2013) of O.

## The "truth object"

Bion (1962, 1965, 1970) called the goal of analysis, "the detection and observation of … [psychoanalytic] objects" (Bion, 1962, p. 68) through at-one-ment with O. One patient of mine had been abandoned by her father as a child when her parents divorced. He recently verbally abused her, blaming her for his own failures. She felt unprotected by her mother, but also, I thought, by me, after a vacation break. She had spent her childhood, her whole life, trying to create a better father, but in fact there *was* no protection from the reality of who her father was, and had always been. After many years of analysis, she has been able to see that the only protection from reality is the awareness that there is no protection from reality. Like it or not, one simply had to accept it. A horrible truth, if one can bear it, is better than the loveliest lie.

We sometimes erroneously think the patient needs a better attachment to a better object, presumably the analyst, when in fact what is required is an attachment to O, to truth, which the analyst introduces to the patient through his own at-one-ment with O. Analytic knowledge then serves to create an ever-changing relationship to a self in the process of becoming. I am considering O to be a metaphysical "truth object", the relationship to which enables that process of mental growth. Again, it is not really an object, for O represents formless dynamic energy, impersonal truths or realities transformed into dynamic *mental* energy, by which process O becomes a subjective experience. The mind's inherent formlessness takes on new forms with each new experience of O.

In relation to this "truth object", the individual becomes an audience for O, receptive to those "thoughts without a thinker" which Bion (1970) associated with impersonal truths we cannot yet contain. It is something like building a home on shifting sands, a kind of shape-shifting, illustrated in the evolving styles of Picasso or the works of writers such as Beckett, where new forms are created to express "new" truths. These are thoughts which finally find a thinker and can take center stage, first in the artist's mind and then in the cultural zeitgeist. O is always a surprise, a notion Frost (1939) expressed in this famous description of poetic creation: "Like a piece of ice on a hot stove the poem must ride on its own melting … it can never lose its sense of a meaning that once unfolded by surprise as it went" (p. 242). The essential, creative self in a process of becoming is an ever-changing internal audience for O, it is a self open to truth—the infinite, formless, unknowable "God" within. This "God" does not see all or know all, it simply *is* all of inner and outer reality, pieces of which one can experience in relation to an internalized infinite truth object.

## Clinical example

This clinical example gives an idea of the process of growth of the "God" within, and the correlated idea of O as a "truth object". I hope to show clinically something of the distinction between O as the Godhead and as the primitive internal God of the superego, in developing from states of mindlessness to mindful existence.

### "Regina"

During "Regina's" ten years in analysis, she has become a respected psychologist, no small feat for a sensitive, often fragile woman raised by a psychotic mother and an emotionally absent father who divorced her mother when she was young. Raised Catholic, she is no longer religious. Recently, her capacity to tolerate feelings of need and vulnerability has increased. After years working in a psychiatric clinic, Regina is in the process of opening a private practice. This has aroused primitive anxieties, which she counteracts by retreating into a womb-like phantasy of a perfect mother, often binging in sweets, as if in possession of a perfect breast.

My approach to dreams, briefly put, includes allowing the elements of the session—associations, feelings, observations, etc.—to wash over me in what often feels like a nonverbal deluge. What I have recorded here relates to the selected fact, that which brings the discursive discourse into a coherent thinkable form, some part of which I can share with the patient.

### Session # 1—(Monday)

This session exemplifies the uncanny experience of O. As I waited for Regina to arrive, I jotted down the word "language" on a piece of paper. "O is silent," I continued, "… we have to hear into the silence, there is no language for O." These were random words, I thought, but as the session progressed I saw this as the crux of the session.

Regina said, "I'm hungry … I felt hungry to see you this weekend too." She described having reached out more to socialize with friends, which "felt good, but difficult". She dreamt:

An Asian woman opened her eyes ... a wise woman.

I was driving to give a man a yoga lesson, although I don't do that work anymore. There was a storm, the road flooded, I thought I should go back, I could get swept away. But maybe the man could be helpful with my new job. I saw a Whole Foods, which was somehow comforting, and I thought I'll be okay ... I kept going.

Regina then stopped. Silence. "I feel frustrated talking so much, like I *have* to talk because I'm so desperate to connect." I said she seemed to feel she had to talk *in order to* connect with me, but then noticed she didn't feel connected to herself *or* to me. She was having trouble using language to say what she really wanted to say, and wasn't even sure what that was. She said, "That's what happened yesterday with my friend, Beth, I was flooding with words which didn't feel connected to what I was saying. Afterwards I felt ashamed, like I'd destroyed something with Beth ... but I know that's ridiculous, she was fine." I said that maybe on another level she felt as if her words did destroy something, as if they weren't words at all but more like waste to get rid of, urine or vomit or diarrhea which would poison me or her friend. "Kidneys do very well in ridding your body of waste," I added, "but that method doesn't work to rid your mind of desperate feelings of wanting to connect and not knowing how." Regina said, "Funny you say that ... Beth's cat just died of renal failure ... she'd been peeing all over Beth." When Regina doesn't know what she's feeling or thinking, I said, all she can do is try to spill them out.

Regina expressed anxiety about her work transition. The Asian woman looked like an admired meditation teacher. About the next dream, she wonders why she was doing her old work. This related to an interpretation last session about the "work" she's done all her life, being a perfect self-sufficient mother, but unable to do the work of growing her own mind. Although she here feels drawn back to that old job of her traumatized baby self, she had enough mental space to remember she could get some "Whole Food" from me on Monday, food for thought which might help her gather up the storm in her mind. Despite the flood of old feelings, the "thoughts without a thinker" (Bion, 1970), she could wait, with the hope they might become something she could think about. In this regard, I thought I was the wise Asian woman, opening my eyes to see *her*, and that she could also open *her* eyes, having internalized the mental functions of attention and containment, the beginning of an authentic capacity to think.

The essential ideas here are Regina's uncertainty about what she is saying, and a dawning recognition of need for a new kind of language and a new container for it, a new kind of mind able to withstand the flood of feelings which heralds an unknown truth—O. Bion (1970) called it "the Language of Achievement", described as "both prelude to action and itself a kind of action" (p. 125). In the previous session Regina experienced me as a killer whose work with her might cause terrifying changes, but I was now seen as the purveyor of truth, "whole food". Her old "job" involved turning to lies, delusions, and omnipotent defenses of being a seemingly self-sufficient mother. Her new job entailed the work of waiting for me so we might together discover the truth.

My "premonition" about language at the beginning of the session seemed to fit with the idea that in the storm of her unfelt, unthought primitive feelings, words seem more like urine or waste than mental products. Why I singled out urine I didn't know, but such "coincidences" may signal some engagement with O, which always comes as a surprise. I cannot prove this was so, nor do I understand it, but by now I do heed these uncanny occurrences which may prove useful in assessing the rest of the evidence.

## The "language of achievement"

How does one learn to speak a "language of achievement", whose words, in service to truth, can express meaning and facilitate communication and *mental* action? Bion differentiates it from a "language of substitution", substituting lies for truth and characterized by meaninglessness and stasis. In analysis, where the primary means of communication is verbal, it is critical to differentiate these two uses of language. In telling me her dream, Regina herself sensed a "language of substitution", not in *what* she said but in *how* she said it. Its unconscious intention was to rid herself of a desperate need for connection, of which she had no knowledge and for which she had no words. Real connection depended on knowing of this need, through words informed by feeling and thought. Her words were intended to rid her of awareness and need for an object, projections of anxiety whose silent obstructive language as the "O" of the session.

The next day, Tuesday, Regina said, "I felt so vulnerable and small after I left yesterday … I fell into crazy … The idea of really learning how to talk … at my age! I need your help with that." What felt "crazy" to Regina's old idealized self was to need my help.

### Session # 2—Wednesday

Regina dreamt that her former supervisor, a rigid oppressive woman, was filling out a form for her. "Then I realized I no longer worked there." In another dream, she was riding her bike home from her old job, and wondered, "What am I still doing here?" The theme about Regina's new and old work was continuing. She associated her bike with freedom, fun, childhood, and I could see her struggling between the primitive "God" of her old internal oppressive "supervisor" and a more evolved ability to think and learn, an internal relationship to truth. In the process of differentiating these states, she oscillated between the painful work of mindfulness, and her mindless loyalty to her "old supervisor". With no mother to serve as representative of truth, she had relinquished her relationship to truth. The absence of an audience for truth activates the necessity for the lie of the perfect parent.

### Session # 3—3 months later

In this session, three months later, Regina announced her reaction upon seeing me. "I feel scared of you. I'm scared that contact with other people will annihilate me … even good feelings with people scare me." She knew no particular reason why I seemed so scary.

> I was at a house, a guy was making an Old Fashioned. I said I'd make my own drink, something healthier called "Vive", made from acai berries. The blender looked dirty, remnants of egg whites in it. The guy wanted one of my drinks but there wasn't enough. I didn't know what to do … .

> I also dreamt that a neighbor's snake got into my house, my kitchen. I was terrified it would kill me and screamed at him for not getting it out.

Regina explained, "I wanted one pleasant drink and didn't want to give him part of it just to get drunk … He looked like my father … he drank a lot." She commented that Native Americans saw snakes as symbols of power. A friend saw fear of snakes as "fear of your feminine power". The neighbor looked like her "dear old friend, Christian". Regina said she used to make smoothies in her blender for breakfast, but now eats egg whites and has lost a lot of weight. While now quite thin, she remains fearful about food, saying, "'Bad foods' like sweets can trigger a binge". Any pleasure or need for something good is abducted by greed or mania and becomes bad.

I thought Regina's dream reflected a profound confusion between good and bad. The issue is not what she eats or drinks, for her primary addiction isn't to food but to the "old fashioned" state of mind, her old method of eating as a means to oblivion, getting "drunk" on good feeling and omnipotence. Like a vampire, this drunken self wants her "Vive", her "life", which he usurps. She fears needing me, becoming addicted to me, and that fear turns me into bad food, gobbling me up in a manic binge which destroys her need, her mind, and me.

From this perspective, the snakes seemed more related to her own "Christian" background than to Native American mythology. The snake's threat in Genesis is knowledge of good and evil, the genesis of consciousness. On some level, truth is her "dear old friend", but I become the evil snake who invades her with this knowledge in lieu of her "old fashioned" drunken unconsciousness. From this perspective, she believes that losing weight rids her of painful need and hunger, and like the earlier evacuations of urine, spares her the work of developing a mind to feel them. Every contact with me is frightening, for each time she must choose between the difficult work of having a mind or continuing to work at destroying it. As Bion put it, "Wisdom or oblivion, take your pick." The religious reference seems to encompass the struggle between her devotion to the old primal superego God—toward magic and omnipotence and away from knowledge—and her inclination toward truth and the growth of her mind.

*Session #4 (next day)*

In this last session, the next day, Regina's choice is brought into stark clarity. After not binging for many months she had a weekend of binging and insomnia. She dreamt:

> I was at the house I last lived in with my father, but I was sleeping on the living room couch. My stepmother was making noise in the kitchen, and then my grandfather came home and sat drinking in the living room. "Can you go to your bedroom?" I said, "I need to sleep." He said no. I became hysterical. "Can't anyone understand my needs? Why won't anyone help me?!" My stepmother didn't know which side to take. Finally my dad said he'd talk to him.

Confused and vulnerable, Regina spoke of not feeling understood by her family. She connected her grandfather to her father, who always drank at night. "Hung over" after binging on sweets, her voice sounded dead and detached. I found myself feeling confused. In her dream she was the good girl desperate for her needs to be heard by her oblivious parents. However, since the alcoholic father offers to help, perhaps I was the oblivious parents, ignoring her need to be oblivious, to remain asleep. I then become the snake, interfering with her "drunken" bliss, awakening her to her internal war—to be mindful of or oblivious to her needs, "To be or not to be". Unfortunately, having been awakened too early by the trauma of a psychotic mother, victimized by the "noise" of her insanity, Regina had killed off her connection to her family, her feelings, and her mind, thereby victimizing herself. She is finally having to see that perfect, sweet little girl as disdainful of me and everyone who might help her. Devoted to her ideal mother/superego/God, there was no room for the development of self aligned with truth.

## Summary

I have described the relationship to a metaphysical internal "object," an attachment to truth (O). It is the basis of learning, the foundation of mental health and the growth of a dynamic self or mind in a constant process of becoming. This metaphysical self, inherently formless, is given new form with each new experience of truth or reality. Essentially, the individual becomes an audience for O, for those "thoughts without a thinker" (Bion, 1970) which come to us to be thought if we can become a receptive audience for truth. One's relationship to this metaphysical object/self gives a sense of continuity to the ever-changing self.

Nietzsche (1886) wrote, "Convictions are more dangerous enemies of truth than lies" (p. 63). The illusion of certainty simplifies reality in the hope of making it manageable. Instead it deadens reality and the mind capable of contact with truth. The lies which shrink the truth also shrink the mind.

Fairbairn's idea of internal objects as essentially "bad" objects was discussed in view of the idea that the healthy mind takes O as its object. This "truth object" is distinguished from the analytic object in that it is the goal, not only of analysis, but of creative mental life in general. One becomes the audience for O, receptive to those thoughts without a thinker, which allow access to new ideas.

One patient, who endured serious trauma in infancy, was terrified of making contact with those early feelings, and was therefore terrified of my interpretations. After many years in analysis he began to feel relieved by the interpretations—still terrified but relieved. There is always some fear in contact with O, with the unknown universe of the mind, but if one is interested in mental development, one is called upon to embrace the truth, despite the danger.

## References

Applebaum, D. (Ed.) (1995). *The Vision of Kant*. Rockport, MA: Element.
Bion, W. R. (1962). *Learning From Experience*. New York: Basic Books.
Bion, W. R. (1965). *Transformations*. In: *Seven Servants* New York: Jason Aronson, 1977.
Bion, W. R. (1970). *Attention and Interpretation*. London: Karnac.
Bion, W. R. (1974). *Bion's Brazilian Lectures, I, Sao Paulo, 1973*. Brazil: Imago Editora.
Bion, W. R. (1977a). Lecture. Los Angeles.
Bion, W. R. (1977b). The past presented. In: *Memoir of the Future*. London: Karnac, 1991.

Bion, W. R. (1978). Private clinical seminar. Kenter Canyon, Los Angeles.
Blass, R. (2011). Introduction to "On the value of 'late Bion' to analytic theory and practice". *International Journal of Psychoanalysis, 92*: 1081–1088.
Bolle, K. (Trans.) (1979). *The Bhagavad Gita*. Berkeley: University of California Press.
Borgogno, F., & Merciai, S. A. (2000). *W. R. Bion: Between Past and Future*. London: Karnac.
Britton, R. (2011). The pleasure, reality, and uncertainty principles. In: C. Mawson (Ed.), *Bion Today*. London: Routledge.
Fairbairn, W. R. D. (1943). The repression and the return of bad objects. In: *Psychoanalytic Studies of the Personality*. London: Routledge, 1990.
Fairbairn, W. R. D. (1952). *An Object Relations Theory of the Personality*. New York: Basic Books.
Freud, S. (1927). *The Future of an Illusion. S. E., 21*: 3–56. London: Hogarth.
Freud, S. (1930). *Civilization and its Discontents. S. E., 23*: 3–137. London: Hogarth.
Freud, S. (1933a). Lecture XXX, Dreams and Occultism. *New Introductory Lectures. S. E., 22*: 31–56. London: Hogarth.
Freud, S. (1933b). *New Introductory Lectures. S. E., 22*: London: Hogarth.
Frost, R. (1939). "The figure a poem makes." In: J. C. Oates (Ed.), *The Best American Essays of the Century*. New York: Houghton Mifflin, 2000.
Grotstein, J. A. (1995). Orphans of the "Real". *Bulletin of the Menninger Clinic, 59*: 287–311.
Grotstein, J. A. (2000). *Who Is The Dreamer Who Dreams The Dream?* London: The Analytic Press.
Grotstein, J. A. (2007). *A Beam of Intense Darkness*. London: Karnac.
Grotstein, J. A. (2013). Private conversation. Los Angeles.
Hawking, S. (1988). *A Brief History of Time*. New York: Bantam Books.
Kassner, R., Meyer, M., & Wurst, G. (Eds.) (2006). *The Gospel of Judas*. Washington, DC: National Geographic Society.
Nietzsche, F. (1886). *Human All Too Human*. In: W. Kaufman (Trans.), *The Portable Nietzsche*. New York: Viking Penguin, 1954.
O'Shaughnessy, E. (2011). Whose Bion? In: C. Mawson (Ed.), *Bion Today*. London: Routledge.
Pagels, E. (1989). *The Gnostic Gospels*. New York: Vintage.
Reiner, A. (2009). *The Quest for Conscience and the Birth of the Mind*. London: Karnac.
Rilke, R. M. (1978). *Duino Elegies* (Trans. D. Young). New York: Norton.
Sumner, A. (1983). "Every Breath You Take". On the album: *Synchronicity*. Netherlands: A & M Records.
Symington, N. (1994). *Emotion and Spirit*. London: Karnac.
Symington, N. (2004). An exegesis of conscience in the works of Freud. In: *The Blind Man Sees: Freud's Awakening and Other Essays* (pp. 30–44). London: Karnac.
Taylor, D. (2011). Commentary on Vermote's "On the value of 'late Bion' to analytic theory and practice". *International Journal of Psychoanalysis, 92*: 1099–1112.
Vonnegut, K. (2011). *The Last Interview: And Other Conversations*. New York: Melville House.

CHAPTER THIRTEEN

# Making contact with psychotic and autistic phenomena: container/contained and autistic transformations

*Celia Fix Korbivcher*

"In war the enemy's objective is so to terrify you that you cannot think clearly, while your object is to continue to think clearly no matter how adverse or frightening the situation. The underlying idea is that thinking clearly is more conducive to being aware of 'reality' to accessing properly what is real. But being aware of reality may involve being aware of the unpleasant, because reality is not necessarily pleasing or welcome."

—*Bion*, 1987, p. 248

"(…) autistic children are afraid of the 'black hole' of 'not being'. Losing the sense of existence is far worse than dying. In dying, at least a body is felt to be left behind. In losing the sense of being, nothing is left. (…) Annihilation is the worst threat of all, because it means extinction of the psychic sense of 'being'."

—*Tustin*, 1990, p. 39

## Introduction

Some patients in our clinical practice present more developed mental organizations, whereas others display more primitive ones. It is important that the analyst identify the level of mental development in which the patient is operating at each movement in the analytic session, that is, whether he is functioning on a neurotic, psychotic, or autistic level. Each of these levels has different characteristics and requires the analyst to use specific approaches.

Even patients in whom the neurotic part of the personality prevails, may present important psychotic nuclei that have been created in order to avoid painful contact with an ongoing real situation. When this occurs, the analyst does not find anyone with whom to communicate.

There are other patients who also operate predominantly with the non-psychotic part of the personality (Bion, 1957), but who maintain certain impenetrable nuclei, which prevent real changes occurring during the analytic process. In such patients, certain mental aspects remain inaccessible (Tustin, 1986; Klein, S. 1980). They present, predominantly, bodily manifestations that do not acquire representation. These manifestations often express important primordial experiences which were never contained or transformed and for which the patient failed to develop a verbal language to communicate. The degree of primitivism in autistic and psychotic phenomena can provoke strong pressure on the analyst's mind, disturbing his capacity to think and to maintain an analytical vertex.

The aim of this article is to reflect on how to establish contact with and contain psychotic and autistic phenomena, while under this primitive pressure. For this, I resort to Bion's theory of transformations (1965) as an observation method of the mental phenomena in the analytical session, highlighting among Bion's different groups of transformations the projective transformations, transformations in hallucinosis. Autistic transformations (Korbivcher, 2001, 2005b) will also be considered.

In projective transformations and transformations in hallucinosis, the psychotic phenomena prevail, whereas in autistic transformations, autistic phenomena predominate. Special attention is given to the analyst's mind under the pressure of these types of transformations. Clinical vignettes of two patients, Nina and Luiza, are presented, illustrating psychotic phenomena and autistic phenomena respectively. Their material will help readers to distinguish these two different kinds of phenomena and reflect upon how to make contact with the areas of the mind to which they relate.

## The psychotic phenomena

As Bion turned his focus to the thinking process, he created different models of the mind as part of his clinical apprehensions and theoretical developments. In 1957, he proposed the concept that the personality presents a psychotic and a non-psychotic part. This was the starting point for Tustin's hypothesis (1990, 1992) of an autistic part of the personality. In 1962, Bion went further and proposed that the analyst's task is that of learning from emotional experience. With *Transformations* (Bion 1965), he explored a psychoanalytic observational method applied to phenomena brought up in the session by the analytical relationship. In this latter theory, he expanded the classical analytical field of knowing reality, and introduced the dimension of *being* the reality (O). Transformations in knowledge (K) are seen as an intermediate step to transformations in becoming the reality (O), which he now proposes as the ultimate aim of a psychoanalytical work. This multidimensional approach to the mind offered us a basis to develop the idea of other transformations, the autistic transformations (see Korbivcher 2001, 2005b)—side by side with the neurotic transformations (rigid motion) and the psychotic transformations (projective and in hallucinosis) (Braga, 2009).

In *projective* transformations, the prevailing mechanisms are splitting and projective identification. This prompts the mind to work like a muscle, projecting into the object undesirable parts of the *self* in order to obtain relief from unbearable mental pain. In transformations in *hallucinosis*, as Bion (1965) points out,

> The patient whose transformations are effected in the medium of hallucinosis might almost have as his motto "actions speak lauder then words" with its hint of rivalry as an essential feature of the relationship. The general picture the patient presents is that a person anxious to demonstrate his independence of anything other than his own creations. These creations are the results of his supposed ability to use his senses as organs of evacuation which are able to surround him with a universe that has been generated by himself: the function of the senses and their mental counterpart is to create the patient's perfect world. Evidence of imperfection *ipso facto* is evidence of intervention of hostile envious forces. Thanks to the patient's capacity for satisfying all his needs from his own creations he is entirely independent of anyone or anything other than his products and therefore is beyond rivalry, envy, greed, meanness, love or hate; but the evidence of his senses belies his pre-determinations; he is not satisfied. (pp. 136–137)

Bion also says that:

> Rivalry, envy, greed, thieving, together with [a] sense of being blameless, deserve consideration as invariants under hallucinosis. (p. 132)

Bion emphasizes that the presence of this mechanism, even in patients in whom the non-psychotic part prevails, is more frequent than we may recognize. When subjected to high levels of intense pressure, such patients operate by projective transformations and transformations in hallucinosis (Korbivcher, 2001, 2005b).

## The autistic phenomena

According to Tustin (1984, 1986, 1990, 1992), autistic phenomena appear mainly in individuals with exacerbated sensitivity. They manifest extreme auto-sensuality. For these individuals, awareness of bodily separation from their primary object occurred abruptly in infancy or early childhood and before they acquired the capacity to bear it. They experienced the separation as if parts of their own body had been torn, bringing feelings of annihilation, of internal holes, of "black holes". Such experiences lead them to withdraw to a "protective shell" where they remain absorbed with auto-sensual activities, protecting themselves from unbearable experiences of fragmentation, obliteration, and vulnerability. In the autistic area, the notion of object is different from that of the neurotic and the psychotic parts of the personality. The notion of internal or external object is absent, since its representation at the psychic level does not occur, nor are fantasies linked to object representations. The relations between me and not me occur through sensations obtained by contact with the object instead of through the fantasies that may emerge. Such contact results in relations with sensation objects; autistic objects and autistic forms.[1]

I have previously proposed (Korbivcher 2001, 2005b) the inclusion of autistic phenomena, the sense dominated phenomena, in the theory of transformations along with the other groups of transformations suggested by Bion, constituting a new group of transformations: the autistic transformations. These autistic transformations develop in an autistic realm, which implies absent recognition of the internal and external objects. The relations between "me" and "not-me" happen through sensations obtained by contact, sensations that do not acquire representation in the mind. The invariants in the autistic transformations are "absent affective life", "affective emptiness", "auto-sensual activities" with autistic object and autistic forms.

If we use the theory of transformations as a reference, our understanding of autistic phenomena will be modified. The analyst becomes involved in the context of the emotional experience shared with the patient, and his observations emerge as a link from a chain of successive movements deriving from the pair's interaction, (Korbivcher, 2001, 2005b). The proposal of autistic transformations allows the analyst, based on his emotional experience, to identify autistic phenomena in neurotic patients and so he has a chance to affect them. However, it is important to emphasize that the introduction of autistic transformations in the theory of transformations adds a sense dominated phenomenon, the autistic phenomenon. With this, the field of observation in the session is widened to an area where there is no mental representation and relations through "sensation objects" prevail.

Autistic transformations belong to a separate universe, an autistic area, organized by specific laws, different from those of neurosis and psychosis. In neurotic and psychotic areas, according to Bion (1962), the emotional links L, H, K, and their negatives, permeate any relationship that connects objects. If we agree that, in the autistic area, there is no notion of internal or external object, we may presume that in this area there is an absence of emotional links. This is perhaps an area of "non-links". The dimension of the mind to which autistic transformations belong is of "existing" and "not existing" and not K or –K, as occurs in the groups of transformations proposed by Bion. Autistic phenomena would belong to an area close to beta elements. Both share fairly similar characteristics, although there is between them a difference in quality.

As Bion defined them, beta elements are sensorial elements that were not transformed at the psychic level by the alpha function and therefore are not likely to be used for thought. They are sensorial stimuli that have not been digested, that are unloaded, expelled, with the intention of freeing the mental apparatus of the accumulation of tension. There is a barrier made of beta elements—the beta screen—which is constituted by an accumulation of beta elements.[2] Autistic phenomena, on the other hand, are characterized by their static nature of belonging to the inanimate world. We can suppose that, similar to alpha and beta elements, which when grouped give rise respectively to the contact barrier and the beta screen, the grouped autistic elements create a protective "autistic barrier". The individual seeks protection through this autistic barrier and, with auto-sensual activities, generates his object himself, an object with autistic characteristics (Tustin, 1984, 1986). Unlike beta elements, autistic elements do not function to provide relief through discharge, but offer protection in situations in which the individual is in a state of terror facing the threat of psychic non-existence[3] (Korbivcher, 2008a, 2008b, 2013).

Bion (1992) hypothesized the existence of a primordial area of phenomena, the tropisms area that constitutes the "matrix of the mind":

> Tropisms are the matrix from which all mental life springs. For maturation to be possible, they need to be won from the void and communicated. Just as a breast, or its equivalent, is necessary for the infant life to be sustained. The vehicle of communication—the infant's cry, tactile and visual senses—is engaged in order not only to communicate but also to control the tropism. If all goes well the communication, by projective identification, leads (as Melanie Klein (1946) has described) to the deposition in the breast of the tropisms that the infant can neither control, modify, nor develop, but which can be so controlled and developed after they have been modified by the object. If this breaks down, then the vehicle of communication, the contact with reality, the links of every kind of which I have spoken, suffer a significant fate. This applies particularly to the communicating particles that are felt to lie with their enclosed tropisms, rejected by psyche and object alike … the tropism … is enclosed within the vehicle of communication itself, be that sound, sight, or touch. (p. 47)

Through the notion of tropisms, Bion points towards the existence of an area of primordial phenomena prior to beta elements, an area in which there is only the movement of approximation and removal of the organism in relation to a stimulus source. It is an area that has an expecting object that will modify tropism (Grotstein, 2005). As Bion asserts, this area constitutes a matrix from which the whole of mental life sprouts and the personality is organized. We may suppose from this concept that when the individual is born—or even before that—he brings with himself the disposition to search for an object. I wonder whether this tendency would be a preconception of a breast, but only at a biological stage, prior to the emergence of psychic life.

The individual who operates with tropisms expects to find an object with the possibility to modify it. We know that plants need light to develop; their leaves move naturally towards the light. In the absence of light they may not develop and even perish. I question if we can make an analogy between autistic states and plants that are unable to find light. In this way, I am arguing that autistic states are located in the infant's early tropisms—but tropisms that have been frustrated by not finding an object. The autistic state is therefore the consequence of moving towards an object and then not being able to find it.

Bion claims (1992) that if the individual cannot find a breast into which to project tropisms the result will be "a disaster that takes the form of loss of contact with reality, apathy or mania"; I think this is connected to Tustin's (1984, 1992) "premature psychological birth": a situation in which a particularly sensitive child is driven to separate prematurely from the object. Such a child will develop a second skin (Bick, 1968, 1986), which allows her to experience a state of pseudo-independence from the object (Bick, 1986) as a means of protecting herself from the threat of the loss of psychic existence.

Could we suppose that "the apathy", "the loss of contact with reality", to which Bion refers with regard to the loss of an object in which to project tropisms, could be manifestations of a state in which an autistic barrier is developed? An autistic second skin arises because there is no object into which the baby can project its tropisms. So, autistic phenomena are connected with tropisms as a search, a demand, a direction, and expectation, but where these don't find an object (Korbivcher, 2008a, 2013).

### The analyst's mind under the pressure of container/contained

As we know, the analyst, as well as his patient, has a mind of his own, and in spite of this mind being his main working tool, he remains exposed to the vicissitudes of his emotions, as would any human being. Let us imagine the analyst being subjected to an experience of strong pressure on his mind. Would he not use mechanisms similar to those of his patient?

Like the patient, the analyst also has primitive parts in his mind, a psychotic part, areas without representation and an autistic part of his personality. Facing situations of anguish, the analyst can also create "another patient" in his mind, coercing the patient to attempt to operate with resources unavailable at that moment so as to ignore his true condition. In view of the pressure exercised by the autistic manifestations on his mind, the analyst may lose the perspective of his own existence.

For the analyst, this situation is difficult to bear, since it requires the capacity to tolerate his own condition of non-existence. Very often an abyss is formed between the analyst and the patient, each one remaining self-absorbed, living in a universe of their own, without making contact. Under this circumstance, fatigue and apathy may predominate on the analyst's side, or he can entertain himself with activities linked to his own body. At other times, the analyst can get involved with the enjoyment of the act of talking, even giving long speeches unrelated to the patient, speeches that obviously meet more his own needs than those of the patient. Facing a state without emotion, the analyst may also hold onto theories in an attempt to obtain some reference and with this, mitigate his feeling of nothingness.

Doubtless, the analyst would have the alternative, even under the strong impact of the patient's communication, to create a space in his mind, to contain the situation, and with his capacity of reverie and alpha function, think about it, give it a meaning and offer it to the patient. However, it must be pointed out that all these reactions in the analyst's mind are not necessarily a result of successful projective identification phenomena. If the analyst is not recognized by the patient as a separate object in whom the patient projects his emotions, then the analyst may feel that he doesn't exist for his patient. (Korbivcher, 2001, 2005b). It is nevertheless hoped that, in contrast to his patient, the analyst would use his analytical training and self-observation to become aware of his mental state and rescue his capacity for thinking.

### Clinical material

Nina, twenty-five years old, is a successful professional. When invited to enter the consulting room in the session I am going to narrate, she seems to be in a bad mood. She puffs and stamps her feet as she walks in. She throws her handbag on the chair, throws herself onto the couch and lifts up its back. In a fairly aggressive tone, she talks about her hatred for a friend who had not invited her to participate in a project with him. She adds, very irritated: "That's because I don't belong to the land of Caras.[4] It is because I don't move around in a helicopter."

I tell her that I don't understand what she is saying. She immediately explodes, shouts, becomes irritated, as if complaining because I should know what she was talking about. I mention that I notice that she is taken by an intense state of mind created by herself, but she does not seem to be listening. I later tell her that she is living a state of terror when she becomes aware that we are separated and that I may not know what she is talking about. She reacts and becomes furious.

While we talk, she becomes involved in pulling the cuticles of her fingers with her pointed nails. In other moments, she lifts the nail of one of her thumbs with the nail of the other thumb, as if she were going to pull off the nail with a lever. It seems her intention is to provoke emotions in me by doing that. I am intensely taken with the scene and decide to turn my chair around to avoid seeing what she is doing, so as to be able to continue thinking. I tell her that she seems to be threatened when she notices that I am not inside her and that I cannot know exactly what is happening, and as a result she makes everything explode, like pieces flying through the air. She says: "Of course, you are stupid, you don't understand!!!"

Her reaction again affects me greatly. I make an effort to contain my emotions and not react. I tell her that this seems to be the way she needed to be organized in life to establish relationships in order to not feel so desperate, similar to what had just happened here a short while ago.

She interrupts me, puffing and shouting: "You see! It's not possible!!! I know all this already, and so what? You're not telling me anything new!" I add that she seems like a gladiator who has to instill fear in everyone, provoking others the same way she does with her fingers, to avoid getting in touch with her own nothingness, her fear, her terror.

My words seem to touch her and, calmer, she replies in a friendly tone: "I feel more like a beggar than a gladiator." I tell her that perhaps now she is able to bear the situation and remain closer to what she really feels, that perhaps she feels fragile, helpless.

André, an eight-year-old boy, has schooling problems. His parents seek my help with this complaint. He is intelligent, but very distracted and doesn't focus on tasks. He is a handsome boy, well developed for his age, but with lifeless eyes. He seems very passive and submissive. On entering the room, he opens the toy box, picks up small cars, and throws himself on the couch, turning it into a kind of a race track where the cars go around several times. He emits sounds of a car engine interspersed with narratives of stories related to those movements. (One of the stories is about two brothers; each one has his own car and both compete in a rally. Afterwards, he talks about a widowed father, who travels with his son, and also about two couples of boyfriends and girlfriends who travel together.) I try to attach myself to the content of the stories, but it is difficult for me to stay connected, because I am struck by an intense state of torpor and sleepiness. The atmosphere becomes still, lifeless. I try to be in touch with him, but realize that he is totally absorbed in this activity, seeming to ignore my presence.

In a following session, André, in the midst of a lifeless state, fills up the garbage can with water and slowly places several toys from his box inside the can and a large amount of shredded paper. He stirs it and says it is a "soup". He seems absorbed with the circular motion of the water inside the can. The atmosphere in the room is of emotional emptiness, very difficult for me to bear. In a session some time later, André arrives with a livelier eye, telling me enthusiastically about his swimming school. The subject is exhausted and he then starts a drawing. He soon abandons it, saying he has no idea what to do. He plunges into a state of recoil, ignoring my presence.

With some effort, I can go back to connect myself to him and tell him that he just seemed to be full of ideas about the swimming school and that maybe he could also find some ideas now for his drawing. He seems to be interested in my speech and resumes drawing. To my surprise, sometime later, he asks: "Do you know the library of the Dead Sea? It is a library where they keep the maps of the Dead Sea, pieces of plaster, vases, all that's left".

I say: "But why did it become dead?"

He shows the drawing of the sea, the sunbeams. He says that the sun hit the sea and dried it all up leaving just salt, so there is no more life there. I say he is telling me that sometimes he feels like this Dead Sea, lifeless, with nothing inside, not knowing what to draw. He asks me if I knew that there are places where archaeologists excavated mountains and found some pyramids, with drawings on them, and people communicated through these drawings. I tell him this is how we are communicating today. "It seems that just a short time ago, everything was kind of dead inside you, but after we talked, it is more alive."

## Comments

Nina arrives for the session immersed in a state of profound turmoil. Unable to contain this disturbed state in her mind, she discharges the tension through actions: she throws her purse on the chair, throws herself on the couch. Nina apparently realizes the indiscriminate state in which she finds herself and decides to raise the head of the couch to a vertical position. She seems to need to raise a concrete barrier to separate herself from the analyst.

Nina claims that her state is due to the fact that she was not included in a certain event because she does not belong to the "Island of *Caras*", which made her feel of little importance. Not understanding what she is saying, the analyst asks for clarification. This triggers a rupture in the precarious balance of the patient, who cannot tolerate the fact that the analyst is a person separate from her. Facing the experience of abandonment at that moment, Nina transforms the real image of the analyst into another image of her own creation. She transforms the analyst into someone who, as she describes, is "stupid, doesn't understand". Puffing and shouting, she adds: "You see! It's not possible!!! I know all this already, and so what? You're not telling me anything new!" The emotion in the room is intense. An atmosphere of superiority, triumph, and rivalry from the patient towards the analyst predominates. Parallel to that, a non-verbal manifestation with the nails appears.

With this activity, Nina seems to have the intention to somehow strike the analyst. The analyst in fact becomes very disturbed with the violence of the situation. When she informs the patient that she "seems like a gladiator who has to instill fear in everyone, provoking others the same way she does with her fingers, to avoid getting in touch with her own nothingness, her fear, her terror", she triggers a change in Nina's emotional mood, and in a more subdued tone, Nina says: "I feel more like a beggar than a gladiator."

Most of the time, Nina violently unloads her undigested contents on the analyst's mind, triggering in the analyst fear and threat. With that, Nina seems to avoid in herself experiences of abandonment and terror. This seems to be the way she organizes herself in life to feel as though she exists.

André, in contrast, presents himself for the session with a lifeless eye. He develops the racing track game in which the cars go around. He becomes absorbed with the circular movement of the cars on the track and with the sounds that he himself emanates. He recoils in this activity, ignoring the presence of the analyst in the room. In another session, as described, André becomes involved with the movement of the water in the "soup". In the session in which André recoils after claiming he has no idea what to draw, and the analyst reminds him that he does have ideas inside himself, André seems to feel encouraged to abandon his protective maneuvers and can nominate his internal state through the metaphor of the Dead Sea. He is then able to dream and, like Bion, compare the analytical work to that of the archaeologist: As André says: "the archaeologists found pyramids while excavating mountains. There were drawings on them, and people communicated through them." Maybe André is referring to a primordial mental stage, which was buried and is now being reached.

## Discussion

As we can observe, in both clinical materials the emotional experience of the analyst is different. Both patients operate most of the time with the neurotic part of the personality, although Nina displays important psychotic phenomena, and André, autistic nuclei. Both states produce a strong pressure on the container/contained relationship. Nina displays the prevalence of transformation in hallucinosis and projective transformations, and André, autistic transformations. The atmosphere in the room with Nina is intense. There is movement and violence of emotions. With Nina, the analyst is invited to hallucinate the products created from her mind. With André, the atmosphere experienced is of absence of emotion, static and emotionally empty. The analyst feels she does not exist for André during the session.

It is noteworthy that with both patients the analyst is able to establish some contact, in spite of the strong pressure directed against the container/contained relationship.

Nina displays bodily manifestations, pulling her nail cuticle. She triggers an intense emotional experience in the analyst. With the violence of the situation with Nina, the analyst becomes extremely disturbed to the point of avoiding eye contact. André, on the other hand, produces circular movements with cars. With André, there is boredom, lack of interest, lethargy.

Although the autistic phenomenon may superficially appear similar to the phenomenon of hallucinosis, both differ in nature, as we observed. The patient immersed in autistic states neither includes nor excludes the analyst's figure in the session, but rather, ignores his presence. The patient operating in transformations in hallucinosis transforms the figure of the analyst into another kind of object created by himself, ignoring the real qualities of the analyst's existence. In autistic transformations, the patient remains absorbed with sensations generated in his own body, so as to maintain a state of continuity with the object. In transformations in hallucinosis, in contrast, the patient remains immersed in his own hallucinated universe, a world created by himself, independent of reality.

The quality of the emotional experience of the analyst in both situations is also different. In autistic transformations, the analyst's emotional experience is that of emptiness, of emotional absence and this stimulates the analyst to evade, whereas in transformations in hallucinosis, the atmosphere in the room is intense, full of emotions. In transformations in hallucinosis, the analyst is invited to hallucinate with the patient the products of his mind´s creation. As already mentioned, the invariants in both transformations are different.

A last point to be discussed relates to the question: how may the analyst contact the patient when he finds himself facing projective transformations, transformations in hallucinosis, and autistic transformations? When faced with projective transformations, the analyst becomes impacted by the violence of the patient's projections on his mind, as seen in Nina's case. The analyst tries to contain the situation in order to maintain his thinking condition. With his reverie and capacity for alpha function, the analyst tries to transform these projections into a meaning that he then communicates to the patient, waiting for an opportunity to inform the patient that his experiences are creations of his own mind and do not correspond to real facts. This can help the patient contain those unbearable contents in his mind, and no longer have to expel them. Eventually, this can help the patient become aware of his state of hallucinosis.

With regard to autistic transformations, the analyst's task is to try to penetrate the autistic barrier, introducing himself as a live element, and to approach that inanimate world giving it psychic life. In order for the analyst to reach the patient, the autistic barrier needs to have some vulnerable points, and a transit between autistic states and states in which the mind operates. This experience will possibly allow the patient to transit through mental areas, without feeling so vulnerable and terrorized (Korbivcher, 2008a).

Situations such as the one described with Nina places us, as Bion (1987) mentions in the epigraph of this article, "in front of someone whose objective is to terrorize us to prevent us from thinking clearly. However, our objective is to continue thinking clearly in spite of the situation being adverse or frightening" (p. 248). In contrast with André, I think that if there were an objective, it would be, as Tustin says in the epigraph, that of protecting himself from the worst of the threats, the loss of the notion of his existence. For this, André isolates himself in his world of sensations, acquiring a sensorial existence through them.

Patients like André and Nina often throw us into an inaccessible universe, without known references for guidance. However, I think that these can possibly stimulate us to develop a privileged condition for work, requesting to function most of the time with the "negative capability" (Bion, 1970), investigating the material offered by that particular system of mental functioning through the discipline "of absence of memory and without desire" (Bion, 1967).

## Notes

1. Autistic objects are characterized by experiences with hard objects and by the contact with borders. The awareness of the absence of the object is covered by the autistic object, so that the feelings of terror coming from its absence are suppressed. The autistic forms consist in sensorial experiences that acquire forms. They are entirely particular forms of that individual, not shared with others. They are experiences with soft objects and with body substances felt as comforting and calming. These forms acquire a soothing function, providing through their physical action, rudiments of the notion of limits, containing a space in their interior (Tustin, 1984).
2. In the beta screen, (Bion, 1962) in which a contact barrier could be developed, what is observed is its destruction. This happens by an inversion of the alpha function, that is, those elements that form the contact barrier are dispersed and become beta elements, increased by remains of ego and superego, deprived of all the characteristics that separate them from the beta elements; these are the bizarre objects. The strength of the grouped beta elements has the power to provoke emotions in the analyst, affecting his condition to think and his analytical capacity.

3. It is necessary to point out, however, that by proposing autistic transformations, I am dealing with mental configurations with autistic characteristics rather than with pathological autism. Similarly to how Bion (1965) emphasizes hallucinosis phenomena by proposing transformations in hallucinosis, which are not hallucinations, I propose autistic transformations distinguishing between autistic phenomena and pathological autism.
4. *Caras* is a Brazilian magazine that features celebrities and socialites.

## References

Bick, E. (1968). The experience of skin in early object relations. *International Journal of Psychoanalysis*, 49: 484–486.

Bick, E. (1986). Further considerations on the function of the skin in early object relations, *British Journal of Psychotherapy*, 2: 292–299.

Bion, W. R. (1957). Differentiation of the psychotic from the non-psychotic personalities. *International Journal of Psychoanalysis*, 38: 266–275.

Bion, W. R. (1962). *Learning from Experience*. London: Heinemann, 1991.

Bion, W. R. (1965). *Transformations*. London: Karnac, 1984.

Bion, W. R. (1967). Notes on memory and desire. In: R. J. Langs (Ed.), *Classics in Psycho-analytic Technique*. New York: Jason Aronson.

Bion, W. R. (1970). *Attention and Interpretation*. London: Karnac, 1984.

Bion, W. R. (1987). Making the best of a bad job. In: *Clinical Seminars in Brasilia and São Paulo and Four Papers*. Abingdon: Fleetwood Press.

Bion, W. R. (1992). *Cogitations*. London: Karnac, 1991.

Braga, J. C. (2009). Personal communication.

Grotstein, J. S. (2005). Personal communication.

Klein, M. (1946). Notes on some schizoid mechanisms. *International Journal of Psychoanalysis*, 27: 99–110.

Klein, S. (1980). Autistic phenomena in neurotic patients. *International Journal of Psychoanalysis*, 61: 395–492.

Korbivcher, C. F. (2001). A teoria das transformações e os estados autísticos. Transformações autísticas: Uma proposta. *Revista Brasiliera Psicanálise*, 35: 935–958.

Korbivcher, C. F. (2005b). The theory of transformations and autistic states. Autistic transformations: A proposal. *International Journal of Psychoanalysis*, 86: 1595–1610.

Korbivcher, C. F. (2008a). Bion e Tustin. O referencial de Bion e os fenômenos autísticos. Uma proposta de aproximação. *Revista Brasiliera Psicanálise*, 9: 407–443.

Korbivcher, C. F. (2008b). Bion e Tustin. Le trasformazioni autistiche. In: *Identificazione e trasmissione psichica fra gli adulti e Il bambino. Quaderni di psicoterapia infantile*. Roma: Borla.

Korbivcher, C. F. (2013). Bion and Tustin. The autistic phenomena. *International Journal of Psychoanalysis*, 94: 645–665.

Korbivcher, C. F. (2010). *Transformações autísticas. O referencial de Bion e os fenômenos autísticos*. Rio de Janeiro: Imago.

Korbivcher, C. F. (2013). *Autistic Transformations: Bion's Theory and Autistic Phenomena*. London: Karnac.

Tustin, F. (1984). Autistic shapes. *International Review of Psychoanalysis*, 11: 279–290.

Tustin, F. (1986). *Autistic Barriers in Neurotic Patients*. London: Karnac.

Tustin, F. (1990). *The Protective Shell in Children and Adults*. London: Karnac.

Tustin, F. (1992). *Autistic States in Children*. London: Routledge.

# PART IV

CLINICAL/THEORETICAL: TWO

*Editors' introduction*

Ferro's paper, an incredibly rich and generous contribution, invites readers to *feel* what it might be like to participate in and experience the process of psychic transformation from sense impressions to images and thought. Here, theory and practice are happily intertwined in a living language. Something very sophisticated is presented in a simple and "human" way that allows readers to journey through Bion's revolution, which, according to Ferro, is "comparable to the French Revolution" in the sense that after Bion, nothing looks as it had before. There is a sea-change, in which the aims of psychoanalysis have shifted from an emphasis upon the discovery of contents to the development of narrative and oneiric functions.

Essential to this endeavor is the "play of characters", which reflects the emotions that circulate in the field. Ferro's "cast list" includes a fascinating series of characters, some of whom are totally unexpected: "mismash or nebula of proto-Somites, proto-devils, proto-Mortimers", "hamburgers, rump steak, fillet steaks"; movies: *Star Trek, La Strada, The Silence of the Lambs*; novels: *Crime and Punishment, Anna Karenina*; places: Moulin-Rouge; people: Mrs. Giacometti, Laura, Francesca, Luigi, and so on, in a kaleidoscopic and vertiginous sequence. We are magically transported and enveloped in the dream of the session. Why? Because we *always* give meaning to existence, we come into existence, by dreaming it; and our patients are more or less stuck in a nightmare or, as Ogden says, were never really able to dream. Dreaming in analysis is accomplished by becoming attuned to and with the patient and expanding conscious and unconscious narratives towards new potentialities, different worlds, new capacities: improving the metabolism and "digestive" capacities of the mind and founding a basic emotional grammar.

Cartwright's contribution revolves around a simple but powerful concept: Bion's formulation of the container-contained. His central idea is that "container-contained configurations represent emergent relational capacities occurring in different areas of a multi-dimensional analytic field." What these processes are aimed at, at various levels of complexity (non-symbolic, preverbal and symbolic), is transforming emotional experience or O into thought. Stated in other terms, the aim of the analytic work is to allow the subject a happy negotiation of sameness and difference. The author also affirms that in order to understand these "containing systems", field theory and non-linear dynamics system theory may prove very useful. But the paper is also valuable for the way in which Cartwright succeeds in providing us with convincing clinical examples of how to put to work creatively these fine conceptual instruments.

The body-mind relationship is at the center of the following three papers. In the first, Lombardi deals with it from to point of view of Bion's concept of O. Lombardi offers the reader a clear account of this concept, saving it from any spiritualistic, religious, mystical "Bionism" and treating it as a real analytic tool: simple and powerful at the same time. As well as the body, O is always unpredictable, developing and beyond full verbalization. It cannot be spoken but only lived, felt or *become*. So O seems a concept that Bion forged to oblige the analyst not to forget the centrality of emotions, as they arise—as Lombardi quotes from Damasio—"from maps of body states". Consequently, when the author writes that the formless void state of O "is actually *empty only cognitively*", we clearly understand that considering O is a way not to overshadow the sensorial/semiotic dimension of experience, which is constitutively not-thematizable. For analysts, this means that we shall be called again and again to reconnect the mind to its bodily roots, to avoid abstract thinking, and to think in the presence of emotions. This becomes the model of both the ideal way of the analyst's functioning within the session and of the kind of psychic functioning that we seek to help the patient to attain. As Lombardi shows in a telling vignette, what counts is that the analyst tries to use his own sensations and attune to the pre-symbolic levels of experience in order to help patients to re-establish a better body-mind relationship. In this context the transformative capacity of dreaming is also discussed in a masterly way.

In her paper, Bronstein uses Bion's concept of a primitive proto-mental system, later developed as a *somato-psychotic*, to advance a hypothesis about the nature and dynamics of psychosomatic illness. She extends Bion's idea that a foetal part and its relative sub-thalamic fears can live persistently in the adult as a split-off entity, to the particular kind of dissociation between body and mind that is active in these painful situations. In two beautiful vignettes, Bronstein describes how a conglomerate of beta elements (which lack the capacity for linkage) or unrepresented states of mind can be projected as a beta screen into the body in order to defensively regulate the distance from the object. A tough "over skin" is then put in place in order to protect a thin and fragile psychic skin. Usually these illnesses derive from failures in the mother's capacity for containment and in "lovingly accepting" and transforming the baby's unprocessed sense data. That is why it is so important to elaborate theoretical tools that enable us to listen to this ongoing "semiotic" communication—which has a powerful impact on the analyst's countertransference; to learn to let oneself be touched both "physically" and emotionally.

A clinically oriented approach is also present in Abel-Hirsch's contribution, which, from the title, would seem a more theoretical one. What the author aims at is precisely to find a clinical usefulness even for abstract ideas. In fact we all immediately refind our own experience in her examples of patient A—"all body"—and patient B—"all mind". The first is the kind of patient that cannot tolerate the idea of a creative parental couple and so defends against any vital contact; the dissociation between body and mind is obtained through a "shallowness of mind", a lack of vitality and mortifying every authentic form of curiosity regarding the relationship. For the second, instead, the mind, only *his*, is all that can be "trusted" and she "'over-thinks' everything."

Abel-Hirsch engages here with the same problem dealt with by Bronstein, but from a different perspective. What is focused on is still a good intercourse between psyche and soma, but seen as constituting a couple, "a twosome", that must come to be "suffered" by the patient. This couple is reminiscent of other "twosomes": the parental couple, external and internal reality, and so on. The author argues that a template for all "twosomes" may be provided by the preconception of the parental couple. So the working through of oedipal issues (how to accept a sustainable separation from the object) can illuminate and transform the relationship between mind and body, whose strength is a source of internal support for the subject, and vice versa. Tolerating the unknownness of the parental couple helps to tolerate that of the relationship between mind and body. Being able, in her countertransference, to enact being the mind with one patient and the body with the other, helped both patients to decrease their sense of guilt and the persecution stemming from the unknown and to reach a better somato-psychic integration.

Last but not least, in a moving vignette, Salomon Resnik shows us again his theoretical creativity and clinical talent and his capacity to dialogue even with the most severe patients in a deeply human and light (Chagallian) and inspired visionary way. The basic theme of his paper, a tribute to Bion as also the old friend and supervisor he was, is how to reach the essential integrity of intellect and affect that is desirable in the construction of meaning. What we need as human beings and what we need to help our patients to acquire is an *intelligentia sentiente* (sentient intelligence), "sensible" ideas, the Winnicottian psycho-somatic collusion. Resnik describes how, when the mind isn't able to tolerate very violent emotions, a flight of thoughts can take place. Thoughtful feelings are expelled into an empty and infinite space, alienated as unthought emotions. The subject is left with *a-motional* (instead of e-motional) thoughts, with thoughts that are motionless (not moving/or moved), stuck thoughts, thoughts deprived of the living aura of emotions. It is here that the analyst is called upon to make his mind available; to be deeply receptive, willing to resonate with the patient and put an end to the war in the mind from which the patient may be suffering; to help the patient to rediscover the link between sensoriality and thoughts and bring him back to the original nest where he was born and from which he may grow and flourish.

CHAPTER FOURTEEN

# Changes in technique and in the theory of technique in a post-Bion field model

*Antonino Ferro*

Having initially considered that the patient says something that I am required to decipher, I gradually came to adopt different perspectives, such as the introduction of the increasingly strong concept of relationship, and later the idea of the field and that of transformation in dreaming. The second and third of these remain central to my approach (Ferro, 2009), albeit subject to constant adjustment.

At present, I try to work together with the patient on how to undertake a process of directing and editing narrations and sense impressions that have come to life, or are waiting for life to be breathed into them, in the field.

Bion entitled one of his books *Taming Wild Thoughts*; however, in my view it is a matter not of taming them, but of being able to experience them, and if it is normal to have *Little Women* or *Little Women: The Sisters Grow Up*, it is equally normal to be able to open the way to *Apocalypto*.

Every patient comes to us not with characters in search of an author (we should already be doing very well if that were the case), but with a mishmash or nebula of proto-Somites, proto-devils, proto-Mortimers, and so on (Bion, 1975), which have seldom attained the status of characters. If we already had characters, we should already have analyses that put our capacity for invention and creation less to the test (by "our" I mean that of both patient and analyst).

If a patient who is a well-known surgeon tells us—in analysis—that he has grown a beard so as not to be mistaken, when out in his town, for his brother, who is also a doctor, and who makes spurious diagnoses of non-existent tuberculosis in order to have patients to treat and to become famous for curing them; and if he also reports that his brother is about to embark on his seventh marriage, his first five wives all having died of natural causes/illness/in accidents, while the sixth escaped by getting a divorce in time; then it is not hard to imagine some possible developments. We might think of split-off aspects that will require a prolonged period of negotiation in order to be integrated, so as to bring together the exemplary surgeon and the criminal doctor, the double, the imaginary twin and the secret sharer. However, even in such cases we should beware of having this developing plot in mind, as we should then be blinding ourselves to all other possible stories, to all the nebulae of beta elements which have come together for the moment in that world—for they could fly apart again and, by subsequently re-coalescing in a different way, give rise to a different possible world. So let us take care not to try to foresee how this movie will develop.

When a colleague correctly apprehended the theme of "narcissism" in a patient and followed that thread, he eventually brought the analysis concerned to a satisfactory end. But it took a second analysis to reveal the presence of so many paths "off the beaten track", of so many failures to open up different worlds and breathe life into incarcerated emotions, the outcome being an abiding sense of suffocation with severe asthma attacks, presented by the patient in that second analysis.

Such is all the more the case when a patient comes along "without bringing any characters at all" and these must begin to germinate from a kind of wilderness. The requirement is in effect to allow boredom, silence, repetitiveness, or extreme stupidity to become *La Strada*, *Crime and Punishment*, *The Silence of the Lambs*, or *Anna Karenina*. Some examples can be found in the longer case histories featuring in other contributions of mine (Ferro, 2002a, 2003, 2009).

Some analyses may proceed from the very beginning with characters whom we imagine to be principals and who may subsequently prove to be such; or these characters may simply exit the stage; or else unforeseen and unforeseeable characters may appear. Other analyses, which call for trust, resemble westerns in which it is extremely difficult to gather in the herds making off in all directions and to bring them to the river, to urge them across the ford towards thinkability, and ultimately to transform them into hamburgers, rump steaks, fillet steaks, or the like.

What is Anna's unthinkable world? One perfectly decent session follows another; Anna is a brilliant patient such as every analyst would like to have. But who is Anna? What are Anna's other possible worlds? For the time being, she is a good actress ready to play the part for which the Actors Studio has prepared her—an excellent patient! What unexpressed potentialities could eventually come together? These might even include the possibility—as Poe shows in "The Purloined Letter"—that Anna might become Anna pure and simple and no one else!

I am reminded of the *Star Trek* series which came to be populated by beings from other worlds, having very weird and almost paradoxical physical features: well, we must open ourselves up to such "monsters" if and when they are present, or, as Bion does in *A Memoir of the Future* (1975), to Somites, Mortimers, stegosauruses, and so on.

So we should, in my view admittedly, lend an ear to what the patient says, does, and feels, but should also keep another ear (or eye) always open to the nativity of something previously unthinkable or unthought. Even if not all patients require this from us, they are entitled to it if that is their wish; perhaps that is the difference between analysis and psychotherapy. Analysis is a journey of adventure in search of the source of the Nile, Indiana Jones, or, in other words, a taste for travel and discovery; whereas psychotherapy is "I feel bad and want to feel better, but let's keep the work involved to a minimum." There is nothing to prevent exchanges between these two approaches at any time.

Apart from certain invariants, I am many, and some of these many are prevalent—at least for the time being or *sic rebus stantibus*. Other potentialities may come to life, as in *I Am Legend*, at night and in the dark, and do their best to devour the dominant identities.

A patient's granny, Eufemia, was a good grandmother, a good mother, and a good woman. She had given birth to three moderately unhappy children and brought them up; and her kitchen featured aluminium pans (in those days, pans were made of aluminium and were exposed on hooks on the kitchen wall) that were the finest that had ever been seen. *Eu-phemi* … she who speaks well and is blessed.

But who was Granny Eufemia? She had a floating kidney (*mobile* in Italian). *La donna è mobile* (woman is fickle—also *mobile* in Italian). She wore a girdle to hold her "floating kidney" in place; if she had put on a red girdle, would it have become a wasp-waisted corset and would she have danced the cancan at the Moulin-Rouge? Alternatively, what else might this "kidney" have done once it was no longer held in check by the most containing girdle that had ever, ever been seen?

However, if a woman came to me for analysis and mentioned the problem of her floating kidney, what worlds should we be able to open up? And if another were to tell me in her very first telephone call that she lives in the Milan district of Inganni ("deception" in Italian)? Again, what of another disturbing character from another patient's childhood: Mrs. Giacometti, married to a scientist, a militant in an ultra-orthodox catholic-communist party, who ran away from home with a black jazz trumpeter and swindler by trade? Should we "hold in check" that fickle/floating wasps' nest, swarming with beta elements, or, deploying the minimum necessary defenses, open up an initial possibility of transforming the wasps into bees?

In one session, a patient reports that he has dreamt of the caretaker at his holiday home who wore his sunglasses the wrong way round—that is, on the back of his neck. I immediately imagine the sun behind him, but does it mean that he feels sunset time looming before him, or that he sometimes feels blinded by my interventions, which are too glaringly bright or blinding on the back of this neck? I have no way of knowing the answer immediately; we shall have to wait and see what route will gain the upper hand.

Meanwhile, however, we thus observe one of the functions of a dream—as a fantasy grabber, or rather an instrument for casting characters that cannot otherwise easily be reached: the dream has brought into the analysis the character of the "man with sunglasses on the back of his neck", and the dream we shall be able to have of the session will enable us to locate this character and put him in context, to facilitate editing of the film co-produced with the patient.

Following the report of an exchange of coins for plastic tokens in a supermarket, a comment by the analyst might bring on the character of the "cheat", perhaps triggering a sequence in which someone wants to protect the back of his neck from seeing painful visions (i.e., wants to cheat the back of his neck) … but that is only one of the vast number of possible hypothetical developments. Again, if the patient were then to say: "Today my father asked me to lunch, and then the sun came out", this could be seen as confirming the postulated plot (someone has transformed sense impressions into food), and the climate of the session would take a turn for the better. In this way, by trial and error and stop-go editing, the dream of the session comes to life with a character cast in his role by the patient's dream, another cast on the basis of a reverie, and yet another brought directly by the patient. In other words, we first have to go shopping (that is, undertake the casting) and then cook our purchases, thus generating the dream of the session.

Just before a Christmas holiday separation, a patient says she has "twisted" a muscle and is in great pain … The pain thus enters the session. She then adds that she is furious (*malgirata* in Italian—literally "mis-turned"). That is to say, the patient is unwittingly saying that she is furious/"twisted" owing to separations that inflict pain on her. All this must of course find a way of becoming embodied in a story that will progress from a zero level of transformation—when she tells me that she is furious and in pain—to transformative levels in accordance with the activation of the directing/editing function, which, over and above the content, will be able to develop the micropoietic and macropoietic capacity of the field.

Pure deciphering, or assembly of pieces of a jigsaw puzzle, is sometimes possible, but in such cases a great deal of work will already have been done, and the characters will solely await narrative editing. For instance, Laura begins a session by saying that she is full of well-being and feels really good. She goes on to mention two consultations in an intensive care ward, concerning a boy waiting for a heart transplant and a girl suffering from dyspnoea and hardly able to breathe pending a lung transplant.

In this case, I felt that I had enough information (the patient had already supplied "dream sequences") and that I could therefore tell her that, whereas this on the one hand reminded me of one of those highly optimistic advertisements for a healthy children's snack, on the other she seemed also to be focusing on problems of the heart and telling me that she felt suffocated by something—something that prevented her from completely filling her lungs with air. From then on, the patient herself was able to develop these two themes, which seemed to be awaiting the availability of a road that, once traveled, would enable her to disentangle her emotions and give shape to her discontents and doubts concerning "choices of the heart" and her needs for freedom and autonomy.

To sum up, I see that my technique is very close to row C of the grid. As for rows E and F, I leave them aside (or perhaps I use them only as an internal, personal, and provisional reference point), in order as far as possible to remain on a level involving the sharing of row C (myths, dream thoughts, and alpha sequences).

If a very inhibited, lethargic patient talks about a catafalque (*catafalco* in Italian), I am immediately attracted by the element of the *falco* (Italian for "falcon")—something extremely vital that is swallowed up, locked away and put to sleep in the claustrum. Even if I do not tell the patient this, from then on I shall be looking for ways of attuning myself to the "falcon".

Similarly, I am strongly attracted by what I have called "semantic nests"—that is, places within the spoken words that include high, and different, potentials for communication.

If I should at some point imagine that a patient has been abused, my vertex would be: in what way might I have been abusing him, or might the "falcon" be abusing (or have abused) him? However, something from a different external or temporal historical reality can be transformed only to the extent that it comes to inhabit the present field.

If a classmate by whom a patient feels bullied makes his appearance in a session, I cannot—as long as an analysis, or the maintenance of the setting, makes sense—fail to see this as a form of functioning adopted in a place within the field and acted out by the patient himself (as a potentially disturbing identity) or by me (as a disquieting presence for him).

If an expert analyst finds herself cutting short a session with a patient suffering from selective mutism, I am bound to imagine that the analyst is undergoing a kind of silent abuse, so that she wishes to remove the abused container (herself) from the abusing content.

If a patient were to tell me that he is collecting and arranging all the bricks (*mattoni* in Italian) scattered all over the terrace in order to construct something, I see them as the *matte* (Italian for mad or bad) parts which the patient is trying to arrange and make usable for a project.

If one is somewhere along row C, there is always the possibility of "dreaming" or "visualizing other possibilities with the eyes of the mind or the alpha function". If an inhibited, hyper-controlling patient mentions a "button" that is about to fall off, I shall surely think of the huge emotional explosion of which he is afraid, and shall let myself be guided by the semantic/olfactory trails that every story and everything else brought by a patient leave in their wake.

I recall a little girl's drawing of the trunk and crown of a tree, which immediately appeared to me as a lava-spewing volcano, and which after two years of therapy took the form of a landscape visible through an open window from which a large number of small trees with "lava" crowns could be seen: the huge proto-emotional volcano had been broken down into lots of containable little volcanoes, as if it had been possible to remove the storm elements from the hurricane of beta elements and transform that hurricane into discrete aggregates, now containable and thinkable in terms of different and representable emotions.

### A case of acting out as an undreamed (and recovered) dream

Francesca, a patient in her fifth year of analysis, arrives for her session at her usual time of 5.30 pm, but I notice that I had thought it was 6.30 pm and had set everything up for the supervision group that I have been holding for years at that time. What is more, in my certainty that a member of the group (who resembles the patient) is arriving, I say: "Hi". I immediately realize my mistake, and the disorientated patient stares at the capacious entrance hall, which is arranged quite differently from its usual layout, with the armchairs in a circle, the hallstand in a different corner, and extra chairs.

The patient grasps my mistake and begins to talk about her father's absentmindedness and unreliability: this has now got so bad that he has inadvertently put on his wife's hat, and so on.

For a moment I panic, although nothing like that has ever happened to me; I think of ageing, and of being very busy. But then I "see" the situation from a different perspective: for some time now, the patient has been wondering whether to present herself this year for the initial selection interviews as a candidate. The decision is of course hers, but do I feel deep down that I should give her a green or a red light?

So now we have the answer: I see the patient differently, I see a colleague to whom I say "hi", I see her in the context of supervision and not of analysis: my traffic light is green.

Next day, the patient mentions the major restructuring in hand at her workplace and, in particular, the need to repair the clocks, which have not worked for a long time. We realize that the patient is in her fifth year of analysis, and she says she feels ready to go for the interviews. In a partial self-disclosure I tell her that we should move to New York for ten minutes, after which we can immediately return to Europe.

The patient then tells me that she would begin her CV with the words: "I am the elder of two brothers." I show her that it is time to make up her mind: she is a woman, not a man, and it is time to shed all the ambiguities that have kept her plans out of time, including the idea of getting married and having a child. This would involve rearranging the furniture in her home to make room for her future child's cot (*lettino* in Italian)—as well as to make room for her future patients' couch (also *lettino* in Italian), I add.

The patient goes for the interviews a few months later.

### The demolished bell tower: a co-constructed dream

An approximately thirty-five-year-old patient tells me in irritation that her mother has said to her: "You are old enough now not to put off the important decisions in your life any longer …" In the next session she says that she feels irritated without knowing why and that her boyfriend has been even more irritated. After a silence, I respond: "Do you want me to tell you the dream your boyfriend had last night?" "What do you mean?!" After a moment of paranoia, she says: "Did you hear us talking at the bar while we were having breakfast!? How do you know that my boyfriend had a dream and that he told me it?"

"Well, tell me, do you want to hear it or not?" "Yes, all right," she answers.

"Here is the dream: there was one of those old demolished church clock towers that are being rebuilt, and the builders were hoisting into position a clock that at first had no hands (like the one in *Wild Strawberries*); then the hands were fitted and showed twelve o'clock." (All this resulted from my visual imagination, triggered right at the start of the session.)

The astonished patient says: "No! I don't believe it! Carlo's dream went like this: 'I dreamt of an old demolished church with a bell tower that was being rebuilt, and you were there waiting for me.'" I reply: "Usually it's the groom who waits for the bride, but the other way round is all right too."

This unconscious, partly serious, "dreamlike dance" led us to return to the subject of the mother, of time, and of mourning for time. The patient then tells me—and I feel this is important—that the clock was showing 12, and not 7 am or 9 am, but not 5 pm or 8 pm either: it was time to act. The implicit message was obviously that she should accept her responsibilities—marriage, children, existential decisions, the time of fertility, the time of mourning for omnipotence. The Church in our culture stands for the marking of time: baptism, marriage, funerals, and so on.

### Luigi and the rifle: dreaming the symptom

Luigi is a severely obsessional librarian. At our very first interview, he says he has a father with an aortic aneurysm and a paralysed uncle. (This suggests to me two different forms of functioning in the patient, one incontinent and the other that immobilizes him, as in his obsessive rituals.) He goes on to tell me how he spends ages "cleaning", "sweeping", and tidying up the garden lawn, where animals sometimes dig "holes".

In this ritual-filled world (the rituals being practised both at work and at bedtime) he seems to have one area of freedom: his hobby of hunting. He has to look after two dogs, clean his guns, and organize the various hunts. He goes on to describe his grandfather's terrible experience during the war when he found that his house had been destroyed by a bomber, killing his entire family. He then returns to the subject of his highly complex cleaning rituals (meanwhile I cannot help associating the hunting with the bomber [the Italian word *caccia* means both] and the death of his whole family).

In the next session he refers to Mario Tobino's famous book *Le libere donne di Magliano*, about women patients in a mental hospital (introducing the subject of madness?), and then mentions an inexplicable tic: whenever he feels tense, he raises his right shoulder and moves it backwards. A friend tells him it looks like he is "signalling a jack to his partner in [the card game of] *briscola*". He then launches into a long account in which the words "funeral" and "hunting [*caccia*] rifle" constantly recur.

At this point everything comes together in my mind, like a jigsaw with the pieces previously scattered higgledy-piggledy. The raising and backward movement of the right shoulder is precisely the effect of the "recoil" of a rifle: Luigi is a kind of killer, who constantly eliminates anyone who makes him feel tense. We cannot see the rifle, but what remains is the recoil, the cleaning rituals after every crime, the holes dug in the garden so as not to leave any trace of the buried bodies. When the rage is at fever pitch, he takes off in his bomber (*caccia*) and kills everyone in sight.

So here we have the dream that I was able to dream on his behalf. We now need to observe the development of these themes together: we shall see the Quentin Tarantino function and shall then have to decide what to do with this Django Unchained, dressed as a well brought-up librarian.

Having reached this point, I must now present an outline of my model, whose origins lie in the intersection of the post-Bion field and the post-Baranger field.

The upheaval wrought by Bion (1962, 1963, 1965) was comparable to the French Revolution: nothing has been the same since. Its cardinal point is that the unconscious is constantly in the throes of formation and transformation, and is secondary and subsequent to the relationship with the Other. Nameless anxieties, proto-sense impressions and proto-emotions, projected and evacuated into the Other's mind, are transformed into alpha elements by the Other's function of digestion and metabolism, the Other being the caregiver, group of alpha functions, or analyst; perhaps I should say the field rather than the Other. These entities are visual building blocks (pictograms)—although they could also be associated with all the other senses—which, when linked together, give rise to waking dream thought. Alpha elements will then be constantly repressed, laying the foundations of the capacity to remember, and hence to forget, and forming the "contact barrier", or boundary between conscious and unconscious. All this is known. What is less familiar, on the other hand, although mentioned by Neri, Ogden, and Grotstein (2007), is that some beta elements penetrate this barrier and escape the process of alphabetization. These—the quanta of proto-emotions and untransformed sense impressions—are, in my opinion, the principal focus of interest in analysis. It is these quanta that give rise to the tsunamis, whirlwinds, and gales of beta elements which, if not adequately transformed, lie at the root of the most severe pathologies.

## Origins of the image

In psychoanalysis, the kingdom of the image is the dream, or has perhaps been the dream, at least since Bion provided us with a model of the mind in which images (or "pictograms" [Rocha Barros, 2000]) continuously arise through the so-called alpha function, which continuously transforms into images all the sense impressions that pervade us, irrespective of their provenance. The sequence of images thus formed somehow calms and soothes the mind whenever this transformation is successful.

Of course, the choice and construction of the "pictogram" and its sequences are extremely subjective. It is like the depiction of a "subject" by Degas or, say, Caravaggio, Monet, Chagall, Picasso, or whoever. This, then, is the first locus of the mind's creativity: the transformation from beta into alpha through the alpha function.

We now come to the second locus of creativity in the mind—namely, the manner, which is also extremely subjective, in which the sequence of pictograms (waking dream thought) is "narrated", or put into words, by means of an infinite number of literary genres. These are the narrative derivatives of the pictograms (or of the alpha elements). Where some of these pictograms are projected outwards, they retain their characteristic dreamlike quality, constituting the visual flashes referred to on many occasions by Meltzer and later by myself (Ferro, 1992).

Another example, in which projection is more violent, is transformation in hallucinosis, when a patient projects pictograms on to someone else and then sees them as emanating entirely from that other person.

However, let us now consider further my model of the mind. During the daytime, we store up a vast quantity of pictograms (of alpha elements), and it is then up to a "super alpha function" to perform a kind of secondary pressing/weaving of the stored material, eventually yielding the dream images that will constitute the most thoroughly digested productions of our apparatus for thinking thoughts.

Tellingly, Ogden holds that the aim of psychoanalysis and the work of the psychoanalyst consist in dreaming those dreams, in transforming storms of sense impressions into images, where the patient has been unable to do this by himself. It follows that another aim of analysis is to develop the capacity to "generate images", to create dreams where there were previously symptoms (that is, sense impressions set as it were in concrete).

Of course, that is not all there is to the "visual" element in analysis. There is also the wide-ranging aspect of drawings produced in analysis—not necessarily only in child analyses—which, by analogy with narrative derivatives, can be seen as graphic derivatives of waking dream thought. At any rate, a session is in most cases structured as a dance between narrations with a visual character, reveries, metaphors, and dreams.

The major difference between "conversion" and "somatization" in my model is that, while the former involves the discharge of balpha elements, with which fragments of narrative derivatives are therefore correlated, the latter concerns the evacuation of "pure" beta elements that have not undergone incipient processes of mentalization or metabolization. Whereas the former include quanta of "thinkability" or proto-pictograms and proto-sequences of balpha, with possible immature chains of narrative derivatives, the latter have not been subject to any process of mentalization at all (Ferro, 2002b, 2005, 2009).

Furthermore, while the analyst can sometimes assign scraps of meaning to the former, the latter confront him with "upstream" problems, involving a substantial deficiency (albeit with "lumps" and "holes") of the instruments leading to mentalization.

When pure beta elements are evacuated, we are in a kind of theatre with no light and no sound, containing a burst pipe constantly leaking sewage that will eventually form a sac and give rise to various psychosomatic pathologies.

If the evacuation takes place at a later stage, the stage will be in a half-light, with a minimum of sound interruption, so that we can attempt the construction of a degree of meaning—that is, it will then already be possible to work on the contained (whereas in the former case the work must precede what is actually contained). Of course, some pathologies arise further along the path towards mentalization.

Projective identification is a natural attempt to relieve the burden on the mind by projecting disturbing states resulting from fragmentary sense impressions into the Other's mind. If that mind is receptive, it will not only be permeable to these, conveying a sense of dimensionality (depth), but will also offer a sense of temporality, due to the relatively predictable alternation of concave and convex sequences: besides receptivity, there will be the capacity for transformation and progressive alphabetization of the projected (beta) elements that, when transformed (alpha), will become the building blocks of thought. The principal change in psychoanalysis in the last few years has been the transfer of attention from the contents of the mind to the development of the instruments for thinking, feeling, and dreaming.

From this point of view, the two key points involved in the development of a mind will be development of the container and of the "dreaming ensemble"—that is, the entire range of activities concerning the dreaming functions of the mind: the alpha function, reveries, night dreams, and the super alpha function (Grotstein 2007, 2009).

In the view of Ogden (2009), a symptom—any symptom—is the result of a dream not dreamed or, in other words, of a scar-like accumulation of beta elements, to constrain which various defense mechanisms (that is, symptoms) may be deployed pending their deconcretization and eventual dreaming. Such a dream, in that author's view, corresponds to a process of digestive metabolization, which gives rise to the first elements of thought and emotion by way of the formation of unconscious images (pictograms).

There are various kinds of reveries: flash reveries if they are instantaneous; feature-length reveries when different moments of reverie are linked; and the continuous process of assumption and transformation carried out without any element of consciousness.

The seeds of recovery or therapeutic factors variously described in different models are closely bound up with the foregoing.

It is important to note that all the above must always take place within the structure of the so-called "field". In the field, an analytic session in my view takes the form of a dream of the minds involved, in which stories originating from different places and times, outside the field itself, arrive, are diffracted and overlap (Ferro & Basile, 2009). The shared experience is to permit the circulation of emotional states, affects, thoughts, and characters together with the analyst (who is also a place in the field), who guarantees and safeguards the setting, while also facilitating dreamlike activity in the analytic couple. A session is played out on the level of a mutual dream, both when the patient "dreams" (if he can) the analyst's intervention or his mental state, and when the analyst "dreams" the response to give to the patient. The more this response is "dreamt", the more it will help to constitute, and mend any deficiency in, the patient's alpha function. The analytic field is in effect the "unsaturated waiting room" that accommodates emotions, proto-emotions, and characters pending their channelling towards their saturated destination in the relationship or construction.

From a different perspective, the field is made up of all the lines of force, all the proto-aggregates of proto-emotions, proto-characters, and characters floating in the virtual space of the field, as they gradually assume solidity, color, and three-dimensionality. Patient and analyst are in effect joined by a number of elastic bands, or possible narrative lines, while more and more "clips" are attached to them, comprising the field's "casting" of what was previously indeterminate.

What matters in this last field model, which tends to take a dreamlike form, is the development of the field's capacity to dream, leading to the transformation and introjection of functions. The field contains unconscious, or non-mentalized, forms of functioning that undergo constant transformation into thinkability by way of the phenomenon of casting and transformation in dreaming.

In this model, the focal point of analysis is, significantly, the development of the capacity to dream, and not just work on repression or splits. While the ensuing hypotheses are in my view convincing, they call for further research, along the lines of the work of Norman (2001) and Salomonsson (2007).

## *Basic emotional grammar*

Many pathologies involve an alteration of the basic emotional grammar, which is organized on the basis of simple concave/convex sequences:

∪∪∩ .... ∪∪∩∩∩∪∪∪ ....

This basic grammar consists in the alternation of receptivity and penetrativity, which constitutes the emotional foundation of any more complex emotional or affective grammar: "You accept me/you reject me/I accept you/I reject you". This is underlain by the constant interplay of projective identifications and reveries.

This "scansion", as it were, remains the basic fabric, which tends to stabilize, and on which there form layers, like veils and eventually carpets, of subsequent experiences that will be organized along the same lines as the basic rhythm.

One patient expresses all this through the progressive use of the *b-athroom*, where he finds the receptive space for the evacuation of anxieties (Meltzer's toilet-breast). Later there appears the convex feeding space of the elegant *b-ar* with many kinds of brioches. Then comes the *b-arrier*, which represents a limit and will later develop into *b-ellowing* in fits of rage.

We therefore have:

resulting from the rhythmic alternation of projection and reception.

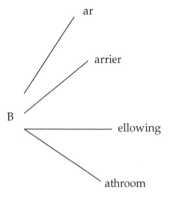

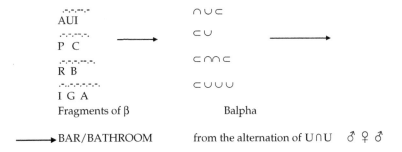

It is a simple matter to translate this into more complex form.

However, such proto-structures will for a long time trace out the path of development taken by the relevant type of mental functioning.

Possible problems are an excess of convexity:

∩∩∩∩∩∩∩ (absence of reverie/receptivity)

or an excess of receptivity:

UUUUUUU (absence of ♂ and turbulence).

Another problem arises from the possible dissociation between the content of the underlying sequence—for example, ∩∩∩∩∩∩∩∩—and the signals emanating from other channels, such as a mother who is closed off mentally but nevertheless smiles. This situation lies at the root of many pathologies—especially the "three Ds" (dyslexia, dysgraphia, and dyscalculia). A possible exercise might be to draw a diagram of the underlying sequence of these basic affective codes.

## References

Bion, W. R. (1962). *Learning from Experience*. London: Karnac Books.
Bion, W. R. (1963). *Elements of Psychoanalysis*. London: Karnac Books.
Bion, W. R. (1965). *Transformations*. London: Heinemann.
Bion, W. R. (1975). *A Memoir of the Future*. London, Karnac, 1990.
Ferro, A. (1992). *The Bi-Personal Field: Experiences in Child Analysis*, London: Routledge, 1999.
Ferro, A. (2002a). *Seeds of Illness, Seeds of Recovery: The Genesis of Suffering and the Role of Psychoanalysis* (Trans. P. Slotkin). Hove: Brunner-Routledge, 2005.
Ferro, A. (2002b). Some implications of Bion's thought: The waking dream and narrative derivatives. *International Journal of Psychoanalysis, 83*: 597–607.
Ferro, A. (2003). Marcella: the transition from explosive sensoriality to the ability to think. *Psychoanalytic Quarterly, 72*: 183–200.
Ferro, A. (2005). Which reality in the psychoanalytic session? *Psychoanalytic Quarterly, 74*: 421–442.
Ferro, A. (2009). Transformations in dreaming and characters in the psychoanalytic field. *International Journal of Psychoanalysis, 90*: 2009–2030.
Ferro, A., & Basile, R. (Eds.) (2009). *The Analytic Field*. London: Karnac.
Grotstein, J. (2007). *A Beam of Intense Darkness: Wilfred Bion's Legacy to Psychoanalysis*. London: Karnac.

Grotstein, J. (2009). *But at the Same Time and on Another Level: Clinical Applications in the Kleinian/Bionian Mode*. London: Karnac.

Norman, J. (2001). The psychoanalyst and the baby: A new look at work with infants. *International Journal of Psychoanalysis, 82*: 83–100.

Ogden, T. H. (2009). *Rediscovering Psychoanalysis: Thinking and Dreaming, Learning and Forgetting*. Hove: Routledge.

Rocha Barros, E. M. (2000). Affect and pictographic image: the construction of meaning in mental life. *International Journal of Psychoanalysis, 81*: 1087–1099.

Salomonsson, B. (2007). "Talk to me baby, tell me what's the matter now." Semiotic and developmental perspectives on communication in psychoanalytic infant treatment. *International Journal of Psychonalysis, 88*: 127–146.

CHAPTER FIFTEEN

# Containing systems in the analytic field

*Duncan Cartwright*

The meeting of minds in the analytic setting requires the constant negotiation of fragile tensions between having a mind of one's own and making mental and emotional contact with the patient. Each meeting opens up a unique intersubjective experiential field that requires transformation in order to expand capacities for thinking and feeling. Multiple entry points, multiple transformations, are possible depending on our positioning and immersion in the field.

I understand Bion's formulation of container-contained relations to represent a basic relational unit for conceptualizing how transformation occurs or becomes possible. Bion thought that container-contained configurations connote "abstract representations of psychoanalytic realizations" (1962b, p. 90). As with all great theoretical contributions, the idea is simple but its impact is profound. One entity (container) external to another (contained) interact, resulting in a number of possibilities: the container fails to contain, the container is exploded by its contents, the contained fails to interact or perhaps establishes a parasitic link, depleting the container. Many other possibilities exist, including, of course, the idea that container-contained interaction leads to mutual growth or gives rise to a third object. As an abstraction the configuration is applicable in infinite ways depending on one's perspective: emotions contain words, the analyst contains the patient's dream-thoughts, people are contained by their cultures, our bodies contain emotions, my attitude may contain my family, with the reverse also applicable, and so forth. It is also possible to think about how this sets up multiple interactions between different configurations where they themselves become contained or container. We can imagine a complex dynamic nesting process (Billow, 2003), expanding cycles and interactions that set up complex containing systems. Of course, the experiential field itself can be seen as a container (Civitarese & Ferro, 2013) but it is also contained by society, the histories of its subjects, and so forth.

Within the analytic field the containing function of the mother's or analyst's mind represents a combination of container-contained relations most readily referred to in clinical practice. Bion (1962a) wrote about the role of the mother's container function in psychic development as follows:

> Normal development follows if the relationship between infant and breast permits the infant to project a feeling, say, that it is dying, into the mother and to reintroject it after its sojourn in the breast has made it tolerable to the infant psyche. If the projection is not accepted by the mother the infant feels that its feeling that it is dying is stripped of such meaning as it has. It therefore reintrojects, not a fear of dying made tolerable, but a nameless dread. (Bion, 1962a, p. 306)

How this actually occurs, the process of "making tolerable", containing, and then returning the projection, has been understood in different ways. But as Caper (1999) points out, despite its popular use in psychoanalytic jargon, such a formulation still remains remarkably under-theorized. That was over twenty years ago, and although there have been some very useful developments in this area (e.g., Civitarese, 2012; Ferro, 2005, 2009; Grotstein, 2007; Ogden, 2004), it still remains fertile ground for other considerations. One such consideration involves emphasizing the radical relational qualities of the container-contained dynamic. I read Bion (1977a) as doing just this in *The Grid*:

> The breast [container] and the mouth [contained] are only important in so far as they serve to define the bridge between the two. When the "anchors" usurp the importance which belongs to the qualities which they should be imparting to the bridge, growth is impaired. (p. 26)

This might be related to Bion's (1977a) emphasis on transcending caesuras, in this case transcending caesuras between the container and contained. It emphasizes the configuration's interactive, emergent, and reciprocal qualities. We lose the point if we focus on just the "anchors", the container or the contained. Here we are closer to questions about how we focus on the *bridge*, attend to its confluence, and understand its properties in the analytic field.

In this chapter I want to develop the idea that container-contained configurations represent emergent relational capacities occurring in different areas of a multi-dimensional analytic field. This is helped by modeling the development of psychic experience on some ideas from non-linear dynamic systems theory. My understanding is that containment systems (interacting with alpha function, PS<->D, alpha elements, and beta elements) emerge at different levels of complexity as attempts to articulate emotional experience (O), "unknowable reality" as a thing-in-itself. As Grotstein puts it: "everything hinges on the outcome of the interaction between O and the container" (Grotstein, 2007, p. 163). I explore the idea that containment systems exist as mutated functions at different levels of emotional experience, with all having in common the function of negotiating the pulse of "sameness" and "difference", symmetries and asymmetries, in the analytic field. For my purpose, I explore containment systems as they exist at three levels: non-symbolic, pre-verbal, and symbolic. Most of these ideas stem from Bion's thinking, some more developed than others. Discussing psychoanalytic concepts using non-linear thinking may amount to rather dry theoretical abstractions, experience-distant and difficult to realize or use in clinical work. I try to address this somewhat by exploring a case that has helped me explore and develop some of my thinking in this area.

## Non-linear dynamic systems and the analytic field

My understanding of "containing systems" combines Bion's observations with field theory (Baranger & Baranger, 2008; Baranger, Baranger, & Fiorini, 2011; Civitarese, 2012; Civitarese & Ferro, 2013; Ferro, 2005) and non-linear dynamics systems theory (e.g., Ghent, 2002; Grotstein, 2007; Marks-Tarlow, 2011; Quinodoz, 1997; Seligman, 2005). The analytic field refers to the idea that analysis is conducted "within an intersubjective relationship in which each participant is defined by the other. In speaking of the analysis, we are referring to the formation of a structure which is a product of two participants in the relationship but which in turn involves them in a dynamic and possibly creative process" (Baranger, 1993, p. 16). The analyst and patient produce an intersubjective field of experience bigger than the sum of its parts. We might conceptualize analytic experience as follows:

> The analyst and patient meet each other at conscious and unconscious levels of experience, creating multiple tracks that organize inchoate sensory experience, the components of thought (alpha elements), verbal communications and consequent interpersonal processes. It is also possible to think about how different tracks of experience might influence each other, in turn, generating emergent experiences. Here, non-conscious interpersonal processes, psychic functions and processes, internal objects and so forth, form a complex influencing system. From this perspective the ability to hold unbearable psychic states in mind so that they become thinkable and meaningful is dependent on complex psychical and interpersonal processes that occur at different levels, each level having non-linear influences of the other. (Cartwright, 2010, p. 12)

The basic assumption here involves the idea that sensory experience, thoughts, phantasies, and associated psychic processes reverberate through a multidimensional field, creating fractal-like patterns that find different levels of representation and function. While in some areas of the field distinctions between internal and external reality emerge as important aspects of clinical experience, at other levels of experience these distinctions hold no currency. The field is populated with presences, characters, props, animate and inanimate objects, bastions, barriers, different feeling qualities, and so forth. All contribute to an intersubjective derivative commentary on the current evolving emotional reality (O) in the session.

I think that the theory of the analytic field is usefully extended by emphasizing its non-linear qualities. I want to emphasize the following aspects:

1. Multiple influences (external and internal, at varying experiential levels) are able to produce new *emergent* emotional experiences in the intersubjective field.
2. The field is self-organizing, generating fractal-like patterns of experience that have reciprocal influences on other aspects of the field. Ferro's (Ferro & Basile, 2011) notion of "inclusiveness"

is an example of these self-organizing qualities where any element in the field is imbued with characteristics of the field as a whole.
3. The field is open to continuous input, is context sensitive and unique to its particular interpersonal context. Given this, as Seligman (2005) points out, "questions of technique depend on the particular properties of the analytic system at any given moment" (p. 295).
4. In non-linear systems differences between structures, elements, functions, and processes cannot be easily made as they all stand in for one another, reflecting the natural ambiguity of the experiential field.

Much of Bion's thinking makes implicit reference to the above qualities. Alpha function, for instance, the mind's unknown "psychological transformer", operates on multiple levels of experience, suggesting the existence of a graded or multi-dimensional field comprising beta elements and alpha elements that have undergone a range of different transformations. Here, sensuous experience, proto-thoughts and proto-feelings (derivatives of alpha elements), more developed thoughts, operate simultaneously in different dimensions of the field. Within this, container-contained configurations and PS<->D operate in endless reciprocal, interchangeable, cycles (Bion, 1970), while "binocular vision" and the "reversible perspective" are evocative reminders of how multiple perspectives operate in the system awaiting the emergence of a self-organizing "selected fact" (Bion, 1962a).

In addition, the idea that psychic elements, functions, processes, and psychic structures may serve multiple functions and are not easily distinguishable is a common feature of Bion's work. As Grotstein (2013) has pointed out, the mental apparatus involved in thinking and dreaming, alpha function, container-contained, the contact barrier, PS<->D, negative capability and the "selected fact", caesuras and transcendence, and the binocular perspective, all appear to be cognates of each other: they share similarities and even stand in for each other, yet represent "differing facets of a unified, composite function" (2013, p. 123). For example, the fragmentation of alpha elements or dream-thoughts (PS) may become a barrier or caesura to new experiences, but it may simultaneously act as a container for other experiences. This may, in turn, form a contact barrier or a beta screen depending on other factors in the system. In this process, sensory and psychic elements take on some of the qualities of each other while remaining sufficiently distinct. In non-linear dynamic terms, psychic experience is organized around the principal of self-similarity (Marks-Tarlow, 1999) which has the effect of generating some degree of psychic stability in an otherwise chaotic system (Seligman, 2005).

All the above suggests a model of mind that operates like a complex self-organizing system where emphasis is placed on the *self as process*, rather than it being the product of psychic contents or static structures (Grotstein, 2007; Marks-Tarlow, 1999, 2011). This leaves us with questions about the central drivers behind "selves in process". For Bion, the most fundamental invariant in his theoretical system is organized around the drive to transform O (ultimate unknowable reality), the "formless infinite", into personal truths. Grotstein (2004) has put forward the idea that this constitutes a "truth drive" superordinate to the libidinal and death drives. With this in mind, we can think of oscillations between becoming O (or moving close to O) and representing it (K or Knowing) as constituting a central pulse in the field. This is compatible with Eigen's (2011) idea that all experiences are made up of distinction-union tendencies.

Tensions in the experiential field between sameness-difference, symmetry-asymmetry, symbiosis-individuation, integration-disintegration, the unknowable and the known, to name a few, all represent distinction-union tendencies, bimodal tensions aimed at accommodating, digesting, or evading emotional experience.

## Containment systems

In what follows, I want to consider the idea that container-contained configurations represent another variation of the distinction-union tendency that finds representation at different levels of psychic complexity. My main point is that the configuration works to negotiate experiences of "sameness" and "difference" in different ways depending on the level of complexity in the intersubjective field. From this perspective, it is possible to think of containment systems as being cognates of each other or variations of a function. For the purpose of discussion I have borrowed Bucci's (1997a) distinction between non-symbolic, pre-verbal, and symbolic experiences as a way of "framing" the various areas of the field that otherwise act in unison. I will use a case to try and illustrate the clinical utility of my abstractions.

### Non-symbolic process and the proto-container

Non-symbolic activities in the field involve the pre-reflective processing of sensory patterns or gradations of continuous experience through perceptual, affective, and motoric channels (Bucci, 1997a). A number of authors, from different perspectives, have begun to explore the idea that non-symbolic formats create elemental connections between subjectivities (e.g., Alvarez, 1992; Bruschweiler-Stern et al., 2002; Gallese, 2005; Trevarthen & Aitken, 2001; Tronick et al., 1998). Bion (1961) thought that proto-mental activity of this kind was driven by unformulated experience that led to "the instantaneous involuntary combination of one individual with another" (p. 153). It is "characterized by behavior in the human being that is more analogous to tropism in plants than to purposive behavior …" (p. 153). Similarly, Meltzer (1986) sees the proto-mental system as "habitual, automatic, unintentional" (p. 38), where boundaries between internal and external reality do not exist. We might say that in this area of mind the group is in the individual as much as the individual is in the group; distinctions between inside and outside cannot be made.

Bion introduces the term "beta elements" to represent hypothetical units of experience, unknowable in themselves, generated by sensory impressions that have the capacity to imprint or influence proto-mental capacities. Although beta elements are mostly referred to as "accretions of stimuli" fit for evacuation and projection (producing meaningless behavior, hallucinations, and psychosomatic disorders), Bion also thought of them as the basic building blocks of experience (Ogden, 2004), representing the hypothetical "stem cells" of experience. They occur in the immediacy of engagement with another, prior to representation in the mind, forming non-conscious analogical traces, affective contours emerging from the processes of interaction itself. Given this, is it possible to think about these experiences as proto-containing? Could it be that these non-symbolic experiences form the preconceptions, precursors, of the containing function represented in higher dimensions of the field? This would mean that proto-containing experiences are emergent phenomena.

In *Cogitations*, Bion (1992) speculates about the indigestible near-physical qualities of beta elements assuming the role of a container:

> Are "undigested facts" then used in the process of "digesting" other facts? Is their "indigestibility" a quality that renders them useful for this function, as if it were some kind of container for an eroding liquid which must be able itself to resist the erosion by its contents? (p. 52)

Although Bion never develops the idea of what "digesting" capacities occur at this level of mind, in *Elements of Psychoanalysis* (Bion, 1963), he puts forward the idea that beta elements undergo processes of agglomeration and dispersal that essentially mimic psychic mechanisms responsible for thinking proper. In his words, dispersed beta elements "may be regarded as an abortive prototype of a container" (1963, p. 40).

Elsewhere I have argued that Bion's ideas about a proto-mental system and his peripheral thoughts about the edifying role of beta elements may be linked to the generation of proto-containing experiences. I see proto-containing capacities as emerging out of the imitation of action-movement systems and attempts to organize experiences of "sameness" and "difference" in the experiential field (Cartwright, 2010). Below I summarize the main points of my speculations:

1. Non-symbolic sensory processes are orientated towards object seeking and tracking based on action-movement systems, tactile and auditory input. This involves the sensory processing of frame-by-frame repetitions and routines in an interactive field involving eye contact, gesticulations, changes in posture and facial expressions, non-verbal aspects of speech, the way gestures and sounds mirror or complement each other.
2. These pre-reflective effects and actions generate a sense of "being" through "doing" or "doing together". In this sense Winnicott's (1988) idiom "being before doing" is reversed in the proto-mental system.
3. Primary intersubjectivity is produced through processes of imitative identification (Gaddini, 1992) and embodied simulation (Gallese, 2005). This constitutes the "unthought" sensory background of the meaning-making subject and shapes the way internal reality forms and the quality of internal object relations.
4. The constant repetitions of action and movements in the non-symbolic field may be understood as "a primary means of apprehending or 'knowing' the object within the constraints of a psychic system that lacks complex dimensionality. It represents a crude manifestation of K, our best effort at 'thinking', a primitive counterpart of representational thought" (Cartwright, 2010, p. 125).
5. In this process, sensory impressions, beta elements, are organized or agglomerate around experiences of "sameness" and "difference", absence and presence of the object. This leads to the "patterning" of beta elements, leaving non-conscious analogical affective traces on the proto-mind.
6. The lack of negation and discrimination at this level of mind means that "sameness" and "difference" are not experienced as discrete or separate entities. Rather, they are experienced

as different points in a field, fluctuations of emotional intensities. There are no caesuras in the proto-mental system. This leads to psycho-physical experiences of a "sense of flow" or "moving along" inseparable from immediate interaction itself. Movements between "sameness" and "difference" create a pulse or a sense of rhythm that, in turn, produces reliable temporal shapes and feeling contours (Alvarez, 1992; Maiello, 2001). These might be understood as barely describable "pressures" similar to Stern's (2000) description of "vitality affects".

7. Following Bion, we may speculate that beta elements mimic or take on the natural intensities of external reality. They also mimic aspects of psychic reality in "abortive" or simulated attempts to integrate or contain experiences. In this way we may think of the existence of a "mimetic function" in the proto-mental system as a primitive counterpart of alpha function. The "mimetic function" represents an elemental means of apprehending the object by taking on its form. It aids in the formation of transient "adhesive identifications" (Bick, 1968) with the object.
8. Proto-containing experiences have an edifying role in the experience field. But because rhythmic, repetitive experiences are produced at a non-symbolic level, they give rise to a sense of being carried by interaction or by something "other". At a phenomenological level they are felt to "exist outside the self" (Bucci, 1997b, p. 159), perhaps cradling the self and other in interaction. Musicians refer to a similar experience when they describe a selfless sense of being carried by the rhythmic repetitions of the music.
9. These experiences may be thought of as representing a "potential third" emerging out of the interactive process itself (Maiello, 2001).
10. Projective identification makes little sense at this level of mind as it lacks the dimensionality to make use of internal/external differentiations or associated phantasies that drive the projective process.
11. Qualities of the proto-container, including the mimetic function, have referential impacts on other modes (subsystems) of generating experience. Conversely, proto-containing capacities can be impacted by more highly developed mental systems.

Given the dominance of symmetrical processes in the proto-mental system, proto-containing experiences remain ineffable and outside the realm of thought (Matte Blanco, 1988). When alpha function processes these kinds of experiences they are sequenced as continuous streams or affective contours of feeling, the emergent background flow of a self-resonating-with-the-other. Perhaps it is best represented by the sense of feeling lost in the musicality and timelessness of interaction or conversation. This is part of Winnicott's (1965) "environmental mother", but here emergent feeling states from the interactive process itself are being emphasized. The musicality and rhythm of interaction represents the emergence of something out of nothing. It seems to me to represent a primordial preparatory state for containing the "no-thing", thoughts, some "thing" that is not there. I turn now to considering how some of these speculations appear to be met with realizations in the clinical setting.

> Sarah came to see me in an attempt to deal with acute anxiety states that kept her from socializing with others. Although she was functioning well at work, at night she was often overwhelmed with anxiety and a sense of disintegration that she tried to control using alcohol.

In one of our first meetings, she described herself as "numb" to her own experience and appeared to live a duty-bound existence, aspiring to "correct" ways of being a mother and a wife. At one point, looking back on her inability to feel, Sarah remarked, "It wouldn't matter if I was raped by four men, I wouldn't feel a thing".

At a non-verbal level my experience was characterized by a number of particular features. Firstly, as I listened, as we discussed things face-to-face, I noticed that I was constantly trying not to focus on what I can only describe as a kind of "deadness" behind her eyes. I was fond of Sarah and looked forward to our sessions but there existed a kind of uncomfortable difficulty between us that I spontaneously tried to avoid. I felt like I was searching for a "lightness" or "aliveness" in Sarah. Indeed our discussions appeared to be lively, but there was little depth of feeling or reflection. Although during sessions I appeared engaged, I noticed how little space there was for reflection and reverie. Sarah worried about not being able to "take things in" from our sessions. This appeared to precipitate a deep sense of unarticulated shame and "stupidity" that was often managed using humor. I also noticed that I failed to recall much about our meetings.

As the therapy progressed, some dominant positions in the analytic field appeared to emerge. I was aware of worrying about exacerbating Sarah's anxiety and thought that I felt persecutory towards her. At other times, I felt I was pulled into the analytic field as some kind of "truth seer" and that everything I uttered was tantamount to an unwavering "truth" that Sarah could take on in a whole, undigested form.

I experienced our interaction as pressured and rushed, although we appeared to meaningfully connect. When I think about it now, it seemed we were enacting a kind of "hurried dance", as if we were trying to get everything covered before a storm hit or something dreadful happened. The storm usually took the form of a collapse of symbolic meaning where words were experienced as concrete real objects. These occurrences appeared to cause considerable anxiety between sessions, leaving Sarah preoccupied and repeating things I had mentioned in previous sessions as if trying to remain focused by clinging to "known facts" about herself.

On one such occasion, Sarah talked about feeling "lost" like her father. She explained that she would often disappear into herself and not hear what others were saying. When I wondered out loud about her experience with me, she said it was different because "we talked a lot". She said she was sometimes worried that her face would give away a sense of "lostness". In conversation I noticed that I hesitated and avoided using the word "lost" (not understanding why) but eventually said, "At least we can talk about this lost part of you". This apparently benign statement had catastrophic effects on the analytic field. It had the effect of freezing or deadening relatedness, seizing up the rhythmic flow of conversation. Perhaps more aptly described, my experience was one of creating a crater in the analytic field through which we both disappeared. Later, Sarah described these moments in terms of an overwhelming fear that "words became the whole of me and I felt like I disappeared".

Recovery from these states took the form of Sarah deferring to me, taking whatever I said as indisputable fact, in turn, overriding her own experience. These moments appeared to be captured by a sense of her mimicking me in order to restore some form of coherence. On one occasion she felt I was "talking slowly" and that this was somehow part of my intended technique and she attempted to do the same. On other occasions she would want to use the exact words I had used in a repetitious way. After experiencing the pressure to give her something that she could use as "truth", I found myself thinking about how difficult it must have been for her previous therapist to not lapse into giving instructions on how to live her life. Indeed much of Sarah's recollections of her previous therapy involved mantras on how to be herself, how to decorate her house, how and where to travel.

Sarah also used a number of other repetitive strategies in an effort to restore a coherent "sensory floor" (Ogden, 1992) to her experience. Most prominently, between sessions, she would ruminate and repeat things I said to her, talk to herself in the hope that the words would "eventually go inside and become part of me". Sarah would also rub her skin and use bodily sensations (often related to having a full bladder) to remind herself of her bodily presence. I supported her need to repeat things the way she did, sensing it remained an important way of maintaining some sense of coherence.

Returning to Bion's thoughts about hypothetical beta elements and proto-containing capacities, I understand the analytic field in the above account to be organized around affective resonances related to "lively" and "dead" eyes, two tracks of experience. As I try to connect with Sarah (and avoid my experience of deadness behind her eyes), I fall into an apparently meaningful but rapid conversation that feels safe and predictable. A rushed affective-time contour binds us through the rhythm of our interaction, creating a particular shape to proto-containing experiences. Here, beta elements, as well as proto-emotions and proto-thoughts (alpha elements), are entrained in a dance of continuities, carried by transient forms of adhesive identification and "difference" as we follow each other. But the affective build-up in the session is sometimes too much for the proto-container to bear. It amounts to a rupturing of proto-containing experiences and the emergence of thoughts and feelings that take on near-physical qualities in the room. It seemed to mark the eruption of "dead eyes" in the intersubjective field and a sense of "lostness" becoming real between us. This would play out between us through a series of concrete fearful exchanges organized around "symbolic equations" (Segal, 1981). Often my attempts to enquire about her internal world were met with a compounding fear that there was no "inside" and "outside", or a feeling that she did not have an "inside". Sarah would also describe micro-dissociative experiences linked to a sense that her thoughts and feelings did not feel like her own. When I happened to repeat some of her words, or tried to reflect on her experience she was met with a destabilizing realization that they were *her* thoughts. My words appeared to generate a kind of secondary shock to the system. "Can thoughts give you a heart attack?" she once asked. On another occasion she asked, "Can something from the outside really be inside me?". Later, when she was able to articulate some of this using her waking dream-thoughts, she recalled the terror of feeling like she was disappearing into her father's eyes, terrifying confusions she experienced between being asleep and being dead, and worries that her face looked "stiff" and dead.

My experience during sessions intrigued me. Although we engaged in a meaningful way, this did not seem to stop the escalation of overwhelming affect in other areas of the field. It was as if our joint alpha function capacities were quickly overwhelmed, giving rise to unmetabolized affective states that agitated her and could not be sufficiently contained. Eventually this led to Sarah experiencing words in a near-physical way, shutting down her capacity to think. Put another way, words appeared to lose their discriminating qualities as symmetrical pressures (Matte Blanco, 1988) on the field began to dominate, leading to a situation where words and her sense of self could not be separated.

I understand Sarah's reaction to the breakdown of proto-containing capacities to represent an attempt to use sensory experience to create a claustrum-like container where rhythmic, interactive non-symbolic experiences, along with proto-thoughts and proto-emotions, are related to as near-physical objects for the purpose of generating boundaries around the self. Here, emergent, interactive proto-containing experiences, complete with qualities of mimicry and repetition, are annexed for use by an isolated self to generate some sense of sensory coherence. I think this process describes a kind of "beta mentality" (Cartwright, 2010) where proto-thoughts, "undigested facts" or "balpha" elements (Ferro, 2000, 2005), are used to mimic reality so as to avoid learning from experience. It amounts to a cut-and-paste mentality where "being like" others takes the place of "becoming" one's feeling and thoughts (Bion, 2005). In keeping with thinking about the mind as modelled on non-linear dynamic systems that reflect different qualities of experience, balpha elements represent "partially digested beta elements that refer back to a ruminative pre-digestion that has not been finished" (Ferro, 2000, p. 104).

Sarah's concern about not being able to take things in and my lack of retention appears to relate to Bion's ideas about the retardation of alpha function being linked to deficits in notation, attention, and memory. In addition, deficits in alpha function and the production of alpha elements compromise the psyche's ability to discriminate between unconscious and conscious experience, as well as between external and internal reality. In Sarah's case, this appears to be associated with the build-up of unprocessed experience that overwhelms alpha function, giving rise to unmanageable "pressures" in the transference-countertransference and the production of semi-processed balpha elements that reduced our interaction to an exchange of "undigested facts".

### The containing function: pre-verbal process, reverie, and negative capability

At a level where greater dimensionality can be conceived, introjective and projective processes connect separate subjectivities in the field. Along with this, increased discrimination between internal and external reality, and an awareness of the interiority of self and other, defines the parameters of the container-contained configuration. Viewed from the perspective of dynamic systems, we could say that projective identification is an attempt to locate uncontainable psychic pain elsewhere in the field; a solution to dealing with ruptures in proto-containing experiences or a build-up of uncontainable affect and primitive mentation. Following Matte Blanco (1988), the build-up of unmetabolized affect has the effect of "symmetrizing" the interpersonal field, in turn, making the attribution of one's own mental states to another possible. Communication through projective identification is, however, always to some degree bi-logical in the sense that the object also has to be seen as somewhat separate or different (asymmetrical) to achieve a sense of ridding the self of unbearable experience. This way of thinking is consistent with my understanding that projective identification represents a particular way of organizing and dealing with tensions between "sameness" and "difference" in the analytic field which, in turn, needs to be complemented by the analyst's containing function.

Bion (1962b) makes the analyst's containing function an "essential feature of Melanie Klein's conception of projective identification" (p. 3). The containing function has been understood in varied ways in the literature (Alvarez, 1992; Britton, 1992a; Caper, 1999; Ferro, 2005; Grotstein, 2007; Hamilton, 1990; Lafarge, 2000; Meltzer, 1986; Mitrani, 2001; Ogden, 2004, 2007). I understand it to represent an intersubjective transformational process whereby proto-thoughts and feeling (alpha elements) that are projected into the field are rendered "thinkable" and meaningful as they gather narrative coherence. Here, alpha elements represent unique personalized snapshots of emotional experience (O). In Bion's words, "$\alpha$-elements may be presumed to be mental and individual, subjective, to a high degree personal, particular, and unequivocally belonging to the domain of epistemology in a particular person" (Bion, 1992a, p. 181). Alpha elements await a thinker to organize them so that disparate thoughts become a meaningful commentary on current emotional experience.

My sense is that the analyst's (and patient's) containing function is best understood using Bion's notion of a "balanced outlook" (1959, p. 313) as a starting point. In order to transform projective identifications into more tolerable and thinkable forms, the therapist/mother has to be immersed in the projective field in order to use his or her reverie to detect and contain emotional occurrences in the interactive process. But this, in my view, has to be balanced (Bion's "balanced outlook") with properties that demonstrate a "limiting function", realistic boundaries around what can be contained and thought about.

I see the containing function as an emergent capacity represented by the analyst's ability to balance opposing tensions in the field between immersion ("sameness") in the field and the capacity to retain a mind of his own ("difference"). Bion refers to the former as a process of the analyst "becoming the analysand" (Bion, 1965, p. 146), a process that stimulates what Cassorla (2009) refers to as "dreams-for-two" that help "name" and process unarticulated experience. I refer to this aspect of containing as the analyst's role as "dream object" in the field. The latter refers to the many ways the analyst demonstrates a capacity for independent thought, an aspect of the analyst's mind that remains relatively unmoved by the patient's projections. Previously, I have developed Caper's (1999) term, the analyst's role as "proper object", to refer to this function. But I am also referring here to additional aspects of the analyst's function that help steady and circumscribe the emotional field. For instance, Ferro (2005) sees the analyst as sometimes functioning like a "dam controller", steadying the analytic field by controlling the flooding effects that unprocessed experiences might have on the field.

Sarah would readily talk about many aspects of her life, but I was often left with a strange sense that her thoughts "came from somewhere else"; like she had marked herself absent and someone else was doing the work. This appeared related to the lack of "personalization" of her experiences. When I tried to respond by making observations in the spirit of getting her to reflect on the content of her associations, she would respond by treating my statements as absolute truths about herself, in turn arresting the containing process. This initially had the effect of shutting down thinking and the ability to tolerate thoughts from a separate mind. It led to experiences of invasion or intrusion in the field which I sometimes embodied. This changed however, when I was able to alter the way I engaged with Sarah.

Sarah started a session telling me that she had been absent-minded and had taken the wrong route to see me. I asked her why it was the "wrong" route. She said it took her through a dangerous part of town and this made her worry that criminals would "come in" and steal her car. She went on to say that she also worried that her absent-mindedness made her a "bad mother", although she tried very hard "to do what the books said". She explained that she baked "gingerbread men" with her children but was unsure of the recipe. Still discussing her children, Sarah recalled having to often check on them while they slept to make sure they were still breathing. She hastily went on to tell me about a time when her father slept while burglars entered the house. She felt that his remaining asleep saved him from attack. At this point Sarah reported having a sudden image of her father being strangled by the intruder. She worried that I would think she was mad for thinking such things. During the session I found it difficult to have access to my own thoughts but, as I listened to her pacey associations, I had an image of Sarah running; I thought about gingerbread men running before they got snapped up by an intruder. I tried to talk to her about a sense of intrusiveness that appeared to dominate the session along with references to how to escape (the O of the session). I was careful not to focus too much on the dangerous or destructive aspects of her derivatives, or transference aspects, as I sensed it would overly distress her. Nevertheless, Sarah appeared shocked by my noticing this. She worried that she was intrusive, she tried to work out a "recipe" for how she could stop others being intrusive; she wanted to know how to think like me in order to address "the problem". The word "intrusive", with its associated feeling states, appeared to overwhelm us both. Towards the end of the session Sarah went on to talk about a friend who she admired for living on her own and needing no help from others. She recalled running away from home at an early age in order to escape a depressed and intrusive mother but also felt that she had never managed to escape her. I heard these statements as references to experiencing my interventions as intrusive, while at the same time, taking them on as immutable facts.

Although partial interpretations of some of these aspects of our experience served to differentiate aspects of the field (bad intrusive objects that make her feel stupid, a need to escape, etc.), most of the time it felt like I was delivering some kind of astonishing fact that she quickly took up in a very concrete way and used it to replace or devalue any previous thoughts she had had on the subject. While promising meaning, her thoughts were quickly downgraded to fixed, immutable, near-physical objects that had little influence on expanding the emotional field. In short, aspects of our dialogue could not be used as "food for thought". This led to fantasies in me of remaining mute, voiceless, in the session and I feared that she would somehow never understand me.

I thought about these difficulties as representing failures in containment where dangerous intrusive aspects of the field could not be rendered "thinkable". Instead, aspects of reverie or waking dream-thoughts were downgraded to form an "abortive container" made up of bal-pha elements (Ferro, 2000). Pertaining to this particular fragment, almost everything was perceived as being intrusive or intruded upon, based largely on symmetry, leaving little room for other considerations and leaving little distinction between internal and external experience.

For these reasons, I held off from interpreting Sarah's need to fill the field with split-off aspects of herself that were linked to an "intrusive danger". Although it was sometimes difficult to keep up with Sarah's hurried discussion, I tried to remain open to her attempts at keeping the discussion alive, light, and free of real feeling, allowing her to make contact with me while I got caught up in the field. While doing so, I often found myself recalling Alvarez's (2010) notion of attending to "the self that is left behind" rather than simply focusing on metabolizing projected contents (in Sarah's case, dead, intrusive, terrorizing aspects). I thought that the quick "dance" in which we were embedded started to make contact with a different part of the field, a "hurried girl left behind". While listening I found myself trying to check the flow of associations simply by inquiring regularly and asking for clarification. Instead of trying to interpret content and motivation, I was more interested in attending to the "rush in the field" that seemed linked to an increase in anxiety. I made simple comments like "We have discussed a great deal, I find myself thinking about …", "Do you find we go really fast through things here, I sometimes do", "I didn't quite follow what you meant". Interventions of this nature appeared to have little immediate effect on the analytic field. But, to my surprise, a few sessions later, Sarah caught herself in mid-sentence, after many associations, saying, "I can't believe I do this! There are so many thoughts, I just had a sense that you can't possibly follow this all!" This marked her first attempt at reflecting on our minds in the process, the start of her "seeing myself, seeing you", as she put it. Sarah started to talk about her memories of having to get things hurriedly done while looking after her siblings and how overwhelmed she felt with the responsibility "of looking after little babies". My reverie was filled with images of her as a faceless child surrounded by out-of-control children, and I was reminded again of her running away from home as a teenager. "It is like there are so many baby thoughts in the room," I said, "it is difficult to know how to manage them." To this she replied, in a humorous way, "I could just kill all the little babies there are too many!"

In the next session Sarah said that her "killing babies" statement had filled her with fear and she had been preoccupied with the idea that she could actually kill something (it felt real and not just a thought). We found ourselves having a meaningful conversation (demonstrating more access to feeling states and reflection) about fearing the impact her feelings would have on others/me. Sarah reported a dream with some trepidation: She is sitting by a swimming pool (a pool seen from my practice) and she has just given birth to a baby "the natural way". The baby is held by me, barely alive with the umbilical cord still attached. I congratulate her. She is exhausted and responds "in some kind of slow alien language" (like a slowed down movie) and is worried that I will have to clean up the "afterbirth" in the pool.

In the session we discussed the possibility of the baby representing the birth of her own genuine thoughts in the session, with me trying to help, though she was worried about the impact (the afterbirth) this would have on me (I was anxious about seeing it as "our baby" and delivering another shock to the system). She seemed relieved by this understanding, but also worried about how "alien" she felt with others. She worried about the impact this had on her daughters because she felt she shut down feelings and "faked-it-to-make-it as a mother". Sarah's new-found ability to reflect on mental states had the effect of slowing down interaction, allowing us a more nuanced and circumscribed experience of "alien" feelings linked to a sense of feeling "dead" to others. Being able to hold these thoughts in mind led to her identifying a sense of shame and associated needs to hide behind others. She was also able to appreciate the triumph of having her own thoughts, while being mindful of her anxiousness about their impact on others.

The above fragment was somewhat of a watershed moment in terms of expansion of the analytic field and the revival of a more robust containing presence, where images of Sarah's "alien self", fears about her own destructiveness and her ability to care and feel, start to become "thinkable". It led to narratives about being intruded upon, suffocated by a maternal object, and a sense of feeling left out and ridiculed. Images of adopted children, abandoned babies, fake or copied objects used to avoid feeling, helped further develop contact with parts of herself that were previously mute, unbearable presences in the field.

Initially, there was little room for meaningful contemplative thought, despite the fact that Sarah produced a great deal of analytic material. I would say that the depth of my immersion in the field was too overwhelming for Sarah. In Matte Blanco's (1988) terms, components of the field were quickly "symmetrized" making it difficult for her to experience me as a separate object in the field. In short, although our interaction gave rise to waking-dream thoughts (my function as "dream object") we could not contain them as Sarah was unable to make use of me as a "proper" discrete object.

Later on, through changing my position in the field, I think I was able to steady "the rush" in our interaction through my function as a "proper object", checking the flow of associations either through action (inquiry) or attention. This had the effect of circumscribing an area of experience that could undergo containment and transformation (Meltzer, 1986). Secondly, it had the effect of implicitly demonstrating what a mind needs in order to think, complete with the need to tolerate frustration until meaningful thoughts occur. Finally, containment needs to work off a consensual reality (in Sarah's case, the idea that "the rush" makes it difficult to think and feel). By drawing attention to what appeared to be close to a consensual reality I am, in effect, also controlling my level of immersion in the field. I think of this position in the field as the analyst "taking care of the way things are", reflections on a consensual reality about common sense views that help circumvent an insistence on meanings that oversaturate the field.

The analyst's containing "proper object" function appears linked to Alvarez's (1992, 2010) idea about attending to introjective capacities ("the self left behind") as opposed to just focusing on disowned, split-off aspects of the self. It appeals to the non-psychotic aspects of the personality (Bion, 1957). As Alvarez has pointed out, contact with these aspects of the self promotes agentive qualities while split-off aspects are permitted to temporarily reside in the field (or in the analyst's mind). This also has the effect of holding off from stifling the containment process with saturated "all knowing" interpretations about projected contents.

My positioning in the field appeared to both open up and circumscribe a place for "dreaming", allowing for some form of emergent meaningful experience to arise. Perhaps we can say it opened up a negative space, a space to be filled with waking dream thoughts. Much has been written about "negative capability" and it links to stimulating reverie (e.g., Civitarese, 2012; Civitarese & Ferro, 2013; Ferro, 2005; Grotstein, 2007). I will not elaborate much here. I see it as linked to the analyst's capacity to use himself as "dream object". In Sarah's case, waking dream-thoughts about babies, baby thoughts, killing babies, faceless figures, all provide meaningful commentaries on our intersubjective experience. The "gap" in the field also allows for renewed powers of observation, and reflection gives rise to new (albeit half-living) ways of thinking along with fears about alien presences and their impact on others. This kind of dream-work (day and night) helps contain and render "thinkable" constricted and undeveloped aspects of the field. It amounts to the difference between having facts and knowledge about something (uncontained) and feeling it, becoming it, so it can be used to further emotional development. Expanding the container function in the intersubjective field becomes most evident when more narrative coherence appears to emerge around "selected facts", in turn, leading to less pressure to use evacuative projective identification as a form of action. As was the case with Sarah, it was accompanied by growing curiosity about her internal world and a renewed awareness and ability to feel. This also meant being able to make better use of the natural ambiguity of fictionalized experiences as they emerged in the field (Civiterese, 2012).

In terms of containment systems, I would say that proto-containing experiences between us, the repetitive "rushed" rhythm, allowed some form of elemental connection, in turn, allowing for containing proper to emerge (i.e., the use of reverie alongside the "proper object" function). Although experiences in the field still carried some "shock value" representing the rupturing of proto-containing capacities, this was diminished by being able to hold things in mind in a more bearable way. Furthermore, it had the effect of slowing down the interaction, altering the proto-container after being processed and re-entering the field.

The work of containing systems is iterative, reciprocal, and selective, leading to aspects of the field undergoing transformation at different tempos and in unforeseen ways. In Sarah's case, for instance, the arrival of meaningful "thinkable" thoughts appeared fused with attacks on the self ("shock" from an alien presence) that felt too "real" to think about. Her dreams, certainly in the initial phase of the therapy, appeared to bear the characteristics of both alpha elements and balpha elements. To digress a little, I understand "balpha dreams" to be closer to "flashes" of mentation that make dreams feel like an imposition. Some elements of the dream are felt to be too real and still possess near-physical qualities around which balpha elements can maintain some sense of self-integrity. They have some representational qualities when the dream is taken in its entirety as a "snapshot" of the experiential field. For instance, Sarah was worried, after having her dream, that she had really sat at the pool that appeared in her dream. These kinds of dreams are often felt to represent an alternative reality that has been received from somewhere else. It is as though the dream has us, rather than us having dreams. I see them as existing on the borderline between Bion's (1992) conceptualization of evacuative and introjective dreamwork processes. To return to Sarah, her "birth dream", as she described it, shared some of these qualities but also allowed some of its elements to undergo transformation. Perhaps in the spirit of Bion's "abortive container" and in line with the idea of emergent containing systems, we can say that sequences of balpha elements may act like an "abortive container" for the growth of alpha elements or the later development of dream-thoughts.

## Symbolic process: the symbol as container

Symbolic processes represent emergences in the field that act like highpoints or "epochs" that bind the experiential field at a higher level. Symbols "have properties of reference and generativity; they refer to and represent other entities, and they can be combined to generate infinite varieties of composite images and meanings" (Bucci, 1997b, p. 159). Symbolic representations can be linked to Bion's emphasis on fictionalizing experience where metaphorical processes become an essential part of being able to think. To quote Bion (1977), "metaphors can be the ghosts of ideas waiting to be born" (p. 418). If metaphors are the ghosts of ideas, I would see symbols as their transient homes or meeting places. Symbols emerge out of the analytic couple's ability to tolerate negative capability long enough so as to allow the "selected fact" to emerge. This represents the essence of the work of the symbol: to integrate similarities and conjunctions across fragments of experience (PS or differences) in a way that develops new ways of containing and thinking. The symbol represents transient movements to D (integration) which inevitably requires tolerating the differences between objects as well as the ineffable nature of experience itself. From this point of view the use of symbols not only involves mourning the loss of the object, but also involves mourning the loss of O. We can approach O through knowing (K), "become" it momentarily, to some extent, but it is always beyond us; we can never know the full sense or meaning of O.

Symbolic representations act as nodal points in an ambiguous nonlinear meaning-making process. Following Bion (1992), symbols are best understood to represent hypotheses that push thinking along and inspire curiosity. This is very different to an approach that attempts to decode symbolic material in a "top-down" manner, using chains of associations. Symbols are also not preordained, they emerge out of interactive, real-time experiences, in an unpredictable way and represent "private" configurations that link patient and analyst (Ferro, 2000). From the perspective of containment systems, symbols appear to emerge out of commensal container-contained configurations before they themselves become containers of the analytic couple.

> Sarah complained of feeling exhausted after "interacting with others", and worried that over the weekend the blank expression on her face gave away her "lost strangeness". As I listened, I found myself counting backwards, "5, 4, 3, 2, 1". I am reminded of a Bowie song, "Space Oddity". I thought: "Oddity or odyssey?", "Is it odd?", "Is it space? Am I lost in space?". I told her that it must be exhausting feeling that others see a strangeness in her and I recalled her "alien" dream. I asked her what is "strange". She said she went away for the weekend with lots of kids. She had the thought that she could not allow the children "to get inside her". I thought of alien babies and abductions. Sarah told me she coped by "running away" from the children now and then. She recalled a time when she stopped eating due to invasive surgery. As she says this, she reminds me that her words feel strange to her, as if they are not hers: "They feel dangerous because they are not mine", she said. "What is yours?" I asked. She replied that she felt her children were her own and recalls having to check on her daughter during the weekend to see if she was still "alive and well". I interpreted that she fears intrusions from others will have a deadly effect on her so it is important to keep checking. She agreed and says, "Yes, otherwise they become me". Sarah then reported "a strange dream" and looked embarrassed: She, as an adult, has a nappy on, but the faeces inside it is not her own. She wipes the outside of the nappy to hide any evidence of it. All the time she is thinking that she should just get a new nappy. Sarah feared that I would interpret the dream by saying she "is full of shit". We spoke about the faeces not being her own and she worried that I would see "the mess" as hers. We also talked about the possibility of "covering up" or finding a new nappy (which feels out of reach). I thought about my words and interpretations feeling too foreign to her and therefore excreted.

In the following session, Sarah reported she had watched a horror movie with her family, something she had never been able to do before. We spoke about her willingness "to take a look". She reported that the real horror came from cat noises she heard in the night that sounded just like a baby screaming. She thought that was why she dreamt of babies: Her daughter finds an abandoned foreign baby. She wonders if it is human and sees that it is. Her daughter wraps the baby in a plastic bag thinking she is helping. But she is suffocating the baby. Sarah, in anger, helps by taking the baby and putting it on her chest. After recounting the dream Sarah expressed relief that she could care. The words "imposter alien baby" emerge in my mind. I told Sarah that my mind seemed to focus on an "alien imposter baby" somewhere in the background while we spoke. "Yes", she replied. "I didn't know if it was human, that was the biggest fear". We entered a discussion: What does one do with an alien baby? Will it contaminate us? How does one care for an alien baby? Should one care? Perhaps it is better to kill it because others would think it dangerous and strange. Sarah recalled a memory of a psychiatrist asking her if her talking to herself was "inside or outside her head". She thought the psychiatrist felt she was mad and she became so anxious she had to be hospitalized. It was only herself and a friend, she recalled, who thought that it was not about "madness".

After a pause in the session, Sarah reflected on how much more "grounded" she felt, wanting less to run away. At some point I affirmed that she felt alive in the discussion, more herself. A thought flashed through her mind which she disclosed with surprise: "The aliens have landed, they must have babies". I suggested that she fears that if she is herself, I would experience her "baby" thoughts as strange and alien. I added that she would rather take on my thoughts to keep things safe.

Two sessions later Sarah reported a fantasy she had while driving to the session. She felt as if she was bringing a baby to therapy, but it is not her baby. She felt relief when she thought "it could go under the couch" so *she* could talk to me.

In the above account, "imposter alien baby" appears to emerge as a symbol linked to a "selected fact" between us. In keeping with a model based on non-linear dynamic systems, it represents an "attractor state" (Grotstein, 2007). The "selected fact" organizes shafts of interest between us, relating disparate themes of strangeness, occupation, intrusion, destructiveness, care, ambivalence, self-annihilation, shock and deprivation, confusion, and the near-physical qualities of her experience. It allows disparate emergences to cohere, particularly experiences about intrusive presences and foreign bodies that Sarah tries to cover up. Put another way, the symbol brings us closer to O where we can experience fictions of O as a personal "thinkable" presence in the field. We could say it carries, or knits together, disparate aspects of the field so it can undergo further development by alpha function. Furthermore, the symbol, as a container, also helps sequestrate aspects of the field so that other elements can emerge or be reconfigured. In Sarah's case, the "alien baby" begins to occupy a more distinct place in the field, undergoing many transformations. It had less of the shocking qualities that were previously tangible, although they were still there. But this allowed other experiences prominence in the field. In particular, this involved the emergence of narrative derivatives related to her "copying reality", cutting and pasting it, as a substitute for her own feared internal reality. In one session, she reported a dream that resembles some of the transformative elements of "dreams that turn over a page" (Quinodoz,

1999): Sarah decides to go to a new restaurant, but decides "not to eat yet". She anxiously goes home to a single flat and finds a large blue parrot in the room (mimicry as a substitute), she removes the beak and the parrot is killed. Out of its belly emerges a baby parrot. Sarah realizes that the chaotic wallpaper on the walls is easy to remove. Detailed development of the dream is not necessary here. I use it as an illustration of how other aspects of the field began to push for symbolic representation and integration. In Sarah's case it related to attending to and transforming breakdown elements of the proto-container referred to earlier, balpha elements based on mimicry that had various influences at different levels of complexity in the field. Here, the dream appears to illustrate how they undergo a fascinating "thinkable" transformation as Sarah grew more curious and less persecuted by internal "imposter states".

Bion (1962a) thought that the "selected fact" emerges out of the intersection between two models: the analyst's own meaning-making and the model implicit in the patient's experience. It also depends on the patient's and analyst's capacity to generate a third object that expands their ability to think. The third object represents the products of both minds producing a commensal symbol. For Bion (1970), commensal container-contained configurations represent "a relationship in which two objects share a third to the advantage of all three" (p. 95). In my view, the emergence of the symbolic third sets up a dynamic nesting process where patient and analyst are either contained by the "third", or contain it, in turn, expanding psychic dimensionality. Within these dialectical movements the symbol itself becomes the container. This is similar to Britton's (1992b) notion of "triangular space" (p. 86) where mother and infant tolerate a creative influence alongside having to deal with attendant anxieties linked more clearly to the depressive position. The commensal container depends on relinquishing control of the object and tolerating difference and separateness. This can only take place if the analytic couple feels contained by the affective contours created by non-conscious proto-containing experiences.

The symbol holds the fractal qualities of the system as it organizes itself around distinction-union experiences. Here, asymmetrical relations evident in projective-introjective symbiotic relatedness are partially resolved by the creation of a third. Put another way, symbolic processes momentarily unburden symbiotic relatedness, allowing the analyst's and patient's reverie to reconfigure in a different way. For example, in Sarah's case, the gradual integration of "the mimic" into the field (represented by a parrot, as well as a chameleon and a copying clown), allows other "characters" to gain prominence. It shifts the analytic field where waking-dreams thoughts about an "invisible deadness inside", penetrating missiles, fantasies of debris freed from the body, gain prominence.

What breakdown products occur at the symbolic level? I noticed with Sarah, when she spoke to me about her fantasy of bringing a baby to therapy, I wanted to joke with her about the baby not being able to fit under the couch. I was very aware that this would shock her, make her feel the baby was "too real". I thought about my place in the field as representing some kind of malevolent jester wanting to attack elemental symbolic activity while hiding behind humor. Attacks on the emergent containing capacities of symbolic activity appear to be one area of potential breakdown in the field. A second occurs when selected facts, represented by symbols, become saturated and lose emotional value. They take on fanatical characteristics and cannot be given up or transformed. In terms of emotional growth, they become "dead symbols", resistant to the continuous reworking of alpha function. In its place, symbolic objects, previously rich with meaning, become the repositories for undigested facts and assertions of fixed truths. For instance, I imagine this happening for Sarah if the "imposter alien baby" starts to be seen as the sole reason or "recipe" for all her difficulties and ceases to be a transient representation of experience that can be thought about. Here, the container cannot be broken up and reconfigured along with the evolving emotional context (O).

One final point: Perhaps it goes without saying that in demonstrating containment systems in the field, much of the transformative work takes place in the transference, within the microtransformations of dialogue, not necessarily through interpreting it (Ferro, 2005, 2009; Ferro & Basile, 2011). I am referring here to saturated interpretations that often have the effect of creating caesuras in the field. There are many examples of oral and anal themes, signs of splitting, and so forth, emerging in the transference in this case. But I tend not to interpret them as discrete elements, objects or defenses, I rather allow them to undergo transformation through expansion of dialogue, expansion of the container, as it is represented in the many dimensions of the field.

## Conclusion: birth attendants in the analytic field

> "… births keep occurring and we cannot keep up with them. We can only live them in a piecemeal fashion, a little here, a little there, sometimes a little more. And every bit of this kind of living makes a difference to the quality of the whole."
>
> Eigen, 2011, p. 12

In *The Italian Seminars*, Bion (2005) tells us: "You have to *dare* to think and feel whatever it is that you think and feel, no matter what your society or your Society thinks about it, or even what *you* think about it" (p. 13). I read this as testament to how we have to allow the emancipatory aspects of the field, with all its non-linear workings, to work through us. In this chapter I have tried to show, theoretically and in clinical work, how containment systems function to make this a possibility. Proto-containing capacities, the use of reverie and symbolic process are all transformative in different ways (themselves transforming each other) as they negotiate "sameness" and "difference" in the field. They represent fractals of the container-contained configuration shaped by the self-similarity of mental and proto-mental processes. As analyst and patient wait for emergences in the intersubjective field, to borrow Eigen's (2011) eloquent words, they act like "birth attendants", co-presences, "necessary for the birth to happen, although neither [know] of the pregnancy until the baby [is] born" (p. 12).

## References

Alvarez, A. (1992). *Live Company: Psychoanalytic Psychotherapy with Autistic, Borderline, Deprived and Abused Children*. London: Routledge.

Alvarez, A. (2010). Levels of analytic work and levels of pathology: The work of calibration. *The International Journal of Psychoanalysis*, 91: 859–878.

Baranger, M. (1993). The mind of the analyst: From listening to interpretation. *The International Journal of Psychoanalysis*, 74: 15–24.

Baranger, M., & Baranger, W. (2008). The analytic situation as a dynamic field. *The International Journal of Psychoanalysis*, 89: 795–826.

Baranger, M., Baranger, W., & Fiorini, L. G. (2011). *The Work of Confluence: Listening and Interpreting in the Psychoanalytic Field*. London: Karnac.

Bick, E. (1968). The experience of the skin in early object-relations. *The International Journal of Psychoanalysis, 49*: 484–486.

Billow, R. M. (2003). *Relational Group Psychotherapy: From Basic Assumptions to Passion* (Vol. 26). London: Jessica Kingsley.

Bion, W. R. (1957). Differentiation of the psychotic and the non-psychotic personalities. *International Journal of Psychoanalysis, 38*: 266–275.

Bion, W. R. (1959). Attacks on linking. *The International Journal of Psychoanalysis, 40*: 308–315.

Bion, W. R. (1961). *Experiences in Groups*. London: Tavistock.

Bion, W. R. (1962a). *Learning from Experience*. London: Karnac.

Bion, W. R. (1962b). A Theory of thinking. *International Journal of Psychoanalysis, 43*: 306–310.

Bion, W. R. (1963). *Elements of Psychoanalysis*. London: Karnac.

Bion, W. R. (1965). *Transformations*. London: Heinemann.

Bion, W. R. (1970). *Attention and Interpretation*. London: Tavistock.

Bion, W. R. (1977). *A Memoir of the Future: The Past Presented* (Vol. 2). London: Karnac.

Bion, W. R. (1977a). *Two Papers: "The Grid" and "Caesura"*. London: Karnac.

Bion, W. R. (1992). *Cogitations*. London: Stylus.

Bion, W. R. (2005). *The Italian Seminars*. London: Karnac.

Britton, R. (1992a). Keeping things in mind. In: R. Anderson (Ed.), *Clinical Lectures on Klein and Bion* (pp. 102–113). New York: Routledge.

Britton, R. (1992b). The Oedipus situation and the depressive position. In: R. Anderson (Ed.), *Clinical Lectures of Klein and Bion*. London: Routledge.

Bruschweiler-Stern, N., Harrison, A. M., Lyons-Ruth, K., Morgan, A. C., Nahum, J. P., Sander, L. W., et al. (2002). Explicating the implicit: The local level and the microprocess of change in the analytic situation. *The International Journal of Psychoanalysis, 83*: 1051–1062.

Bucci, W. (1997a). *Psychoanalysis and Cognitive Science: A Multiple Code Theory*. New York: Guilford Press.

Bucci, W. (1997b). Patterns of discourse in "good" and troubled hours: A multiple code interpretation. *Journal of the American Psychoanalytic Association, 45*: 155–187.

Caper, R. (1999). *A mind of One's Own: A Kleinian View of Self and Object* (Vol. 32). London: Routledge.

Cartwright, D. (2010). *Containing States of Mind: Exploring Bion's' container model in psychoanalytic psychotherapy*. London: Routledge.

Cassorla, R. (2009). Reflections on non-dreams-for-two, enactment and the analyst's implicit alpha function. In: H. B. Levine & L. J. Brown (Eds.), *Growth and Turbulence in the Container/Contained: Bion's Continuing Legacy*. Hove: Routledge, 2013.

Civitarese, G. (2012). *The Violence of Emotions: Bion and Post-Bionian Psychoanalysis*. London: Routledge.

Civitarese, G., & Ferro, A. (2013). The meaning and use of metaphor in analytic field theory. *Psychoanalytic Inquiry, 33*: 190–209.

Eigen, M. (2011). *Contact with the Depths*. London: Karnac.

Ferro, A. (2000). Sexuality as a narrative genre or dialect in the consulting-room: A radical vertex. In: P. Bion Talamo, F. Borgogno & S. Merciai (Eds.), *W. R. Bion: Between Past and Future*. London: Karnac.

Ferro, A. (2005). *Seeds of Illness, Seeds of recovery: The Genesis of Suffering and the Role of Psychoanalysis*. London: Routledge.

Ferro, A. (2009). *Mind Works: Technique and Creativity in Psychoanalysis*. London: Routledge.

Ferro, A., & Basile, R. (2011). *The Analytic Field: A clinical Concept*. London: Karnac.
Gaddini, E. (1992). *A Psychoanalytic Theory of Infantile Experience: Conceptual and Theoretical Reflections*. London: Routledge.
Gallese, V. (2005). Embodied simulation: From neurons to phenomenal experience. *Phenomenology and the cognitive sciences, 4*: 23–48.
Ghent, E. (2002). Wish, need, drive: Motive in the light of dynamic systems theory and Edelman's selectionist theory. *Psychoanalytic Dialogues, 12*: 763–808.
Grotstein, J. S. (2004). The seventh servant: The implications of a truth drive in Bion's theory of O. *The International Journal of Psychoanalysis, 85*: 1081–1101.
Grotstein, J. S. (2007). *A Beam of Intense Darkness: Wilfred Bion's Legacy to Psychoanalysis*. London: Karnac.
Grotstein, J. S. (2013). Dreaming as a "curtain of illusion". In: H. B. Levine & L. J. Brown (Eds.), *Growth and Turbulence in the Container/Contained: Bion's Continuing Legacy*. Hove: Routledge.
Hamilton, N. G. (1990). The containing function and the analyst's projective identification. *International Journal of Psychoanalysis, 71*: 445–453.
Lafarge, L. (2000). Interpretation and containment. *International Journal of Psychoanalysis, 81*: 67–84.
Maiello, S. (2001). On temporal shapes. The relation between primary rhythmical experience and the quality of mental links. In: J. Edwards (Ed.), *Being Alive: Building on the Work of Anne Alvarez* (pp. 179–194). London: Brunner-Routledge.
Marks-Tarlow, T. (1999). The self as a dynamical system. *Nonlinear Dynamics, Psychology, and Life Sciences, 3*: 311–345.
Marks-Tarlow, T. (2011). Merging and emerging: A nonlinear portrait of intersubjectivity during psychotherapy. *Psychoanalytic Dialogues, 21*: 110–127.
Matte Blanco, I. (1988). *Thinking, Feeling, and Being*. London: Routledge.
Meltzer, D. (1986). *Studies in Extended Metapsychology: Clinical Applications of Bion's Ideas*. Strathclyde, Perthshire: Clunie.
Mitrani, J. L. (2001). "Taking the transference": Some technical implications in three papers by Bion. *The International Journal of Psychoanalysis, 82*: 1085–1104.
Ogden, T. H. (1992). *The Primitive Edge of Experience*. London: Karnac.
Ogden, T. H. (2004). On holding and containing, being and dreaming. *The International Journal of Psychoanalysis, 85*: 1349–1364.
Ogden, T. H. (2007). *This Art of Psychoanalysis: Dreaming Undreamt Dreams and Interrupted Cries*. London: Routledge.
Quinodoz, J. M. (1997). Transitions in psychic structures in the light of deterministic chaos theory. *International Journal of Psychoanalysis, 78*: 699–718.
Quinodoz, J. M. (1999). "Dreams that turn over a page": integration dreams with paradoxical regressive content. *International Journal of Psychoanalysis, 80*: 225–238.
Segal, H. (1981). *The Work of Hanna Segal: A Kleinian Approach to Clinical Practice*. New York: Jason Aronson.
Seligman, S. (2005). Dynamic systems theories as a metaframework for psychoanalysis. *Psychoanalytic Dialogues, 15*: 285–319.
Stern, D. N. (2000). *The Interpersonal World of the Infant: A View from Psychoanalysis and Developmental Psychology*. London: Basic Books.
Trevarthen, C., & Aitken, K. J. (2001). Infant intersubjectivity: Research, theory, and clinical applications. *Journal of Child Psychology and Psychiatry, 42*: 3–48.

Tronick, E. Z., Bruschweiler-Stern, N., Harrison, A. M., Lyons-Ruth, K., Morgan, A. C., Nahum, J. P., et al. (1998). Dyadically expanded states of consciousness and the process of therapeutic change. *Infant Mental Health Journal, 19*: 290–299.
Winnicott, D. W. (1965). *The Maturational Processes and the Facilitating Environment*. London: Hogarth.
Winnicott, D. W. (1988). *Babies and their Mothers*. London: Free Association.

CHAPTER SIXTEEN

# The hat on top of the volcano: Bion's 'O' and the body–mind relationship

*Riccardo Lombardi*

"The inescapable bestiality of the human animal is the quality from which our cherished and admired characteristics spring."

—W. R. Bion, 1970, pp. 65–66

In this work I shall be attempting to indicate parallels between Bion's O and the body–mind relationship—which I have explored on various occasions in the light of my clinical experience—setting out my own variations on several theories of A. B. Ferrari, which assign a central position to the body as the concrete original object (Ferrari, 2004, Lombardi, 2002). The theoretical and conceptual spheres represented by Bion and Ferrari do, of course, differ, since they are grounded in diverse perspectives, but the two men's thinking can reveal some interesting points of interaction and, given the fact that Ferrari was a student of Bion's in Brazil, they can give us an indication of how some of Bion's theories might be developed.

In his theory of the eclipse of the body, Ferrari maintains that mental functioning is initiated by the cooling down of primitive raw sensoriality, which was originally incandescent and overwhelming. Maternal—or analytic—reverie contributes to lowering the sensory tension, but the actual operation of putting the sense data into perspective takes place inside the infant or patient. Ferrari discriminates between a horizontal relationship between the analyst and the analysand and a vertical body–mind relationship: they are both constantly present, but distinguishing one from the other points the way to a specific working through on the vertical axis in all those cases in which this represents the patient's most urgent needs and can further analytic development.

The phenomena of intersection between mental notation and sense data are a constant point of reference for mental activity. As regards Bion's emphasis on symbol formation, Ferrari stresses that the body continues to be present even during the most abstract mental processes: it is only temporarily eclipsed by the mind's activity, but is ready to re-emerge in the foreground with its overwhelming structural ethological baggage on any occasion of intensification of emotions. Thus what is sacrificed by Ferrari is the distinction between thought-friendly alpha elements and thought-hostile beta elements, and especially the viability of the body-mind relation, which, when functioning, creates the conditions for access to thought or, on the contrary, blocks access when it has shut down.

While for Bion (1962) thinking always takes place in the presence of feelings, Ferrari favors the microphenomena of sensory perception to the more developed interaction between feeling and thought. Thus, the eclipse of the body has the advantage of being a hypothesis oriented specifically towards the way the body and the mind interact, focusing on the areas in which most primitive phenomena responsible for mental functioning are organized. In this sense Ferrari's hypotheses seem particularly up-to-date, since they foreshadowed the most recent findings in neuroscience that reveal a close connection between awareness of the body and the ability to feel—emphasizing that "feelings are likely to arise from maps of body states" (Damasio & Carvalho, 2013, p. 146)—and consider our bodily self-experiences determinant for the understanding of intersubjectivity (Gallese & Ebisch, 2014).

Bion's psychoanalytic contribution unsurpassably develops the thought-centered analytic perspective introduced by Freud. At the same time it marks a blockage point, such that psychoanalytic research can acquire new impetus and explore new horizons *only* by starting from the pre-mental generative levels: the body, in short, can become the new starting point of psychoanalytic explorations (Ferrari & Lombardi, 1998).

So we shall now consider some areas of intersection between Bion's ideas—his O hypothesis in particular—and the body-mind relationship.

## The mystery of a constant conjunction

Bion reminds us of the need for a "constant conjunction" within the analytic setting, although it might take us years to understand what it is in our experience of analysis that is doing the conjoining and what exactly this conjunction means. This puts us in mind of how the analyst must constantly bear the anxiety of the unknown, together with a "becoming" that contains certain terrifying characteristics: "of all the hateful possibilities, growth and maturation are feared and detested most frequently" (1970, p. 53). It is from this central presence of the unknown that there ensues the disproportion between the massive engagement required by analysis and the scarcity of means at our disposal for explaining to ourselves and communicating what is happening.

The anxieties that are called forth in the analyst can be so strong that they activate a tireless quest for external approval, a "popular repute" that reassures the analyst that his analytic ability is not in question. Bion is trenchant on the subject, as he considers "popular repute" to be "notoriously fickle and unreliable, and unsuited for use as a foundation for any judgement" (1970, p. 62): a point of view that is decidedly polemical for the analytic current that cleaves ever more closely to the notion of the identity of analytic capacity with institutional power (Lombardi, 2006).

One cannot deny that there is something defensive about a certain verbal "Bionism", in which it seems that "the container extracts so much from the contained that the contained is left without substance ... An illustration would be the word used as a metaphor until the background is lost and the word loses its meaning" (1970, pp. 106–107). Reference to Bion is thus in danger of serving to *deactivate* the explosive nature of the psychoanalytic experience, rather than to *develop* it, so that—to paraphrase Bion himself (1970, p. 78)—we can fear that Bion "risks being loaded with honours and sinking without a trace".

The endurance of darkness and mystery is most particularly necessary when dealing with so-called severe cases which confront us with our limitations in the matter of translating and communicating our analytic experience, given that the "available verbalizations do not provide the psychoanalyst with appropriate formulations" (1970, p. 63): a problem which is made all the more complex by the fact that, when we seek to transmit our clinical experience, "no vertex at present recognized is adequate" (ibid.). So psychoanalysis cannot survive except in a context that is open to the quest for new vertices that are in line with the experience of our most extreme analysands. In his attention to the toleration of mystery and uncertainty, Bion seems to be a direct heir of the Freud who loved the midnight gloom described by Goethe:

> *Nun ist die Luft von solchem Spuk so voll,*
> *Dass niemand weiss wie er ihn meiden soll*
>
> (Now is the air with horror's brood so dense
> That no hope flickers of deliv'rance hence) (*Faust*, Part II, Act V, Scene 5)

### Bion's O

In an attempt to open psychoanalysis towards new horizons, Bion summons up the Kantian concept of the thing-in-itself and suggests that psychoanalytic events cannot be known directly. O denotes the "ultimate reality, absolute truth, the godhead, the infinite" (1970, p. 26) of the psychoanalytic experience, which cannot be known "in itself" since it is "darkness and formlessness". O has, however, the potential of "becoming" and of being knowable (K) at a certain point of its evolution.

If the analyst becomes O, he is capable of becoming acquainted with the events that are a development of O; and this particular "becoming O" has to do with Being, rather than with knowledge. The analyst cannot *know* the patient's O, but can *be* the O that corresponds to that O (Bion, 1970, p. 27). Since "Being" is involved, the interference of lying takes on ontological, even more than cognitive, characteristics, so that "there can be no genuine outcome that is based on falsity" (Bion, 1970, p. 28).

Memory and desire are an obstacle to becoming O to the extent that they introduce an element of saturation that stands in the way of at-one-ment with O. In the case of memory, the element of saturation introduced is an obstacle to the free unfolding of mental functioning: "an analyst with such a mind is one who is incapable of learning because he is satisfied" (Bion, 1970, p. 29). Similarly, sense conditioning—derived from the desire that the patient be well—is damaging. By avoiding memory and desire "the psycho-analyst and the analysand achieve a state in which both contemplate the irreducible minimum that is the patient" (1970, p. 59) and develop a faith in a "psychoanalytic experience which remains ineffable" (1970, p. 35). Failing to follow the "difficult discipline" (1970, p. 56) connected to the suspension of memory, desire, and knowledge "will lead to a steady deterioration in the powers of observation whose maintenance is essential" (1970, p. 51).

In its tendency to counter the force of sensual desire coming from the pleasure principle (Freud, 1911), the experience of O introduces a series of important features:

- an observational framework for the analyst and a discipline that is not subject to personal will;
- an approach to unknown internal experiences in a context of intersubjective syntonization;
- a temporal syntonization that opens to a continuous updating in the context of the session and of the analysis;
- an obstacle to intellectual control;
- a specific focus on unknown phenomena that should be explored.

From his psychotic patients, Bion had learned to recognize the danger lurking in symbol saturation, which leads to transforming all acts into symbolic acts, with a possible delusional outcome. The tendency towards constant symbolization represents a serious danger for the functioning of a so-called normal mind as well: when the analyst keeps himself constantly anchored to his knowledge and his symbol-forming ability, he or she falls into a "premature saturation", which impedes the experience of an unsaturated mind and the development of the normal process of symbol-formation (1970, p. 68).

Bion's misgivings about the operation of memory and desire seem to extend to all cognitive activity when he cautions his readers not to assume they can reach O through knowledge: "At-one-ment with O would seem to be possible through the transformation K->O, but it is not so" (1970, p. 30). This reveals important implications about the role one should attribute to feeling and to the body-mind dialogue, which I shall be exploring in the next section.

The marginalization of knowledge (K) in a universe dominated by O should have important implications for psychoanalytic training as it is provided in seminars. This training is only too often reduced to mere cognitive activity with strict monitoring: indeed in some psychoanalytic societies attendance is now required at an established schedule of seminars, and candidates are subject to annual evaluations. This emphasis on the mandatory nature of knowledge and on well-policed inspection—which was conceived essentially to rear new generations of a "ruling caste" which is "not by nature fitted to have direct experience of *being* psychoanalytic" (1970, p. 73)—can have nothing but harmful effects on successive generations, given the current state of psychoanalysis, already afflicted with conformism and a lack of creativity.

Borrowing a concept from Keats, Bion focuses on "negative capability", "that is, when a man is capable of being in uncertainties, mysteries, doubts, without any irritable reaching after fact and reason" (John Keats, quoted by Bion, 1970, p. 125). He also underlines the role of "patience", by means of which the analyst can "relate to what is unknown", even for long periods. Exercising "patience" leads to "security", in which the analyst becomes able to put together his scattered observations, think symbolically, and produce interpretations (1970, p. 124).

## Bion's O and the body-mind relationship

I believe that the emphasis—introduced by Bion—on the unsaturated condition can be traced to the experience of one's relationship with one's own body and with sensoriality as ontological conditions of one's belonging to oneself and to one's ethological matrix. The mental experience of the body is characterized by continuous evolution and change—as is the case with the condition of "becoming" that Bion describes for O—since the world of sensations is in constant and unpredictable motion.

In this sense it seems to me that Bion's scrutiny of O leads his gaze to a condition that in certain ways corresponds to the body-mind relationship: and surely Bion is admitting that there is a relationship between O and feeling when he says that "its presence can be recognized and *felt*" (1970, p. 30; my italics). Obviously this does not mean that Bion's vertex is directed towards the body-mind relationship, since it is declaredly focused on mental functioning *tout court*: but nevertheless this observation of his about O and what is felt is still significant because it takes him back to a more human and subjective dimension of feeling.

In fact Bion's insistent emphasis on the ineffable meaning of the psychoanalytic experience and on O as "ultimate reality, absolute truth, the godhead" leaves his approach open to an interpretative tendency of a spiritualistic, religious, even mystical nature, even though it is evident from his whole output that his work is distinctly empirical in method. Hence it seems to me that a dialectical juxtaposition of Bion's propositions and the "ineffable" dimension of physical sensations as an expression of the deepest and most concrete levels of the unconscious might broaden the pragmatic implications of his hypotheses.

My attempt to effect a meeting between O and the body-mind relationship might seem less paradoxical if we were to think of the importance that Freud attributed to the relationship between the body and the unconscious (cf. 1915a, 1915b, the correspondence with Groddeck), even in the conclusion to the *Outline of Psychoanalysis* (1940), in which he states, "there would thus be no alternative left to assuming that there are physical or somatic processes which are concomitant with the psychical ones and which we should necessarily have to recognize as more complete than the psychical sequences, since some of them would have conscious processes parallel to them but others would not. If so, it of course becomes plausible to lay the stress in psychology on these *somatic processes*, to see in them *the true essence of what is psychical*" (1940, p. 157, my italics). It is in this sense that we can see the experience that Bion calls O as connected—with full respect for the difference in the implied vertices—with the concrete levels of the unconscious (Freud, 1915b), as well as with the body, understood as the primary object of the mind (Ferrari, 2004).

Bion stresses the importance of reaching the unsaturated condition characteristic of O, by tolerating the depression and feelings of persecution that are associated with it. If we alter the vertex and take a look at the area involving body-mind that Bion explored, we might conclude that the "unknown, incoherent, formless void" state of O (1970, p. 52) is actually empty only cognitively, if it corresponds to approaching the subject's sensory world. Approaching one's sensations coincides with the void to the extent that we are speaking of an area that is difficult to describe or define and structurally alien to thought (Lombardi, 2009a, 2009b). The feeling of persecution that Bion describes as deriving from elements of an O in evolution can then be viewed, alternatively, as the expression of the experience of approaching the overwhelming and incandescent nucleus of primitive sensations, which is unknowable and unthinkable precisely because it is structurally alien to thought.

On the other hand, Bion was anything but unaware of the motive power that the body represents for the mind: it was not by chance that he felt that "the inescapable bestiality of the human animal is the quality from which our cherished and admired characteristics spring" (1970, pp. 65–66). The analytic experience becomes a decisive challenge for the development and awareness of the animal and bodily matrices of the personality: "love, hate, dread, are sharpened to a point where the participating pair may feel them to be almost unbearable" (1970, p. 66). Thus there seems to be no doubt that Bion was aware of the propulsive role played by the investigation of the connection of the mind with its bodily matrices (cf. also Lombardi, 2008). But then how ever did Bion come to place this repeated emphasis on the value of the mental level to the point of setting it against the sensory dimension?

## Differentiation between sensory and mental

If we are to increase our understanding of this question we should not forget that Bion was interested first of all in revaluing an orientation towards thinking; his reference point is Freud's hypothesis (1911) of the two principles of mental functioning, according to which the pleasure principle involves a sensual pressure towards fulfillment, which is in contrast with setting in motion an orientation towards thinking, based on the capacity for tolerating frustration and the containment of motor discharge. With this presupposition in mind, we can observe that Bion was interested in contrasting the mental and the sensory dimensions, relegating the role of the body to the sphere of the pressure of desire and its satisfaction. As Bion consistently pursued this line, he inevitably left unexpressed the active role that the experience of the body plays in constructing the ego and in the differentiation of the personality: an absolutely central role, as Freud had indicated that "the ego is first and foremost a bodily ego" (1923, p. 26), further specifying, in a note added in 1927 to the same work, that "the ego is ultimately derived from bodily sensations, chiefly from those springing from the surface of the body. It may thus be regarded as a mental projection of the surface of the body, besides, as we have seen above, representing the superficies of the mental apparatus" (1923, p. 26).

In keeping with an approach comprising the opposition of the two principles of mental activity, Bion considered that "the "act of faith" has no association with (…) sensation" (1970, p. 35) and that "the central phenomena of psychoanalysis have no breakdown in sense data" (1970, p. 35). Bion meant thereby to emphasize that symbol formation requires a distancing from the sensory level: from this perspective the revaluation of the sensory level would in fact expose thought to a risk of confusion with sensation and desire, whereas thought must quite properly accentuate its difference from the sensory level and from the domination of the pleasure principle: otherwise it would be unable to have any containment function for sensory and affective events.

Thus, for the sake of conceptual clarity, we must keep the two components of the body-mind relationship well differentiated: whereas, at the first level—as Bion underscores—we must free ourselves from the restrictive conditioning of sensory data dominated by the pleasure principle if we are to approach mental activation, at the second level—that needs a specific working-through in primitive mental states—there must be activated a functioning body-mind relationship, as a prerequisite for the setting in motion and continuation of mental functioning. This involvement of sensory data is necessary, both as a safeguard against the danger of self-referential and abstract thinking that loses all connection with the concrete levels of the personality, and as a protection of an orientation towards thinking in the presence of emotions, which Bion (1962) considered fundamental.

An exclusive emphasis on the phenomena of thought and the analytic relationship, such as can occasionally be seen in certain followers of Bion, runs the risk of obscuring the role of the sensory dimension which perforce accompanies the phenomena of thought—those basic ineffable experiences that can at times be so urgent that "the participating pair may feel them almost unbearable". Spotlighting this "almost unbearable" sensory dimension that arises from the relationship with sensations and feelings can lead to a more effective value of the contributions of the individual subjectivities of analyst and analysand: each is, in fact, endowed with a different constitutional sensitivity to the impact of sensations and emotions, so that they tend to develop different characteristics of thought on the abstract plane. As regards the importance of mental activity that develops on the evolutive axis of body, affect, and thought (Lombardi, 2009a), the very concept of "thought without a thinker" risks fostering the erroneous notion of *disembodied* thought, in which the role of feeling is secondary and unimportant. With this assertion I do not, of course, intend to deny the argumentative value that this hypothesis can, in other ways, have in the context of Bion's theory of thinking.

## *The hidden tsunamis of the analytic encounter*

When we are facing clinical experience, we discover that one of the extreme aspects of the challenge that work with so-called serious cases offers us derives from the almost unbearable ineffable sensations we discover within ourselves, at the border between the unconscious and the conscious, as a result of the broadening of experience consequent upon our relationship with the analysand. Failing to recognize the development of our own emotional life as it takes place in the analytic relationship can lead to impasse in the evolution and growth of the analysis.

Facing our feelings can involve the risk of fragmentation, with ruptures on the mental and physical sides, when the analyst is not up to working through, internally, the great sensory and emotional burden to which he or she is exposed. The famous sequence in *Alien* (R. Scott, 1979) comes to mind, in which Kane, played by the actor John Hurt, is contaminated by the creature and, prey to choking and convulsions, suddenly gives birth to the monster Alien, who (fatally) lacerates him as he emerges. Similarly the analyst who is not prepared to recognize as her own the new feeling which is being activated by the analytic relationship, is in danger of being the object of an alienating laceration on the part of her sensations.

On the sensory level, we find that we are discovering within ourselves a new world, which has those terrifying and evolutive characteristics that Bion assigned to O. We discover that *we*—inside ourselves—are the patient in front of us. This opening up of the analyst to an otherness in herself becomes the condition of the patient's being able, in his turn, to recognize himself within himself: a condition which is necessary but not sufficient, given the possibility that the analysand may balk at the attendant internal evolution.

These sensations have a specifically invasive quality as well as a specific weight that must be borne, and they have a decisive effect on the analyst's personal order and indeed life. When the difficult analysands under her care number more than one, the situation creates a burden on the analyst that has multidimensional implications, because of both the multidimensionality connected to profound emotions (Matte Blanco, 1988) and the multiplicity of analytic relationships that are in play. The evolution that takes place on the sensory level in the analyst involves the tolerance of unknown phenomena with explosive characteristics that last until some representative and symbolic definition is found.

By way of example, I shall briefly mention the case of Giovanni, a frigid analysand who was particularly impermeable to emotions. This impenetrability was most evident on the occasion of his return from the Far East, when he told me, without the least ruffle of his glacial comportment, that he had been somewhere that was involved in the violent tsunami of December 2004: an event that is still impressed on the collective memory as one of the most catastrophic disasters of the modern age, with hundreds of thousands of victims in Asia and Africa. Giovanni and his family had managed to get themselves to safety on their hotel terrace, whence they could witness the devastation wrought by the tsunami. Unsettled by the information, I nevertheless continued to listen to Giovanni's account, which he delivered with the inflection and control of someone who is describing the delivery of today's edition of the newspaper, instead of an overwhelming natural happening which placed his own life in serious danger.

Sometime later I awoke in the night in the grip of a terrifying nightmare, in which a gigantic lion leapt at my head, his jaws gaping. The next day Giovanni told me about a strange dream in which he was sitting in a room when he became aware of an unfamiliar presence just behind him: indeed, out of the corner of his eye, he could just make out the form of a lion's body, whose head was hidden.

This bizarre and unforeseen parallelism of our two dreams revealed a complementary progression of the analytic couple towards an approach to very intense feelings of hatred. For my part, the direct confrontation with the lion's head showed that I was exposed to a more direct and conscious contact with the hatred of which the patient was just beginning to have an indirect inkling, opening himself then gradually to a conscious working through. The situation finally became explicit when, after some weeks of psychoanalytic work, my unflappable analysand told me about having had an extremely violent impulse to fling his little son, only a few months old, out the window, when he had him in his arms. The urge had been sudden and very intense and he had "miraculously" managed to contain it: this discovery had left him profoundly worried about the disastrous consequences of such an act. From that moment, Giovanni's condition of emotional insensibility began to recede little by little, until it left him space for a more normal working through of his emotions.

This clinical illustration may perhaps give some idea of the burden the analyst must bear during all those long phases in which the relation to sensations and feelings is built up in the analytic relationship, following a progressive incubation which only a few indirect elements rise to the conscious level: nonetheless these "almost unbearable" sensory pressures take root within the analyst, a condition for a gradual approach to them and for their working through in the analytic setting.

I should like at this point to move on to another clinical case, and to explore in greater detail some moments of its analytic development, starting from a dangerous condition of acute psychosis. In this case, it will become manifest that there had to be an at-one-ment—not by any means easy for the analyst—with swamping violent emotions. We shall also see how the analysand initially lacked not only the ability to contain motor discharge, but also the resources that derive from an internal container, of which the body is the first concrete representative. I hope it may serve as an example of how, in a clinical context, Bion's vertices of O and of the container-contained relationship can prove to be intertwined with the vicissitudes of the body-mind relationship, thus extending the implications of psychoanalytic intervention and increasing the comprehension of clinical cases.

## *Karl*

Karl was apparently icy and impassive, but from what he related it emerged that he was capable of turning into a volcano in full eruption that threatened to destroy everything around it. When he began his four-session-a-week analysis he showed the characteristics of a delusional state alternating with moments of lucidity, with intensely paranoid experiences at work and attacks of uncontrolled fury which put various people at risk, even his own family: on one occasion he came close to killing his baby son with the ferocity of his blows. In these violent situations Karl entered into action automatically and was completely incapable of containing the impulse to act.

The initial work in analysis was very difficult because Karl felt that whatever I said was hostile. For my part, I felt a great internal weight and I followed with considerable anxiety and concern the situation of this patient who was at risk of doing concrete harm through his attacks. In my dreams of that period I found myself in enormous refrigerators in the midst of hanging animal carcasses dripping with blood. These slaughter-related dream experiences seemed to represent my own O, in which hatred had infinite and lethal features: something that corresponded to what the patient was experiencing on his side in a very concrete way as a conjunction of frost and rage.

One day during a session I happened to move in my chair, producing a noticeable noise. Karl reacted with impatience and irritation, saying that he could not bear noises of that sort, and that he could not understand where they came from. I forced myself to overcome my immediate reaction, which would have led me to deny my physical presence, just to avoid confronting Karl's hatred. I said to myself that I couldn't not exist physically, so that making no noise was not a thing I could ask of myself.

And so I answered Karl, saying that it was I, in fact that it was my body that had produced that noise: clearly he had no idea that there could be an actual body that was capable of producing noises. Used as I was to his reactions of scornful intolerance, I was astonished to hear him placidly say that he was feeling more at ease on the couch.

It is interesting to note the analysand's positive reaction to a working through based on a non-symbolic, concrete level that referred to an actual body. We had started from the perception of a noise produced by my body, followed by his irascible exclamation. My comment, then, instead of offering a symbolic interpretation of his reaction as an expression of aggressive transference towards my person, had brought us back to the concrete bodily level that had generated it. Evidently the concrete level based on a recognition of the body met the analysand's need, giving rise to that positive reaction, so unlike the annoyance he would generally express when I sought to introduce a more symbolic level of elaboration, which ran the risk of widening the fracture of dissociation from his own body instead of mending it.

This episode proved to be decisive, because thenceforth Karl embarked on a working through focused on localizing his bodily presence. During the next session it happened that a beep was emitted by the pager in Karl's pocket: he took it out to look at it. Then he said it had never occurred to him that his body also produced beeps, or signals that he could receive and in some way place. It seemed to me an interesting development of the preceding session, with the difference that this time it was *his* body that was producing sensory signals, not mine. He also demonstrated that he was capable of connecting the beep sound to other undefined signals coming from his body: bodily signals waiting to be received by his mind.

This model reappeared in subsequent sessions, to the point that when he felt submerged by mental confusion, he activated the beep of his pager, which helped him to track down his bodily presence and begin to be aware of something moving inside of him. This working through led to greater attention to his bodily needs, like the need for rest and for sleep, which he was in the habit of ignoring completely. His first awareness of his body and of what was moving inside of it, together with increasing respect for his need for rest, led to clinical improvement and to a first containment of emotional violence.

This working through, which placed Karl in relationship to himself and to his actual body, opened the door, not by chance, to the first forms of self-representation, so that, in a later dream, Karl saw himself before a mirror: but in the dream his face appeared without a mouth. The dream gave rise to no associations, but it did anticipate a phase centered on the working through of his sense perceptions regarding taste, from which there arose a greater containment of his feral impulses towards disembowelment.

## A few comments

This material shows how the psychoanalytic office can constitute an undifferentiated space in which the sensations of the participants in the analytic relationship are superimposed on one another: a "massive body" that the working through enables, to give birth to the subjective experience of the analysand's body. So we see how, in a mobilization of experience characterized by sensory predominance and non-symbolic, pre-verbal levels, the analyst's intervention can be oriented towards concrete and non-symbolic levels, emphasizing the analysand's discovery of sensations and of his body, and helping to set up his internal body-mind relationship:

while working in this manner the analyst can make use of the events that occur in the horizontal analyst-analysand relationship (his intolerance of the movements and noises originating in my body) so as to highlight the analysand's vertical body-mind relationship (his hatred and denial of sensations and of his body).

Thus a first internal relationship is set up in the analysand—a prerequisite for the discovery of an internal space—and there can then be containment of the patient's fragmenting tendency to expand aggressively and "omnipotently" outside himself. These developmental steps lead us back to some interesting reflections of Bion on the elaboration of O and the passage from a formless infinite in the "omnipotent" patient to his more realistic and finite perception of himself.

Bion writes that "The individual's realization of a gulf between his view of himself as omnipotent and his view of himself as an ordinary human being must be achieved (…) as in ordinary analysis" (1970, pp. 76–77).

Karl's "omnipotence" involved the absence of any limits regarding his violent impulses: this conspired with his unbearable helplessness about recognizing his limits as a person and within his actual body.

Bion continues: "In the first stage there is no real confrontation between the god and the man because there is really no such distinction. In the second stage the infinite and transcendent god is confronted by the finite man" (1970, pp. 76–77).

In the sequence above, "the infinite and transcendent god" of Karl's violence finds, "concretely", a container, when he recognizes in my body the source of the irritating "noises". The discovery of the body can in fact make possible a first passage from an omnipotent, transcendent, and infinite dimension of the emotions to a more realistic conception, according to which, impulses—even if they are experienced as infinite—belong to a finite body, to a finite man, and hence are themselves finite.

The prerequisite of this working through is the analyst's willingness to develop his own O which corresponds to the patient's, so that I found myself first of all bearing an indistinct "felt" weight of unthinkable violence, after which I passed on to a phase in which the infinite world of my violent impulses found representation in my dreams of carcasses that dripped with blood. Thus it became possible to refrain from interpreting Karl's hatred, when he was faced with the noises originating in my body, in terms of the transference. Such an interpretation would have driven those emotions he was already having trouble dealing with back inside him, now aggravated by a dangerous guilt-infused coloration. If the analyst is willing to recognize as his own the savage hatred belonging to the infinite level, he can accept joint possession of the very hatred that the patient is experiencing, and be open to the recognition of his actual body. Thanks to this relational exchange mediated by the analyst's reverie, the analysand discovers that infinite hatred is connected to an actual body and hence to an actual and finite man.

In this context both of clinging to the infinitude of a sensation, and of uncertain access to a "finite" conception of affects and of oneself, Karl's missing mouth in the dream in which he saw his reflection in a mirror seemed to make visible the missing integration between the fact of the body and mental experience, so that the body and its sensory emanations were sealed, like a body without a mouth, without any form of connection with the external world or with mental phenomena. Most significantly, Tustin (1981) pointed out the importance of bodily orifices in autistic children and the profound terror of recognizing the natural cavities that make the child aware of her own sensory self, her own separateness, and the existence of the world.

## The hat on top of the volcano

Karl's further development in analysis, which brought him closer to an awareness of his body, is significantly represented by a dream he had after he had lived through a frustrating situation that earlier would have led him to explode in violent acting out. Instead of behaving aggressively, this time Karl showed that he was capable of dreaming. "There's quite a short fellow with a big top hat in his hand. He approaches a kind of pyramid with smoke coming out of its apex, as if it were a volcano, and he puts the hat over the smoke. The hat begins to act like a fireballoon, and starts to rise. The fellow is still anchored to his hat and finds that he's being raised into the air, and then he returns to earth, describing a semicircle."

This dream was accompanied by marked physical participation, so that, in the course of that same night, Karl was seized by a sudden fever which left him prostrate.

I said to Karl that when he felt stirred up by hatred, he managed to discover that there is a way of recognizing the explosive volcano within himself, by orienting his mind to recognize his internal sensations. Karl reacted by saying that the weakness he had felt was unbearable, so I pointed out that the counterweight of this physical weakness was the mental strength he was beginning to discover within himself as he dealt with his hot and explosive emotions. At this point he began for the first time to associate experiences of a depressive nature, particularly those having to do with memories of his childhood and the family he came from.

The dream shows how an intense sensory current headed towards muscular discharge managed to find a check, thanks to a new frame of mind, so that Karl actively prepared to accept his internal sense experiences. His new frame of mind is seen to be at work when he begins to approach the volcano and then places his mind/hat over the fumes emanating from the pyramid. The smoke from the volcano does however show that we are dealing with live, incandescent material, something that is burning and could explode, as he had observed in his experience of episodes of violence.

Although it took place quite a bit later, we shall now consider a development that was very significant, in part because of the way it was transmitted by a dream, in which Karl sees himself sitting on a potty, such as is used by small children. Through the doorway he can see a very beautiful woman, whom he finds attractive and with whom he would like to have sexual relations, but he prefers to allow himself the time to finish his bowel movement, instead of interrupting it to run after the woman.

This dream displays Karl's further integration in his relationship with himself, such that he is capable of favoring the needs suggested by his bodily functions rather than the satisfaction of his sexual desires. Karl had been dominated by a propensity for control of what was outside him: his relationship with himself was completely overshadowed by his tendency to move in a world of concrete objects to be controlled and possessed, in which human beings were also ranked as inanimate objects. In this dream, on the other hand, he makes progress with his ability to relate to a physical, actual self, as he tolerates his connection with the temporal requirements of his body, in this case his intestinal functions.

*A few comments*

Karl was distinctly wanting not only in muscular containment, but also in his capacity to think abstractly. To give you an idea of his concreteness: I recall that Karl once arrived for his session in a rage because he had seen a television program in which a public figure spoke well of his own analysis, saying that it had profoundly changed him: Karl was furious with a psychoanalysis that manipulates people and transforms them into someone else. The metaphoric meaning of change as evolution completely escaped him: he grasped only the concrete aspect of change, which for him was the same as manipulation and depersonalization.

The dream about the hat on top of the volcano thus seems to represent his approach to his own personal O, with decisive developmental, and also terrifying, characteristics, together with his assuming a transcendent position (Bion), such that the patient discovers that he is capable of mental transformations. The dream hat's upward movement seems to evoke a first separation from concreteness and a start of abstraction, associated with a containment of paranoia and an orientation towards the depressive position.

At the same time the hat/mind's drawing nearer to the burning and fuming manifestations of the body catches an elaborative movement of the eclipse of the body (Ferrari), through which the patient sets in motion a mental orientation towards recognition of the body itself and of emotions, so that the chaotic pressure of the emotions can begin to find containment.

The later dream about defecation on the potty and sexual attraction gives us a further stage of body and mind integration, whereby the patient succeeded in conceiving of himself with a differentiated inside—with a stomach and a digestive system that became the model of independent mental functioning. There had been a great developmental step forward since the earliest phases of the analysis, in which a spatial definition of Karl's body just did not exist, and also since the first attempts at self-representation, in which his anxiety banished his mouth from the dream representation because it was an element of intolerable vulnerability, and further, since when his body assumed the geometric and impersonal features of a pyramid that was on fire inside.

By this time Karl was able to recognize his bodily needs and to show respect for interior space and for time, which was connected with the experience of his body: thus he achieved a first in the vertical body-mind relationship linked to excitatory satisfaction and to discharge. The dream sequence with the choice between sexual gratification and respect for the body's time requirements makes it possible to differentiate between a more evolved level connected to sexual desire and a more basic organizing level connected to the space-time of the body and to its needs, on which level the patient is ready to recognize his own actual body as the basis of an incipient humanization.

We first looked at Bion's criticism of sensoriality and desire, which leave one open to the risk of saturating the mental apparatus. From this tossing of excitatory desire and the bodily senses into the same category there seemed to arise the danger that Bion might have been "throwing the baby out with the bath water", to the point of considering everything connected to the body as antagonistic to mental functioning. But here we can see how Karl succeeds in differentiating between, on the one hand, sexual desire (the pleasure principle) and, on the other hand, a basic respect for sensoriality, linked to his own body-mind relationship, to temporality and to loss (the reality principle), that is, to parameters capable of fostering integrated mental functioning that opens the door to the depressive position.

## Conclusion

In this work I have attempted to bring together two concepts—Bion's O and the body-mind relationship—with some of their ramifications, leaving the very different vertices just as they are. Considering them together makes possible a clearer placement of Bion's contribution to the exploration of the mysterious experience of our sensations and of corporeity, as well as their decisive influence on our understanding of the development of the mind. Without denying that Bion's vertex is oriented towards mental functioning, I feel that recognizing those components of his thinking connected to the body and sense experience can perhaps help to free our reading of his approach from an intellectualistic tendency, which could easily get in the way of "patience" and the "negative capability", as well as the activation of our resources of common sense and evidence.

An example of working through according to Bion's ideas about O in conjunction with the activation of a body-mind relationship seems to me to have been offered unwittingly by a piece on late Bion by Rudi Vermote (2011), in which the patient's Ts (O) are described in relation to a dream in which he sees "protrusions in his belly, like tumors which were growing fast. Later these became bulbs pushing through his skin, and his abdomen becomes a field of tulips". In this material there emerges, it seems to me, a clear bodily component as a result of Bion's approach. Vermote also reports the dream of another patient, in which an object that is rooted inside the patient's body is extracted from behind the patient's sternum.

I find evidence, in both fragments of material, of a strong pressure from the body heralding the patients' integrated evolution, in which the body can play a part in the analytic relationship and in a representative dimension, becoming a foretoken of mental development. Nonetheless we must acknowledge that Vermote completely overlooks the reference to the body-mind relationship, both in dialogue with these patients and in his scientific reconstruction. Taylor (2011), in his commentary, underlines the risks inherent in Vermote's approach, in which a patient's responses have too much of an aura of mystery, thus inhibiting analytic thought and limiting the development of the analyst's understanding of the patient. For my part, I believe that an explicit reference to the setting in motion of a body-mind relationship could, in both cases, have introduced a hypothesis—to be verified empirically with the analysands—, thus offering a parameter of comprehension of the evolution that was under way: a comprehension whose absence is rightly regretted by Taylor.

What I have learned from my experience with Karl—which I have also found with many other patients—is that placing the hat/mind on top of the incandescent volcano of the body involves the cost of contact with the sensory world, which often leads us to the limits of our human resources for managing and containing: it is, all the same, the resonance with the profound vibrations of our corporeity that organizes our capacity for empathy and makes possible a more than superficial understanding of the patient's world. I hope that the perspective I have presented here can contribute to a greater openness of clinical vision, as well as to an increased flexibility in interpreting Bion's contribution on thinking.

## References

Bion, W. R. (1962). *Learning from Experience*. London: Karnac.
Bion, W. R. (1970). *Attention and Interpretation*. London: Karnac.
Damasio, A., & Carvalho, G. B. (2013). The nature of feelings: Evolutionary and neurobiological origins. *Nature Reviews Neuroscience, 14*: 143–152.
Ferrari, A. B. (2004). *From the Eclipse of the Body to the Dawn of Thought*. London: Free Association.
Ferrari, A. B., & Lombardi, R. (1998). Il corpo dell'Inconscio *MicroMega, 3*: 197–208.
Freud, S. (1911). Formulations on the two principles of mental functioning. *S. E., 12*. London: Hogarth.
Freud, S. (1915a). Instincts and their vicissitudes. *S. E., 14*: 117–140. London: Hogarth.
Freud, S. (1915b). The unconscious. *S. E., 14*. London: Hogarth.
Freud, S. (1923). *The Ego and the Id. S. E., 19*. London: Hogarth.
Freud, S. (1940). An outline of psychoanalysis. *S. E., 23*. London: Hogarth.
Gallese, V., & Ebisch, S. (2014). Embodied simulation and tact: the sense of touch in social cognition. Read at the Roman training program of Italian Psychoanalytic Society, 1 Feb.
Lombardi, R. (2002). Primitive mental states and the body. *International Journal of Psychoanalysis, 83*: 363–381.
Lombardi, R. (2006). Passioni e conflittualità nelle istituzioni psicoanalitiche. *Rivista di Psicoanalisi, 52*: 191–212.
Lombardi, R. (2008). The body in the analytic session: Focusing on the body–mind link. *International Journal of Psychoanalysis, 89*: 89–109.
Lombardi, R. (2009a). Body, affect, thought: Reflections on the work of Matte Blanco and Ferrari. *Psychoanalytic Quarterly, 78*: 123–160.
Lombardi, R. (2009b). Through the eye of the needle: The unfolding of the unconscious body. *Journal of the American Psychoanalytic Association, 57*: 61–94.
Matte Blanco, I. (1988). *Thinking, Feeling, and Being*. London: Routledge.
Taylor, D. (2011). Commentary on Vermote's "On the value of 'late Bion' to analytic theory and practice". *International Journal of Psychoanalysis, 92*: 1099–1112.
Tustin, F. (1981). *Autistic States in Children*. London: Routledge.
Vermote, R. (2011). On the value of "late Bion" to analytic theory and practice. *International Journal of Psychoanalysis, 92*: 1089–1098.

CHAPTER SEVENTEEN

# Bridging the gap: from soma-psychosis to psychosomatics

*Catalina Bronstein*

> "… our two enemies Soma and Psyche. Sometimes the two characters do not share the same body; each contributes a real physical and imaginary component."
>
> —*Bion*, 1979, p. 565

Psychosomatic illnesses face us with both theoretical and clinical challenges. The subject of psychosomatics spreads across many disciplines, and within psychoanalysis itself we encounter many different ways of conceptualizing psychosomatic illnesses. The understanding of the interaction between body and mind, and theories on infant development and of what is believed to be at the "origin" of psychic life, inform the different theoretical approaches to psychosomatics (Bronstein, 2011; Taylor, 1987; Aisenstein & Rappoport de Aisemberg, 2010).

Bion contributed to the understanding of psychosomatic illnesses in different ways. I will address here two aspects of his theory that I think are of great help in the understanding of these processes. The first one has to do with his proposition of a proto-mental system, which he later developed into what he called the "soma-psychotic". The second one is connected to his notions of contact barrier and beta screen.

## Containment, projective identification, and the proto-mental system

Bion's notion of maternal containment had both a profound theoretical and clinical impact. Bion developed his ideas of container/contained as a contribution to the understanding of the mechanism of projective identification. His model has close links to his theory of mental development in that it describes the impact that the early interaction between infant and mother has on the infant's development of a capacity to think. Containment is the capacity that an individual (for example, the mother) has to receive projective identifications from another individual (i.e., the baby), which she can then sense and use as communications from him, transform them, and convey them back to the baby in a modified form (Riesenberg-Malcolm, 2001).

In 1946, in "Notes on some schizoid mechanisms", Melanie Klein wrote about the articulation of anxieties and defenses that constitute the "paranoid-schizoid position" defined as such for the first time in this paper. In order to minimize the anxiety stemming from the death drive the infant defends himself by splitting and projective processes (Klein, 1946). In this paper Klein describes the projection of "bad" parts of the self into the primary object. In the infant these bad parts of the self are invariable unconsciously linked to parts of the body. For example, the infant can identify hated parts of the self with bodily excrements. In 1952 Klein described this process in greater detail:

> Together with these harmful excrements, expelled in hatred, split-off parts of the ego are projected on to the mother, or as I would rather call it *into* the mother. These excrements and bad parts of the self are meant not only to injure but also to control and to take possession of the object. In so far as the mother comes to contain the bad parts of the self, she is not felt to be a separate individual but is felt to be *the* bad self. (Klein, 1952, p. 30, italics in original)

Projective identification thus involves an unconscious phantasy of ridding the self of unwanted and psychically dangerous aspects of the self (though good parts of the self can be projected too). This phantasy includes the aspect of identification, in that the object who is the recipient of these projections is felt to carry them (Bell, 2001; Klein, 1946; Spillius, 1988).

Bion's innovation was to propose that projective identification was not just an evacuatory defensive process that the infant uses in order to deal with anxieties of annihilation, to get rid of an excess of unprocessed sense-data, of unbearable aspects of the mind and to control the object (Bion, 1962a). It is also part of a primitive form of thinking and the basis on which the process of unconscious communication between mother and infant gets established. It is an emotional experience, an unconscious activity of the mother.

In Bion's words, during the sojourn in the good breast the infant's projections "are felt to be modified in such a way that the object that is re-introjected has become tolerable to the infant's psyche" (Bion, 1962a, p. 90).

> Another important point is that if the mother cannot tolerate these projections the infant is reduced to continued projective identification carried out with increasing force and frequency. (Bion, 1962b, p. 115)

His mechanism therefore needs to encounter a receptive mother who can not only tolerate the manifestation of inchoate emotional experiences and raw sense impressions (which he called beta elements) but who can also be lovingly accepting of the projections even when they bring anxiety. This process is fundamental for the infant in order to be able to transform the raw sense impressions into alpha elements that can be used to form dream-thoughts and to develop a capacity to think and to "bridge the gap between sense-data and appreciation of sense-data", rather than just evacuate and evade psychic pain (Bion, 1962b, p. 117).

It seems important to mention here the relevance of the mother's capacity to contain and process not just the potential meaning of the infant's unformed communications but also the *intensity* of the projections that she is dealing with.

In order to understand this process more fully we need to take into account not just the role of the mother's reverie and her capacity for containment but also the newborn's "proto-mental state". In his work on groups and as part of a basic assumption group mentality, Bion postulated the existence of an early "proto-mental" system where physical and psychological or mental processes are not yet differentiated.

> I have postulated the existence of a proto-mental system in which physical and mental activity is undifferentiated and which lies outside the field ordinarily considered profitable for psychological investigation (Bion, 1952, p. 236).

He indicated that such primitive experiences can still be actively functioning in the adult (Bion, 1952, 1961). The proto-mental matrix involves beta elements that are indistinguishable from bodily sensations.

In Bion's words:

> I shall suppose the existence of a mixed state in which the patient is persecuted by feelings of depression and depressed by feelings of persecution. These feelings are indistinguishable from bodily sensations and what might, in the light of later capacity for discrimination, be described as things-in-themselves. In short Beta-elements are objects compounded of things-in-themselves, feelings of depression-persecution with guilt and therefore aspects of the personality linked by a sense of catastrophe. (Bion, 1963, p. 40)

Bion thought that emotions from the proto-mental matrix could reinforce, pervade, and even dominate the mental life of the group. The operations of the proto-mental apparatus closely correspond to Freud's description of the primary process, one in which the ego does not construe mental representations of emotional experiences but construes them instead as bodily states also reacting to them with bodily states (Meltzer, 1984). When emotional experiences (beta elements) are not processed into symbolic representations leading to dream-thoughts, they will be evacuated. One of the possible routes for evacuation is via psychosomatic disorders (Bion, 1961, 1962a; Bronstein, 2010b, 2011; Meltzer, 1984; Ogden, 2009).

The notion of "proto-mental" was further developed and extended by Bion into the concept of the soma-psychotic. In his later works (1979) Bion developed the idea that the fetus can experience prenatal emotions and that might even try to

> rid itself both of the sense when they become sensitive to changes of pressure in the watery medium, and of the feelings, "emotions" of sub-thalamic intensity … (Bion, 1979, p. 563)
>
> The foetus premature personality "continues its life in uneasy proximity with his post-mature lodger in the same physical soma. Sometimes the psycho-somatic partner demonstrates his soulful qualities; sometimes his soma-psychotic demands acknowledgment and recognition of his physical and psychotic gifts. (Bion, 1979, p. 564)

Bion's proposition is that some prenatal parts of the personality can tend to become split off and remain without the means for mental representation (a soma-psychotic level of mental life).

I personally think that Bion's description of the soma-psychotic functioning of the fetus, more than elucidating what might be actually happening before the caesura of birth, is a helpful description of the dissociation that we encounter in psychosomatic processes, a dissociation where the body is felt to be disconnected from the mind and carries its own way of "thinking", dealing with anxiety mainly through evacuation and projective identification. It is a state of dissociation by which early experiences have never reached the possibility for proper symbolic thinking but remain active through and via the body and bodily illnesses.[1]

We could think of the above as a state that is within the realm of unrepresented states of mind or the pre-psychic (or proto-psychic) (Levine Reed, & Scarfone, 2013). However, I think that this phenomenon is not totally outside psychic representation and that is very close to Susan Isaacs's description of the early, raw unconscious phantasies that are registered and lived out in and via the body (Isaacs, 1948; Riviere, 1936) and that Brierley described very aptly:

> The child must sense the breast, for instance, before it begins to perceive (i.e. recognize) it, and it must feel its sucking sensations before it recognizes its own mouth. ... Freud said "The ego is first and foremost a body-ego" but it would seem that there might be advantages at this stage in saying that the ego is at first a series of sensation-egos, part-body part-object nuclei. (Brierley, 1937, p. 262)

These early unconscious phantasies are linked to perceptions of the internal physiological and biological processes of the infant. Isaacs stresses the non-visual character of these phantasies, which the baby feels concretely as pleasure or pain (Steiner, 2003). I think that we can describe this phenomenon as one that is within the realm of early unconscious phantasies that have been experienced in "somatic ways" and have never reached the possibility of accessing symbolic meaning but that still carry "psychic" meaning in a proto-symbolic way and manifest themselves in *semiotic* ways[2] (Bronstein, 2012). I am referring here to early experiences that might look as if they are part of an "inaccessible unconscious" but that are actually lived in and through the body.[3] The actualization of these early psycho-somatic or, following Bion, "soma-psychotic" relations to the primary object can have a powerful effect on the analyst's countertransference. The patient's physical rigidity, the need to create a special psycho-physical space between patient and analyst, the tone and "temperature" of voice, the "don't touch me" quality of communication, can have considerable impact on the analyst. These are levels of semiotic communication which coexist with a greater capacity for symbolic thinking and verbal communication (Bronstein, 2012; Civitarese, 2013).

Mr. A sought help because of difficulties in his relationship to his wife. He had had two previous therapies but he felt that they did not really help him. Mr. A suffered from psoriasis. His condition was quite visible, for example, on his scalp, sometimes on his hands. I was aware of the psoriasis from the first interview but Mr. A did not mention it then. From the very beginning I felt that his psoriasis was something that we were not meant to talk about. I initially thought that Mr. A was denying pr perhaps just ignoring the existence of the psoriasis because it caused too much anxiety. He did not say anything about it for many months.

The psoriasis was an obvious presence in the session and at the same time it did not exist. I realized that Mr. A was not consciously avoiding the subject. It felt far more like a deep split, a dissociation between his mind and his skin. Whilst his skin did not seem to exist, his body did come up in his discourse via his permanent sense of tiredness, a word that he used to express both psychic and physical states of mind (he was tired because he did not manage to sleep well, he was tired of his job, he was tired of arguing with his wife, he was tired because he got up too early for work, he was tired because he had to pay too many bills, he was tired because he had to move furniture around at home, etc.). It felt to me that he was tired of "life", that he suffered from a state of pervading depression which he was not conscious of and that the word "tired" was used to try to make sense of it as well as being a way to try to communicate this to me, I think in the hope that I would help him make sense of his sensations (while I was often seen, as well, as a tired object). Beyond his tiredness his discourse could be described in the same way as Marty defined the "pensée opératoire", an endless account of what he needed to do, what he was going to buy, etc., but without any distinctive emotional connotations.

While the expression of his tiredness seemed to be his way of trying to express something that he could not verbalize in any other way, it was also an appeal to me to "do" something about it (help him "move the furniture around", stop the internal and external arguments, show I was not tired of him, etc.). I felt that he actually projected his depression into his body that was now carrying the tiredness he felt in his relation to his objects. In phantasy, his body was equated to the tired object, to a depressed mother (Segal, 1957). I felt that the psoriasis belonged to a different order. It just did not seem to exist, as if apparently did not have any psychic meaning. At one point, something he said in a session made me feel that I could make a connection to his skin and to his psoriasis. When I made this connection he said:

> I spoke a lot about the psoriasis in my first therapy. I don't have anything more to say about it. I said all there was to say. I do what the doctor told me I should do, that's it!

This was not said with either anger, irritation, or anxiety. It was a "fact" for me to know about and to accept. It felt like it was a "dead end", a closure in respect to the possibility of generating thoughts, or even to the possibility of becoming curious and wanting to know more about it. There wasn't any awareness that I might be curious or interested to know about what he had thought or discussed in his other therapy. Even though thoughts might not be yet there, what seemed to be lacking was the idea of a mind receptive to the possibility of thoughts coming into it. And in particular that my mind could be different from his other therapist's mind and I might be able to entertain different thoughts to the ones he already had or had been given. Rather than a K-L link (a "coming to know", connected to the notion of an epistemophilic instinct and a move towards exploration) it seemed to be more like a minus K link.

And still, I felt that the "nothing to say—psoriatic skin" occupied an important place in the session, that its existence appeared in a different way to the one manifested by his tiredness. While I felt that I should not *touch* it in any way, I was permanently aware of it. I became too conscious of an issue that functioned like a "no-go" area and that I should not interfere with. But I could not forget it either and it was still constantly present.

This could be seen as the enactment in the transference of the splitting between a safer object: one who can contain the raw emotional/skin aspects of the infant (the other psychotherapist) and an actual unsafe me in the session.

But following Bion I am more inclined to think that what was having an effect on me was the result of Mr. A's "proto-mental functioning" that could not find its way into the symbolic process (not even as a symbolic equation) but was experienced and manifested instead in semiotic ways that had a deep effect on my countertransference.

In Bion's description of the pro-mental system,

> Since it is a level in which physical and mental are undifferentiated, it stands to reason that, when distress from this source manifests itself, it can manifest itself just as well in physical forms as in psychological. (Bion, 1961, p. 102)

From a phenomenological point of view this carries similarities with what Green described as a decathexis (Green, 1983) and with Marty's notion of "essential depression" (Marty, 1967, 1968). However, I think that the unmentionable skin disorder was the way in which Mr. A lived out early unconscious phantasies in connection to a mother who could neither touch him nor tolerate to be touched by the baby, both physically and emotionally. To be "touched" was felt to bring a sense of psycho-physical danger between him and me. His mother was a disturbed woman who could not offer him any sense of safety (she herself was a severe phobic and could not tolerate to be close to her child). His diseased skin was what made me aware that I had to be cautious and careful as if I would be touching a very fragile psychic-skin[4] that could barely contain him. But at the same time, the extra layers of skin, his thick skin, also made me feel that it would not be easy to get close to him. Closeness and distance, temperature, thickness and thinness in the relationship to the maternal object were felt and expressed via his skin condition.

The symptom (not just the psoriasis but the "nothing to say about the psoriasis") was a communication at a semiotic level of sensations of danger and the need to regulate the distance from the object that had never been integrated but that exercised a powerful effect on my countertransference.

As well as the development of a sense of continuity between somatic and emotional manifestations of experiences and representations that can be used for thinking, the proto-mental needs to encounter what Cortinas calls an ideo-grammar to be able to become psychical (Cortinas, 2009). There might be many different reasons why this ideo-grammar cannot be developed. This certainly includes the lack of a capacity for maternal reverie, and states where the mother projects her own unresolved conflicts into her child, as well as the infant's own sensitivity and his intolerance of frustration.

## Contact barrier and beta screen

"… [the] blood spoke in her cheek … [as if] her body thought … "

Bion, quoting Donne, 1990, p. 41

In the shift between the paranoid-schizoid and the depressive positions repression takes over from splitting as the leading mechanism. Bion looks on repression as a contact barrier, not a caesura, the possibility of a constant ongoing transformation between the beta and alpha elements (Bion, 1962a, p. 26). The contact barrier can be seen as a structural concept as well as a function that enables the constant transformation of beta elements into alpha elements. The contact barrier is responsible for the preservation of the distinction between conscious and unconscious, is what separates conscious from unconscious mental processes. It is produced by alpha function and therefore composed by alpha elements

> The man's alpha-function whether in sleeping or waking transforms the sense-impressions related to an emotional experience, into alpha-elements, which cohere as they proliferate to form the contact-barrier. … The nature of the contact-barrier will depend on the nature of the supply of alpha-elements and on the manner of their relationship to each other. They may cohere. They may be agglomerated. They may be ordered sequentially to give the appearance of narrative (at least in the form in which the contact-barrier may reveal itself in a dream). They may be ordered logically. They may be ordered geometrically.
>
> The term "contact-barrier" emphasizes the establishment of contact between conscious and unconscious and the selective passage of elements from one to the other. On the nature of the contact-barrier will depend the change of elements from conscious to unconscious and vice versa. (Bion, 1962a, p. 17)

The contact barrier enables constant transformation and symbolization. Sense impressions need to change into alpha elements for use in "dream-thoughts" which can then be used for thinking and for storage into memories and dreams. This will enable the individual to have continuous contact with his unconscious which is necessary in order to be in contact with external reality as well (Segal, 2001). When this process fails a beta screen is formed—a cluster of beta elements, an agglomeration of sense impressions—that is impermeable and blocks the communication between conscious and unconscious. Though it can sometimes achieve a certain coherence these cluster of beta elements can masquerade a coherence that does not exist and present itself clinically as a confused state or a confused outpouring (Bion, 1962a).

Bion discussed the replacement of the contact barrier by a beta screen mainly in connection to psychotic functioning where the reversal of alpha function takes to the destruction of the contact barrier and does violence to it. It is not just a return to beta elements but a forming of bizarre objects. Differently from alpha elements, beta elements lack a capacity for linkage with each other, but they can agglomerate and evoke responses from the analyst which are heavily charged with countertransference. For example, in the psychotic, the associations that form part of the beta screen are intended to provoke a response in the analyst's emotional involvement, rather than thinking.

> [T]hanks to the beta-screen the psychotic patient has a capacity for evoking emotions in the analyst and are related to his need to produce an emotional involvement. (Bion, 1962a, p. 24)

There are many instances in analysis when the fluidity between conscious and unconscious—a contact barrier—is replaced by a rigid agglomeration of beta elements that can sometimes masquerade as a coherent discourse. This can be sometimes seen in patients who resort to an evacuative discourse, flooding the analyst with a barrage of meaningless talk. Other times, the beta screen takes the form of action. This is often the case in adolescence, when the adolescent feels at the mercy of uncontrollable impulses that might not be able to be contained and thought about. Compulsive action in its various forms (such as shoplifting, self-harming, binging and vomiting, etc.) serve the purpose to evacuate the mind so as not to feel the anxiety that results from psychic conflict, in particular, anxiety that is originated by the workings of the superego and that confronts the adolescent with feelings of guilt, blame and shame (Bronstein, 2010).

Another instance where we can find the formation of a beta screen is in patients affected by severe psychosomatic illnesses where the part of the ill body seems to carry the projections of unprocessed beta elements and can form a beta screen.

Martha, a fifteen-year-old girl, had suffered from severe eczema since birth.[5] When she was three years old her mother died. At this point she developed a serious generalized eczema and she had to be admitted to hospital for several months. Martha longed for an ideal mother who she imagined would make her anxiety—and her eczema—disappear. But this idealized picture of her mother was contrasted by a far more persecuting fear of being pulled into a hole underneath her bed by her dead mother. Martha was constantly scratching; sometimes she tore dead pieces of skin with her mouth. She felt she did not have a "body": "I don't have a body. Just bits of dry, dead, rotten pieces of skin". I think that Martha felt that she was carrying, or rather embodying, the dead mother. This was making her feel in a state of terror, as she felt that her body was not her body. At the same time, this was also her way of keeping her mother alive, not by remembering her, not by mourning her, but by living in her mother's skin. The masturbatory pleasure-pain of caressing and scratching provided both the confirmation that she carried her mother within herself as well as the proof that she was not her mother, that she was still alive. I think that her belief that she was living in her mother's skin made her feel suffocated and claustrophobic, which could have been one of the reasons why she desperately needed to tear her skin off or drove her into fits of scratching as if she had become allergic to her own skin (her scratching sometimes became out of control and triggered a generalized inflammatory reaction that required admission to hospital).

In her sessions Martha flooded me with a totally evacuative discourse that did not allow for any pause or any introspection and that I felt had more the intention to keep me at a distance rather than to have a meaningful contact with me and with her own thoughts. I felt that Martha often experienced me as the maddening mother who was going to pull her into death (I think that for her, psychic disintegration was equated to death). But my persecution of her was also connected to her seeing me as a harsh superego who was reproaching her for her hateful feelings towards her mother. At these moments her discourse became an outpouring, an evacuation of beta elements, necessary for her psychic-physical survival, an attempt to rid the psyche of thoughts which were felt to be persecuting "things", a beta screen.

I think that in phantasy, the evacuation of hateful aspects of the self/object was followed also by their projective identification into the skin that was then felt to persecute her from within and that was needed to be kept under control. Rosenfeld described this phenomena as the formation of a "psychotic island" (Rosenfeld, 2001).

Martha seemed to be imprisoned in a system of bodily sensations (Ogden, 1989). It was only through the containment and understanding of the magnitude of her anxieties and of her need to evacuate her mind that very slowly she could start to tolerate some "thoughts" and the beta screen started to become replaced by alpha elements. The move to a greater capacity to think goes together with a capacity to tolerate psychic pain. Slowly, scratching decreased, Martha's eczema improved and she started to find words to express her sadness for her lost mother.

## Notes

1. The importance of dissociation in psychosomatics was underlined by Winnicott who wrote that "The illness in psycho-somatic disorder is not the clinical state expressed in terms of somatic pathology or pathological functioning (colitis, asthma, chronic eczema). It is the persistence of a split in the patient's ego-organization, or of multiple dissociations, that constitutes the true illness" (Winnicott, 1966, p. 510).
2. Kristeva called them "metaphors incarnate" (Kristeva, J., 2004).
3. Antonino Ferro's notion of "balpha" elements is important in that there might not always be as clear a distinction between alpha and beta elements as it is often described. They might be "psychically present" but cannot be used for thinking (Ferro, 2009). Bion also wondered whether there could be elements called "gamma", "delta", and so on to describe gradually less psychic and more physical elements in the grid (Bion, 1990, p. 41).
4. Bick proposed that in the newborn infant the parts of the personality must be held together (contained) by the skin functioning as boundary. In cases where there are difficulties in maternal containment she described a "second skin formation" that would provide the needed sense of cohesiveness of the skin's surface. We can think of Mr. A's skin functioning in this way (Bick, 1968).
5. This case was discussed in the chapter "Psychosomatics: the role of unconscious phantasy" (Bronstein, 2010b).

## References

Aisenstein, M., & Rappoport de Aisemberg, E. (2010). *Psychosomatics Today: A Psychoanalytic Perspective*. London: Karnac.
Bell, D. (2001). Projective identification. In: C. Bronstein (Ed.), *Kleinian Theory: A Contemporary Perspective* (pp. 125–147). London: Wiley.
Bick, E. (1968). The experience of the skin in early object-relations. *International Journal of Psychoanalysis, 49*: 484–486.
Bion, W. R. (1952). Group dynamics: A re-view. *International Journal of Psychoanalysis 33*: 235–247.
Bion, W. R. (1961). *Experiences in Groups*. London: Tavistock.
Bion, W. R. (1962a). *Learning from Experience*. London: Tavistock.
Bion, W. R. (1962b). A theory of thinking. In: *Second Thoughts* (pp. 110–119). London: Heinemann, 1967.
Bion, W. R. (1963). *Elements of Psychoanalysis*. London: Heinemann.
Bion, W. R. (1979). The dawn of oblivion. In: *A Memoir of the Future* (pp. 429–576). London: Karnac.

Bion, W. R. (1990). *Brazilian Lectures*. London: Karnac.

Brierley, M. (1937). Affects in theory and practice. *International Journal of Psychoanalysis, 18*: 256–268.

Bronstein, C. (2010b). Psychosomatics: The role of unconscious phantasy. In: M. Aisenstein & E. Rappoport de Aisemberg (Eds.), *Psychosomatics Today* (pp. 63–76). London: Karnac.

Bronstein, C. (2011). On psychosomatics: The search for meaning. *International Journal of Psychoanalysis, 92*: 173–195.

Bronstein, C. (2012). Finding unconscious phantasy in the session: recognizing form. UCL Conference on unconscious phantasy, London. To be published in *International Journal of Psychoanalysis* (in press).

Civitarese, G. (2013). The inaccessible unconscious and reverie as a path of figurability. In: H. B. Levine, G. S. Reed & D. Scarfone (Eds.), *Unrepresented States and the Construction of Meaning: Clinical and Theoretical Contributions* (pp. 220–239). London: Karnac.

Cortinas, L. P. (2009). *The Aesthetic Dimension of the Mind: Variations on a Theme of Bion*. London: Karnac.

Ferro, A. (2009). Psychosomatic pathology or metaphor: problems of the boundary. In: *Mind Works: Technique and Creativity in Psychoanalysis* (pp. 73–106). London: Routledge.

Green, A. (1983). The dead mother. In: *On Private Madness* (pp. 142–173). London: Karnac, 1996.

Isaacs, S. (1948). The nature and function of phantasy. *International Journal of Psychoanalysis, 39*: 84–90.

Klein, M. (1946). Notes on some schizoid mechanisms. *International Journal of Psychoanalysis, 27*: 99–110.

Klein, M. (1952). Notes on some schizoid mechanism (slightly reworked). In: *Developments in Psychoanalysis* (pp. 292–320). London: Karnac, 1989.

Kristeva, J. (2004). *Melanie Klein*. New York: Columbia University Press.

Levine, H. B., Reed, G. S., & Scarfone, D. (Eds.) (2013). *Unrepresented States and the Construction of Meaning: Clinical and Theoretical Contributions*. London: Karnac.

Marty, P. (1967). Régression et instinct de mort: hypothèse à propos de l'observation psychosomatique. *Revue Française de Psychanalyse, 31*: 1113–1133.

Marty, P. (1968). A major process of somatization: the progressive disorganization. *International Journal of Psychoanalysis, 49*: 246–249.

Meltzer, D. (1984). A Klein-Bion model for evaluating psychosomatic states. In: *Studies in Extended Metapsychology* (pp. 34–37). Strathclyde, Perthshire Clunie, 1986.

Ogden, T. H. (1989). On the concept of an autistic-contiguous position. *International Journal of Psychoanalysis, 70*: 127–140.

Ogden, T. H. (2009). On talking-as-dreaming. In: *Rediscovering psychoanalysis,* (pp. 14–30). London: Routledge.

Riesenberg-Malcolm, R. (2001). Bion's theory of containment. In: C. Bronstein (Ed.), *Kleinian Theory. A Contemporary Perspective* (pp. 165–180). London: Whurr.

Riviere, J. (1936). On the genesis of psychical conflict in earliest infancy. *International Journal of Psychoanalysis, 17*: 395–422.

Rosenfeld, H. (2001). The relationship between psychosomatic symptoms and latent psychotic states. In: F. de Masi (Ed.), *Herbert Rosenfeld at Work. The Italian Seminars* (pp. 24–44). London: Karnac.

Segal, H. (1957). Notes on symbol formation. In: *The Work of Hanna Segal* (pp. 49–65). Northvale, NJ: Jason Aronson, 1981.

Segal, H. (2001). Changing models of the mind. In: C. Bronstein (Ed.), *Kleinian Theory: A Contemporary Perspective* (pp. 157–164). London: Wiley.

Spillius, E. B. (1988). *Melanie Klein Today: Developments in Theory and Practice, Vol 1: Mainly Theory.* London: Routledge.

Steiner, R. (2003). Introduction. In: R. Steiner (Ed.), *Unconscious Phantasy* (pp. 1–66). London: Karnac.

Taylor, G. (1987). *Psychosomatic Medicine and Contemporary Psychoanalysis.* Madison, CT: International Universities Press.

Winnicott, D. W. (1966). Psycho-somatic illness in its positive and negative aspects. *International Journal of Psychoanalysis, 47*: 510–516.

# CHAPTER EIGHTEEN

# A Note and a Short Story

*Nicola Abel-Hirsch*

What follows are two short comments arising from Bion's work. The second of the two comments is based on a passage from his novel *A Memoir of the Future*, and I have called it A Short Story. It was in fact a thought about short stories that led to this whole piece. In psychoanalytic writing we do not usually have a format that would allow us to write a shorter piece, rather than a paper—short story, rather than a novel. And yet, I think it likely that others might have a similar experience to me, whilst reading Bion, of coming to a "short-story" length realisation or question that could be fruitful to share. This may be truer now than ever, because it is my impression that we have usefully clarified the broad systems of thought arising from Bion's work, to some extent leaving "the devil now in the detail". Like many readers, I find myself going back to the same paragraph or even sentence (and repeatedly skipping over the same paragraphs or sentences that I can't understand). The following comments have arisen from two such paragraphs, one from Bion's work *Elements* and the second from the work of fiction written towards the end of his life *A Memoir of the Future*.

### A Note—Is maternal reverie different to analytical alpha function?

The paragraph that prompted this note is as follows:

> To summarize: Detachment can only be achieved at the cost of painful feelings of loneliness and abandonment experienced (1) by the primitive animal mental inheritance from which detachment is effected and (2) by the aspects of the personality that succeed in detaching themselves from the object of scrutiny which is felt to be indistinguishable from the source of its viability. The apparently abandoned object of scrutiny is the primitive mind and the primitive social capacity of the individual as a political or group animal. The "detached"

personality is in a sense new to its job and has to turn to tasks which differ from those to which its components are more usually adapted, namely scrutiny of the environment excluding the self; part of the price paid is in feelings of insecurity. (Bion, 1963, p. 16)

The first thing that struck me is the comment towards the end of the quote that the "'detached' personality is in a sense new to its job". As analysts we are trained to do a particular kind of work—arguably this is a new kind of work for the mind. By contrast, maternal "reverie" is an old kind of work, as old as the species, and perhaps not even correctly described as work at all.

In order to go further in to the possible differences between maternal reverie and analytical alpha function I want to introduce Bion's concept of the "container" to the discussion, and in particular, the question of how the space in the container comes into being. Bion provides us with a visual image of the process of containing through his reference to a reticulum (any reticulated system or structure/a network of intercellular fibers). Of the reticulum, he says the gaps are the sleeves, and the threads forming the meshes are emotions. The gaps are made available by the meshes of emotion, and from this point of view, the emotional capacity of the mother to be available to her baby, and the emotional capacity of the analyst to be available to the patient have much in common. But there is another aspect of how mental space comes into being, in relation to which the two are quite different. In his later work *Attention and Interpretation* Bion comments that mental space comes into being through the experience of the absence or loss of what was there before (1970, p. 10). This idea is also, importantly, in his earlier, seminal "A theory of thinking" (1962) in which he states that the first thought comes about in the space created by the experience of the absence of the breast. Does the mother experience a loss in order to be available to the baby, does the analyst experience a loss in order to be available to the patient, and are they the same? Both mother and analyst "consent to be invaded" and to "feel, think and share the emotions contained in such projection, as if they were a part of his own self" (1991, p. 21). A loss experienced by the mother is that of meeting the needs of her own (non-mothering) self. For the mother, this is somewhat ameliorated by her identification with the baby and the meeting of her own infantile needs through her care of the baby. In a good enough situation she is also cared for by the father and there is some analogy to this in the analyst being cared for within her analytic identity/community. The key difference is that the analyst is not to forget that she is alone. The analyst is intended to *not* identify her own infantile needs with the patient.

To return to the quote above:

To summarize: Detachment can only be achieved at the cost of painful feelings of loneliness and abandonment (1) by the primitive animal mental inheritance from which detachment is effected and (2) by the aspects of the personality that succeed in detaching themselves from the object of scrutiny which is felt to be indistinguishable from the source of its viability.

I think Bion is saying that in order to be available to the patient, we as analysts have to learn how to turn away from our own primitive animal self. I am suggesting that this is different from what a mother does naturally in reverie, because we do not simultaneously identify our primitive animal self with the patient, as a mother does with an infant. As a result of this "new job" the primitive animal part of the self feels abandoned, and even the part looking out towards the patient is unsure of its viability.

When the young Freud was learning how to use his mind differently, he reports experiencing a loneliness. Some have questioned whether, in his psychoanalytically formative years, Freud was as lonely as he claimed. It is sometimes implied that he was exaggerating his loneliness to augment a picture of the heroic nature of the task. It is possible, however, that there was a loneliness caused by his repositioning himself internally, in a way that allowed a new kind of attention to be directed externally. I quote Freud from one of his early letters to Fliess:

> Every now and then ideas dart through my head which promise to realize everything, apparently connecting the normal and the pathological, the sexual and the psychological problem, and then they are gone again and I make no effort to hold onto them because I indeed know that neither their disappearance nor their appearance in consciousness is the real expression of their fate. On such quiet days as yesterday and today, however, everything in me is very quiet, terribly lonely. I cannot talk about it to anyone, nor can I force myself to work, deliberately and voluntarily as other workers can. I must wait until something stirs in me and I become aware of it. And so I often dream whole days away …. (Freud to Fliess, December 3, 1897 in Masson, 1985)

To my knowledge Bion does not, himself, differentiate between maternal reverie and alpha function. He drew on maternal reverie to illustrate what he was then exploring about projection into the object, as a communication to be borne, and returned transformed. Since Bion's original thinking a possible problem that has arisen, however, is that we may have too great an emphasis on the infant/mother model, and overlook the other roots of Bion's seminal concept of container/contained. Bion begins his published thinking about container/contained with his experience as an analyst of psychotic patients, one of whom complained that Bion's understanding/ interpretation of his (the patient's) material was refusing ingress of the patient's projections in to the analyst (Bion, 1958). Another primary source of Bion's developing understanding of alpha function is discussed in a recent paper by Larry Brown, who shows that "simultaneous with working out this new theory of dreaming, Bion also revisited his World War I experiences that had remained undigested and all these elements coalesced into a selected fact—his discovery of alpha function" (Brown, 2012).

The "Short Story" to follow, is about something else. This seems strange in comparison to writing a paper, but this experimental format does allow for points to be explored and debated in their uniqueness, in a way which may allow the threads to find their points of intersection with another single point.

## *A Short Story—about the mind and body*

TERM: I am mind and my mental membranes make me able to reach far beyond my feet …
EM: Now you have muddled me. I shall be body; forever I shall gird at your mind.
MIND: Hullo! Where have you sprung from?
BODY: What—you again? I am Body; you can call me Soma if you like. Who are you?

MIND: Call me Psyche—Psyche-Soma.
BODY: Soma-Psyche.
MIND: We must be related …
BODY: … It is the meaning of pain that I am sending to you; the words get through—which I have not sent—but the meaning is lost.
MIND: What is that amusing little affair sticking out? I like it. It has a mind of its own—just like me.
BODY: It's just like me—has a body of its own. That's why it is so erect. Your mind—no evidence for it at all.
MIND: Don't be ridiculous. I suffer anxiety as much as you have pain. In fact I have pain about which you know nothing. I suffered intensely when you were rejected. I asked you to call me Psyche and promised to call you Soma.
SOMA: All right Psyche; I don't admit that there is any such person other than a figment of my digestion.
PSYCHE: Who are you talking to then?
SOMA: I'm talking to myself and the sound is reflected back by one of my fetal membranes.
PSYCHE: Your fetal membranes! Ha, ha! Very good! Is that your pun or mine?
SOMA: It's the only language you understand.
PSYCHE: It's the only language you hear. All you talk is pain.
SOMA: All you respect is pain or lack of it. The only time I can get anything over to you is pain-talk from the hills. (Bion, 1993, III, pp. 433–434)

In this conversation we hear reference to the language of the body and the language of the mind—two different languages. We are more used to conceiving of the mind/body relation in terms of the representations of the body in the mind. Bion has the body speaking its own language—it's "pain-talk from the hills".

Descartes states "I think therefore I am". His "I"—his "self"—is located in his mind, the body viewed as a mechanistic container. Animals, and perhaps by implication human beings' animal nature, are seen by him as lacking "bodily intelligence" including feelings. In contrast to Descartes, Freud places the body at the center of "I-ness". The first ego is a "body ego". The bodily rooted drives place demands on the mind. Freud was convinced that psychical excitation must lie in a physical factor that was sexual. Sexuality (not "sex" but the profound conceptual and physical phenomenon conceived of in *The Three Essays*) was manifest in the psychical realm (in the form of affectively charged sexual ideas), and manifest somatically (in the form of an excitation within the nervous system).

The primary link between body and mind in Freud's model of the body/mind relation is sexuality. By contrast, in the above quote, the primary link we see in Bion's model of the body/mind relation is one of K, the "knowing" of the mind by the body and the body by the mind.

In clinical practice I have found that some patients experience themselves as either all mind, or all body (I am simplifying matters). This seems to happen when the patient has attempted to put either his or her own mind or his or her own body in the place of the primary object. If it is the mind that is the attempted substitute for the primary object, the "self" becomes over-identified with mental activity, whilst the body is disavowed. If it is the body that is the attempted substitute for the primary object, the patient may complain of a shallowness of mind, and be overly reliant on the containment provided by their physical being.

One would expect that as the patient became more contained in the analysis, we would begin to see an improved relation between the patient's own mind and body (now released from the attempt to be a substitute for the primary object), and this does seem to be the case in the limited number of examples I have knowledge of.

*Patient Pb—"all body"*

Pb's presenting concern was what she described as a "shallowness of mind". Dialogue between us was quickly halted with comments like "that's not very pleasant", and she had little curiosity. Her dreams were experienced as foreign objects and brought for me to think about, rather than for her and me to engage with. She distrusted what she saw as the inexactitude of associations and experienced "associating" to be an unwelcome, onerous task. She was sure that the only way to proceed was for me to do the thinking, although in fact this was also what she feared. A unifying thought for me was that it seemed there could be no couples, and in this context I began to consider the relationship between her mind and body and internal and external worlds as also being "couples".

Pb was preoccupied with her body, on which she felt very reliant as a kind of bastion. She was deeply suspicious of me, but as she began to feel more contained in the analysis an incident occurred that is, I think, illustrative of an increased dialogue between her mind and body. Pb, unusually, went out for the evening with a man who sounded to be attracted to her in a strong and sexual way. In the middle of the night she awoke, "hot". The "heat" seemed to be a rudimentary "bodily" communication—with the potential then to be named and thus be the site of a dialogue between the language of the body (in this instance, heat) and the language of the mind (in this instance, the naming of desire).

*Patient Pm—"all mind"*

Pm described his capacity to think as more important than anything. His own mind was all that he "trusted". He behaved as if I did not have a mind myself. He anxiously and exhaustingly believed that he must think for me, and manage the analytic situation for us both.

Just as Pb, above, "undersized" her thinking, Pm can speak in overreaching terms. My impression is that in childhood a main defense was to know as much as he could—in particular about anything painful and frightening. As a result he has an unusual capacity to go into painful emotional "worlds", but he can also "over-think" these.

I began to notice a repeating phenomenon in my countertransference in which I would go off in my mind, not in an associative way, but more as an escape. I became interested in the fact that I could not "rest" between thoughts, whilst at the same time remaining with him. I began to talk to him about *his* experience of my pausing after something has been understood (from my point of view this would be to allow for the next potential avenue to emerge). He hated the idea of my resting. He said he never rested, and only believed he ever would be able to when absolutely everything was done. He would either have "to be severely injured and unable to move, or dead" before he could rest. Shortly after this, a dream he had, in which he took my chair, helpfully enabled us to robustly address his putting himself in the place of the primary object (or, correspondingly, as the material was unfolding, the oedipal couple). Following this, and for the first time, he remained in the waiting room for me to collect him, instead of hastily appearing in the corridor down which I was walking. He said he had been off in his thoughts and hadn't heard me coming. There was an element of dismissiveness in this, but more importantly something had happened between us that was not being controlled by his anxiously attentive mind. He had let me collect him. Some days later I heard that he had been able to rest at home (rather than only collapse in exhaustion). He had sat back in his chair and "for once" let his thoughts wonder freely. This appearance of his own alive body, which could contain him in waiting and resting, seemed to have happened at the same time as his becoming more aware of/trusting in, my having a mind myself in which I am able to contain him.

The language of the body in the examples is heat and rest respectively; that of the mind, naming and freely associating. Bion's imaginary dialogue of the body and mind set the scene for my conceiving of the two languages of mind and body, neither defining the language of the other.

A further thought to be held as a working hypothesis is whether the mind-body relation is specifically affected by the Oedipus complex. Freud's account of the Oedipus complex foregrounds sexual desire rooted in the body. In the resolution of the complex the child both "gives up" the parent as the sexually desired object, and introjects parental authority into his own self (superego). The child is thus both withdrawing bodily sexual desire back from the object, and at the same time gaining a strengthened, more independent mind. Might we consider that the body of the young Oedipus (male or female), into which the sexual desire for the object has been withdrawn, could now depend more on the containment provided by their own mind, and the mind (now more independent of the object) to depend more on the containment of the body. Does a healthy experience of the oedipal couple facilitate the "coupling" of the mind and body in the child? This can be further investigated clinically, in the manner of the examples given above.

## Conclusion

Bion, perhaps more than any other analyst, attended to "spaces". In "A Note", I ask whether maternal reverie and analytical alpha function are in some ways different. I suggest that in maternal reverie the mother can identify with the baby in a way that as analysts we attempt *not* to do with our patients. This requires us to turn away from a primitive animal part of ourselves (with all the inherent difficulties this causes us) in order to provide a "space" for the containment of the patient. Our training fits us to do this. I suggest that Bion's account of why feelings of loneliness are part of this work, may throw light on the loneliness Freud reports experiencing in his discovery of a psychoanalytic way of working.

The "Short Story" begins with Bion's imagined dialogue between mind and body. Bion gives a fictional account of the crossing of a gap—perhaps the most discussed gap in Western philosophy—that between mind and body.

Analysis is a relatively recent craft. It draws on age-old capacities, of course, but as an apprenticed craft, it is relatively recent. In the Bion quote which forms the base of "A Note", the mind is being adapted to a "new job". In the second quote—that of "A Short Story"—mind and body speak, each in its own language. Rather than the mind/body link being seen to be primarily that of sexuality, as in Freud, we imaginatively see the mind/body linked by K (the mind "knowing" the body and the body "knowing" the mind).

## *References*

Bion, W. R. (1958). On arrogance. *International Journal of Psychoanalysis, 39*: 144–146.
Bion, W. R. (1962). A theory of thinking. *International Journal of Psychoanalysis, 43*: 306–310.
Bion, W. R. (1963). *Elements*. London: Karnac, 1984.
Bion, W. R. (1970). *Attention and Interpretation*. London: Karnac, 1984.
Bion, W. R. (1991). *Cogitations* (F. Bion, Ed). London: Karnac.
Bion, W. R. (1993). *A Memoir of the Future*. London: Karnac.
Brown, L. J. (2012). Bion's discovery of alpha function: Thinking under fire on the battlefield and in the consulting room. *International Journal of Psychoanalysis, 93*: 1191–1214.
Masson, J. M. (1985). *The Complete Letters of Sigmund Freud to Wilhelm Fliess 1887–1904*. Cambridge, MA: Harvard University Press.

CHAPTER NINETEEN

# Flying thoughts in search of a nest: a tribute to W. R. Bion

*Salomon Resnik*

*Flight of ideas*

In the 1950s, I was able to attend Bion's seminars and group supervision. Then, for several years, I had personal supervision with him. Later on, as friends, we were able to discuss some fascinating topics. He helped me to develop my own ideas concerning the nature of psychosis, some of which I shall share with readers in this chapter. In particular, I wish to address a number of different kinds of symptoms that are related to the flight of ideas or "aerial thoughts". It is as if, in trying to think, some thoughts fly off, out of the thinker's control. Some patients seem to have the impression of being empty of thoughts and indeed of feelings. They have a sense of being "full of emptiness". In fact, we cannot speak normally about thoughts deprived of feelings. Thinking is an emotional, unifying or unified experience.

Xavier Zubiri (1980), the Spanish philosopher related to José Ortega y Gasset, spoke about *"inteligencia sentiente"* (sentient intelligence). In schizophrenia and in "obsessional" psychosis, mental and verbal thoughts are usually deprived of all feelings. They become, in my experience, *a-motional* (where *a-* signifies the absence of something). The concept of "a-motion" implies that thoughtful feelings are deprived of motion (movement), as though the capacity to experience thoughtful feelings was paralysed and deprived of all life. Sometimes in psychopathological cases, thoughts fly away by themselves, in a persecutory situation or climate (*Stimmung*) of the mind.

As Bion (1992) noted, sometimes thoughts are too violent or too forceful to be contained by the "mind-nest". One can imagine that they can be also expelled violently by the mind (becoming what Bion called "violent emotions", 1992, p. 249). The skull, where the mind is supposed to live, becomes a sort of "nest of disturbed or disturbing thoughts". Thoughts born in the mind can be conceived of as well-contained. When this is the case, we could say that the maternal function of the containing skull-mind is operating correctly. Winnicott often wrote about the good enough containing mother. The "good enough containing skull" could be thought of as a cradle or nest of proto-mental or mental experience. Sometimes thoughts are fused or confused with contradictory ideas, like an inner war in the mind; this is particularly the case in schizophrenia. In such a situation, a given thought will attempt to expel a contradictory one, as if it was being experienced concretely as an enemy.

### *Envious black crows: thoughts in the same nest*

In my work on Vincent van Gogh (Resnik, 2012), I emphasize the envious feelings of a split part of his mind, experienced as dark rays—or dark crows (in one of his last paintings)—attacking the bright yellow rays. These devastating envious inner attacks in Vincent's mind are personified by the dark crows (in the shape of a dark V, that of "Vincent") attacking the enlightening yellow field. Envious thoughts are destroying his own creative work at the time when he was beginning to sell his paintings and to be recognized in France as a true artist.

The content of the mind can be sometimes an inner war situation, in which some thoughts/warriors are trying to escape or to be saved, like Ulysses on his way to his original nest, Ithaca (*sein Heimat*).

In a state of crisis of the system of thoughts (ideas), an expelled or escaping thought will try to find a new harbor, a new nest. That is very difficult, because there is only one basic nest. Thoughts may then become wild and mad when they are far from their original nest-mind, leading to the experience of feeling lost "out in open space".

### *Cloudy floating thoughts and their transformations*

Bion (1997) suggests to me the idea of thoughts becoming wild: do they become "wild" when they are left on their own? When they are still little creatures or almost proto-mental? Is the ideal thinker, sitting in a "royal" chair, waiting for thoughts to come or rather just by thinking the thinker is implicitly created? (I explore this more fully, below, in the section entitled

"Thinking and the thinker"). A thirty-three-year-old schizophrenic patient of mine, whom I shall call Philip, was unable to speak and to think. In one session, he said:

"It's cloudy today. There's no sun."

I could see that the sun was in fact shining, so I asked him:

"Where are the clouds?"

He answered: "In my mind."

After a while, he said that he could see some tiny corpuscles in the mist.

"Are they thoughts?" I asked him.

"No," he answered, "It's something *before real thoughts* [proto-mental]. They are more ancient than you suppose."

"That is very interesting," I replied.

Philip went on: "As the cloud becomes more dense and more solid, it becomes a kind of solid wall."

"A petrification of something proto-mental, little ideas being born?" I thought to myself.

After a pause, Philip added: "If you think that I'm hiding behind a wall, you are wrong. I am *inside* that wall, trapped in it, *walled* in."

Then he seemed to calm down, and spoke about the sheep-like clouds in the sky announcing that rain is coming. In Italian "sheep-like clouds" suggest also that a slight shower of rain is about to fall: *pioggia a catinelle*. In Philip's mind there is a jump, a flying-away of inner cloudy thoughts, not-quite thoughts or just freed corpuscles expelled into the cloudy sky … But then they are trapped when the cloudy sky becomes petrified.

I thought, and Philip suggested it to me as well, that the petrified thoughts or proto-thoughts, if liberated, could become naked little thoughts, lost in the openness, lost in the cosmos … Later on, he described another phenomenological state of mind, in which the misty or cloudy confused, de-petrified thoughts could become more fluid and change into feelings or rain-tears … A painful moment … Would his suffering mind then be able to cry? Would the tears shed change into humanized little crying creatures? I was both observing and participating in that very intense transference experience, one that was also highly creative.

Philip was also quite gifted in communicating "sentient thoughts" through drawings.

One day he came with his father, who said: "He's not talking today, he's uncommunicative". But as Philip was moving his hands, I interpreted: Philip was trying to say with his hands something that his mouth did not want to pronounce.

"Maybe you'd like to draw?" I asked him, in order to help him to express himself without taking the risk of coming out of his closed world, his closed mouth. His hand then became a kind of expansion or extension of his talking mind. This phenomenon often occurs with autistic patients, as I have been able to experience. It can also function as an autistic defence in schizophrenia, as Bleuler (1923) suggested, when he spoke about a "dereistic" world.

Do schizophrenic patients think? Bleuler put forward the idea of *autische denken*, that is, they are able to think but in a de-realistic manner, one that lies within their own specific reality.

In Philip's drawing, the clouds look like hands, a sort of chain of "thoughts", one after the other; are they helping each other, "giving a hand" to one another? (Philip also took part in a therapeutic group of psychotic patients.)

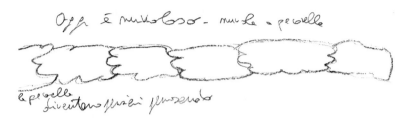

In a later session, he said to me: "Today, it's sunny." "Where?" I asked him. "In my mind: in fact I can think." Out-of-doors, the sun was indeed shining, and he made childish drawings in which he was trying to grab the living rays of the sun, the "king" of his universe.

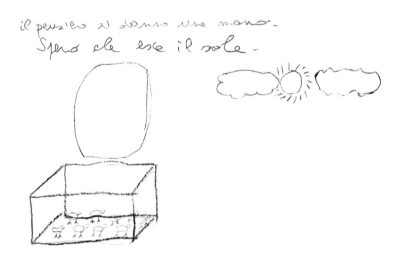

There is also a box—and at the same time a chair—inside which are "sheep-thoughts" (could this be the "royal" chair of the idealized thinker?). Are thoughts waiting perhaps for a shepherd, therefore paralysed and/or astonished? The sheep-like clouds have changed in fact into little sheep inside a closed rectangular mind/chair. Where are the flying, lost thoughts? Can they find a resting-place? An obsessional, rigid one—a square-shaped, non-flexible aspect of the mind, a square nest?

### Thinking and the thinker

Philip was beginning to think for himself and to give meaning to his thoughts and thoughtful feelings.

"How is it that you are able to think now?" I asked.

"Just by thinking ..." was his reply. The gerund is very important to Philip, like in the Spanish poet Antonio Machado's work.[1] In the *act* of thinking, a pathway appears, as well as the thinker. There would seem to be a vivid transformation in which motionless or paralysed images, feelings, or thoughts, become *moving*: e-motional instead of a-motional.

Phillip's discussion of his chair drawing and its evocation of the concept of motion led me to hypothesize that his head, his "skull", sometimes became a protective warm nest, a circular container, with circular thinking, rather than a square one.[2] In that case I felt that his thoughts were able to feel alive and therefore at ease with one another; they became full of (e)motions; they could "be moved" and be "moving" for me in his presence, as was actually the case.

According to Philip, a thinker is created—and makes his way—by the very act of being able to link together solitary, lively, and fluid thoughts—in other words, becoming able to think and to express feelings through *mental* walking.

Are living fluid thoughts trying to get into some kind of relation with one another and become a thinking group or a world in itself? What are the energies, the forces, as Freud said, that can give life to the inner world? That can enable thoughts to talk among themselves? Sometimes, however, competition and a spirit of inner war can be powerful, particularly in cases of a split, tense, and therefore aggressive self.

## *Thoughts in conflict: where is the thinker?*

One day, Philip did a drawing in which competing thoughts/creatures were football players. From an archaeological point of view, they were players from another time, a rather eccentric one perhaps—there was no ball, unless perhaps it was hallucinated.

In the painful pathos of this football pitch drawing, the paralysis is aimed perhaps at avoiding movement, which might turn out to be a killing motion if the spirit of the ancient, perhaps pre-historical, wartime was still there.

Looking in detail at part of that drawing, this is what we see—an image of a prehistoric engraving. It reminded me of the archaeological discovery of engravings on the stones and rocks of Emmanuel Anati's work.[3]

Looking at Philip's drawing in terms of "prehistoric players", the outlook changes. It is as though an inner cultural primitive background of the mind is appearing in a playful setting. That might help up us to understand the origin of playing and "games" in our own inner world, a world in which images are perhaps masks of primitive thoughts.

"Playing" can turn into something combative or competitive among members of the same team, or in the mirror image of the team (symmetrical thinking). We could also try to understand, following Bion's idea, the different kinds of "transformation", pathological transformations.

How can cloudy, primitive, and perhaps competing thoughts, coming out of a mist or being liberated from their state of being walled-in, develop into a potential internal team looking for a playful dialogue?

I have elsewhere suggested, *à propos* of Vincent van Gogh's own drama, that internal competition or envy can have tragic consequences (Resnik, 2012). This has to do with object relations, both internal and external; a context of relationships and of language appears. Is thinking part of a living network of thoughtful feelings? Is the network a juxtaposition of different spheres or periods belonging to our internal and external cultural history? Memory is made up of traces or sensitive engravings on the matter of the mind coming out of an avoidable exchange between the inner and the outer worlds. This is what I suggested in my recent book, *The Archaeology of the Mind* (Resnik, 2011) in which, following the ideas of Semon[4] (1921), and Aulagnier (1975) with her idea of the "pictogram"[5], I was able to elaborate upon a theory in which sensory impacts become undifferentiated from early wounds. All of this, taken together, encourages us to consider the origin of pain and pleasure, perhaps undifferentiated from each other or coming together in a confused way. The newborn child (perhaps even the fetus) is probably sensitive to any sensual experience still undifferentiated but leaving, all the same, its mark or wound. Suffering is certainly one of the earliest experiences in life.

## Phenomenology of the transference

Philip's experience of a living and fascinating phenomenology of the transference situation bears witness to elements that are probably related to the origin of thinking in relation to sensoriality and the construction of an imaginary world. The little particles or "atoms" that Philip described (in the manner of pre-Socratic thinkers such as Democritus) change the nature of matter and its atoms, according to the different states of his emotional world. Antonin Artaud (2004), the great French poet, used to say that, for him, anatomic and atomic bodies were interrelated. Condensation, mist, and nebulosity take us back to the concept of a primary confusional state (in which the ego cannot yet recognize understanding and misunderstanding), which in turn is related to the proto-symbolic state, or proto-mental in Bion's conception.

The sensory perceptive experience, according to Julia Corominas (1993), is very important for getting in touch with the infant's primary development. Philip's different states of mind were related, as I suggested earlier, to different states or proto-historical and historical levels of his unconscious memory.

I believe that the geography of our memory and the scars of our wounds become mnemic marks of primary sensory experiences. Taken together, those wounds give shape to a sort of orographic relief map of our intimate history.

When Philip drew a group of sheep looking for a shepherd, it brought to mind Nietzsche's idea according to which "madness is a herd that has lost its shepherd".

Recently, Philip has been talking quite a lot about how he would like to take hold of the rays of the sun in order to be strong, saying at the same time that he felt envious of the king's son—and in his drawing he shows his fist.

In the phenomenology of Philip's thinking, the idea of a wound appears when a strong wind troubles and hurts his mind, that is, when he feels traumatized by those elements of nature. Between the nature of the mind and bodily existence, thoughts can be conceived of as creatures that can change, even though at times they may be paralysed and at others full of life; friendly or competitive, they can be kept alive and mobile. What sometimes dominates is disorder and discord between feelings and thoughts—when thoughtful feelings become alienated. In such a case, the mind, as a place for thinking, may feel a need to reorganize the setting and to build up a new network in which ideas will be held and kept alive.

266  THE W. R. BION TRADITION

In schizophrenia, discordant and disorganizing tendencies dominate; this inspired Chaslin (1912), the great French psychiatrist, to use the term *"folie discordante"* for what Bleuler (1923), in 1911, called "schizophrenia". Bleuler felt that what Chaslin called "discordant madness" was a good description of what he himself was calling schizophrenia.

## Depression in time

Philip used to be hospitalized in a mental health unit once a year—always, more or less, in June. Once he began to participate in the analytical group with other psychotic patients, he attempted to cope with his living time. Sometimes that was painful and he needed help to contain the pain—perhaps in a container made up of friendly hands that, together, would make up a chain. He had to face up to his normal depression and feelings of loss, and therefore to mourning processes.

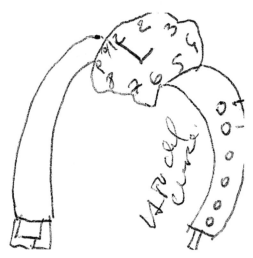

He made the above drawing. It is a wristwatch, a painful one, which looks like a boy who is suffering, with lots of wounds on his left arm, and his arms hanging down. He is trying to hold—or to be helped to hold—his living time, in a depressed chronological state: this happened in June.

Philip was able to express his depressive position, but he could not hold on to it with his arms. He needed many hands or arms around him to co-operate in this containing function until he became able to cope with his own feelings—for instance, feelings of loss and pain concerning his narcissistic wounds: not being loved "magically" by a girl whom he never approached. Above all, in his depressive position, he understood that he was indeed mentally ill and out of contact with reality. He began to define the "holes" that he felt, saying that that was when people began to criticize him, in voices that he was perhaps hallucinating.

Nevertheless, he felt the need to communicate and the wish to be appreciated and loved both by the group and by people in general. He felt guilty at the idea that he was perhaps very demanding towards his parents and upsetting them with his recurrent breakdowns. The fact that he did not have another one was an expression of affection towards his family and towards me.

Philip was able to fly away from his mind and to put his feelings and thoughts in the shape and nature of clouds floating in the sky.

My aim in this paper is to deal also with the flying thoughts that were expelled by his mind.

Bion spoke about flying thoughts becoming lost and "wild". This is what I wrote in a paper of mine published (in French) in 1998, "*Pensées sauvages en quête d'abri*" ("Wild thoughts in search of a shelter"): "Wild thoughts emigrate from their nest and are subjected to the vicissitudes of the life and death drives. They become feelings or thoughts lost in the forests of the cosmos."

Flying thoughts expelled into the open feel abandoned; they become wild because they do not know where to go and where their appropriate nest is.

Normally, in psychosis, patients who rid themselves of their inner persecutory object experience unbearable depressive feelings and do not recognize their own expelled thoughts when they want them to come back and be re-introjected. In his book *Invasive Objects*, Paul Williams (2010) describes these as "intruding violent introjections", which in fact should be seen as self-re-introjections or disturbing emigrants that are not recognized as such. Lost thoughts flying about are often not recognized by the mother-nest. Let down and with no aim, they behave like lost birds that are going mad. When they are not tamed, according to Bion (1997), this stops them from returning to the mind of their "creator". I believe that the "brain" must also be tamed, in order to be less hard and recognize those infant-thoughts. Sometimes, these can seem to be persecutory invaders, perhaps coming from another planet. Patients may hallucinate aliens in the street. But when we ask them to describe these alien beings, often we discover that they have some resemblance to the patients themselves. In such a case, patients need to be helped to recognize that the aliens are part of themselves, parts that had been expelled and transformed into intruding figures.

In fact the effectiveness of the therapeutic process in psychosis lies in helping the patient to transform wild thoughts into tamed, friendly ones, which once again can belong to the mind or the nest where they were born.

If this does not take place, they may again turn into wandering astronaut-birds lost in an open cosmic space. If the brain recognizes them and takes them back in—that is, if they return home—the mind becomes richer and able to think more normally. However, the original thinker in whom those thoughts were born does not always recognize them, so that the struggle is renewed between a new immigration and forced emigration.

Pathological projective identification, as described by Melanie Klein (1946),[6] is a very useful concept. Although people may try to be and to exist inside another place or object, nobody ever gets his true identity inside any other person's "skin".

Melanie Klein was inspired by Julien Green's (1949) novel, *If I Were You*, in her attempt to share her understanding of projective identification. The hero of this novel, Fabien Especel, was searching for a new identity. He could not tolerate being inside his own skin. He wanted to be in the skin of someone whom he could admire, someone who aroused feelings of both admiration and envy. The object of envy becomes an admired or idealized object, and that is what he wanted to become. This is the case in psychosis, in which the patient wants to wear the mask of the character that she admires enviously. Fabien tried to get inside the people who were working with him and whom he used to admire. But he was never happy. When he was someone else, he still wanted to be another person whom he admired very much. He could never be entirely happy; to some extent disappointed, but also partly happy at being himself again, he returned to his own body—but too late, for he was dying.

One of the problems with psychotic patients is that sometimes they cannot break free of the mask of the idealized object or character; they become trapped. They lose the opportunity of being themselves again. That was what happened to Fabien in Julien Green's novel.

## Conclusion

My aim in this chapter has been to share with the reader something of my understanding of psychosis and its relation to Bion's formulations and thinking, as well as to illustrate my feelings and the patient's feelings when we try to help each other in our difficult task of working together in a therapeutic situation. I wanted also to show how involved we were in this painful and fascinating experience of discovery, in that adventurous journey inside the unconscious transference situation with psychotic and non-psychotic patients. At the same time, I intend this paper to be the groundwork for research into proto-mental and mental phenomena, partly founded on Bion's ideas. I have attempted also to suggest some new points of view on the subject, which, I hope, will enrich this adventurous experience in a way that will make this research of some use to the reader.

## Notes

1. Antonio Machado (1875–1939) the great poet from Seville writes (in *Caminante no hay camino*):

    *Caminante son tus huellas*
    *el camino y nada más;*
    *caminante, no hay camino*
    *se hace camino al andar.*

    *Traveller, the road is only*
    *your footprint and no more;*
    *traveller, there's no road,*
    *the road is your travelling.*

    I am grateful to my wife and collegue Ana Taquini Resnik, for this reference.
2. See "Geometrical thinking", in Resnik (2011).
3. Anati is a well-known archaeologist in Valcamonica (Italy), where he founded a research center on prehistoric Camuno culture. I myself was fortunate enough to be there during a congress on prehistory, and to discuss with him and his colleagues ideas about prehistoric art and its cultural background.
4. Richard Wolfgang Semon (22 August 1859, Berlin—27 December 1918, Munich) was a German evolutionary biologist, who believed in the inheritance of acquired characters and applied this to social evolution. His ideas of the *mneme* (based on the Greek goddess, Mneme, the muse of memory) were developed upon early in the twentieth century. The *mneme* represents the memory of an external-to-internal experience. He suggested the idea of a written or engraved irritable substance in the mind.

Semon's book *Die Mneme* (Semon, 1921) directly influenced the Mnemosyne-project of the idiosyncratic art historian Aby Warburg.
5. The French psychoanalyst Piera Aulagnier spoke of the pictograms of the unconscious. I personally believe that the original sense-perception (or *mneme*) is a painful mark, an imprint that pricks the substantially fragile matter that is our mind.
6. In the beginning of the 1960s, there was a meeting at the British Institute of Psychoanalysis and Mrs. Bick asked me to find all the references and discuss them, with the idea of a future publication. Paula Heimann on that occasion emphasized her idea of forceful projection into the object, in the case of projective identification, and I agree to some extent with this.

## *References*

Artaud, A. (2004). *Œuvres*. Paris: Gallimard.
Aulagnier, P. (1975). *The Violence of Interpretation: From Pictogram to Statement*. Routledge, London 2001.
Bion, W. R. (1997). *Taming Wild Thoughts*. London: Karnac.
Bion, W. R. (1992). *Cogitations*. London: Karnac.
Bleuler, E. (1923). *Lehrbuch der Psychiatrie*. Berlin: Julius Springer.
Chaslin, P. (1912). *Éléments de Sémiologie et Clinique Mentales*. Paris: Asselin & Houzeau.
Corominas, J. (1993). *Psicopatologia e sviluppi arcaici*. Roma: Borla.
Green, J. (1949). *If I Were You*. New York: Harper.
Klein, M. (1946). Notes on some schizoid mechanisms. *International Journal of Psychoanalysis, 27*: 99–110.
Resnik, S. (2011). *An Archaeology of the Mind*. Scurelle (TN): Silvy.
Resnik, S. (2012). *L'arte del dettaglio. Sulle rocce di Capri, van Gogh, Pan ed Egon Schiele*. Capri: Edizioni La Conchiglia.
Semon, R. (1921). *The Mneme*. London: Allen & Unwin.
Williams, P. (2010). *Invasive Objects*. New York: Routledge.
Zubiri, X. (1980). *Inteligencia Sentiente: Inteligencia y Realidad*. Madrid: Alianza Editorial.

# PART V

A CLINICAL EXCHANGE

*Editors' introduction*

In 2012, a meeting took place in Marrakech, Morocco in which a small group of analysts from all three regions of the IPA met to engage in clinical discussions under the broad heading of "a Bion conference". One of the important subtexts of the conference was the creation of an opportunity for dialogue between French- and English-speaking analysts, intended to broaden appreciation of the different cultural contexts in which Bion's ideas had taken root and been developed. The clinical exchange taken from that meeting and presented here reflects both the depth and the spirit of the discussion. As readers will discover, Nastasi offers a very moving and poetic description of moments from the analysis of a deeply troubled and disturbing patient. Levine uses the opportunity of this elegantly presented case material to explore the intersubjective dimension of the analytic process, as reflected in the analyst's reverie, the communicative aspect of projective identification, and the intersection of two unconscious minds in the service of representation, mentalization, and the creation of mind and meaning.

CHAPTER TWENTY

# A silent war: dreading recovery*

*Antoine Nastasi*

Twenty minutes to eight. Eight o'clock is the agreed time of his sessions, three times a week. He was ringing my doorbell insistently; I was still getting ready. One day, when I went to fetch him in the waiting-room, I realized that, while he was waiting for me, he had gone to the toilet—in a very violent way. I was assaulted by the stench and, in the grip of a silent kind of nausea, I felt afraid.

She's been dead now for a long time. Every evening, the same scenario. At bedtime, all through his childhood, his mother would tell him to come into her bedroom. There, he was caught up in the combined effect of depression and the heat of terrifying desires. As she became more and more drunk, his mother told him of her private feelings; she shared with him her secrets and her extreme pain, she became less able to maintain any sense of decency or wear her clothes properly. The memory of childhood infidelity tormented him. At that time, they lived in the south of the country. Invited to a friend's house, he was held back by that friend's mother while they were beside the swimming-pool, but he ran off, not daring to be even later than he already was—his mother was waiting for him, but that woman was attractive and the thirteen-year-old boy that he then was felt panicky for a short while.

I often made links between the times when he was bathed in sweat, smelling of alcohol, lost in a quite extraordinary agitation and trying to get back to normal via an attempt at seduction that brought to mind the smell of urine and dirty underwear. I often made links between that style of being—because it was not a case simply of isolated incidents—and that powerful memory. The very long beginning of that analysis was marked by the smell of sweat, the dampening

---

*Presented at the March 2013 Bion in Marrakech conference, Marrakech, Morocco.

of the couch, the alcohol about which he never said a word, and the absolute impossibility of any respite.

One fragment of a vague dream did, however, remain present for quite some time. In the mist, a watchtower, men in rags—he was among them—waiting for some scraps to eat; the queue was a long one, and danger was everywhere. I could feel disgust at this cannibalistic, bloody, and excremental universe. The feeling of not being able to break free of the substance that was sticking to us. He spoke of the Stalag, which, in my mind, I linked to Cormac McCarthy's *The Road*. My trousers and his are stiffened by a packet that, through both its material aspect and its smell, gets front and back all mixed up.

The glimmer of another world, of another body, of another father begins to light up the sessions and he meets Basil. They will subsequently live together. The patient's days are those of a senior executive—exhausting. He writes, tells me about his short stories, quotes extracts from his poems and stages a one-man show. He goes off on a theater tour while at the same time travelling all over the world for the multinational company he works for. He feels invaded by Basil, but he accepts that promising sign of life. They buy a priory and his never-ending busy life becomes even more intense due to the work that has to be done, the gardening, inviting family and friends … They replant the hedges; I point out to him the fact that hedges and embankments represent, in a cultivated landscape, the primitive forest. He is very pleased with that image; he tells me how he discovered the complex biotope of these fragments of a forest, species of animals, the range of flora, preserved specimens, and above all how it spreads out all over the land, how that preserved liveliness of the borders spreads into the plots of land.

**11 June**. I had an argument with Basil. I feel I'm not being understood. I wonder if I have some tendency towards being paranoid. The whole world is against me. I feel threatened. And there's the feeling of not being able to talk, of having to shout. It's as though I were reacting to something that happened a very long time ago. As if I were using the weapon that I ought to have used in the past. I'm going round in circles, I can't see any way out, unless it's a kind of responsibility. As though I had to remember in order not to collapse, or else I have an oversized ego. I'm speaking only about myself, as if I were at my own bedside.

I spoke to my father. I hadn't spoken to him since the time when I got angry with him. I was pleased that he was worried about me.

– Does that calm down what you call paranoia?
– Yes, it's as though he acknowledged something, a kind of acknowledgement of his inadequacy. If he can take something on board, then I can too.
– Being in his rightful place.
– Yes, exactly.
– Maybe you're afraid that I won't be able to take things on board?
– It has to do with my father and with Basil, not with you. It's here that the main thrust of all the violence should be expressed. Three male characters. I don't like people telling me what to do. Basil—am I with the right person? Yet it's the best thing that's happened to me in such a long time. He's lively, he exists—and that's a good thing. It's as though the need for acknowledgement is less powerful now.

When I came here, I thought that I was either mad or a genius—I didn't want to be just normal. I wanted to be everything for my mother. I wanted to be everything—her adviser, her lover. I thought that that was what was expected of me—to be everything for someone. Basil holds his own, he loves me but he's not going to accept everything that I say or do. And that, too, reassures me.

I realize that this is the first time I've told you that I'm capable of not wishing someone well. I'm going through a stage in which I'm redefining the image that I have of myself.

- The child you once were went beyond the boundaries of his place as a child.
- That child was quite fearsome, and manipulative, ready to do anything to catch people's attention. When I was a child, I dreamt of having some kind of illness or disability that would make people look at me, draw their attention, their compassion.

I think that I existed because I made my mother worry. I have the impression that I'm a hypocrite, wrapped in a false image of myself. There is in me a wish to destroy Basil, to wound him in what he is. I'll have to be careful, because I'm really putting our relationship to the test.

**12 June**. I was wondering if you were feeling okay. I saw a programme about how homosexuals have been perceived over the centuries. That did me good. A forty-year-old man said that he felt dirty. I thought of illness, the wish to be disabled, as though I were saying: "Look at me, I'm different".

- You were wondering if I was ill?
- Yes, I didn't make the connection. Yesterday, I said to myself, when I was telling you about Basil, that perhaps you wanted to be the only person with whom I have any kind of relationship. Maybe you feel disappointed at not taking up all the space. Illness was when it became possible to express feelings, to have a kind of merging-together relationship. As though illness did away with the prohibition against physical contact. With my mother, illness made physical contact possible once again.
- So your mother might have fallen ill once you'd grown up.
- I myself was very late in giving any concrete expression to my own desires—I was twenty-two. I wondered why I'd remained a child for so long. Being just as she was, not getting any older. I'm relating that to what I said about keeping to one's own place. Staying in a kind of childhood, with no sexual relationship, protected me, even though, later, I did take risks.
- Protected you from illness?
- From illness, from AIDS, from death—but it mutilated me too. I have just now understood that that means that no sexual relationship can exist without death.
- As though death had been here for a long time.
- I don't understand—what do you mean "here"? In this room?
- In this analysis.
- Hmm, yes, I think … I remember saying here, a long time ago, that when things are aroused, it's both sides that are aroused at the same time—Eros and Thanatos. But I understand that there is no race against death, it's a case of "living with" … It's as though you were telling me

that this work will soon be over. Staying in childhood is one way of dying. Such a terrible fear about sexuality, not growing up …
– And the dread of violence …
– And of the violence that is part of it. Destruction and wrecking. Wrecking—that makes me think of my mother's stomach. The failed Caesarean meant that her body carried the mark of sexual intercourse …
– That ruled over your birth.
– Hmm, hmm … Is that not linked to the idea of death? In fact, I've always been interested in the word "maieutics".

**15 June**. In the taxi coming from the airport, I said to myself that none of this was doing any good. Is it possible to make a mess of an analysis? End up in a kind of disintegration? If I had met somebody, I would have smashed his face in. In a sort of extreme aggressiveness. I again felt as though I were a victim, and I don't want to have that idea. I have a kind of suppressed violence, I'm afraid it'll just sweep me along.

– Yes.
– Anyway, it wants out. With Basil, it's as though feelings of humiliation were never far off. A feeling of being treated like a child, being looked upon like a child. No matter how slight the criticism, I feel deprived, denied. Like a child, and I can't stand it, it makes an intense violence burst out, one that is quite disproportionate in terms of the actual situation. I'm thinking of when, as a boy, I came down for breakfast and said: "Dennis isn't here? But he slept here overnight." My father went into a rage saying that I knew perfectly well that Dennis hadn't slept here—that was true—and I just broke down; I had no idea where I was or what I could do to calm down my father's anger. It's as though I wanted to hit somebody, like in that film in which the hero gives out a loud cry that cleans everything up. Throw all of it outside myself.
– Why was Dennis there at that time?
– Because he was a friend. I'd met him at judo. When we were competing, we didn't hurt each other. My father somehow felt embarrassed by Dennis. Maybe I wanted to let my father and mother know that I had my own world, my own territory.
– Dennis was elsewhere, not in the center of your parents' world.
– The center?
– Yes, in the center of the bed, as it were.
– Hmm. In gymnastics, we had to climb the rope, a knotted rope … The stupid teacher saying "On you go, on you go" all the time. I couldn't do it. On one occasion, I did manage, I was right on top, my penis rubbing against the rope, how delightful. Up there, my arms were letting go, I was afraid I'd fall down. Once back on the floor, I ran to the toilet because I was afraid I was going to pee everywhere. Something important had just occurred.
– Here also, perhaps?
– Yes, I was thinking that too.

**22 June**. The image of the little boy on the rope. I said a knotted rope, but in fact it was smooth, there were no knots. Knots have sexual connotations. Something knotted together there.

My grandmother died. It was as though that didn't mean very much to me. We three brothers inherit our mother's share—there's a conflict with one of our aunts who wants to sell off the furniture. That argument with her got me back on my feet, because I hadn't been feeling well. Basil's in Russia; I don't like cooking for just myself. I don't feed myself properly, it's like a throwback to my childhood.

- About that knotted rope—did you have one image or several images?
- It was as though I had escaped from myself, I could see myself. And here too I see myself. Terrible weakness, my arms failing me, the movement of the rope turning round, and the effort that I'm putting into holding on to it, the rest of them all sitting on the floor underneath. I imagined that, when I got back down, they'd all be laughing at me.
- Holding on means not being swallowed up into the void.
- Not being swallowed up by something that comes from within and carries you away. At that point, I learned to beware of myself because there was something going on inside me that I couldn't control. You can never be sure of what might happen inside yourself. The idea of an imposture is running through my mind—maybe that has something to do with the rope thing. Right now, I'm here but I'm not here, not present. I'm scared about not being able to control things. I live against my will. Something more powerful than me is expressed through all of that. I'm constantly making the effort to preserve a kind of facade, so as not to be frantically running away. Impossible to control a desire.
- You can't have an erection to order!
- You can't have one to order. I don't know why I used the word "desire".
- Maybe the rush to go to the toilet wasn't just a matter of wanting to pee.
- Yes, maybe it was an orgasm. The urgent need to have walls. Later—street urinals, smells, pornographic drawings, places for pick-ups even though I didn't want to. An underground dimension. As though things that are underground have to be placed in the sunlight to dry them out; wounds.
- Here.
- Yes, here. Bring out things that are damp. I was thinking of an excavation—today my grandmother will be buried. Three weeks ago, I saw my grandmother—she'd forgotten that we were supposed to be having lunch together. We were all in the kitchen, she came in and said that she'd suffered a lot, that my grandfather had become chronically depressed after the death of his brother during the First World War. She said: "If I had known, I'd never have married him". Also, my father's father was depressed too. I feel I want to take refuge in that inheritance.
- Taking refuge in something unsteady brings to mind the rope: let it all go.
- Yes, yes, as if the struggle were being played out again. Something unsteady; that's exactly it.
- It's also as though desire could carry everything along with it, and that some attempt had to be made to contain oneself.
- Desire is a threat to consistency, it's unsteadiness and perhaps imposture too. Being torn between two things. Education with respect to desire, I never had any of that. It's a kind of explosion that shatters everything. And you have to struggle to stick things back together again.
- Did the teacher hold the rope?

– No, he would just smile, in a mocking kind of way, he could see I was struggling. He saw my helplessness and my desire, and he was watching me. The word that comes to mind is "sardonic". I don't remember his face, I just remember someone standing there. There's a kind of key between his look, the rope, and my ecstatic pleasure. Something gets knotted together there. The fact that it was a man is important ... and, too, the fact that it was in public. He seemed to be saying: "Look, look ..." There's something to do with the shape of, with marking the boundary of desire. One part of the key is that my desire had no shape. It's something of a paradox, but that's how it is. I have to become an adult. My grandmother's death will help me.

**20 July**. It's the first time I've felt summertime to be like something unknown. There's the idea of abandonment, and that's strange. When I got up this morning, I thought to myself that I had changed you into a guardian.

– So now you can allow yourself to feel abandoned?
– Hmm. I feel really good when I've got something to do in the morning and in the afternoon, when in-between there's some space just for me.

**3 September**. My father's been hospitalized for his depression. I find it difficult to love him. The old lion is on his knees. A strange feeling—maybe we hit on him too much. He told me he'd spent his life running away, trying to avoid trouble. I said that I preferred that kind of talk to his so-called heroism. He said he felt that he was to blame for my mother's death. He had prohibited her from going to see a "shrink" who might have been able to help her. He said he was jealous of me, of everything, of his grandchildren. It's very difficult to help somebody you don't love.

– As if fear could subside when we reach the point where we have feelings that frighten us: "I don't love him," you say ...
– When did we lose each other? Did I ever love him? It's all a bit too much.

**4 September**. I know that the end of the analysis will impose itself on me and that it won't be my decision but a shared one. Wanting to walk without crutches. I used to hear my mother say that: cigarettes, alcohol, medication.

– There is perhaps a difference between that kind of dependence and a dependence that links you to other people?
– My relationship with Basil is strong and simple, and that helps me to have some confidence in myself. It's because I can feel that link that I want to free myself of other kinds of dependence. We used to be very much in love, but at the same time anxious—now things have calmed down.
– The other person is less dangerous?
– Yes, let's say that the other person is able to love.
– Hmm ...

– I was with my father. Basil came up and said that he didn't want me to get into a terrible state. He cares about me … and in fact I don't think I've ever known that before. As things progress, there is the feeling of being oneself on the crest of the wave.

**7 September**. Something came into my mind at the door, there: "It was quite an adventure". Yesterday, at the theater, the play was *Six Characters in Search of an Author*. I thought of the characters saying: "We are more alive than you are". Like here: characters wanting to act in a tragedy and waiting for an author. One of the characters says: "You can't imagine how painful it is to be playing the same thing all the time". The author gets completely taken over by his characters. And there are also the characters that the author refused. I've written poems that I've never managed to show anyone. There is a link between the work I'm doing here and the launching of that collection. I thought that the day I publish it, my work here would be over.

**10 September**. As she was dying, my mother said to me: "See what your father did to me". I thought that she would have deserved to be happy. She was happy when she was young. There's still something terrible between my father and me. I'm trying to get things straightened out between us. When that will indeed be the case, I don't know what will happen. Does forgiveness exist in psychoanalysis?

– Maybe one day we can say to ourselves that we can spend our lives actually living it rather than looking for revenge?
– Yes, is it a nice enough path to follow in order to become more and more free? How am I to leave you?
– Become more and more free?
– Yes, I met someone again, quite by chance, I was very pleased. Parts that are reconciled, things that come together again. Maybe it is indeed all about giving up revenge. But you first have to feel it, experience it, the desire for revenge. Maybe that's the major stumbling-block with religion.

**11 September**. As I was on my bicycle on my way here, I thought of Basil sleeping.

– The present, life in the present.
– Yes, dilate and restore the present. Something anchored, something quite physical. I thought of what Mitterrand said about Rocard: "He wanted to be president, but he never wanted to be a candidate". It brings to mind what's taking place here—to be a man implies that you're ready to fight. In our society, there is a kind of connivance between politics, the media, culture and the world of economics.
– Connivance—an unnatural alliance.
– Vagueness, non-separation?
– Yes.
– A mass that cannot be differentiated … The similarity between homosexuals and Jews is that they're always on their guard. In our building, all the neighbours invite one another, everybody's welcome in our flat, but I do feel that that could change so very quickly, regime

change … My existence does not go without saying, it's as though I were living something that is bestowed on me.
- So the progress you're making in your life and in your analysis might be taken away from you?
- Yes, I try to reassure myself, but …

**14 September.** My relationship with my mother was very dense. If losing that means life or death, it's as though you could say: "I'm behind what I say" or "Look at who's behind what I say". Getting into a relationship that doesn't entail a commitment could lead to losing oneself.

- To not existing.
- Yes, not existing … The discovery, when she died, that words are both powerful and powerless, that they are no substitute for life. I said to myself that I'm speaking like you do.

**18 September.** Pierre Guyotat's work—and *Coma* especially—which has been with me for so long, now resonates as though it were some way off. I said to myself that I was no longer depressed. You can write while you're outside of yourself, when you are a tree or an animal. Guyotat said: "The splendour of that language kills me".

- Some way off?
- Yes, but I still feel some kind of nostalgia. It's not what I'm experiencing at the moment, but I could go through it again. It has to do with fate. It would be nice to live one's whole life in that kind of condition. I would like to write something that would begin with: "I never went back to the cemetery". I'm thinking of the cemetery in the Massif Central, the white gravel, contrasting with the surrounding forest. Guyotat raised the question "Oeuvre or life?"—I'd prefer to answer "Oeuvre and life". But that way of putting it is artificial. You have to have dinner with the devil before you know that you never want to do it again. Maybe I feel that I exist, but that's not the word. A kind of energy that is coming back. Like the idea of a wave, and you have to stay on top of it for as long as you can. Because you know that in the end it'll collapse. I feel terrified at the idea that analysis might take my oeuvre away from me. Created from clay, like God. Being the guardian of what is sacred. Maybe the distance is simply relative.

  I'm afraid to talk about Guyotat or Pessoa, because I'm afraid that what I say might come about in reality; that words precede life, and carry us along with them. A cloud that precipitates into rain. At some point, there's a kind of crystallization, and words become life.

- That's very frightening.
- The fear that words become life. That book of poems, I must have it published, but it's hard for me to let it out of myself, hand it over, deliver it. "Deliver" is a very biblical word—God delivers his son to other men. Christ is God's word, the word is uttered, let out.
- The word uttered is feared.
- Yes, let out in the midst of wild animals, set loose by the father. God delivering his son to other men—it's both an abandonment and an act of love.

**25 September.** A nightmare: I was sleeping beside someone—and that someone was my father.

**1 October.** The work of analysis has made me more human, and that's a good thing as regards the inhumanity of solitude. But has it not taken the edge off things?

**2 October.** As I was coming upstairs, I thought about my garden, the shrubs that I have to plant and all that. And I said to myself: "Go slowly". When I went to my mother's funeral, I travelled by car, making the most of the journey, listening to music and looking at the surrounding countryside. There was some beauty within all the pain. It was one way of experiencing loss to the utmost.

- In all that slowness, there was perhaps being built up some differentiation between her and you.
- One was still alive, the other was dead. Time solidifies difference.
- Leaving slowly.
- Infusing; you have to learn not to eat too quickly.
- Give separating the time to exist, because there is also everything that we keep.
- Accept the slowness of the flesh. There is something very productive about the mind-body duality, it's a very resourceful tension. I don't remember who it was who said "the murmur of the body to the spirit" or "what descends into the body".
- You seem to be hinting also at the articulation between masculine and feminine.
- The androgyne before separation. I bought a book about the life of a transsexual.
- There's separation, the journey to go to your mother's funeral and the separation between masculine and feminine elements inside oneself.
- Yes inside oneself, because there's an acknowledgement of difference within oneself: is it possible to be consistent?
- Yes.
- In a unity that is not oppressive?
- Yes.
- "In my Father's house there are many mansions"—does that mean that in each of us there are a lot of different parts?
- It implies that, at least for some of those parts, it is possible to be close to one's father's house.
- Yes, the father's "house" could be understood to be his "presence".
- The opposite would be everything broken up.
- The possibility of the father's presence lets us see the end of terror … and the possibility of being pardoned as long as feelings can be shared. It's almost domestic or carnal. What I said there has to do with experience: making room without being overwhelmed.

**5 October.** I don't want to see my father completely down. And I don't want to confront him. He built himself up like that; we're not going to pester him now about it. I feel closer to my father than to my brothers, I realize that now. It's as though I was in a different position from that of the block made up of my brothers and their wives.

- Separating from an undifferentiated block!
- Maybe living implies being different.
- Yes.

– The idea is to remain non-aligned. Alignment is deadly. Differentiation is a process that hurts, because to some extent it is also a tearing-apart. Am I not also talking about tearing myself away from you?

**9 October**. Now that my problem with filiation has moved a bit into the background and is more settled, I'm wondering more about paternity. The cards have at last been reshuffled. I read *The Diary of a Transsexual*. Without going as far as that, I feel that some degree of reconstruction is possible. Like a piano on which we gradually become able to use all the keys. I savor the silence.

– Is it a new silence?
– It's very new, it's a navigation, the pleasure in letting things go their own way, in letting ideas just come into your head. Moses's skin was black; that must remind me of my childhood in Africa. My childhood has now been reconstituted … Maybe tranquillity doesn't take the edge off whatever is really sharp. It's the "over and beyond" that interests me.

**15 October**. I'm worried about losing myself and just letting everything go. There's something beautiful in an inner rebellion. I mean, not taking things as they seem to be. The road I've been following for some time now is life-giving, but it is also one of giving up things.

– Perhaps, in spite of the excruciating pain, the boy at the top of the rope was dominating the world?
– I don't know if it was the world, but he was certainly dominating something. He was dominating the world because he had taken refuge up there so as not to suffer any more. And—it's not easy, but out of that isolation, something was going to be created. What was the "trade-off"? To live by giving something that I don't want to give? It's as though the choice was between living and creating. But I changed the creation into something divine. I came close to it, but I never really got to know it.
– There wasn't only the fear of giving up something, there was also that of rebellion.
– Yes, the fear of rebellion has always been present, but I made the choice of putting myself at risk, of being provocative. In the midst of terror, there's some kind of ecstatic pleasure.
– Terror?
– The fear of being, I'm looking for the right word … of being in a kind of absolute solitude, in a kind of inhumanity, as though I was convinced that I could be self-sufficient. It's a strange idea, a bit romantic, feeding on the elation of literature … Like you said, the boy on the rope, it was both a terrible pain and a high degree of ecstatic pleasure.
– As he said this, the poem, "So Many Constellations," by Paul Celan (2001) came into my mind:

"I know./I know and you know, we knew,/we did not know, we/were there, after all, and not there/and at times when/only the void stood between us we got/all the way to each other."

## Reference

Celan, P. (2001). "So Many Constellations". In: *Selected Poems and Prose of Paul Celan* (trans. J. Felstiner). New York: Norton.

# Dreaming into being

# A response to Antoine Nastasi*

*Howard B. Levine*

I would like to begin by thanking Antoine for bringing this material and congratulating him for the work he has been able to accomplish with a very difficult, disturbed, and disturbing patient. I will attempt to use these sessions to illustrate and explore the intersubjective dimension of the analytic process, as reflected in the analyst's reverie, the communicative aspect of projective identification, and the intersection of two unconscious minds in the service of representation, mentalization, and the creation of mind and meaning. In order to do so, I will use and describe my reactions to this case material to illustrate the assumption that the text performs an unconscious action of mobilizing something within the mind of the reader—as the patient's discourse does to the mind of the analyst in the analytic setting—and as Freud said about the drives, "makes a demand upon the mind for work." This demand is for psychic regulation and tension relief through the creation of meaning and order out of the inchoate; for mentalization of the pre- or proto-psychic; for alpha transformation of excess and unruly beta elements; and for the construction of narrative. It is an innate, quintessentially human process that I have elsewhere (Levine, 2012) called "the representational imperative".[1]

When the case material arrived, I had not yet met Antoine and I was not familiar with his thinking or way of working. I only knew that I was expected to offer a response, hopefully in some "Bionian" way, that the audience might find "useful," "helpful", or perhaps "interesting." The title of our congress, "Fear and Conflict," was so general that I had no idea what to expect or what would really be expected of me. And yet, I can honestly say that I do not believe that I was worried, because I have given clinical discussions before large audiences many times before.

---

*Presented at the March 2013 Bion in Marrakech conference, Marrakech, Morocco.

The task was familiar and I waited for the material with a quiet, confident expectation, without giving it much thought. (Here, we might draw the analogy to the state of mind of the analyst awaiting the patient's arrival, a quiet expectation without memory or desire.)

When it did arrive—on Christmas Eve, like a holiday present—I put it aside with the intention of reading it after the New Year. At some point, however, my curiosity got the better of me and I could not resist opening it up and taking a look inside. I saw the title, passed quickly over it without really registering its meaning or considering its import, and began to read the first paragraph. It had a deep and immediate effect upon me. I was greeted with an almost assaultive string of words and the powerful feelings and images that they provoked: "war", "dread", "insistence", "intrusion", "violence", "assault", "stench", "nausea", "fear" ... And this was just the first paragraph! My God, I thought. What have I gotten myself into? I felt helpless, overwhelmed, filled with a sense of dread and I quickly shut the document on my computer wishing to return to more pleasant things.

This, then, was who and what I was confronted with: my introduction to this patient, a man, who, by the way remains nameless. Is he then a cipher? A ghost? Someone, something unformed and not yet mentalized? Or perhaps someone defined by his very namelessness, as in nameless dread?

As I sat with this initial experience, I no doubt sought to reassure myself as I recalled that as a medical student on a psychiatric service, I had a teacher who would conduct patient interviews in the following way: the patient would be brought in without any previous history or discussion. The professor, who I'm sure was not aware of Bion in the least, would greet the patient, conduct an initial interview for no more than two minutes, ask the patient to step outside, and then ask the audience of psychiatric residents, students, and other trainees to attempt to derive the patient's diagnosis, symptoms, and history from what that they had initially observed or could conjecture. After ten to fifteen minutes of this "myth building" exercise, the patient returned for a more extensive, traditional interview. Each time, the audience was surprised to learn how much had been revealed and could be inferred from even the tiny sample of initial data.

There is something in the spirit of that exercise and in my description of my own initial reactions to this material that is quintessentially Bionian. The listening and observing stance, the use of the analyst's self as a kind of receiving instrument for unconscious data, the preconditions for reverie, which include openness and negative capability (the capacity to tolerate ignorance). Each moment, if we are open to discovery and not put off by the disturbing nature of what we may find, we may encounter something different or new. This is what Bion advocated when he urged us to try to listen without memory, desire, or predetermined "understanding" and to make room for wild thoughts. He wanted us to take the word, "unconscious", seriously, so as not to be lulled into expectations that pull us inexorably back towards consensually validatable external reality or towards the familiar or the known. In *Attention and Interpretation*, he reminded us that what patients really need to hear from their analysts are things that they are truly unconscious of, because otherwise, they will be hearing about something that they can hear from someone else or that they may already know (Bion, 1970).

Although Bion did not use the term, "intersubjective", his concepts of alpha function and container/contained transformed our ideas of the analytic encounter and presented us with a model of psychoanalytic process, therapeutic action, and psychic development that was profoundly intersubjective in its characterization of how the minds of two people can interact affectively and unconsciously to perform the work of figurability and mentalization. Although not always given sufficient credit, I believe that his formulations were at least parallel, if not central, to certain concepts in French psychoanalysis, such as Green's "working as a similar other"; De M'Uzan's "chimera"; Widlocher's "third"; and of course the Botellas' description of *figurabilité*; etc. Each of these authors is attempting to name and describe the unconscious, co-constructive movement that can take place within the dyad—mother–infant; analyst-analysand—and that catalyzes and/or accomplishes a movement from pre- or proto-psychic to psychic, from beta to alpha, and from unrepresented, vague, and inchoate sensori-motor "inscriptions" to specific, verbalizable, represented mental states.

This is territory and a description that I assume most, if not all, of you are familiar with and that Nino Ferro and his colleagues, in particular, have expanded upon in their field theory: the extent to which at every moment, we are, along with our patients, not just empirical observers, but perched at the edge of a deeply intuitive creative process. The latter is not simply the embodiment or the uncovering of hidden archeological strata. Rather, it is very much the product of two minds linked together, engaged in the process of creating and evolving, "characters in search of an author", where participants spontaneously alternate in their roles of "transmitter" and "receiver". Initially, and perhaps more dominantly, the analyst will prove a bit more "authorial" than the patient, especially if, diagnostically, the patient resides farther from the neurotic-normal spectrum. But both participants will contribute the emotional raw material out of which the analytic field that they inhabit and construct will be composed.[2]

For the analyst, this is a blessing and a curse. It means that the opportunity to be a significant participant in the patient's psychic development is always present. It also means that the analyst will perforce be caught up in emotional storms and upheavals; that these will be both induced by the encounter with the patient and evoked from within the analyst's own vulnerabilities; projected and/or triggered by and "borrowed" from the internal world of the patient. Consequently, the conditions under which the analysis must be conducted will often be quite chaotic, not unlike the First World War battlefields to which the young tank commanding Bion was subjected. The problem then is "How to keep your head when all about you those are losing theirs?" Sometimes literally, as well as figuratively. Or as Bion once said, "How to make the best of a bad situation."

So here, with this patient, it was not "love at first sight", but rather repulsion, disgust, or perhaps even hatred. At first encounter, he is someone I do not think that I can stand, do not wish to get close to, prefer to turn away from. How interesting! For me, for Antoine, for the audience. How to make sense of this? How will we stand him? How does his analyst stand him? And with so much violence, revulsion, eruption, and despair in the picture, how does the patient stand himself?

Reading further, there is an air of great tension, high drama, an almost literary quality to the text. But then, almost immediately, with the appearance of Basil, there is a calming down that occurs. The "bloody, cannibalistic, excremental universe" of a post-apocalyptic Cormac McCarthy novel gives way to landscapes of the imagination, as we learn that the patient writes poems and stories, is involved with the theater, and is creating a home with Basil.

Concurrently, the analyst produces a metaphor: "hedges" and "embankments" are intentionally introduced as symbols of the primitive wild into a cultivated and domestic landscape. This seems to me to be an image of the linking and containing work that the analysis must accomplish. Surely, it is the product of the analyst's having absorbed and transformed the patient's projections; an act of *figurabilité*, the expression of alpha function, followed by the publication of an interpretation as an act of re-presentation. The patient responds (June 11) by introducing the pair: mad/genius and describing the manic wish to be *everything* for mother, "adviser, lover", anything but "normal". (The latter perhaps refers to reality and its limits.)

We next hear that Basil, with whom the patient has begun to live, "holds his own". Loves the patient, but has his limits. This reassures the patient (June 11). But the next day (June 12), the patient fears that the analyst will resent Basil's presence: "Perhaps you wanted to be the only person with whom I have any kind of relationship." The plausibility of this fear was supported the previous day, when the analyst made a "typical" transference interpretation, "Maybe you're afraid that I won't be able to take things on board", and the patient saw fit to correct him: "It has to do with Basil and my father, *not* you" (italics added).

This sequence seems quite instructive. We could view the transference interpretation as "incorrect", or correct but off in its timing, correct, but defended against by the patient, etc. From another perspective, however, the analyst's response may be seen as actualizing the narcissistically possessive mother in the transference and the field—what Ferro would call "casting". It is reminiscent of Freud's comment that one cannot slay an enemy in effigy and illustrative of how we unconsciously conspire with and respond to the patient to help bring those "enemies" on to the analytic field of battle.

The second half of the June 12 session contains some very heady discussions of sex and death, sex and violence, the metaphor of "maieutics", etc. In one part of me, it evokes a momentary envy: "God, why don't I have patients who can talk like this?" But on the heels of that thought, a remark made by Harry Stack Sullivan appears: "God save us from an analysis that is going well!"

I suspect that at least two important developments are occurring here:

1. Envy has more clearly entered the field in the form of this reader's reaction (countertransference).
2. The patient has responded to the analyst's remark by intensifying his performance for the analyst. He is now in the role of the "brilliant analysand"; the kind of patient about whom the analyst will think and treasure and write papers. Perhaps even the kind of patient one might chose to talk about at a conference in Morocco! Whatever else may be going on, this seems to bring to the fore within the field the living out of the drama of the narcissistic mother and the precious, golden child (enactment).

In the sessions that follow, sessions with reference to the rope-climbing incident from childhood, there seems to be too much going on to make real sense of: missed sessions, grandmother's death, childhood memories, etc. Perhaps the important message is in the process rather than any specific content. Some of the patient's remarks seem like super intellectualized analytic interpretations of the kind a patient wishing to be seen as "good" or "pleasing" might make—for example, a knotted rope somehow seems sexual.

Many of the fragments evoke images of being out of control: losing hold of the rope and crashing down in a humiliating heap; running to the bathroom with an almost uncontrollable need to pee or perhaps masturbate; the wild and exciting world of hidden, transgressive sexual encounters in public restrooms. Is the patient begging for containment? Perhaps the excitement of possibly realizing the narcissistic idealized state in the primitive mother transference is overwhelming him.

Despite these florid exchanges, the patient complains of feeling like an imposter (June 22) and not being present, Notably, it is the day of the grandmother's funeral and there is not one word, reflection, or feeling that we might think of as being appropriate to a death in the family …

The thread of the narrative ends here, without further mention as we jump to July 20 and the impending summer break in a very abbreviated report of a session. While it is true that one cannot report everything in a presentation such as this, we are being a shown a patient who omits mention of anything emotional connected to his grandmother's death and that is followed by an editorial truncation. Is the unconscious message here a vehement protest against sadness and mourning?

When the patient returns from the summer break, there is some support for this possible line of interpretation. There are references to real time passing connected to love and loss of love, to father's waning health and strength and, on September 7, to characters in a play wanting to escape from timelessness, wanting to have their play evolve, to take part in a tragedy, but needing the help of the author (analyst?) if they are to enter real time and escape the pain of endless, sterile repetition. Incredibly, these thoughts are followed by the patient's recognition that someday the analysis must end!

Three days later, this movement becomes more prominent when Antoine says to the patient, "Maybe one day … we can spend our lives actually living … rather than looking for revenge." To which the patient replies, "Yes, is it a nice enough path to follow to become more and more free?" And then poignantly adds, "How am I to leave you?"

The latter theme then seems to go underground, as Antoine comments instead on "Becoming more and more free." Is there a feeling here about letting go and ending that has temporarily led the analyst to join the patient in the suppression and avoidance of loss? If so, that collusion is only temporary. What seems to be at stake is how and where the patient will live his life: in fantasy, mania, and grandiosity or in the real world of love and loss. Thus, on September 18, the patient describes, in a speech that alludes to his manic grandiosity and god-like aspirations, the fear that analysis will take something precious away from him. He calls that something, "oeuvre", but I suspect it is his infantile grandiose narcissistic self he fears losing; the possibility of being "everything" for his mother or her stand-ins.

Despite this anxiety, by October 1 and 2, the patient can acknowledge the gains of analysis— he has become more human—and, via the memories of his mother's funeral, goes a bit further with the necessary work of mourning: not only her loss and the future death of father that is signaled by the latter's failing health, but his need to accept many different kinds of limits and disappointments: time and its passage, differentiation, separation, and the inevitable end of the analysis:

> "Differentiation is a process that hurts, because to some extent it is a tearing apart. Am I not also talking about tearing myself away from you?" (October 5)

> "The road I've been following for some time now is life-giving, but it is also one of giving up things." (October 15)

The session and this presentation end with a powerful moment of insight. The "ecstatic pleasure" of his narcissistic grandiose aims can only come at the cost of a terrible isolation, an "absolute solitude" that is "inhuman". Antoine ends with a quote from the poet, Celan. I am reminded of a phrase from the Hebrew Bible that is used in the Atonement service at Yom Kippur: "Choose Life!"

## Notes

1. Jean-Claude Rolland (1998) has similarly written of a "compulsion to represent".
2. This was a point that I was moving towards when I suggested that the analyst's subjectivity and countertransference reactions were two sides of the same coin (Levine, 1997).

## References

Bion, W. R. (1970). *Attention and Interpretation*. London: Karnac, 1984.
Levine, H. B. (1997). The capacity for countertransference. *Psychoanalytic Inquiry, 17*: 44–68.
Levine, H. B. (2012). The colourless canvas: Representation, therapeutic action and the creation of mind. *International Journal of Psychoanalysis, 93*: 607–629.
Rolland, J. -C. (1998). *Guérir du mal d'aimer*. Paris: Gallimard.

# St. Sulpice

# A reply

*Antoine Nastasi*

As Howard has correctly surmised, this patient wanted to be my best patient, just as he was his mother's *chevalier*. Indeed, his whole attitude was heroic. Was that heroism an attempt at avoiding non-existence? Was it a dramatization, a dramatic construct[1] that enabled him to preserve some form of existence?

In presenting him, perhaps I ran the risk of being in the same position as he was—simultaneously holding on to the rope and drawn towards the void. Is it possible, at times, to forget meaning and be surprised by form? A form that is linked to the void, as Celan's (2001) poem[2] would seem to suggest? Those renewed contacts take place in the shadow of nothingness. In my theoretical representations, the image of a monster plays a major role. I think that this is linked to the idea of nothingness, and perhaps even derives from it.

Intersubjectivity, the passing of material from one to the other in the transference encounter—it is indeed important to take these elements into account. In my theoretical reverie, as I put it elsewhere, there is a monster that "[…] is placed at the interstice between continuity and discontinuity … It is an organizing element that does not invalidate the essential (continuous) discontinuity […] It lies just where the passing occurs, while at the same time emphasizing the gap that it embodies" (Nastasi, 2004).

It seems to me that the fear of something within the self that is undifferentiated is very much to the fore here—the fear of the inevitability of going through some degree of non-differentiation. The beginning of the clinical presentation may bring to mind not only anality, but also an element of the mixing-together that is part of the transference encounter. This relates to a primitive form of contact (physical, emotional) in the course of which different kinds of material are mixed together.

I too wondered why, in this report, my patient remained nameless. Perhaps it has something to do with non-differentiation and the impact that this had on the intersubjective element. But since that time a name has appeared. With Basil, he found an alcove in the wall behind the altar in the priory chapel. When they dug into it, they saw first of all a hand holding a book, then a sixteenth-century statue—a polychromatic statue of St. Sulpice, with no head. He was enthusiastic and spoke of it as a kind of solidifying of foundations. In the wake of all this, two childhood memories began to surface:

– a missing incisor, atrophied. He saw in it a sign of feebleness, of femininity and of something androgynous; at the same time, it evoked the image of a man, a caveman with bared teeth;
– a tree-stump on which he hammered to the point of making it disappear.

I pointed out that he was trying to destroy an ancestral figure, a monster that was moving between us. An androgynous cave-dweller with bared teeth. I added that St. Sulpice and the monster were two aspects of the same character.

He replied: "I would not have wanted to be my father—that boy really was a monster."

## Notes

1. "Dramatic construct is the alchemy of what is built up, destroyed and in all cases revealed in the encounter, simultaneously with what is there presented (or fails to be presented) as though on a stage. It is also what is created in the form of elements that are displayed and dramatized, thus bringing into play the world of myths" (Nastasi, 2006).
2. "… were there, after all, and not there
   and at times when
   only the void stood between us we got
   all the way to each other …"

## References

Celan, P. (2001). "So Many Constellations". In: *Selected Poems and Prose of Paul Celan* (trans. J. Felstiner). New York: Norton.
Nastasi, A. (2004). Le passage et le monstre. In: *Communication n° 76*. Paris: Seuil.
Nastasi, A. (2006). Le transfert fragmentaire. Le tragique, le monstre, le fragment. In: *Enfances*. Paris: SPASM.

# PART VI

## SENSE, MYTH, AND PASSION

*Editors' introduction*

Readers of Bion have often found his writing style enigmatic and elusive. This may have resulted from the fact that while he was very deliberate about the specificity and exact meaning of what he hoped to convey, he was equally, if not more so, eager to challenge and stimulate the minds of his readers, so that they could come to their own understanding and use of whatever he had chosen to say to them. Thus, his style of writing illustrated a basic principle that informed his attitude towards his work with patients and a belief in the essential importance of learning from one's own experience.

One of his more famous and oft quoted statements appears in *Elements of Psychoanalysis*, (Bion, 1963), where he states that "psychoanalytic elements and the objects derived from them have … extension in the domain[s] of sense [myth and passion]" (p. 11). We have chosen this remark as a starting point for reflections and "imaginative conjectures" that explore, interrogate, and expound upon this assertion. Thus, we offer readers the responses of three authors, each of whom feels that their ways of working with and thinking about patients are deeply influenced by and engaged with thoughts and ideas derived from Bion.

Civitarese recognizes a central paradox in Bion's assertion about sense, because Bion (1970) was later to make clear the view that the object of psychoanalytic inquiry was not one that could be reached or apprehended empirically through the *bodily* senses. Hence, he sees Bion as seeking out "an alternative sensoriality" that is not of the physical senses. Given that "the facts of psychoanalysis cannot be seen with the sense of sight, heard with that of hearing, touched with that of touch, smelt with that of smell, or tasted with the tongue—in other words, that they are invisible and immaterial facts, even if concretely determined by cerebral events" (Civitarese,

Chapter Twenty-one), what was needed and what Bion sought and found in Freud was a "a model of a sense organ that is conceptual rather than anatomical" (ibid.).

Levine's essay on myth further extends the idea of a conceptual sense organ, as he examines "myth-making" as an aspect of the transformational change that can evolve from the intersubjective engagement of the minds of the patient and analyst. This creative, catalytic, and co-constructive effort is an illustration of Bion's theory of container/contained, with the "beliefs" that arise in one or another of the participants being seen as heuristic "myths", potential elements of psychic reality that can function dynamically as constructions, as described by Freud in his classic paper of 1937.

Migliozzi's exploration of passion is accompanied by an extended clinical example of her analysis of a very disturbed, psychotic, and suicidal adolescent. Citing Meltzer, she reminds us that passion is a component of the catastrophic change that must inevitably accompany true and significant psychic growth and development. Although passion may appear as unruly and disruptive when seen from the perspective of the patient's disturbed and disturbing conflicts, she wisely reminds us that at its more positive pole, "passion implies the experience of intensified emotions, sublime-transient, and exists within the vitality of the human experience in everything we do" (Migliozzi, Chapter Twenty-three). This more positive pole in the dialectic of passion is illustrated in the quality of her stance, which is filled with the passion and commitment that must accompany true analytic engagement and that informs her determination to be an analyst for her patient. In her view, it is the passion for truth that underlies and informs the genuine intuition and receptivity from which develops trust in exploring the unknown.

*References*

Bion, W. R. (1963). *Elements of Psychoanalysis*. London: Heinemann.
Bion, W. R. (1970). *Attention and Interpretation*. New York: Basic Books.
Freud, S. (1937). Constructions in analysis. *S. E., 23*. London: Hogarth.

CHAPTER TWENTY-ONE

# Sense, sensible, sense-able: the bodily but immaterial dimension of psychoanalytic elements

*Giuseppe Civitarese*

Bion began his career as a theorist of psychoanalysis with a strongly epistemological approach. His initial intention was to develop a scientific theory of the psychic functions with a view to resolving the confusion of the various psychoanalytic tongues. He eventually relinquished the aim of "mathematizing" psychoanalysis—that is, of raising it to a higher level of formalization—but never abandoned the wish to base it on secure foundations. Yet this quest paradoxically took the form of exploring an alternative sensoriality to that of the senses. Given that the facts of psychoanalysis cannot be seen with the sense of sight, heard with that of hearing, touched with that of touch, smelt with that of smell, or tasted with the tongue—in other words, that they are invisible and immaterial facts, even if concretely determined by cerebral events—Bion's focus shifted on to the type of sensibility required for grasping these facts. For this reason, he often quotes Freud's statement (1900, p. 594) that consciousness is the "sense-organ for the apprehension of psychical qualities", because Freud is thereby furnishing a model of a sense organ that is conceptual rather than anatomical. The following brief review of Bion's principal writings will illustrate the successive stages in the development of his theory.

*Sense, sensuous*

In *Experiences in Groups* (1961) the word "sense" occurs some thirty times. In most cases it refers not to the senses but to a psychical quality, as in everyday phrases such as the sense of responsibility, inferiority, disillusionment, hostility, vitality, independence, security, incapacity for understanding, and so on.

In *Learning from Experience* (1962) it is found about a hundred times—very often in phrases such as sense(-)impression(s), sense(-)data, or the "sense of reality", but also, and in particular, in Freud's formulation of consciousness as the "sense-organ for the apprehension of psychical qualities". This latter is manifestly the conceptual foundation of Bion's personal vision of the subject, which he constructs in his next book.

For in *Elements of Psychoanalysis* (1963), the word "sense" appears on some fifty occasions, but now takes on a complete and consistent theoretical meaning. Already in the very first pages, Bion states that an element of psychoanalysis—in a word, something that can be deemed a fact of psychoanalysis and is susceptible to interpretation—should extend simultaneously in the domains of sense, myth, and passion:

> Psycho-analytic investigation formulates premises that are as distinct from those of ordinary science as are the premises of philosophy or theology. Psycho-analytic elements and the objects derived from them have the following dimensions.
>
> 1. Extension in the domain of sense.
> 2. Extension in the domain of myth.
> 3. Extension in the domain of passion.
>
> An interpretation cannot be regarded as satisfactory unless it illuminates a psycho-analytic object and that object must at the time of interpretation possess these dimensions. In view of the importance I attach to these dimensions I shall discuss each of them in detail.
>
> Extension in the domain of sense need not detain us long. It means that what is interpreted must amongst other qualities be an object of sense. It must, for example, be visible or audible, certainly to the analyst and presumably to the analysand. If the latter presumption turns out not to be the fact the grounds for the presumption must be such that the failure in correspondence must be regarded as significant in itself. Put in another way when the analyst gives an interpretation it must be possible for analyst and analysand to see that what he is talking about is something that is either audible, visible, palpable or odoriferous at the time. (Ibid., pp. 11–12)

While Bion seemingly disposes quite hastily of the dimension of "sense", this impression is in fact misleading, because his meaning is not at all clear, as immediately emerges from the continuation of the relevant page. He begins by describing myth as something that allows the analyst to engage in "model making", to construct a "personal myth" for experience; it is not a theory—a model of a ship helps us to understand how it is built, but is not the ship—and so mythologies could be seen as "bad theories". He also refers to myth as the "'as if' component"—that is, a virtual dimension, a dimension of play or fiction. He then links it to "passion", which he strips of that word's customary implication of violence, emphasizing instead the *necessary* intensity that must be attained by the link to the object, whether it be of love, hate, or knowledge, if it is to be significant: a patient's expression of anger toward the analyst does not necessarily imply the presence of passion between the two parties, but suggests Merleau-Ponty's idea (Carbone, 2011, p. 19, translated) of the "institution of a *between* the two". In a surprising twist, the discussion of "sense" thus once again becomes interwoven with the other two entities:

*the evidence that passion is present that may be afforded by the senses is not to be taken as the dimension of passion.* That is to say, if the angry tone of the patient is judged to be evidence of hate it must not be assumed that passion has been discerned as a dimension of a psycho-analytic object, H in fact. Evidence may be afforded by the senses, in such an episode, that can be correlated with the evidence, *sensuous perhaps but not sensible*, of passion. *Awareness of passion is not dependent on sense.* For senses to be active only one mind is necessary: passion is evidence that two minds are linked and that there cannot possibly be fewer than two minds if passion is present. Passion must be clearly distinguished from counter-transference, the latter being evidence of repression. (Bion, 1963, p. 13, emphasis added)

Hence extension into the domain of passion means that there are two minds, that these two minds are linked by an emotional bond, and that a kind of third, or intermediate, area forms between the two. These brief indications already demonstrate that sense, myth, and passion cannot be separated because they are thoroughly interwoven with each other, together defining not only the elements of psychoanalysis and of interpretation—in Bion's view, interpretation should be characterized by these three aspects—but also the attitude of the analyst. Interpretation should be a narrative, a myth in the sense of the mythopoietic ability to generate new and original representations of the world, almost a poetic text, an understanding that cannot be separated from its sensible expression; it should be passionate, and hence not abstract or intellectual, and provide for an initial moment of pain, equivalent to becoming the O of the session; and, lastly, it should arise from the emotional experience shared with the patient—from intuition of the emotional truth prevailing at that point in time. Passion stands first and foremost for the love, like that of a mother for her child, that the analyst must come to have for the patient—not only because of the gift of "biological" birth, but because the analyst will then have truly "adopted" the patient, or invested the patient with his love, as all parents should with their child. However, it also stands for the capacity to "absorb"—almost in a metaphoric act of "exorcism"—the other's pain (to become "O") and hence the willingness to "suffer" that pain.

While extension into the domain of myth expresses the idea that we make sense of the world linguistically, by narration, extension into the domain of sense signifies that knowledge must be embodied—that is, based also in the body. "Becoming the patient's" O means thinking with the body, knowing aesthetically, and being receptive to the emotions pervading the analytic field. This knowledge must not be abstract, but must instead be based on the understanding that springs from sens/a(c)tions (and not solely on the perceptions of the sense organs). What in Freud are the drives become in Bion the emotions; but the emotions always spring from a relationship of love, hate, or knowledge with the other: relationship—the other (as well as the Other, with a capital, or in other words the unconscious symbolic matrix created by sociality) is always involved, and is involved from the start. So sense stands for the body, for sensoriality, and not for a sense organ. It also means that there is never any such thing as a pure perception. Perception is always anchored in memory, in the imagination, in the body. Sense refers to a concept of truth as shared emotional truth. As Lombardi puts it, "Bion's statement that *one thinks only in the presence of emotions* is absolutely uncompromising; and the following statement is equally uncompromising: 'Reason is emotion's slave and exists to rationalize emotional experience' (Bion, 1970, p. 1)" (Lombardi, 2012). By itself, passion cannot yet account for how to think—that is, also to think with the body.

Oddly enough, in *Transformations* (1965) Bion in effect reverts almost completely to a non-specific use of the word "sense" (which occurs in that work just under a hundred times), once again employing it in accordance with everyday usage. However, in a couple of quite memorable passages he does give a more precise definition of the word, as previously adumbrated in *Elements*, as the "inward eye", or "seeing in imagination"—as, if you will, the *tactus intimus* of classical antiquity (Gagliasso, 2001, p. 768).

> If the reader visualizes a point or a line, without representation of it on paper, he does something that has been variously described as "using his inward eye", "visualizing", "seeing in imagination", etc. I consider this activity to depend on a "mental counterpart of the sense of sight". Similarly the "bitterness" of a memory is dependent on a mental counterpart of the alimentary system; similarly with others including the reproductory system.
>
> The "inner" reproductory system, as I may call the mental counterpart of the reproductory system by analogy with the "inward eye" of the mental counterpart of the visual system, must not be confused with awareness of reproductive activity any more than visual images that are related to the activity of the mental counterpart of sight are to be confused with objects of sight. *The mental counterpart of the reproductory system is related to premonitions of pleasure and pain.* The second source of confusion may lie in my use of the term vertex. I am unwilling to use a term such as "point-of-view" because I do not wish to be reduced to writing "from the point of view of digestion", or "from the point of view of a sense of smell" when the distinctions between metaphorical and literal usages are fine yet difficult to preserve. (Bion, 1965, p. 91, emphasis added)

This passage is noteworthy, too, in showing the extent to which Bion considers the body and sensoriality to be situated in the mind. The mind is seen, as it were, as a virtual body, with organs and processes equivalent in all respects to their physical counterparts. Sight is the most intellectual of the senses. Bion therefore draws attention to the need to introduce the concept of the "vertex", in order to relativize the other senses that are more closely connected with corporality and to restore some additional space to them. Furthermore, he imagines the functioning of the mind as analogous to that of the body, describing it as a "mental" digestive apparatus, a "mental" reproductive apparatus, and so on.

### Sensible, sense-able

In the second passage of *Transformations* that I wish to discuss, Bion introduces the idea of hallucinatory manifestations as a dimension of analysis and of the sens-ible ↔ sense-able oscillation (i.e., the oscillation between what can be seen with the senses and what can be intuited with the senses; intuition admittedly needs senses, which are our window on the world, but only obliquely, indirectly, and with mediation).

> The analyst must be able to detect signs of projective identification in a field which, relative to that which obtains in classical theory, is, as it were, multidimensional [...] the analyst is in a position analogous to that of a listener to the description of a work of art that has been implemented in materials and on a scale that is not known to him. It is as if he heard the description of a painting, was searching on a canvas for the details represented to him, whereas the object had been executed in a material with which he is unfamiliar. Such a patient can talk of a "penis black with rage" or an "eye green with envy" as being visible in a painting. These objects may not be visible to the analyst: he may think the patient is hallucinating them. But such an idea, perhaps sound to the view of a psychiatrist, is not penetrating enough for his work as an analyst. *Hallucination may be more profitably seen as a dimension of the analytic situation in which, together with the remaining "dimensions", these objects are sense-able (if we include analytic intuition or consciousness, taking a lead from Freud, as a sense-organ of psychic quality)*. (Ibid., p. 114, emphasis added)

This passage is Bion's most extreme and most courageous attempt to conceptualize the nature of the facts of analysis and how to perceive them. In just a few lines he completely overturns our usual perspectives. The psychoanalytic equivalent of painstaking, recordable observation in the exact sciences is the capacity to hallucinate the object!—provided, of course, that this takes place in an analytic setting and against a background of myth and passion. This point was to take on an even more prominent role in *Attention and Interpretation* (1970): hallucination is stripped of its negative aspect if it is both the expression and the medium of unison with the patient's emotional reality (O).

Hallucination is thus seen to be withdrawn from the objectivizing approach of the psychiatrist and becomes a royal road to intuition; this proposition was to reach its full flowering in *Attention and Interpretation* with the concept of "transformation in hallucinosis" (see Civitarese, 2014a).

In *Attention and Interpretation*, Bion (1970) uses the word "sense" seventy-six times with reference to the world of space and time of the sense organs' perceptions (usually in the form of "sense impressions", "sense perception", or "sense data'; then as the "sense of loss" with regard to the definitory hypothesis; the "sense of gratification" afforded by hallucination; the "sense of freedom" derived from acting-out; and in the phrase "in the sense that"). He again stresses that psychical qualities cannot be apprehended with the senses, but only with a counterpart of the senses. In order to be real and true, the analyst must be "at one with the reality of the patient. Conversely, the more he depends on actual events the more he relies on thinking that depends on a background of sense impression" (ibid., p. 28). He must be receptive to the O of the session and capable of being in unison with O; he must cultivate a form of "mental fitness" (ibid., p. 41): the shunning of memory and desire is analogous to the avoidance of activities harmful to physical fitness (memory too, after all, being connected with the senses). The analyst's tactical aim, instead, is to enter into a state of "sleep akin to stupor".

> Desire, memory, and understanding are based on sensuous experience, expressed in terms whose background is precisely the same experience and which are designed for use related

to that experience. They are vitiated by the same defect as are formulations based on a background of inanimate reality when they are applied to biological reality. Anxiety, depression, persecution are not *sensed* (though common usage sanctions an analogical use of the term 'sensed' in a context in which it is not appropriate). The nearer the analyst comes to achieving suppression of desire, memory, and understanding, the more likely he is to slip into *a sleep akin to stupor*. Though different, the difference is hard to define. The sharpening of contact with O cannot be separated from an increase of perception, in particular of elements of K; this *sensuous sharpening is painful although partial and mitigated by the general obliteration of sensory perception*. The residual sensory perception, often auditory and restricted to particular kinds of sound, is responsible for inducing a sharp and painful reaction (similar to the startle reaction seen in babies). (Bion, 1970, p. 47, emphasis added)

Bion is clearly not referring here to Proustian involuntary memory, the dreaming memory that is the stuff of analysis (Bion, 1970), but to the precise memory of facts, events, and data—the exact counterpart of the perception of objects in external space. The data accruing from the senses are rejected to the point that the analyst must *actively* forget that today's patient is the same as yesterday's. To behave otherwise would be constitute "a collusive relationship intended to prevent emergence of an unknown, incoherent, formless void and an associated sense of persecution by the elements of an evolving O" (ibid., p. 52).

This is an extremely important point: deliberately abstaining from attributing a sense to things entails an immediate increase in anxiety and in the sense of guilt. That is why we defend ourselves by the institution of stocks of memories or by memories decanted into "institutions"—from monuments to festivals, from Parliament to psychiatric hospitals, from the "Complete Works of …" to marriage, and so on—all of which are ways of avoiding the new. Yet we cannot do without them, lest we plunge into a state of chaos. After all, "institution" also signifies the act of starting something for the first time; of introducing something new—"the foundation of …" The point is to preserve the salutary tension between the already given and the new.

In that sense the Genius and the Mystic, figures that surprisingly come alive in the pages of Bion, are not merely bit players on the social stage, but also, obviously, functions of the analyst's mind in a session. More particularly, they might also express the dialectic of "sens-ible" versus "sense-able", of what memory constantly "institutes" of the things presented to it by the senses versus what can be seen only with the *tactus intimus*—as if for the first time, with a sense of surprise, fear, and awe (note the phonetic symbol for this last word—/ɔ:/—and its similarity to O).

> Intuitive power cannot develop because it is hindered by such obtrusions of "sense". The institutionalizing of words, religions, psycho-analysis,—all are special instances of institutionalizing memory so that it may "contain" the mystic revelation and its creative and destructive force. The function of the group is to produce a genius; the function of the Establishment is to take up and absorb the consequences so that the group is not destroyed. (Ibid., p. 82)

As our brief review shows, the theme of the senses verges on obsession in Bion's works. What is the situation? On the one hand, he never ceases to emphasize that we can do nothing with the senses (which saturate memory and desire); while, on the other, he insists that what matters is the present, the here-and-now of the session, what is before everyone's eyes. He is manifestly implying the existence of an intimate connection between visible and invisible sensoriality. The non-sensible is the part of the sensible that is invisible to the senses. It would be sensible if we had senses that could see the ultraviolet or hear ultrasound. Non-sensory objects are non-sensory owing to our limitations, not because they do not exist. That is why Bion so often invokes subthalamic emotions, vestiges of fetal life, or of the inaccessible unconscious. In a passage of *A Memoir of the Future: The Dream* he writes: "The important senses may be the 'microscopic'—'ultra'- and 'infra'-sensuous" (1975, p. 99).

The concept of the "vertex", mentioned earlier, expands the area of the observable: Bion reminds us that there are in fact five senses and that, however absurd or odd it may seem to say "from the point of view of the sense of smell", the phrase actually makes perfect sense.

Bion is thus moving in several directions. Whereas on the one hand he maximizes the area of the sensory (to include also the non-*sensible* but *sense-able* sensory), and even extends it to the non-sensory, on the other he knows that the senses compete with each other: seeing obscures hearing and hearing obscures vision. So here we have the idea of negative capability as an instrument for raising the human reagent to the highest possible level. Hence in order to apply maximum gain to the signals of the non-sensory area we must set that of the sensory sphere (memory and desire) to zero. We ultimately deny the senses (i.e., we put them out of mind): "Many people are so lifeless that I could stare in silent admission that I did not believe the evidence of my senses" (1975, p. 4). Some theories seem to us to be so true when they have gained acceptance that they become blind ("Melanie Klein …"). Another outcome of Bion's journey here is his anti-scientific, anti-establishment, anti-British, and anti-religious polemic: institutions are all potential forms of blindness. At the end of his thoroughly original journey, Bion concludes in felicitous Kantian style: "Without intuition they were empty; without concept they were blind" (1975, p. 33), together with the notion of "not sight […] but insight" (ibid., p. 34).

All this suggests to me an interpretation of the concept of thought without a thinker. Might it not be, precisely, the "unthought known" (Bollas, 1987)—what the body (not another part of the mind) knows but the mind does not? Things that may be, but of which one cannot speak? The pre-reflective horizon of *Dasein* considered by Heidegger to determine at all times the way we experience reality? Conversely, thought without a thinker could be understood as abstract thought, not anchored in the body and in a single individuality.

As stated earlier, the facts of analysis cannot be seen but can be intuited. The need for a scientific approach to which Bion draws attention leads him to develop a theory of observation in psychoanalysis. Hence the central importance, for him, of the ill-treated grid. An excellent interpretation of Bion is given by Ferro (2009), who invokes the concepts of the field and of waking dream thought to evolve a radically novel way of seeing the facts of analysis. Ferro's approach can be summed up in the central concept of "transformation in dreaming", which entails a fundamentally anti-realistic vision (within the context of material reality), directed precisely to the development of this ultra-microscopic vision that heightens the inner vision. Transformation in dreaming suspends the past, the future, and external reality in order to concentrate on a here-and-now magnified at the maximum possible resolution. If there is any problem with transformation in dreaming—recursively with respect to its own inherent requirement of de-concretization—it is that of knowing how to use it after having forgotten it.

The same requirement applies in the post-Bionian field model to the other two elements of the triad, myth and passion (see the contributions in this book of Levine and Migliozzi respectively). Myth is the history narrated in the form of narrative derivatives of waking dream thought, while passion is availability for and receptivity to being touched by the other, to resonate with and cathect the other: a mother loves her child with reverie, or, in other words, reverie is inconceivable if detached from a link of love (which, however, also entails "healthy" hate), akin to the "psychiatric condition" that for Winnicott (1956, p. 302) constitutes the phase of "primary maternal preoccupation". The following remarks by Henry Moore about himself (2002, p. 198) can perfectly well be applied also to Bion and Ferro: "My sculpture is becoming less representational, less an outward visual copy, and so what some people would call more abstract; but only because I believe that in this way I can present the human psychological content of my work with the greatest directness and intensity." Now let's listen to Bion in the light of Moore's considerations:

> Under a certain vertex-by which of course I mean a vertex that is so "uncertain" that I do not even know what it is-the visual image of the sensuous, Euclidean objects appears to have been expelled, "projected" from *behind* the eyes onto the world of objects in *front* of the eyes. Under one perspective the observer sees, takes in, a horse which he cannot put in his mouth but *can* take in through his eyes […] Sometimes the flow is a focal point behind the eyes out-to the horse, say; sometimes the "perspective", that is to say, the "flow", is reversed. Sometimes these flowing objects come in waves, sometimes in quanta, sometimes a feeling is described under a vertex as "helplessness", sometimes as "God". The "perspective is reversed". (1975, pp. 163–164)

To facilitate understanding and acceptance of his audacious technical proposition, Bion often cites the example of imaginary numbers, which eventually had to be invented to allow mathematics to expand. On other occasions he quotes Freud (Bion, 1975, p. 176), who, in revising his seduction theory, similarly needed to invent the unconscious for himself—that is, "to entertain the idea that events which had never taken place could have serious consequences." Further examples are the importance of the rest in music, or that of empty spaces that attract light in a sculpture ("act as a trap for light", ibid., p. 190).

Ultimately, it is the sensual dimension of the elements of psychoanalysis that constitutes Bion's radical overturning of Freud's paradigm of dreams in analysis. The transformation in hallucinosis resulting from consideration of this dimension broadens the spectrum of oneiric manifestations in a psychoanalytic session, so that hallucinosis takes its place alongside and prior to reverie and transformation in dreaming.

## Stupor and hallucinosis

### "OMSA—what fantastic legs!"

I remembered that Olga had worked in the past as a sales representative, in particular in the field of lingerie and more specifically of nylon stockings. For some months this had been my constant belief. Every so often the character of the *calzettara*—an Italian word meaning both a purveyor of hose and a pipsqueak—would crop up, especially in certain instances of healthy joking. However, she now mockingly reminds me in surprise and amusement that I am wrong: she used to sell not nylons but orthopedic stockings! I realize that I had "hallucinated" and that I was now enabling myself to wake up from my dream (and thereby to transform the hallucination "into a dream"). The differences between the two occupations are plain: one, which I had confused with that of another female patient of mine, is bound up with the world of feminine seduction (a mysterious and threatening world for Olga); while the other relates to illness, invalidity, and the loss of any element of seductiveness. Yet my false memory had allowed me to intuit something important about our relationship: an aspect of seduction might be present as a character of the analytic field, albeit well concealed by the symptoms of illness—or, from a more classical point of view, by Olga's symptoms—whose existence had hitherto gone unnoticed by both of us. I had not been alerted by her constant complaints about a symptom that made her unattractive (she was losing her hair), which I now saw as a kind of negation. Usually, though, if we only know how to read it, a symptom "shouts out" its truth: in this case, the truth of someone who had not succeeded in seducing her love objects and had felt rejected since birth. The intuition had resulted from a misunderstanding—as is always characteristic of a symptom—that had arisen before our very eyes. It was due not only to a perception by the sense organs, but instead to their complete suspension. In the end it was as if we had said to ourselves, as in the Kessler twins' famous advertisement on the Italian TV program *Carosello*, "OMSA—what fantastic legs!"[1] (After the event this could also be seen as a form of functioning *à deux* by analyst and patient). Might this be regarded as something akin to healing? The seductiveness in question had nothing to do with eroticism, but concerned the incredible beauty that children ought always to possess in their parents' eyes.

All in all, then, in addition to free association, Bion invites us to deploy the power of imagination to fill in the gaps of reason, to make the invisible visible and the unrepresentable representable. To this end, he uses stylistic elements derived from English literature of the Romantic period (Coleridge, Keats, and Shelley)—in particular, the symbolic matrix of the aesthetic of the sublime (Civitarese, 2014b). The theme is the same as with transformations in hallucinosis. "Sense-able" has more to do with hallucinosis than with the correct perception of the senses, because it brings all the analyst's emotionality to the intuition. It is the ultimate destination of Bion's reflections on the nature of the objects of psychoanalysis and at the same time our most breathtaking application of the unconscious as a probe for putting us in contact with the other.

*Note*

1. See https://www.youtube.com/watch?v=-2qw7nyVGvc

*References*

Bion, W. R. (1961). *Experiences in Groups*. London: Tavistock.
Bion, W. R. (1962). *Learning from Experience*. London: Heinemann.
Bion, W. R. (1963). *Elements of Psycho-Analysis*. London: Heinemann.

Bion, W. R. (1965). *Transformations: Change from Learning to Growth*. London: Heinemann.
Bion, W. R. (1970). *Attention and Interpretation*. London: Tavistock.
Bion, W. R. (1975). *A Memoir of the Future: Book 1: The Dream*. Rio de Janeiro: Imago Editora.
Bion, W. R. (1992). *Cogitations*. Ed F Bion. London: Karnac.
Carbone, M. (2011). *Amore e musica. Temi e variazioni*. Milan: Mimesis.
Civitarese, G. (2013a). The grid and the truth drive. *Ital. Psychoanal. Annu.*, 7: 91–114.
Civitarese, G. (2013b). Bion's evidence and his theoretical style. *Psychoanal. Q.*
Civitarese, G. (2014a). Transformation in hallucinosis and the receptivity of the analyst. *International Journal of Psychoanalysis* doi: 10.1111/1745-8315.12242. (Epub ahead of print).
Civitarese, G. (2014b, in press). Bion and the sublime: Roots of an aesthetic paradigm. *International Journal of Psychoanalysis, 95*: 1059–1086.
Ferro, A. (2009). Transformations in dreaming and characters in the psychoanalytic field. *International Journal of Psychoanalysis, 90*: 209–230.
Freud, S. (1900). *The Interpretation of Dreams. S. E., 4–5*. London: Hogarth.
Gagliasso, E. (2001). La traccia del corpo nelle metafore cognitive. *Rivista di Psicoanalasi, 47*: 767–777.
Lombardi, R. (2012). Il corpo nella teoria della mente di Wilfred R. Bion http://www.consecutio.org/2012/02/il-corpo-nella-teoria-della-mente-di-wilfred-r-bion/ (accessed September 26 2013).
Moore, H. (2002). *Writings and Conversations*. Berkeley: University of California Press.
Winnicott, D. W. (1956). Primary maternal preoccupation. In: *Through Paediatrics to Psycho-Analysis* (pp. 299–305). London: Hogarth, 1975.

# CHAPTER TWENTY-TWO

# Myth, dream, and meaning: reflections on a comment by Bion

*Howard B. Levine*

In *Elements of Psychoanalysis*, Bion (1963, p. 11) states that "psychoanalytic elements and the objects derived from them have ... extension in the domain[s] of sense [myth and passion]" and follows (pp. 11–13) with a brief description of each of these terms. In regard to myth, he acknowledges that he finds it difficult to give readers "a satisfactory explanation" of what he means and adds in a footnote "the problem relates to the discussion of row C ["Dream Thoughts, Dreams, Myths"] of the grid" (p. 12). He then offers the following example:

> Suppose that a patient is angry. More meaning is given to a statement to that effect if it is added that his anger is like that of a "child that wanted to hit his nanny because he has been told he is naughty." (p. 12)

In offering this characterization, Bion tells us that he is *not* proposing "a genetic exposition" or construction. That is, the statement about nannies is neither a general "theory that small boys hit their nannies if they are called naughty" (p. 12) nor a particular statement about the historical truth of *this boy's* past experience, real or imagined. Rather, Bion enigmatically tells us that although this statement is

> akin to the type of statement that philosophers contemptuously dismiss as mythologies when they use the term pejoratively to describe bad theories" [he, Bion,] "*require[s] as part of analytical scientific procedure and equipment statements of this kind*. They are not statements of observed fact, or formulations of a theory intended to represent a realization: they are statements of a personal myth." (p. 12, italics added)

He further asserts that:

> Unless the experience of the psycho-analytical object is accompanied by a formulation by the psycho-analyst of a statement that has this type of component it lacks a necessary dimension." (p. 12)

How are we to understand this cryptic, perhaps ironic, endorsement of "bad theories'? What clinical sense are we to make of it? Does Bion mean to say that an interpretation is apt to gain more attention or carry more force or impact if it is accompanied by a narrative metaphor (personal myth) with its unique "penumbra of associations"? If so, to whom does the personal myth belong? The patient? The analyst? The pair? In this essay, I will attempt to examine certain passages from *Attention and Interpretation* (1970) and *Cogitations* (1992) in order to address these questions from a contemporary vertex. In particular, I will argue that such statements of "personal myth" are particularly powerful containers and conveyers of emotion, reflect the subjectivity, emotional engagement, and therefore "passion" of the analyst, are useful to approximate previously unarticulated aspects of the non-dynamic unconscious of the patient, and may serve as catalysts of an emotional turbulence, which "makes a demand for work" upon the minds of the analytic couple.

To restate this in a language commensurate with contemporary field theory, the "personal myth", the emotional turbulence, and the resulting dream-work and/or narrative structure that the turbulence evokes may, depending upon the vertex of observation, variously be seen as belonging to the patient, the analyst, or the field.[1] If the process of myth-making and myth-telling takes place in a way that is tolerable to the patient and remains within the capacity for containment of the patient, the analytic couple, and/or the field, then the patient may be more ably helped to make contact with, "suffer", think about, and learn from the truth of her experience. While the views that I shall propose may be felt by some to go beyond those that Bion intended, I feel justified in my hypotheses, because they are developed from the implications of his writing and through use of the very tools that he bequeathed to us.

At the risk of oversimplifying and with Bion's theory of thinking and view of the psychoanalytic situation in mind, I would like to summarize the perspective from which I shall be speaking by suggesting that the challenge faced by both analyst and analysand is how to maintain composure and a competent, functioning psyche (how to "continue to think") in the face of an adverse, painful, and a potentially traumatic (overwhelming, mind numbing, or fragmenting) reality ("catastrophic change"; terror; "nameless dread"). How to come into contact with and continue to face ("suffer") the truth of one's existence (O), while keeping intact one's capacity to think and allowing oneself to experience enough of that "Experience"[2] so that one may learn from it and one's psyche may grow. How to keep the relationship between mind (♀) on the one hand and thought, feeling, and/or perception (♂) on the other salutary and productive in the face of contents (potential experiences and psychic "facts") that are almost painfully unbearable and threaten to become disruptive and even destructive to the mind that must try to contain them.[3]

Bion's (1963) descriptions in *Elements* of sense, myth, and passion contain certain assertions that I shall take as clues. The first concerns the dimension of sense, which apparently refers to literal and concrete *sensuousness*. This is not "sense" in the sense of "making sense" or being meaningful, but rather something that is empirically verifiable by resort to the data of the senses:

> when the analyst gives an interpretation it must be possible for analyst and analysand to see that what he is talking about is something that is either audible, visible, palpable or odoriferous at the time. (p. 12)

This assertion is puzzling when contrasted to what Bion (1970) will later say in *Attention and Interpretation*:

> the realities with which psycho-analysis deals, for example fear, panic, love, anxiety, passion *have no sensuous background*, though there is a sensuous background (respiratory rate, pain, touch, etc.) that is often identified with them and then treated, supposedly scientifically. (p. 89, italics added)

While it is possible that Bion changed his view in this later writing, I think it more likely—and perhaps useful—to assume that he has changed his intent and vertex of observation. In the earlier statement, Bion seems to be referring to the concomitants (the sensuous background) of emotional states rather than the states themselves. These concomitants (respiratory rate, tachycardia, sweating, somnolence, etc.) can be empirically observed (felt, smelt, heard, etc.) and used as evidence in relation to the presence and quality of a psychoanalytic object of investigation (emotional state of mind). The situation is similar to the relation that obtains between an atomic particle and its path through a cloud chamber: the presence of the particle may be inferred by virtue of the path that may be observed, but the thing-in-itself is never seen.

Having something empirically validatable to refer to in the session may prove persuasive or tactically useful in alerting a patient to something or convincing a patient to accept or consider some bit of information (K) about himself. However, whether that information or its communication will prove *transformational* may be a very different matter. That Bion (1970) is concerned with the transformational in his later writing is made clear by the context (Chapter Nine, Ultimate reality, pp. 87–91), in which the later quote appears. There, he writes:

> What is required is not a[n evidentiary or empirical] base for psycho-analysis and its theories but a science that is not restricted by its genesis in knowledge and sensuous background. It must be a science of at-one-ment. (p. 89)

The latter term, "at-one-ment", is associated with the patient's *being* (O or Experience) rather than knowledge about that being (K or experience) and may be approached or approximated in more traditional terms, but never fully described, by phrases such as "trial identification", "empathy", or the temporary permeability of ego boundaries that may occur during reverie when the analyst's unconscious is in contact with that of the patient. Each of these denominations attempts to describe some aspect of the unconscious, intersubjective linkage that arises within the analytic couple in the process container/contained.

Bion's assertion about at-one-ment is consistent with his belief that:

the term "science", as it has been commonly used hitherto to describe an attitude to objects of sense, is not adequate to represent an approach to those realities with which "psychoanalytical science" has to deal. Nor is it adequate to represent that aspect of the human personality that is concerned with the unknown and ultimately unknowable—with O. (Bion, 1970, p. 88)

Is it possible then that in *Elements*, Bion was speaking *tactically* when he included the domain of the senses and in *Attention and Interpretation* he was speaking more strategically—existentially and *transformationally*—when he cautioned against too great a reliance on the data of the senses in relation to transformations in O? Recall that in *Elements*, he was insisting upon the essential inclusion of a kind of statement that he says philosophers would pejoratively dismiss as '"bad theory". Bad theory, perhaps, from the perspective of objective empirical science, because it would be judged as too intuitive, metaphoric, or subjective a formulation on the analyst's part and not the result of a careful following of the implications of the patient's (saturated) associations? But a philosopher's "bad theory" may be an analyst's mobilization of something alive within the analysis. Recall Green's (2005) discussion of the treatment of states of psychic deadness, where he says:

> Sometimes, paradoxically, it will be less damaging to the process to allow a lively counter transference reaction to be expressed, even if negative, in order to gain access to the internal movements animating the analyst. These are all evidence of ... spontaneity ... having more value for the patient than a conventional pseudo-tolerant discourse which will be experienced by the patient as artificial and governed by technical manuals. (p. 35)

I can imagine in Bion's example that in response to the "nanny" remark, his patient might silently snort and think "What rubbish! Where in the world did *that* come from? Surely that's *your* idea and not my own ..." But perhaps the mobilization of affect in that kind of response is precisely the value of the comment and Bion's point: that even if the immediate affect mobilized is negative and dismissive, there is deep meaning and transformational power in being thought about in so personal and intimate a way; in being presented with an idea coming from within the psyche—and here I would remind us of the literal translation of this word = *soul*—of the analyst; that the analysis must *require* such statements on the part of the analyst, statements that go beyond that which is empirically verifiable by reference to objective sensations and facts that are fixed (saturated) in their meaning. Put another way, transformational analysis may require and even spring from the personal, the intuitive, the subjective, the metaphoric.

Remember that Bion's third essential domain is that of passion, the awareness of which "is not dependent on sense" (1963, p. 13), and which stands as "evidence that two minds are linked" (p. 13). Given all that Bion has taught us about the communicative dimension of projective identification, the intersubjective development of alpha function, the psyche, and the processes of container/contained, is it not possible that what Bion is seeking to convey in describing the necessary value and role of the *analyst's* "personal myth" about the patient is the importance of the patient's being with an analyst who has such a myth, as a reflection of a passionate commitment to understanding and engaging in the analytic process? Just as a quickened pulse and respiration may be a sign of an emotional state of fear, the formation of a personal myth about the patient's mental state may be a sign of having received and absorbed the patient's projective identifications, lent alpha function (a highly personal part of the analyst's mind/self) to a process of container/contained, and established an intersubjective connectedness with the inner world of the patient, all of which is reflected in the analyst's reverie and capacity to dream as yet undreamt aspects of the patient into being. To pursue this further, it will be useful to turn to *Cogitations* (Bion, 1992).

In an entry dated February 18, 1960, Bion (1992) makes the following observation about dreams, dream-work, latent content, and alpha:

> Freud assumed that the interpretation, the latent content, was the origin of the dream, and that it had been worked on by the dream-work to produce the dream. *I say the origin is an emotional experience—perhaps even an experience that is emotional and nothing else* [italics added]—and that this is worked on (rationalized?) to produce the dream, the manifest content as we know it, and that it is the *analyst* who then does the *interpretation* [original italics] to produce the so-called latent content. Then what validity or significance is to be attached to his product, the latent content?" (p. 135)

Earlier, on 21 August 1959, he had written:

> It is very important that the analyst knows not what *is* happening but that he *thinks* it is happening. That is the only certitude to which he lays claim. (p. 70)

We must consider the meaning and implications of these two entries.

To begin with, notice how Bion revises Freud's theory of the pathway of dream-work and dream-thoughts. For Freud, the dream begins with a psychic fact; an organized latent dream thought that has come into psychic existence, been repressed, continues to exert pressure on the psyche and achieves vicarious expression in the dream by becoming linked to and expressed by the more innocuous manifest images of the dream. For Bion, the dream begins with "an emotional experience—"perhaps even an experience that is emotional and nothing else." What can he mean by this? I would suggest that Bion is referring to "an experience", perhaps an experience, that does not by itself constitute, but may *precede*, the creation or registration of, a psychic element or fact.[4] If I am correct, then the dream may originate in an emotional experience, presumably a beta element, or, if we dare to hypothesize its existence, something "prepsychic" (Green, 2010), that is even less, or "other", organized, more primitive, somatic without psychic registration or representation, "an experience that is emotional and nothing else". The analyst's mind, through contact with the patient—unconscious to unconscious; receptive to projective identification; empathy; etc.—is activated (alpha function) and creates an image (alpha element), which in turn can be used to generate a thought in the form of a narrative fragment, metaphor, or personal myth through which the analyst captures his surmise concerning some quality of the patient's emotional state ("like that of a 'child that wanted to hit his nanny because he has been told he is naughty'"). Once this myth is constructed, felt, or articulated within the mind of the analyst—that is, once the analyst feels "certain" that this is what he thinks is happening—it may be used as data ("signals from the field") to adjust the analyst's internal listening stance and degree of activity, saturation of intervention, etc. (Ferro, 2002) or used as the basis of an interpretation that may be given directly to the patient ("Your anger at X is like that of a child that wanted …").

If the analyst chooses the latter course, then he must be aware that the interpretation given may not be a statement of *fact* about the patient's life, but only a statement of fact about the analyst's belief at that moment.[5] It is up to the patient to "decide" whether or not the analyst's interpretation is "true," "meaningful", or "useful." This decision is not necessarily a conscious, *intentional* decision, or some form of search for correspondence between the analyst's conjecture (construction) and the patient's repressed, organized memory, but more a matter of whether the conjecture is taken in by the patient, bears fruit, has a positive effect on the analytic process etc. The transitionality of the situation that obtains between analyst and patient—the analyst indirectly offers, the patient can accept or not—is similar to Winnicott's placing a reflex hammer in the visual field of an infant or making a "squiggle" in his drawing games with children. In offering an interpretation based on a personal myth, the analyst is offering something to the patient, which may or may not create or contribute to the creation of the latter's latent dream thoughts!

Bion's question about the "validity" or "significance" that can be assigned to the product of this dream-work might be restated as, "To whom does the latent dream thought belong?" And the answer might be that although from one perspective it may seem to begin in the mind of the analyst (personal myth), one cannot say to whom the latent dream thought belongs, any more than you can say whether the infant's transitional object is "me" or "not-me".

In contrast to Freud, who had the well-structured psyche of the neurotic in mind and so described an analyst who *uncovers* or *decodes* a pre-existent, hidden, or otherwise formed, but disguised thought, Bion, who was more attuned to the unstructured parts of the psyche, is describing instead how the analyst produces, catalyzes, or creates such thoughts for and with the patient through the act of interpretation. I believe that it is for this reason that Bion's note of 21 August 1959 emphasized that the analyst cannot say what *is* so, only what he is certain that he *believes* is so. In relation to the non-repressed unconscious, the unstructured parts of the patient's mind, the analyst's certitude cannot concern the factualness of what the analyst suggests are the patient's latent dream thoughts. Certitude may only relate to the analyst's degree of belief about what he *thinks* that those latent dream thoughts might be. Thus, for Bion, in so far as it touches on the not yet known or articulated O of the patient, every interpretation must implicitly contain the following caveat:

> I quite realize that my view may be entirely wrong, but I do know that I am certain at any rate that *this* is my view. (Bion, 1992, p. 70, original italics)

If we now recall that for Bion the dream-work goes on continuously, during wakefulness as well as sleep—indeed, "is concerned with, and is identical with, unconscious waking thinking designed, as part of the reality principle, to aid in the task of the real, as opposed to pathological, modification of frustration" (Bion, 1992, p. 54)—then we can see that the resulting view of the analytic process, particularly in relation to the non-repressed unconscious, *requires* that the analyst create and offer his beliefs or "personal myths" ("my view") to the patient about the patient, the unfolding analytic relationship and the analytic process in the form of interpretations and that this action helps organize and thereby create elements (latent dream thoughts, waking and asleep) in and of the patient's unconscious.

The epistemic transitionality of the resulting situation—that is, the fact that the question, "Whose myth or latent dream thought is it?" cannot be answered—is a reflection of both the depth of the analyst's identification with the patient and the intersubjective link ("passion") that must exist between them as a result of their being connected by the process:

> Patient's projection of unmetabolizable emotional turbulence (beta elements and perhaps even more primitive forms of turbulence, "experience that is emotional and nothing else") –> analyst's receptivity (reverie) –> absorption of the patient's projective identifications –> analyst's exercise of alpha function –> analyst's transformation of absorbed projections (representation) –> re- presentation of now- transformed elements to the patient in the form of interpretation (publication of the analyst's personal myth/latent content of the patient/ field).

I would like to conclude with some final thoughts on the implications of Bion's work for our understanding of the unconscious. As Freud (1915, 1923) indicated in his writings, the dynamic or repressed unconscious, which he described so ably in his theory of neurosis and the dream, is only a small, finite sector of a larger, domain, which Bion (1970) proposed was formless until acted on and transformed, infinite, ever expanding and therefore unknowable in its fullest extent. Hence, Bion's distinction between Experience (O) and what can be known about it (K).

The fluidity of potential form that follows from the ineffable, ever-expanding nature of the unrepressed unconscious produces a situation of narrative possibility that may be analogized to that of the hermit crab, who needs a place in which to live, cannot secrete or build a dwelling structure of its own and so occupies whichever nest or shell of another sea creature fits and is handy for survival. The vast variety of available "shells" comprises the set of possible narrative dialects for the elaboration and expression of alpha elements. It is this plasticity of possible expression that authorizes the analyst as myth-maker for and with the patient and makes intersubjective co-construction not only possible, but necessary.

To offer still another myth, as Bion (e.g., 2005) has done in some of his "thalamic" speculations, one could imagine that the intersubjective use of alpha function and the communicative dimension of projective identification, indeed, the psyche itself, evolved as a way to protect the individual from and modulate the impact of the disorganizing threat, agony, onslaught, and "too much-ness" of raw existential Experience (with a capital E). With this in mind, we might even say that Bion's choice of the term, "passion", contains associative overtones drawn from the Christ story ("passion play"), in which facing a torturous experience of crucifixion and death is the only prelude to salvation. Perhaps then, behind the choice of the word "passion" we hear the voice of the tank commander trying to explain what it takes to try to face life and manage the inevitability of mortality and loss.

## Notes

1. That is, they often appear to observers in the part of the field called, from the field perspective, "the analyst".
2. Elsewhere (Levine, 2011) I have attempted to distinguish raw, existential Experience of a kind that extends beyond the capacity to be fully known by writing that word with a capital "E". This is to contrast it with the kind of felt or known part of that Experience, which we colloquially refer to as "experience" and which I write with a small "e". To further illustrate the distinction, I offer that "Experience is to experience as O is to K."
3. The basis for this "traumatic view of reality" has been hypothesized as relating to Bion's experiences as a tank commander in the First World War (Souter, 2009; Szykierski, 2010).
4. The question of whether or not a beta element is to be considered "psychic" or "pre-psychic", that is, of the mind, but perhaps in a different, more archaic register than alpha elements and thoughts or outside the mind and not yet psychic, will not be considered here.
5. The exception to this statement may be when the analyst offers a construction concerning a past event in the patient's life that is thought to be forgotten. In such a case, if the analyst's conjecture is factually correct, then the analyst may be stating what turns out to be a statement of fact. However, its truth value at the point of conception and interpretation may only be what the analyst *conjectures* or believes to be true.

## References

Bion, W. R. (1963). *Elements of Psycho-Analysis*. In: *Seven Servants. Four Works by Wilfred R. Bion*. New York: Jason Aronson, 1977.
Bion, W. R. (1970). *Attention and Interpretation*. London: Heinemann.
Bion, W. R. (1992). *Cogitations*. London: Karnac.
Bion, W. R. (2005). *The Tavistock Lectures*. London: Karnac.
Ferro, A. (2002). *In the Analyst's Consulting Room*. Hove, East Sussex: Routledge.
Freud, S. (1915). The unconscious. *S. E., 12*. London: Hogarth.
Freud, S. (1923). The ego and the id. *S. E., 19*. London: Hogarth.
Green, A. (2005). *Key Ideas for a Contemporary Psychoanalysis*. Hove, East Sussex: Routledge.
Green, A. (2010). Thoughts on the Paris school of psychosomatics. In: M. Aisenstein & E. Rappoport de Aisemberg (Eds.), *Psychosomatics Today: A Psychoanalytic Perspective* (pp. 1–45). London: Karnac.
Levine, H. B. (2011). The colourless canvas: Representation, therapeutic action and the creation of mind. *International Journal of Psychoanalysis, 93*: 607–647.
Souter, K. M. (2009). The war memoirs: Some origins of the thought of W. R. Bion. *International Journal of Psychoanalysis, 90*: 795–808.
Szykierski, D. (2010). The traumatic roots of containment: The evolution of Bion's metapsychology. *Psychoanalytic Quarterly, 79*: 935–968.

CHAPTER TWENTY-THREE

# Passion

*Anna Migliozzi*

"But I would suggest that one whole area of emotion has yet found no place in our body of theory (...) I am speaking of passion."

—*Meltzer*, 1986

Bion named passion as an essential component of any psychoanalytic interpretation, along with sense (that which is empirically observable) and the expression of a personal myth (narrative metaphor). Meltzer (1978) agrees that passion has not received sufficient recognition or specific delineation within the corpus of our theory, and noted that passion is often taken for granted as simply "a very intense emotion", a quality of love or hate. In contrast, passion represents a state of turbulence derived from the conflict between newly evolving emotions and mind states and old residual organizations of our internal world. Therefore, it should not surprise us when Bion (1962) puts the vicissitudes of emotions into the very center of psychoanalytic thinking and offers a radically new view of the analytic process, transforming our sense of the relationship between patient and analyst, to one which favors the development of an apparatus for thinking and the capacity to produce dream-thoughts.

Emotions and reason have often been considered oppositional: with reason calculating, guiding, and thinking and emotion inflaming, overwhelming, and blinding. Without attempting to obfuscate reason by pushing it towards irrationality, emotions are fundamental to the proper functioning of our rational faculties and moral action. As Ogden (1991) reminds us, passion gives meaning and sense to our human experience. If we attempted to separate passion from meaning, we would be in danger of creating an individual without energy, "... an entity for research of an attachment or devotion unlinked to, or separate from its biological appearance ..."

(Ogden, 1991, p. 363). Therefore, finding a place for emotion within the construction of mind has been a struggle.

In psychoanalysis, some see passion as resistant, illusionary, triumphant, or devastating. It exists within a bizarre conjunction between life and death, energy and destruction; impatient to build up myth and tear it down. Passion implies the experience of intensified emotions, sublime-transient, and exists within the vitality of the human experience in everything we do. Passion, when connected to Eros, is exemplified by the mother's unconditional love and is essential for growth and development of the psyche.[1] One also cannot help recall the imagery of the passion of Christ, whose suffering and love washed clean the sins of man.

I think that Bion *intentionally* chooses passion, perhaps one of the most controversial and multidimensional words we may encounter in psychoanalysis, because he believes that psychoanalysts, "… have to invent the language" in order to discover a method of communication for their material which is, not visible and not palpable. He leaves space for everybody to find a definition by themselves, using their own ideas in their own way (Meltzer, 1990). So, we are left to struggle with words, in order to develop a personal articulate and accurate vocabulary. "… Use them very sparingly, very exactly, only in order to say what you mean" (Bion, 1985, p. 5). It is not sufficient to rest within the security of our fixed terminology in the description of our psychoanalytical experience; rather we must journey forward in the exploration of what can be revealed.

Aware that this word cannot capture the essence of experience and only approximate its mystery, Bion lets meaning gradually accrue within a creative dialogue between patient and analyst, avoiding a precise definition of this, "very inadequate word" (Bion, 1978). The analyst must develop a capacity to see what "… your intuition enables you to see" (Bion, 1978, p. 7).

In this way, passion is not restricted to the realm of sexual desire—"… Sex is a name, but none of us 'sees' sex, though it is a word we often use …" (Bion, 1991, p. 206)—nor to the theater of love—"… When someone says 'I love', the rules of articulate speech apply to 'speech' not to 'loving'" (Bion, 1991, p. 208).

Bion states, "It may seem that by introducing passion I am repeating what I have said already by including the L, H and K, as elements. This is not so; by passion I mean one of the dimensions which L, H or K must possess if it is to be recognized as an element that is present" (p. 12). He brings together elements that have apparently no connection and reveals an unsuspected coherence, offering a double dimension to passion: an emotional process, which develops rapport, and a phenomenological element, which creates meta-concepts (Meltzer, 1978). As such, passion would be the activator of vital experiences, allowing for deep comprehension and promoting other more elaborated expressions of mundane existence and human creativity.

The capacity to perceive the beauty and mystery of life through intimate human relations emerges from a combined vision of the conflict between L, H, and K and −L, −H, and −K (Meltzer, 1986, p. 17). We could hypothesize that Passion (P), necessarily present in the analytical field, strengthens the intuitive and receptive capacity between patient and analyst and favors the transformation of the experience from $\beta$ elements (raw sensory data) to $\alpha$ elements (units of meaningful experience). "… By a mysterious creative act of mind the data of the various senses are introduced into the container (…) when the thirst for knowledge and the dynamism of concern for one's love objects (…) can produce a dream image in which meaning is trapped, like light in a diamond" (Meltzer, 1986, p. 102).

Within the psychoanalytic setting, passion is "… evidence that two minds are linked and that there cannot possibly be fewer than two minds if passion is present" (Bion, 1963, p. 13). As we know, the baby experiences this primary emotional link through the receptive and containing mind of his mother and every future encounter would be created by the introjection of this link. Thus, passion ties, transforms, and develops the awareness of the emotions themselves, which are shaped in a communication that produces knowledge about oneself and one's own internal world. It becomes one of the elements which constructs the apparatus for thinking, supports the ability to dream, creates rapport with and reflects true contact with objects, promotes processes of psychic growth, and creates an emotional and effective intrapsychic, interpersonal, and intersubjective tuning process. When the patient attempts to deal with intense, often quite primitive emotions provoked by the immediate contact with the analyst, the analyst must deal with powerful and disturbing phantasies that are evoked in him by the patient's projections and, probably, may find herself colluding with the patient's attempts to escape.

Passion enables the analyst to develop her psychoanalytical intuitive knowledge, attitude, and disposition, which then resounds emotionally within the couple, "… with intensity and warmth though without any suggestion of violence" (1963, p. 12). Inextricably linked to reverie, passion depends on the analyst's $\alpha$ function and is in effect an expression and a way of loving: "… when the mother loves the infant what does she do it with? […] my impression is that her love will be expressed by reverie" (Bion, 1962, p. 35).

The capacity for reverie—"the dream comprehension which teaches a language and constructs thought" (Oneroso & Gorrese, 2004, p. 112)—is an alternation between hearing, feeling, and imagining, our future capacity to think/dream. Reverie is connected to a rapport with an object, a mother or analyst, who is able to provide love and passion, trust and hope, the constitutive elements of the mind.

Reverie and projective identification work along a continuum, offering the possibility, through absorption and digestion of the patient's anxiety, to transform into thoughts that which has been and has yet to be experienced. Through words, the analyst, who has incarnated passion without being overwhelmed, offers the patient a bearable truth.

> … psychoanalysis is a joint activity of analyst and analysand to determine the truth; that being so, the two are engaged—no matter how imperfectly—on what is in intention a scientific activity. (Bion, 1992, p. 114)

In the analytic session, passion helps the couple cope with what otherwise might seem unbearable; recreating, bringing to light, what was previously unknown and not yet representable; and allowing the couple to remain emotionally alive to scrutinize the process. The emotional turbulence that is produced exposes both patient and analyst to catastrophic experiences of change that reflect, anticipate, and catalyze what has not yet come into being. Thus, Being is a drama and passionate Being a drama amplified, "as many forces which appear under many disguises" (Bion, 1991, p. 645).

The analyst using passion as her conscious and unconscious perceptual organs, the former offering a possible interpretation, the latter not requiring one, integrates the two perspectives, which enables the analyst to form models and abstractions, offering elucidation and multiple points of view to the patient who is unable to do so for himself (Sandler, 2005).

Bion recognizes passion as a necessary element and part of the *intersubjective* process by which the analyst, "… subconsciously [allows him or herself] to be a [willing] subject of the subconscious experiment of the other" (Ogden, 1994, p. 10). Moreover, he considers passion a fundamental aspect or quality of O, the ultimately reality, the unknown.

> … "Passionate love" is the nearest I can get to a verbal transformation which "represents" the thing-in-itself, the ultimate reality, the O, as I have called it, approximating it. (Bion, 1991, p. 183)

In this sense, Bion (1970) encourages us to use our intuition to see through misleading aspects of reality and reach a state of mind unsaturated, as mystics and poets know very well. The "mystic" experience is a particular mental state, not tied to anything in particular, free to be in contact with what is emerging in the session. Therefore, it would appear that he is asking us to give up our strict rationality in favor of a more blurred position which embraces absence of clarity, uncertainty, and knows how to pause and remain there until needed.

"… Bion left behind the saturated pre-conceptions of the psychoanalytic establishment and ventured inward in a soul-searching, mystic journey … What emerged perhaps become the state of the art in psychoanalytic metatheory and metapsychology" (Grotstein, 1996, p. 130) and in that way, he "… is providing a model of mysticism abstracted from his psychoanalytic experience of the interplay of interpretation, projection, containment and resistance. But this is a psychoanalytic model of mysticism and not a mystic model of psychoanalysis" (Caper, 1998, p. 420).

The practice of psychoanalysis is largely dependent on intuition of what has been felt within the moment of discovery. Of course, we have to be able to transform what we have intuitively felt into a formulation. This formulation, allowing us to link analysis to knowledge, does not pretend to be true in the "hard" sciences way, but only true in the emotional sense.

In the case that follows, I will attempt to illustrate some of the vicissitudes of passion in both patient and analyst, the disturbances and turbulence it causes and the defenses it arouses, including the identification with the patient and his objects and the resulting "suffering" needed to make contact with and help catalyze transformations in a very disturbed young boy.

### Secret window

When he came to our first encounter, D, a fifteen-year-old boy, did not look like an adolescent to me. He was tall, obese, and imposing. He wore a large-brimmed hat pulled low over his head and dressed in an old-fashioned style. Shuffling slowly into the room like an elderly person, he carried an atmosphere with him that was tense and heavy and I felt a sense of coldness.

An image flashed into my mind of Mort,[2] the protagonist in the film, *Secret Window*, based on a novel by Stephen King. In the film, the protagonist (and the spectator) discovers that he moves into a heretofore unrecognized murderous identity when he puts on the hat. I pushed aside the immediate visual association but the link between Mort and D remained unelaborated in the back of my mind and I felt an apprehension that made our encounter awkward. This old man-young boy seemed to challenge my capacity to listen. I felt blinded and breathless. The emotional storm in our initial impact and the desire to reject him was, in turn, the beginning of an engagement that would bring together two very different individuals.

D filled me in on general details of his life that he either felt were the most important or that he may have assumed I most wanted to hear. He seemed oppressed by a tyrannical superego, which terrorized him. His parents did not appear to be emotionally present within him and his only significant rapport was with his maternal grandfather, who had treated him like an adult. While his grandfather had stimulated his mathematical and logical intelligence, he had also terrorized him, by drilling him with oral tests and slapping him if he was too slow to respond or made an error. His grandfather had died only several months before our first encounter. It seemed to me as if D's body was occupied by a bitter old man, thereby denying both the reality of his own selfhood and of his grandfather's death.

D had a good rapport with his teachers, who were impressed by his intellectual capacity. He said he wanted to become a doctor and specialize in pathological anatomy, so that he would be able to dissect human bodies.

D's parents sent him to analysis, because they were worried he wanted to commit suicide. Although D had agreed to see a psychoanalyst four times a week, he was like a military soldier, only offering curt replies to direct questions. Considering his reticence to talk and his ability to shut out others, including me, it was not clear how aware he actually was of being in analysis. He asked me to question him, in a drill-like fashion, so that he might be able to give me responses, which on the one hand, might have reflected his desire to control the session and, on the other hand, might have been his attempt to deflect me away from him.

The atmosphere during the session was extremely tense and impersonal and I felt like it might explode or collapse at any moment. I was tense and fidgety and, unusual for me, I had difficulty finding a comfortable sitting position. We remained seated facing each other until D asked me if he "could lie down on the couch for a while". After he did so, the tension seemed to lessen and D appeared to be more at ease. Despite this, I felt the session still contained a powerful sense of uncertainty and impending storm.

Later on, D began to occasionally miss sessions, phoning to tell me that he had been "held up and would not be able to come". During these absences, I reflected on D, free of his glare. He had casually mentioned that he spent many hours drawing bunkers in various forms and sizes. It seemed to me as if the bunkers were a clue to something separating us, which we would have to deal with. They seemed to encapsulate him, keeping him away from me or, indeed, anyone who might challenge his version of reality.

Once these thoughts took form in my mind, I asked him if his sketching was so important to him that it kept him away from our encounter. D looked surprised by my interest and he listed, in great detail, the drawings he had recently been doing. "Drawing is not the most suitable word," he said. For D, his elaborations were reality as he wished it to be.

As I began to discover, his reality was both magnificent and horrific. Within his construction, he was a famous scientist who lived in a very special castle where he conducted sadistic experiments. When he got lost inside this scenario, he often cut himself, becoming excited at seeing his own blood spurting out.

"With the scalpel, I cut myself. I missed my veins. Unfortunately! But I spurted blood everywhere. It didn't seem so terrible or serious to me. I did it, that's all!"

At times, he even became overtly suicidal.

"When I see an open window I feel an irresistible impulse to throw myself out of it or I feel compelled to cut my throat. It would only take a second."

He had split himself off from reality, retreating into a phantasy world and reifying this retreat through his drawings, using his body as the theatre upon which his sadistic experiments were played out.

Sometimes, he also imagined cutting up female patients. He periodically replayed the same scenario where he was in a bunker-morgue in a dilapidated hospital, full of blood. In one scenario, he created a beautiful nose for a woman he was operating on, but then was filled with an irresistible urge to destroy her face, because it was flaccid and sagging. In a German accent, a voice told him she was not quite dead, even though she was nailed to the table.

In another scenario, a little girl led him down a dark corridor. She had a poodle with her. D ordered her to kill it. She cuddled it and cried but D insisted. The little girl twisted the dog's neck and broke it. At that moment, D said he felt excited.

To say I was horrified and in obvious difficulty, is not simply a statement of circumstance. I felt that I should have spoken, and yet, at the same time, I was aware of how difficult it would have been to say something that didn't sound as if it came from a petrified analyst who, overwhelmed by the intensity of these sadistic scenarios, had lost her capacity to think.

In retrospect, I had become enraptured by his stories, overwhelmed in one part, but also stirred. I struggled to remain in touch with myself and my feelings of terror while trying to digest these images and put into words how his "other", alien identity was attempting to overtake the analysis. I told him that I understood how difficult it was for him to tell me about these phantasies and now I realized why he had avoided me by missing sessions, because he feared that I would reject or recoil from him, because he was too disturbed. D confirmed this and said he was trapped inside this world and he was afraid of losing all touch with reality.

"What is worrying me is that I have begun hearing voices and I get uncontrollably furious."

Only then did I feel comfortable enough to say that we shared this concern, because these frightening images came from an alien world.

D responded by talking more openly to me about this world where visions of blood, mutilation, and slaughter brought out fierce impulses in him to control and brutalize himself and others. D had been isolated since he was a child, had never played with children of his own age and was terrorized by them. Subsequently, he had never had friends and expressed a ferocious hatred towards young and fragile people. It was as if a perverse sadistic identity had colonized him, offering him identification with an older and more powerful authoritarian scientist.

Paradoxically, in actual fact, D was neither destructive nor aggressive towards me, perhaps because he regarded me as little more than a spectator. He projected his own fragile and suffering self into me, allowing his cruel magnificence to come forward. We were both hunted down by and subjected to his sadism.

I hypothesized that D's bloody phantasy[3] rituals were an expression of his need to purify the world of its imperfections. D was trapped within and terrorized by his own horror without any way of escaping. I asked myself why I had initially been so aloof with him. I now recognized in myself an analyst who had not been completely receptive to his words. Perhaps there was more that he could not talk about.

With this in mind, I said to him that his attempts to cut me out of his hidden world may have been a way to protect our analytical relationship while he stood in the distance, observing. However, I was not satisfied with the limitation of my words, which did not completely express our fear of getting close to each other. I moved warily and cautiously in order to avoid missing something.

At this point, D told me that he remembered terror and hate had always been within him and came from his mother who, like a military general, froze him with her glance and her metallic voice.

I realized that I had been dragged into acting like a mother who could not show joy to her own new born baby, but only reflected a suspicion and fear. D had absorbed the idea that there was, perhaps, something wrong with him or that he might do something which would be irreparable. He had carried this idea into our relationship and he believed that he was horrible and worthless in my eyes. In fact, I had been devastated by the horror of his inner world and was unable to *love* him. I should have been more receptive, and courageous enough to get closer to him. I realized from my unconscious rigid bodily reactions that "he had frozen me". In so doing, we had both actualized, and I had enacted, "the military general mother". It was only through the awareness of my own conscious and unconscious feelings that I was able to defrost the eyes that had encased me and regard D through the passionate eyes of a warmer, more containing analyst.

Some days later, he arrived at session and found the door slightly more open than usual. D asked me, "Is everything alright, doctor?"

At that moment, I realized that he had the capacity to worry about me. I began to envision him as a good enough child. I imagined him as a child attached to a mother who could not recognize his capacity to love her. Perhaps he now felt that I was more able to face that terrible indigestible block of ice that he carried within him. I pushed aside my aversion and suspicion and defrosted my own conventional modes of response.

I said that he had been startled to see me so open towards the world and ready to welcome him without hesitation. Maybe he expected me to be a rigid psychoanalyst who feared losing control of the situation and thus needed protection against his destructive impulses. He may have asked himself, if his analyst could be so open-minded, maybe he could trust in her.

D responded that during the day he had felt the need to talk to me. The pressure on him had been so heavy that if he had not arrived on time to session, he felt as if he would have gone *mad*.

I said that he hoped to find an analyst capable of understanding him, one who was not horrified by his terrible and distressing words.

He responded he was only one of my patients placed on a shelf inside my studio.

He expressed a deep desire to be placed within my gaze while he maintained a privileged position of distanced observer. Even though he considered himself an object of my observation,

I believe that this development marked the beginning of his willingness to actually be in analysis.

## Discussion

It would seem that if we can tolerate our own emotional experiences, then we can use our alpha function to find representations and narrative structures to describe even the most primitive, disturbing, or chaotic experiences. "… But the structure of the personality, with its heavy armoring of conventional modes of response, often intervenes to prevent this from occurring" (Meltzer, 1986, p. 11).

For this reason, a central task of psychoanalysis is to capture the experience of what it feels like for the analyst to be with the patient and for the patient to be with the analyst at a particular juncture (Ogden, 2004). The capacity to know someone is "being able" to resound to the truth of our experience with our own true self (O/Reality/Experience) and through a vision which clarifies obscurities and obscures clarifications, move towards, though never fully achieve, closure in relation to what might be emerging (Billow, 1999, 2000; Grotstein, 2007).

> "We [analysts] must be able to have these strong feelings and be able to go on thinking clearly even when we have them". (Bion, 1978, p. 187)

This oscillation between what we know and what we don't know, what we feel and what we think, constitutes the substantial part of what it means to use passion in the clinical session.

In the beginning, D and I were not tuned in to each other. D froze any elements of humanity, both within himself and within me. He praised destruction and hatred towards helpless people and sought pleasure in blood and violence. Part of me would have liked to push him away, considering him too unpleasant or even impossible. He had encased me in ice in the same way that he himself had been frozen by the cold glances and metallic voice of his internal mother.

These (β) elements, through the oscillation among passion, intuition, and reverie, are transformed into Knowledge (K), creating the possibility for future transformations into dreams and other narrative structures. Since dreaming is a form of α function, it "… consequently is responsible for the maintenance of sanity itself" (Ogden, 2004, p. 289).

At a certain point, I had a dream: I am at my computer trying to write. I feel a sense of impediment. D arrives and sits down beside me. He looks at me and smiles. I am reassured and I am able to carry on.

After having reflected upon the dream, I felt comforted by the feeling that I was able to work and that we could suffer together and give meaning to our emotional experience.

D's appearance in my dream enabled me to recognize that even in his sadistic, psychotic madness, we were—or had the potential to be—a working couple, and passion was genuinely necessary in the exploration and experience of how we would undergo and endure our personal metamorphoses. Through my receptivity, I had become genuinely meaningful to D, thereby allowing us to create an analytical coupling in which our two minds became linked for future elaboration.

From then on, I was consciously aware of my own body armor, which had protected me from his emotional insults. My barriers were not about D, but about my own sense of self-preservation. The metal between us had been perforated and I could more readily allow D to put his horrific agony into me so that I could absorb his anxiety, transform it and re-present it back him.

"In order to introduce meaning into this processes and thereby assist in their elevation into the sphere of symbol formation, thought, judgment and decision, it is necessary that the therapist perform alpha function of which the patient is incapable" (Meltzer, 1986, p. 36).

Subsequently, D told me about a dream he had:

> "… I am in a car with my parents and we are driving through a terrible place, a land desolate and frozen. Ice everywhere, a horrible sight. I am sitting in the back seat. I am freezing to death because I am covered with ice and under the ice I am wearing a suit of armor. Freezing cold. I ask them to stop the car because I want to remove the ice. So I throw myself out of the car. There is a man. Maybe he is a blacksmith and together we try to find a way to remove the ice. The man gives me a hammer. We begin removing the ice and the suit of armor by hitting them with the hammer. Little by little, I feel better and better. When the ice shatters, I open the armor. I feel warmth. The landscape has changed. There is no ice. It is autumn. Trees with yellows leaves. My parents have left me behind. I start running, trying to reach my parents but they are very far away. I feel sad."

I interpreted his dream as an indication that we had been frozen within a protective armor, which made the landscape of analysis desolate where nothing could have grown. I had been in danger of adopting a comfortable stance designed to keep,

> … out the cold so that we will never have another thought, never be upset by somebody else's thoughts, may be very comfortable, but it does not allow space for the development of new ideas. (Bion, 2005, p. 84)

Through loving eyes, we hammered away at the ice and armor until we found something that was still alive.

Passion works within us as something that pushes us to experience what is unknown and unarticulated. As a mother conveys to her baby the joy of his birth and growth, the analyst conveys a real, genuine intuition and receptivity from which develops trust in exploring the unknown. The relationship, both physical and emotional, between mother and child, is a creation that has a life of its own and nurtures the ability to develop other creative relationships. The analyst, like the mother, encourages her patient's development by weighing how much experience is appropriate and, when it is appropriate, defending him from catastrophic exposure.

In order to tune into the patient's emotional mind, the analyst must be tuned into her own. The analyst is in a continuous internal relationship with herself, with her own analyst, teachers, favorite authors, etc., and her psychoanalytical myths. This also includes her doubts, real or imaginary, hopefulness and distrustfulness, compliance and reluctance.

This is whom the patient encounters when he comes to analysis. The coupling process of two minds—patient and analyst—coupling enables both to cope with anguish and transform it, and thus engenders a mutually creative relationship. Through the suffering of passion, the analyst registers and holds in her being the unsymbolizable, unknowable, inexpressible and shapes it into the symbolizable, the knowable, and expressible dimension of experience K-›O in which the couple can exist.

As Bion (1985) said,

> We are not obliged to become inhumane, unable to love and hate. We must always maintain the capacity to feel love and hate and all the others that follow." (p. 30)

## Notes

1. Passion could become a propulsive force which leads to change and reanimates the vitality in a patient, which had been crushed too soon, not allowing her to be able to love in real life (Freud, 1915; Rappaport, 1956; Bloom, 1975–76; Meltzer, 1974; De Masi, 1988; Bolognini, 1994; Bollas, 1994).
2. *Secret Window, Secret Garden* is one of four novellas published in the Stephen King book, *Four Past Midnight*, in 1990.
3. Spillius, E. B. (2001). Freud and Klein on the Concept of Phantasy. *International Journal of Psycho-Analysis, 82*: 361–373.

## References

Billow, R. M. (1999). LHK. *Contemporary Psychoanalysis, 35*: 629–646.
Billow, R. M. (2000). Bion's "Passion"; the Analyst's Pain. *Contemporary Psychoanalysis, 36*: 411–426.
Bion, W. R. (1962). *Learning from Experience*. London: Tavistock.
Bion, W. R. (1963). *Elements of Psycho-Analysis*. London: Heinemann.
Bion, W. R. (1965). *Transformations: Change from Learning to Growth*. London: Tavistock.
Bion, W. R. (1970). *Attention and Interpretation*. London: Tavistock.
Bion, W. R. (1978). São Paulo clinical seminars. In: *Clinical Seminars and Four Papers* (pp. 121–220). Abingdon: Fleetwood Press, 1987.
Bion, W. R. (1985). Seminari Italiani. Roma: Borla. Reprinted in: Italian Seminar. London: Karnac, 2005.
Bion, W. R. (1991). *A Memoir of the Future*. London: Karnac.
Bion, W. R. (2005). *The Tavistock Seminars*. London: Karnac
Bloom, L. (1975–76). Ellenberger on Freud's aphasia: Fact and method in the history of science. *Psychoanalytic Review, 62*: 615–637.
Bollas, C. (1994). Aspects of the erotic transference. *Psychoanalytic Inquiry, 14*: 572–590.
Bolognini, S. (1994). Transference: Erotised, erotic, loving, affectionate. *International Journal of Psychoanalysis, 75*: 73–86.
Caper, R. (1998). *The Clinical Thinking of Wilfred Bion* by Joan and Neville Symington. *International Journal of Psychoanalysis, 79*: 417–420.
Corrao (1992). *Modelli psicoanalitici. Mito Passione Memoria*. Laterza: Roma, 1992.

De Masi, F. (1988). Idealization and erotization in the analytic relationship. *Rivista di Psicoanalisi.*, *34*: 76–120.

Ferro, A. (1992). Modelli psicoanalitici. Mito Passione Memoria Laterza, Roma 1992.

Ferro, A. (2010). The work of confluence: Listening and interpreting in the psychoanalytic Field. *International Journal of Psychoanalysis*, *91*: 415–429.

Freud, S. (1915). Observations on transference-love (further recommendations on the technique of psycho-analysis III). *S. E.*, *12*. London: Hogarth.

Grotstein, J. S. (1979). Demoniacal possession, splitting, and the torment of joy: A psychoanalytic inquiry into the negative therapeutic reaction, unanalyzability, and psychotic states. *Contemporary Psychoanalysis*, *15*: 407–445.

Grotstein, J. S. (1996). Bion's transformations in "O", the thing-in-itself and the real: Toward the concept of the transcendence position. *Journal of Melanie Klein and Object Relations*, *14*: 109–141.

Grotstein, J. S. (2007). *A beam of Intense Darkness: Wilfred Bion's Legacy to Psychoanalysis*: London: Karnac.

Meltzer, D. (1974). Narcissistic foundation of the erotic transference. *Contemporary Psychoanalysis*, *10*: 311–316.

Meltzer, D. (1976). Temperatura e distanza come dimensioni tecniche dell'interpretazione. In: *La comprensione della bellezza e altri saggi*. Torino: Loescher, 1981.

Meltzer, D. (1978). *The Kleinian Development, Part III: The Clinical Significance of the Work of Bion*. Strathclyde, Perthshire: Clunie.

Meltzer, D. (1986). *Studies in Extended Metapsychology: Clinical Application of Bion's Ideas*. London: The Roland Harris Trust Library.

Meltzer, D. (1990). *The Claustrum*. London: Karnac.

Oneroso, F., & Gorrese, A. (Eds.) (2004). *Mente e pensiero: Incontri con l'opera di Wilfred R. Bion* Napoli: Napoli.

Ogden, T. H. (1991). An interview with Thomas Ogden. *Psychoanalytic Dialogues*, *1*: 361–376.

Ogden, T. H. (1994). The analytic third: Working with intersubjective clinical facts. *International. Journal of Psychoanalysis*, *75*: 3–19.

Ogden, T. H. (2004). An introduction to the reading of Bion. *International Journal of Psychoanalysis*, *85*: 285–300.

Rappaport, E. A. (1956). The management of an erotized transference. *Psychoanalytic Quarterly*, *25*: 515–529.

Sandler, P. C. (2005). *The Language of Bion: A Dictionary of Concepts*. London: Karnac.

# PART VII

## LATE PAPERS AND BASIC CONCEPTS

*Editors' introduction*

Brown's paper on Bion's "Notes on memory and desire" (Chapter Twenty-Four) introduces the reader to one of the main theoretical and technical features of a post-Bionian psychoanalysis. Why "post-"? Because—very interestingly—Brown reads Bion's contribution in the light of contemporary field theories (Italian and North-American) and of the Boston Change group. The first serves him well in shaping a lively clinical vignette in which the working through in the here and now is illustrated. This takes the form of a narrative-building endeavor shared by the analytic dyad. The reader can follow the appearance, on the stage of analysis, of meaningful characters: the Crushed Computer, the Cyborg, the Tyrant, the Philosopher King, the People-Going-Away, and so on. On the scale of the micro-metric interaction between patient and analyst the characters are derivatives and already transformations of raw emotions ignited in the emotional field of the session, or, differently said, in the intermediate world stemming from the inevitable and ongoing unconscious communication between the analytic dyad.

Following the life of these characters allows the couple to experience at-one-ment (Bion) or a "lived experience" or "dreaming into existence" (Ogden); to make "real contact" (Joseph). In this way Brown underlines how, with Bion, a shift, from contents to containers or psychic function and, consequently from the past of the infantile neurosis towards what is being newly lived and constructed in the here-and-now of the clinical encounter, takes place. The goal of the cure becomes to develop a capacity to represent or think. These perspectives are rendered even more convincing if read through the lens of the "Change Group" theories about the so-called "now moments" or the "moments of meeting", which can elicit a "dyadic expansion of consciousness", even if differences have to be emphasized regarding their use of the concept of the unconscious.

Vermote's comment on "Emotional turbulence" helps us to better understand the play of characters already mentioned by Brown. These are the products of, and at the same time the first forms in which, emotional turbulences appear. In the never-ending flow of life, they arise from the friction between the human bodily and psychic surfaces on one side and the real, the unknown, the infinite, O on the other. Appropriately, Vermote points out the importance that style takes on for Bion. As illustration, his own text not only tells but shows, and so asks the reader, in the very act of reading, to live an experience of "meeting" with the text that will go beyond the rational or logical to allow what is intuitively relevant to emerge.

This appreciation of the text as performative as well as communicative recognizes that the act of reading has to produce emotional turbulence if something valuable is to be achieved from it. What this requires on the side of the reader is to give him or her self entirely to the text and to renounce what is already known. Here Bion joins a prestigious philosophical tradition, from Socratic irony to Husserlian *epoché* to Derridean deconstruction; and with the same impressive radicalism that is the mark of the genius. What is requested from the analyst in order to make contact with "psychoanalytic objects" is to be capable of standing in intuitive states of mind. The reference to artists' experiences or artworks can be useful: here Da Vinci and Hokusai.

In regard to the analytic attitude, Vermote mentions that a certain modesty is necessary. This theme implicitly recurs as a core issue in the other late papers. For example, Cairo, in response to the brief and for her very influential paper, "Making the best of a bad job", recounts a telling clinical vignette in which she shows how emotional turbulences can become emotional storms that can prevent the analyst not only from intellectual understanding, but also from "at-one-ment" and "becoming the O" of the patient. The remedy, for her, meant accepting to see herself as the patient saw her (as the "bad object"), not defending against this and taking full responsibility for the disturbance and pain her analytic presence had mobilized and caused.

Often a "bulwark" is formed when the analyst does not accept to make the best of a bad job, that is "to be" the bad object, and only attempts to interpret the patient's (transference) misunderstandings. Thus, Cairo meditates on how prematurely returning the enraged and terrifying patient's projections via interpretation was actually cruel. The point is that the "light pollution" of theory can easily blind the therapist to what is potentially emerging from the darkness of the unknown. So in this case, the "bad" in the title of Bion's paper not only refers to the "impossibility" of the analytic profession, as Freud pointed out, but also to the need to accept being cast into the role of the "bad guy" on the analytic stage. Bion constantly warns us how this acceptance may be much more difficult to achieve than we might think.

In the language of the caesura paper, this acceptance could be reformulated, in terms of learning to use non-pathological splitting when confronted with the choice between several options. Sosnik argues that a non-separative logic is necessary to tolerate all the paradoxes, which are the hallmark of psychic life. One of the caesuras that need to be transited is between pre-mental areas of the personality and the mental ones. Some of the questions that Bion challenges us with and that Sosnik addresses are these: Are there sub-thalamic fears that continue to operate post-birth? Are there some forms of mentation or of pre-mental emotional life already active in the embryo? If so, how might these unrepresented states of mind influence development and show up in analysis? What is the role of physical action in signaling their presence?

In addition, Sosnik points to many other caesuras that may constantly arise as "barriers of calcification" and that the analyst may be challenged to transverse. For example, between there and here, then and now, the different roles in analysis, knowing and not-knowing, and so on. So the discourse of "Caesura" clearly implies a discourse on method, intended by Bion to give theoretical tools to the analyst in order to help him or her to remain open to the emotional turbulences—or, as we saw, storms—represented by the new idea or the unknown.

Levine follows with a meditation on O, the ineffable and not fully knowable "thing-in-itself" that is the always elusive core of existential reality for both analyst and patient as individuals, and of the relationship that is continually emerging and evolving between them. For Bion, the concept of O was intimately connected to the clinical centrality and pursuit of the psychoanalytic object, the necessity of the analyst's trying to achieve a state of reverie and listening without memory, desire, or intention, and the allowance of the emergence of something truly new and creative within and between the analytic couple, even if it was accompanied by the terrors of change and the unfamiliar known as catastrophic dread. Levine further suggests that for Bion, introducing the concept of O into psychoanalytic theory and discourse was a way of alerting analysts to the constricting tendency of prior discoveries and of systems of thought, such as psychoanalysis itself. In so doing, Bion provided analysts with "a provocative reminder offered in a constructive way to help us to think about and interrogate the truth of our existence."

It is a felicitous happening that this series of comments on Bion's late papers and concepts ends with Chuster's text on "Evidence", because we find in it one of Bion's rare and precious clinical illustrations: two sessions with a patient, where Bion shows how his inability to transcend the caesura brought the therapy to a dramatic end. This experience raises for Bion and for us a major epistemological question: If the psychoanalytic object is believed to lie beyond the reach of sensuous experience and is accessible to the analyst only via intuition, what is the evidence for its existence?

Chuster's paper deals with the obstacles to this process of intuition: words and language itself, temporal split, emotional turbulence; and, then discusses the use and positive benefits of imaginative conjectures and intuition. He stresses the point that creative imagination, which is essential to approach the complexity of the human mind, is "not only the capacity to combine elements that are provided by the patient. It is the capacity to create new forms with these given elements." This is a disciplined and artistic-like activity—we also say that Medicine is an art—, which includes the emotional dimension of aesthetic experience combined with "rationally plausible presumptions". If the caesura between these two realms is well enough transited, then we can hope that each term of the binary opposition works as a safe anchoring for the other.

# CHAPTER TWENTY-FOUR

# "Notes on memory and desire": implications for working through*

*Lawrence J. Brown*

> "[The analyst] should withhold all conscious influences to his capacity to attend and give himself over completely to his 'unconscious memory'."
>
> —Freud, 1912, p. 112

> "The psychoanalyst should aim at achieving a state of mind so that at every session he feels he has not seen the patient before. If he feels he has, he is treating the wrong patient."
>
> —Bion, 1967, p. 273

Recollecting one's repressed childhood conflicts has been a mainstay of classical psychoanalysis and in "Remembering, repeating and working-through" Freud (1914) discussed how many patients "remember" their early conflicts through actions:

> the patient does not remember anything of what he has forgotten and repressed, but *acts* it out ... As long as the patient is in the treatment he cannot escape from this compulsion to repeat; and in the end we understand that this is his way of remembering. (p. 150, original emphasis)

Although these repetitions are a resistance to memory, they simultaneously are a pathway to recovering the forgotten past through the development of a transference neurosis by which the analysand's illness becomes "not an event of the past, but as a present day force" (p. 151). Thus, Freud regards the inevitable repetitions as an invaluable tool to help the patient work through

---

*Expanded version of a paper given at the International Psychoanalytic Association Congress, Prague, 2013.

his infantile past since that troubled history is played out again in effigy through an "artificial illness" (p. 154) in the here and now of the transference neurosis. However, the transference neurosis develops slowly, as though it had a timetable of its own, and the analyst "has nothing else to do than wait and let things take their course" (p. 155). Freud counsels patience with this process and the analyst must curb any tendencies that distract him from paying exclusive attention to what is on the patient's mind in the moment. Freud's advice in this paper elaborates his recommendations two years earlier (1912) that the analyst must adopt a stance in which his unconscious is a "receptive organ" to the analysand's communicating unconscious and that he, the analyst, ought to give himself over to his "unconscious memory".

In my view, there are many aspects of Bion's work that have their origin in ideas that remained inchoate in Freud; partially developed proposals that seeded Bion's genius and which he nurtured in creative and unexpected ways. For example, Bion appears to have been greatly influenced by Freud's (1911) paper, "Formulations on the two principles of mental functioning"[1] (Brown, 2009, 2011), and significantly reworked the concepts of the pleasure and reality principles to promulgate a theory of dreaming that broadened Freud's first contributions (Bion, 1962, 1992; Brown, 2012, 2013; Grotstein, 2009). Similarly, with regard to clinical practice, though Bion does not refer specifically to "transference neurosis", he writes as though he has taken Freud's recommendations very seriously and builds on these in unique ways. What is most evident to me in "Notes on memory and desire" is Bion's unequivocal emphasis on the here-and-now of the session that is implicit in Freud's (1914) notion of the transference neurosis as a "present day force" (p. 151), but which Bion brings into bold relief as the centerpiece of his technical recommendations. Furthermore, where Freud (1912) advises the analyst "to give himself over completely to his 'unconscious memory'" (p. 112) and "let things take their course" (1914, p. 155), Bion (1967) speaks of an evolution in the session that emerges effortlessly in which "some idea or pictorial impression floats into the mind unbidden as a whole" (p. 279).

These parallels notwithstanding, Bion parts company with Freud by his seemingly ahistorical approach to the session. Where Freud would stress the important vitality of repetition, Bion (1967) is concerned that each session should be fresh in order for there to be "less clogging of the sessions by the repetition of material which should have disappeared" (p. 273), resulting in a livelier analytic pace. Furthermore, Bion states that the analyst following his "rules" will notice that

> [t]he pattern of analysis will change. Roughly speaking, the patient will not appear to develop over a period of time but *each session will be complete in itself*. "Progress" will be measured by the increased number and variety of moods, ideas and attitudes seen in any given session. (p. 273, italics added)

To my mind, this raises an important dilemma: if, as Bion says, we must unclog the sessions of repetition and that "each session will be complete in itself", how are we to understand the process of working through? And, if progress is to be assessed solely through evolution within individual sessions, how are we to regard the established analytic practice of measuring progress by the working through of various transference/countertransference configurations over the course of many years? I will now present some analytic material to help us further think about this apparent paradox.

### Edward: stuck at a threshold

Edward, a friendless and socially awkward nine-year-old began analysis because of intense panic, which, when he was younger, was manifest as significant separation anxiety. A brilliant student who academically outshone his talented peers, Edward was also a loner whose only reliable companion was his beloved computer. He was eager to display his very impressive knowledge and occasionally I "consulted" him with questions about my computer. One August when he was eleven years old, shortly after my vacation and two weeks before school was to begin, I received a panicked call from his mother that Edward had "melted down". Indeed, that was an apt term because when I saw him he was so terrified that he was barely able to speak, only able to say, "My computer crashed and I lost everything." Although he was consciously referring to the computer's files and documents, the underlying message was clear—that everything holding his world together was gone. I thought, but did not say, that this terror must be the current version of his earlier panic. We were able to talk about how he and his computer were an intertwined unit, like a cyborg that was part human and part machine, and also about his anxiety in starting a new school year. These discussions were very helpful and he was able to regroup emotionally in order to begin school.

I did not share with Edward my association to his earliest separation anxiety for several reasons. Typically, he was exceedingly cerebral and his affects were always muted and/or banished through his impressive intellectual strengths; therefore, finding him in a rare state of emotional vulnerability, albeit one of intense panic, was an opportunity to reach him at a moment of affective aliveness. In addition, more "traditional" interpretations that linked the present with the past were usually dissembled by Edward through arguments that skewered the logical basis of my interventions that had been reduced to a jumble of meaningless words. Thus, I approached each session as a unique experience which enabled the analysis, in certain instants, to be a "lived experience" (Ogden, 2010). Gradually these experiences of "real contact" (Joseph, 1985) in individual sessions accrued over time and created in my mind a more or less coherent sense of Edward's inner world, that is, what Ogden (2004a, 2004b) terms "dreaming into existence".

Now, three years later, I find Edward, a plump and physically immature fourteen year old, standing motionless at the threshold between the waiting room and my office when I open the door for the session. He does not appear frozen with anxiety, but rather seems to be casually standing in place. When I ask what is going on, he says "I'm thinking": he isn't sure whether he will come into the office or not. I comment that his feet are exactly positioned in the middle of the door frame at the threshold of my office as though he can't decide what to do. Edward then steps into the consulting room, lies on the couch, and I ask what had just happened. He says he is experiencing the same problem at home: that he feels compelled to stand midway at the doorjamb before he leaves one room to enter another; however, he is not feeling anxious but rather, perched in this in-between place, has a sense of calm. I say that we have been talking about how scared he is to "grow up" and that it seems being stuck at the threshold coming in today expresses his worry about moving out of the relative comfort of being young to the frightening mysteries of being a teenager; that he wants to me see with my own eyes how he is stuck. This comment feels obvious to me and Edward says he thinks I am right, though he shows little emotion. Nevertheless, this "symptom" quickly disappears in a few sessions.

Some weeks later, Edward tells me about the powerful and crippling anxiety he is feeling while doing homework. He then collapses into an anxious mass of tormented tears, self-hatred, and impotent rage, saying that his life is over. He is terrified because his panic is so overwhelming that it is difficult to read and he is spending six hours or more each night doing his homework. I also am feeling utterly helpless and that I have little to give him: even when I offer interpretations gingerly, Edward pulls himself into a fetal position and weeps loudly, nearly howling in the grip of some unbearable inner torment. He says he is only able to do his homework when his mother sits next to him and I realize he needs my silent presence as a non-intrusive analyst. I suggest that he bring in a book to read in the session for us to try and get some perspective on his difficulty reading. He brings in Plato's *Republic* that is assigned in one class and reads a portion about the difference between a leader who is a tyrant and the more munificent Philosopher King and suddenly a pall comes over his face accompanied by a chilling shiver. It is the notion of the punishing tyrant that frightens him and I say I think he lives under constant threat from a tyrant inside him with no gentle Philosopher King inside his mind to protect him. For the first time in many weeks Edward relaxes and, patting the couch like an old friend, stretches out comfortably with an audible sigh of relief.

Edward's anxiety remains very forceful but now, armed with the metaphor of the Tyrant and the Philosopher King, we are able to begin to make sense of what haunts him. Through his tears and panic, he tells me that he only received one B during his school career and all the other grades were As and A+s; now he is terrified that because of his overpowering anxiety his grades will suffer. I say that the tyrant part of him must be very unhappy with that, which brings forth a torrent of plaintive tears and the revelation of his private fear that "it would be the beginning of a slippery slope and I'll end up living in a card board box." I say there's no Philosopher King in his mind to argue against, and protect him from, this cruel tyrant; adding that sitting close to his mother and reading here with me gives him the safety and protection he cannot feel when he's alone. He is palpably calmed by this interpretation and there is a sense in the hour that we have arrived at an important emotional truth (Bion, 1994: Grotstein, 2004). In the months that follow, Edward and I learn a considerable amount about the tyrant part of him and his phantasy of being an omnipotent Philosopher King, themes that once contained devastating emotion but whose meaning we are beginning to come to understand.

## Discussion

My analytic work with Edward illustrates the apparent paradox about how one works through repetitive painful affective patterns when the focus is on the evolution in each session rather than on the overall arc of the analysis. I condensed nearly five years of analysis and described the various forms in which his anxiety was manifest: Edward's early separation anxiety, his sheer terror at age eleven when his computer crashed, his getting stuck halfway between the waiting room and my office at fourteen years old, and his horror that with one B grade his life would end in ignominy. In my view, there was an important working through during this period of time, but a qualitatively different sort than the classical notion of "working through". For Freud, it was an infantile neurosis, organized in early childhood and then repressed, that, under pressure from the repetition compulsion, was replicated over and over in action because it could not be remembered. However, in Edwards's case, there was no structured infantile neurosis but there was instead a periodic destructive threat to his world that looped unpredictably from an unknown corner of the void like an unnamed comet. In this connection, working through consists of a gradual process of helping the patient bring meaning to unrepresented experience in order that, as Bion states, "Out of the darkness and formlessness something evolves" (1967, p. 272).

Edward's profound anxiety was simply a powerful affect that made an unstructured appearance at certain periods in his life that loosely had something to do with separations and transitions. I realized early on that offering "traditional" interpretations, such as his anxiety about crossing the threshold into adolescence, were typically met with a bland "that could be right" but with no connection to the overwhelming anxieties that persecuted him. I believe that he took great comfort from being physically near to me, as he was with his mother at his side during homework, and also that I was a containing companion who helped him bear the unthinkable anxieties that tormented him. It was especially vital that I could tolerate, and could share in, Edward's paralyzing helplessness when reading was so difficult for him. It was an experience of at-one-ment that Bion (1970) describes, which the patient senses, and is an important step in the transformation of unrepresented affects into meaningful psychic events. In patients like Edward, I believe this is an essential first step that ultimately leads to the later capacity for the working through that Freud discussed, which requires an organized and symbolically formatted template, that is, the infantile neurosis that prefigures the transference neurosis.

In a series of papers, da Rocha Barros (2000, 2002, 2011) has explored the connection between dreaming and working through. He notes that Freud's theory of working through was predicated on the assumption that an adequate symbolic capacity was sufficiently intact in the patient to permit the transformation of affects into dream thoughts. Da Rocha Barros (2002) states that

> it is through the process of building up symbols in the dreamwork that part of the process of working through takes place ... [because] fresh symbols are created that widen the capacity of the person to think about the meanings of his/her emotional experiences. (p. 1085)
>
> However, these "fresh symbols" created through dream-work, or Bion's (1962) alpha function, are not yet thought processes, since they are expressed in images rather than in verbal discourse and contain powerful expressive, evocative elements. (2002, p. 1087)

These comments are relevant to the point in Edward's analysis, during our reading of Plato's *Republic*, when the Tyrant and the Philosopher King were discussed in the book. These figures became "powerful expressive, evocative elements" that served as representatives of aspects of his inner object world. In the language of Ferro's (2002, 2006, 2009) work, these were "characters in the field" that signified the affects of the here-and-now emotional field in which Edward and I were immersed. The emergence of the Tyrant and the Philosopher King were the outcome of that component of working through that transformed emotions into what Ferro calls affective holograms[2] and these characters gave Edward and me a beginning language to continue the working through process of newly defined themes that had evolved "Out of the darkness and formlessness" (Bion, 1967, p. 272).

In discussing the "Wolfman's" dream as an example of *Nachtraglichkeit* by which an earlier childhood experience was given psychological meaning by the later dream at four years old, Freud commented that

> Indeed, *dreaming is another kind of remembering, though one that is subject to the conditions that rule at night and to the laws of dream formation.* (1918, p. 51, italics added)

This statement seems to suggest a role for dreaming in bringing emotional meaning to dormant experiences that now, having been given representation through "laws of dream formation" (condensation, symbolization, displacement, etc.), may be "remembered". Bion's (1962) observation that these "laws of dream formation" are continuously active while we are awake and asleep has greatly impacted current psychoanalytic thinking that underscores the omnipresence of a psychic function[3] that constantly transforms raw emotional experience[4] into meaningful psychological events. However, I think it is incorrect to say that previously unrepresented states, now transformed through alpha function, are "remembered", as Freud says, but rather that they are made available for thinking for the first time. In this regard, the appearance of the Philosopher King and the Tyrant in Edward's analysis was a vital step forward because it gave us two meaningful characters (representations) to embody affects that previously were without shape and form, existing only as nameless somato-sensory bombardment. As da Rocha Barros (2002) has stated, these images "are not yet thought processes ... [but] contain powerful expressive, evocative elements" (p. 1087) that promoted further elaboration in Edward's analysis.

Freud's (1914) concept of working through assumed the existence of an organized infantile neurosis constructed from symbolic elaborations of childhood conflicts and compromise formations. Anna Freud (1970) added that

> [s]een from the developmental point of view, the infantile neurosis can represent a positive sign of personality growth; a progression from primitive to more sophisticated reaction patterns ..." (p. 202)

However, in patients like Edward, this "progression from primitive to more sophisticated reaction patterns" has not occurred, leaving the analysand vulnerable to invasions of "nameless dread" (Bion, 1962). In such situations, I believe that working through occurs on both the macro level over a period of time as well as on the micro level in which "each session will be complete in itself" (Bion, 1967, p. 273). The analysis must first proceed on the micro basis, inhabiting each session as a seemingly isolated outpost, like a string of islands that are later brought together into a unified nation. From the large-scale vantage point, the analytic work aims at containing the anonymous terrors plaguing the patient and helping to build and/or strengthen the "apparatus for thinking" (Bion, 1962) necessary for symbolization, that is, to give a face to the analysand's fear. Once accomplished, as when Edward offered the characters of the Tyrant and the Philosopher King, the analytic pair can engage more interpretively with each other and collectively face the pain which now has an identity.

These "isolated outposts" are the building blocks from which the analytic pair can construct a narrative of the patient's emotional life. The initial linking together of these elements occurs within the mind of the analyst as a sort of construction (Freud, 1937), a working hypothesis about who the patient is, that Ogden (2004a, 2004b) has termed "dreaming the patient into existence".

For example, at the beginning of Edward's analysis, I knew from his history that he had been frightened of separations as a young child, but there was no way to access this in the sessions until one hour in which I needed to leave my office for a minute to get some more paper for drawing. Edward grew terrified and asked me not to leave, but he did not know what frightened him. I was able to give a name to the fear, "people going away", that enabled us to speak about it and it was the start of our developing a narrative about his psychic life. Later on, when his computer crashed, I could add that he felt like a cyborg, which was another denotation of his inner experience of himself. Further on in the analysis, when he was stuck on the threshold of my waiting room and office, I added that change was very frightening to him; however, my comment did not have any meaning to Edward emotionally. Nevertheless, it registered quite profoundly for me as I witnessed his paralysis in the moment that facilitated a more complex view in my mind of what was overwhelming him, which could best be described as, "Edward, now heading into adolescence, frozen and terrified of change and separation that could lead to his complete and utter collapse." However, his apparatus for thinking thoughts was still too impaired to tolerate the affects associated with my inner view of him, so my "dream" of him, of necessity, remained my speculation.

Edward's capacity to represent his internal world through reference to the Tyrant and the Philosopher King was a significant leap forward in his growing ability to use symbols to convey his emotional inner life and illustrated da Rocha Barros' (2000) observation that

> [w]hat is felt as internal pressure must be transformed at first through images, and then into a broader channel of expression made up of words, in order to become part of our process of thinking. (p. 1097)

It is important to note that these *characters* (the Tyrant and Philosopher King) were Edward's creation: he brought them into the session and these represented two different emotional currents that initially were "felt as internal pressure" but now signified two discreet internal objects that prefigured later transference manifestations. This forward movement also resulted in the growth of a more deeply enriched analytic process in which both Edward and I were engaged in an unconscious intersubjective exchange (Brown, 2010, 2011) that spontaneously created new meanings. Thus, he had evolved to a point at which he could form the emotionally evocative image of fearing that he would collapse and end up living in a cardboard box.

Edward's figures of the Tyrant and Philosopher King comprised a vital instance in the analysis and it brought to my mind the work of the Boston Change Process Study Group[5] (henceforth,

"Change Group") (2010, 2013) that places great emphasis on analytic encounters that create *now moments* described as

> short subjective units of time in which something of importance bearing on the future is happening in the dyad. ... Clinically and subjectively, how analyst and patient know they have entered a new moment, a moment distinct from the usual present moments ... is that these moments are unfamiliar, unexpected in their exact form and timing, unsettling or weird. (2013, pp. 735–736)

These moments typically produce some turmoil in the ongoing mood of the analytic dyad that initiates an action by the analyst, whether an interpretation, an enactment or even a response of silence. The Change Group views such moments as opportunities for change, though the analytic pair may at first wish for a return to the status quo; however, the analytic situation at such times is ripe for the emergence of new patterns of relating that have advanced in a nonlinear way. Indeed, the appearance of the Philosopher King and Tyrant signaled such a pregnant moment that catapulted Edward and me into a new terrain: the emergence of a greater capacity for symbol formation and a "broader channel of expression made up of words" that da Rocha Barros (2000) described.

Much of what the Change Group sees as essential in analysis is consistent with the ideas that I have been discussing, though there are some important differences. Their concept of now moments is a significant contribution that links with some of Bion's ideas of the importance of the here-and-now as well as his concept of the *caesura* (Aguayo, 2013; Bion, 1977), which marks the sudden change from one mode of being/relating to another, creating an experience of newness and even disorientation. Similarly, Bion's (1970) notion of the inevitability of *turmoil* when change occurs connects with the Change Group's emphasis on how unsettling the appearance of new ways of relating may feel. In addition, the Change Group's underscoring of nonlinearity is consonant with the perspectives offered in this chapter; however, there is a major difference in how these two points of view diverge—the understanding of unconscious processes and their role in therapeutic change.

I (Brown, 2010, 2011) have been outlining a model of change that first and foremost hinges on a constant unconscious communication between the psyches of patient and analyst that either aims to uncover repressed unconscious contents or to transform unrepresented affective experience into symbolized and emotionally meaningful experience. Projective and introjective processes are the thoroughfares along which unconscious to unconscious communication travels and alpha function in the analyst and patient is responsible for encoding and decoding unconscious messages. In my view (Brown, 2009), this process is at work constantly but, since it is unconscious, it is difficult to access except through one's reveries and counter transference phenomena. Furthermore, working through involves changes in the unconscious, which is comprised of phantasies that are registered discursively as well as existing as yet unprocessed emotional experience.

I find that the Change Group tends to underemphasize the role of unconscious processes in their work and that when the unconscious is mentioned (though rarely), it is a different notion than the one promulgated in this chapter. Instead, they speak of "nonconscious" happenings, "implicit relational knowing", and "implicit relational exchanges"; the latter concept referring to

> the assumption that the patient and analyst are generally working hard to intuitively grasp each other's implicit intentions and directions. Conversation between them occurs continuously. (Change Group, 2013, p. 729)

This quote conveys an impression that accentuates conscious dialogues, though the wording "implicit relational knowing" seems to suggest an unconscious aspect. Similarly, the Change Group refers to

> [i]mplicit experience [that] is not necessarily dissociated experience, unformulated or repressed, and the goal of working with it is not to transform it into an understanding within the reflective verbal sphere. (p. 734)

If an experience is not dissociated, unformulated, or repressed, then the only other option is that it is a conscious experience, but I don't think this is what the authors mean. It would be helpful to the reader not familiar with their argot to have these terms more completely defined.

## Conclusion

This chapter has explored the impact on our understanding of the process of working through of Bion's emphasis that each session is an entity unto itself and that the analyst ought to approach each clinical hour without memory and desire. I have suggested that working through, especially when dealing with unrepresented experience, occurs on a micro and macro basis. The micro basis involves working in the immediacy of the clinical here-and-now moments with the assumption that, over a period of time, themes in individual sessions will cohere into meaningful narratives. Working on the macro basis, on the other hand, involves the analyst being mindful of the overall arc of the analysis with an eye on developing transferences and countertransference over a long period of time. A clinical vignette from the analysis of a deeply troubled latency age boy is offered to explicate working from both of view—micro and macro. Finally, some similarities and differences between the model proposed in this chapter and the standpoints of the Boston Change Process Study Group have been examined.

## Notes

1. This work is cited more than any of Freud's other papers.
2. Or affective pictograms according to da Rocha Barros (2000).
3. Alpha function.
4. The reader is referred to the recent book, *Unrepresented States and the Construction of Meaning: Clinical and Theoretical Contributions* (2103), edited by Levine, Reed, and Scarfone, for a more detailed discussion of these processes.

5. This group consisted of Nadia Bruschweiler-Stern, Karlen Lyons-Ruth, Alexander C. Morgan, Jeremy P. Nahum, Bruce Reis, Daniel Stern, and Louis Sander.

## References

Aguayo, J. (2013). Wilfred Bion's "Caesura": From oral to published text (1975–1977). In: H. Levine & L. Brown (Eds.), *Growth and Turbulence in the Container/Contained: Bion's Continuing Legacy* (pp. 55–74). London: Routledge.

Bion, W. R. (1962). *Learning from Experience*. London: Heinemann.

Bion, W. R. (1967). Notes on memory and desire. *Psychoanalytic Forum, 2*: 270–273.

Bion, W. R. (1970). *Attention and Interpretation*. London: Heinemann.

Bion, W. R. (1977). "Caesura". In: *Two Papers: "The Grid" and "Caesura"* (pp. 35–56). London: Karnac, 1989.

Bion, W. R. (1992). *Cogitations*. London: Karnac.

Bion, W. R. (1994). *Clinical Seminars and Other Works*. London: Karnac.

Boston Change Process Study Group. (2010). *Change in Psychotherapy: A Unifying Paradigm*. New York: Norton.

Boston Change Process Study Group (2013). Enactment and the emergence of new relational organization. *Journal of the American Psychoanalytic Association, 61*: 727–749.

Brown, L. J. (2009). The ego psychology of Wilfred Bion: Implications for an intersubjective view of psychic structure. *Psychoanalytic Quarterly, 78*: 27–55.

Brown, L. J. (2010). Klein, Bion and intersubjectivity: Becoming, transforming and dreaming. *Psychoanalytic Dialogues, 20*: 669–682.

Brown, L. J. (2011). *Intersubjective Processes and the Unconscious: An Integration of Freudian, Kleinian and Bionian Perspectives*. London: Routledge.

Brown, L. J. (2012). Bion's discovery of alpha function: Thinking under fire on the battlefield and in the consulting room. *International Journal of Psychoanalysis, 93*: 1191–1214.

Brown, L. J. (2013). The development of Bion's concept of container and contained. In: H. Levine & L. Brown (Eds.), *Growth and Turbulence in the Container/Contained* (pp. 7–22). London: Routledge.

da Rocha Barros, E. M. (2000). Affect and pictographic image: The constitution of meaning in mental life. *International Journal of Psychoanalysis, 81*: 1087–1099.

da Rocha Barros, E. M. (2002). An essay on dreaming, psychical working out and working through. *International Journal of Psychoanalysis, 83*: 1083–1093.

da Rocha Barros, E. M., & E. L. da Rocha Barros (2011). Reflections on the clinical implications of symbolism. *International Journal of Psychoanalysis, 92*: 879–901.

Ferro, A. (2002). Narrative derivatives of alpha elements: Clinical implications. *International Forum of Psychoanalysis, 11*: 184–187.

Ferro, A. (2006). Clinical implications of Bion's thought. *International Journal of Psychoanalysis, 87*: 989–1003.

Ferro, A. (2009). Transformations in dreaming and characters in the psychoanalytic field. *International Journal of Psychoanalysis, 90*: 209–230.

Freud, A. (1970). The infantile neurosis: Genetic and dynamic considerations. In: *The Writings of Anna Freud, Volume VII* (pp. 189–203). New York: IUP.

Freud, S. (1911). Formulations on the two principles of mental functioning. *S. E., 12*: 215–226. London: Hogarth.

Freud, S. (1912). Recommendations to physicians practicing psycho-analysis. *S. E.*, *12*: 109–120. London: Hogarth.
Freud, S. (1914). Remembering, repeating and working-through. *S. E.*, *12*: 147–156. London: Hogarth.
Freud, S. (1918). From the history of an infantile neurosis. *S. E.*, *17*: London: Hogarth.
Freud, S. (1937). Constructions in analysis. *S. E.*, *23*: 255–270. London: Hogarth.
Grotstein, J. (2004). The seventh servant: The implications of a truth drive in Bion's theory of O. *International Journal of Psychoanalysis*, *85*: 1081–1101.
Grotstein, J. (2009). Dreaming as a "curtain of illusion": Revisiting the "royal road" with Bion as our guide. *International Journal of Psychoanalysis*, *90*: 733–752.
Joseph, B. (1985). Transference: The total situation. *International Journal of Psychoanalysis*, *66*: 447–454.
Levine, H., Reed, G., & Scarfone, D. (Eds.) (2013). *Unrepresented States and the Construction of Meaning: Clinical and Theoretical Contributions.* London: Karnac.
Ogden, T. (2004a). An introduction to the reading of Bion. *International Journal of Psychoanalysis*, *85*: 285–300.
Ogden, T. (2004b). This art of psychoanalysis: Dreaming undreamt dreams and interrupted cries. *International Journal of Psychoanalysis*, *85*: 857–877.
Ogden, T. (2010). On three forms of thinking: Magical thinking, dream thinking, and transformative thinking. *Psychoanalytic Quarterly*, *79*: 317–347.

CHAPTER TWENTY-FIVE

# On Bion's text "Emotional turbulence": a focus on experience and the unknown

*Rudi Vermote*

This brief paper on emotional turbulence (Bion, 1976) "and its counterparts" might equally have been entitled "Caesura", in line with Bion's final formulations concerning invariance and transformations and the idea that the same pattern is apt to be present both before and after a catastrophe (Bion, 1965). Faithful to his approach of focusing on the unthinkable, the unfamiliar, and the alien in the unconscious, Bion treats the subject of emotional turbulence in an indirect, circumferential way. He eschews logical deduction and refuses to settle for the reassuring "discovery" of what is familiar and already known, preferring instead to allow his associations to lead him and the reader in many different unfamiliar, but very productive directions. In addition to its content, the very *form* of the text offers readers an illustration of Bion's ways of thinking and working analytically in his last period (so-called "late Bion") in relation to encountering and discovering that which was previously unknown.

In the beginning of the text, Bion explicitly asks the reader not to start from previous knowledge, but to begin from an experience. More specifically, to start from some personal experience that is better left open and that should not be interpreted. He further specifies that it is best to take an experience that is not too strong—lest the mind be triggered to defend itself or close itself off. That is, he encourages the reader to engage with the text in the same way that he advises analysts to proceed in the clinical setting: waiting till a selected fact and its associated patterns and connections emerge.

Indeed, Bion sees the mind as something premature, a poor thing that in terms of both evolutionary potential and regulatory capacity is relatively undeveloped; something that is, so to speak, imposed on the alimentary system. He links the constellation of defense—resistance-repression—with the notion of caesura. The question then becomes how we can observe and be in contact with an experience, without closing ourselves off to it. Bion gives several examples of phenomena that we tend to close off, because they are too strong (e.g., like a personality that cannot be contained by a person, or problems relating to primordial experiences that originate in the prenatal period when the psyche was barely established).

## Opening and closing

Apart from this, Bion emphasizes how being blinded by excitation, desire, and the senses may have a closing effect. His suggested solution about how to deal with this problem is at first sight more Socratic and less mystical than one often thinks in relation to the late Bion. His being Socratic consists of questioning and maintaining his inquiry, even while radically focusing on the unknown. To illustrate, he offers the example of how we can be plunged into the unknown by a simple childlike question, such as "What is a cow, Daddy?"

Bion also warns us that there is great urgency in trying to encounter the world from the vertex of approaching and discovering the unknown. In his view, there is far too much development of what he calls "the monkey trick business"; that is, using our intelligence for seemingly practical adaptation, but really in the service of the pleasure principle. Thus, he notes that the "monkey trick business" has led to the stockpiling of nuclear missiles, presumably for defensive purposes, but which are now so abundant that they can allow us to destroy the world ten times over.

The question and its answer are not only urgent, but also, when directed at what is truly unfamiliar and unknown, can be anxiety provoking and dangerous, just as they were for Socrates. Bion warns us how quickly the mental attitude of resisting easy and familiar explanations and keeping one's mind open to the truly unknown can get closed down. Even an illuminating insight that emerges from his way of looking at one moment can then paradoxically be used to close down thought and stifle openness to discovery at the next.

The defenses martialled against the anxiety of not-knowing can take many forms, including a tendency to fill the empty space of our ignorance and uncertainty with concepts that function as paramnesias. It is telling that in the grid, Bion put "psychoanalytic theory" in the same column as defenses and the lie, warning us of the extent to which our very theory may function as a filler, obstructively and deceptively. Bion preferred trying to keep the question open as a continued stimulus to thought and investigation despite—and *because* of—the emotional turbulence that that openness can produce. Hence he often quoted Maurice Blanchot's (1969, p. 15) phrase: "La réponse est le malheur de la question" (Bion, 1978, pp. 21–40; 1980, p. 116; 2005, p. 8, p. 30). When he was asked in a seminar about projective identification, a concept that was central to his Kleinian formation, his way of working, and his theory of the analytic process, he answered that it does not mean a thing (Bion, 1990, p. 56). Why? Because as a concept, it tended to become reified and thus to shut down thought and inquiry rather than open it up.

Bion developed an "alchemical formula" for creativity and for dealing with the multitude of variables of a session: (PS<->D, container/contained, selected fact) (Bion, 1963). In this text, he makes the sobering remark that even when an analyst works with this formula in an intuitive state of mind, he relies on splitting and then brings parts together and by chance. He compared this once with "the game of snakes and ladders" (Bion, 1977), in which we only know the outcome after the fact. It is possible that a correct interpretation can stop growth and a bad interpretation can lead to a new experience or to a new thought that opens the mind to true discovery. It is a sobering thought to realize that we cannot know in advance the effects of our interpretations.

Bion does not leave us anything to hold on to; even the caesurae-resistances that he depicted as something that we should try to transcend may be potential necessary conditions for emotional growth. Resistances are also necessary as stabilizing structures in the mind that preserve us from psychosis and become lost in the infinitude of mental space (Bion, 1970). Thus, one needs some points of closure (resistance or caesurae) to be able to function psychically. Being aware of this necessity is the difference between an insane (closed to the unknown and clinging to a sterile delusional thought) and a sane psychotic (who has awe for the unknown) (Bion, 1967). Bion gives the example of Rimbaud, who listened and could tolerate being open to the inarticulate, to what Bion described as the proto-mental matrix (Vermote, 2011, 2013, 2014). The exercise for the analyst however, is to lessen resistance and to become what Keats called a "man of achievement".

The following clinical vignette took place after my reading and maybe because I had been reading "Emotional turbulence":

> A patient told me that he read in a newspaper that a car bomber was identified, because his face was melted into the metal of the car. The analysand was shocked that his friend told him that he could understand this. We could have tried to understand the meaning of the shock through identification with his own feelings of despair or adolescent memories, or by psychoanalytical concepts of splitting, death drive, etc., but these would all have been closures of the effect that the powerful image was producing. Even if these approaches were true—they would have tended to close down ("saturate") the dimension of the unknowable of the phenomenon, the experience in the session of this image of the mould of a face in the metal of an exploded car that killed other people.

What struck me in the session was that the analysand was particularly lively in talking about this cruel and deadly phenomenon. He associated to death masks, to the mask of the twin of Louis XIV, who was exiled and imprisoned within an iron mask, because he was a threat to his brother, and to the leather mask of Hannibal Lecter, which restrained his cannibalism; a mask to stop a drive.

Via these associations and what was evoked in me, we found ourselves moving in an imaginary world, partly shared: the TV series, "Breaking Bad", which unexpectedly opened up to Bacon's *Pope Innocentius*, and then to the power of sexuality and its effect on mentalization and to splitting off parts that revealed themselves in this negative of a face, a metal skin. The experience, and chance, led us to this unexpected outcome. The image remained a selected fact. The power of the image was strong enough to open new chains of association and thought and to break through the container into which, for the sake of understanding, they were initially put. All these elements could be placed in different categories of the Grid and were leading us to see a pattern in the life of the patient, which was in constant movement. This seeing was in itself an emotional experience.

## Movement and turbulence

Bion has an underlying faith that patterns of connections (conjunctions) that are not perceptible *per se*, exist in this world. For example, anxiety may be present and exist before its consequences (rapid heartbeat, sweating, etc.) are noticed and experienced as such (Bion, 1970). The mental attitude of being totally open to experience, and not hoping to grasp at meaning nor trying to understand, makes possible a contact with this dimension of a world that transcends what one can perceive.

Bion compares this unknowable psychic reality with the void and formless infinite of Milton's *Paradise Lost*. We may link this with his notion of the proto-mental matrix, the hallucinatory layer described in other places in his writing (Vermote, 2011). It is an undifferentiated, non-represented zone from which elements emerge that may become representable. In Bionian terms: O moves to K, from infinity to finitude. The contact with this unknown zone is an experience that Bion described as "becoming O" or a "transformation in O", although even these terms tend to become saturated these days.

Bion suggests that intuition is the organ of perception for this contact, and, in order for the latter to function at its maximum, one has to train (even in everyday life) to focus on what is unknown by trying to achieve a mental state that is as much as possible denuded of desire, memory, understanding, and coherence. These are all factors that restrict and close intuition for the sake of having a feeling of control and safety. This is why Bion (following Hume, 1735) sees reason as the slave of the passions (Bion, 1965) and thinks that reason is of little help to the analyst who is trying to get in contact with this unknown reality that moves us.

In "Turbulence", Bion refers to great artists, who can tap into this unknown invisible reality, this infinite void, which is not governed by verbal thought. Leonardo da Vinci, for example, was fascinated by turbulence, which he saw as an important aspect of life, perhaps even as an expression of life itself. Great artists succeed, paradoxically, through the creation of their art objects in putting this movement into immovable forms that remain eternal. Think, for example, of the Ryōan-ji garden in Kyoto, which in its total rest reflects an eternal movement, or Da Vinci's depiction of the turbulence in water and in curling hair. We see the same genius in his *Mona Lisa*, which leaves a mysterious impression upon being seen. Through his art, Da Vinci was able to transmit something invisible in such a way that we are still able to experience it so many years later; a genius who asked that at his funeral his casket be followed by forty beggars, reflecting his basic attitude of having nothing to hold on to.

Another artist that reached this state and depicted turbulence in an unforgettable way is Hokusai. In a postscript to his work *One Hundred Views of Mount Fuji*, he writes:

> From around the age of six, I had the habit of sketching from life. I became an artist, and from fifty on began producing works that won some reputation, but nothing I did before the age of seventy was worthy of attention. At seventy-three, I began to grasp the structures of birds and beasts, insects and fish, and of the way plants grow. If I go on trying, I will surely understand them still better by the time I am eighty-six, so that by ninety I will have penetrated to their essential nature. At one hundred, I may well have a positively divine understanding of them,

while at one hundred and thirty, forty, or more I will have reached the stage where every dot and every stroke I paint will be alive. May Heaven, that grants long life, give me the chance to prove that this is no lie.

What is striking in this description is the modest, open, non-thinking attitude and the faith to be able to be in contact with "what is" and knowing this in a way that is absolutely without thought. Again, Da Vinci's and Hokusai's way of expressing is close to what Bion found expressed in Keats' "language of Achievement", which is different from a symbolising language, but is closer to "pure experience" (Nishida, 2001), a language that not only expresses, but *does something*, breaks through a crust.

## Essences

Seeing the essential nature of things, the so-called structure, seems to refer to a-sensuous constant conjunctions. They are perceived in reality, but accompanied by an experience of something that is behind, beyond, or at least that is not clear to the untrained painter. It is a way of seeing-becoming, not merely a matter of better technique. The connections, conjunctions, or, as Hokusai says, "the essential nature", remains the same through different levels of transformations. These constant conjunctions are more important to Bion than "meanings". The conjunctions remain the same within the constant flow of ever-changing representations of them. Even more, it is this flow that makes it possible to discern them. Bion (1962a, 1962b, 1963, 1965, 1970) also calls them "psychoanalytic objects". We can grasp them intuitively in an indirect way or, in Bion's (1963) terms, we need three grid categories to apprehend them. They can evolve from the undifferentiated zone, when we are intuitively open to allowing them to do so. However, this evolution is not self-evident. We tend to block contact with the unknown by reason, by caesurae. This blockage can be disrupted by the power of nature, for instance—this is what Kant called the Sublime—but this seldom happens. We must train ourselves to be open and receptive to moments of this contact and to transcend the caesurae that may obstruct it. What is the essence of our personality, our small life that ends and which is nothing compared to the large movement that Von Weizsäcker called "Das Grosse Leben" (The Great Life) that goes on and on and never dies?

The idea of life in movement and flow was already expressed in Heraclitus' *panta rhei*, everything flows, and, one may add: everything remains the same. The water is never the same, but the river remains. A rock is composed of electrons moving with an astronomical speed in an empty space (when the surface of an atom is compared to a football field, then an electron has the size of a pinpoint, and the nucleus the size of an orange) and still, from the outside, a rock gives an appearance of solidity and permanence in our minds. From a physical vertex everything in our body moves: the atoms, the cells with their pumps, the blood and other fluids, not to forget the brain with its 200 trillion possible neuronal connections (more than the number of stars in the Milky Way). Only from the surface can we deduce movements by EEG, fMRI, and PET scan. These are all statistical data that may take visual form, but show the electric currents which reflect connections made up of increased glucose oxidation and blood flow in specific parts of the brain with different activities organised in networks.

Most of these movements and flows may show turbulence, such as epileptic fits and dysregulations of the blood flow, vomiting, shock, or ejaculation, and so on. But what of movements in our psychoanalytic models? Freud suggested movement and displacement of energy in his "Project", in the primary process, and a binding of energy by verbal thought in the secondary process. In Klein's (1935, 1946) model we have the movement of introjection-projection, projective identification, and a stream of phantasies. For Bion, there is movement in the PS<->D oscillation, in exchanges in the container-contained, and in the transformations and changes that he describes as catastrophic, close to turbulence, and that are reflected in his grid.

The late Bion takes us a step further. The zone of psychic functioning, which he called infinite (and it is possible here to make links with neuroscience—Vermote, 2013, 2014) has deep down within it a state of rest. In this infinite zone exist psychic constant conjunctions, close to the Platonic Forms—which, for Bion, are not just external, as they are for Plato, but internal as well. They are "unmovable movers", to use an expression of Eckhart (2010). They are the unchanging essences that determine the constant flow of transformations that take the form of images, hypotheses, narratives, dreams, and actions. In short, they are essences within the emotional turbulence that makes up our lives. The aim of psychoanalysis is to render the patient his essence as we may see it from a point close to infinity (Bion, 1970).

## Conclusion

We are mentally immersed in a constant flow that Bion compared with the mythical river Alpheus. He discerned elements in that flow that may move in different directions and, as vectors, meet or not. The flow shows resistances and turbulence and catastrophic changes, as in growth. We cannot grasp this, or come in contact with it by understanding. We may only experience it from a mental state that approaches the infinite, becoming it, which in Bion's words means that we may let O find K. One can only *let* this happen, not seek to make it happen.

> What is to be sought is an activity that is both the restoration of god (the Mother) and the evolution of god (the formless, infinite, ineffable, nonexistent), which can be found only in the state in which there is NO memory, desire, understanding. (Bion, 1970, p. 129)

## References

Bion, W. R. (1962a). A theory of thinking. In: *Second Thoughts*. New York: Jason Aronson, 1967.
Bion, W. R. (1962b). *Learning from Experience*. London: Karnac, 1984.
Bion, W. R. (1963). *Elements of Psychoanalysis*. London: Karnac, 1984.
Bion, W. R. (1965). *Transformations*. London: Karnac, 1984.
Bion, W. R. (1967). *Second Thoughts: Selected Papers on Psychoanalysis*, New York: Jason Aronson, 1984.
Bion, W. R. (1970). *Attention and Interpretation*. London: Karnac, 1986.
Bion, W. R. (1976). Emotional turbulence. In: W. R. Bion & F. Bion (Eds.), *Clinical Seminars and Four Papers*. Reading: Radavian Press, 1987.
Bion, W. R. (1977). Caesura. In: *Two Papers: "The Grid" and "Caesura"*. London: Karnac, 1989.
Bion, W. R. (1978). *Four Discussions with Wilfred Bion*. Strathclyde, Perthshire: Clunie.
Bion, W. R. (1980). *Bion in New York and São Paulo*. Strathclyde, Perthshire: Clunie.

Bion, W. R. (1990). *Brazilian Lectures*. London: Karnac.
Bion, W. R. (2005). *The Tavistock Seminars* (ed. F. Bion). London: Karnac.
Blanchot, M. (1969). *L'entretien infini*. Paris: Gallimard.
Eckhart, J. (2010). *Meister Eckhart. Over God wil ik zwijgen. Preken en traktaken (I do not want to talk about God; Sermons and treatises* (Trans. C. O. Jellema). Groningen: Historische Uitgeverij.
Hume, D. (1735). *A Treatise of Human Nature*. London: Penguin Classics, 1985.
Klein, M. (1935). A Contribution to the psychogenesis of manic-depressive states. *International Journal of Psycho-Analysis, 16*: 145–174.
Klein, M. (1946). Notes on some schizoid mechanisms. *International Journal of Psychoanalysis, 27*: 99–110.
Nishida, K. (2001). *Uber das Gute. Eine Philosophie der Reinen Erfahrung*. Frankfurt am Main: Insel Verlag.
Vermote, R. (2011). On the value of "late Bion" to analytic theory and practice. *International Journal of Psychoanalysis, 92*: 1089–1098.
Vermote, R. (2014). Transformations et transmissions du fonctionnement psychique: approche intégrative et implications cliniques. *Revue française de psychoanalyse, 78*: 389–404.
Vermote, R. (2015). *Reading Bion*. London: Routledge. In publication.

# CHAPTER TWENTY-SIX

# On "Making the best of a bad job"

*Irene Cairo*

As analysts, when we think of what we have learned, what envelops our minds most? What marks us and makes us the bearers of experiences that are ineffable, and yet allows us to keep ourselves open to the emotional impact of our patients, while tolerating the loneliness that our work demands? I reflect on these notions as I begin to consider and reappreciate a paper by Bion in the manner he himself did with his writings in *Second Thoughts* (1967), a text that has had an enduring influence on my thinking and rethinking about my work.

My purpose here is first to define the aspects of this paper that have resonated most with me. I will then try to illustrate with a clinical experience the tormented encounters that are so often evoked in our consulting rooms, and try to reconstruct some of the pathways that I followed to "make the best of *my* bad job". Finally, I will try to relate my experience to my own development in terms that I hope will be understandable to colleagues, and readdress the old issues I present in this communication, reframing them along the lines of my current clinical thinking.

Before ever reading Bion's paper, "Making the best of a bad job" (1979), I was already fascinated by the title, with its implication of the inevitable imperfection of our task. The impossibility of achieving what may once have been our ambitious aims still affects me. Undoubtedly though, if taken too far, this title can cast too melancholy a shadow over our capacity to respond to our patients. Then, when I finally did read the paper, I responded to its first paragraph with an emotional shock.

> When two personalities meet, an emotional storm is created. If they make sufficient contact to be aware of each other, or even sufficient to be *un*aware of each other, an emotional state is produced by the conjunction of these two individuals, and the resulting disturbance is hardly likely to be regarded as necessarily an improvement on the state of affairs had they never met

at all. But since they *have* met, and since this emotional storm has occurred, the two parties to this storm may decide to "make the best out of a bad job". (1979, p. 321)

The realization of its truth, the instant recognition of the concept of "an emotional storm", doesn't just live in my memory, but remains intense in successive readings.

The ideas that Bion expressed here have had reverberations in all my clinical thinking, and also in my personal life. These have led in turn to many reflections on the consequence of this understanding. How and when are we permeable to this storm? I am not thinking only of defenses, in the ego psychology sense of the term, those lies of the mind, as Bion (1970) named them. I am thinking, rather, of the need to preserve our capacity, or capacities, to be what I would call *selectively permeable*. In my consulting room, the two personalities who meet do so out of a very specific purpose, but outside the consulting room, when encountering an other, even if the personalities that meet have very different and conflicting purposes, the storm may be just as inevitable.

Later on, Bion writes: "In war, the enemy's aim is so to terrify you that you cannot think clearly ...." (1979, p. 322). And there is the parallel with the encounter with the patient ... I have come to learn that it is also possible and indeed probable that outside the consulting room, the other personality may also terrify me or at least try to terrify me. Despite my intentions not to make use of my clinical capacity outside of a therapeutic context, my capacity to develop imaginative conjectures, and indeed my capacity to "intuit", may be just as necessary outside the office as inside. (And perhaps even more so!)

I have discovered that I cannot let myself be too vulnerable in either setting. I have to remain capable of recovery when "the enemy" succeeds in immobilizing me. And most significantly, I cannot, of course, protect myself so successfully that I am blinded to the other's intentions.

Other aspects of Bion's paper jump out at me in their immediacy: the speculation on the alleged superiority of the waking state over the sleeping state still has a silent but profound and continuous impact on me. These reflections culminate in the question of deciding what state we shall choose for interpretation.

For the clinical illustration I will use, dream language plays an important role. In regard to dream discourse, the different psychoanalytic schools refer to codes and symbols for deciphering a strange language, as well as for understanding universal symbols and private meanings. But perhaps those are old constraints, which lock up our imagination and silence our creative voice. Bion himself urged readers to try to forget him after reading him, so that what they may have gained from the encounter might become more unique and personally meaningful.

So, returning to the question I raised at the beginning, I believe that what allows us to grow as analysts is a gradual, almost imperceptible, interweaving of experience and reflection, both within the session and outside, and, most challenging, the growing awareness that we have such minimal control over our own thinking. Within our clinical setting, this requires then, as Bion (1970) showed us, both "patience" (p. 124) and "faith" (p. 321). To frame more precisely the issues that attract my interest, I will address one specific and complex aspect of our field of observation regarding the choices we have to make use of that field.

Bion's extraordinary illumination of the clinical process as something that takes place between two people, his imagery, such as the enemy who is trying to terrorize us, ends in clinical interventions that aim at describing precisely the inner states of the patient. Many modern Kleinians focus specifically on the interaction, internally raising the question "What is the patient trying to do to me?" or "Who—or what—am I at this moment for the patient?" Bion's exquisite sensitivity leads him to a somewhat different place. Though I have no doubt that his description of the emotional storm involves his understanding of what goes on in the analyst's mind as well as in the patient's, this particular paper seems to privilege what occurs in the patient. This is always more apparent in the sicker patients. We see it clearly in the description of some of his clinical cases, such as "The imaginary twin" (1967, p. 3). There, the succinct, so often brilliant, interventions aim at a description of what Bion perceives is going on *within* the patient, specifically of course, relative to the patient's emotions and capacity to think. This is a refinement of, and an important addition to, classical Kleinian work.

My comments then, are framed by distinguishing, both in the theoretical understanding and in the technical implications, the two kinds of phenomena—those that occur in the depth of the patient's mind and those that occur in the *communication* between the two personalities. I believe, of course, that there is no "objectless" thinking, but that both theoretically and technically we address ourselves at times to the inner experience and at other times to the message.

It may be inferred from what I described earlier that the focus on the patient's inner process becomes a greater necessity with the sicker patients. This would be consistent with the distinction between evacuative and communicative projective identification. But sometimes the severity of the disturbance may so worry and mislead us as to not let us detect the communicative aspect, despite its being there. I believe this may have happened with the patient I describe here. I think in retrospect that I addressed myself too singularly to something in him, and less to something that he was trying to communicate and that was latent and had not yet emerged between us.

P was twenty-eight and single when he started his five-times-a-week analysis. Obsessional and phobic symptoms had imprisoned him in a life devoid of any pleasure. Awkward in all relationships and shy, sometimes cruel to the women in his life, he restricted his work life to a dreary sterile job, where what would later emerge as his creativity and talent were definitely hidden.

In the first few years of his analysis, weekend separations resulted in violent acting out, where he would use drugs, seek prostitutes, provoke fights, sometimes with a pimp, be assaulted, beaten up, and come in injured, even disfigured, when he appeared for the Monday sessions. Why did the violence of his feelings about separation explode in this brutal expression against himself?

After a few more years in analysis many things had changed in his outside life. He had started a successful line of work, his relationships with women were freer, and he could begin to be more open and vulnerable. He didn't have a steady long-term relationship, but did have some romantic or sexual "interests". In the transference, no recognizable erotic or romantic feelings that could have been called oedipal emerged. But we could see defenses emerging, in the form of disparaging comments about me. He once referred to his physical image of me saying, "You look like E.T." When asked about this image further, he, a bit embarrassed, said, "Well, smallish, big eyes, cute actually." On one occasion he described the plot of a movie in which the actress, Julie Andrews, plays a psychotherapist and a male patient either has an affair with her or dreams of it (his description was ambiguous). It seemed to me that there was a blatantly clear transferential meaning in this communication, but he was, characteristically, not aware of it.

In the next session he reported a dream. He was at a party with me, and wanted to introduce me, but he couldn't remember my name. He kept introducing me as "Mrs. Edward Blake". His (perhaps intellectualized) associations were about the poet William Blake. I suggested that the reversal of that name, Blake Edwards, a director, is the name of the real life husband of the actress, Julie Andrews.

Several lines of exploration followed from this dream. The temptation of course was, and still may be, to think of the language of this dream as obviously both expressing, and disguising, a clear oedipal wish. Some of the exploration led us indeed in that direction. But I had, even then, an additional awareness of something blurred and incomplete.

I was curious about a particular aspect of the representation. Why was the disguise of the name a *reversal*? What required to be turned around, or inside out, or upside down?

In another dream he had "a speech impediment". Analysis of that dream led to my foreign accent. Why, then, did he have to identify with me in a *problem* of mine? Why did he attribute my "speech impediment" to himself?

Was there a blurring of boundaries between us? From early on, did I convey a fragility that made him especially restrained in the experience of his negative feelings toward me, thereby condemning him to self-destructive acts? And what of Mrs. Edward Blake? Was that an allusion to a reversal of our positions that he longed for? And what did the speech impediment, or perhaps my being a foreigner, represent? All of these thoughts may refer to what I call a "classical" vertex of observation, simply what goes on in the patient's mind. Those aspects were explored, commented on, as events that were taking place. But there was more, something that I was not able to think clearly about until very late in his analysis, and that had to do with a deeper message to me, and my difficulties in receiving it. The communicative function of his actions was certainly not totally lost on me, but it was difficult to understand or hold on to.

In reflecting on this material, I had been aware of the brutal intensity of what went on in his mind and the potential violence between us. Yet his destructive aggression always turned against himself in physical acts, and thus my terror for him, for his safety, I believed, often immobilized me: I was not able to think clearly enough, and definitely not able to think *for* him. I curiously never feared for my safety. There were instances of fragmented associations, of "blank" moments, that let me glimpse the severity of the disturbance in thinking that was underneath his symptoms—a disturbance that in retrospect I did not yet have sufficient composure or tools to address.

The ending of the analysis, though planned ahead with over a year's time, revealed depths of his rage that while not new, shocked me, because I had believed they had seemed sufficiently explored and worked through. Yet the glimpse I had of his unreadiness to terminate, was not sufficient to postpone the ending. And so we did end what, at the time, I thought was a limited but "good enough" analytic process.

Years later, P came back for further treatment without a clear cut precipitant. Rather, it seemed that he returned because of his awareness of a diffuse emotional isolation that had recurred and that prevented him from forming a sufficiently strong and stable intimate relationship.

In this second analysis, we had occasion to revisit the main issues that had occupied us. What struck me first was the new and different awareness I had now of *my* role in all of our interactions. The most glaring was my taking cognizance, for the first time, of the intensity of my own attachment to him, which prevented me from fully accepting and containing his projections. Where I had seen in the Mrs. Edward Blake dream his oedipal longings, as well as his wish for our roles to be reversed in terms of power, I could now see that I had held him too close for me to see clearly enough; where the "speech impediment" may indeed have revealed his identification with me, now I could see that language represented the most obvious arena of our connection, and thus could be confused between us. Perhaps the dream also condensed his unconscious recognition that there were important things neither he nor I could articulate. I also realized now that his words of rage had a distinctly painful resonance in me.

Now, the reversal of the name Blake Edwards suggested more severe aspects of his pathology. Indeed, in the violence he expressed against himself there was the strictness of his mandate against directing any violence at me, which I had thought about and explored, as considerable work on superego analysis. I also had the perception of our boundaries as so blurred that I knew I was being tortured as well as him. But the sadistic superego, visible not only in the brutal sadomasochistic behavior, but also in perverse activity, in his seeking prostitutes, and in periods of addiction, had components I had not seen. My understanding of primitive modes of thinking grew, as my immersion in Bion's ideas had grown, and I could see more clearly the basic "cognitive" issues that permeated the material and the process. I had now an awareness of a disorientation in something more basic: a "misunderstanding" of the parental union, in the sense described by Money-Kyrle (1968). The attack that was evident in the symptomatic regressive violence of a long period of the prior analysis was really an attack on *our* confused union, and, as was gradually revealed in the second analysis, such attack was a major obstacle to his own creative development.

But perhaps the most glaring aspect of the problems in our work together, the one that involves not simply a theoretical reassessment but a technical precept, was my difficulty in accepting that I was indeed the bad object that was merged with a part of himself, the part that he was trying to project. This resulted in a form of collusion that I had not been aware of, perhaps a "bulwark" as described by the Barangers (2008). No matter how compassionate, kind, and accepting I believed myself to be, I could see now that in the prior analysis, in a sort of caricature of Kleinian technique, I had prematurely returned his projections to him, and that action *was* cruel. Not just felt by him as cruel but truly and objectively cruel. I had difficulty in really seeing myself as he saw me in the most intensely convulsed periods of analysis, as the drug he was addicted to or as the prostitute who took his money, but saw other patients and left him on weekends and certainly did not suffer the way he suffered. When I had interpreted, a part of me had remained outside the intensity of our connection. This was so even when I thought I glimpsed some of his cognitive difficulties, and even when I addressed what I believed was his message. I had not been a sufficiently containing object.

So, those lies of the mind I referred to earlier, started with my own. Perhaps I believed in my technique to the detriment of my deeper emotional understanding. My brief intuition of something incomplete, if I had respected it, might have led me to further exploration. An exploration that I could now undertake but earlier I could not tolerate. Now I perceived how the masochistic side of his violence, displayed outside, not only would inevitably be turned into sadistic actions against me, but actually *had been* turned against our work together. I believe also that in the past, aspects of my own sadism may have reverberated in my confused understanding, so that I could not tolerate holding a perception of myself as truly the current instigator of his violence. Technically, it is very different saying "You feel as if what you're doing is my fault" from internally acknowledging "It *is* my fault. I am in the position of power, and I am the current cause of your suffering and thus of this behavior."

In fact, in this case, the description of his inner state would have had to include much more of the tortured aspects of his relationship with me. Was I blinded by old concepts of regressive defenses against oedipal wishes? It seemed clear only now that the issue was not simply one of oedipal wishes. Oedipal wishes were confused, distorted into a caricature. Yes, no doubt there were oedipal longings in the Julie Andrews/Blake Edwards material, but those oedipal wishes were a pretense, a *defense* actually, against more primitive wishes, violent wishes of merging. A merging that I myself may have desired.

The name reversal had perhaps hinted at the more real nature of the problem. Fragments of other moments, in which he remembered feelings of exclusion and abandonment and of potential or real violence from his parents, colored whatever libidinal forces were at play. And neither he nor I had fully understood the boundaries of our positions in the session. It had been impossible for me to see myself in the caricature he presented of me, because I could not tolerate seeing the outline, the shadow, on which that caricature was based.

The speech impediment was not just on a superficial level an identification with me in my accent, of course, but also with the prohibitions he internalized against verbalizing a particularly violent, explosive destructive force, and an allusion to the way I was seen, perhaps as an alien, dangerous object, incapable of holding his projection.

By the time he returned to treatment, my tolerance for the brutal projections had changed sufficiently so that now we were both better able to survive this second analysis! The ending we traversed now contrasted with the first. A capacity for tenderness was expressed in his verbal communication in the analysis, and revealed in his own life. A few years after the end of analysis he sent me a brief letter with a photograph of himself, his wife, and their twins. He included a catalogue of a show of his artistic work.

In a moving article, written about anti-therapeutic factors in the analyst, Rosenfeld (1987) emphasizes how patients so often keep trying and trying to make us understand. We miss the message, but they insist. We don't get it, and they tell us again. Can we say that P came back to see if this time I would get it? Certainly there was some of that.

Now, undoubtedly, my initial "bad job" had a possibility of redemption. As analysts, we are rarely so lucky. So, looking at the aspects of the paper that I described at the beginning, can I say that I had made the best of a bad job? The storms of the meeting of our two personalities reverberated throughout the entire analysis, but can we say that my initial understanding was not sufficient to overcome my terror? In the first period of analysis, he had succeeded in terrifying me in a way that growth was prevented. In part my terror blinded me. My tolerance for anxiety, certainly the anxiety of not knowing and not understanding, was now definitely greater.

Finally, was the sleep state more important for understanding than the waking state? The dreams had been very important clues to the deeper issues. In looking back, the ideographs were more revealing than any associations and conscious verbal communication, but they had to await my capacity to contain them. I believe that our capacity for containment, which is certainly never measurable, grows gradually, obviously through reanalysis, also through new readings, also thanks to our exchanges with colleagues, and, most certainly, perhaps primarily, thanks to our patients.

## *References*

Baranger, M., & Baranger, W. (2008). The analytic situation as a dynamic field. *International Journal of Psychoanalysis, 89*: 795–826.
Bion, W. R. (1967). *Second Thoughts*. London: Karnac, 1984.
Bion, W. R. (1970). *Attention and Interpretation*. London: Karnac, 1984.
Bion, W. R. (1979). Making the best of a bad job. In: *Clinical Seminars and Other Works* (pp. 321–323). London: Karnac, 1994.
Money-Kyrle, R. E. (1968). Cognitive development. *International Journal of Psychoanalysis, 49*: 691–698.
Rosenfeld, H. (1987). Some therapeutic and anti-therapeutic factors in the functioning of the analyst: In: *Impasse and Interpretation* (Chapter Two) London: Tavistock.

CHAPTER TWENTY-SEVEN

# Reflections on "Caesura" (1977)

*Rogelio Sosnik*

In the context of re-reading "Caesura" thirty-seven years after Bion's presentation at the Los Angeles Psychoanalytic Society in June 1975, I want to quote Edna O'Shaughnessy's work (2005), "Whose Bion?": "That there are different readings on Bion's works is a tribute to its originality and richness; even re-readings reveal, as they do with any classic work, new things previously missed."

In other words, going back to Bion's papers always involves an emotional experience that opens up new ways to work with ideas and to create new concepts. In this chapter, I will try to describe what this pro- and e-vocative paper triggers in me as a reader and also as a clinician. The subject deals with basic theory of the mind, extending fundamental metapsychological concepts, as we always find in Bion, with his conjectures and intuitions grounded in and evolving from the emotional experience of clinical psychoanalysis.

As the reader will know, "Caesura" is one of the last works that Bion wrote. As such, it shows the evolution of his conjectures about the clinical situation. In what follows, I will try to connect it with other moments of his thinking, and show the questions that this paper evokes for me with regard to the problems that he refers to during the development of the text.

As always with Bion's writing, its multidimensional quality offers different facets for the reader to think about and the opportunity to err in the attempt to fragment it in order to "digest" its content. As Bion says, the universe of discourse within which this paper is confined comes from different disciplines (Psychoanalysis: S. Freud; Philosophy: M. Buber; Mysticism: St. John of the Cross).

From Freud (1926): "There is much more continuity between intra-uterine life and earliest infancy than the impressive caesura of the act of birth allows us to believe."

From Buber (1958): "The prenatal life of the child is a pure natural association, a flowing toward each other, a bodily reciprocity; and the life horizon of the developing being appears uniquely inscribed, and yet also not inscribed, in that of the being that carries it; for the womb in which it dwells is not solely that of the human mother" (Bion, 1989, p. 36).

"Every developing human child rests, like all developing beings, in the womb of the great mother, the undifferentiated, not yet formed primal world. From this it detaches itself to enter a personal life … But this detachment is not sudden" (p. 37).

"… In his mother's womb man knows the universe and forgets it at birth" (p. 37).—

In this regard I think that Bion goes on to specify what the "primal" means to him at this time. At the beginning of his psychoanalytic development, working with groups and defining the configuration of the basic assumption group as the primitive and the work group as the sophisticated, thinking group, he described the essence of developmental conflict as the conflict between basic emotional states and thinking processes. The meaning of the pre-mental states that, before, we found in the basic assumption group is now defined by the introduction of the "embryonic intuition", following Freud on the continuity between prenatal and post-natal thought.

This appears as the central subject of "Caesura". But is it so? Is it part of his research on the evolution of O, and the effect on the mind of the "un-thought thought"? Or it is a new idea that synthesizes and helps to make sense of his theory of thinking (K link) while expanding his elaborations of the differences between knowing, (transformation in K) and knowing about, that is at the center of the process of "becoming" (transformation from O To K), and at the same time introducing new ideas about the nature of psychoanalytic activity?

I quote him: "Has this discussion any practical value for a psycho-analyst? It is a question which I fear may be provoked by my stress on practice rather than theory" (p. 55).

Bion applies the concept of caesura to many different functions at different conceptual levels. For example, it refers to:

1. The separation between different parts of the personality;
2. The separation that exists between different mental states (e.g., from being asleep to being awake, from the more primitive to the more evolved and sophisticated);
3. The separation that exists between two personalities when they meet, as in the analytic encounter; and
4. The separation that verbal language, playing with different meanings, introduces in terms of communication within ourselves and with the other.

I quote again: "Rephrasing Freud's statement for my own convenience: There is much more continuity between autonomically appropriate quanta and the waves of conscious thought and feeling than the impressive Caesura of transference and counter-transference would have us to believe. So …? Investigate the Caesura; not the analyst; not the analysand; not the unconscious; not the conscious; not sanity; not insanity, but the Caesura, the link, the synapse, the transitive-intransitive mood" (p. 56).

So, in his fashion, Bion proposes we take caesura as a model (caesura of birth), while considering the clinical situation with the patient, in which the shift from one mental state to another is the problem at stake. He also proposes we take it as a reality, a clinical reality to be faced by us as psychoanalysts, after working through our own resistance, to accept the fluctuations of our mental states that differ from the ones that "we like to think we can always present to our fellows" (p. 53).

In my reading, a central methodological point that Bion makes in the paper is the fact that the analyst, in order to make an interpretation, has to use a non-pathological splitting when he has to make a choice between a number of consciously entertained ideas. This involves inhibition of other ideas, while at the same time he is facing a partial aspect of the patient's personality that exists as a whole. Therefore his recommendation, "Any attempt to classify the material with which we have to deal should be regarded as provisional, or transitive, that is to say, part of a process from one thought or idea or position to another, not a permanency, not a halting spot at which the investigation is ended" (p. 43). "The problem for the practicing analyst is how to match his hunch, or his intuition, or his suspicion, with some formulation, some conceptual statement ... The analyst's role, in other words, is one which inevitably involves the use of transitive ideas, or ideas in transit. The analysand, likewise, is attempting through his free associations to formulate an experience of which he is aware" (p. 44). "As things are at present, giving an interpretation means that the analyst has to be capable of verbalizing a statement of his senses, his intuitions and his primitive reactions to what the patient says. This statement has to be effective as a physical act is effective" (p. 44).

"There are any number of different Caesuras. How are they to be traversed? We must reconsider the transitive characteristic of the free association and the interpretation. Each free association and each interpretation represents a change in the situation which we psycho-analyze" (p. 49).

We know that Bion was very careful in introducing new terms in his language because of the distortions that the penumbra of associations creates in communication. So I wonder why Bion feels it is necessary to introduce "Caesura" into his canon at this time in his thinking. Was he motivated by his need to objectify "wisdom" as an evolution of O and connect it with "embryonic intuition", following the Jewish myth?

I believe that the analyst's capability to differentiate the quality of mental states from the more primitive to the more evolved, and to distinguish them from the psychopathological mode of mental functioning, are implicit points that he is making. His major concern in "Caesura" is how to reach earlier mentation, recognize it, how to penetrate "caesuras" in order to open up new levels of mentation that will contribute to mental evolution. In this regard, Bion's intuition about the pre-mental emotional life of the fetus opens an implicit question: When is the personality born? Is caesura a new door to traverse in order to reach new levels of mentation in our patients, to integrate earlier mental states that compose their personality? There is an implicit equation between mental development and freedom to navigate different mental states, freedom gained by the increased capability to hold and contain different aspects that the personality possesses.

Bion takes from Freud the model of the personality as composed of levels of consciousness (organized in a way that is similar to the layers of an onion), which are reflected in the actuality of the session by what have become free associations. These associations were once interpretations that in past times were conscious but now are unconscious. The role of the analyst to entertain ideas in transit by exerting negative capability is the clue to the method to traverse caesuras and follow the evolution of the expanding personality.

Nowadays it is accepted that the human embryo is capable of some form of mentation, although it remains a mystery as to how and when that mentation begins and what this mode of functioning would look like. Bion speaks of a "sub-thalamic" intensity in emotional states that belong to a pre-mental area of the personality and are seeking expression as well as discharge in the form of action. Such conjectures lead us to think about when and how the personality is born.

Following Bion's theory of the thinking apparatus, at birth, after the "catastrophic" fact of the delivery, mentation starts when the infant projects fragments of his previous mental states in a disorganized fashion. By taking them in, and transforming them into alpha elements, the mother's mind in her "reverie" starts to organize the inchoate (beta) elements into a modulated state of mind. The internalization by the baby of this modulated state (now composed of the mother's alpha elements), creates the contact barrier that gives to the baby's mind the possibility of functioning at two levels: conscious and unconscious. This, by the way, defines and implies the caesura that exists between the two modalities of mental functioning.

While the contact barrier is in the process of forming, it will act as a container of preconceptions that initiate the process of thinking. These preconceptions are part of and compose the prenatal mentation (Freud's *Ur-phantasie*) that will evolve into unconscious phantasy as the personality becomes organized. The functions of the breast, as a mediator for the organization of unconscious phantasies and as regulator of the projective identification modalities, provide the "continuity" between the pre-mental states and the new experiences of connections that the baby is starting to acquire as he learns from his experience. This is how Bion, before "Caesura", hypothesizes and understands the birth of the personality. The processes of projection and introjection described by Melanie Klein, and the resulting changes in the quality of the mechanism of projective identification, are seen as a way to deal with the strong emotional states (anxieties) that the baby is facing.

It is through the repetition of these processes and the oscillation, PS<->D, that the "caesura" of the newborn mental state is traversed. Is Bion here introducing new content with the concept of caesura? Is it old wine in a new bottle simply rephrased within the language of his own canon or is it a departure from previous conjectures about the evolution of O (ultimate reality) that he refers to, as many authors (Grotstein, 1983; Paul, 1997; Pistiner de Cotiñas, 2007; Vermote, 2013) have suggested?

In looking for a response to these questions, and trying to find a difference from previous conceptions, wondering if that difference exists or if we are seeing only an expansion of those previous conceptions, I was struck by the fact that Bion goes back to aspects of the personality that are still composed of physical states, which manifest themselves in terms of impulses, some of them subtle, some of them strong (sub-thalamic potency), and which need to be transformed into mental states in order to contribute to the process of "becoming". This implies that Bion is in fact offering a new approach that comes from his hypotheses concerning O.

When Bion first observed psychotic patients using pathological projective identification to unburden their minds of excessive stimuli, he described their use of their musculatures to rid themselves of thoughts and ideas that carried or induced a strong emotional charge. Using the thinking apparatus in reverse, they transformed these ideas into movements that created an impression in those who received them. He thus called attention to the way that verbal communication, specifically speech as action, can become a tool used to exert mental pressure on the recipient to whom it is addressed.

In the "Caesura" paper, Bion's major concern has become how to make links between mental states that express themselves in physical actions and the part of the personality that had evolved out of the earliest exchanges with the primary object: the mother's mind and body. In offering this new vertex of observation, however, Bion also creates a problem for the practicing analyst: how to differentiate psychotic functioning from an underdeveloped mental state looking for expression, which, if it is achieved, will allow the personality to keep developing.

When we work in the direction of mental integration, we have to distinguish between, on the one hand, the avoidance of mental pain and intolerance of frustration that triggers rejection of mental states on the part of the psychotic mental functioning, and, on the other, the more primitive mental states that need to be integrated and become a source of amplification of the capability of the personality in "becoming". We then have to face "catastrophic change" in both instances. These issues are relevant in connection with our current concerns about represented and unrepresented states of mind (Levine, Reed & Scarfone, 2013).

What is the origin and nature of the unrepresented? Does it belong to earlier states of mind, to the "unborn" part of the personality, or is it the expression of the aspect of the self that had been split by an intolerant earlier ego? If the latter is the case, do we face the same level of work for the psychic apparatus in the process of integration as we do in facing other levels of psychic work, such as resolving unconscious conflicts, reclaiming repressed memories, or healing psychic splits? How do we approach the primitive, still impulsive, unrepresented material and what kind of links are we going to establish when working in this direction?

As Bion suggests in "Caesura", by providing conscious, verbal thought to underdeveloped and earlier states of the mind, we are providing the chance to include a non-pathological latent or potential mental state that is looking for expression into the psyche, and creating and integrating new levels of mental states into the rest of the personality.

The major obstacle to traversing caesuras consists in facing "catastrophic change", which comes about as a result of the modification and expansion of the container. This is similar to what happens when psychotic patients have to reintegrate parts of their personalities that have been split off. Integration requires facing depressive anxiety, in order to allow the oscillation PS<->D to be re-established.

Nowadays, we have dissimilar approaches to these unrepresented mental states, which derive from different conceptions of the way that presentations, representations, and symbol formations play a role in the configuration of the structure the mental apparatus. We also have different ways to reach and integrate—or reintegrate—them with the rest of the personality. Is Bion providing us with a new door to think and understand the complexity regarding the source of the "unrepresented"?

If the source of this unrepresented state of mind is the still "unborn" proto-mental preconception that can be transformed by the presence of the external object (mother's/analyst's reverie function) into a thought contained within the mind, this will differ from the consequences of the attack on linking that the psychotic personality may launch as a result of the intolerance of "reality", psychic or material. This difference describes two very different situations, in which the qualities of the container function that the analyst must provide are very different.

When Bion describes "any part of the human mind which still betrays signs of an 'embryological' intuition", he talks about "feelings that I could describe as envy, love, sex, hate, but which seem to have an intense and unformed character" (1989, pp. 42–43). In this regard, he says, "the best that the patient can do is to give effect to feelings which are feared for their intensity, magnitude and obtrusiveness compared with those feelings which most people are used to regard as normal" (pp. 42–43).

During the "Italian Seminars" (2005) that took place in Rome, in July 1977, two years after he presented "Caesura" in Los Angeles, Bion was elaborating the concept that he decided to include in his vocabulary. In Rome he was reflecting on the differences that exist between the mental state that is open to receive-conceive a "new thought" (negative capability) and the destiny that the "new thought" (new meaning) suffers while in connection with the rest of the personality. He expresses clearly his dissatisfaction, saying: "the Freudian architectonic requires readjustment, particularly in the direction of leaving room for growth" (p. 12). And then: "While we are trying to elaborate a system of thought or a system of analysis, we have to be aware that we are also excreting a kind of "calcification" which is going to make that thoughts become more a prison than a liberating force" (p. 12). "I think it is helpful to forget all our theories and our desires, because they are so obstructive that they become an impressive Caesura which we cannot get past. The problem is how to let the germ of an idea, or the germ of an interpretation, have a chance to grow and develop" (p. 12).

By including caesura as a new concept, Bion was working in that direction. Clearly at this moment, Bion's preoccupation had been on the destiny of the "new meaning". Mental growth depends on the transformation that the personality "suffers", by the inclusion of that "new meaning" and the new sense of reality that it implies. In this regard, caesuras that can be traversed and be functional during the process of digestion of the "new idea", also can have a negative quality in terms of processes of "calcification" (opacity of memory and desire).

So now I come back to the problem of the unrepresented, primitive mental states and the connection of those states with the most evolved states of the personality.

There is a dual aspect of the definition of the caesura: the one that connects ("there is more continuity …") as a bridge between the primitive (intra-uterine) and more evolved states of mind (coming from the living experience), and the one that interposes, by organizing "memory" in terms of a process of "calcification" of meaning.

That leads us to the problem of how we conceptualize "memory" within the structure of the mental apparatus.

From Freud we have the conception of the structure of the psychic apparatus as an organization based on memory traces of past experiences of satisfaction, regulated by different levels of repression, caesuras. The "desire" finds expression in recharging the hallucinatory experience of satisfaction in which the unrepresented, still unorganized impulse is still on the borders of the ego structure.

Then we have Bion's radical conception of the psychic apparatus as an evolution of the development of meaning, the expansion of the capability to hold and contain new meaning, departing from preconceptions that are part of the embryo's intuition, which will evolve during his life in learning from experience.

Is Bion contradicting Freud, or is he sharing with him the same concerns regarding the evolution of ego functions, by his concerns on "calcification" processes? Is he saying that too much saturation leads to too much "knowing" instead of "being" and "becoming"? In Freud we encounter the existence of caesuras, levels of repression, as organizers of the mental apparatus. In Bion, the opposition between transformation in K and transformation in O, seems, at the moment of "caesura", to have a central place.

Perhaps the dilemma is not such, because each refers to a different aspect of the human personality, and the way that the mind works. One is connected with "contractual" qualities, how we learn to "be" with the other, and the other is connected with how to "become" ourselves, the result of the digestion of our experiences in life. There is a functional caesura that we have to keep remaking all the time between those aspects while we keep evolving.

I see the evolution of the mental apparatus from the vertex of the thinking process in this way: it starts with preconceptions (looking for an object and the expectation of a meaning), then the transformation of those preconceptions during the meeting with that object (e.g., the breast) into "unconscious phantasy". That is, preconceptions involve implicit meanings, latent in impulse, affect, and sensation (Isaacs, 1952) that have the potential to evolve into phantasies, when "scaffolded" by visual images, and then word representations.

Thus, Bion highlights two different roles that caesuras may have: when they are traversed, they can contribute to the expanding of the mind, as a container that holds new meanings, and which, in that way, continues to grow; when they are not traversed, they may function as a barrier or calcification used as a refuge to avoid "new meaning", and prevent the "messianic idea" from being born. It is in the first sense, in his inclusion of caesura as link, the one that must attract and guide the attention of the analyst while in the session, that Bion provides us with a new direction in the way that we participate in the analytic process.

As the reader can see, most of my reflections on "Caesura" arise from my concern as a clinician. But was that Bion's intention in introducing it? I doubt it. I think that his major concern, as always, had been about psychoanalysis as a "thing in itself", a human activity with the potentiality of contributing to human evolution, and not as a series of rules and methods to constrain the potentiality that the human mind possesses. And with "Caesura" he was amplifying that, trying to help us at the conceptual level to keep open to the "un-known", the "new experience" that contains the "new idea" that can be presented to us on a daily basis during the clinical situation.

## References

Bion, W. R. (1989). *Two Papers: "The Grid" and "Caesura"*. London: Karnac.
Bion, W. R. (2005). *Italian Seminars*. London: Karnac.
Buber, M. (1958). *I and Thou*. New York: Scribner.
Freud, S. (1926). Inhibitions, symptoms and anxiety. *S. E., 20*: 75–175. London: Hogarth.
Grotstein, J. S. (1983). *Do I dare to disturb the universe? A memorial to W. R. Bion*. London: Karnac.
Isaacs, S. (1952). The nature and function of phantasy In: M. Klein, P. Heiman, S. Isaacs & J. Riviere (Eds.), *First Developments in Psycho-Analysis*. London: Hogarth.

Levine, H., Reed, G., & Scarfone, D. (2013). *Unrepresented States and the Construction of Meaning*. London: Karnac.
O'Shaughnessy, E. (2005). Whose Bion? *International Journal of Psychoanalysis, 86*: 1523–1542.
Paul, M. I. (1997). *Before We Were Young*. Binghamton, NY: PDF publications.
Pistiner de Cotiñas, L. (2007). *La Dimensión Estética de la Mente*. Buenos Aires: Ediciones del Signo.
Vermote, R. (2013). *Reading Bion*. London: Routledge.

# CHAPTER TWENTY-EIGHT

# Evidence*

*Arnaldo Chuster*

As human beings, we are always dealing with random possibilities, chance occurrences, and statistics. But for each of us, our individuality is not random. The unique singularity of each individual is part of what reflects and comprises the essence of human life. It is intrinsic to the complexity of the human mind and must be taken into consideration as an aspect of every psychoanalytical observation.

This complexity, however, presents analysts with a challenging question: how to select a fact that furnishes proof or gives ground for an interpretation among the many hazards that translates our singularity?

In order to answer this question one needs to imagine that there is something that is called individuality that provides evidence. What we are or what we have been as an individual cannot be created with elements obtained from random circumstances. It derives from our personal history, which, in its turn, has a main influence that came from something that is called "unconscious". One needs to achieve those elements in order to arrive at the evidence of the singularity that presents to our observation. This is the subject of the paper, "Evidence", which Bion presented for the first time on July 23, 1976 at the British Psychoanalytical Society.

The paper is part of a series called "Four papers" (1987), each of which highlights details of Bion's final thoughts about transference and countertransference that were advanced in the paper "Caesura" (1977).

The term *caesura* as used by Bion fundamentally conveys the quality of something constantly new and unknown moving in the work of analysis. Thus, when he quotes Freud—"There is

---

*\*The Heritage Illustrated Dictionary of the English Language* (New York: McGraw-Hill, 1975) defines "evidence" as: the data on which a judgment or conclusion may be based, or by which proof or probability may be established.

much more continuity between intra-uterine life and earliest infancy than the impressive caesura of the act of birth allows us to believe" (1976b, p. 59)—he introduces the vigor contained in the meanings of generation and upbringing, links and transit, birth and death, hidden and explicit, blindness and perception of the unexpected. But whenever or wherever it occurs, caesura refers to something that emerges with a twofold movement: (counter-trans)–ference (Chuster, 2013).

In "Evidence" Bion introduces the subject through the clinical material of a patient (about whom we know nothing), who makes the following statement:

> "I remember my parents being at the top of a Y-shaped stair and I was at the bottom … and …". (1976, p. 312)

Bion reports that this was all that the patient said. There were no further associations. He then adds:

> I waited, and during this time I, as usual, had plenty of free associations of my own (which I kept to myself because I am supposed to be the analyst). (1976, p. 312)

It is worth noticing how Bion's clinical sensitivity helps him to refrain from disturbing the process by introducing something that can be seen as a closed statement, which could provoke a blank that might serve as a space for saturation with memories. He takes the patient's speech openly; works with it like a dream in order to recover its imagistic dimension:

> It occurred to me that this was like a verbal description of a visual image, simply a Y-shape. The thing that struck me straight away about a statement that was so brief, so succinct, and stopped short at that point, was that it must have a lot of meaning that was not visible to me. What did in fact become visible to me I could describe by writing "Y". Then it occurred to me that it would be more comprehensible if it was spelled, "why-shaped stare". The only trouble was that I could not see how I could say this to the patient in a way which would have any meaning, nor could I produce any *evidence* whatsoever for it—excepting that this was the kind of image that it called up in my mind. (1976, p. 312)

The task of the analyst is that of listening to what is provided by the patient. But this task also includes the work of the imagination of the analyst, as he looks for evidence in psychoanalysis. Imagination—or as Bion many times stated it, image-in-action,—refers not only to the capacity to combine elements that are provided by the patient. It is the capacity to create a new form with these given elements. In a certain way, one uses the same elements that were provided by the patient, but Bion's idea of the shape is that it must be new. He said it many times and in different ways that one should try to observe in every session the new and the unknown; what is already known is false or irrelevant (1970).

> So I said nothing. After a while the patient went on, and I started producing what seemed to me to be a fairly plausible psychoanalytic interpretations. Thinking about this later, I imagined

a Y-shape which, when pushed in at the intersection of the three lines, would make a cone or a funnel. On the other hand, if it was out of the intersection, then it would make a cone shape sticking out or, if you like, a breast shape. In fact it was an evocative free association on the part of the patient as far as I was concerned, but I was still lost because I had no idea of what I could say that would reveal an interpretation, and would also be comprehensible to the patient. In other words, could I possibly be perspicacious and perspicuous? (1976, pp. 312–313)

Bion's vertex is very clear: one may not know what is happening but it is possible to provide a description of the situation while inviting the patient to think about it and then proceed with listening.

In the following session it came to Bion's mind what he had previously thought; then he said to the patient:

"I suggest that in addition to the ordinary meaning of what you have told me—and I am perfectly sure that what you said means exactly what you meant—it is also a kind of visual pun." The patient replied: "Yes, that's right. But you've been a very long about it." (1976, p. 313)

The interpretation produces a response that brings the analyst back to a situation where there is nothing to be done except to keep listening in an attempt to go beyond something that was for a moment considered evidence upon which to build an interpretation: a visual image with a double meaning; while one meaning is perceived, the other escapes.

Now the question is: what was the *evidence* that the patient was giving me, and what was the *evidence* that I saw, or thought I saw, for the interpretation? It is all very well for the patient to say, "Yes, that's right." I believe him. But I do not know why he thought it was right, or why it was right. In fact I don't know what the *evidence* is for that statement. (1976, p. 313)

As always, Bion maintains a basic Socratic stance: as much as we may think we know, the less we may know. As Bion was fond of quoting (e.g., 1970), "*La réponse est le malheur de la question*" ("The answers are the misfortune of the questions.").[1] Bion's questions are always opening to imaginative conjectures, even as they match with rationally plausible presumptions.

One may venture theoretically that the clinical material suggests the movement of preconceptions: the breast, and behind the breast the sexual united couple is searching for a realization that creates a conception. One can see those elements merging with the visual set and finally the whole situation is expressing the patient's conception of the analytical link. This conception could be the evidence provided, although there are many others, like the ambiguity of the patient in the polarization: voyeurism-exhibitionism. Nevertheless, Bion does not enter into those conjectures that may saturate the field with routine interpretations. His work privileges the transience in the link that is centered in the idea of "O" (1965), which emphasizes the uncertainty that is always inherent in our observations.

The subject of evidence raises many questions about the analytical capacity to observe, and correlates Bion's ideas about transference and countertransference as an exclusive link that can be summarized in six topics:

1. The observational model used by Freud since the creation of psychoanalysis based on his experience with Charcot: to observe an unknown situation till some pattern emerges and therefore can be interpreted. "I learned to refrain my speculative tendencies and to follow the forgotten advice of my master Charcot, that is, to look at the same things again and again until they themselves began to speak" (Freud, 1914, p. 22).
2. Is the interpretation capable of nurturing the curiosity and the care of the patient for himself at the same time that it provides a continuity of the observation?
3. The experience of psychoanalysis contains elements that can be verbalized and others that cannot. It is both categories of elements that contribute to the perception of evidence.
4. The development of the quotation from Freud in "Inhibitions, Symptoms and Anxieties" (1926, p. 138): "There is much more continuity between intra-uterine life and earliest infancy than the impressive caesura of the act of birth allows us to believe". Bion said that Freud did not go much further with his quotation and in a general way seems to minimize it. Bion describes the two sides of the caesura as a two-fold movement, which functions as a valuable source of thinking.
5. Bion shapes once more his version of Freud's statement: "I have thought of it in terms of trying to dismiss memory and desire—memory as being the past tense; desire, a future tense. In other words trying to start a session with as nearly blank a mind as one can get—which is not altogether very near because one has such an enormous past history between the time that one is born and the present day; such an extraordinary amount has been learned since becoming an inhabitant of a gaseous medium, the air" (1976, p. 314).
6. The presence of questions about the origins of the mind: At which moment does the mind start to exist? Is there an embryonic mind? If so, how does this embryonic mind work? What is the archaic debris that persists in the grown up individual? How to observe and communicate it if it does exist? One can see these questions as an enlargement of the preconceptions theory related to the analyst's state of mind of imagination and capacity to create an interpretation.

Although the analytical field is a field of words and language, this feature in itself is the first obstacle to reaching analytic evidence. Therefore, it brings to the discussion the singularity of the analyst and his capacity to use and understand his own words while working with this twin-fold configuration: obstacle/communication.

> For this reason I think that each analyst has to go through the discipline—which cannot be provided for him by any training course that I know of—of forging his own language and keeping the words that he uses in good working order. I do not think it has to be a particularly profound vocabulary, or particularly broad—it may be a quite narrow one—but it is very important that it should be the one that he chooses for himself. Nobody can tell you how you are to live your life, or how you are to think, or what language you are to speak. Therefore it is absolutely essential that the individual analyst should forge for himself the language which he knows, which he knows how to use, and the value which he knows—knows so well that he can detect, when he gives an interpretation and the analysand repeats it with a slight change on intonation or emphasis, that although it sounds as if it is a repetition, in fact it is not. (1976, p. 315)

The second obstacle to reaching evidence is the temporal split found in every communication with words. Is it the patient that communicates a delay of the interpretation or is Bion inviting the patient to think of the temporal splitting?

> This is where the *practice* of analysis is so appallingly difficult: if you say nothing, you leave the patient to assume that he has correctly reported what you have just said to him; if you draw his attention to the difference, you leave yourself open to the accusation that you are being pedantic and fussy, complaining about what he has said when he really repeated exactly what you said to him. You can point out, "You can't have repeated exactly what I said to you because this is about one and a half minutes later; time has been passing since I spoke to you, so what sound just like I said, in fact cannot be. You either understood what I meant—in which case there is nothing further to be said about the matter; either it was correct or it wasn't—or you are now saying something else." (1976, pp. 315–316)

The third obstacle is emotional turbulence. Bion suggests that the ideal image of that turbulence should be the description made by Leonardo Da Vinci in his diagrams, Shakespeare with his writing, Francis Bacon with his epistemology. Maybe the three of them could be represented by Kant's aphorism: how to introduce a blind intuition into an empty concept or vice versa. It is worth noting how a basic feature of *A Theory of Thinking* (1962a) is always present: psychoanalysis for Bion is a practical response to philosophical questions (that is, questions of life).

From the moment an intuition weds a concept a new dimension is created, but who will define this dimension with the validity of a fact or declare it as evidence? For instance, a thought may be validated as a *fact* just because it is present. But this does not mean that we should stop our inquiry. If a thought is present it may be true or false. Its truth status is something that may be established only by the analytical pair.

On the other hand, the closest one can get to a fact in psychoanalysis is a feeling. A feeling could achieve a sense of evidence, because it gives a sense of certainty. But a feeling could also be connected to some unknown fact. This unknown may be a kind of amnesia or someone may try to fill the lack of knowledge with a paramnesia. The human mind may find countenance through both. Bion was fond of Kant's observation that every intuition without a concept is blind, and every concept without intuition is empty. A psychoanalytical theory that offers a concept to reify or promote blind or mistaken intuitions may be transformed into a paramnesia: something that is used to fulfill an unbearable emptiness, what Bion often called "our bottom of deep ignorance."

It is this bottom of ignorance that questions all rationality as something that characterizes human essence. What brands the human essence is precisely the creative imagination on its way to deal with this bottom pit of ignorance. It is this movement that allows us to say that the human beings are first of all psychological creatures. Yet humans are also equal and constitute a society and each society likewise has its own history. One cannot find a stationary "present" even in the most primitive society. Present time is always created by a past time. Our present is always historical. As psychoanalysts, one has the difficult task to describe something about the present moment without having the advantage of the artists who "can use esthetics as a universal language".

> I must confess that I do feel, partly I suppose because of my prejudice, that in analysis we are dealing with *something*, something that is very difficult to describe. The artists have a great advantage because they can resort to the aesthetic as a universal linguistic. The defects of verbal communication were clearly discerned about two thousand years ago by Plato: in the *Phaedo*, describing the trial of Socrates, he points out what a great disadvantage it is that in spite of the fact that Socrates and Phaedrus can apparently talk very accurately and precisely, they are actually using extremely ambiguous terms. I do not see that we have made much progress in that regard in the last two thousand years. (1976, p. 317)

Many trends in philosophical thinking repeat that there is no essence of the human being. This negative statement is totally inadequate. There is a nature in human essence (O) that is possible to formulate and speak of, as well its transformations. This nature is precisely the ability or the possibility to create new forms of social and individual existence. It is easy to verify this assertion by reflecting upon our institutions, idioms, literature, art, science, and mystical ideas.

The psychoanalyst is always confronted with his patient's creations, which may be called private myths (1962a). The task of the analyst is that of trying to formulate a myth that fits to the patient myth.

> If we consider that there is a thing called a mind or a character, is there any way in which we can verbalize it which is not a complete distortion? The mathematicians talk about "quantum intermediacy", something unknown in between; we can imagine some sort of screen onto which these various elements project themselves. For example, Picasso paints a picture on a sheet of glass so that it can be seen from either side. Using my hand, I suggest something of this sort: look at it from one side; there is a psychosomatic complaint; turn it round; now it is soma-psychotic. It is the same hand, but what you see depends on which way you look at it, from what position, from what vertex—any term you like. But does one look at the character from any direction at all? I cannot see how this problem is to be solved except by the particular analyst. It is no good anyone trying to tell you how you look at things—no one will ever know except you. (1976, p. 318)

Two levels, two faces of the same hand or two sides of the same coin point to the same direction: imagination and thoughts. Both create a chain of feelings, thoughts and ideas where the psychoanalyst must use his imagination:

> Let us take flight into fantasy, a kind of infancy of our own thought. I can imagine a situation in which a nearly full-term fetus could be aware of extremely unpleasant oscillations in the amniotic fluid medium before transferring to the gaseous medium—in other words, getting born. I can imagine that there is some disturbance going on—the parents on bad terms, or something of that sort. I can further imagine loud noises being made between the mother and the father—or even loud noises made by the digestive system inside the mother. Suppose this fetus is also aware of pressures of what will one day turn into a character or a personality, aware of things like fear, hate, crude emotions of that sort. Then the fetus might omnipotently turn in hostility towards theses disturbing feelings, proto-ideas, proto-feelings, at a very early

stage, and split them up, destroy them, fragment them, and try to evacuate them. Suppose this caesura takes place and the infant is subjected to the trauma of birth, and the further trauma of having to adjust to a gaseous medium. I can imagine the fetus being so precocious, so premature that it tries to get rid of its personality to start off with, and then after birth—still being highly 'intelligent', if that is correct term—is able to learn all the words and phrases which people consciously use. In the very severe, very obtrusive situation such as one I have in mind, that person learns well the difference between right and wrong; the M'Naghten Rules (the governing decision as to criminal responsibility of the insane) present no difficulty whatever. But as far as he is concerned he may preserve a mind at the deeper level which knows nothing about that, but which might nevertheless have well-established feelings of guilt. I have been amazed to see the way in which you make a faintly disapproving sound to a baby; it will wince as if it had been subjected to an almost intolerable accusation. Has the baby a kind of well-established "conscience"? What is one to call it? (1967, pp. 318–319)

How can we translate those very primitive elements? Language is a creation that allows us to have access to a logical dimension that formulates all kind of proverbs, poetry, metaphors, but mainly it formulates the idea of a reality that is called the mind. Does anyone "see" the mind? What is the *evidence* that a mind does exist? All one can say is that a mind is not accessible through the senses but through an indirect form, a kind of a marriage between knowledge and human action.

> I have invented terms of my own private purposes like, "sub-thalamic fear" meaning the kind of fear that one would have if no check on it was produced by the higher levels of the mind. A patient may in fact be subject to tremendous feelings of fear. I remember one who was quite articulate, in fact articulate enough to make me think that I was analyzing him rather well. Indeed the analysis did go extremely well, but I was beginning to think that nothing was happening. However, the patient checked all that. After one session he went home, sealed up all the crevices throughout his room, turned on the gas, and perished. So there was my highly successful analysis—a very disconcerting result indeed, and no way of finding out of learning for myself what exactly had gone wrong, excepting the fact that it had undoubtedly gone wrong. (1967, p. 319)

No matter the vast legacy of Freud and his followers, it is impossible to infer a society from the substrate that is called psyche. Complexity and uncertainty impeach such an attempt. Obviously, anyone can psychoanalytically interpret *aspects* of society, showing that they correspond to unconscious schemes that satisfy unconscious desires. This is true because society must always reflect the search for meaning that characterizes the psyche. But society in itself is totally alien to the psyche. This is why the socializing process is so painful and lasts so long. One can observe this in babies that cry at night without a concrete reason. They had food, they are not wet or with any discomfort. They simply discovered that the reality does not bend to their will. Suppose that this baby became a grownup and discovered this very late in the course of an analysis; he may find out that nothing can be done to save him from a painful thing. He may then realize a conception that there is no escape, only death. The problem for the psychoanalyst is to find that *evidence* and communicate it to the patient before a disaster occurs, or reoccurs, if one had already taken place in the distant past.

> Supposing we are in fact always dealing with some kind of psychosomatic condition. Is it any good talking to a highly articulate person in highly articulate terms? Is it possible that, if feelings of intense fear, self-hatred, can seep up into a state of mind in which they can be translated into action, the reverse is true? Is it possible to talk to the soma in such a way that the psychosis is able to understand, or vice versa? …. We may be dealing with things which are so slight as to be virtually imperceptible, but which are so real that they could destroy us almost without our being aware of it. That is the kind of area into which we have to penetrate. (1967, pp. 319–320)

## Note

1. This is a phrase from Maurice Blanchot, which was quoted to Bion by André Green.

## References

Bion, W. R. (1962a). A theory of thinking. In: *Second Thoughts* (pp. 110–119). London: Heinemann, 1967.
Bion, W. R. (1962b). *Learning from Experience*. London: Heinemann.
Bion, W. R. (1965). *Transformations*. London: Heinemann.
Bion, W. R. (1970). *Attention and Interpretation*. London: Tavistock.
Bion, W. R. (1976). Evidence. In: *Clinical Seminars and Four Papers*. London: Karnac. 1994.
Bion, W. R. (1977). Caesura. In: *Two Papers: "The Grid" and "Caesura"* (pp. 9–39). Rio de Janeiro: Imago.
Bion, W. R. (1987). Four papers. In: *Clinical Seminars and Four Papers*. London: Karnac, 1994.
Chuster, A. (2013). Transference—or caesura? In: R. Oelsner (Ed.), *Transference and Countertransference Today* (pp. 215–235). London: Routledge.
Freud, S. (1914). On the history of the psycho-analytic movement. *S. E., 14*: 7–66. London: Hogarth.
Freud, S. (1926). Inhibitions, symptoms and anxieties. *S. E., 20*: 75–175. London: Hogarth.

CHAPTER TWENTY-NINE

# Is the concept of O necessary for psychoanalysis?*

Howard B. Levine

> "The analytic situation itself, and then the psycho-analytic occupation or task itself, are bound to stimulate primitive and basic feeling in analyst and analysand … Love, hate, dread, are sharpened to a point where the participating pair may feel them to be almost unbearable: it is the price that has to be paid for the transformation of an activity *about* psycho-analysis into an activity that *is* psycho-analysis"
>
> —Bion, 1970, p. 66

O is the term that Bion used to refer to the moment-to-moment existential reality that each of us inhabits by virtue of our existence. It is a term whose meaning intersects that of "the unconscious", because by definition O is only partly knowable, noticeable, or capable of being reflected upon, despite the fact that for each of us and in each moment it is fully 'lived'. In that sense, some part of O is and will remain outside of conscious awareness—that is, evade our knowledge and awareness about it—even while it is what we are and what we become. It is important to note, however, that the part of O that remains beyond consciousness, is not repressed, but is *unrepresented*, unformed, and in some part will remain so. The O of our experience is an important component of what I have described elsewhere (Levine, 2013) as the "unstructured unconscious" (p. 43).

From the historical vertex, O may be seen as related to and an elaboration of Freud's description of "the actual" and "the umbilicus of the dream", that universe of ineffable, non-dynamic unconscious "things" (*das ding*) that have yet to be structured or organized to the point where

---

*This chapter originated in a talk given at the International Bion Conference held in Los Angeles, California on October 25, 2014.

they may be known and expressed in words. Within Bion's own theory, O is also closely allied to the oscillation between PS<->D and to the recommendation of trying to achieve a listening stance without memory, desire, or intention.

While O cannot ever be fully known, there is always a part of O that is potentially emergent and in process of transformation. This forms a reservoir of developmental potential that each of us can and must draw upon as we move forward in life. From the vertex of psychoanalysis as a therapeutic praxis, this emergent potential is an important component source of the "'truth" that Bion (1970) felt the psyche needed, the way the body needs alimentation, in order to grow.

> Psycho-analytic procedure pre-supposes that the welfare of the patient demands a constant supply of truth as inevitably as his physical survival demands food. (Bion, 1992, p. 99)

Any examination of O must include the question of its relation to the unconscious and development of the psyche. And for Bion, the exploration—and later the creation and expansion—of the unconscious was the proper subject of the analyst's attention. In fact, he was quite clear that the analyst's greatest use to the patient lay in being able to talk to the patient about that of which the patient was not yet aware. It is important to emphasize that in so doing, Bion was not suggesting that the analyst had a privileged position in regard to knowing "the truth" of any given situation. Rather, Bion believed that what the analyst could offer the patient was at best an opinion, an alternative view or perspective, a *belief*, that if it was successful, might disrupt and decenter the patient and that the patient might come to find useful.

Bion (1970) links O to religious and philosophical concepts, such as "the Godhead", Ultimate Reality, Kant's "thing-in-itself", and Plato's ideal form. These are concepts that point to things that are assumed to exist, but remain directly unknowable in their essence, and can only be recognized by the effects that they produce. To the extent that O is in some part unknowable, it is an epistemological conjecture that would seem at first glance to have little immediate relevance to clinical psychoanalysis. Traditionally, in the latter, it is the repressed and otherwise formed but defended against elements of the dynamic unconscious, the once known but now forgotten, hidden, or disguised memories, desires, phantasies, wishes, conflicts, fears, defenses, etc., that have been the traditional subject of analytic interest.

How then do we understand Bion's decision to introduce this concept into his theory and into general psychoanalytic discourse? What might his intentions have been? Is the concept of O useful or necessary? And if so, in what ways?

We know that Bion was a careful writer, with a highly developed sensitivity to the meaning and connotations of words and language. It is reasonable to assume that in introducing the concept of O (in *Elements of Psychoanalysis*, 1963), he did so with a specific intention in mind. But since he never explained this intention, we are left to conjecture what it might have been or why he felt that this term was necessary.

In his Tavistock seminars, Bion (2005) was asked about O and responded by saying:

> I find it useful to suppose that there is something I don't know but would like to talk about; so I can represent it by an O, or a zero, or a nought, as a sort of place where something is, but that I am very unlikely ever to get to understand. (p. 33)

At first glance, this kind of statement might be taken more simply as a caution about the arrogance of too much certainty and as advice to keep one's options open in regard to learning something more about one's patient.

However, Bion's next comment is a reminder of what he felt was an inevitable limit to empirical knowledge.

> I think one is a prisoner of the information that one's senses bring—sense of touch, sight, hearing and so on. I don't think, though, it is a good thing to suppose that there is nothing except what is open to our senses. (Ibid., p. 33)

This comment is reminiscent of a position that Bion (1962) advanced as early as *Learning From Experience*, where he said:

> The problem presented by the psycho-analytic experience is the lack of any adequate terminology to describe it. (pp. 67–68)

It also takes us back to *Attention and Interpretation* (Bion, 1970), where he begins his Introduction with a powerful indictment of the rational.

> Reason is emotion's slave and exists to rationalize emotional experience. (p. 1)

Bion's caution is based upon the belief that words and verbal formulations are inadequate to fully convey or describe the psychoanalytic object or the subtleties of emotional experience, because words and verbal formulations have "developed from a background of sensuous experience" (p. 1), while the domain of psychoanalysis exists beyond that which may be apprehended by the senses.

In 1970, he definitively asserted that:

> … psychic qualities, with which psycho-analysis deals, are not perceived by the senses. (Bion, 1970, p. 28)

Hence, his argument that in contrast to the physician, whose praxis is dependent on empirical observation, that is, the "realization of sensuous experience" (Bion, 1970, p. 7), the praxis of the psychoanalyst is dependent upon "experience that is not sensuous" (Bion, 1970, p. 7).

> The realizations with which a psycho-analyst deals cannot be seen or touched; anxiety has no shape or colour, smell or sound. For convenience, I propose to use the term "intuit" as a parallel in the psychoanalyst's domain to the physician's use of "see", "touch", "smell", and "hear". (Bion, 1970, p. 7)

A good deal of *Attention and Interpretation*—and indeed of Bion's later writings—attempts to convey something about "experience that is not sensuous" and its relation to the birth of new ideas and the creation of the psyche, to examine some of its implications for analytic practice, and to prepare the analyst's mind for an encounter with the non-sensuous domain of psychic reality and all the attendant terrors and difficulties that that encounter may entail.

Bion concludes his answer to the seminar question with a plea for each of us to face the terror of the new and the not yet known, to make room for wild ideas, and cultivate the conditions under which they will be allowed to germinate and take root, in order to see what will develop (Bion, 2005, pp. 34–35).

What I believe Bion is struggling with in this passage—and indeed throughout a good deal of the work of his later period—in addition to finding words to describe the ineffable, is the problem of how new ideas can be "born(e)" in both senses of the word. "Born", in the sense of coming into being, and "borne", in the sense of being suffered, tolerated, and kept fresh and alive in the face of the pain of human self-awareness and existence.

Emotional growth requires learning from experience and frequently depends upon the participation of another. These are "facts of life" that assault our fantasies of omniscience (to learn means accepting that we did not know) and omnipotence (none of us are totally self-sufficient; our minds need an Other in order to grow) and are apt to produce reactions of intense envy and hatred. Add to that the terrors inherent in the disorganization that may precede a reorganization required to grow and achieve something new, and we can more deeply appreciate Bion's (1970) assertion that:

> Of all the hateful possibilities, growth and maturation are feared and detested most frequently. (p. 53)

These problems are further compounded by the inherent conservatism of the Establishment and its internalized representative, the human ego. Bion was keenly aware of how much confusion and uncertainty was inevitably present in the analytic situation and of the dialectical relationship and tension that exists between the possibility of making new discoveries and the inevitable tendency of the human psyche (ego) to assimilate whatever is foreign, strange, or unfamiliar to that which is previously known.

This tendency can often be of great value in helping us make sense of a patient's discourse or presentation, because it provides a structure and series of meanings that can orient the analyst in what is apt to be the incomprehensible "blooming, buzzing confusion" of the analytic encounter. Alternatively, it may prevent the analyst from observing new relationships that may obtain between the elements of experience, because it shapes observations along pre-established and familiar lines.

The paradoxical position of this tendency presents an enigma for the analytic enterprise, since for Bion, the whole purpose of the analyst's presence in the analysis is to offer the patient something new; that is, some observation or interpretation that the latter had not yet recognized, because it was unconscious or had not yet achieved saturation and verbalizable form:

> The analyst must focus his attention on O, the unknown and unknowable. (Bion, 1970, p. 27)
>
> … to spend time on what has been discovered is to concentrate on an irrelevance. What matters is the unknown and on this the psycho-analyst must focus his attention. (Ibid., p. 69)

To do so will hopefully prove transformative in allowing both patient and analyst to precipitate a new and evolving state of being.

> O does not fall in the domain of knowledge or learning save incidentally; it can "become" but it cannot be "known". It is darkness and formlessness but it enters the domain of K when it

has evolved to a point where it can be known, through knowledge gained by experience, and formulated in terms derived from sensuous experience; its existence is conjectured phenomenologically. (Ibid., p. 26)

It is not that the analyst has a superior purchase on "the truth" of the moment, but rather possesses the potential of offering a different belief, opinion, or perspective that may be decentering, transformative, catalytic, or useful to the patient in some other way. Hence, Bion's clinical admonition to try to achieve a listening stance without memory or desire, his description of the tension between selective fact and overvalued idea, and his discussion in *Attention and Interpretation* of the inevitable conflict that is apt to occur between the mystic and the group.

The tension that exists between the known and the not yet knowable, and the dialectical arc that oscillates between them, remain as significant problems for our field, which should perhaps concern us most when we assemble for a Bion Congress. While transmission of knowledge and sharing of ideas are vital for the growth of our profession, is there not a danger in *sanctifying* certain authors and their perspectives, creating a new Bionian Establishment that will then stand in opposition to true emergent discovery? As Bion has often noted, there is a world of difference between talking about psychoanalysis and actually doing and experiencing it. I would add that there is much that goes on in each of our so-called analytic hours that could be called "talking about psychoanalysis" and that moments of actually "doing psychoanalysis" are precious and few!

The danger, as Bion taught us, lies in the inherent dynamics and mental functioning of the group and in the personal ego. Each offers adaptation, stability, and security in return for a kind of orderly sameness—even stagnation—that comes about as it assimilates new, strange, and potentially disruptive experiences to that which is already known. The uncertainty, ambiguity, and even terror of the analytic situation can foster a tendency or wish to reach for the familiar. This tendency can extend to the defensive creation and use of analytic theories and orthodoxies.

In *The Tavistock Seminars*, Bion (2005) wrote:

> You only have to ask yourself what you do individually in a situation where you feel completely lost; you are thankful to clutch hold of any system, anything whatever is available on which to build a kind of structure. So from this point of view it seems to me that we could argue that the whole of psychoanalysis fills a long-felt want by being a vast Dionysiac system; since we don't know what is there, we invent these theories and build this glorious structure that has no foundation in fact—or the only fact in which it has any foundation is our complete ignorance, or lack of capacity. (p. 2)

He later cautioned:

> What happens to your feelings, opinions, ideas and theories when, as here, we all come together? They would appear to be sunk without a trace, swallowed up in the group where we would hope to get some kind of discussion or clarification of the problems with which we have to deal. But the curious thing is that as soon as we are contained in the group, it seems to be very difficult indeed to go in the direction of developing thoughts or ideas or feelings of our own; we are dominated by a need to be like everybody else and to think what everybody else

thinks and feels—although how to tell what everybody else thinks or feels may be something we would find very difficult to formulate. (Ibid., p. 74)

In relation to ideas that are creative, new, or revolutionary, ideas that have the potential to arouse the terrifying anxiety inherent in the possibility of true emotional growth that Bion called "catastrophic change", the ego tends to function as a "fifth column", as it joins with the Establishment in a tendency to neutralize and vitiate the revolutionary and new by co-opting them and making them "commonplace" and "common knowledge".

In Bion's later writings, the struggle between the Mystic and the Group, the new idea and the already accepted familiar and previously known, is always the key. The problem is that each needs the other, even as it fears their disruptive and/or constraining influence (Bion, 1970).

> The function of the group is to produce a genius; the function of the Establishment is to take up and absorb the consequences so that the group is not destroyed. (p. 82)

At any moment, the determining factor will be the invariant relationship that obtains between them. Will it be commensal, symbiotic, or parasitic? Will the new and revolutionary idea continue to exist within the Establishment in ways that preserve the tension between them and the growth enhancing dialectic it can foster? Will each part of the dialectic function in ways that are distressing but ultimately mutually enriching (symbiotic) or at least permit and preserve the revolutionary power of the new idea (commensal), or will that power destroy or be destroyed (parasitic)?

It is a testament to Bion's genius that he saw that these questions apply to any relationship of container/contained in which growth and new creation, attended by the threat of catastrophic change, is necessary or possible. This includes the areas that are of crucial interest to those of us attending this conference: the analytic relationship and the ongoing relationship between the analyst and his or her view of analytic theory.

In *The Tavistock Seminars*, Bion (2005) acknowledged this when he noted that psychoanalysis:

> ... is one of these situations that start as the possibility of freeing the mind of its chattels, but very rapidly become a shell, an exoskeleton. And then it is difficult for any sort of development to take place unless room has been left in the skeleton for the further development of the creature inside.
>
> We are perpetually dealing with this difficulty. As we try to express or formulate our findings ... so we also excrete a kind of shell around them, a layer of knowledge that we can neither penetrate nor break out of. And very soon we get to the point of thinking, "Well, I don't want somebody to start arguing with me, because they may say something and I shall have to think again." It is much nicer to feel we are establishing a kind of authority that can't be questioned and then is an impenetrable shell inside which we lie snugly and simply deteriorate. (p. 33)

From this perspective, the concept of O places at the heart of psychoanalytic practice and theory the paradoxical value of the enigmatic and the unknowable and underlines the importance—and even the necessity—of "negative capability" (the analyst's tolerance of uncertainty and ignorance) for long periods of time in the pursuit of existential truth. It is a provocative reminder offered in a constructive way to help us to think about and interrogate the truth of our existence. And truth, for Bion was of the utmost importance.

As Samuel Johnson wrote in a letter to Bennet Langton, which Bion quoted with appreciation and approval:

> Whether to see life as it is, will give us much consolation, I know not; but the consolation that is drawn from truth, if any there be, is solid and durable; that which may be derived from errour must be, like its original, fallacious and fugitive. (Bion, 1970, p. 7)

By locating the problem within the analyst, within psychoanalytic theory, and within our very profession, itself, Bion was not only speaking to clinical necessity and the near impossibility of the analytic task, but I believe he was also leaving us with a continuing warning about the seductive appeal of stasis and the dangers and even the potential arrogance of "knowing". In that sense, perhaps the very idea of a "Bion Congress" is a terrible incongruity! I suppose it depends upon what each of us may be able to make of it. That remains to be seen …

## *References*

Bion, W. R. (1962). *Learning From Experience*. London: Heinemann.
Bion, W. R. (1963). *Elements of Psychoanalysis*. London: Heinemann.
Bion, W. R. (1970). *Attention and Interpretation*. New York: Basic Books.
Bion, W. R. (1992). *Cogitations*. London: Karnac.
Bion, W. R. (2005). *The Tavistock Seminars*. London: Karnac.
Levine, H. B. (2013). The colourless canvas: Representation, therapeutic action and the creation of mind. In: H. B. Levine, G. S. Reed & D. Scarfone (Eds.), *Unrepresented States and the Creation of Meaning: Clinical and Theoretical Contributions* (pp. 42–71). London: Karnac.

# PART VIII

## GROUPS

*Editors' introduction*

Bion's contribution to the theory and functioning of groups remains at the heart of contemporary psychoanalytic understanding of group dynamics and the individual's relationship to the various social systems within which human life is inevitably embedded. Whereas Freud formulated his group dynamics from the perspective of repression and the Oedipus complex, as he imagined the latter lived out dramatically by the primal horde, Bion expanded Freud's theory by focusing upon psychotic anxieties and the inevitable pressures toward regression that participation in group life produced in its individual members. Bion argued that these powerful, disruptive forces mobilize primitive defenses such as splitting, projection, and projective identification and lead to manic responses characterized by unconscious phantasies of miraculous and salutary changes and cures that will come about through dependency, pairing, or fight/flight responses.

In addition to Freud (1921), the foundations of Bion's thinking about groups included the work and ideas of Wilfred Trotter, John Rickman, and the knowledge that he acquired in combat as a tank commander in the First War and in the famous Northfield experiments working with shell-shocked soldiers during the Second World War. Lessons learned from the latter form an important core of Bion's (1959) famous volume, *Experience in Groups*.

In the essays that follow, readers will be introduced to the basic outlines of Bion's theory of groups and the unique vocabulary that he created to help describe the powerful dynamic forces that are inherent to group participation. They will also see how four leading psychoanalytic thinkers—Shields, Hinshelwood, Erlich, and Kaes—have extended and applied Bion's foundational work to analytic group therapy, the study of group dynamics and relations, and to the analysis of culture, social systems, and large group phenomena in general. At the heart of each of these applications lies the essence of Bion's (1959) vision of group relatedness that he described in the following terms:

> … in his contact with the complexities of life in a group the adult resorts, in what may be a massive regression, to mechanisms described … as typical of the earliest phases of mental life. The adult must establish contact with the emotional life of the group in which he lives; this task would appear to be as formidable to the adult as the relationship with the breast appears to be for the infant; and the failure to meet the demands of this task is revealed in his regression. (pp. 141–142)

On the other hand, if this encounter can be successfully managed, then group participation holds out the prospect of "finding the capacity to engage in necessary grief work in response to our shared encounter with the inevitable limitations of human experience that may pave the way to hope of transformation of raw experience into fulfilling creative work together." (Shields, Chapter Thirty).

## References

Bion, W. R. (1959). *Experiences in Groups*. London: Tavistock.
Freud, S. (1921). *Group Psychology and the Analysis of the Ego*. S. E., *18*: 65–144. London: Hogarth.

CHAPTER THIRTY

# Affect, reverie, mourning, and Bion's theory of groups in our time

*Walker Shields*

"What'er the theme the maiden sang as if her song could have no ending ..."

—Wordsworth, W., 1807a, "The Solitary Reaper"

"Bear free and patient thoughts."

—Shakespeare, W., 1608, *King Lear*, 4.6.80

## Introduction

More than ever before, in our time we face the inevitable impact of participation in the large group context of our world in its entirety. Wilfred Bion's theory of groups offers an approach to study many of the problems and opportunities that emerge within that experience (Bion, 1959; Shields, 2001; Turquet, 1975). Yet it is difficult to apply Bion's ideas since one must then face a variety of emotional challenges. Engagement with these challenges inevitably requires mourning at the level of the group as well as within the individual. However, when groups and their members find ways to mourn together, they may discover bridges to emotional connection and imaginative collaboration across previously impassable boundaries of difference (Ogden, 2008, 2010b; Rioch, 1970b; 1971; Volcan, 2006). In this paper, I will explore three of the challenges one encounters in the application of Bion's approach.

## Three challenges from Bion's theory of groups

First, "if responsibility is anywhere, it is everywhere" (Rioch, 1971, p. 171). Each individual and each subgroup exists in continual covert as well as overt mutual interdependence with the entirety of the group context of which they are a part. There is interplay at every level between the responsibilities of leaders and followers in every group such that individuals and groups earn their leaders for good or for ill. In the words of any group relations consultant, groups get the leaders they deserve.

Second, there are problems that can only be comprehended and addressed by building hypotheses about the unconscious functioning of the entire social system of which each individual is a part. Alternatively, group participants remain imprisoned in non-rational and often destructive isolationist patterns from the past. However, the construction of such hypotheses requires the group participant to relinquish attachment to a familiar perspective based on conscious experience in individual relationships. Furthermore group participants must also engage in a process of mourning during which they assume responsibility for previously disowned and projected parts of the self or of one's subgroup.

The heart of Bion's approach to the study of groups (1946, 1959; Bion & Rickman, 1943; Rickman, 1957), is his invitation to use reverie or "waking dream thoughts" to construct "group-as-a-whole" hypotheses or metaphors for the unconscious functioning of the social system in its entirety. While engagement with these hypotheses may require the mourning of old cherished beliefs, they also may provide open, unsaturated images and/or narratives to invite further narration and exploration with discovery of new imaginative terms for relating in the world in place of repetition of many futile and relatively sterile, egocentric struggles from the past.

Third, the notion that human beings and/or the subgroups to which they belong exist as self-sufficient agencies is an illusion. This illusion represents the attempt to disavow the primitive affects about dependent needs and related anxieties stimulated by our inevitable, even if reluctant, experience of membership in the large group or community context. We are apt to abhor such primitive affects; we are apt to attempt to disavow and disown them, and then to project them on to others, particularly others who may appear different from ourselves. As a result, we may have difficulty finding the capacity to engage in necessary grief work in response to our shared encounter with the inevitable limitations of human experience that may pave the way to hope of transformation of raw experience into fulfilling creative work together.

It is the unique potential for collaboration in depth that has allowed human beings to survive as a species and even to thrive, in contrast to the mastodons of the archaic past. Yet this potential remains only a potential. Bion's theory of groups and his theory of thinking pose important problems as well as point towards creative opportunities.

I will now continue with a brief overview of Bion's theory of groups and his theory of thinking (Bion, 1962; Brown, L., 2011; Ferro, 2002, 2006; Ogden, 1997a, 1997b; 2001; 2004a, 2004b, 2004c; 2008; Symington & Symington, 1996). I will follow with examples to illustrate and explore the emotional challenges listed above as well as make reference to the creative opportunities in Bion's approach. Lastly, by means of a study group held in response to a selection of imaginative literature, I will illustrate how access to reverie in the group context may promote mourning and deepening of collaboration within a group.

## *Overview of Bion's theory of groups*[1]

Bion famously summarized as follows: "… in his contact with the complexities of life in a group the adult resorts, in what may be a massive regression, to mechanisms described … as typical of the earliest phases of mental life. The adult must establish contact with the emotional life of the group in which he lives; this task would appear to be as formidable to the adult as the relationship with the breast appears to be for the infant; and the failure to meet the demands of this task is revealed in his regression," (Bion, 1959, pp. 141–142). By regression Bion referred to inevitable emergence of powerfully influential yearnings for emotional connection and non-rational unconscious phantasies about the meaning of group life derived from the earliest, most undifferentiated phases of development in the minds of all group participants. It refers to the management of these affect-laden experiences by unconscious patterns of disavowal, splitting, and projection. These patterns include unconscious communications that influence all participants and may determine the behavior of individuals in the group as well as the structure and functioning of the group-as-a-whole. Bion emphasized that this phenomenon was inevitable and led to emotional bonding organized around the unconscious attitudes or assumptions shared by group participants and projected on to the leadership of the group.

**Basic assumption group**: An abstract term to refer to the nature of the unconscious organization of a group in response to inevitable unconscious yearnings, anxieties, phantasies, and beliefs of group participants. These include depressive and/or persecutory anxieties and/or more primitive fears of annihilation or loss of individual identity and distinctness through merger with the group. Elliot Jaques, a colleague of Bion's, wrote that all social systems form as defenses against the primitive anxieties of the group and its participants (1955). A group's basic assumption is just that … the common, implied, fundamental unconscious belief of group members about the group's agenda that binds them to the group (in contradistinction to the consciously agreed-upon "primary task" … see below).

Bion suggested three characteristic examples of unconscious, basic assumption group structure: dependency, fight-flight, and pairing (Rioch, 1970b). While basic assumption themes may provide unconscious energy to accomplish group tasks, unrecognized and unexplored basic assumption activities are apt to block the capacity of the group and of group members to think effectively and solve the problems of the group in its environment.

**Large group phenomena**: The potential for fragmentation of thought in response to intense anxiety that may emerge in any group in which the individual may not establish consistent face-to-face contact with all other participants … any group larger than ten or twelve members … as in a small circle of family members. Coherent person-to-person communication of any depth may become lost in a "large group" with greater and greater vulnerability to the influence of early yearnings for security and primitive phantasy, including fear of annihilation. The individual may feel his or her sense of identity is severely threatened under these circumstances (Shields, 2001; Turquet, 1975). As a result, there is a natural inclination to avoid awareness of one's relatedness to one's large group context. Conversely, there is a natural and even healthy inclination to focus on individual relationships and small groupings to avoid excess stimulation of one's inner world and associated fears that may arise in response to attending to one's relatedness within the large group context.

The nightmarish emotional experience the individual seeks to avoid, of being lost or hopelessly overwhelmed and homogenized in "large group phenomena", is illustrated vividly by Remarque in his novel, *All Quiet on the Western Front* (1928). Terrified and caught in a foxhole in the midst of the conflagration between armies and among and within men on the Flanders salient during World War One, Remarque's main character longs desperately for the sound of the voices and footsteps of his comrades in the trenches. Perhaps Bion himself, leading his tank crew on the Flanders front during World War One, may have had a similar and indeed unforgettable experience (Bion, 1982; Bleandonu, 1994; Brown, 2012). Consciously or not, Bion may have devoted the rest of his creative life to the attempt to resolve its meaning.[2] Bion recognized eventually that large groups in their entirety, as well as any and all of their members, may become vulnerable to processes of fragmentation of thinking including primitive disavowal, splitting, and projection with destructive consequences.

**Primary task**: What any group must accomplish in order to continue to survive or exist in its environment ... the fundamental and rational purpose for the survival and productive work of the group. The primary task is a consciously agreed-upon objective that may link participants in creative work on their own behalf. Dedication to a creative primary task may reduce the likelihood of regression towards a destructive group process and promote instead the growth and well-being of all participants. As soon as an aggregation of individuals has an acknowledged shared primary task, it becomes possible to examine its overt patterns of communication and decision-making but also to develop hypotheses about what covert influences might lead it to function in non-rational ways (basic assumption patterns), that either obstruct or possibly even enhance the accomplishment of its task in its environment. The primary task of a group may often be explicitly stated in a few words, for example, "to build automobiles". But more important in leadership is what might be called "a sense of task", learned from experience over time, that takes into account the complexities and opportunities for the group in its pursuit of its work within its larger human and world environment.

The importance of the concept of "primary task" first became apparent to me while leading hall meetings on an inpatient treatment unit in a psychiatric hospital. I discovered it was extremely valuable to ask the group repeatedly the question, "Why are we here". Subsequent discussion among patients and staff then helped all of us find "our backbones" with regard to the emotional and thoughtful work we were there to do.

**Work group**: Bion suggests that there are always two organizations to a group that coexist simultaneously and interact dynamically with each other: the work group and the basic assumption group. The term work group describes how the group may be organized into roles, structures, and activities in order to accomplish its primary task in contrast to the basic assumption group that is organized in accord with unconscious and often non-rational assumptions about the purpose of the group. Most important in the structure of the work group is the extent to which it exists in open communication and interplay with its environment as well as the extent to which the group is open to self-scrutiny.

**The "group-as-a-whole hypothesis"**: Bion invites the group participant to use access to reverie or waking dream thoughts derived from lived emotional experience in role within the group to arrive at a new vertex of thought, an imaginative conjecture about one's unity with the entirety. Such an imaginative hypothesis links one's experience in role within the work group with a conjecture about the unconscious functioning of the entirety, the level of the unconscious basic assumption according to which the group functions, that may be contrary to the consciously agreed-upon group task. Such a conjecture is merely a metaphor and not a statement of fact. Nevertheless, a group-as-a-whole hypothesis, though it may appear speculative and even paradoxical, may provide an evocative image or unsaturated narrative that leads to valuable further exploration and collaborative discovery of new creative terms for relating in place of repetition of futile battles of the past. In the dyadic analytic setting it is access to reverie that enables the psychoanalyst to build hypotheses about the emerging unconscious intersubjective relationship (Brown, 2011; Ferro, 2009; Levine, Forthcoming; Ogden, 1994) of the analytic pair. Bion's interest in the group-as-a-whole hypothesis links with his subsequent studies of the role of reverie in the growth of the human thinking apparatus.

## Overview of Bion's theory of thinking[3]

Bion concisely stated the core of his theory of thinking in one sentence: "The mother's capacity for reverie is the mother's receptor organ for the infant's harvest of self-sensation gained by its conscious" (1962, p. 116). Ogden observes that Bion's theory of thinking describes the potential for growth-producing conversations to occur on "the frontier of dreaming" (Ogden, 2001), within the mind of the individual and/or within relationships between the individual and others. He summarizes the nature of Bion's central metaphor, "the container/contained" (Bion, 1962, p. 90), as follows: The container/contained "is a process, not a thing. It is the capacity for the unconscious psychological work of dreaming, operating in concert with the capacity for preconscious dreamlike thinking (reverie), and the capacity for more fully conscious secondary-process thinking. Though all three of these types of thinking … unconscious dreaming, preconscious reverie and conscious reflection … are involved in the containing function of the mind, Bion views the unconscious work of dreaming as the work that is of primary importance in effecting psychological change and growth" (Ogden, 2004c, p. 1356).

Ogden emphasizes that in order to promote development of the apparatus for thinking about lived emotional experience and for doing psychological work … the container (mother, analytic therapist) must be capable of reverie. Reverie enables the containing agent to be able to receive, accept, metabolize, and return to the infant or patient "the emotional experience that he is unable to process on his own, given the rudimentary nature of his capacity for function" (ibid., p. 1357).

## Affect: the coin of the realm

Human beings are connected most deeply with each other and with themselves by affect. Bion, himself, emphasizes, "… [the container/contained] when disjoined or denuded of emotion, [diminishes] in vitality … [and approximates] … inanimate objects" (1962, p. 90). Grotstein (2000, p. 282), observes "it all boils down to [Bion's] utmost belief in the centrality of emotions as the nucleus of our 'heart of darkness' and of our very being." For Bion, Grotstein continues, reason is the slave of affect. Conscious and unconscious affects constitute the primordial and universal language of all human relationships from birth throughout life.

Modell writes in *Psychoanalysis in a New Context*, "Affects are not pleasure-seeking but object seeking" (Modell, 1984, p. 30), and "the communication of genuine affect is the communication of need" (ibid., p. 2). The establishment of relationships in which there may be communication of need and the discovery of the opportunity for emotional rapport is essential for well-being and even for the sense of identity itself throughout life. Modell then describes the "illusion of self-sufficiency" as a defense against affective meanings about the need for connection with others that the individual cannot integrate within the sense of self (1975, 1984, p. 38). This illusion may play an important part not only in dyadic relationships but also in human social systems of all sizes.

Access to affect requires access to the body. In the absence of communication between mind and body there can be no connection with the world outside the self, no relationship that is experienced as alive and real. As Lombardi describes, (2002, 2003), the issue of relatedness between mind and body must be addressed before thinking about emotional experience in relationships with others separate from the self may take on meaning and purpose. Primitive mental states in response to intense affect may occur in the midst of group life in which there is dissociation between mind and body with impairment of thought and communication about emotional experience. In other words, in order to have creative access to reverie in the group context one must have, within the self or in one's relationships with others, good-enough holding to maintain connection between mind and body as well as sufficient containment to promote development of the capacity for creative use of reverie.[4]

### The paradox of reverie: selflessness leads to empowerment

By allowing identification with the entirety of which one is a part, reverie paradoxically transports the individual to a state of inner selflessness that may lead to the calm that comes with humility and to the empowerment that comes from attaining an open perspective to address the tasks of the social system to which one belongs. We know that in a dream or in our dream thoughts we are all the characters in the dream; we are also the dreamer who dreams the dream; we are also the dream narrative in its entirety. In our dream thoughts the entirety and the self become one. From this perspective it becomes possible to explore many diverse hypotheses about the functioning of our minds in our world (Grotstein, 2000). Rioch (1971, p. 175) refers to this transition in thinking as the 180 degree turn in which the individual relinquishes the struggles of an isolating egocentric perspective to discover this new sense of authorization by finding the meaning of his or her potential involvement in the social system as an entirety.

However, to make this transition requires the experience of mourning attachment to old rigid beliefs and ways of relating to others. It requires a kind of grief work as one takes up responsibility for and ownership of bits of one's experience that formerly were projected on to other individuals or subgroups. This task becomes an important part of the work of the group just as mourning is an essential element of growth in individual psychoanalysis. Paradoxically, this process of grieving patterns of relatedness based on the egocentric views of the past may lead to a startling new sense of empowerment and calm. As Edgar kindly says in encouragement to his blind father, who is gaining new inner perspective and calm through suffering on the blasted heath in Shakespeare's *King Lear*, "Bear free and patient thoughts!" (*King Lear*; Shakespeare, 1608, 4.6.80).[5]

Bion's theories invite us to recognize that to speak from one's experience in this way on behalf of the work of our groups is to take up leadership in whatever role one finds oneself, to assume responsibility, and to work with authority with potential benefit for the groups in which we live as well as for the life within our own individual minds. One's working group-as-a-whole hypothesis is also the mirror of the functioning of one's own inner world (Rioch, 1971).

The discovery of this authorized empowerment within oneself on taking up leadership on behalf of the group is the paradox of selflessness in the group context. "Human beings are never more fulfilled than when they are united to a whole … perhaps it is a small inkling of this total union which makes the experience in a working group committed to a common task so fulfilling … it is not possible to do this unless … the individual [knows] … that he himself, on his own authority, has made the commitment to put his competence in the service of the common task" (Rioch, 1971, p. 177).

In the following examples, I will examine how if individuals attempt to "turn each to his own way" (Rioch, 1971), to disavow the emotional consequences of their inevitable overt and covert involvement in the groups and communities to which they belong, they may become even more vulnerable to misadventure than if they attempt to engage in learning about responsible group membership and leadership.

## Examples and applications

### Threats to identity leading to isolation and violence

Written shortly after the murder of a U.S. ambassador to a North African republic, Coll wrote a "Comment" article, "Days of Rage", in *The New Yorker Magazine*, (Coll, 2012, pp. 21–22). He critiqued a previous passionate and evidently influential portrayal in 1990 by the historian Bernard Lewis of "a surge of hatred rising from the Islamic world … a rejection of Western civilization as such". Coll also recalled the comment of a former prominent Western political leader: "They hate our freedoms".

Coll proceeded to question these two expressions of raw, undigested reactive emotional judgment. He wrote, "… the notion that a generalized Muslim anger about Western ideas could explain violence or politics from Indonesia to Bangladesh, from Iran to Senegal, seem[s] deficient." He offered evidence to the contrary and then suggested, "Free speech in a digital public square—not fringe violence—is what's new under the Mediterranean sun. And with free speech comes provocation." To this summary I would add: "And heightened vulnerability to primitive reaction in place of thoughtful response".

As I read this piece that described the impact of internet communication, which expands and deepens our involvement in the large group context of the world beyond our familiar experience of face-to-face relationships, including our relatedness with Africa, Asia, and the Middle East, I began to reflect once again about my own painful but vital learning experience as a member of a Tavistock group relations conference in Leicester, England twenty-five years ago (Shields, 1986). At this group relations conference my experience left me stunned by the new vision I began to hold of myself and of my place in the world. As I think of it now, I still feel a certain shock as I reflect about my own feelings of helplessness with respect to the issues that we all explored in that event.

Following Bion's model for the study of learning from experiences in groups, participants and consultant staff in Tavistock group relations conferences engage in the here-and-now exploration of covert as well as overt relatedness with each other in the context of the groups they form. In this model there is particular reference to how participants handle issues of authority, leadership, and responsibility in their groups. In short, these conferences study processes of overt and covert intersubjective communication and interplay, including not only collaboration but also patterns of denial, splitting, projective identification, and related modes of organizing experience as paranoid/schizoid, depressive, or manic disavowal. All participants, both staff and conference members, attempt to explore the nature of the social system they create in the conference itself as an overarching educational institution.[6]

The greatest learning in such events comes from the attempt potentially shared by all participants to collaborate in the development of hypotheses that link individual affect-laden experience with study of covert as well as overt processes in the group in its entirety that may promote or inhibit or even destroy the primary shared educational task. The unique power of this application of Bion's theory comes from the humbling attempt to build hypotheses together from reveries in response to the "lived emotional experience" of each individual in whatever role he or she may assume about the functioning of the group-as-a-whole as an educational institution, in other words as a social system taken in its entirety.

On this particular occasion in the inter-group study event, the conference membership divided spontaneously into three groups, presumably with the task of studying overt and covert themes in our relatedness with each other. Some members chose to form one or the other of two groups that became highly organized and proficient in articulating their meanings as well as in selecting officers. Those who joined a third group found they could not elect leadership. They fought among themselves, and generally barely remained unified except for their fierce attempt to hold on to the territory they occupied in the conference hall. I was initially quite proud to be a member of one of the highly organized groups. We selected delegates and negotiated with each other about how to study the issues we had decided to study. We believed we were demonstrating how to function as a sophisticated work group and believed the consultant staff would be delighted at our progress and the profundity of our thinking about our work.

Then, suddenly, the third group abruptly broke into our midst, insulted our intelligence, and loudly expressed their outrage about our self-satisfied arrogance and how we had ignored them while being so preoccupied with our own assumed sophistication. The abruptness and even violence of their intrusion into our calm and thoughtful deliberations led to a counter response of outrage on our part as our presumably excellent discussions were severely disrupted. We wished to retaliate by drafting a formal complaint to the conference director of how they had disrupted the work of the conference in its entirety.

At this point, the senior staff consultant for this exercise offered a group-as-a-whole hypothesis to all of us in this event, including participants in all three groups. He called to our attention the fact that several months before this conference a bomb had been exploded in a nightclub in a major city in northern Europe by a terrorist group that represented an isolated North African republic led by a dictator known for atrocities towards subgroups in his nation and violations of human rights. This consultant invited us to consider the following group-as-a-whole hypothesis following Bion's theory of groups: All three groups had recreated together the situation that had occurred on the continent two months before. By our preoccupation with our own presumed success and by our neglect of our relatedness with the third group, those of us in the two presumably well-functioning groups had not only isolated and shamed the third group. We had also created a circumstance in which they could only express their relatedness towards us by violence. Furthermore, we had evacuated our own raw energy into them and our own deliberations had become sterile, empty, and lifeless.

We had drawn ourselves more and more into an illusion of our own sophistication and superior value. In fact, we were closing ourselves from the depths of our own experience of ourselves as individuals as well as from our own greatest imaginative resources. In the language of Bion and Klein we had projected our own rich but raw energy that had made us uncomfortable into the third group while depriving them of our own capacity for coherent discourse. Our own difficulty within our two groups was projected across a boundary of difference from ourselves into the world that lay outside our familiar boundaries.

Reflecting today on Modell's recognition of the importance of the communication of genuine affect, I later recognized we had constructed a cocoon around ourselves, a grandiose illusion of self-sufficiency (Modell, 1984) that attempted to deny our own vulnerability and need for connection with others different from ourselves. In so doing we had isolated ourselves from the third group and had thereby robbed ourselves of part of ourselves, including the opportunity to work creatively with our own raw energy that we had projected into the third group. This illusion also denied our own experience of the threats to our identity as individuals and as a group created by the growing impact of our inevitable and inexorable participation in the large social system context of the world.

As noted by Pierre Turquet, (1975), in the absence of the attempt and the opportunity to connect, differentiate, and communicate coherently and in some detail with others separate from oneself, one loses the capacity to maintain one's sense of a unique and secure individual identity. One becomes more and more vulnerable to being consumed by an unconscious and thoughtless homogenization with the large group to which one belongs. Affect-laden communication in whatever form is an expression of need for connection and dialogue. If so interpreted, even in the midst of conflicting viewpoints, it may become a path towards creative collaboration. Alternatively, if it is rejected and not considered to be a vital communication about interrelatedness within the entire social system, it may lead towards more and more alienation and eventually more and more destructive enactment. [7]

*The terrorist within*

Bion's theories invite us over and over to explore the possibilities for learning and growth that may emerge when we succeed in owning that which we have previously evacuated into others, even when ownership requires accepting the experience of shame or guilt and finding the way to necessary grief work. While the following example is quite miniature in comparison to events on the large political stage, nevertheless it may illustrate important principles not only about the application of Bion's theories in the group context but also about the nature of reverie itself.

Some years after the above-mentioned conference, while serving on the consulting staff in another group relations conference, I was participating in a staff group meeting during a major conference event. At the time of this staff meeting, we were beginning to notice the relatively dry and excessively logical nature of our own dialogue and that of the conference membership in the group events up to this point. Ordinarily, during staff discussions I am soft-spoken and deliberate in my manner. However, on this particular occasion, I became abruptly and rudely angry with two colleagues who I felt had paired into an exciting subgroup quite separate from the remainder of the conference staff. Less in my awareness, but vastly more important, were deeper feelings of exclusion from collaborative connection with the conference director and meaningful involvement with others in the task of the conference.

My angry emotional outburst was sufficiently intense as to startle the other members of the staff group and for a time seriously to interrupt and fragment our work together. It was difficult for us to study the meaning of this interaction together at the time. Eventually, I succeeded in recognizing that I had evacuated raw material from within myself, which was mine, to manage into others in the staff group. As I began to acknowledge and accept responsibility for my emotional voltage, I began to feel deep guilt and grief over my outburst. Finally, I was able to apologize and begin to explore the meanings of my outburst not only for the group-as-a-whole but also in terms of my own inner world.

I had recognized to my horror my own capacity to play the part of an emotional terrorist in the midst of covert projective processes in the group. Within my inner world, my previously concealed feelings of longing for fulfilling connection and helplessness had sought release as rage. I had chosen to evacuate this energy rather than to find a way to contain and transform it into thought about my emotional experience ... not only about my own internal world but also about the circumstances in which we found ourselves as a social system taken in its entirety.

Fortunately, after bearing the pain of shame, guilt, and particularly an acute sense of grief over these recognitions, I was able again to rejoin the group dialogue. We were able to use our experience with each other as a staff group towards the goal of promoting learning about covert as well as the overt themes with the membership in the conference as a social system taken in the entirety.

In retrospect, I might have built an imaginative conjecture or group-as-a-whole hypothesis (Shapiro & Carr, 1991), based on discovery of my own role in the group process as "terrorist". Finding a suitable pictograph to invite and negotiate the shared construction of a narrative about the experience together I might have said something like, "I found myself feeling excluded, helpless, ashamed, and enraged until I realized that I had been blind to the fact that, like a sheep following a magical shepherd, I was waiting for the conference director to show me the way rather than finding my own resources and energy to work with all of you on our shared learning task together. Instead I had erupted like a volcano or a terrorist." With this hypothesis about my own experience in role I might have invited others to join me in the construction of a shared hypothesis about our functioning as a group.

It may be necessary to maintain a degree of insulation from the intense emotions that relate to our inevitable participation in groups of all sizes in order to accomplish many of the activities of our daily lives. Furthermore, most people reserve the word hatred for those situations in which they feel their most destructive thoughts and phantasies seem justified by immediate reality circumstances, circumstances in which they feel profoundly exploited or abused. On the other hand, in the group context we remain vulnerable to the bursting forth of such intense affect and the consequences of not being prepared to study such experiences. Particularly with reference to the large groups to which we belong, now, in this age of internet communication, we have even more of a large group experience at our fingertips but one out of reach of familiar forms of face-to-face communication (Shields, 2000). Such experience of the world beyond our immediate environment may threaten our sense of identity more than ever before. In such circumstances individuals and groups may turn to follow leaders with blind dependency and thereby become vulnerable to violent and thoughtless enactment in order to avoid the experience of responsibility for unfamiliar affects and to attempt desperately to maintain a coherent sense of their identity and value. Alternatively, they may detach from their need for connection within an illusion of self-sufficiency that leads to progressive isolation from others and even from the most important resources within themselves or within their own group. The issue is how to develop the capacity to think about circumstances that evoke such powerful feeling, as opposed to imprisonment in one or another of the above reactive patterns that block learning and growth in the capacity to engage in creative relationships. In fact, the attempt to acknowledge, explore, and think together about personal experience at the level of the group context of which we are a part may not only expose our deepest vulnerabilities to our awareness, it may also lead us to new creative opportunities for life together.

## The importance of mourning in the group context

On the basis of wide experience studying approaches to violent social conflict across international boundaries of difference involving large ethnic groups in many countries around the world, the psychoanalyst Vamik Volkan describes what he calls the use of the "Tree Model" in a book entitled *Killing in the Name of Identity: A Study of Bloody Conflicts* (2006). Using this model, Volkan and his team seek to address psychological processes that have led to destructive consequences between large ethnic groups with rigidly defended boundaries around their sense of identity and value. Beginning with exploration of the background issues that contribute to the conflict as if they are roots of the tree, Volkan designs small dialogue groups as if they are the trunk. These groups are led by seasoned group conveners and offer an open agenda to allow members of separate ethnically different groups to come together and speak spontaneously with each other of their experiences much as an analysand is invited to associate freely about memories, thoughts, and feelings in the analytic setting. These dialogue groups eventually begin to address memories and affect about the "chosen ethnic traumas" of each group, which have often been transmitted for centuries across generations.[8]

As such dialogue groups deepen and become more personal, there is movement beyond resentment toward a grieving process with regard to the ethnic traumas. The group members begin to share a mourning process and become aware of emotional bridges with each other based on recognition of common human emotional themes shared by all. As the trunk of the tree, the dialogue groups offer members the opportunity to move beyond stereotypic reactivity towards discovery of alternatives to old bitterness, isolation, alienation, and even ensuing violent enactment. In Volkan's tree model the participants of these dialogue groups become branches that may reach out into the community to communicate to others about potential growth of new attitudes. Volkan emphasizes the importance of finding ways to enable mourning of the recurrent ethnic themes. To aid in this process he recommends establishment of monuments to facilitate an open process of mourning for losses from the past often transmitted across many generations.

Salvio (2012, 2013) describes the dedication of a magnolia tree in Palermo, Italy, as a monument in memory of Giovanni Falcone, an anti-Mafia magistrate who was assassinated 1992 in a car bombing, along with his wife, Francesca Morvillo, and their escorts. The Falcone magnolia tree in Palermo continues to provide opportunity for public mourning and potential development of non-violent yet effective creative responses to Mafia violence by the community. Other monuments that live on in the minds of succeeding generations include the Lincoln Memorial, the Vietnam Memorial, and the Holocaust Museum in Washington, DC.

While Volkan does not suggest that it is possible merely by these means to remove vulnerability to violent enactment between diverse human social systems across boundaries of difference, he does emphasize the importance of engagement in such group processes that may lead through the acknowledgment of suffering to a process of mourning, much as in an individual psychoanalysis, in order to free participants to move towards creative alternatives to the old, futile struggles of the past. When group participants engage in a process of mourning together, a sense of human kinship may develop across boundaries that previously were impassable.

### *An illustration of the power of reverie and mourning in the group context*[9]

I have designed a series of exploratory study groups to be offered in conference workshops for mental health professionals to examine and illustrate the impact of derivatives of dream thoughts, including not only remembered dreams and daytime reveries but also selections of imaginative literature, on thinking about lived emotional experience in the group context (Shields, 2009). Initially, I was inspired by Bion's theories but also by Winnicott's "squiggle" interview technique (1964–1968), in which he offered his own spontaneous and incomplete line drawings, derivatives of his own imagination and dream thoughts, to begin an associative interview with a given patient. I have explored how selections of great poetry might bring group participants to respond, from the realm of their own reveries, with each other.

When a poet writes a poem that resonates with generations of listeners, it becomes a reverie that may link generations of listeners in an ongoing deepening conversation on "the frontier of dreaming" (Ogden, 2001). Wordsworth's "The Solitary Reaper" (1807a) is just such a poem. Furthermore, as noted above, when people can find a way to access their reveries and deep feelings of grief together, they may find access to common human mortal experience and new pathways for creative bonding with each other. In this way, great imaginative literature may provide a deepening and integrative function for our culture, as dream thinking may for the individual. Like a container/contained, the poem becomes a timeless, open, unsaturated "group-as-a-whole interpretation". The following is an example of a study group designed to invite and explore the potential for such conversations at the level of dream thoughts, affect-laden memories, and ongoing lived emotional experience in response to such a selection of literature.

Using a study group format in the manner of Bion (Rioch, 1970a, 1970b; Shields, 2009), I consulted to a group of participants to examine and explore feelings, memories, and reveries elicited by reading Wordsworth's "The Solitary Reaper" (1807). I read the poem aloud twice at the beginning of the one-hour study group. In this way the reading of the poem stimulated an open response from twelve group participants as they sat in a small circle together with me as their consultant. During this study group I consulted exclusively to the group in its entirety (the group-as-a-whole), in the here-and-now, and with respect to covert as well as overt responses to the poem. In this way my interpretations were to remain both unsaturated and yet consistently to invite attention to the images of the poem as pictographs for a potential open evolving emotional narrative by all participants and by the group-as-a-whole. Wordsworth's "The Solitary Reaper" is a lyrical ballad of four verses:

> Behold her single in the field
> Yon solitary highland lass
> Reaping and singing as she works
> Stop here or gently pass
> Alone she cuts and binds the grain
> And sings a melancholy strain.
> Oh listen for the vale profound
> Is overflowing with the sound.
>
> No nightingale e're did chaunt
> More welcome notes to weary bands
> Of travelers in some shady haunt
> Among the Arabian sands.
> A voice so thrilling n'er was heard
> In springtime from the cuckoo bird
> Breaking the silence of the seas
> Among the farthest Hebrides.
>
> Will no one tell me what she sings?—
> Perhaps the plaintive numbers flow
> For old, unhappy, far-off things
> And battles long ago:
> Or is it some more humble lay,
> Familiar matter of today?
> Some natural sorrow, loss of pain,
> That has been and may be again?
>
> Whate'er the theme, the Maiden sang
> As if her song could have no ending;
> I saw her singing at her work,
> And o'er the sickle bending;—
> I listened motionless and still;
> And, as I mounted up the hill,
> The music in my heart I bore,
> Long after it was heard no more.

After hearing the poem read aloud twice and slowly by me, there was a long silent pause. Then very gradually, two or three of the participants began to speak softly and tentatively at first and then more and more directly of deep grief over lost loved ones. One spoke with deep feelings of a son who died of leukemia in early adolescence. Another responded tearfully, speaking of the death of her husband following a long illness during early mid-life. Then yet another spoke about the deteriorating health of a beloved elderly parent. Soon others also joined with further examples, not "of battles long ago" but of "natural sorrow, loss, or pain" emerging in the here-and-now about their personal lives. Apparently, the music of Wordsworth's words and the image of the solitary highland girl cutting and binding the grain and singing a melancholy strain had invited them to bring such feelings to each other. As we approached the last fifteen minutes of the here-and-now study group, I wondered more and more about my own experience in role as consultant.

Following Bion, I searched for my own reveries about my part in the entirety of the group. First, I imagined myself as the highland girl, the reaper herself! I feared that I represented only death itself to the study group members, the reaper with her inevitable scythe that harvests all that has been growing as fodder for some incomprehensible final purpose or perhaps for some ominous obscure Armageddon. Or did I represent the woman who comforts or even provides nourishment in a time of loss? My anxiety grew. I thought perhaps I had selected this poem to struggle with my own fears of loss of loved ones dear to me or about personal limitations and disappointments or growing recognition of my aging process or my own eventual death. As I anxiously examined these thoughts within myself, I discovered the extent to which I felt an intense desire for comforting, intimate, physical contact and soothing. Initially, I found it difficult to think about the meaning of this palpable physical longing in my body. Then I discovered I was repeating certain lines from the poem over and over in my mind, lines which came from the end of the poem: "And as I mounted up the hill, the music in my heart I bore, long after it was heard no more." Quite spontaneously I spoke these lines to the group.

In response several members spoke of recollection of moments when hearing music or being sung to by a beloved family member brought well-being even in the midst of moments of fear or deep sorrow. One mentioned the power of listening to favorite selections of classical music while recovering in a medical ICU following a serious automobile accident. Another recalled her joy on being sung to at bedtime while far away from home as a child by a favorite aunt. In the midst of these comments several others began to acknowledge with much feeling the importance of their relationships with certain of the group members from their lives outside of the group not previously acknowledged as such.

A reflective review discussion followed the "here-and-now" portion of the workshop. During this "there-and-then" review discussion one of the participants began our conversation by recalling a line from Wordsworth's "Ode", "… soothing thoughts that spring from human suffering".[10] He observed how such soothing seems to occur when one discovers one is not suffering alone but may feel one's connection on a very personal level with others through the acknowledgement of such feelings together.

Another repeatedly asked me to comment on my impression about the image of "the solitary reaper", which was haunting her still. Her inquiry reminded me of my own anxiety while in role as consultant. My first response to her inquiry was to recall my hypothesis that the group had unconsciously invited me in my role as consultant to be both the mysterious reaper as well as the poet entranced and yet mystified by her song. As I responded to this inquiry, I suddenly realized that during the group itself, without any conscious intention, I had restricted all my interpretations to lines from the poem! In effect, I had clung to Wordsworth and to the poem itself. And, in fact, Wordsworth's poem had held me. I had not previously decided to consult to the group in this fashion. In a sense, Wordsworth's poem had become a holding and containing environment not only for the group participants but also for me in my role with regard to these primordial themes about mortal human experience. The poem itself had become a group-as-a-whole interpretation for me! And yet in a larger sense, as I wondered further about the image and music of the solitary reaper in the poem, I recognized I was not able to provide satisfactory cognitive understanding in response to the inquiry of this group member.

And yet, as a derivative of his own dream thoughts, perhaps Wordsworth's poem with its image of the young girl as "the solitary reaper" brought all of us to a deeper degree of connection with each other, to mourning about similar experiences we all share in our lives within the entirety, and hence to imaginative resources we had not known before, a place that was as mysterious as it was beautiful.

## Notes

1. For further elaboration of Bion's theory of groups and its application in the study of social systems the reader is referred to Rice, 1965; Rioch, 1970b, 1971.
2. Brown explores Bion's description of his war experiences, including those during the Battle of Amiens, and their link to the development of his theory of thinking in "Bion's discovery of alpha function: Thinking under fire on the battlefield and in the consulting room" (2012).
3. For further elaboration and discussion of reverie and Bion's theory of thinking the reader is referred to Bion, 1962; Bleandonu, 1994; Brown, 2011; Ferro, 2002, 2006); Grotstein, 2000; Ogden, 2004a, 2004b, 2004c, 2010b); O'Shaughnessy, 2005; Symington and Symington, 1996.
4. Ogden describes the nature of good-enough holding and containing to enable transformative work with dream thoughts (2004a, 2004b, 2004c, 2010b).
5. Ogden, (2004, 2010a), describes how the analyst may provide the necessary containment to allow the analysand to dream what was previously un-dreamable and as a result imagine an alternative to the futile struggles of unconscious internalized early object relationships such as those described by Fairbairn.
6. For detailed descriptions of the design of Tavistock group relations conferences the reader is referred to Miller, 1989; Rioch, 1970a, 1970b, 1971; Shapiro and Carr, 2012; Shields, 2001.
7. Lombardi (2002, pp. 368–369) describes the importance of harmonious conversation between mind and body for a secure sense of identity. The relationship between mind and body may become severely distorted in the midst of anxiety generated during engagement in the large group context.
8. Volkan (2006) also describes "chosen ethnic glories", moments of ethnic heroism, as important in the organization of the group's identity.
9. Corrao (1981) compares the work of dream thoughts in the group mind, which he calls gamma function, with alpha function in the individual mind.
10. Wordsworth's (1807b) "Ode: Intimations of Immortality from Recollections of Early Childhood".

## References

Bion, W. R. (1946). The leaderless group project. *Bulletin of the Menninger Clinic, 10*: 77–81.
Bion, W. R. (1959). *Experiences in Groups and Other Papers*. London: Tavistock.
Bion, W. R. (1962). A theory of thinking. In: *Second Thoughts: Selected Papers on Psychoanalysis* (pp. 110–119). New York: Jason Aronson, 1967.
Bion, W. R., & Rickman, J. (1943). Intra-group tensions in therapy: Their study as the task of the group. *Lancet, 242*: 678–682.
Bion, W. R. (1982). *The Long Weekend: 1897–1919* (Ed. F. Bion). Abingdon: Fleetwood Press.
Bleandonu, G. (1994). *Wilfred Bion: His Life and Works, 1897–1979* (Trans. C. Pajaczkowska). New York: Other Press.
Brown, L. (2011). *Intersubjective Processes and the Unconscious: An Integration of Freudian, Kleinian, and Bionian Perspectives*. New York: Routledge.
Brown, L. (2012). Bion's discovery of alpha function: Thinking under fire on the battlefield and in the consulting room. *International Journal of Psychoanalysis, 93*: 1191–1214.
Coll, S. (2012). Days of rage. *The New Yorker Magazine*. October 1, 2012.
Corrao, F. (1981). Struttura poliadica e funzione gamma. *Gruppo e Funzione Analitica II*, 2.
Ferro, A. (2002). Some implications of Bion's thought. *International Journal of Psychoanalysis, 83*: 597–607.
Ferro, A. (2006). Clinical implications of Bion's thought. *International Journal of Psychoanalysis, 87*: 989–1003.
Ferro, A. (2009). Transformations in dreaming and characters in the psychoanalytic field. *International Journal of Psychoanalysis, 90*: 209–230.
Grotstein, J. (2000). *Who is the Dreamer Who Dreams the Dream: A Study of Psychic Presences*. Hillsdale, NJ: Analytic Press.
Jaques, E. (1955). Social systems as defence against persecutory and depressive anxiety. In: M. Klein, S. Isaacs & J Riviere (Eds.), *New Directions in Psychoanalysis*. London: Tavistock.
Levine, H. (Forthcoming). The transformational vision of Antonino Ferro. *Psychoanalytic Inquiry*.
Lombardi, R. (2002). Primitive mental states and the body: A personal view of Armando B. Ferrari's concrete original object. *International Journal of Psychoanalysis, 83*: 363–381.
Lombardi, R. (2003). Catalyzing the dialogue between the body and the mind in a psychotic analysand. *Psychoanalytic Quarterly, 72*: 1017–1041.
Miller, E. J. (1989). Tavistock Institute of Human Resources Occasional Paper # 10: The Leicester model: Experiential study of group and organizational processes. London: Tavistock.
Modell, A. H. (1975). A narcissistic defense against affects and the illusion of self-sufficiency. *International Journal of Psychoanalysis, 56*: 275–282.
Modell, A. H. (1984). *Psychoanalysis in a New Context*. Madison, CT: International Universities Press.
Ogden, T. H. (1994). The analytic third: Working with intersubjective clinical facts. *International Journal of Psychoanalysis, 75*: 3–19.
Ogden, T. H. (1997a). Reverie and interpretation. *Psychoanalytic Quarterly, 66*: 567–595.
Ogden, T. H. (1997b). Reverie and metaphor: Some thoughts about how I work as a psychoanalyst. *International Journal of Psychoanalysis, 78*: 719–732.
Ogden, T. H. (2001). *Conversations at the Frontier of Dreaming*. Northvale, NJ: Jason Aronson.
Ogden, T. H. (2004a). An introduction to the reading of Bion. *International Journal of Psychoanalysis, 85*: 285–300.
Ogden, T. H. (2004b). This art of psychoanalysis: Dreaming undreamt dreams and interrupted cries. *International Journal of Psychoanalysis, 85*: 857–877.
Ogden, T. H. (2004c). On holding and containing, being and dreaming. *International Journal of Psychoanalysis, 85*: 1349–1364.

Ogden, T. H. (2008). Bion's four principles of mental functioning. In: *Rediscovering Psychoanalysis: Thinking and Dreaming, Learning and Forgetting*. London: Routledge.

Ogden, T. H. (2010a). Why read Fairbairn? *International Journal of Psychoanalysis, 91*: 101–118.

Ogden, T. H. (2010b). On three forms of thinking: Magical thinking, dream thinking, and transformative thinking. *Psychoanalytic Quarterly, 79*: 317–347.

O'Shaughnessy, E. (2005). Whose Bion? *International Journal of Psychoanalysis, 86*: 1523–1542.

Remarque, E. M. (1928). *All Quiet on the Western Front* (Trans. A. W. Wheen). New York: Fawcett Crest.

Rice, A. K. (1965). *Learning for Leadership*. London: Tavistock.

Rickman, J. (1957). *Selected Contributions to Psychoanalysis*. New York: Basic Books.

Rioch, M. J. (1970a). Group relations: Rationale and technique. *International Journal of Group Psychotherapy, 20*: 340–355.

Rioch, M. J. (1970b). The work of Wilfred Bion on groups. *Psychiatry, 33*: 56–65.

Rioch, M. J. (1971). "All we like sheep …" [Isaiah 53–6]: Followers and leaders. *Psychiatry, 34*: 258–273.

Salvio, P. (2012). Eccentric subjects: Female martyrs and the anti-mafia public imaginary. *Italian Studies, 67*: 397–410.

Salvio, P. (2013). Julius Silberger Award Lecture: "To tarry with grief": Spontaneous shrines and the public memorialization of death in Palermo." Boston Psychoanalytic Society and Institute. Boston, Massachusetts, April 10, 2013.

Shakespeare, W. (1608). *King Lear*. In: R. A. Foakes (Ed.), *Arden Edition of the Works of William Shakespeare*. London: Methuen, 1997.

Shapiro, E. R., & Carr, A. W. (1991). *Lost in Familiar Places: Creating New Connections Between the Individual and Society*. New Haven: Yale University Press.

Shapiro, E. R., & Carr, A. W. (2012). An introduction to Tavistock-style group relations conference learning. *Organizational and Social Dynamics, 12*: 70–80.

Shields, W. (1986). A Massachusetts Yankee in Leicester, England; Experiences at Tavistock Group Relations Conference; An application: Tripoli, April 1986. *Newsletter of Northeastern Society for Group Psychotherapy, 8*: 1–5.

Shields, W. (2000). The virtual universe, the open large group, and maturational processes in the future. *Group, 24*: 33–48.

Shields, W. (2001). The subjective experience of the self in the large group: Two models for study. *International Journal of Group Psychotherapy, 51*: 205–223.

Shields, W. (2009). Imaginative literature and Bion's intersubjective theory of thinking. *Psychoanalytic Quarterly, 78*: 559–585.

Symington, J., & Symington, N. (1996). *The Clinical Thinking of Wilfred Bion*. London: Routledge.

Turquet, P. (1975). Threats to identity in the large group: A study in the phenomenology of the individual's experiences of changing membership status in a large group. In: L. Kreeger (Ed.), *The Large Group*. London: Karnac.

Volkan, V. (2006). *Killing in the Name of Identity: A Study of Bloody Conflicts*. Charlottesville, VA: Pitchstone.

Winnicott, D. W. (1964–1968). The Squiggle Game. In: C. Winnicott, R. Shepherd & M. Davis (Eds.), *Psychoanalytic Explorations* (pp. 291–317). London: Karnac, 1989.

Wordsworth, W. (1807a). The solitary reaper. In: *The Collected Poems of William Wordsworth* (introduction by A. Till). Hertfordshire: Wordsworth Editions, 1994.

Wordsworth, W. (1807b). Ode: Intimations of immortality from recollections of early childhood. In: *The Collected Poems of William Wordsworth* (introduction by A. Till). Hertfordshire: Wordsworth Editions, 1994.

# CHAPTER THIRTY-ONE

# Containing primitive emotional states: approaching Bion's later perspectives on groups

*R. D. Hinshelwood*

An anecdotal story is that towards the end of his analysis, around 1952, Melanie Klein told Bion to stop bothering about groups and to concentrate on psychoanalysis proper. Whether that is true or not we will never know. But it seems that for whatever reason, he did turn from groups, and recast his group theories into psychoanalytic ones.[1] His re-view—that is a new view, not a review—is to say that when an individual engages in a group he regresses to primitive levels of functioning, so that we can understand the emotionality, sensitivity, and irrationality of groups in terms of the primitive levels of mental functioning to which the individual is reduced by entering a group. That then allowed Bion to reinterpret the basic assumptions and group dynamics in the general terms of the primitive mechanisms that Klein had discovered and described.

In this chapter, I shall reconsider Bion's progress in group thinking, from those early days through to 1970, and his late "manifesto" on what he thinks psychoanalytic knowledge to be. It is a rough ride, as Bion frequently changed direction. In Meltzer's admiring words,

> ... the quality that distinguished Wilfred Bion, and which marks his passing from us with such serious consequences for psychoanalysis—perhaps for the world—was his capacity to tolerate caesura after caesura, to weather what he called "Catastrophic Change". (Meltzer, 1981, p. 13)

However, it is not clear whether his readers can follow the pattern of his conceptual journey. We tend to get stuck on one or other of the particular phases—shall we say the Tavistock approach—or perhaps the seemingly mystical contemplation of O in his late years. I shall pick only parts of this meandering journey.[2]

## The early group projects

Bion respected very few people, but one he did respect was Trotter, and exposure to Trotter's ideas was probably highly significant (Trotter, 1916). Trotter's thesis was that people gather in "herds" from inherent causes. It is practically in the genes, and it is this inherited gregariousness from which sensitivity to others arises. This inherent property of the herd, as a part of the material substance of human beings, comes through as Bion's idea of "group mentality" with which he started his series of papers between 1948 and 1951, collected in *Experiences in Groups* (Bion, 1961).

Bion had started at the Tavistock Clinic in 1933 as an associate to train in psychotherapy. The founder of the Clinic (in 1921), Hugh Crichton-Miller, promoted an integrative approach (Dicks, 1970)—that is, a bio-psycho-social one. Here we are concerned with the psychosocial aspects of that integration (see Suttie, 1924).

From 1948, Bion contributed a series of papers reporting empirical observations. In this he was influenced considerably by John Rickman who was Bion's first analyst from 1938 to 1939 (Vonofakos & Hinshelwood, 2012); and later by Eric Trist, and Trist's acquaintance with Kurt Lewin (Trist & Murray, 1990).

During their military service during the war (1939–1945), Bion discussed with Rickman the work at the Officer Selection Boards, and one gets the first impression of Bion's group thinking (Bion, 1946). They argued that if you want to find the men with most leadership qualities, then put the candidates for selection together in a group, assign them a task, and then observe who emerges as leader, like the figure from the ground. This was very successful. The first so-called "Northfield Experiment" (Bion & Rickman, 1943) is well documented (Pines, 2000; Lipgar & Pines, 2003), and is strong evidence of the mentoring function that Rickman assumed during war time with his ex-analysand. The "experiment" took place in 1943 in a military hospital for soldiers who had suffered mental breakdown while on active service, and was written up as a joint paper with Rickman (Bion & Rickman, 1943). This is a brilliant reconceptualization of the psychiatric work of a military hospital. What, they asked, is the aim of the rehabilitation of soldiers? Their answer was that it was to restore morale to a group of soldiers so that they could return to the task of fighting the enemy. Then, whilst languishing in a hospital, what was the soldiers' enemy? Bion answered that the enemy was neurosis. The organisation of the ward should therefore be geared to a collaborative (group) combat with that enemy, under the authority of an experienced leader—the psychiatrist, Bion himself. This was such a radical revision of a hospital's task (as he would later realize, from a dependency culture to a fight-flight one) that his ward was rejected by both the military and medical authorities, and closed within six weeks (see Main, 1975)!

Nevertheless, his originality greatly impressed many people, especially psychoanalysts such as Ronald Hargreaves, head of military psychiatry at the War Office (Hinshelwood, 1999). It also impressed those at the Tavistock Clinic when he returned there, and he was charged with researching group dynamics, a new field defined by Lewin and introduced to the Tavistock by Trist (see Trist & Murray, 1990). Bion's work started with Trotter's notion of group mentality as a biological given. We have a description of Bion's first study group at the Tavistock, on

January 1 1946, reported next day in a letter to John Rickman. The group included professionals and lay staff (clerks as he called them), about thirty in all:

> I opened the discussion by saying I wanted to know how many people would like to form a guinea pig group and what hours we could appoint for meetings and what fee we should pay the Clinic. I then stopped.
>
> Everyone seemed a bit sheepish and then a few people started talking to ease the tension. Leonard Browne said, could you give any indications about how groups behave? To which I replied, Just like this.
>
> Another awkward pause followed. And then further questions to all of which I responded with non-committal grunts. The group hunted round a bit and then Dr. Stein took the floor to explain, since I wouldn't, what he thought Dr. Bion wanted. The group fell on this with gratitude and Dr. Stein took over the group. Then they petered out again. Then the topic of Dr. Bion cropped up, but without much assistance from Dr. Bion. A certain amount of heat began to be generated at this point and I then intervened to point out that they were angry with me because it was becoming clear that when I had said "group therapy" I meant "group" therapy and not therapy by Dr. Bion. I said that when I hadn't taken the lead they had first fallen back on themselves and had then squeezed Dr. Stein into the job since I wouldn't. After this things followed pretty conventional lines with Maberly's hostility and anxiety becoming more and more marked every minute. I may be wrong but I am pretty sure Maberly was present as a spy from the enemy's camp. (Letter from Wilfred Bion to John Rickman, January 2 1946, see Vonofarkos and Hinshelwood, 2012, p. 89)

Bion's ironic descriptions are characteristic, and they foreshadow those in his series of seven papers on the experiences he culled from these study groups. He had three years of these experiences until he left the Tavistock in 1948. Interestingly, the first three of his papers, "Experiences in Groups I, II, and III" (see Bion, 1961) were often ironic and idiosyncratic descriptions of pieces of dialogue from the groups. These set out to emphasize a paucity of sophistication, simplistic thinking, and downright prejudice posed as knowledge. He demonstrated in line with Trotter that the group life of humans is not rational. However, this is a rather limited conclusion, and by the third of his papers he began to unpack the idea of group mentality, revising the concept by substituting three irrational assumptions, each of which could be the basis for a specific group culture. It is as if the nature of the human mind is inherently programmed in its material base, its proto-mental origins, to link up with similar assumptions with others in the group. The group was pervaded by one or other of the assumptions adhered to by all individuals in the group—we know these assumptions as dependency, fight-flight, and pairing. In his role running these study groups he preferred to remain above the irrational assumptions, and believed he had that ability, unlike the other members. He felt he could stand for something different, more rational. So, he differentiated another modality of group culture not so enslaved to the three assumptions. This he called the work group.

This contrast of group emotionality and individual reason came from Trotter. To put it another way, the individual is capable of being emotionally active and irrational in a group but as an individual he is capable of rationality. Being in a group, therefore, an individual is in conflict between himself as a rational individual and himself as a group member. As Bion put it, "The individual is a group animal at war, both with the group and with those aspects of his personality that constitute his groupishness" (Bion, 1961, p. 168). These papers form the body of the collection in 1961, *Experiences in Groups*. Then came one of Bion's dramatic revisions, one of his caesuras.

## Re-viewing

When he qualified as a psychoanalyst in 1951, he joined a younger generation of Kleinian analysts that included, Hanna Segal, Herbert Rosenfeld, and also Roger Money-Kyrle and Elliott Jaques. Bion became known as one of the foremost in applying Klein's ideas to working with psychotic patients, reported in Klein's paper on schizoid mechanisms (Klein, 1946). Under the influence of this work with psychotic anxiety and primitive mechanisms of defence, he revised his basic assumption theories.

He began his revision, as part of the festschrift for her seventieth birthday (in 1952). In his "Group dynamics: a review", he reinterpreted the hitherto inherent basic assumptions in terms of psychological mechanisms, and employed Klein's primitive psychotic mechanisms of splitting, projection, and introjection. At that point, Bion moved, we could say, from being a group therapist to a group psychoanalyst. The paper was itself revised in 1955 (Sanfuentes, 2003); and it challenged Freud in a loyally Kleinian way. It later became the final chapter in *Experiences in Groups* (1961).

## The family group

Freud, and especially his 1921, *Group Psychology*, applied the theory of the Oedipus complex to social psychology. He started by making the point that a full regard for the Oedipus complex constructs the individual as a locus within various loves, jealousies, murderousness, and so on. He wrote:

> In the individual's mental life someone else is invariably involved, as a model, as an object, as a helper, as an opponent: and so from the very first individual psychology, in this extended but entirely justifiable sense of the words, is at the same time social psychology as well. (Freud, 1921, p. 69)

Freud's "phylogenetic fantasy" was originally described in his *Totem and Taboo* (Freud, 1913). He postulated an historical event that has gone into the mythology of most tribes, the murder of the tribal chief, the king, with an ensuing brotherhood banded together out of guilt. This then became a character trait increasingly installed into the nature of the human being according to the Lamarckian principle of the inheritance of acquired characteristics. It resurfaces not just as a common myth, but as the actual lived relations in groups. Freud clearly distinguished two libidinal bonds in a group which derived from early family experience and phantasy: (a) a rivalry towards the leader, and (b) a guilt-ridden equality amongst the members. These are the complex double bonds that are likely to be found in groups that resemble the family—relations with the leader/father, and relations amongst the members/siblings. So much for Freud's speculations.

## The part-object group

Bion, using his empirical observations, saw a group in different psychoanalytic terms. Klein's discovery of the primitive mechanisms allowed him to reinterpret the basic assumptions and group dynamics in more primitive terms:

> It will be seen from this description that the basic assumptions now emerge as formations secondary to an extremely early primal scene worked out on a level of part objects, and associated with psychotic anxiety and mechanisms of splitting and projective identification. (Bion, 1961, p. 165)

These intra-group mechanisms render the individuals anonymous, and the group indifferent to them as individuals. He goes on to say,

> … the basic assumptions appear to be the source of emotional drives to aims far different either from the overt task of the group or even from the tasks that would appear to be appropriate to Freud's view of the group as based on the family group. (Bion, 1961, p. 189)

Bion is hypothesizing aims that contrast with those connected with oedipal conflicts and anxieties. Explicitly he is referring to the aim of defending against psychotic anxiety, not with repression, but with the primitive defenses of splitting, projection, and projective identification. These defenses are problematic. They defend against the psychotic anxiety, but they also provoke it. Psychotic anxiety in Klein's terms is the fear the ego has of disintegration, fragmentation, and ultimately of annihilation. That dismantling of the ego is exactly what also happens as a *result* of splitting, projection, and projective identification. This is the dilemma of the ego—that in some people, in some situations, it may only have defenses against annihilation that actually enhance its annihilation.

In that situation, the ego is extremely dependent on an external object that can represent the coherence of the ego, the containment of the anxiety or annihilation and death, and the maintenance of sophisticated mental functioning. The problem for the group is that the individual is no longer properly able to feel in existence, and comes to feel as if he were detached or split-off from the group. And often, in the reality of group functioning, individuals appear to play single functions—the destructive one, the guilty one, the lightening conductor that defuses everything, and so on, including Bion's claim to hold the rational work-oriented role. Continuing:

> But approached from the angle of psychotic anxiety associated with phantasies of primitive part-object relationships, described by Melanie Klein and her co-workers, the basic-assumption phenomena appear far more to have the characteristics of defensive reactions to psychotic anxiety, and to be not so much at variance with Freud's views as supplementary to them. In my view, it is necessary to work through both the stresses that appertain

> to family patterns and the still more primitive anxieties of part-object relationships. In fact I consider the latter to contain the ultimate sources of all group behaviour. (Bion, 1961, p. 189)

Bion is categorical that, despite an attempt to acknowledge Freud's view of the groups as family relations, psychotic anxiety and primitive defenses are the "ultimate source" of all the behaviour in groups and of groups. At this point his loyalty to Klein is total.

The version of groups as psychotic experiences of the mind is one in which each member performs a function (in the group) relatively isolated from the functions that others perform. This dismembered quality of the group has more lately been developed by others, especially in the dynamics of large groups; for instance Turquet (1975) and his exploration of the existential problems of self, or Hopper (2003) and his notion of "massification."

## Group therapy as containing

Back in the 1960s, whilst President of the British Psychoanalytical Society (1962–1965), Bion seems to have been interested in the group behavior of the Society itself, and he spent the rest of his life interested in (probably concerned with) how people in general communicate to each other their experiences and knowledge. He turned in the 1960s to consider thinking, learning, and communicating one's knowledge. One trial he made was to invent a mathematical notation for experiences, the grid (Bion, 1963), intended to enable debate across the psychoanalytical schools of conceptual thought. It was not successful.

Bion's "psychotic", part-object model of groups leads to a particular understanding of group cultures. Stemming from his later work with psychotics, in particular his idea of their attacks on linking (Bion, 1959), it was the capacity for people to link together in social or interpersonal interaction that led to the theory of alpha function and of containing (Bion, 1962). The key passage from which Bion takes off is:

> The analytic situation built up in my mind a sense of witnessing an extremely early scene. I felt that the patient had experienced in infancy a mother who dutifully responded to the infant's emotional displays. The dutiful response had in it an element of impatient "I don't know what's the matter with the child." My deduction was that in order to understand what the child wanted the mother should have treated the infant's cry as more than a demand for her presence. From the infant's point of view she should have taken into her, and thus experienced, the fear that the child was dying. It was this fear that the child could not contain. He strove to split it off together with the part of the personality in which it lay and project it into the mother. An understanding mother is able to experience the feeling of dread, that this baby was striving to deal with by projective identification, and yet retain a balanced outlook. This patient had had to deal with a mother who could not tolerate experiencing such feelings and reacted either by denying them ingress, or alternatively by becoming a prey to the anxiety which resulted from introjection of the infant's feelings. (Bion, 1959, pp. 312–313)

In this model of infancy there are three possibilities; (a) when all goes well, (b) when mother denies the projected feelings ingress, or, in effect, blocks the projection, and (c) when mother does allow the projection but she becomes a prey to them and goes to pieces, losing her mental balance.

There are thus three different relations between container and contained, one fruitful, and two intolerable and defensive. It is important for the theory of containing that we include the cases where containing fails as well as when it succeeds. Our question then is whether these kinds of successful or failing containing relationships occur in a group, and what to do about the failure.

I shall now give very brief vignettes of therapeutic groups, which exhibit the three different states.

In the well-functioning relationship, both the container and the contents adapt and mould in response to each other, so that both are able to develop and "grow". This I call a *flexible* container.

The second process is a group culture where the container is so rigid that it does not allow "ingress", so there is no real expression of the contents, which are then simply molded to the containing space. That is to say, the individual must *rigidly* conform, so both he and the group bleach any meaning out of the intolerable feelings.

The third possibility is when the contents are so vibrant and explosive that the container is disabled or blown apart. I refer to this as the fragile or *fragmented* container.

I shall briefly exemplify each of three kinds of group culture; the flexible, the rigid, and the fragmented containers (more detailed clinical descriptions are given in Hinshelwood, 1994).

## Flexible containing

In this group, the atmosphere is not necessarily friendly. Clearly the participants grasped the importance of what was being described, and *felt* in ways which connected them to each other.

> Two men in a group were discussing a trivial detail about some maintenance work on a car that belonged to one of them. A described his difficulty with a rusty bolt. B talked about how he had once had the same problem and had solved it by hitting the bolt with a hammer; he seemed pleased with himself. Another, third man, C, gave a slight laugh and remarked on B's hint of pride. A looked startled and then a little angry, as he realized that he had given B the opportunity to be pleased with himself. He told B that it was no solution to hit the bolt with the hammer and explained why. Clearly he now wanted to put B down. Two women in the group were looking on with some fascination at this male sparring. One said "Men!" with mock exasperation. The other said her husband had returned from a football match recently with a bruise on his cheek which he had refused to talk about.

Experiences of rivalry and prowess were exchanged and accurately responded to by the members, each in their own way. The male rivalry and psychological bruising was not harmonious, respectful, or friendly, but members were reading each other accurately. It is this quality of being "in tune" that I am emphasising, each *feeling the tune* of the one who is speaking.

## A rigid group

In another group there is not the same kind of emotional meeting. Individuals follow on each other's comments in a quite different way—they absorb themselves in their own experience. They only tangentially connect, on a more cognitive level, without reading each other's feelings.

> In another group a woman, X, described an event in which her husband had had a row with her mother. Another woman, Y, waited just until this story had finished, and immediately asked for the dates of a forthcoming holiday break. They had been announced recently. The therapist pointed out how Y had cut across the first woman's story. She had also cut out her own memory of the dates. Y immediately turned to enquire of someone else. A man started to talk about his mother-in-law, seemingly following the first woman, though clearly absorbed only in his own tale—more to do with seeking out a mother for himself because in childhood he had spent long periods separated from his own mother.

In this culture, there is a considerable cutting across each other, or using another's communication to divert to one's own thoughts without linking into the other person's state of mind. The apparent link to the mother-in-law problem for X's wife, and for the last speaker, is not accurate. They are different stories with quite different affective tone. Despite plenty of talk, there is no emotional linking.

This rigid form of containing displays a property which may be significant. It is a strict holding together so that the individuals form an aggregate, or agglomeration. As Bion remarked about schizophrenic thought,

> thanks to this employment of projective identification, he cannot synthesize his objects: he can only agglomerate and compress them. Further, whether he feels he has had something put into him, or whether he feels he has introjected it, he feels the ingress as an assault, and a retaliation by the object for his violent intrusion into it. (Bion, 1956, p. 346)

The group it seems makes this same kind of inadequate integration, agglomerating its parts rather than truly integrating them. It is a desperate attempt perhaps to *be* a group. This process has a connection with the third culture of containing, the fragmented group. It is as if the rigid but still unintegrated aggregation is a reaction intended to avoid fragmentation/annihilation (as if rigidity were a group defense).

## The fragmented container

Finally, a group may simply not contain the impact of an individual's own state of mind. Then the group loses its coherence, structure, and function completely:

> A rather stiff woman, R, spoke briefly and emotionally about certain sexual practices her husband demanded of her, and which troubled her. She appeared unemotional when divulging

this. An embarrassed silence fell on the rest of the group. The therapist pointed out how the feeling was redistributed—the woman's feeling disappeared and the others felt her embarrassment. Then a man, S, started talking in a moral way about perversions in general and about the wicked ways of the world, and his own mournful misfortunes. His insensitivity to others and to their embarrassment provoked annoyance. Another man, T, said that S was dominating the group. A quarrel began. T became more and more loquacious with his list of complaints about S, the insensitive man. As this excited anger increased, S shrank into a hurt protest under the accusations. T, the angry accuser, suddenly jumped up out of his seat and stood over S, pointing his finger and jabbing at S as if firing each accusation from a gun. When he stopped his accusations, T was quite still for a moment. Then as if deeply embarrassed he abruptly left the room. There was silence and only a few innocuous comments were made before the end of the group.

There is a high level of emotional tension, anxiety, and anger in this session. It is passed around from one to another with an increasing force, ending with the scene at the end as if emotional bullets were being fired into the insensitive man. The unresponsiveness led to more and more powerful emotions being expressed by T as his violence increased. This was beyond the capacity of the group to contain. The character of the containing vessel, the group, became more and more helpless.

## *The invariant in groups*

Bion's later phases of development can elaborate this kind of group agglomeration. In the early 1960s, his search for a means of abstract communication amongst psychoanalysts took him to consider the mathematical abstracts used by natural scientists, especially physicists. The failure of the grid as a usable abstracting device led him further, and by 1965, he had discovered the mathematics of transformations.

His book *Transformations* (Bion, 1965) applied some of this mathematical theory to psychoanalysis. Central to the mathematical theory is the idea that something perceived from different angles looks different, like a circle that can appear as an ellipse. Yet something remains similar in the two perceptions. Mathematically what remains the same is called an "invariant".

The idea of an "invariant" appears to be a potential solution to the differences between psychoanalysts' varying perceptions of their patients. Indeed, Bion also considered the different perspectives of analyst and patient, or patient and relative, and so on. The important element is that there is an invariant that is common to each person's experience of the patient. And moreover, Bion seems to have recognized in the idea of an invariant something that is over and above (or maybe inside) mere sensory perception. This possibly took him back to an early interest in Bergson (Torres, 2013). Bergson had described his own method as "intuition", which went beyond mere perception and could gain access to the thing-in-itself (*Ding an sich*). This was a direct challenge to Kant who claimed we are all limited to merely a perspective on things. In *Transformations*, Bion first starts to use the term "intuition", and also, to emphasise this new form of knowledge, he talked of moving from K (knowledge from sense impressions and rational thought) to O (a direct intuitive knowledge of a thing in itself).

If this applied to the difference in psychoanalytic perspectives, then a patient described from two points of view will have some invariant features. These invariants Bion could begin to think of as something beyond the perspective of a single point of view. It is like the parable of the six blind men and the elephant—each depends on touch, one thinking he is touching a tree, one a serpent, one a wall, etc., etc. Whatever the partial appreciation, there is still a whole elephant. Bion appears to have been inspired to think that this whole could be the elusive "thing in itself". This put Bion onto a whole new track in which he explored intuition as a method to go beyond separate psychoanalytic perspectives.

For the rest of his life he explored what O might mean—the direct intuitive awareness of the essential invariance that is beyond perspectives. Much of this exploration concerns the "internal group" within a person's mind (Menzies Lyth, 1981), an exploration that formed the major aim of the three novellas, the three parts of *A Memoir of the Future* (Bion, 1975, 1977, 1979). The interaction between the state of the internal objects and the state of the social group of which the person is a part, had been a feature of the application of psychoanalytic ideas to organisations (e.g., Jaques, 1953, 1955; and see Hinshelwood, 1987).

But how does this affect therapeutic work in groups?

There is an important consequence arising from Bion's newly found perspectivism when we apply it to the "psychosis" view of groups. If a group comes to represent, in part, the split-up functions of a mind, then can we regard this as a set of individual points of view around the group? This is a complex phenomenon to investigate. In abstract terms, he considered the possibility of considering something with different functions of the mind. Somewhat eccentrically, he used the term "common sense" to cover this kind of event, when different senses collaborate to build a more complete picture of whatever is sensed (Bion, 1963), like the combination of the blind men discovering an elephant. It is less eccentric when applied to groups if the parts of the group mind come together in a more integrated way to create a group activity to which all contribute, engaging in something like psychic teamwork.

If that is a useful extension of Bion's "psychosis" idea of a group, then we need to make examination of the kind of linking between individual part-minds in a group. They need to link in such a way as to conform to the idea of common sense that is to be some alternative experiencing of some common invariant. In the examples I have given, the invariant is something at an experiential level, rather than cognitive and rational; more specifically the first group, the flexible one, showed a coming together of group members in an emotionally integrated arrangement.

The other two groups, even the one rigidly sticking together, demonstrated the aggregation of parts, not integrated but observing an awareness of others with whom they linked at the most shallow level. It was so shallow that they could be regarded as disengaged from each other, except that they clung together. It seems to me that this phenomenon of sticking together resonates with various other psychoanalytic and object relations notions, including Bick's idea of the skin and its substitution in secondary skin phenomena (Bick 1968; Briggs, 2002; also consider Anzieu's notion of the group envelope as a kind of group skin—Anzieu, 1990).

Implicit here is the understanding of the specific kind of anxiety in groups. Klein's (Bion's) designation of it as "psychotic" anxiety is important. The rigid clinging is a part, it would seem, of a constant invariant in groups, the anxiety about disintegration—not an oedipal anxiety, but an anxiety about survival. Groups and organisations are notorious for ensuring continuous existence even when their function and task has been superseded by others. It is the concluding hypothesis of this chapter that the invariant in groups is the problem of survival versus fragmentation and annihilation. The antidote to this fate, and the anxiety about the fate, is twofold. One is to form a culture of rigidly clinging to the group and other members, as in the second example of group culture, the rigid group. The other strategy is to institute a different culture, one based on more genuinely integrated sets of functions, as demonstrated in the first group vignette.

## Conclusion

Extending Bion's later views on invariants to the linking phenomena within groups, points to a specific focus for group therapy. It needs attention to group cultures and the characteristic linking that is dominant at any one moment. In a particular group, we pay attention to the commonality—shallow or deep, integrated or aggregated.

There has always been a debate within group therapy about making interpretations of the individual's dynamics, or interpreting the group dynamics of the group as a whole. Perhaps it is not an either-or choice. Rather one could focus on how well the individuals are knit together, each contributing a specific function, that overall creates an integrated "common sense", a set of links that makes the whole more than the sum of the parts. Or, conversely, how the individuals manage to subvert such unconscious teamwork.

It would seem appropriate to take into account the nature of the anxiety that besets people in groups. This I have described, following Bion's later interest in transformations, caesuras, and catastrophic change, as an invariant, which affects all the individuals in common. It is not a neutral experience, but a frightening one of going out of existence in a process of dispersal. As Klein much earlier has noted, the response to such an anxiety of annihilation, as she called it, was to resort to mechanisms of splitting and projection which enhance the experience (and then the fear) of going to pieces.

Bion drew on a whole series of ideas from various sources and at different times (Torres & Hinshelwood, 2013) in ambitious attempts to solve a range of problems—some no doubt his personal ones, but explicitly the problems of psychoanalytic knowledge and debate. His proclivity for drawing on new ideas inevitably left him short of time and opportunity to develop the fertile new lines of thought. In this chapter I have tried to extend one area of Bion's thinking, his interest in group psychology. I have taken the step of emphasizing his notion of the invariant between different perspectives—that which goes beyond sensuous experience and rational thought. It reveals itself in the intuitions about the reach and depth of integration—or of fragmentation.

## Notes

1. He modified the text somewhat when it was published as the final chapter in his *Experiences in Groups*, in 1961.
2. After his first clinical papers on the psychoanalysis of schizophrenic patients, in the mid-1950s, he concentrated on a conceptual model, or rather, conceptual models in the plural: his theory

of thinking and linking, and then containing, as well as his epistemological work on the communication between analysts, the notation of the grid, on transformation and invariants, and ultimately his interest in intuition as opposed to sensory perceptions. See also Hinshelwood (2013) to consider what can be developed today.

## References

Anzieu, D. (1990). *A Skin for Thought*. London: Karnac.
Bick, E. (1968). The experience of the skin in early object relations. *International Journal of Psychoanalysis*, 49: 484–486.
Bion, W. R. (1946). The leaderless group project. *Bulletin of the Menninger Clinic*, 10: 77–81.
Bion, W. R. (1952). Group dynamics: a review. *International Journal of Psychoanalysis*, 33: 235–247. Revised 1955. In: M. Klein, P. Heimann & R. Money-Kyrle (1955) (Eds.), *New Directions in Psychoanalysis*. And 1961. In: Bion, W. R. (1959), *Experiences in Groups*. London: Tavistock.
Bion, W. R. (1956). Development of schizophrenic thought. *International Journal of Psychoanalysis*, 37: 344–346.
Bion, W. R. (1959). Attacks on linking. *International Journal of Psychoanalysis*, 40: 308–315.
Bion, W. R. (1961). *Experiences in Groups and Other Papers*. London: Routledge.
Bion, W. R. (1962). *Learning from Experience*. London: Heinemann.
Bion, W. R. (1963). *Elements of Psycho-Analysis*. London: Heinemann.
Bion, W. R. (1965). *Transformations*. London: Tavistock.
Bion, W. R. (1975). *A Memoir of the Future, Book One: The Dream*. Rio de Janeiro: Imago.
Bion, W. R. (1977). *A Memoir of the Future, Book Two: The Past Presented*. Rio de Janeiro: Imago.
Bion, W. R. (1979). *A Memoir of the Future, Book Three: The Dawn of Oblivion*. Rio de Janeiro: Imago.
Bion, W. R., & Rickman, J. (1943). Intra-group tensions in therapy. In: W. R. Bion (1961), *Experiences in Groups and Other Papers* (pp. 11–26). London: Routledge, 1961.
Briggs, A. (Ed.) (2002). *Surviving Space: Papers on Infant Observation*. London: Karnac.
Dicks, H. V. (1970). *Fifty Years of the Tavistock Clinic*. London: Tavistock.
Freud, S. (1913). Totem and Taboo. *S. E.*, 13: 1–161. London: Hogarth.
Freud, S. (1921). Group Psychology and the Analysis of the Ego. *S. E.*, 18: 65–144. London: Hogarth.
Hinshelwood, R. D. (1987). *What Happens in Groups: Psychoanalysis, the Individual and the Community*. London: Free Association.
Hinshelwood, R. D. (1994). Attacks on the reflective space. In: V. Shermer & M. Pines (Eds.), *Ring of Fire: Containing Primitive Emotional States* (pp. 86–106). London: Routledge.
Hinshelwood, R. D. (1999). How Foulkesian was Bion? *Group Analysis*, 32: 469–488.
Hinshelwood, R. D. (2013). Bion's nomadic journey. In: N. Torres & R. D. Hinshelwood, (Eds.), *Bion's Sources: The Shaping of his Paradigms*. London: Routledge.
Hopper, E. (2003). *Traumatic Experience in the Unconscious Life of Groups: The Fourth Basic Assumption: Incohesion: Aggregation/Massification or (ba) I: A/M*. London: Jessica Kingsley.
Jaques, E. (1953). On the dynamics of social structure: a contribution to the psycho-analytical study of social phenomena deriving from the views of Melanie Klein. *Human Relations*, 6: 3–24.
Jaques, E. (1955). Social systems as a defence against persecutory and depressive anxiety. In: M. Klein, P. Heimann & R. Money-Kyrle (Eds.), *New Directions in Psycho-Analysis* (pp. 478–498). London: Tavistock.
Klein, M. (1946). Notes on some schizoid mechanisms. *International Journal of Psychoanalysis*, 27: 99–110.

Lipgar, R. M., & Pines, M. (Eds.) (2003). *Building on Bion: Roots, Origins and Context of Bion's Contributions to Theory and Practice.* London: Jessica Kingsley.

Main, T. (1975). Some psychodynamics of large groups. In: L. Kreeger (Ed.), *The Large Group* (pp. 57–86). London: Constable.

Meltzer, D. (1981). Memorial meeting for Dr. Wilfred Bion. *International Review of Psychoanalysis, 8*: 3–14.

Menzies Lyth, I. E. P. (1981). Bion's contribution to thinking about groups. In: J. S. Grotstein (Ed.), *Do I Dare Disturb the Universe?* Beverley Hills: Caesura Press.

Pines, M. (Ed.) (2000). *Bion and Group Psychotherapy.* London: Jessica Kingsley.

Sanfuentes, M. (2003). Group dynamics: a review. In: M. Pines & R. Lipgar (Eds.), *Building on Bion: Roots* (pp. 118–131). London: Jessica Kingsley.

Suttie, I. (1924). The development and evolution of mind: biological v. psychosocial interpretations of the ontophylogenetic parallelism. *Journal of Neurology and Psychopathology, 5*: 133–145.

Torres, N. (2013). Intuition and ultimate reality: Bion's implicit use of Bergson's and Whitehead's notions. In: N. Torres & R. D. Hinshelwood (Eds.), *Bion's Sources: The Shaping of his Paradigms.* London: Routledge.

Torres, N., & Hinshelwood, R. D. (Eds.) (2013). *Bion's Sources: The Shaping of his Paradigms.* London: Routledge.

Trist, E., & Murray, H. (Eds.) (1990). *The Social Engagement of Social Science, Volume 1.* London: Free Association.

Trotter, W. (1916). *Instincts of the Herd in Peace and War.* London: Unwin.

Turquet, P. (1975). Threats to identity in the large group. In: L. Kreeger (Ed.), *The Large Group* (pp. 878–144). London: Constable.

Vonofakos, D. & Hinshelwood, R. D. (2012). Wilfred Bion's Letters to John Rickman (1939–1951). *Psychoanalysis and History, 14*: 53–94.

CHAPTER THIRTY-TWO

# Bion and the large group

H. Shmuel Erlich

In the historical timeline of psychoanalytic exploration of groups and social phenomena, the large group (LG) actually comes before the small group (SG). Freud's seminal and ground breaking work, "Group psychology and the analysis of the ego" (1921) is more correctly translated as "Mass psychology and the analysis of the ego". In this work Freud explores the phenomena of large, unruly, and regressive groups, expanding his earlier effort to locate the origins of oedipal rivalry and guilt in the myth (or inspired construction) of the prehistoric primal horde (1913). Yet his work on the psychology of the "mass" or the "mob" pertains as well to highly structured and well-organized groups, such as the Church and the Army. With this extension Freud implicitly links the two polarities that are so representative of the phenomenology of the LG: On one hand, "the mass", an unstructured and regressive entity, and on the other, an organized and institutionally collaborative large number of people who function as a productive and goal-oriented work group. Later on, in "Moses and Monotheism" (1939), Freud amplifies another major theme in the creation and dynamics of the LG, which consists of leadership and followership: he attributes the formation of groups to the emergence of a leader who replaces or usurps the individuals' ego-ideals with his own. The leader thus creates the group of followers and imbues it with his ideas, goals, and ethics.

Already present in Freud's pioneering work are thus the germinal issues and questions that pertain to the large group: What are the similarities and differences between a structured and an unstructured (or spontaneous) large group? When we speak of LG, do we have in mind an organization or an institution, a political party or movement, or a haphazardly formed crowd, momentarily united in some encompassing regressive process? What are the forces operating within such large group entities? Are the pertinent dynamics those of leadership and followership, which are relatively easily identifiable, or are there unique dynamics that characterize large groups? Is the LG necessarily regressive or explosive in nature, or can it also be highly regimented and structured?

Obviously these are issues of definition quite familiar to social psychologists. I do not intend to go into such definitions and categorizations. For the purpose of the illustrations I have in mind and the exploration of their links with Bion's work, I propose two rather simple characterizations: a large group is one in which the number of people simultaneously present exceeds what can be easily encompassed or taken in face-to-face; and while it may have certain external boundaries, it manifests little or no internal structure.

Bion's (1961) contributions to the understanding of and work with group processes developed out of his and his colleagues work with small, face-to-face groups (initially called therapeutic groups) and not with large groups. It is therefore interesting to note the way in which his observations and methodological stance have permeated the work with large groups. At the same time, additional lines of theoretical input have been interwoven with Bion's, resulting in what may be rather loosely described as the currently influential methodology of convening and working with large groups.

If I am allowed a gross oversimplification, I would suggest that Bion's legacy in this area finds expression in the adoption of two major guiding principles: First, that the phenomena to be observed is that of the group-as-a-whole (also referred to as the group mind), shifting the focus away from individual group members and their intrapsychic dynamics or clinical issues. Second, the stance of the group "taker" is not one of leader, authority, or therapist, but of a consultant, a social anthropologist, or participant-observer. This stance has been conceptualized as being situated on the group's boundary, thus being both in it and out of it at the same time. This stance has also been described as associated with taking the leadership role (Miller & Rice, 1967), running the risk of being identified and labeled as the enemy, with the attending consequences (Erlich, 1997), and as analogous to the position of the psychoanalyst (Erlich, 2003a).

A number of conceptualizations of the LG are available in both theory and practice, representing increasingly sweeping and encompassing dimensions (Lipgar & Pines, 2003). The most typical, perhaps somewhat basic, LG is probably the one which has become a standard component of Tavistock group relations conferences: Here it includes the entire membership (typically varying between thirty and eighty) with two to four consultants. Its place and frequency within the conference roughly parallels that of the small groups. In keeping with the primary task of group relations conferences, which usually is to provide opportunities to learn about group and organizational processes through their experience within the conference institution, both the LG and the SG are study groups, with the task of learning about the group process as it unfolds. In this model of group relations conferences the LG serves as a variant group format, which, due mainly to its overwhelming size, pulls in the direction of particular dynamics, such as splitting and splintering, struggling against losing one's identity, defensively becoming a singleton or being merged with the mass (Turquet, 1975). The two basic assumptions that have emerged subsequent to the three originally described by Bion (FF, P and D)[1]—that is, oneness (Turquet, 1974) and me-ness (Lawrence, Bain, & Gould, 1996)—are very much related to these experiences in the LG. Interpretations and interventions by the consultants are directed at such experiences and processes and emergent themes related to authority and leadership.

Other themes may of course emerge and be addressed as well, such as current events and the social, political, and historical antecedent issues represented by the membership. It is important to emphasize, however, that the primary task is still the study and learning about LG processes as such through one's own immediate experience.

There are, however, additional variants of LG of which the widest common denominator is that they do not take place within the typical GR conference. Two different modes can be distinguished in this connection: First, the LG takes place within an atypical GR conference that is an adaptation of the usual GR format. Second, the LG is a free-standing event, perhaps taking place within a larger meeting or conference, which however is not a GR setting. In what follows I will illustrate both of these variations.

My first example comes from the series of conferences that received the title: "The Nazareth Conferences", since they first took place in the city of Nazareth in Israel. The full title of these conferences was: "Germans and Israelis—The past in the present" (Erlich, Erlich-Ginor & Beland, 2009a). These conferences addressed the residues of the Holocaust within Germans and Israeli Jews, in order to investigate how these residues affected the personal and professional lives and functioning of either group. The underlying assumption was that each group suffered from the traumatic effects of the Holocaust, whether as victims, perpetrators, by-standers, or their offspring, and that each group needed the presence of the other in order to work on its own traumatic residues.

The stages leading up to these conferences involved the realization as well as the determination that the group relations approach and methodology would provide the most suitable way to go about such a meeting. With the help of Eric Miller of the Tavistock Institute, one of the leading authorities on GR methodology and thinking, a specially adapted design evolved. Unlike the usual GR conference, this design recognized and addressed the *a priori* existence of two distinctly identified nationality groups within the conference.

The enormous anxiety generated by the fantasies about this conference was reflected in two major deviations from the usual GR design. One of them was that, at least initially, the conference aimed exclusively at psychoanalysts on both sides. The governing idea was that psychoanalysts, by virtue of their training and professional attitude, would be able to contain and work with the turbulent feelings that were anticipated. Interestingly, the conference that was based on this assumption and restrictive definition of membership never took place. The conference that actually took place the following year widened the scope of invited membership, and this dynamic of expanding membership has continued to evolve in the subsequent conferences (Erlich, Erlich-Ginor & Beland, 2009a).

Undoubtedly, the attempt to restrict the membership to a single professional category stemmed from the tremendous anxiety that characterized the early stages of the planning and evolution of the conference. There was, however, another manifestation of the anxiety associated with the anticipated encounter of Germans and Israeli Jews: the design of the conference left out completely the customary LG. The rational for this deviation from the usual GR model was stated quite openly: it was the fear that the LG, by its very regressive pull, would generate such an enormous emotional upheaval that it might not be possible to contain and work with it. In place of the LG, a number of plenaries were scheduled, in which all staff and members participated. The structure of a plenary, in which staff and members are seated in two distinct configurations, is naturally much more controlled and contained. It was quite evident, however, that this containment was also to an extent suppressive and difficult to work with.

The paradoxical point I wish to stress is the anxiety associated with and generated by the LG. It was so overwhelming that even one as experienced as Eric Miller was loathe to experiment with it in a setting that promised (and often was) quite volatile, despite the fact that on the whole the membership consisted of highly trained and disciplined people. This defensive exclusion undoubtedly bears testimony to the threats inherent in the LG or projected on it, even within the relatively contained and controlled structure of a GR design. It also needs to be pointed out that in the course of time, after the first three conferences, and as staff grew more experienced with this conference design and dynamics, the LG was reintroduced into the conference. As is often the case with fantasies, the actual LG experience, though intense and difficult at times, was much more workable and beneficial than anticipated. The most recent conference (2012) in this series, which addressed the theme of "European perpetrators and victims—then and now", contained a highly variegated membership, of east and west Europeans and others, of varied professional backgrounds, and a LG in which victimhood became the coveted object, with competition for what might be termed the recognition and acknowledgment of having the greatest amount of suffering and victimization. While the LG was at times very emotional and at others produced dreams and fantasies, it was well contained, perhaps even too much so.

My second example comes from a couple of LGs that took place as free-standing events, that is, not within a GR conference. In both these cases the LG took place within the frame of the biannual congress of the International Psychoanalytic Association (IPA). The IPA Congress is devoted to scientific presentations, discussion, and exchange, and has never included an experiential event within its frame. The first time this took place was in the Berlin Congress in 2007. It was introduced in response to the invitation and wishes of the congress organizing committee, who felt strongly that the return of an IPA Congress to Berlin for the first time since World War Two was fraught with significance and powerful feelings, for which they wanted to provide an outlet as well as a container. There were actually a great many presentations that addressed emotional subjects related to the Holocaust, the war, and its aftermath. Yet the only event which had no clinical or intellectual contents and provided a container for the direct expression of thoughts and feelings was the LG, which we titled: "Being in Berlin" (Erlich, Erlich-Ginor & Beland, 2009b).

The Berlin LG had a great impact and was attended by hundreds of people. Many described it afterwards as "the heart" of the congress, and there was great interest in and much gratitude for it. Yet it was not without problems: the authorization of the three consultants to the event was never quite clear. The physical venue and boundaries of the group repeatedly came under attack and shifted daily. The shortage of time (three daily sessions lasting sixty minutes each) did not allow for working through or adequate closure. Some of these problems were inherent and would come up again in the next example. Yet there is no doubt that for the many people who participated in it, it was a most meaningful experience.

The second example is of a LG that took place several years later and once again within the frame of an IPA Congress, this time in Prague (2013). The theme of the congress was "Facing the pain", and the LG event was named in relation to that: "The pain of being and becoming an analyst—here, there and everywhere". Unlike the Berlin LG it was not solicited by the organizers but rather suggested by the prospective consultants. In spite of the learning that has accrued from the Berlin event, once again it was surrounded by many organizational difficulties. These again had to do with the fact that an IPA Congress is structured in ways that are suitable for scientific presentations and discussions, such as lectures and panels, but is not geared to an experiential event such as a LG. Indeed, as I said, Berlin was the first time such an event was part of the congress program. Yet once again, many attended the event on each of the three days it took place, in spite of the competition by so many other simultaneous events, the numbers reaching one hundred participants and more.

Of the many themes that came up in the Prague LG I want to single out one that had to do with the use of the microphone. The organizers provided amplification equipment and wireless microphones, in order to enable participants to be heard, since the lecture hall in which the group took place was large. The use of the microphone, and the dynamics created by its being passed around and asked for by speakers, created and imposed a kind of structure and orderliness, as people would politely wait for their turn and the microphone to be handed over. At some point, a movement arose within the membership as a rebellion against this "artificial" structuralizing of the LG. It seemed as if people longed for a touch of disorder, perhaps even some chaos that might allow for greater intimacy and immediacy of experience, even if this would result in other difficulties. In association with the congress title, it may be regarded as an expression of the pain of feeling estranged and isolated by modern technical advances and gadgets and longing for a more direct, perhaps even a more primitive or primal, experience which the LG might provide.

## Discussion

The examples I cited cover a range of different LG applications in different settings. There are certainly more such settings that could be described, since LGs are often part of contemporary meetings of various sorts, especially those dealing with group and organizational processes. We may note that the interest in and focus on the LG has grown considerably in recent decades. Yet the theoretical understanding of the LG seems to have lagged behind its practical applications. What may we say that we have learned about LG process and implementation? How does this understanding relate to Bion's and others' legacies?

Bion's perspective of the group-as-a-whole, especially as it relates to the group's leaders or facilitators, that is, the group's transference to whoever is perceived to be in a leadership role, has been enormously seminal in working with the LG. It is at times uncanny to observe the group, beyond individuals' inputs, as if it is some sort of huge, primeval, even prehistoric creature, moving about. What comes to mind is the vision of a dinosaur roaming through ancient landscapes and jungle vegetation, on the lookout for prey and food, yet at the same time watchful and suspiciously on guard against dangerous predators. Its movement may be slow, deliberate, even monotonous and boring, until suddenly a mad rush begins and the great mass moves swiftly in some unforeseen direction with a speed that leaves one breathless. The consultant or facilitator is the small figure riding on top of this creature, risking falling off, becoming disoriented, and falling prey to its voracious appetite. Lacking any bridle, there is no way in which he or she may be capable of guiding the beast in some direction. The consultant is therefore in the observer's position, noting and communicating the direction the movement has taken, the speed of advance, the dangers that are being avoided, and the hopes for a solution. Hopefully he communicates these insights in a language understandable and meaningful to the beast. If we think not of a consultant but a real leader, his challenge is precisely the ability to bridle the beast, to guide and manipulate it in the direction he wishes. It is obvious that this works much better in authoritarian settings and totalitarian regimes and far less well in egalitarian and democratic ones. Yet even democracies are never immune from being thus manipulated, because when a democracy yields to becoming a LG, it quickly becomes this prehistorical dinosaur.

Perhaps the image invoked can supply an answer to why the LG is so anxiety provoking. Bion's insights into unconscious group processes, in terms of the basic assumptions he named and described, operate in the LG as well as in the SG. But they are not enough, nor can they be sufficiently adequate for the LG. Basic assumption groups are the underlying, mostly unconscious fabric, which impedes the group's assumption of its goal as a work group. This is true of the SG, but cannot be applied to the LG. The LG, by definition, can never really become a work group, unless two conditions are met: the group submits itself to a leader who is capable of dominating and guiding it in the direction he stands for; and the group undergoes substantial internal restructuring, typically of some hierarchical order. Examples of the former abound in history and permeate the present. The latter may be exemplified by any large organization, and best fits the army, the church, and even the university. All of these huge organizations can only function if the masses of people in them are fairly rigidly organized within a hierarchical structure. Only under such conditions can a LG function as a work group in which the abundance of energies may be channeled toward a unified and specific goal.

Granted that the LG, left unstructured and with no organization imposed on it, can become a work group only very briefly and fleetingly, if at all, it still needs to be explicated why it is so anxiety provoking. In any LG there may be some who speak, seize a momentary leadership position, only in order to be shot down and replaced by others. But there are also many who remain in some way immobilized, who never find their way in, so to speak, and remain on the group's periphery (physically as well as mentally), who are overwhelmed and dumbfounded by what is going on, and emerge from the experience bewildered and confused. While this voiceless experience may be more difficult to contain and deal with, it may nevertheless be more in tune with the underlying chaos and senselessness of the LG than those who assume a more participant and "knowing" position. Often this sort of knowledge is more reminiscent of Bion's –K than of K. The experience of speechlessness represents the primitive aspects of the herd, of being carried along passively, without any effective control of one's direction and destiny.

This experience of losing control over one's destiny is deeply frightening. It is particularly frightening to modern man because of his illusion of having considerable control and even choice over oneself. Indeed, as Turquet (1975) pointed out, the only defense against the merger with the group and the loss of one's identity is to remain outside it and become a singleton. Difficult as that may be under certain circumstances, it also pretends to obviate the LG phenomenon and hence the anxiety it generates. It seems to me that as modern man moves towards greater individuation and self-expression, the LG experience becomes increasingly dangerous and anxiety provoking. As one consequence, there is a growing need and attempt to deny it and refrain from it. At the same time, however, it becomes clearer how this trend towards individuation, not to say narcissistic encapsulation, becomes increasingly coupled with feeling isolated, detached, and not-belonging. Paradoxically, this oscillation leads back to re-finding and losing oneself in some mass movement.

Bion described the tragic dimension of human existence as the conflict between two inherent and fundamental aspects of the human being: that of being a herd animal which can fully exist only within a matrix with others; and that of possessing an individual subjectivity that only knows itself and seeks to follow its own individual course. While this is true of man's existence in any size group, this conflict is nowhere as poignantly met and experienced as in the large group. The example described above of the conflict around the use of the microphone illustrates both sides of this conflict: on one hand, the wish to be heard clearly and dominantly, and in some way asserting one's individuality of thinking and reflection, that may be achieved by means of structure and social rules; and on the other hand, the wish for immediacy of belonging, wishing to go beyond the flimsiness of social structures and technical means of "closeness" (being better heard) that actually promote distancing.

We may thus identify two sources for the anxiety generated by the LG. The first is the one ordinarily associated with it, namely the fear of regression, of the elemental intensity of affects and drives, and of the potential destructiveness inherent in the unruly mass. This source is closer to Freud's description of the psychology of the mass. It conjures up the specter of the id with its seething cauldron of untamed sexual and destructive urges and drives. The relatively unstructured setting, together with the overwhelming numbers, threatens with loss of control, regression, and the emergence of all that is primitive, repressed, and contained by the social veneer of civilized society. It is this anxiety that ruled the LG out of the early design of the German-Israeli encounter. The fear in that case was that a LG setting would be unable to contain and control the regressive eruption of hate, violence, retribution, and murderous fantasies, making it virtually impossible to do any work. This example also demonstrates how the anxiety associated with the LG actually contaminated the thinking and the design of the conference, creating collusion aimed at leaving out the difficult feelings and fantasies that made the encounter so necessary. Clearly, in this instance all the fears of the encounter became focused on the LG. Perhaps this was rightly so, since one way of regarding the Holocaust is to see it as a gigantic LG happening, in which one LG fears and hates another and sets out to annihilate it. The fear of the encounter was perhaps the fear of the repetition of this calamity associated with the LG.

The second source of anxiety is quite different and is more related to Bion's notion of the human animal. The conflict Bion sees, as was mentioned, is between the individual subject's subjectivity, which pulls him in the direction of separateness and autonomy, and his herd instinct, which pulls him towards losing himself in the multitude, merging and finding shelter and security within the larger social entity. Bion regards this conflict as inherent to the protomental level of human existence, which in turn gives rise to the basic assumptions group fantasies and behaviors.

I would like to add a further dimension to this conflict. My work on the two modalities of experience, although inherent to the individual psyche, is pertinent to this level of group and social phenomena (Erlich, 2003b, 2013). Briefly stated, I hypothesize the universal presence of two different yet complementary experiential modalities, which simultaneously process raw sensation and perception into psychically available material. This is very reminiscent of Bion's statement regarding alpha and beta functions: he hypothesizes an alpha function whose task it is "to convert sense data into alpha elements and … provide the psyche with the material for dream thoughts … the capacity to wake up or go to sleep, to be conscious or unconscious …" (1967, p. 115). I suggest the existence of two transformational functions, rather than a single one. These two parallel modalities transform raw experience into psychic experience that can be recognized and mentalized. But the different nature of the transformational processes gives rise to different experiential end-products or contents. One modality is characterized by the separateness of subject and other (object), hence the experience is one of wishfulness, of desire for the object and the need for it in order to find satisfaction (as in drive wish and fulfillment). The other is characterized by the unity or fusion of subject and other (object), hence the experience cannot be one of wish (which implies the otherness or separateness of subject and object) but of fusion, merger, and oneness. It is the existential component of feeling alive and connected and part of something larger than the circumscribed and isolated self. There are further implications to this theoretical construction which I will not go into here.[2]

How is this related to the LG and the anxiety it produces? Bion's notion of the inherent duality of the human being, in terms of separateness and merger, is complementary to the two experiential modalities I described. While these modalities operate constantly and in all situations, the LG actualizes them and causes them to clash and conflict. The pull of the LG, often openly stated, is towards losing oneself in it, allowing the self to merge and fuse with the overwhelming quantity and energy the group offers. At times this merger is willingly accepted and provides an experience of peace and tranquility. At other times, however, it is experienced as a threat to one's individual existence, one's identity and capacity to think and perceive adequately and realistically.

The group is therefore simultaneously experienced as enormously seductive and threatening. The anxiety it engenders is that of the seductive pull and the simultaneous reticence evoked by the experience of the earliest maternal presence. It is an anxiety that touches on the very essence of what it is to be and feel alive, to be aroused and wanting, and yet also to be frightened and aversive to the overwhelming presence one cannot do without.

These conflicting experiences and contradictory movements in the LG are the source of upset, feeling ill at ease, not quite oneself, wishing strongly to join while simultaneously wanting to escape and be alleviated. The LG is thus feared in reality as well as in fantasy, and the two become hopelessly enmeshed.

The experience in many LGs may perhaps not divulge these deep-seated dynamic conflicts. The people present are well-spoken, well-meaning, and seriously engaged in making sense of what is happening. Yet often there is an overt attempt to render the presence of consultants into a management function, indicating the underlying anxiety born of the conflicts I described. The wish is thus clearly for a protective and containing agency that will introduce control and order and spare one the agonizing difficulty experienced, consciously or unconsciously, of being pulled in two directions and risking the loss of one's integrity.

There have been many other avenues to understanding what transpires in a given LG. For instance, depending on the nature and title of the specific setting or conference, there has been a trend toward political and/or social interpretation of what goes on. There may of course be great similarity and direct reference to some current event or political issue. Naturally, these possibilities have much appeal as well as direct implications and relevance. Yet it seems to me, analogously to such issues arising and being introduced in a psychoanalytic session, that they represent and express precisely consciously available concerns and dilemmas. The challenge is to relate these more conscious layers of experience to the deeper and more primitive ones. As always, this should not be broached and interpreted with any violence. At the same time, it would not serve the purpose of learning through one's experience in a LG if the consultants were seduced into remaining fixated at the level of current issues and events, as these may actually hide the deeper anxieties produced by being in a LG.

In conclusion, I have described some of the prevalent current uses of the LG and how these may be related to two major insights into LG processes, namely those of Freud and Bion. I have attempted to link the great anxiety commonly associated with and engendered by the LG with these seminal contributions and the somewhat different, yet complementary, directions they point in. I suggest that this anxiety stems from two sources: the frightening regressive potential of the LG on the one hand, and the powerful seductive pull it exercises on the other. The regressive aspect may be captured in terms of Freud's vision of the unconscious and its mighty influence. The seductive and threatening attraction is related to Bion's insight into the dual nature of man as individual and herd animal. I have extended this by introducing the two psychic modalities of transforming experience, which involve, simultaneously, separateness and fusion. The LG is the arena in which these processes come into existence most poignantly, as powerfully conflicting, diametrically opposed pulls and forces which the individual both craves and fears.

## Notes

1. FF = fight/flight; P = pairing; D = dependency.
2. For a fuller presentation see Erlich, 2003b. More references are to be found there.

## References

Bion, W. R. (1961). *Experiences in Groups*. London: Tavistock.
Bion, W. R. (1967). *Second Thoughts*. London: Karnac.
Erlich, H. S. (1997). On discourse with an enemy. In: E. R. Shapiro (Ed.), *The Inner World in the Outer World: Psychoanalytic Perspectives* (pp. 123–142). New Haven: Yale University Press.
Erlich, H. S. (2003a). Working at the frontier and the use of the Analyst. *International Journal of Psychoanalysis, 84*: 235–247.
Erlich, H. S. (2003b). Experience—What is it? *International Journal of Psychoanalysis, 84*: 1125–1147.
Erlich, H. S. (2013). *The Couch in the Marketplace: Psychoanalysis and Social Reality*. London: Karnac.
Erlich, H. S., Erlich-Ginor, M., & Beland, H. (2009a). *Fed with Tears—Poisoned with Milk: The Nazareth Group-Relations-Conferences: Germans and Israelis—The Past in the Present*. Gießen: Psychosozial Verlag.
Erlich, H. S., Erlich-Ginor, M., & Beland, H. (2009b). Being in Berlin: A Large Group experience in the Berlin Congress. *International Journal of Psychoanalysis, 90*: 809–825.
Freud, S. (1913). Totem and taboo. *S. E., 13*: 1–161. London: Hogarth.
Freud, S. (1921). Group psychology and the analysis of the ego. *S. E., 18*: 69–143. London: Hogarth.

Freud, S. (1939). Moses and monotheism: Three essays. *S. E., 23*: 7–137. London: Hogarth.
Lawrence, W. G., Bain, A., & Gould, L. (1996). The fifth basic assumption. *Free Associations, 6*: 28–56.
Lipgar, R. M., & Pines, M. (2003). *Building on Bion: Branches, Contemporary Developments and Applications of Bion's Contributions to Theory and Practice*. London: Jessica Kingsley.
Miller, E. J., & Rice, A. K. (1967). *Systems of Organization*. London: Tavistock.
Turquet, P. (1974). Leadership: The individual and the group. In: E. Gibbard, J. Hartman & R. Mann (Eds.), *The Analysis of Groups* (pp. 75–91). San Francisco: Jossey-Bass.
Turquet, P. M. (1975). Threats to identity in the large group. In: L. Kreeger (Ed.), *The Large Group: Dynamics and Therapy*. London: Constable.

# CHAPTER THIRTY-THREE

# The influence of Bion on my research*

*René Kaës*

## Introduction

I came into contact with Bion's thought somewhat belatedly, even though, when I began to take an interest in the problems of groups, trying to understand, with the help of psychoanalysis, how they functioned, Bion's work on groups had only just been published in France.

I was interested in three aspects of groups: first, I thought, as the research studies of that time led me to conclude, that it was necessary to consider the group as a whole in order to understand its specificity; second, that it was also indispensable to consider the group as an object of drive investments and representation, as Pontalis (1963) had proposed, and as a psychic structure within each one of us; and third, that it was important not to forget that it is a component element of social space and that this form and this elementary structure comprise a psychic determination in so far as it informs the psychic space of the group and that of the subjects who are its members. My project was complex and ambitious, nourished and sustained by my psychoanalytic experience, but also by my initial training and orientations of research.

At the end of the 1950s and at the beginning of the 1960s, at the time when Bion had brought some of his own work together into the volume *Experiences in Groups* (1961), after studying psychology and sociology, I worked on the social representations of the culture of French workers. I had chosen to take a group approach to the formation processes of social representations, and was interested in the relationship between these and individual representations. The focus of interest then switched towards the psychoanalytic approach to groups, the foundations of

---

*Translated by Andrew Weller.

which had just been outlined by J.-B. Pontalis (1963) and D. Anzieu (1966). My own analysis helped me to work on the more personal aspects of my interest in groups. Anzieu had also just founded, in 1962, the CEFFRAP[1]: so I joined them, finding in this emerging institution the atmosphere of team work and the stimulation from which my own research has benefited for half a century.

Even though it was Anzieu who took the initiative of having Bion's book translated into French by E. L. Herbert as *Recherches sur les petits groupes* (1965), Bion's ideas on groups were ignored, put to one side, or reduced to a few summary propositions for quite a long time.[2] This "ignorance" can be examined from several points of view, which I shall resume in broad outline, less in order to seek to justify it than to contribute some thoughts on the cultural context of the influence that a powerful body of thought can exert on another when it is in the process of constituting itself, particularly in another cultural space.

From my point of view, three main factors prevented Bion's work on groups, and the influence he had on French psychoanalysts interested in this form of practice, from being taken into consideration earlier. The first is of a cultural order and concerns not only Bion but also Winnicott, who was equally "discovered" late in France. The French psychoanalytic culture of rationality, the cult of Freudian orthodoxy, and the exclusive focus on the adult individual is at odds with the psychoanalytic culture of the English school, which is more empirical and open (not without conflicts) to an extension of psychoanalysis to the treatment of children, psychotic patients, and disorders of intersubjectivity.

The second factor is related to the conditions of emergence of the "question of the group" in the context of the tensions and splits which shook the French psychoanalytic movement in 1953, 1964, 1969, and 1980, causing certain orientations to break up into multiple psychoanalytic groups. These conflicts, and the use of splitting to resolve them, revealed certain dimensions of the functioning of psychoanalytic groups and institutions, which had already been operative since the origin of the psychoanalytic movement. This return of the non-elaborated repressed turned group psychoanalytic research and practice into instruments capable of revealing what still had to be excluded from the field of psychoanalysis by powerful defensive alliances. Those psychoanalysts who ventured into this domain were marginalized or worked in a sort of suspect clandestinity.

The third factor has its specific value, but is combined with those that I have just mentioned. I would describe it as a phenomenon of withdrawal that characterizes a group in its phase of discovery and creation. This process provides its members with the security of group belonging, supporting the process of self-appropriation of its object of research and fulfilling the illusory and foundational function of the found-created object. The history of discoveries, beginning with that of psychoanalysis, provides quite extensive evidence of this process. This factor may acquire a prevalent weight when, in the face of a "state of siege", the need to form an alliance against an enemy imposes itself or, more precisely, when a basic "fight-flight" assumption predominates.

The format of this chapter imposes limits on me concerning the description of these three factors and obliges me, in particular, to leave out a finer discussion of the introduction of Bion's ideas in France.[3]

I want now to focus on the subject of this chapter. Although I have been asked to speak about the influence of Bion on my research, I am not sure that I will constantly use this term; it is more likely that I will speak of correspondences, of confluence, of "bridges" and passages which were established even before the references to Bion's thought became more manifest and explicit for me, and articulated with my own approach. In order to establish this recognition of the similarities and true influences, I will begin by proposing to the reader a brief overview of my research into groups.

## Overview of my research into groups

In the first period of my research, I contributed to the necessary undertaking characteristic of the foundational classical models of the psychoanalytic approach to groups, namely, of describing and conceiving the group as a specific entity endowed with its own psychic formations and processes, as it is defined by the Freudian notion of *Gruppenpsyche*. Pichon-Rivière, Bion, and Foulkes each conceived of the group in this way and expressed its characteristics in different models.

The model that I constructed is different. It is probably different because the questions I was concerned with were different from those that my predecessors, Pichon-Rivière, Bion, Foulkes, and their successors, had tried to resolve: I was living in a different context of psychoanalytic culture.

### A model of the group: the group psychic apparatus

At the end of the 1960s, I outlined a model that could still only give an incomplete account of the construction of group space. The principal proposition of the model that I called the group psychic apparatus[4] (Kaës, 1976a) is that the group is constructed on the basis of psychic formations that each member of the group mobilizes in order to forge links or bonds with the other members and to form a new, common, and shared psychic space. When this common and shared psychic construction has taken place between the individuals constituting this group, there is not simply a collection of individuals, but a group, with specific phenomena. It comprises a non-differentiated and a differentiated level of investments, of object-relations, and of defense mechanisms.

The model of the group psychic apparatus is an ergonomic model in the sense that it accomplishes a particular psychic work: it produces and processes the psychic reality of a group, in a group. It is constructed as an apparatus for binding and transforming the psychic contributions of its subjects so as to produce a specific psychic reality that is irreducible to that of the individual psychic apparatus: it is not an extrapolation from it. In this sense, it has its own formations and its own processes.

However, the difference between this model and those that preceded it resides in the fact that it distinguishes in the group three spaces and three levels of organisation of unconscious psychic reality and not just one (the group as an entity): that of each subject, that of the relations between them, and that of the group. The model I am proposing articulates their relations in the group as a whole. This model integrates complexity and implies the existence of several types of organizers. To ensure the passage and transformation between the individual psyches, the space of intersubjective relations, and the group space, the group psychic apparatus comprises specific operators. Two concepts describe the principal ones.

### The organizers of the combination and adjustment[5] of the psyches: internal groups and psychic groupality

I have called psychic groupality a general property of psychic matter: its associativity. The psychic matter electively mobilized in the intrapsychic space of the participants is an organized matter whose structure is that of internal groups that associate elements (drives, affects, representations, objects) linked by a law of composition. In this way I describe and qualify the primal fantasies, the oedipal and fraternal complexes, bodily and psychic imagos, and all the configurations of internal objects obtained by the different modalities of identifications. Certain internal groups are acquired through introjection, others are inherent to the primordial organisation of unconscious psychic matter, while others, such as the psychic groups described by Freud, are constitutive of the primordial unconscious. All these groups of the "inside" are the expressions of psychic groupality.

The form, the structure, and the function of these internal groups are mobilized in the group process: they are unconscious psychic organizers of the adjustment (or assemblage) of the psyches. I have commented on several occasions and from different angles on how a group organizes itself on the basis of a phantasmatic organizer, whose generic structure is described by the statement: "A parent is seducing/menacing a child".[6] A group psychic organizer such as this fantasy accomplishes several actions: it mobilizes, channels, diverts, distributes, and binds the psychic energy, identifications, fantasies, and mechanisms of defense of the group members. The process of combination/adjustment that it organizes is accomplished through distortions, displacements, condensations, and diffractions of psychic matter.[7]

The process of combination/adjustment takes place in two principal modes: an isomorphic mode of adjustment between an internal group and the real group, both formations tending towards an identity or, in R. D. Laing's (1969) terms, a co-inherence characteristic of a psychotic mode of grouping; and a homeomorphic mode of adjustment which maintains the gap and the difference between the internal groups and the real group. These two modes can co-exist or substitute each other.

### Linking and unconscious alliances

A second concept describes the specific operators of the process of adjustment: linking and unconscious alliances. A bond (*lien*) is what binds several subjects together in an ensemble that is irreducible to the subjects who constitute this ensemble. A bond has its own psychic consistency. Its logic is a logic of the correlations of subjectivities. Its formula could be stated as follows: "Not one without the other, without the alliances which underpin the links between them, without the whole that contains them and which they construct, which binds them mutually and which identifies them in relation to each other".[8]

Unconscious alliances are a constitutive condition of linking. They are one of the principal formations of the psychic reality of the ties or bonds that are formed between several subjects in a couple or in a group. I have distinguished several types of unconscious alliances: some are structuring (such as the narcissistic contract, the alliance of Brothers, the symbolic alliance with the Father, the contract of renunciation vis-à-vis the direct realisation of instinctual aims); others are defensive (the negative pact), and among these we are faced with alienating and pathological alliances (shared denial, the perverse pact, incestuous narcissistic alliances); and yet others are offensive.

I would like to dwell for a moment on the defensive alliances: their aim is to keep repressed, rejected, denied, or erased whatever, between each of the subjects of a bond, may endanger the bond between them. But this aim is duplicated by other aims of an individual order: the alliances support whatever each individual, for his own reasons, has to repress, deny, or reject. The tuning that results from this is most often unconscious, and these unconscious tunings are co-constitutive of the unconscious of each person. In this way, unconscious alliances participate in the structuring of the life of each subject in so far as he or she is a subject of the unconscious and a subject of these alliances. By virtue of their structure and function, unconscious alliances are thus destined to produce unconscious material and to remain unconscious.

Group psychoanalytic work

On the basis of this brief analysis and with these concepts, how can one describe what underlies the group experience? The group puts to work the identifications, the narcissism, and the imaginary dimension involved in the construction of a group, and in the processes which lead each person to be a member of it, to be affiliated to it. Each person, according to his structure and history, is mobilized, affected, and transformed in these processes of construction of the group, inasmuch as it is these processes that have contributed to his formation as a subject of the unconscious. That is why I have posited a partial but decisive equivalence between the subject of the unconscious and the subject of the group.

Psychic work is required for participating in the group experience: this work confronts the subject with the intersubjective and group conditions of his own formation as a subject. Psychoanalytic work in the group situation is the invention of new forms of self and of new processes of its accomplishment.

This work is a discovery: it is marked both by pleasure and suffering. Painful episodes occur when, in the group process, we have to deal with the "loosening" of ideals, of alienating identifications, of the desire for mastery, and of the unconscious alliances which sustain them, with regard to their aim of making oneself or the other "conform" to a norm. In the process of training, each person is challenged by the diverse modalities of illusion: individual, group, institutional. Each one, alone and with the others, can then experience which major resistances have opposed the appropriation of his process of becoming a subject, once it has been possible to elaborate the confrontation with the unknown that is inherent to any change of form.

Group work is thus an opportunity for deploying and working on the identificatory collages which are provoked in certain subjects through adhesion to group ideals or norms. Each person can then have the experience that the group arouses the desire to take possession of something that does not belong to oneself but to another, that this other is an object of envy but an object constitutive of identification, with the risk of a false-self identification if the process of introjection of the transformations that it implies is insufficient.

## My relations with Bion's thought

As I pointed out in the introduction to this article, my intention is to discern the areas of correspondence between Bion's psychoanalytic approach and mine and to clarify the influence that he has had on my own research, but also to identify what I see as differences between his approach and my own.

I think that there were several phases in the evolution of my relations with Bion's thought. There was the initial phase when I discovered and recognized correspondences and rapprochements between what I was constructing and certain aspects of his thought.[9] I note a first rapprochement between the "ideological position" that I described in an article of 1971 and the group "mentality". I had not yet read Bion at the time when I wrote this article, but in my book on ideology (1980), I gave a large place to Bion's work.

### Presence of Bion in my first model of the group psychic apparatus

A first contact with Bion's *Experiences in Groups* at the end of 1971 was an opportunity for me to make occasional references to Bion in my thesis of 1974, and then in other texts which resulted from it, notably in *L'Appareil psychique groupal* (1976a), published in 1976. But I was not really in a position to put his concepts to use in my elaborations. I included citations from Bion, but what I mentioned, like many of my colleagues,[10] were the basic assumptions, but without doing much with them other than establishing correspondences. My theoretical references were those that I found in Freud and in my colleagues of the CEFFRAP: Anzieu, Béjarano, Missenard, and Pontalis. In fact, I was trying instead to develop my own model.

I am aware, however, of a number of partial corespondences between certain concepts of Bion and those that underpinned the model of the group psychic apparatus that I developed at the end of the 1960s. My major hypothesis was that this apparatus produces a work of binding between the psychic contributions of the participants and that it transforms them into processes and formations that are typical of a group. Although it now seems evident to me, and although I insist on the anonymous and impersonal structure of the primal phantasy, as well as on the fact that the very notion of adjustment describes a similar process, I did not notice the correspondence between this proposition and Bion's hypothesis in which he postulates "a group mentality as the pool to which the anonymous contributions are made, and through which the impulses and desires implicit in these contributions are gratified (1961, p. 50).

I have discovered other correspondences, which I have explained on several occasions, between the concept of basic assumptions and that of unconscious group organizers. I conceive of these on the same clinical bases as Bion: I have observed their organizing function and their alternating mode of emergence and latency, but I do not treat them as defensive systems.[11] A further example: when I describe the manifestations of group mentality in terms of three principal "positions" (ideological, utopian, and mythopoietic), I am not referring here to Bion's thought on group mentality. But I cite the notion of empty thought to describe the dominating anxieties of the paranoid-schizoid position, intensified by the lack of phantasy activity in large groups. I have introduced the notion of alpha on several occasions.

There are indeed partial correspondences and convergences. We have both had—Bion before me—similar experiences which find expression in partially convergent ways of thinking.[12] The model that I have developed is different from Bion's. As I have said, I distinguish three spaces of unconscious psychic reality, and I try to articulate them by identifying, in particular, how group formations are mobilized in the formation of intrapsychic space. Another important difference, in my view, was that I introduced the notion of internal group and the concept of psychic groupality: by qualifying the space of the subject in the group, they open up another perspective which the concept of subject of the group would clarify later.

Later, in other articles and books, I returned to what interested me in Bion's thought. In line with my work on the group psychic apparatus, I would certainly say today that there is a preconception of the group and, more generally, of linking, on the model of the preconception of the breast, according to Bion's hypothesis. This preconception resides in the fundamental psychic groupality, that is to say, in the property of psychic matter to be associated in internal groups. Here, I follow Bion's proposition to the effect that the preconception, once it comes into contact with a realisation that has similar characteristics, is transformed into a conception. It pairs up with the realisation. Today, I would say that what I described as the tuning or adjusting of the psyches under the effect of internal groups that are homologous with the group that is being formed is based on this transformation.

## Bion's influence and its presence in several texts

A second phase in my relations with Bion began in 1976: his influence now underpins several of my elaborations and goes beyond the research into small groups.

### Alpha function and transformation. Container-contained and function

The first paper in which Bion's influence was present more directly was "Analyse intertransferentielle, fonction *alpha* et groupe conteneur" (Kaës, 1976b). The concept of intertransferential analysis accounts for the particularity of the analysis of the transference/countertransference movements induced by the transferences of the members of a group in the common psychic space of two or several psychoanalysts in charge of a group. To develop this clinical concept, I drew on the conceptions of Bion concerning the presence (or absence) of the alpha function in analysts, in so far as they are allied in their work and receive the transferences and their contents in their own space and in their common space. I introduced into the relation container/contained the capacity of the analysts to contain and to transform this relation, which I call the container function.[13]

The basic assumptions are no longer simply mentioned; they are tested by the clinical analysis of several group sequences. I established the correspondences between attacks on linking and the use of fragmentation as a defense described by Springmann (1975). All these references would lead me to conceptualize the group more explicitly as an apparatus of transformation (1986).

The Bionian sources of my major references were supplemented by those from D. W. Winnicott, in particular, his concept of transitional phenomena and objects. At the end of 1976 I had begun to write an introductory study of transitional analysis,[14] which I consider as a mode of psychoanalytic work in analysis and in groups when experiences of early traumatic rupture by analysands have made differentiations and connections between internal space and external space impossible or precarious, creating and maintaining psychotic nuclei. I established bridges between this new approach, already nourished by earlier acquisitions concerning alpha function and the container function, and the more general concept of transitionality as a space of indetermination and creation.

It was also during this period that I took up and developed relations between Bion's conception of group mentality and the notion of an ideological, utopian, and mythopoetic position.[15] I refered to the work of Bion[16] on thinking, alpha function, the transformation or non-transformation of contents. Following Bion, I considered certain configurations of ideology as a system of thought against thinking, as an apparatus for manipulating thoughts and petrifying them. These propositions led me to adopt the idea that ideology is constructed on the basis of an impossibility of containing destructive and painful representations owing to a deficiency in alpha function: a part of the beta elements is projected outside; another part remains encysted in the ideological content, without transformation, for lack of a container.

*Third phase: thinking with Bion*

This third period had already begun with the work on alpha function and the containing function (1976b), and with the resumption of my work on mentalisations and the ideological position. What characterizes it, I think, is that issues related to transformation had begun to exert a greater influence on me.

Transformations and transmission

This is apparent in a study of 1986 titled, "Le groupe comme appareil de transformation" (Kaës, 1986). According to my point of view concerning the three spaces of psychic reality, the work of transformation involves each of these spaces in their interrelations, whether the privileged vertex is that of the singular subject, intersubjective relations, or the group. In this study, my attention is focused on the group, but the problem that interests me is to describe the *processes* of transformation, while taking into account both the level of the group and that of the singular subject: how is the status of the transformation of O, and in O, to be understood when we are dealing with a set of subjects? We do not know much about how Bion applied his theory of transformation to the group. I take an approach which takes into consideration the defensive measures of the group when faced with a catastrophic change that brings each member of the group into contact with the reality of an object or a situation associated with a traumatic experience. The concept of defensive unconscious alliances was beginning to take shape here.

Bion continued to accompany me when, at the beginning of the 1980's, I was working on the processes of transmission of psychic life between generations. My research was published later (1993). In this study, I introduced a distinction inspired by Bion between the transmission of transformable objects and the transmission of non-transformable objects; I established correspondences between the transformative functions of the apparatus for interpreting (Freud), alpha function (Bion), and the function of word-bearer (Castoriadis-Aulagnier, 1975).

Thought, thinking, and the apparatus for thinking

The question of thought and of the process of thinking has permeated my research since my studies on social representations, and then on group thinking as an object of drive investments and unconscious representations. On this point, along with the consecutive contributions of Anzieu and Gibello, the concepts of Bion were very useful for me. What was particularly helpful was the notion of an apparatus for thinking thoughts, which I connected with Freud's apparatus for interpreting in my studies on ideology (1980, pp. 109–115, 122–123, 141–142). They were helpful again when I worked on associative processes and the formation of chains of thought in groups and in analysis (1994). I undertook this study to explore the interweaving of the thought processes of each subject in interference, anaclisis, and facilitation with the thoughts that develop through the group process. By exploring the singularities of the associative process in this way, I continued to qualify the importance of the psychic function of the other, of "more than one other", in the access to language, the use of speech, and the formation of thought: this question was explored and structured by the research of Lacan, Bion, and Castoriadis-Aulagnier. Bion sees the psychic apparatus of the mother as a locus of metabolisation in the Other of psychic contents that are incapable of transforming themselves into thoughts. With her concepts of word-bearer (*porte-parole*) and spoken shadow (*ombre parlée*) (1975), Castoriadis-Aulagnier emphasizes the interpretative and containing function of the accompaniment of the experience of the *infans* by the mother's voice and words. Castoriadis-Aulagnier clarifies her own position in relation to Bion by saying that, for her, the *infans* can only metabolize an object that has first dwelled in the area of the maternal psyche into a representation of its relation to the world. However, it is a fragment of the world, in conformity with the interpretation that repression imposes on the work of the maternal psyche, which is remodelled by it so that it becomes homogenous with the organization of the originary (or primal) and of the primary. The metabolisation concerns the representation of an object shaped by the work of repression in the mother into a representation over which repression as yet has no hold.

These propositions were very helpful to me for analysing the associative process at both the individual and group level. The group, one or several persons in the group, and particularly the psychoanalyst or the group of psychoanalysts, accomplish this function of the fabrication and transformation of thoughts, on condition that the apparatus borrowed from the other is available at the right moment for thinking thoughts. In the clinical analysis of a group, Bion's work on hallucination (1958) was particularly useful to me. I returned to the essential points of his research on transformations (1965, 1967).

### On the polyphony of the dream and the common and shared dream space

The influence of D. Anzieu and J. -B. Pontalis was decisive for me in the interest that I took at a very early stage in the forms, modalities, and functions of dreams in the group and of the group dreams of my patients in analysis. I have given an account of my conception in *La Polyphonie du rêve* (2002), in which I put forward three main hypotheses: that the dream is a polyphonic organisation; that it is the meeting point of several psychic spaces; and, that it has a double "navel", one that plunges into the somatic mycelium of the unconscious and another whose source and elements lie in intersubjective knots. In this exploration, I agree with the ideas of Bion, who considers the dream as a primary form of thought and also that the capacity for reverie of the other, particularly of the mother, is a condition of her baby's capacity to dream. The capacity for reverie, and alpha function, which, according to Bion, is one of the factors involved, are the conditions and the materials of normal dreaming. These propositions and a few others accompany my elaborations on the common and shared dream space in analysis and in groups.[17]

### On linking and unconscious alliances. Their relations with catastrophic experiences and alpha function

It is not surprising that the question of linking runs through my research as a whole: in the processes of intrapsychic linking, intersubjective relations, and the pluri-subjective ensembles. How these three spaces of psychic reality are articulated was the question that I wrestled with for several decades. It was only in 2009 that I brought together my ideas on the relation between internal links and linking between subjects, by taking what I have called unconscious alliances[18] as a guiding thread (Kaës, 2009a). In this book, there are numerous references to Bion. Those that held my attention particularly concern the mechanisms of defense mobilized in linking in relation to *Verwerfung*: the rejection of psychic reality, the involvement of alpha function in the contract of renunciation of the direct satisfaction of instinctual aims, as Freud describes it in 1929, for it seems to me that Bion's concept presupposes that this function exists before the contract can be established. Another reference has allowed me to shed light on the relations between catastrophic experiences and the establishment of structuring or defensive alliances.

### *Other recent work: the group and culture put to the test of psychoanalysis*

My more recent contributions bring together the main axes of my research and explores what I have learnt from psychoanalytic work with groups about psychoanalysis and about new forms of discontent in culture. The first (2007) puts the practice and theories of psychoanalysis to the test of the group when it is a case of thinking about the psychic reality of the singular subject and, in particular, what we know about his unconscious organisation: it draws on detailed clinical material from a group in order to mobilize all the resources of the theory that I have constructed in relation to these three spaces of psychic reality. In this book, in which the presence of Bion is still active, I found myself faced with the question he poses in "Evidence": "How are we to introduce the intuitions to the concepts and the concepts to intuitions?" (1976, p. 243). This question is central to psychoanalytic epistemology.

The second book is titled *Le Malêtre* (Kaës, 2012). Here again, Bion accompanies me in this exploration of contemporary culture in the light of what psychoanalytic work with groups and institutions has taught me, and also in the light of what Bion, but also Winnicott, Bleger, and Anzieu have passed on to us.

*What I owe Bion*

In order to be able to make use of what I learnt from Bion, two experiences were necessary: initially I was unaware of his work, but then went on to find certain correspondences between his thought and my own ideas. It was these correspondences that led me to refer to him, to the recognized power of his thought, which was close, strange, and encouraging for my own work, different from my own preoccupations in some respects, and perhaps even with regard to the choice I made of working on these three spaces that open up a debate about the central object of psychoanalysis. I do not consider myself as a disciple of Bion; rather, I regard him as a predecessor with whom I share an affinity of thought on questions that we have each approached differently.

I have scarcely made any references to Bion in my research on institutions, but I found in his concept of the "Establishment" a way of thinking that has helped me a lot in my own relations with psychoanalytic institutions: the Establishment is a collective defense against new ideas in order to control, master, or trivialize them. Bion says that he puts them to the service of what he calls the lie, which I call a defensive alliance, a negative pact. But he also stresses, at the same time, that the institution transmits the new idea, while distorting it. This optimistic way of thinking appeals to me …

*Notes*

1. Known today as the "Cercle d'études française pour la formation et la recherche: approche psychanalytique du groupe, du psychodrame, de l'institution".
2. Exceptions may be found in O. Avron, J. -C. Ginoux, and J. -C. Rouchy who refer to them in their books and articles (see Avron, 1986, 2009; Ginoux, 1986; and Rouchy, 2009).
3. J. Lacan was one of the first psychoanalysts, if not the first, to recognize W. R. Bion's thought in France. His article in *L évolution psychiatrique* (1947) relates what he learnt in London in September 1945, when he met several psychiatrists and psychoanalysts, including Bion and Rickman (1943) who had published in 1943 an article which marked a milestone in the history of the psychiatry and psychotherapy of groups. Lacan was impressed by the powers of creativity and of methodological demonstration of the two authors: "I have the impression", Lacan writes, "I am rediscovering the miracle of the first Freudian initiatives: finding in the very impasse of a situation the living force of intervention" (1947, p. 300; 2001, p. 101). He describes the institutional context, supports the principle of group analysis, presents the setting and its modifications, relates the therapeutic effects and the major conceptual inventions. Twenty-five years later, concerning the impossibility of "psychoanalysts forming a group", he declared that "he measures the group effect by what it adds in the way of imaginary obscenity to the effect of the discourse" and adds that "nevertheless the psychoanalytic discourse (the path that I choose) is precisely that which can found social ties freed of any need for a group" (Lacan, 1972, p. 31). This declaration has a

more general significance since it lent support to the denunciation by his pupils of the group as a locus of jouissance and imaginary alienation.

Group psychoanalytic practice inspired by Bion's ideas was introduced into France notably by O. Avron, J. -C. Rouchy, C. Pigott, and B. Gibello. An eminent place must be accorded to S. Resnik who invited Bion to hold a seminar in Lyon, then in Paris (July 10, 1978). Resnik has recounted certain moments of these seminars in no. 52 of the *Revue de psychothérapie psychanalytique de groupe* (2009). Among the institutions of psychiatric care, I would like to mention the *Clinique de la Chavannerie,* situated near Lyon and run by Drs. A. Appeau, P. Brunaud, and C. Legrand. Very influenced by the ideas of Melanie Klein and Bion, their approach has been to treat patients suffering from severe disorders in a group setting.

4. Conceived at the end of the 1960s, this model was presented in 1974 in my doctoral thesis, and then published in 1976. There is a similarity there with certain propositions of Bion, whose work was unknown to me at the time. I will come back to this point further on in this chapter.
5. In French *"appareillage"*.
6. 1976a, 1993, 1994, and recently in 2007 under the title *Linking, Alliances and Shared Spaces: Groups and the Psychoanalyst* (International Psychoanalytical Association International Psychoanalysis Library).
7. Most of the participants of this group adjusted themselves to this organizer, then to another; and the passage from one organizer to another constitutes a major aspect of the process of psychoanalytic work in the group.
8. Concerning the models of collective logics of the unconscious, of groups, and of intersubjectivity, see Kaës, 2009b.
9. This is also what Avron (2009) recognizes.
10. In the manifesto publication of our "school", *Le travail psychanalytique dans les groupes* (1972), in which Anzieu, Béjarano, Missenard, Pontalis and myself collaborated, only Béjarano makes some rapprochements with the transference and resistances concerning basic assumptions and the function of the co-leader in pairing. Like most of the authors who cited Bion at this period, he remains very descriptive.
11. For example (ibid., p. 75): "I have formulated the hypothesis that a single primary fantasy is not by itself an organizer of the representation of the group; several fantasies are involved, one of which is sometimes predominant, either at the level of manifest expression or at the latent and repressed level. This idea is very close to Bion's idea that the emergence of a basic hypothesis in a group only represents the visible part of the iceberg: just as one basic hypothesis hides another, a fantasy hides or blocks out another".
12. The same is true for the notion of internal groups for which distinct concepts have been elaborated independently of each other in the work of Pichon-Rivière, Napolitani, and in my own research.
13. I developed this problematic in 2012 by introducing the notion of metacontainer, for example, the institution in relation to the group.
14. Published in a collective work that I edited under the title *Crise, rupture et dépassement* (Kaës, 1979).
15. First identified in my article of 1971, *op. cit.,* and then in *L'appareil psychique groupal* (1976a): these positions are the object of my book on *L idéologie. Etudes psychanalytiques* (1980).
16. Notably to his work on learning from experience (1962a) and on thinking (1962b), on transformations (1965) and the texts of 1967 (*Second Thoughts*) and of 1970 (*Attention and Interpretation*).

17. Although Bion introduced the notion of the capacity for reverie as early as 1962 in his theory of thinking as a function of the maternal Other, his research into small groups is not concerned with dream work in groups.
18. See above a very short exposition of the axis of my work on unconscious alliances.

## References

Anzieu, D. (1966). Etude psychanalytique des groupes réels. *Les temps modernes, 242*: 56–73.
Anzieu, D., Kaës, R., Béjarano, A., Missenard, A., & J. -B. Pontalis, (1972). *Le travail psychanalytique dans les groupes*. Paris: Dunod.
Avron, O. (1986). Mentalité de groupe et émotionnalité groupale. *Revue de psychothérapie psychanalytique de groupe, 5–6*: 67–75.
Avron, O. (2009). L'influence de Bion sur ma clinique et sa conceptualisation: écouter et supporter l'inachèvement, *Revue de psychothérapie psychanalytique de groupe, 52*: 19–29.
Bion, W. R. (1958). On hallucination. *International Journal of Psychoanalysis, 39*: 341–349.
Bion, W. R. (1961). *Experiences in Groups*. London: Tavistock.
Bion, W. R. (1962a). *Learning from Experience*. London: Heinemann.
Bion, W. R. (1962b). A theory of thinking. *International Journal of Psychoanalysis, 46*: 306–310.
Bion, W. R. (1965). *Transformations*. London: Heinemann.
Bion, W. R. (1967). *Second Thoughts*. London: Heinemann.
Bion, W. R. (1970). *Attention and Interpretation*. London: Tavistock.
Bion, W. R. (1976). *Clinical Seminars and Four Other papers*. Abingdon: Fleetwood Press, 1987.
Bion, W. R., & Rickman, J. (1943). Intra-group tensions in therapy. *Lancet, 2*: 678–681.
Castoriadis-Aulagnier, P. (1975). *La violence de l'interprétation: Du pictogramme à l'énoncé*. Paris: Presses Universitaires De France.
Ginoux, J. C. (1986). Le modèle théorique contenant-contenu et ses applications au groupe. *Revue de psychothérapie psychanalytique de groupe, 5–6*: 117–125.
Kaës, R. (1971). Processus et fonctions de l'idéologie dans les groupes. *Perspectives psychiatriques, 33*: 27–48.
Kaës, R. (1976a). *L'Appareil psychique groupal. Constructions du groupe* (3rd edition). Paris: Dunod, 2010.
Kaës, R. (1976b). Analyse intertransferentielle, fonction alpha et groupe conteneur. *L'Evolution psychiatrique, 2*: 339–347.
Kaës, R. (1979). Introduction à l'analyse transitionnelle. In : R. Kaës, A. Missenard, D. Anzieu, J. Bleger & J. Guillaumin (Eds.), *Crise, rupture et dépassement. Analyse transitionnelle en psychanalyse individuelle et groupale*. Paris: Dunod.
Kaës, R. (1980). *L Idéologie. Études psychanalytiques. Mentalité de l idéal et esprit de corps*. Paris: Dunod.
Kaës, R. (1986). Le groupe comme appareil de transformation. *Revue de psychothérapie et psychanalyse de groupe, 5–6*: 91–100.
Kaës, R. (1993). *Le Groupe et le Sujet du groupe. Éléments pour une théorie psychanalytique des groupes*. Paris: Dunod.
Kaës, R. (1994). *La parole et le lien. Les processus associatifs dans les groupes*. Paris: Dunod.
Kaës, R. (2002). *La Polyphonie du rêve. L espace onirique commun et partagé*. Paris: Dunod.
Kaës, R. (2007). *Un singulier pluriel: la psychanalyse à l épreuve du groupe*. Paris: Dunod. [*Linking, Alliances, and Shared Spaces: Groups and the Psychoanalyst* (Trans. A. Weller). London: IPA, 2007.]
Kaës, R. (2009a). *Les alliances inconscientes*: Paris: Dunod.

Kaës, R. (2009b). Lógicas collectivas del inconsciente e intersubjectividad. Trazado de una problemática», *Psicoanálisis de las configuraciones vinculares, 32*: 81–115.

Kaës, R. (2012). *Le Malêtre*: Paris: Dunod.

Lacan, J. (1947). La psychiatrie anglaise et la guerre. *L évolution psychiatrique, 3*: 293–312.

Lacan, J. (1972). L'étourdit. *Scilicet, 4*: 5–52.

Lacan, J. (2001). *Autres écrits*. Paris: Seuil.

Laing, R. D. (1969). *The Politics of the Family*. London: Tavistock.

Pontalis, J. -B. (1963). Le petit groupe comme objet. *Les temps modernes, 211*: 1057–1069.

Resnik, S. (2009). Bion et Foulkes, deux présences en dialogue avec moi. *Revue de psychothérapie psychanalytique de groupe, 52*: 61–70.

Rouchy, J. C. (2009). L'origine d'une pratique d'analyste de groupe. *Revue de psychothérapie psychanalytique de groupe, 52*: 71–82.

Springmann, R. (1975). Fragmentation as a defence in large groups. *Contemporary Psychoanalysis, 12*: 203–213.

# PART IX

## AESTHETICS

*Editors' introduction*

In a book of collected papers dedicated to Bion a section on aesthetics is not incidental but necessary. Why? Because the model of aesthetic experience expresses better than any other Bion's conception of the unconscious and psychoanalysis. In his work the unconscious is seen more and more as a psychoanalytic function of personality aimed at transforming raw emotions and sensoriality into effective thinking, and psychoanalysis itself becomes a kind of artistic endeavor, a *Zwittenart*, as Schiller said, for art and poetry. Something between art and science, a disciplined—that is, theoretically and technically inspired—way to intuit the truth of the therapeutic relationship in the here and now of the session. What counts is not the revelation of some knowledge about the other's unconscious, but the sharing of an integrated (somatopsychic) engagement in expanding the creative capacity of unconscious processes in order to attribute a personal and full meaning to reality.

A major theme throughout Bion's work, one reflected by many authors in this book, is that the ability of the analyst coincides with his capacity to remain receptive to the patient's pre-verbal and verbal communications and to "paint" or "play" for and with him what cannot be said in plain words: appropriately enough, as an artist. Like an artist, what the analyst gives the patient are "good" forms to contain virtually exploding agglomerates of beta elements or unthought emotions. The patient, then, internalizes this new capacity to digest the real. So, in Bion's work, aesthetics is more and more recruited to theorize what at any given moment is happening in the analytic encounter. Vice versa, we gain from Bion's theoretical insights a better understanding of the nature of art *tout court*.

Now, coming to the papers included in the section, Adele Abella recalls the main psychoanalytic models for aesthetic experience: Freud's concept of sublimation, Klein's and Segal's of reparation, and then Winnicott's ideas on the transitional phenomena and space, and she compares them to Bion's view. Then, interestingly she enlists three modern or contemporary artists, Marcel Duchamp, John Cage, and Christian Boltanski. All of them share with Bion a strong urge to open the mind to a new receptivity and to unprecedented thoughts: Duchamp inventing the "ready made" art and overstepping the "tyranny of taste", Cage exploring the resources of totally silent compositions, Boltanski asking the viewer to stare at an unlimited series of blurred images and so pushing to the extreme his effort to perceive a new figure, a pattern, a glimpse of meaning.

Aren't all these examples of "negative capability" or, as much as possible, of putting aside any "already known" prejudices or knowledge, so as to encounter the artistic creation in a state of mind analogous to being without memory and desire? The "work of the negative" implied in Bion's thinking is no less than the idea of a "no-thing", which appears in these examples of "no-painting", "no-music", "no-pictures". Like Bion, Duchamp, Cage, and Boltanski are, each in his own way, radical and original. What we get from Abella's paper is an opportunity to realize how illuminating Bion's ideas can be to intuit the secret work of art and, reciprocally, how intriguing it can be for us to reconsider his theories in the light of these artists' vexing and thought-provoking work.

In their papers, Capello and Molinari follow this same path, but then add a flavour of the post-Bionian psychoanalytic model of field theory. Capello's aim is to illustrate how a number of key innovations introduced by Bion in the practice and theory of psychoanalysis have the potential to help us rethink or re-signify the relationship between psychoanalysis and literature. He starts by offering the reader a brief, introductory outline of the main facets of the past conversations between the two disciplines. Then he focuses more closely on Bion's thought and its development in the work of contemporary analysts including Thomas Ogden, Antonino Ferro, and Giuseppe Civitarese. He underlines the relevance of their contributions to psychoanalytic aesthetics in general and psychoanalytic literary criticism more specifically. In the second part of the article, Capello examines some poems from *Il porto sepolto* (The Buried Harbor), the debut collection of the celebrated Italian writer Giuseppe Ungaretti (1888–1970). What he aims at in his reading is to underline the different ways in which the poems' affective functioning resonates with Bionian and post-Bionian notions, including dreaming and thinking, their relationship with the no-thing, alpha function, transformations, and Ferro's concept of "narrative derivatives" of "waking dream thought".

In contrast to the other authors in this section, Molinari's paper is a clinical paper. This is not common: so many articles on aesthetics in psychoanalytic literature are only theoretical, while, in our opinion it is important to try to better link our understanding of art to our clinical experience. Here we are well served. In analytic therapy, Molinari writes, patient and analyst think together about the same contents over and again before their variation signals greater mobility of thought and a wider range of tools for thinking. However, there are some situations when this evolution does not take place, and this produces a shared feeling of constraint that is difficult to tolerate. Patients with nuclei of autistic withdrawal often use repetition as a helpful defense to avoid catastrophic anxieties. Molinari then draws on some observations about the use of reiteration and seriality in art to transform them into useful tools in the exploration of the analytic field that is formed in these clinical situations.

Starting with some of Bion's ideas, she formulates an hypothesis about the structuring of the function of containment along two tracks, each one appropriate to contain different aspects of experience. The function of containment (♀/♂) supports the evolution of thinking towards symbolic representation, while a form of proto-containement would include experiences of fusion that serve to trace a sensory contour of experience. In normal development the latter form of psychic containement—that does include some processing of the experience—undergoes a relative involution, whereas it remains active in autistic patients and creates a serious hindrance for the evolution of thinking.

Her clinical vignette is evocative. Despite the fact that she is actually *seen* at any session by her analyst, a patient, Elisa, brings her a series of photographs to show how she "really is" and how she'd like to be (and to be seen) and so escape her painful sense of being ugly. From the seriality of the gesture, the analyst succeeds in recovering a true understanding: not only from an intellectual point of view, which would be a way of distancing herself from Elisa, but by letting herself undergo a kind of aesthetic experience through which she rediscovers what seemed only too obvious—that is, the deficit of good mirroring in Elisa's relationship with her primary object.

The repetitiveness of the patient's action of offering her pictures makes the analyst think—in the process of subjectivization—of a basic, dialectic of identity and difference that takes place mainly on a sensorial level. But above all, it is a reverie that helps the analyst to see things more clearly. This is a somehow somatic or bodily reverie. Her own gesture of putting a patient's picture, unusually contained in a frame, into a drawer calls her attention to the role of the "frame". Then the image arrives of an artwork by a contemporary artist, G. Varisco's "Communicating Pictures", showing a set of frames enclosing different portions of empty space and colour. So reverie is the aesthetic epiphany that occurs in the mind of the analyst, but also in the group-mind of the analytic pair (or in the field), which really enables her to look—surprised, moved—in a new caring way at Elisa's face and to find her interesting, seducive, beautiful as never before.

In hindsight, the patient's sterile repetitiveness, inflected in different ways, has become an attempt to communicate with the transformative capacity of the analyst, and her capacity to use her unconscious to dream the emotional problem of the relationship. So the reverie "in action" comes to the fore and the importance in the process of meaning creation, as in art, of the semiotic components—frame, form, body, shapes, rhythms, sounds—and not only (semantic) content that can be grasped directly by the reflective ego.

CHAPTER THIRTY-FOUR

# Using art for the understanding of psychoanalysis and using Bion for the understanding of contemporary art

*Adela Abella*

In this paper I will try to explore the interface between Bion's thinking and art. I will approach this from two opposite directions. First, I will discuss how Bion uses art to understand psychoanalysis. Second, I will follow the other way around: I will examine in which ways Bion's thinking is useful for the understanding of art.

Unlike Freud, Hanna Segal, or even Winnicott, Bion has not developed a coherent and finished model of artistic activity. Furthermore, he has not shown any particular interest in the arts of his time. His references to cultural works are mostly classical: philosophers such as Plato or Kant, poets such as Milton and Keats, tragedians or playwrights such as Sophocles or Shakespeare, mystics such as Meister Eckhart and Saint John of the Cross.[1]

However, in a paradox that might have pleased Bion, although his artistic taste is highly classical, his work proves to be particularly useful for the appreciation of contemporary art. We might thus say that Bion's thinking allows us to creatively expand his work in such a way as to use the tools he has created in order to grow further, and in other directions. This would be nothing more than following his constant invitation: think for yourself, be yourself, find your own way, be respectful of your own personality (Bion, 1974b). Such an incitement towards personal truth and authenticity permeates Bion's writings: "Don't try to understand *me*! Pay special attention to your *emotional responses* to me!" (Grotstein, 2008, pp. 7–8) or "The analyst you become is you and you alone, you have to respect the uniqueness of your personality" (Bion, 1987, p. 12). In fact, Bion's pleading for internal freedom in the use of the thinking of our forebears is a warning against the risk that "acknowledging indebtedness to earlier work" might impede personal creative intuition. This is a central contribution of Bion to the approach of contemporary art. I will come back to this.

## Bion's use of art in the understanding of psychoanalysis

It has been noted (Glover, 1998) that there is an evolution in Bion's drawing on foreign disciplines in order to deepen our understanding of psychoanalysis. One of Bion's main lifelong intentions was to build a method of critical approach to psychoanalytic practice instead of adding new psychoanalytical theories. Briefly summed up, his aim was "to understand our understanding". The difficulty for doing this lies in the fact that psychoanalysis is to be considered as "a thing in itself", unknowable by definition but yet liable to be partially explored through the analyst's experience. In this endless and asymptotic struggle to understand that which can never be fully understood, Bion resorts, at first, to scientific constructs borrowed mainly from mathematics, geometry, biology, physics, and chemistry. A progressive but clear shift may be detected in *Transformations* (1965), where Bion increasingly turns to aesthetics and mystical vertices. The difficulty arises from the fact that Bion aspires to capture the unobserved, the inaudible and the ineffable, the mysterious and the unknowable, that which can only be intuited. Therefore, he comes to pose the central problem in terms of how to convey the ineffable experiences that are both the patient's communications and the analyst's interpretation. For Bion, art provides a number of helpful metaphors for this very special sort of understanding.

Thus, Bion compares the transformations that allow a psychoanalyst to produce an interpretation to the transformations made by the painter from the perception of, say, a field of poppies up to the final picture on the canvas. Thanks to this pictorial image, Bion is able to convey with great efficacy the distinction between rigid transformations and transformations in projective identification: suffice to think about the differences between an impressionist painting and a photograph. The poppies metaphor allows equally to explain the fact that different psychoanalysts may propose different interpretations for a given piece of material: the invariants in a Kleinian transformation will be different than those of a Freudian one, in the same way as a realistic painter retains different aspects of a poppy field than those conveyed by an abstract artist.

The factor that makes Bion increasingly turn towards mystical or artistic metaphors is mainly the problem of the ineffability of psychoanalysis. Thus, he suggests that the capacity to convey the ineffable in words might be seen as a "minor ephemeral art". In fact, even if the analyst works with words, Bion suggests that a psychoanalytical communication is more akin to musical or artistic than to verbal communication. The comparison with an artist draws on two main factors. First, in order to be effective, the analyst's words should be able to make an impact in the same powerful way as a piece of art: "The artist stimulates a reaction in his public … [the interpretation] communicates an *emotional* experience, such as the artist intends to produce" (Bion, 1965, p. 32).

Second, "the interpretation given to the patient is a formulation intended to display an underlying pattern … [which is] similar to some aspects of painting, sculpture or musical composition" (1967, p. 131). The analyst reveals an underlying pattern, which introduces some order and meaningfulness in the previous confusion: it is up to the patient to understand it in his own way. For Bion, the same degree of personal freedom is necessary for the psychoanalyst who should permit himself the conditions required to "see" what is happening. This is not always an easy task: "Some of the difficulty … arises when the psychoanalyst allows the intuition achieved to languish and be replaced by what he has learned" (p. 153). Therefore, confronted with a problem overloaded by experience, Bion pleads for combining respect for tradition and "naivety of outlook", a combination that is usually expected of an original artist.

Bion equally borrows an analogy from the artistic field when he discusses another of his central concerns: the problem of communication amongst psychoanalysts. How can a psychoanalyst convey the ineffable experience that is his relationship with the patient? The hindrance is not only unavoidable "unconscious distortions" of our formulations but the fact that we may communicate that which is superficial and meaningless whereas the essential aspects are lost. Bion speaks in dismaying terms about psychoanalytical literature, which "must be the dreariest and most unrewarding scientific literature" for most readers (p. 129). In fact the dilemma of psychoanalytical communication may be put in these terms: "The report of the session ... must be a literal and incomprehensible jumble or it must be an artistic representation." In order to avoid unbearable and meaningless "verbal jugglery", Bion suggests learning from art's ability to efficiently and freely convey truth. The fundamental idea here is that "certain books, like certain works of art, rouse powerful feelings and stimulate growth willy-nilly" (p. 157). Therefore, psychoanalytical papers, interpretations, and art should act in a similar way: that is, not so much as vectors of information but as stimulants to thought in the recipient.

It has been stated how Bion increasingly evolved, in his late work, towards an unexpected and striking aesthetical conception of psychoanalytical work, the one that explores "the deep and formless infinite" of the unrepresented, undifferentiated level in the pursuit of ineffable truths and which must draw on intuition and faith (Vermote, 2011). Thus, Bion justifies the fictional form of his *A Memoir of the Future* (1975, 1977, 1979) as a device aimed to counter the unavoidable opacity of psychoanalytical jargon: "I was compelled to seek asylum in fiction. Disguised as fiction the truth occasionally slipped through." A parallel arises here between Freud and Bion: the first had expressed, in his later years, a progressive disillusionment with the capacity of psychoanalysis to counter resistances (Freud, 1937). As for Bion, we feel an increasing discouragement concerning the capacity of science and reason to attain truth, a. stalemate that leaves Bion no other issue than to turn towards a literary presentation in the hope that it might *occasionally* allow some truth to "slip through".

## Some classical psychoanalytical aesthetic models

In the preceding section we saw some of the ways in which Bion drew on art in order to better understand psychoanalysis. Illuminating as this may be, in my opinion the question is even more rewarding the other way around. I will now discuss in which ways Bion's thinking may be useful for the understanding of contemporary art. In order to highlight Bion's specific contributions and place his work in the context of the evolution of psychoanalytical thinking, I will first need to briefly sum up Freud's, Segal's, and Winnicott's aesthetic models.

### Freud's aesthetic model

For Freud the basic mechanism involved in artistic activity is sublimation (Abella, 2010). The artist achieves a particular "reconciliation" between the pleasure principle and the reality principle, which grants a partial satisfaction of repressed desires. One central point of this model is the nature of the desires that can be worked out through sublimation. All through his life, Freud thought mainly in terms of genital and partial sexual desires including anality, exhibitionism, and voyeurism. Later on, Freud made two significant additions: first, he included narcissistic needs amongst those that art can gratify, pointing out the fact that, from the very beginning, art had conveyed magical intentions. Second, through the description of the uncanny in fantastic literature, Freud opened up the possibility of understanding the role of destruction and death in the work of art. Thus, the range of emotions and fantasies for which art can provide an outlet broadens out, covering sexuality, omnipotence, and aggression—an extension that is fundamental for the understanding of contemporary art.

A problematic point in Freud's model is the value ascribed to formal means. Freud was personally touched mainly by the ideational contents of a work of art: the wishes, the fantasies, and the conflicts underlying a given piece of art. On the contrary, he confessed to being quite insensitive to formal beauty, which he rather dismissed as having a purely defensive role. In fact, for Freud, in the conflict between pleasure and reality, aesthetic enjoyment allows the sidestepping of moral disapproval: "The artist bribes us with the formal and aesthetic pleasures" (Freud, 1908, p. 153). Thus, we understand Freud's reluctance and distrust towards artists, mainly visual artists, a stance that is clearly posited in the opening sentence of "The Moses of Michelangelo" (1914, p. 211): "I have often observed that the subject-matter of works of art has a stronger attraction for me than their formal and technical qualities, though to the artist their value lies first and foremost in this latter. I am unable rightly to appreciate many of the methods used and the effects obtained in arts." And still more definitely: "Meaning is but little with these men, all they care is line, shape, agreement of contours. They are given up to the pleasure principle. I prefer to be cautious" (Freud & Jones, 1993, February 8, 1914).

The position adopted by Freud concerning formal means leaves an unsolved problem: if formal means are of a secondary and defensive value, and if the meaningful aspect of a work of art lies fundamentally on its subject matter, how can we explain the radical different emotional impact of a masterpiece and a cheap novelette when both of them draw on the same theme? This is a central point concerning the understanding of art. It was the merit of Hanna Segal to propose an elegant solution for such a deadlock.

### Hanna Segal's aesthetic model

Following Melanie Klein, Hanna Segal builds her understanding of the psychological functions of art on the notion of reparation, which is a first major difference with Freud's model (Abella, 2010). Art is no longer seen as a diverted way of partially gratifying sexual desires. On the contrary, aesthetic pleasure is linked to art's capacity to allow the enlivening restoration of the fantasized damages inflicted on the loved object. A second important difference with Freud, intimately interwoven with the first one, is the essential role that Segal attributes to formal aspects for the comprehension of art—an appreciation that clearly stems from her profound love of art.

Segal suggests tragedy as a paradigm for aesthetic experience: the horror of the content is compensated by formal beauty. Thus, art allows "to restore and recreate the loved object outside and inside the ego" (Segal, 1952, p. 197), a process that stands upon a successful work of mourning and ends up in the formation of symbols. This position is summed up by a couple of apparently opposed statements. The first one highlights the role of beauty: "There can be no aesthetic pleasure without formal perfection" (p. 204). The second points to the need of a balance for beauty: "There can be no art without aggression" (1991, p. 92). Aesthetic pleasure thus stems from the simultaneous presence of beauty and aggression in a given work of art. It is precisely this coexistence that allows painful emotions and fantasies to be compensated by the accompanying formal perfection, a marriage that produces an effect of enlivening relief and internal reconciliation.

The notion of the dialectic interplay between beauty and aggression is helpful for the resolution of two important riddles left unsolved by Freud's model. First, it allows us to explain the greater effect of a masterpiece over a cheap novelette, which lies on the revitalizing effect of formal perfection. Second, the inclusion of aggression as an essential component of art is useful to grasp the role of ugliness—a trend that is particularly prominent, even if not exclusive, in contemporary art. Segal is affirmative on this point: "ugliness is what expresses the state of the internal world in depression. It includes tension, hatred and its results—the destruction of the good and whole objects and their change into persecutory fragments." The endpoint of this reasoning is the idea that "both beauty, in the narrow sense of the word, and ugliness must be present for a full aesthetic experience" (1952, p. 205). This coherent and elegant model is thus helpful to understand the presence of ugliness in a work of art inasmuch as beauty succeeds to balance and restore the whole. On the contrary, it fails to deal with art, which does not draw on beauty, especially if we think of beauty "in the narrow sense of the word".

*Other psychoanalytical aesthetic models*

One of the most interesting contributions of Segal's model is the fact that it ascribes psychic value to artistic endeavour. Unlike Freud, who seems to sometimes conceive art as a mundane pleasure-seeking entertainment whose defensive value justifies that he "prefers to be cautious", Segal highlights its enriching potentialities. Following other lines of thinking, some psychoanalysts have developed this same basic idea. Thus, Milner and Winnicott have emphasized the way in which creative and aesthetic experience may foster psychic growth both in the artist and in the public, in the analyst and in the patient (Glover, 1998).

Briefly summed up, Winnicott is more interested in the creative process than in the finished work of art—a position that is consistent with some of contemporary art's preoccupations, as we will see later. Winnicott likens the cultural field to children's play. Both of these enable an experience similar to the baby's experience of illusion inside the transitional space, where the question of the difference between the "me" and the "not me" is not to be posed. The rhythmic interplay between illusion and disillusion allows the baby to work out his omnipotence and helps him to build up the limits of the self. In a similar way, art provides the opportunity to engage in experiences which lead to repeated renewals and enrichments of the self, and of our relationship to external and internal reality (Winnicott, 1971).

One important contribution of Winnicott's model is that it provides the tools for recognizing some ingredients of the aesthetic emotion. This is the case, particularly, of two important elements of artistic experiences: the first is the feeling of fusion with the cultural work. The second concerns the narcissistic gain and elation achieved through a socially acceptable experience of omnipotence, such as playing or engaging in artistic activity. In this way, although by taking a different path, Winnicott joins Segal in the appreciation of art as a healthy and growth promoting activity.

## Using Bion for the understanding of contemporary art

It is far from easy to give a definition of contemporary art. For the purpose of this paper, suffice to say that I will refer to the art that is commonly presented in contemporary museums and art exhibitions all over the world, as well as in magazines such as *Artforum*, *e-flux*, *Frieze*, or *Mousse Magazine*. Some of the trends of present day art are the following: its eclecticism and multi-media presentation, the refusal of classical formal beauty as a pre-eminent criterion for artistic quality, and a strong self-reflexive trend. The latter puts into question almost all fundamental assumptions of the classical artistic establishment, such as the role of the artist, of the artistic institutions, and of the public, or the separation between art and life. We find here the first commonality between contemporary art and Bion, who also radically questioned a number of fundamental issues, such as the goals of analysis or the stance and listening of the analyst.

Given the variegated unfolding of today's artistic field I do not aspire to a comprehensive outlook of its whole panorama. I will instead restrict myself to examine some aspects of the way in which some well-known artists, who have deeply influenced contemporary art, conceive of their work. My choice will fall mostly on some artists with whom I am more familiar, such as Marcel Duchamp, 1887–1968, John Cage, 1912–1979, or Christian Boltanski, born 1944, (respectively Abella, 2007, 2012, 2008).

Of course I do not pretend that the whole eclectic artistic community shares their views, but I think they are fairly representative of a significant part of the field. In parallel, I will discuss the way in which Bion's thinking converges with and/or can illuminate their reflections. As a final step, I will suggest an aesthetic model inspired by Bion's contributions.

### The choice between avoiding and modifying frustration. The role of the artist

In *Learning from Experience* Bion states one of his at-that-time basic assumptions concerning what is essential to psychoanalysis: "the choice that matters to the psychoanalyst is the one that lies between procedures designed to evade frustration and those designed to modify it. That is the critical decision" (Bion, 1962, p. 29). In my opinion, a similar sensitivity informs a frequent debate in the artistic field that puts into question the very role of the artist: should the artist try to communicate something to his public? And if so, what this would be? Should he accept the demand to supply pleasurable artistic events, which allow the public to evade frustration through an escapist and consumerist usage of art? Or should the artist, on the contrary, present creative experiences that foster the discovery of new links with internal and external reality, so that frustration is not evaded but modified?

This choice is sometimes expressed in the artistic field in the following terms: is the artist to defend accepted social values or must he be free to express his personal experiences, fantasies, and emotions? Should the artist try to act on his public, pushing it towards conservatism, passivity, consumerism, and escapism, or, on the other hand, should he foster an attitude of participation, activity, contestation, and emancipation? (Kunst, 2012). The propagandistic aim of art has long been acknowledged, ranging from deliberate and committed projects aimed at indoctrination to more subtle and often unconscious "educative" purposes. At one extreme, we find religious art in the Middle Ages and the Renaissance, during the Third Reich, or in Soviet art,[2] all of them openly searching to convey (and impose) a certain view of the world. However, this is not the sort of propaganda that worries most contemporary artists: it is so conspicuous that the public may defend itself quite easily. Artists are most troubled by the discreet, unnoticeable, and often unwanted but still alienating forms of subtle indoctrination.

Bion is equally sensitive to these risks in psychoanalysis. In *Transformations* he warns about the possibility of sliding "from the domain of communication of knowledge to propaganda", a passage that might be dug out through manipulation of the emotions of the patient or the public. Interestingly, Bion leans here on a comparison with art: "The painter who works on his public's emotions with an end in view is a propagandist … He does not intend his public to be free in its choice of the use to which it puts the communication he makes. The analyst's position is akin to that of the painter … since psychoanalysts do not aim to run the patient's life but to enable him to run it according to his lights and therefore to know what his lights are." Bion recommends that the analyst expresses his truth "without any implication other than it is true in the analyst's opinion" (Bion, 1965, p. 37). Thus the analyst should communicate what he considers is the truth while knowing that it is *his* truth and without any attempt to influence his patient. The analyst is to help the patient to find his own personal truth, not to push him to passively submit to his analyst's truths.

A number of twentieth-century artists have vigorously championed this Socratic avenue. Thus, French artist Christian Boltanski speaks of his work in these terms: "Certain pictures call for nothing but to pray and receive communion, others interrogate. I want to be closer to the latter. I fear art that wants to impose itself upon others: I am as embarrassed in front of certain pictures as I would be in front of a mystic trying to convert others." Therefore, adds Bolstanski: "I try not to impose a direction to the spectator but rather to interrogate him" (Abella, 2008, p. 1131). A similar sensitivity unfolds in musician and performer John Cage when he expresses his dislike of the music made by some great composers such as Beethoven or Handel. The reason is that he finds their music "too emotional, too intentional, try[ing] to dominate people, to impose itself on them … I have difficulty with it because it is so pushy. It has precisely in it what government has in it: the desire to control; and it leaves no freedom for me" (Abella, 2012, p. 722). In consequence, Cage pleads for the respect of personal self-determination: "I don't enjoy being pushed while I'm listening, I like music which lets me do my own listening", a radical freedom that he requests for the artist, the performer, and the public. This passionate craving for autonomy drives Cage to state that a mediocre "happening" might be more useful than the representation of a theatrical masterpiece if it opens up its public to free new thinking. A reflection that is astonishingly close to Bion's convictions when he states that an apparently useless interpretation may be useful if it promotes thinking (Bion, 1967).

Thus, we find a shared sensibility in Bion's stating that the analyst's role is not to run the patient's life but to enable him to run it himself in his own way, in Boltanski's refusal to influence and "convert" his public and in Cage's demanding freedom for a listener to do his own listening.

This fostering of an active and creative attitude by the receiver (patient or public) expresses an important trend in contemporary art that can be summed up by Marcel Duchamp's famous aphorism: "It is the spectators who make the pictures" (Abella, 2007, p. 1046). Interestingly, this artistic aspiration matches a current trend in contemporary psychoanalysis that strives to foster the greatest personal appropriation, avoiding the risks of suggestion, seduction and indoctrination—a trend partly informed by Bion's thought. An example of awareness of this danger may be found in Bion's warning against an analysis that would end up in the patient having gained extensive information about his analyst's theories but no insight at all (Bion, 1963).

## "To thine own self be true"

Bion's refusal of propaganda may be connected with his insistence, from the mid sixties and increasingly with the passage of time, on the search for one's most profound truth, the unattainable and unknowable O. One of Bion's most important and long-lasting convictions is the need of truth for the development and the survival of the mind. The basic idea is that deprivation of truth for the mind is the equivalent of physical starvation for the body: "healthy mental growth seems to depend on truth as the living organism depends on food" (1965, p. 38). The important point here is which sort of truth Bion is speaking about. In fact, Bion advocates not a socially accepted truth, and still less a revealed one, but a personal one, the one that allows coming as close as one can to what one really is. Concerning psychoanalysis, Bion expresses the idea of a deep-seated personal truth that should be attained for an analysis to be successful: "It's difficult to conceive of an analysis having a satisfactory outcome without the analysand becoming reconciled, or at one with, himself" (1970, p. 34).

In the artistic field, a related worry is expressed in terms of the alienating and misleading character of taste. An emblematic figure in this sense is Duchamp denouncing in the sixties "the tyranny of taste" that is socially imposed and leaves no freedom for the individual. Duchamp strongly discredits the physically "agreeable" and "attractive" paintings, "the appeal to the senses" that ends up in what he ironically mocks as the "retinal shudder". In order to fight the extraordinary power of socially imposed taste, Duchamp champions the "beauty of indifference", a dematerialized form of art that relies upon intellectual expression: art must be cerebral, the creative act is an act of thought, not of sensuous pleasure. What matters is the idea: "painting … should have to do with the grey matter, with our urge for understanding" (Abella, 2007, p. 1048). We find here an interesting convergence with Bion's warning against the sensuous: for both Duchamp and Bion what really matters lies at another level and, still more importantly, can be obscured by sensuality, which is too easily accessible and deceptive.

In a similar vein, Boltanski denounces the destructive character of cultural codes that impose a prefabricated image of the world and thus kill off the most personal and genuine aspects of our lives. An example might be his work *Honeymoon in Venice*, carried out in 1975 in collaboration with his companion Annette Messager (Abella, 2008, pp. 1125–1126). Boltanski shows how the photographs taken by a couple, far from reflecting intensely personal experiences, rather translate them into pre-existing clichés. Boltanski denounces the "non-reality of photography" in these terms: "In photography, and specially in the photographs of the amateur, the photographer does not try to catch reality: he seeks to copy a pre-existing and culturally imposed image … The non-professional photographer only shows pictures of happiness, beautiful children running on perfectly green meadows: he reconstituted an image he already knows."

From Cage's view, the problem is that our values about what is worth listening to are heavily loaded by habit and taste, which are a product of tradition and education. This deep-seated conviction drives him to this radical and "pro-(e)vocative" (the term belongs to Bion) statement: "The function of art is to hide beauty: that has to do with opening our minds, because the notion of beauty is just what we accept" (Abella, 2012, p. 723). The last consequence of this line of thought is Cage's suggestion of an attitude of renunciation of "one's desire, taste and memory". It should be noted that these parallels between Cage and Bion are not casual and superficial but are rooted in their profound values concerning, respectively, art and psychoanalysis. Cage's renunciation of desire, taste, and memory, as well as Bion's warning against desire, memory, understanding, or coherence are, for them, nothing more than the basic conditions needed to open up to new fresh truths both in the outside world and in the mind. In this uncertain search, contemporary art meets Bion's proposal of a stance of openness and tolerance, the one that allows to pay attention to "imaginative conjectures", "speculative imagination", "stray thinking", "wild thoughts", "interferences", and "unborn babies".

The avenue would thus be opened to realize Polonius' advice to his son Laertes in Shakespeare's Hamlet: "To thine own self be true", an invitation that appears as a programmatic device both for Bion and for contemporary art.

*Opening our minds to the new, searching the unknown. The problem of truth and lies*

Bion's famous device—"without memory or desire"—aims to produce the conditions in which something new might emerge from the depths of oneself. Consequently, Bion insists on the idea that "any session is a new session and therefore a new situation that must be psychoanalytically investigated [without it being] obscured by an already over-plentiful fund of pre- and misconception". We find here also an interesting agreement between Bion's thinking and twentieth-century artistic aims. The artist who explains this goal in the clearest way is perhaps Cage. All through his life, Cage strongly states the idea that the function of art is to open our eyes and our minds to the "multiplicity and complexity of life" in order to be open to what we could not perceive before. For Cage, the result of this openness to the new will be personal development: "We will change beautifully if we accept the uncertainties of change" (Abella, 2012, p. 720). A similar conception of the function of art may be hinted at in Bion's suggestion that the painter brings a change in his public by allowing them to see things in another way (1974a, p. 96). Thus both music and art in general, have the central goal of stimulating mental growth through a renewed and enlarged perception of the world. Or, put in the evocative language of Bion, of facilitating an illuminating "flash of obvious" (Bion, 1974a, p. 103).

In this search for authenticity, Boltanski directly raises the problem of truth and lies whilst questioning the role of the artist. Boltanski, who understands his artistic activity as a "wild therapy" which allows him to work through his personal problems, wishes to offer the public a mirror where everyone can recognize himself and fantasize in a personal way. Thus he compares a work of art with a child's toy: "toys play for me the same role as art work: a toy represents both a culturally coded representation of the real world and an appeal, for each child who uses it, for different dreams" (Abella, 2008, p. 1130). Therefore, the artist's goal is to make an appeal for dreams but, and this is important, not for just any kind of dream. In fact what Boltanski strives to evoke are not socially imposed, codified, and stereotyped dreams: on the contrary, he is searching for the most personal and deeply authentic ones.

One of Boltanski's preoccupations is the universal human tendency to find what we already know, even to the extent of pushing us to succumb to cultural conventions at the price of eliminating the most authentic aspects of our experience. This leads Boltanski to work on the question of truth and lies. In a number of his works, Boltanski denounces the falsifications operated by photography in a way that reminds one of Bion asserting the falsifications of recording an analytic hour. For Bion, the appearance of truth conveyed by mechanical recording devices is deceiving: the falsification has already been introduced at the very beginning by the simple act of recording. Boltanski conveys something similar.

The problem for Boltanski is that images, and in particular the seemingly more veridical images such as photography, carry a high potential of mystification and lies. Boltanski tries to illustrate this idea by several works presented as autobiographic whereas, he explains, the facts shown are totally false, and given with all kind of false proofs. Thus, in his 1969 book entitled *Recherche et présentation de tout ce qui reste de mon enfance, 1944–1950* (Research and presentation of all that remains of my childhood, 1944–1950), Boltanski recollects some photographs of his family, of his class in 1951, of his cot, of one of his shirts, of his building blocks allegedly recovered in 1969, a spoiled page of his reading book … The spectator is touched by the apparent sincerity of these simple, innocent, and intimate relics … which, confesses Boltanski, belong in fact to his nephew and are therefore entirely false. In the same vein, three years later, Boltanski creates his "Attempt at Reconstitution of Objects that Belonged to Christian Boltanski between 1948 and 1954", based on a sheer contradiction between texts and images: a series of texts provide detailed descriptions of Boltanski as a child—descending a staircase on a certain date, coming back home holding his school bag on another precise date—whilst being illustrated by photographs representing these gestures carried out by … Boltanski as an adult! Boltanski comments: "Photography is used as a proof, and proofs are always false" (Abella, 2008, pp. 1119–1120).

Thus, as Boltanski shows, what has a wide appearance of truth and stands on apparently irrefutable proofs may in fact be entirely false. The thrilling fact is that it is also possible to consider the reverse: a deliberate lie may contain a deep-seated truth. Thus, Boltanski thoughtfully adds: "I believe that it is difficult to separate real from false. In one of my early interviews, I played the role of a young, desperate and tormented young man. While I was speaking I told myself: I am acting well, they believe me … But when I got out, I was terribly depressed, because in fact, it was a truth that I was hiding from myself and that I couldn't tell myself except under the appearance of a game …" (p. 1120)—a thought that makes Boltanski sum up his autobiographical works like this: " what I told you was false, even if in fact it was true". Therefore, there would be several kinds of truth and several kinds of lie, each of them with a particular quality and a specific function. Consequently, we should beware of appearances: a deliberate lie may in fact reveal a hidden truth and a partial truth may conceal a deeper truth. A bridge might be made here with Bion's warning against the danger of seeking a premature solution. The risk would be that a rational and reassuring truth might act as a defence against a hidden, wilder, and therefore feared truth (an idea that Bion expresses in terms of transformations in K obtruding the path towards a transformation in O).

*The working tools for reaching the unknowable*

Briefly summed up, the central, and maybe unsolvable, problem lies in the question whether it is possible to reach a personalized perception and appropriation of external and internal reality. How can both art and psychoanalysis alleviate the crushing weight of tradition, education, and unconscious refusal to face dreaded truths? Is it possible for art and psychoanalysis to work against these normalizing forces that loom over us? Of course we become human by immersion in a given society. The question is: Do these constructive socializing forces allow for some personal freedom? Or else, are psychoanalysis and art condemned to reinforce indoctrination through the subtle workings of the benevolent wish of the analyst to cure his patient or the beautiful proposals of sensitive and creative artists?

It is very touching to follow the thoughtful and effort-laden crusade of Bion, Duchamp, Cage, or Boltanski in the pursuit of "naivety of outlook". Their doubts, their drawbacks, their contradictions have something of an epic quality—all the more so because these unconventional personalities are often aware that their crusade is "doomed to failure". Surprisingly enough, there are such similarities in the ways in which Duchamp, Cage, Boltanski, or Bion have identified and tried to solve the same problems that one wonders if these common preoccupations were not somewhere in the air during the second half of the twentieth century.

A first common point between Bion, Duchamp, and Cage is their advocating a form of self-discipline. This need is formulated in ways that depend on each particular field of activity. Thus, Bion stresses that the analyst must discipline his thoughts in order to avoid being distracted by the senses from intuiting the unknown (Bion, 1967b). As for Duchamp, he embraces a "sensorial asceticism" which aims to "contradict [him]self so as to avoid conforming to [his] own taste"—taste being for him a product of culture and tradition and, so, a disguised form of slavery (Abella, 2007, p. 1048). Similarly, Cage champions an attitude of "silence and emptiness" aimed at the "acceptance of whatever happens in that emptiness" (Abella, 2012, p. 725)—a formulation close to the negative capability advocated by Bion. As it has often been remembered, this "negative capability" had been defined by Keats as the faculty of "being in uncertainties, mysteries, doubts, without any irritable reaching after fact and reason". The important point is that this shared fostering of the need for discipline is not an accidental and meaningless convergence. On the contrary, it stems from the same fundamental reason, that it is a necessary constraint in order to avoid superficial and dead understandings.

A second partly shared trend lies in their referral to science. During what has been called his "epistemological period" (Bleandonu, 1990, p. 145) Bion borrows from scientific fields in order to provide the proper tools for psychoanalysis. The basic idea is to facilitate learning from experience and to enable meaningful communication of new findings. One of the problems is that the matter of psychoanalysis is not of a sensuous nature and, therefore, cannot be grasped through the senses. Bion challenges the use of overloaded and hyper-saturated psychoanalytical jargon, which runs the risk of stifling the analyst's personal apprehension of reality under the weight of the sacralized knowledge transmitted by our forebears. An intrinsic problem is the fact that psychoanalysis must work with words, which are so easily overloaded and "polluted" with meaning that they lose the potential for receiving fresh meanings. Tragically enough, worn-away words may act more as a shield against the experience of one's deepest truth than as a tool for it. Confronted with this serious problem, Bion suggests the usage of mathematical terms that should allow flexibility, rigorous use, and freedom for thinking, all of them demanding that the analyst is not restricted by an obscure penumbra of associations. This avenue ends up in the construction of an ambitious, but finally cryptic, and hard-to-use, grid. Bion's longing is clear: if only we could denude our words, they will be apt to carry new truths. Before the mid-sixties, Bion believes that the proper tool for this purifying goal is science. This is the time of hope.

A hope is also seen in Duchamp's first period. In his fight to escape from the seductive retinal shudder and the deceptive impositions of the tyranny of taste, this artist turns to "scientific" drawing, one of his aims being to "rehabilitate perspective so that it would become absolutely scientific." In his drawings Duchamp strives to imitate architect's plans or geographical maps because they "cannot tolerate any taste since [they are] outside every pictorial convention" (Abella, 2007, p. 1048). Thus, Duchamp aspires to what he calls "the dehumanisation of the work of art", which is the principle of the ready-mades that Duchamp wishes to be "totally and strategically unaesthetic". The fundamental idea is to strip off from the art-work any penumbra of either social or individual meaning in order to free it from predetermined clichés. Tragically for Duchamp, this attempt was to end in total failure. Thus, in 1967, Duchamp announces the imminent death of his ready-mades: "I haven't done any now for a long time … Because anything, you know, however ugly however indifferent it is, will become beautiful and pretty after 40 years, you can be sure … So that is very disturbing for the very idea of the ready-made" (Abella, 2007, p. 1052). This statement drives Duchamp to the idea that a work of art necessarily dies with the passage of time. This happens, adds Duchamp, quite quickly, in around forty years, because people get used to it. Finally, consumed by familiarity, the potential of a work of art to refresh and open up, vanishes away—an idea that is echoed in Bion's warning about psychoanalytical theories becoming debased and stifling as psychoanalysts get accustomed to them.

So, for Duchamp, in the end it is taste that fatally wins the battle, and with the triumph of taste comes the death of a work of art willing to open up to the new, a disillusionment that leaves Duchamp no other issue than the (faked) abandonment of art as early as 1923—he was not yet forty years old. Following this, Duchamp engages in what a critic described as "reaching the limit of the unaesthetic, the useless and the unjustifiable": he works on a geometry of the fourth dimension looking for the "infra thin" and the timeless, he imagines the dictionary of an unknown language whose alphabet would be composed by film endings, he sells shares in a gambling system intended to break the bank at Monte Carlo's roulette … (Abella, 2007, p. 1051).

Cage takes a different path. While expressing his distrust of language in terms very similar to those of Bion, he turns back not to science but towards chance—a tricky maneuver already used by Duchamp. Thus, he restricts himself to composing by following the Chinese divination book *I Ching*, or plays on a "prepared piano" in which all sorts of things are added to the strings: screws, pie plates, books … The aim is always the same: to produce an unpredictable series of sounds, which he sees as a radical way of freeing himself of taste, memory, and desire (Abella, 2012, p. 726).

Boltanski chooses another avenue in his search of an extreme and violent cleaning up of the artistic field, aimed to disencumber it from the artist's personal influence. He proposes "unfocused images where everybody can recognise himself" (Abella, 2008, p. 1130). For this aim, Boltanski draws on the depersonalizing and overwhelming effects of endless multiplication and incantatory repetition. He thus proceeds to hand mold over three thousand little earth balls, searching for the perfect sphere, or carves over nine hundred cubes of sugar in different shapes; at other moments he confronts the public with a long series of unfocused photographs, or with huge heaps of clothes, or with endless lists of names, monotonously read out … Superabundance proves thus to have the same effect as starvation: we are left disoriented and, at least momentarily, deprived of our customary socialized frames of thought.

This is probably the underlying reason why today's artists often refuse to provide any clues to their works. A recent example of this can be found in an interview given in February 2013 by filmmaker Michael Haneke. Speaking about his contribution to a new staging of *Così fan tutte* in Madrid, he says: "I refuse to speak about myself because I have always tried to erase any instructions for the usage of my work … If I do give them, I steal the possibility of a personal interpretation to the audience … You must look and confront yourself with the work, not with the author …" And, on a more personal note: "When I read a book or look at a film I want to know nothing about the author." Gerhard Richter expresses a similar sensibility, when he states: "My pictures know more than I do." In order to allow the public to grasp the unseen, the unfelt, and the unthought, the artist should avoid saturating his work with personal feelings or phantasies—an idea that drives Richter to make the following strong statement: "Paintings which are interpretable, and which contain a meaning, are bad pictures." That which is too easily reduced to pre-existing knowledge, and thus hinders access to the new, is bad art and bad psychoanalysis. Tragically enough, all these attempts seem doomed to failure. At the end of *Transformations* Bion recognises that his efforts have driven him to build a "Lewis Carroll mathematics". Some years later, he acknowledges that the grid is useless for what he intended (Bion, 1974b, p. 53). We feel a catastrophic earthquake in Bion's thinking, and the aftershocks are still perceptible. The man who had labored to build up a scientific method aiming to achieve clear thinking and to facilitate communication, he who made the assault against psychoanalytical jargon, this same man produces, in his last works, a hermetic, mystical, often unreadable and kitsch presentation. Startling paradox, disconcerting nonsense, contradictory statements, rambling chatting, and provocative questions come to the fore, all of them mixed up with illuminating suggestions and enlivening "flashes of obvious". A parallel might be draw with Duchamp's abandoning art, with Cage's *4' 33"*: a silent piece of music, with no sounds at all. The hope of reaching meaningful understanding through reason has vanished and what seemed to be important achievements—the grid, the ready-mades, music itself—must be abandoned. At the end, we see these artists explicitly choosing to refuse communication, in a way that recalls Bion's refusal to answer questions and to be clear and pedagogical. In front of unsolvable obstacles, extreme means may be the unique issue. A salutary electric shock, a violent purging and disinfecting maneuver may sometimes be the only way to enliven mummified and excessively self-satisfied minds. Curiously, both Bion's last works and contemporary artistic provocations arouse similar feelings: amazement, awe, discomfort, passionate refusal, or defensive idealization.

## An aesthetic model inspired on Bion

Following on from what I have described, Bion's thinking provides the basis for a psychoanalytical aesthetic model more apt to the understanding of contemporary art. This model highlights art's capacity to open up our minds to new aspects of external and internal reality in a critical and highly personal way. Thus, art is not seen as a pleasurable entertainment providing escape from frustration. On the contrary, it appears as a growth-promoting activity whose aim is to enable the unknown to be grasped and to achieve mental growth.

In order to foster contact with the most profound and authentic layers of oneself and to allow the deconstruction of ready-made and deceptive truths, a silent, receptive, and negative capacity is requested. This capacity is built on the renunciation of taste, memory, desire, understanding, and rational coherence. Therefore the artist, like the psychoanalyst, may choose to retreat from seduction and indoctrination and even, in extreme circumstances, from the simple fact of communicating when this runs the risk of impeding freedom and "naivety of outlook". Thus, this model supports contemporary artists in the idea of the double potentiality of their field: whilst art can open to the new, it is also possible that "the artist's capacity may enable him to provide, as Plato feared, a substitute for truth" (Bion, 1963, p. 2). Art can open up our minds but it can also seduce and mislead, exactly as can psychoanalysis.

This model differs from the precedent psychoanalytical models in one significant point. We have seen how Freud suggests sublimation as the central mechanism involved in artistic activity, whereas, for Segal, this role is attributed to reparation, and, for Winnicott, to the experience of illusion/disillusion inside a transitional space. We have also seen how, for an important trend in contemporary art, the goal of artistic activity is fundamentally to open up our minds to a new perception of the world in such a way as to foster personal thinking and creativity.

Bion's contributions entirely support the understanding of this particular aim. Following an aesthetic model inspired by Bion's work, art is not only seen as an activity that fosters sublimation or reparation or that provides a space for working out omnipotence. Art is seen fundamentally as a means of favoring new thinking. Bion's notion of unconscious dream thought appears here as a precious tool. The thinking fostered by art is not only, nor mainly, intellectual and conscious knowledge, as Duchamp seems to suggest. On the contrary, what is stimulated by art, and that which can allow real mental growth, is the unconscious current of emotional thought that accompanies and underlies rational thinking, reverie, playing, and dream.

Therefore, art may be seen not as the realm of beauty, seduction, and certainties but as the realm of truth, thinking, and questioning. Far from the intellectual and dehumanized ideal of Duchamp, art provides the means for an unconscious processing of emotions intimately interwoven with the germination of new thoughts. There is still pleasure in contemporary art: nevertheless this pleasure is not exclusively sensuous but includes the joys of thinking and fresh understanding.

Bion's thinking yields another interesting contribution to one of the main preoccupations of contemporary artists. The factors that impede freedom of thinking are not only the cultural codes transmitted by tradition and education. Underlying tradition and education we find a far more pervasive dread: the universal fear of confronting the unknown and the most authentic part of oneself, the tendency to seek refuge in certainty described by Bion. Were we able to lessen social impositions, this more deep-seated constraint would still remain: the reluctance to face "uncertainties, mysteries and doubts". This is a very specific contribution of psychoanalysis to art, one that adds complexity to the problem of personal freedom as seen by artists.

To sum up, we do not only crave pleasure and beauty but, maybe even more importantly, we crave truth in the form of understanding and of deep encounter with the most authentic part of ourselves. In Bion's language, we would say that we need a combination of K and O. Bion's significance is to have shown our vital need for both, a need which is simultaneously feared because of its being paradoxically intertwined with dreadful anxieties. As Bion says: "There seems to be a constant warfare between the attraction of something new and one's own wish to remain in a familiar field or state of mind" (Bion, 1974b, p. 205). Therefore, this aesthetic model allows us to build a bridge between psychoanalysis and contemporary art: a bridge that stands on the understanding that this warfare is the real stuff of both art and psychoanalysis.

## Notes

1. There are, of course, some exceptions, such as H. Poincaré (1854-1912), frequently quoted by Bion, or, occasionally, Picasso.
2. It might be shocking that I put together the art of the Middle Ages and the Renaissance, on the one hand, and the art of the Third Reich and Soviet art on the other hand. I refer here exclusively to their deliberate propagandistic aim with no moral or aesthetic judgment concerning their realizations.

## References

Abella, A. (2007). Marcel Duchamp: On the fruitful use of narcissism and destructiveness in contemporary art. International Journal of Psychoanalysis, *88*: 1039–1060.
Abella, A. (2008). Christian Boltanski: un artiste contemporain vu et pensé par une psychanalyste. *Revue Française de Psychanalyse, 4*: 1113–1136.
Abella, A. (2010). Contemporary art and Hanna Segal's thinking on aesthetics. International Journal of Psychoanalysis, *91*: 163–181.
Abella, A. (2012). John Cage and W. R. Bion: an exercise in interdisciplinary dialogue. International Journal of Psychoanalysis, *93*: 473–487.
Bion, W. R. (1962). *Learning from Experience.* London: Heinemann.
Bion, W. R. (1963). *Elements of Psycho-analysis.* London: Heinemann.
Bion, W. R. (1965). *Transformations.* London: Heinemann.
Bion, W. R. (1967). *Second Thoughts.* London: Heinemann.
Bion, W. R (1967b). Notes on memory and desire. In: E. B. Spillius (Ed.), *Melanie Klein Today, Vol. 2: Mainly Practice* (pp. 17–21). London: Routledge, 1988.
Bion, W. R. (1970). *Attention and Interpretation.* London: Tavistock.
Bion, W. R. (1974a). *Bion's Brazilian Lectures 1.* Rio de Janeiro: Imago Editora.
Bion, W. R. (1974b). *Bion's Brazilian Lectures 2.* Rio de Janeiro: Imago Editora.
Bion, W. R. (1975, 1977, 1979). *A Memoir of the Future (3 volumes).* Strathclyde, Perthshire: Clunie.
Bion, W. R. (1987). *Clinical Seminars and Four Papers.* Abingdon: Fleetwood Press.
Bion, W. R. (1997). *Taming Wild Thoughts.* London: Karnac.
Bleandonu, G. (1994). *Wilfred Bion: His Life and Works.* London: *Free Association.*

Freud, S. (1908). The relation of the poet to day-dreaming. *S. E., 9*: 141–154. London: Hogarth.
Freud, S. (1914). *The Moses of Michelangelo. S. E., 13*: 211–236. London: Hogarth.
Freud, S. (1937). Analysisterminable and interminable. *S. E., 23*: 209–254. London: Hogarth.
Freud, S., & Jones, E. (1993). *The Complete Correspondence of Sigmund Freud and Ernest Jones: 1908–1939*. London: Belknap Press.
Glover, N. (1998). *Psychoanalytic Aesthetics: The British School.* London: Free Association.
Grotstein, J. S. (2008). *A Beam of Intense Darkness.* London: Karnac.
Haneke, M. (2013). http://cultura.elpais.com/cultura/2013/02/12/actualidad/1360680566_058620.html.
Kunst, B. (2012). Precarious audience: on the tension between effort and idleness of judgement in contemporary performance. In: *Juzgar el arte contemporáneo = Judging Contemporary Art.* Navarra: Universidad Pública de Navarra.
Richter, G.: from the documentary "Gerhard Richter—Painting" www.boards.straightdope.com
Richter G.: www.boards.straightdope.com
Segal, H. (1952). A psycho-analytical approach to aesthetics. *International Journal of Psychoanalysis, 33*: 196–207.
Segal, H. (1991). *Dream, Phantasy and Art.* New York: Routledge.
Vermote, R. (2011). On the value of "late Bion" to analytic theory and practice. *International Journal of Psychoanalysis, 92*: 1089–1098.
Winnicott, D. W. (1971). *Playing and Reality.* London : Penguin.

CHAPTER THIRTY-FIVE

# The buried harbor of dreaming: psychoanalysis and literature—towards a Bionian, non-archaeological approach

*Francesco Capello*

> "Senza mai negare le necessità universali della poesia, h[o] sempre pensato che, per lasciarsi immaginare, l'universale deve attraverso un attivo sentimento storico, accordarsi colla voce singolare del poeta."
>
> (Without ever denying the universal necessities of poetry, I have always thought that the universal, in order to be imagined, needs to become attuned to the individual voice of the poet through his active sense of how what is universal is positioned in history.)
>
> —*Giuseppe Ungaretti*, 1970

The kinship of psychoanalysis and literature is, as it were, a certified one. From the beginning, Freud famously resorted to literary works and characters in the attempt to describe his findings on our mental functioning, Oedipus and Narcissus being only the most notable cases in point. It is also telling that, having been (unsuccessfully) nominated twelve times for the Nobel Prize in medicine or physiology, Freud was actually honored in 1930 with the Goethe Prize for literature, and then again nominated (by Romain Rolland) for a Nobel Prize in literature in 1936. Nominations and awards are, of course, significant indicators, and in this case the shift from the domain of the natural and medical sciences to the territory of literature seems to prefigure the progressive migration of psychoanalysis, about fifty years later, from the academic departments of psychology and the faculties of medicine to the departments of literature and the faculties of humanities. (This, at least, has been the main trend in Anglo-Saxon universities). In this respect, it also seems noteworthy that, since the second half of the twentieth century, the discourse of psychoanalysis as a whole has been repeatedly identified by scholars and analysts, including Harris Williams and Waddell (1991), Kirschner (1996),

Harris Williams (2005, 2009), Faflak (2007), and Snell (2012), as a ramification or development of Romantic philosophical and literary approaches to subjectivity.

While these considerations may lead one to wonder to what extent psychoanalysis might be a form of literature, other links between the two disciplines, at the same time deeper and more evident, seem to point to another perspective. This has to do mainly with the way in which psychoanalysis and literature function. Both operate chiefly through words; both foreground (and engage with) the fantasies and the mental life of the people involved in the respective processes; both invariably tend to elicit, though in different manners, an emotional response in the participants, thereby also producing a transformation in the affective field that each participant contributes to create, in the intersubjective act of reading as well as in the consulting room. Such a different emphasis, placed on psychic events, interaction, and transformation, may thus invite one to reformulate in reversed terms the question I posed just above: might, in fact, literature operate in a way somehow comparable to psychoanalysis? I will not attempt to provide an answer immediately, for in view of the affinities that I have briefly summarized there is a more practical question, which is probably best addressed from the outset: what have psychoanalysis and literature done so far with each other and their relationship?

Building on an article by Francis Baudry (1984), Susan Budd (2007) discusses the four approaches that have most significantly characterized the interactions of psychoanalysis and literature until now. In the first, "the analyst treats a novel, play, or poem as if it were a piece of clinical material, ignoring the as-if nature of the literary text and looking at characters as if they were cases. This is perhaps the commonest use made of psychoanalysis in understanding literature" (p. 45). This method has been applied in several ways: for instance in the early reading of Shakespeare's *Hamlet* by Ernest Jones, centered on a rather rigid "interpretation/decryption" of the protagonist's Oedipus complex—but also in Freud's dense and fascinating symbolic decoding of Jensen's novella *Gradiva*. More recently, adopting a post-Kleinian perspective, the Italian psychoanalyst Roberto Speziale-Bagliacca (2000) has offered a nuanced, multi-layered, and highly persuasive reading of Flaubert's *Madame Bovary*, taking the "analysis" of its main character Emma and her husband Charles as a starting point. However, it immediately emerges that Speziale-Bagliacca's focus is not so much on the characters treated as real persons with an autonomous psychic life, as was the case with Freud's and Jones's early attempts, but on the states of mind and relational forms that they come to embody.[1]

In a short epilogue centered on Flaubert's life in relation to his work, Speziale-Bagliacca also ventures into the second approach addressed by Budd, one which has often been deemed especially controversial: "the analyst analyses the text as if it were a form of free association of the author and a guide to his mental life" (p. 46). This is what Freud did with his well-known (and ultimately disavowed) essay on Leonardo from 1910 and what Marie Bonaparte did with her monograph on Edgar Allan Poe's "life and work" (1933).[2] It is frequently argued that this is a sort of psychoanalytic Sainte-Beuveism, making unwarranted, reconstructive claims on a writer's psychic life. However, while in view of the inclination towards reductionism that characterizes several of these studies this seems a fair point in general,[3] it is also true to say, as literary scholar Mario Lavagetto (2005) does, that information on the life of an author may occasionally prove useful for an understanding (*including* a psychological understanding) of the subtext, development, and structure of his or her work. In this respect, Thomas Ogden and Benjamin Ogden (2013) have gone even further in criticizing the claim that the states of mind described, represented, or even elicited by a writer's work might be independent of his personal emotional experience:

> … a writer cannot create in his writing what he is incapable of experiencing in his own life [...]. Fictional characters and themes are not repositories for discrete aspects of the author's unconscious mind, but are nonetheless imbued with certain qualities of thinking and feeling that derive from the psychology of the author. (p. 13)

The author, in this perspective, may therefore no longer be "on the couch"—but he is definitely not "dead" either.[4]

The third manner of engaging psychoanalytically with literature would be to look at the text in its own right, and analyse it in terms of the unconscious mental processes that it draws upon. Here, parallels are often drawn between texts and dreams; the expression of meaning via particular symbols and metaphors, and the idea of a latent content of a text. A prominent analyst who made use of this approach was the former president of the *Società Psicoanalitica Italiana*, Franco Fornari, especially in his later writings from the 1970s and early 1980s (Fornari & Fornari, 1974; Fornari, 1977, 1979, 1984, 1985). A striking example of his method is provided by the line-by-line decoding (informed by Kleinian object-relations theory) of the unconscious structures embedded in the narrative of Alberto Moravia's novel *Agostino* (see Fornari & Fornari, 1974).

The fourth option listed by Budd is that of looking at the emotional impact of the text on the reader. This is an approach developed particularly in the US by the literary critic Norman Holland among others and more recently, in a more analytically informed group setting, by the psychoanalyst Walker Shields (2009).[5]

Practicing psychoanalysts, resorting in their literary readings to one or another of these approaches, have also often turned to literature to understand or explain in more depth their theories on mental functioning, as well as the particular psychic processes they happened to observe in their patients or themselves. Again, it was Freud who pioneered this particular psychoanalytic genre with his essay on "The uncanny" (1919). However, his example was followed among others by Melanie Klein (1955), who used Julian Greene's novel *If I were you* to illustrate her notion of projective identification, and, in a more contemporary framework, by Thomas Ogden (2005), who identified in Borges' short story "Funes el memorioso", a particularly impressive depiction of a psychic state definable (in Bionian language) as "inability to dream". In his re-reading of the tale of *Lisabetta* (from Giovanni Boccaccio's *Decameron*), Giuseppe Civitarese (2010) has also intertwined considerations on the plot and the characters of the novella with theoretical observations on Donald Meltzer's theory of aesthetic conflict and on Julia Kristeva's notion of abjection.

One of the main purposes I had in mind in sketching this general outline was to create the possibility of taking a step back from it and observing the implications of these different facets of psychoanalytic criticism, alongside the assumptions about psychoanalysis that they more or less implicitly convey.

To begin with, the first three approaches listed by Budd share one important feature: in its interaction with literature, psychoanalysis is somehow supposed to take the role of a "hermeneutic picklock". The underlying rationale appears to be that the psychoanalytic method will allow the critic-interpreter to unearth, reveal, or unravel ideas, emotions, and meanings that have been repressed, disguised, or encrypted in the text (or through the text) in its narratives and characters. To be sure, this approach is consistent with a certain set of metaphors traditionally associated with clinical psychoanalysis and the way it has long been understood to work as a therapy. One is reminded of the well-known phrase the Italian historian Carlo Ginzburg (1989) coined in this connection, *paradigma indiziario* (evidential paradigm)—the underlying rationale being that a positivist-minded analyst-detective, focusing on slight but tell-tale hints, retraces the different stages of the development of a symptom, "walking backwards" as it were. By reversing all the defensive, unconscious processes of condensation and displacement, he would then progress from the *phenomenon* of the symptom to the latent *noumenon* of the original problem; and once that problem is brought from the unconscious to the consciousness of the patient, the symptomatology becomes unnecessary as a defense mechanism, and naturally recedes. This idea of "bringing to the light" buried contents is also expressed by another metaphor created by Freud himself: that of psychoanalysis as a form of psychic archaeology.

While this narrative, in itself, may seem plausible and inherently consistent, it is also crucial to point out that few analysts today would wholeheartedly subscribe to the idea that psychoanalysis as a therapeutic process works exactly in such a way. In fact, there is increasingly widespread consensus that what cures patients are not insights into repressed contents alone, however "deep" or well-pitched the interpretations preparing the ground for them might be.[6] Accordingly, in the second half of the twentieth century, psychoanalytic theory based on clinical observation has developed different models of therapeutic action alongside new models of mental functioning in general.

In the model of psychopathology developed by Ferro (1999, 2002, 2006, 2007, 2010) building on Bion's theories on the functioning of the mind, mental suffering is rooted not so much in the workings of repression or innate unconscious phantasies. Repression is, in fact, a potentially useful mechanism, in so far as it creates enough free mental space for us to do conscious thinking. In metapsychological terms, it contributes to form the semi-permeable contact barrier between conscious and unconscious that is indispensable for a healthy functioning of the mind. Mental health problems arise when someone is not able to do unconscious thinking—that is to say, when he does not develop the psychic functions necessary to process the raw sense data and the equally basic powerful emotions swarming around and connected with them.

Such data and un-thought proto-emotions, when they are not processed, cannot be "digested", metabolized, and used for thinking by the mental apparatus; they can only be either evacuated through acting outs and projections, or split off in areas of the mind that become deadened and impervious to access. As is well known, Bion (1962, 1967) used the term "beta elements" in referring to these splinters (or clusters of splinters) of bare, unprocessed reality that incessantly present themselves to our bodies and minds. A well-developed mind processes and transforms beta elements into something different—into affectively-charged dream-images (Bion called them pictograms, or alpha elements) that constitute the individual bricks of which dream-thoughts are made. Just as the alpha function of the mind transforms beta elements into alpha elements, another function, called by Bion "apparatus to think thoughts", subsequently proceeds to assemble strings of alpha elements from which what we ordinarily call thoughts emerge. In contemporary post-Bionian thought, the process whereby raw beta elements are processed and transformed into psychic material available for thinking and then possibly sharing thoughts rooted in emotions is called dreaming. Since we are continuously exposed to reality and external stimuli that require mental processing, we also continuously dream, both at night and during the day. As Ogden (2001, pp. 4–5) points out evocatively, dreams are in some respects like the stars; we can see them only at night, but they keep on shining also during daytime, though concealed by the glare of the sun. Dreaming, in other words, is the necessary bridge between the most primitive and bodily level of our emotions and the ability to think.[7] From this perspective, psychopathology reflects one or more of a set of problems affecting that bridge on some level.

But just how does one develop the alpha function and the ability to dream? In early life, this happens through the relationship with the primary caregiver, usually the mother, who makes her mind available to host the violent projective identifications of the baby (evacuated beta elements). If she is "good enough", as Winnicott would have it, in the majority of cases she transforms this unprocessed psychic material on the baby's behalf through her emotional attunement and her own alpha function. Having done this, through her reactions, verbal and non-verbal, to the baby's evacuations, the mother exposes him to detoxified, more processed and manageable emotions he can now safely re-possess and deal with (alpha elements), and with time hopefully the baby will introject not just the "good fish" of meaning but also the "fishing rod" that will enable him to produce meaning autonomously. In this context, the psychoanalytic relationship is understood as a "second chance" (after infancy and childhood) to develop one's mind with the help of another mind.

Although nowadays the theoretical paradigm shift I have described is often reflected in the technique used in clinical psychoanalysis, so far it has been largely ignored by psychoanalytic literary criticism. This has been detrimental for literary studies, which have missed an opportunity for developing fresh insights in both literature as such and their own analytically informed methodologies; but it has been possibly even more detrimental for psychoanalysis, whose prestige in public discourse continues to be negatively affected by the fact that its representation in academia is often grossly distorted, conveying the idea that very little, if anything at all, has changed since the time of Freud. This seems all the more regrettable when one considers that, from a post-Bionian angle, interest in literature and the arts plays a significant part in the sustained attempt to understand what happens "at the frontier of dreaming" (Ogden, 2001).[8] Indeed, if on the one hand one might state that the aim of contemporary psychoanalytic treatments is to revitalize, develop, or even create the mental functions that allow us to dream, on the other hand art in general (and therefore literature as well) is increasingly seen as an activity that constitutes precisely a performative representation of those functions. In this perspective, the essence of a work of art is no longer a latent meaning or content one can laboriously reconstruct in the way one does with jig-saw puzzles, which only have one "correct" solution; artworks are more like emotion-targeted Rorschach test inkblots, whose meaning, if there is one, resides ultimately in the extent to which they manage to promote or engage with one's ability to make something out of them. Needless to say, the narrative and historical-cultural elements that are the "material fabric" of literary works and artworks in general, are instrumental to such a process of emotional engagement, though content alone is not a sufficient condition for it to take place: what is central is that the artwork presents the reader or viewer with the fact that something is being *made* with that content. An effective artwork will thus be understood not only as the product of the artist's transformative encounter with reality—at one and the same time the outcome and the representation of his dream-work process—but also as something that concurrently (and performatively) engages the viewer's (or reader's) ability to dream his own reality, possibly stimulating such a function. Artworks are therefore texts which also act as "readers of their readers". In other words, if thinking, understood as a subjectively felt experience of producing meaning, elicits in the thinker not just the awareness of a process going on but also of a place where this process takes place (the mind), and if it is safe to state that it is precisely this experience that allows individuals to develop a "theory of mind" (Hinshelwood, 2003), leading to an emotionally rooted sense that other people too have a separate mind, then artworks, by exposing viewers and readers to the artists' process of thinking and dreaming, also inevitably expose them to the existence and the workings of their own minds alongside the specific quality of their potential to dream and think.

It seems crucial to add that the same rationale informs the Bionian theory of psychoanalytic interpretations. Indeed, an interpretation can be said to work well not in so far as it discloses a hidden ultimate truth about the patient, but in so far as it can be used by the latter as a tool to build a more sustainably multilayered point of view on his reality (internal and external); a point of view, in other words, that allows him to create new, more meaningful stories—stories that do not merely reflect a rational or operational way of thinking, but which resonate with emotions in relation to which the patient can increasingly afford to feel more alive without the need to split them off or deaden himself to them. In Ogden's words, a good interpretation (and possibly a good work of art as well) helps the patient to dream his yet undreamt dreams. There is a clear continuity with Bion in this respect:

> He [the artist] is someone who is able to digest facts, i.e. sense data, and then to present the digested facts, my α-elements, in a way that makes it possible for the weak assimilators to go on from there. Thus the artist helps the non-artist to digest, say, the Little Street in Delft by doing α-work on his sense impressions and "publishing" the result so that others who could not "dream" the Little Street itself can now digest the published α-work of someone who could digest it. Vermeer was able to digest the facts in a particular way, or perhaps they were particular facts. (Bion, 1994, pp. 143–144)

Some fine-tuning may be in order here. To begin with, what is essential to the painting as a work of art would not (or at least not primarily) be the Little Street in itself, but the "digestive process" that is shared through the act of its representation. Indeed, it is impossible for us to fathom what perceptions, thoughts, memories, desires, fantasies went through Vermeer's mind in the prolonged act of the conception and realisation of his painting. However, that is not the point. What motivates viewers from an aesthetic (emotional) point of view, even those who have never set foot in Delft, is the engaging capacity of dreaming that is made available, of which the representation of the little street is a material medium of transaction or communication. The content (what is said or represented) is the indispensible physical vehicle that makes the artistic event possible, but does not coincide with it. This distinction between content and function is of course reminiscent of the Aristotelean opposition between matter and form or, on another level and following Bollas (2012), between representation and presentation.[9] Ultimately, the emotional (and therefore not intellectual or rational) concern that is shared by literature, art in general, and psychoanalysis (including psychoanalytic criticism informed by contemporary psychoanalysis) might well be traced back to a common engagement with the

> big-bang represented by the kindling of mental life, which can occur only if there is a relationship with another mind, thus triggering the relevant mechanism: instead of being evacuated, β-elements are taken in and returned transformed into α-elements—in particular enriched with quanta of "alphaness" that will subsequently permit the kindling of an autonomous α-function (Bion, 1962). (Ferro, 2006, p. 4)

Of course psychoanalysis on the one hand and literature and the arts on the other have different aims and functions, and share only part of their tools. Needless to say, they also establish a completely different relationship (in terms of roles and responsibilities) between the person who makes a transformative act available and the person who becomes witness of, and active participant in it. That said, what they have in common at their core may be an interest in intersubjective, transformative dreaming.

As far as intersubjectivity is concerned, a perspective which is becoming increasingly established in the post-Bionian version of psychoanalysis entails a shift of focus from the verbal or non-verbal transactions between the individual members of the analytic couple considered separately (patient and analyst, subject *vs.* object) to a different perspective whereby therapy and transformations are understood to occur within the unique, individual field created at every moment by the interaction of two minds. This field is not simply the sum of two individualities, but is in itself a new subject. By devising the clinical notion of an intersubjective analytic third as the actual subject of analysis, Ogden (1994) actually develops Bion's well-known idea that "when two characters or personalities meet, an emotional storm is created", and that analysis is concerned primarily with that storm in terms of what can be made and what is made of it, aiming in any case to "make the best of a bad job" (Bion, 1979). Attention to what occurs in the field where different kinds of storms are created at every moment is thus a key responsibility of the analyst, who thus has the role of both participant and observer. Thomas Ogden (2001, 2005), and more recently Thomas and Benjamin Ogden (2013) have transferred this standpoint from the clinical context to the activities of reading and criticism:

> in reading a poem, there are two voices acting upon one another: the voice of the speaker in the poem and the voice of the reader experiencing and saying the poem. Consequently, it is not easy to say whose voice one hears as one reads or listens to a poem. The voice heard or made is a voice that is neither exclusively that of the poet nor that of the reader; it is a new and unique voice, a third voice that is generated in the creative conjunction of reader and writer. No two readers of a poem will create the same voice. (Ogden, 2001, p. 42)

The implication is that clearly the second, third, and fourth point in the list provided by Budd—that is, the focus on the voice of the author, of the text, and of the reader—become actually merged into one overarching "field point", intertwining in a more complex and multilayered tapestry the voices of all parties involved in what one may call "the literary event". But there is more. Elsewhere, in addressing the subject of psychoanalytic reading, Ogden (2005, p. 63) goes as far as to argue that

> every piece of analytic writing requires a reader who assists the author in conveying something of what is true, something that the author knew, but did not know that he knew. In so doing, the reader becomes a silent co-author of the text.

Ultimately, from a post-Bionian angle, what is shared by literature, the arts, criticism, and psychoanalysis when they function well—that is, when each of them as a process succeeds in creating and making someone else experience meaning—may well be a productive engagement with the task of (to put it in Bionian terms) thinking thoughts that are still without a thinker. In this sense, truth as an experience pursued and occasionally achieved by psychoanalysis and the arts overlaps to a significant extent with the punctual somatopsychic availability to its own emergence. In this connection, the interpreter both inside and outside the consulting room is "not merely a passive carrier of information from one person to another; he is the active preserver and creator of meaning as well as the retriever of the alienated [i.e., the yet-to-be-dreamt dream, the un-thought thought]" (Ogden, 1986, p. 1). Adela Abella (2010) has noted how John Cage seemed to think very much along these lines, when he once stated that an artistic happening should be like a net to catch a fish the nature of which one does not know.

This idea of encountering and making one's own something which is still unknown or may not yet fully exist, evokes not only the act of discovery together with the excitement and fear that accompany it, but also the very private (though, at its core, relationally rooted) experience of investing an object with personal meaning. At the same time, the unseen yet existing "fish" is also suggestive—in a way that is reminiscent of the Freudian *Fort/Da* of the dialectical relationship between inexistence/existence, or absence/presence, alongside the ultimately elusive, mysterious nature of creation and coming into being. In fact, the latter might be conceptualized as the "slash" or *Spannung* mobilizing those static antinomies.[10] In turn, the mysteriousness of the "original spark" of existence (or meaning) inevitably leads to a more or less implicit questioning of the very possibility of sharing or even talking about the experience itself.

To my mind, these themes are in different ways at the core of the five poems by Giuseppe Ungaretti (1888–1970) I now turn to examine. With the exception of the first, "Eterno" (Eternal), which was published in the avant-garde journal *Lacerba* shortly before Italy's entry into the First World War (May 1915), they were all written by Ungaretti comparatively early on in his experience as an infantry private fighting in the trenches in the Carso area, located in northeastern Italy, on what was then the contended border with the Austro-Hungarian Empire. These war poems were first published in Ungaretti's debut collection, entitled *Il porto sepolto* (The Buried Harbor), 1916. He subsequently went on to expand this initial nucleus into a larger collection (*L'Allegria* [The Joy], 1931), which included later poems written on the battlefield in late 1916 and 1917 alongside others composed in 1918–1919. Due to their unique combination of straightforwardness, intensity, and profound insight into the human condition, as well as to the particularly dramatic quality of their setting, these poems, written almost exactly a century ago, are to this day very well-known and much loved in Italy. Although after this early experience Ungaretti continued his literary journey up until his old age, becoming already when he was still alive one of the most celebrated Italian poets of the twentieth century, the poems from *Il porto sepolto* and *L'Allegria* stand apart from the rest of his works for the way in which they convey the special feeling of a first encounter, with loss, pain, beauty, creativity, poetry, one's internal world. As I will attempt to show, the way in which they both present and represent poetry and creativity resonates with Bion's conceptualisation of the processes of dreaming and thinking in relation to the difficult task of having (and maintaining) a mind—a task whose difficulties, it seems fitting to note, Bion himself experienced first hand in the same years of the Great War as a nineteen-year old officer enrolled in the 5th Tank Battalion on the Western Front.

The lyrical brevity found in "Eterno", the opening poem of *L'Allegria*, characterizes more generally the whole first stage of Ungaretti's poetic itinerary.

> Eterno
> Tra un fiore colto e l'altro donato
> l'inesprimibile nulla
>
> (Between a flower plucked/and one proffered/the ineffable nothing)

One is tempted to imagine that, in placing himself within a common and long-standing poetic tradition, Ungaretti placed this poem *in limine* at the very beginning of the collection because he thought of it in terms of an introduction to, a synthesis of, and, at the same time, a statement on what followed; that is to say, as a meta-reflection on his own poetry and, by extension, on his poetics as well. This hypothesis seems confirmed by the fact that, in the "Introductory note" to his complete works entitled *Life of a Man*, Ungaretti again sets off by referring to and commenting on the significance of this particular poem, connecting it to both his poetic inspiration and the process of his coming into being as a subject (a process which, as the initial reference to "deep wounds" makes clear, is far from easy or painless)[11]:

> Al compianto amico Jean Amrouche, che raccoglieva le mie osservazioni improvvisate per la Radiodiffusion Télévision Française, la prima mia risposta fu questa: "Ma è mettere il dito in piaghe profonde". "Tra un fiore colto e l'altro donato/l'inesprimibile nulla". È un'ossessione che torna, come il lettore vedrà, spesso nel mio canto. È nel significato di quel nonnulla che sembra apparisca la prima presa di coscienza dell'essere stesso che io sono.
>
> (The first answer I gave to my late friend Jean Amrouche, who was then collecting my improvized observations for the Radiodiffusion Télévision Française, was the following: "But this is like rubbing salt on deep wounds". "Between a flower plucked/and one proffered/the ineffable nothing". This is an obsession that, as the reader will see, often comes back in my song. It is in the meaning of that nothing that the first awareness seems to appear of that very being that I am.)

Poetry, Ungaretti seems to say in "Eterno", emerges in an in-between space ("tra", "between")—just like subjectivity, which, as argued above, originates from an intersubjective framework. It also has to do with switching from a position where one appropriates something beautiful and valuable (in what might feel like a "damaging", greedy way: once picked, flowers die) to a different one where one can offer it to somebody else. "But at the same time and on another level" (Grotstein, 2009), this shift might also evoke, metaphorically represent, or even reflect a change from a needy sort of relying and leaning on the mental functions of another person who is able to dream and think, to eventually introjecting them, becoming able to relate to others as a separate, existing individual who *has* something because in the first place he now *is* someone, in the sense that he has a mind.

In any case, the idea of a reversed perspective in relation to an object, that is, of a transformation experienced as occurring in the subject, is central to the first line, and what witnesses, accompanies, or possibly even determines such a transformation is presented to the reader as "inesprimibile nulla". The poem would thus seem to focus on a punctual event of transformation felt as a somewhat unfathomable spark of creation (and, indeed, of poiesis): a spark which resides between the two dimensions of non-existence and existence (or non-meaning and meaning), defining them both. But what exactly is inexpressible in all this, and why?

An initial observation may be that the two measures of nothingness and being are incommensurable. The idea of a nothingness that from the standpoint of being cannot accordingly be talked about ("inesprimibile nulla") could also be associated to the notion of eternity—that is, to the all-encompassing, unspeakable non-time alternative to the time of being and language. In this respect, it is significant that the title "Eterno" is the first in the book. Indeed, due to its liminal position, it breaks the timeless silence of non-existence and, in so doing, transcends dialectically the very meaning it conveys, linked to stasis. Put in another way, from a performative point of view the significance of the word "eterno" in this context is that of a *fiat lux* that, as a dynamic gesture, dialectically contains within itself the transcended representation of its static opposite (the signified eternal stasis of nothingness). However, the domain of subjective experience imbued with emotional meaning is not tied to this kind of logic: there is more to it.

Ungaretti's above quotation follows thus:

> Ecco, sono nato ad Alessandria d'Egitto. […] Alessandria è nel deserto, in un deserto dove la vita è forse intensissima dai tempi della sua fondazione, ma dove la vita non lascia alcun segno di permanenza nel tempo. Alessandria è una città senza un monumento, o meglio senza quasi un monumento che ricordi il suo antico passato. […] È una città dove il sentimento del tempo, del tempo distruttore è presente all'immaginazione prima di tutto e soprattutto. E dicendo *nulla* in particolare ho pensato, difatti, a quel lavoro di costante annientamento che il tempo vi produce. Anche, ho pensato al miraggio che quel nulla e quel tempo abolito avvenga facciano balenare all'immaginazione del poeta, ad una immaginazione che mi fa arretrare fino all'infanzia, quando quei miraggi incominciavano ad essermi consueti.
>
> (Here goes, I was born in Alexandria of Egypt. […] Alexandria is in the desert, a desert where life may as well have been very intense ever since the time of the city's foundation, but where on the other hand life does not leave any trace of its permanence in time. Alexandria is a city without a monument, or better still, almost without a monument which might remind one of its ancient past. […]. It is a city where the sense of time, of time as a destroyer, is present in one's imagination before and above everything else. And indeed, in saying *nothing* [here

Ungaretti refers again to "Eternal"], I thought in particular of that intense, constant activity of obliteration carried out by time. I also thought of the mirage that that nothingness and that abolished time happen to conjure up in the poet's imagination, an imagination that brings me back to my childhood, when I started being accustomed to those mirages.)

A fundamental sense of transience, impermanence, painful change ("time as a destroyer") and death seems to reside at the core of these reflections. Alexandria of Egypt, the poet's city of birth and therefore a key reference point of his early environment, is portrayed as a place where nothing stays and things simply and relentlessly fall apart to be forgotten. An intriguing parallelism links the self-correction "[it] is a city without a monument, *or better still, almost* without a monument which might remind one of its ancient past [my italics]" to the passage "and in saying *nothing* I thought in particular of that intense, constant activity of obliteration carried out by time. I also thought of the mirage that that nothingness and that abolished time happen to conjure up in the poet's imagination, an imagination that brings me back to my childhood …". Indeed, the second passage features an implicit switch from absolute nothingness (represented in the first one by the complete absence of monuments) to a kind of suspended something-ness; the "almost" left unspecified in the first passage, and here a highlighted, italicized *nulla* turning inadvertently into some-thing—a mirage, an illusion, an activity (and an actual product) of the poet's imagination also allowing him to get in touch with emotionally meaningful childhood memories. Paying the painful price of facing nothingness seems to bring something(ness) about, at least in the domain of the internal world.

The extreme experience of fighting in the trenches—which, as I have pointed out, is also where Ungaretti established his identity as a poet—provided him with the opportunity to rehearse this thought in different terms. A case in point is "Pellegrinaggio" (Pilgrimage):

> Pellegrinaggio
> Valloncello dell'Albero Isolato il 16 agosto 1916
>
> In agguato
> in queste budella
> di macerie
> ore e ore
> ho strascicato
> la mia carcassa
> usata dal fango
> come una suola
> o come un seme
> di spinalba
>
> Ungaretti
> uomo di pena
> ti basta un'illusione
> per farti coraggio

> Un riflettore
> di là
> mette un mare
> nella nebbia

(In ambush/in these burrows/of rubble/hour after hour/I have dragged/my carcass/plied by mud/like the sole of a boot/or like the seed/of a thornbush//Ungaretti/man of anguish/you need but an illusion/to take heart//On the other side/a searchlight/turns the fog/into an ocean)

The pilgrimage Ungaretti alludes to is not external, as no actual physical destination of his "dragging himself" is mentioned. Rather, the sounds and words of the poem appear to point to an inner pilgrimage from one state of mind to another. With the exception of the last two lines, the first stanza presents the reader with an extraordinarily bleak, gloomy, persecutory situation. The reference to the ambush and the evocation of gutting, the destruction suggested by the rubble and the image of the poet's living carcass badly deteriorated in the mud of the trenches are all echoed in the Italian original by the interplay of dark vowels and harsh consonants: the unusually frequent "u"s and "o"s in "agguato", "ore e ore", "budella", "usata", and "suola", the conglomerate of coarse consonants in "strascicato/carcassa", as well as the rhyme "agguato/strascicato", in all likelihood reminiscent of another poem, "Veglia" (Watch: see below), also written on the battlefield only a few months before and structured on the rhyming of similar-sounding past participles of verbs conveying uncomfortable or violent meanings ("buttato" [thrown down], "massacrato" [massacred], "digrignata"[snarling], "penetrata"[ripping]). The two final lines of the stanza, however, come as a surprising turning point: "o come un seme/di spinalba" (or like the seed/of a thornbush). Significantly, they are introduced by a disjunctive "o" ("or") which, already in itself, heralds a crossroads at the end of what feels like an unstoppable stream of mud, horror, and despair. The flux of the vowels changes colour by gradually shifting at the pace of two-three in a row[12] ( two "o"s, three "e"s, two "i"s, and two "a"s) from a dark, back "o" to a progressively clearer and front (but close) "e" and "i" and then eventually to the release of a final, clear, and open "a". At a semantic level, the change is even more abrupt: the most unexpected alternative term of comparison to the "carcass" of the poet alongside the deteriorated, worthless sole of a boot, is a seed of hawthorn—the promise, somehow disconcerting at this juncture, of something beautiful and redeemingly white that might one day grow out from the dark mud.[13]

Now, is the fulfillment of this promise simply deferred to the future in the way one is accustomed to think it works with promises, or does the hawthorn seed flourish in the very present beauty of poetry? Is this an indirect confirmation of Stendhal's opinion that the here and now of beauty is "une promesse de bonheur" (Agamben, 1994)? In other words, is this promise its own actual fulfillment, and if so, what would it consist in? Would that be the pleasure of experiencing oneself as able to use one's own imaginative and creative capacities in dealing with internal reality, thereby also reworking one's own emotional perspective in relation to external reality, even the most gruesome? Also, would it be the sense of wholeness and of resilient, sheer existence that derives from experiencing the capacity to preserve such capacities alongside one's ability to dream and think in the face of constant attacks from the outside and (one would imagine) from an inner world severely tested by persecution?

What is certain is that not even here are change and growth free from pain. On the one hand, thought, like the seed, needs to endure a long and painful period immersed in a disorienting, meandering, and threatening darkness (in addition to mud there are the "budella" [guts], a word which also triggers associations with the womb and, given the war scenario, with guts spilling out and no longer—or not yet—contained). On the other hand, at the level of the signifier, the very choice of the poetic and rare term "spinalba" seems to suggest through what might be seen as the implicit conflation of two other nouns that there cannot really be a dawn (in Italian: "alba") without painful thorns ("spine").

The thornbush seed that in "Pellegrinaggio" materializes so suddenly, surprisingly, and, as it were, out of nothing (or perhaps, out of facing nothingness) may remind one of the "miraggio" (mirage) that, equally unforeseen, springs out of the "nulla" in the desert surrounding Alexandria. This connection, while not immediate, seems substantiated by Ungaretti's own associations. First, in the author's notes to "Pellegrinaggio", the one specification he feels it necessary to make is that "la spinalba, il biancospino, prospera in ogni giardino d"Alessandria" (thornbushes prosper in all gardens of Alexandria) (p. 524). In addition, as in the second stanza, Ungaretti proceeds to reinforce in the more descriptive form of a statement what he has said in the first, the potentiality and the promise intrinsic in the hawthorn seed are now called "illusione" ("illusion"), a close match to "miraggio":

> Ungaretti
> uomo di pena
> ti basta un'illusione
> per farti coraggio
>
> (Ungaretti/man of anguish/you need but an illusion/to take heart)

Being human ("uomo"), having an identity ("Ungaretti"), in sum: becoming a subject who has a mind—all of this entails learning to suffer, or how to suffer: it takes to be a "man of anguish" capable of withstanding loss and absence in order to dream and think and host in one's mind a felt experience of something becoming meaningful—something emotionally tangible one can cling to and take courage from. In this light, the first two stanzas can be seen as "narrative derivatives" (Ferro, 1999) of the same sequence of alpha elements: from a long-lasting, inchoate darkness threatening existence (eight lines as opposed to two for the hawthorn seed) to the "flash" of a good-scented, fresh white flower becoming alive; or, again, from a pain that seems to inform the very core of a man's being to the emergence of one significant discontinuity that, however isolated, transient, and tenuous ("illusion"), nevertheless "suffices" (i.e., the mind works like a "good enough" container). The "spark" comes about when, into the blood-drenched mud of the trenches, where the deteriorated, half-dead body of the poet is immersed (referential, historical narrative), the potential image is suddenly superimposed of a sort of primordial broth where a yet incomplete, half-alive seed of a thought (or of a mind) is pushing its way into life. The creatively displacing, metaphoric thinking that governs the associative comparison of the poet's body to the hawthorn seed acts as a bridge that opens up to a different level of Ungaretti's narrative, which is now self-referential and "internal".

The idea of "miraggio"—which, incidentally, floats in the poem as an "oversound" (Ogden, 2001) due to its potential rhyming with two key words actually present in the text (the title "Pellegrinaggio" and the word courage, "coraggio")—is also there in the final stanza. Here the mirage of a sea, inextricably connected with Alexandria's landscape in Ungaretti's imagination (and most markedly at this stage in his life) is projected onto the screen of fog of reality.

> Un riflettore
> di là
> mette un mare
> nella nebbia

(On the other side/a searchlight/turns the fog/into an ocean)

The third stanza feels and operates in a way that is different from the other two. While these, making use of the "narrative genres" (Ferro, 1999) of war images first and then introspection, create the roughly equivalent narrative derivatives of the affective sequence I have described above, the concluding lines seem to move away from this by taking a step forward and talking about the poem itself: about what the pilgrimage is about and where it takes place.

Indeed, the final stanza embodies and at the same time represents the pilgrimage understood as the synthetic, ultimately mysterious slash of creation. It embodies it to the extent that it transforms the first two stanzas by both containing and transcending them. Ungaretti starts off with a war landscape, then moves on to an introspective consideration that makes the emotional meaning of the initial part more explicit, and now returns to a war landscape that, however, appears very different and changed by the whole process. The pace of the lines is slowed down alongside that of action, which is brought to a stillness that feels on hold; the scene appears emptied, the sounds have a less harsh, suspended quality and the sense of indistinction evoked by the enigmatic overlapping of sea and fog is enhanced by the two close alliterations of nasal consonants "m" and "n" (mette un mare/nella nebbia: literally "puts a sea into the fog") creating a flowing, dense, humming continuum. The place Ungaretti now finds himself in (and takes us to) is and is not a scene of war, it is and is not the external reality. On one level, the third stanza shows that the whole poem is, in a Winnicottian sense, a transitional space positioned between the inner world of the subject and external reality—a space where the creative tension engendered by the paradox of engaging with and taking part in both realities can be withstood and made use of to the purpose of the growth of the mind.

The "riflettore" (searchlight) projecting a beam of light into the fog turns out to be working much like a "proiettore" (projector) that, in effect, "puts an image" of something else ("a sea") onto a white screen. The cinematic quality so often attributed to dreams is indirectly evoked here, and one may wonder whether Ungaretti, whose generation had had the first, wondrous encounter with cinema, was inspired by this at some level while writing these lines. However, at the same time, to "put a sea into the fog" also means to put the past (the sea of Alexandria) into the present: to hold on to something inside oneself that is cherished and precious as it is precarious. It is to put together and conflate the internal and the external, one side and the other ("di là" [on the other side]) and also seeing and not seeing, as the glow of the searchlight, bright as it is, seems to actually prevent rather than help seeing *directly* what lies "out there". In fact, that sort of seeing may only be possible through the protective filter of an illusion or a mirage (in Bion's language, the creation of our own subjective reality as opposed to the blinding reality of O). Ungaretti's already quoted "Introductory note" provides further insights into the blinding quality of the "beam of intense darkness" necessary to get in touch with one's inner truth, as well as with the "creative response" (Grotstein, 2007, p. 2) of one's unconscious:

> Nacque a quel modo il gusto e la passione di slanciarmi [...] in miraggi. Era un puerile scoprimento del proprio esistere interiore; insieme, l'"abbaglio di un'immagine, e quasi il nulla, dentro di me, d'una realtà, di quella realtà che più tardi m'occorrerà afferrare, domarla ed avvincermela, di quella realtà rugosa famigliare a Rimbaud. Senza dubbio c'era in quel bimbo, nella sua primordiale inconsapevolezza, una conoscenza perfettissima e imperfettissima d'una realtà intima, segreta, indefinibile, indeterminabile; ed era forse miraggio come quel miraggio che dal deserto ci veniva incontro, e il lucente suo plasma non diffondeva che tenebrore. (Ungaretti, 1970, p. 503)

> (That is how the pleasure and the passion of throwing myself [...] into mirages was born. It was a puerile discovery of one's own internal life; and alongside that, it was the flash of an image, and almost the nothingness, inside myself, of a reality, of the reality which I was later on to grasp, tame, and tie to myself, that wrinkled reality to which Rimbaud was familiar. Without a doubt in that child and in his primordial unawareness there was a very perfect and highly imperfect knowledge of an intimate, secret, indefinable, indeterminable reality; and maybe that was a mirage not unlike that mirage that from the desert came towards us, its glowing plasma radiating nothing else but darkness.)

It is important to stress that the mirage Ungaretti refers to here does not seem to be the hallucinatory kind of gratification which originates from an exclusive or prevalent reliance on the pleasure principle—a gratification, that is, impervious to an engagement with external reality. On the contrary, the last stanza of "Pellegrinaggio" highlights the importance in this respect of "putting one thing into the other", that is to say, to sustain the inevitable tension arising from the encounter of imagination and reality.

From an affective point of view, "Veglia" (Vigil) is structured in a similar way to "Pellegrinaggio", and, just like that poem, it constitutes a kind of "inner pilgrimage":

> Veglia
> Cima Quattro il 23 dicembre 1915
>
> Un'intera nottata
> buttato vicino a un compagno
> massacrato con la sua bocca
> digrignata

> volta al plenilunio
> con la congestione
> delle sue mani
> penetrata
> nel mio silenzio
> ho scritto
> lettere piene d'amore
>
> Non sono mai stato
> tanto
> attaccato alla vita

(A whole night/thrown near/the body/of a slain comrade/his mouth snarling/at the full moon/his clawed fingers/ripping/into my silence/I wrote/letters/full of love//Never did I/so/cling to life)

The poem leads from a prolonged exposure to horror and death ("a whole night") to a sudden shift, a change of direction whose premise seems to lie in the very permanence in the previous state of sustained dread. Indeed, the "mutative spark"—that is, the "slash" of transformation and creation—may well be once again what Ungaretti is mainly, albeit indirectly, focusing on here. The moon that reveals death by silently shining on the dead comrade's deformed face is (and is not) the same moon that then provides the light for writing love letters—much in the same way that mud, in "Pellegrinaggio", was first a life-consuming and then a life-promoting agent. Also, the ghastly echo that bounces from one line to the other of the first stanza in the harsh sounds of words ending in "-ata/-ato" comes back after a significant pause in the last three lines, but having acquired at this point a different connotation: it is no longer associated with words full of snarling "r"s and threatening meanings, but to a sense of continuing being ("stato" [been]) and attachment ("attaccato" [attached]). In a way, it is as if the adjective "attaccato" (attached) was the end product of the process of working through "attaccato", understood as the past participle of the verb "to attack" (implicit in the terrifying atmosphere of the initial part of the poem). Perhaps one of the functions of poetry is that of (re)presenting the role emotions play in this potentially shifting relationship between signifiers and signifieds. As the disjointed, eerie sounds of the first lines give way to the melodious and gently dactylic "lettere piene d'amore", it becomes clear that the more bodily level of music and that of meaning are profoundly intertwined. These "letters full of love", however, also illuminate a difference between "Pellegrinaggio" and "Veglia": indeed, the latter brings to the foreground the importance of relatedness, which in the former is possibly restricted to the relationship with an internal object. Here it is very explicitly the loss of a comrade that leads to an awareness of transience and, through its grieving (Freud, 1915), an increased appreciation of (and loving impulse towards) who and what is there and living.[14]

A similar connection between relatedness, mourning, and creation is found in "Fratelli" (Brothers), an arresting war poem in which the sense of communion that unites separate individuals who share the same mortal fate is restated at the level of the signifier through the alliteration of brittleness and brothers ("fragilità/fratelli").

> Fratelli
> Mariano il 15 luglio 1916
>
> Di che reggimento siete
> fratelli?
>
> Parola tremante
> nella notte
>
> Foglia appena nata
>
> Nell'aria spasimante
> involontaria rivolta
> dell'uomo presente alla sua
> fragilità
>
> Fratelli
>
> (What regiment do you belong to/brothers?//Word trembling/in the night//Leaf barely born//In the quivering air/involuntary revolt/of man present at his/brittleness// Brothers)

Together with the comrades from the other regiment and the somewhat epiphanic feeling of empathy that emerges towards them, "fratelli" also designates the title of the poem: poetry, in this respect, is as much a precious "word trembling/in the night" and a "leaf barely born" as the hawthorn seed was in "Pellegrinaggio". Or also (as minimal, fragile, almost imperceptible things go) as the "nulla" (nothing) in "Eterno" or in "Il porto sepolto" (The Buried Harbor), the poem that gives the title to the collection.

> Il porto sepolto
> Mariano il 29 giugno 1916
>
> Vi arriva il poeta
> e poi torna alla luce con i suoi canti
> e li disperde
>
> Di questa poesia
> mi resta
> quel nulla
> d'inesauribile segreto
>
> (The poet plumbs it and to the light/then rises with his songs/and scatters them//Of this poetry/I'm left with the emptiness/of an endless secret)

Explaining the meaning of the poem's title, Ungaretti talks about two brothers he became friends with in Alexandria when he was around sixteen or seventeen years old:

> Mi parlavano d'un porto, d'un porto sommerso, che doveva precedere l'epoca tolemaica, provando che Alessandria era un porto già prima d'Alessandro, che già prima d'Alessandro era

una città. Non se ne sa nulla. Quella mia città si consuma e s'annienta d'attimo in attimo. […] Non se ne sa nulla, non ne rimane altro segno che quel porto custodito in fondo al mare, unico documento tramandatoci d'ogni era d'Alessandria. Il titolo del mio primo libro deriva da quel porto: *Il Porto Sepolto*.

(They talked to me about a harbor, a submerged harbor which apparently dated from before the Tolemaic era, thereby proving that Alexandria had already been a harbor before Alexander, that already before Alexander it had been a city. Nothing is known about it. That city of mine is consumed and annihilated moment by moment […]. Nothing is known about it, no sign is left of it except for that harbor preserved at the bottom of the sea, the only document from any age of Alexandria to have been transmitted to us. The title of my first book comes from that harbor: *The Buried Harbor*.)

*Il porto sepolto*, whose main subject is explicitly poetry, epitomizes much of what I have highlighted in Ungaretti's other poems from a Bionian angle. The first stanza conflates the narrative derivative seen in "Pellegrinaggio" and "Veglia" (dark > light) with the picking > giving away of "Eterno" (the poet seems fully to take possession of his own songs only when he gets to the buried harbor, and then he becomes able to "scatter" them, to share them). There is also the notion of what is left ("resta") once what was picked up has been given away, that is the capacity to pick and give more, and perhaps of being continuously engaged in the activity of producing meaning by dreaming and thinking one's internal and external reality. Above all, there is a clear sense that the unconscious, our buried harbor, is *not only* a repository of forgotten or repressed childhood memories and experiences which a poet (or analyst) archaeologist is called upon to retrieve: it is also, and possibly predominantly, an unseen but rich harbor, a place *par excellence* busy with continuous transactions and exchanges, arrivals and departures, gains and losses to be reckoned with—*that*, as well as a storage place. In fact, much like Marc Augé's (1995) non-places, its connotation as a space may be subordinate to its functional quality, which of course includes the fact that it allows one to get or get back in touch with the deepest and most primary sources of one's sense of being, among which memories and past life events. Indeed, only the buried harbor of the unconscious makes it possible for us to dream, moment by moment, a proto-emotional and proto-sensorial reality that is much like a city which "is consumed and annihilated moment by moment". The secret, inexhaustible riches of the buried harbor are then ultimately the process of dreaming that "nulla". A no-thing that, in "Eterno", is called "ineffable" for a reason that is perhaps attuned to a consideration Anish Kapoor has expressed in a recent paper on his work delivered by Gregorio Kohon at the Institute of Psychoanalysis in London (January 22, 2014): "With respect to my artworks I often have nothing to say—but it is in that nothing to say that there is everything to do".

## Notes

1. It seems to me that Adam Phillips (1998) fails to consider precisely this point when, in his negative review of Speziale-Bagliacca's book, he criticizes Speziale-Bagliacca's engagement with the characters of the novel by making the (per se indisputable) point that "fictional characters are made with words. Neither King Lear nor Charles Bovary ever had a childhood".

2. A more contemporary advocate of this "patographic" approach in the field of Italian Studies is the literary critic Elio Gioanola. See in particular Gioanola (1991).
3. See Civitarese (2012) and Capello (2014).
4. Focusing on the cases of Orwell, Dickens, Chekhov, and Kipling, Leonard Shengold's (1989) well-known book *Soul Murder*, though informed by a very different psychoanalytic theoretical standpoint, also stresses in a similar way the importance of real-life events in the development of an author's main (narrative) preoccupations, themes, and even style.
5. A broader, "culturalist", and rather idiosyncratic approach, which is also worth mentioning, is that of the Italian *francesista* Francesco Orlando, who in his well-known and (at least in Italy) highly influential *Per una teoria freudiana della letteratura* (1965) argued that literature could be understood as a compromise formation allowing writers to engage with the conscious and unconscious resistances and censorships enforced by the dominant cultural and moral values of their time.
6. Gaburri and Ambrosiano (2003, 2013) and Granieri (2011) show from a Bionian perspective how the interpretation/insight dynamic does not always represent the only or the most important therapeutic factor.
7. It is from this perspective that the title of Giuseppe Civitarese's most recent book, *Il sogno necessario* (2013), can be best understood.
8. In this respect, also see Civitarese (2014) and Harris Williams (2009). While the two authors have a rather different take on Bion's thought, they both emphasize the crucial role of the aesthetic component in the psychoanalytic experience.
9. See Bollas (2012, p. 6): "I shall distinguish between the 'presentational' and the 'representational', between self-presentation and self-representation. Presentation (in any context) is the *form* of a being or a communication; representation refers to the *content* of a communication."
10. See in this respect Civitarese (2008).
11. Throughout his life, Ungaretti consistently connected the development of his poetry with his own development as a person. The title of his collected works, *Life of a Man*, is telling in this respect, together with passages such as the following two, taken from the aforementioned "Introductory note": "quelle poesie sono ciò che saranno tutte le mie poesie che verranno dopo, cioè poesie che hanno fondamento in uno strato psicologico strettamente dipendente dalla mia biografia: non conosco sognare poetico che non sia fondato sulla mia esperienza diretta" (1970, p. 511) [those poems are just like the poems I came to write after them, that is, poems grounded in a psychology closely related to the story of my life: indeed, I do not know any kind of poetic dreaming that is not linked to my direct experience]; "Le sue poesie rappresentano dunque i suoi tormenti formali, ma vorrebbe si riconoscesse una buona volta che la forma lo tormenta solo perché la esige aderente alle variazioni del suo animo, e, se qualche progresso ha fatto come artista, vorrebbe che indicasse anche qualche perfezione raggiunta come uomo" (p. 528) [His poems therefore represent his tormented pursuit of formal perfection. However, it should also be acknowledged once and for all that form torments him only because he wants it to reflect the variations in his soul, and if he has made some progress as an artist, he would want this to indicate that he has achieved some degree or form of perfection as a man]. In the second passage Ungaretti refers to himself writing in the third person. This aspiration on Ungaretti's part seems related to what Jacobs (2011, p. 982) argues about novelists: "'story after story, novel after novel, an author returns to familiar issues and to familiar problems, presenting them each time in a new setting and with a new cast of characters. The theme, however, and the underlying concerns that cause its repetition remain essentially the same. They remain the same, that is, until some change

takes place in the inner world of the author; until, in other words, through the process of writing, some solution to or working through of the problem has been achieved". I would add, "through the process of writing" or any other process which may subsequently become reflected in the author's writing. Ungaretti's poems in the Italian original are reproduced with permission of c 2015 Mondadori Libri S.p.A. I also thank Diego Bastianutti for allowing me to quote his English translations of 'Eterno', 'Pellegrinaggio', 'Veglia', and 'Il porto sepolto'.

12. The "u" from "un" is not pronounced because of the synalepha.
13. The idea of white is also present at the level of the signifier in both the Italian names of the thornbush: biancospino and the Latinate form used by Ungaretti, spinalba.
14. Of course, "writing letters" could be understood also as an implicit reference to the creative act of writing poetry, which further highlights the relationship between mourning and beauty.

## *References*

Abella, A. (2010). Contemporary art and Hanna Segal's thinking on aesthetics. *International Journal of Psychoanalysis, 91*: pp. 163–181.
Agamben, G. (1994). *L'uomo senza contenuto*. Rome: Quodlibet.
Augé, M. (1995). *Nonplaces: Introduction to an Anthropology of Supermodernity*. London, Verso.
Baudry, F. (1984). An essay on method in applied psychoanalysis. *Psychoanalytic Quarterly, 53*: 551–581.
Bion, W. R. (1962). *Learning from Experience*. London: Heinemann.
Bion, W. R. (1967). *Second Thoughts*. London: Heinemann.
Bion, W. R. (1979). Making the best of a bad job. In: *Clinical Seminars and Other Works* (pp. 321–323). London: Karnac, 1994.
Bion, W. R. (1994). *Clinical Seminars and Other Works*. London: Karnac.
Bollas, C. (2012). *China on the Mind*. London: Routledge.
Bonaparte, M. (1933). *Edgar Poe. Étude psychanalytique*. Paris: Denoël.
Budd, S. (2007). Reading and misreading. In: L. Braddock & M. Lacewing (Eds.), *The Academic Face of Psychoanalysis* (pp. 33–51). London. Routledge.
Capello, F. (2014). Psicoanalisi e critica letteraria: dall'applicazione alla conversazione. *Rivista di psicoanalisi, 2*: 405–432.
Civitarese, G. (2008). Caesura as Bion's discourse on method. *International Journal of Psychoanalysis, 89*: 1123–1143.
Civitarese, G. (2010). Abjection and aesthetic conflict in Boccaccio's (L)Isabetta. *Journal of Romance Studies, 10*: 11–25.
Civitarese, G. (2012). *Perdere la testa*. Florence: Clinamen.
Civitarese, G. (2013). *Il sogno necessario*. Milan: FrancoAngeli.
Civitarese, G. (2014). *I sensi e l'inconscio*. Rome: Borla.
Faflak, J. (2007). *Romantic Psychoanalysis: The Burden of the Mystery*. New York: SUNY Press.
Ferro, A. (1999). *Psychoanalysis as Therapy and Storytelling*. London: Routledge, 2006.
Ferro, A. (2002). *Seeds of Illness, Seeds of Recovery*. London: Routledge, 2005.
Ferro, A. (2006). *Mind Works: Technique and Creativity in Psychoanalysis*. London: Routledge, 2008.
Ferro, A. (2007). *Avoiding Emotions, Living Emotions*. London: Routledge, 2011.
Ferro, A. (2010). *Tormenti di anime. Passioni, sintomi, sogni*. Milan, Cortina.
Fornari, F. (1977). *Il Minotauro: psicoanalisi dell'ideologia*. Milan: Rizzoli.
Fornari, B., & Fornari, F. (1974). *Psicoanalisi e ricerca letteraria*. Milan: Principato.
Fornari, F. (1979). *Coinema e icona: nuova proposta per la psicoanalisi dell'arte*. Milan: Il Saggiatore.
Fornari, F. (1984). *Psicoanalisi della musica*. Milan: Longanesi.

Fornari, F. (1985). *Carmen adorata: psicoanalisi della donna demoniaca*. Milan: Longanesi.
Freud, S. (1915). On Transience. *S. E., 14*: 305–307. London: Hogarth.
Freud, S. (1919). The uncanny. *S. E., 17*: 219–256. London: Hogarth.
Gaburri, E., & Ambrosiano, L. (2003). *Ululare con i lupi*. Turin: Bollati Boringhieri.
Gaburri, E., & Ambrosiano, L. (2013). *Pensare con Freud*. Milan: Cortina.
Ginzburg, C. (1989). *Clues, Myths, and the Historical Method*. Baltimore: Johns Hopkins University Press.
Gioanola, E. (1991). *Psicanalisi, ermeneutica e letteratura*. Milan: Mursia.
Granieri, A. (2011). *Corporeo, affetti e pensiero. Intreccio tra psicoanalisi e neurobiologia*. Turin: UTET.
Grotstein, J. (2007). *A Beam of Intense Darkness: Wilfred Bion's Legacy to Psychoanalysis*. London: Karnac.
Grotstein, J. (2009). *"But at the Same Time and on Another level": Psychoanalytic Theory and Technique in the Kleinian/Bionian Mode*. London: Karnac.
Harris Williams, M. (2005). *The Vale of Soulmaking: The Post-Kleinian Model of the Mind*. London: Karnac.
Harris Williams, M. (2009). *The Aesthetic Development: The Poetic Spirit of Psychoanalysis: Essays on Bion, Meltzer, Keats*. London: Karnac.
Harris Williams, M., & Waddell, M. (1991). *The Chamber of Maiden Thought: Literary Origins of the Psychoanalytic Model of the Mind*. London: Tavistock/Routledge.
Hinshelwood, R. (2003). Group mentality and "having a mind". In: R. Lipgar & M. Pines (Eds.), *Building on Bion: Roots. Origins and Contexts of Bion's Contributions to Theory and Practice* (pp. 181–197). London: Jessica Kingsley.
Jacobs, T. J. (2011). Insights, epiphanies, and working through: on healing, self-healing, and creativity in the writer and the analyst *Psychoanalytic Quarterly, 80*: 961–986.
Kirschner, S. R. (1996). *The Religious and Romantic Origins of Psychoanalysis: Individuation and Integration in Post-Freudian Theory*. Cambridge: CUP.
Klein, M. (1955). On identification. In: *Envy and Gratitude and Other Works 1946–1963* (pp. 141–175). London: Vintage, 1997.
Lavagetto, M. (2005). Svevo, la psicanalisi, la crisi della critica. Intervista a Mario Lavagetto. *Allegoria, 17*: 50–51.
Ogden, B., & Ogden, T. (2013). *The Analyst's Ear and the Critic's Eye: Rethinking Psychoanalysis and Literature*. London: Routledge.
Ogden, T. (1986). *The Matrix of the Mind: Object Relations and the Psychoanalytic Dialogue*. Northvale, NJ: Jason Aronson.
Ogden, T. (1994). *Subjects of Analysis*. London: Karnac.
Ogden, T. (2001). *Conversations at the Frontier of Dreaming*. London: Karnac.
Ogden, T. (2005). *This Art of Psychoanalysis: Dreaming Undreamt Dreams and Interrupted Cries*. London: Routledge.
Orlando, F. (1965). *Per una teoria freudiana della letteratura*. Turin: Einaudi.
Phillips, A. (1998). Paging Dr. Freud. *The New York Times*, June 7 1998.
Shengold, L. (1989). *Soul Murder: The Effects of Childhood Abuse and Deprivation*. New Haven: Yale University Press.
Shields, W. (2009). Imaginative literature and Bion's intersubjective theory of thinking. *Psychoanalytic Quarterly, 78*: 559–586.
Snell, R. (2012). *Uncertainties, Mysteries, Doubts: Romanticism and the Analytic Attitude*. London: Routledge.
Speziale-Bagliacca, R. (2000). *Adultera e re: un'interpretazione psicoanalitica e letteraria di "Madame Bovary" e "Re Lear"*. Turin: Bollati Boringhieri.
Ungaretti, G. (1970). *Vita di un uomo. Tutte le poesie*. Milan: Mondadori.

CHAPTER THIRTY-SIX

# Communicating pictures: aesthetic aspects as a developmental tool for the container-contained interaction

*Elena Molinari*

The verb "to repeat" in its Latin etymology means "to go again toward somebody" (Oli, 1971). Thus, to repeat refers to going through a space for an encounter to occur and it opens the possibility—regardless of all potential failure—for reasonable hope of success at the next attempt. So, in its original meaning the verb "to repeat", rather than a linguistic act, as we usually think of it, seems to refer to a bodily experience, similar to what the infant lives, where space is, above all, what separates him from his mother's arms. Learning how to walk is an ability that is learned by trial and error and enables the child to go through a physical, as well as a potentially anxiety-ridden, space separating him from the other person.

Something similar to walking towards the other is experienced in analysis, when the analysand gives to the analyst's lack of understanding yet another chance, as the former repeats—at times in the same way, at times slightly differently—what has not been understood. It is not only a matter of tolerating frustration, but mostly of being able to create some form, narrative, or play aiming at reaching the other.

It is quite a different experience when the analyst shares the reiteration of gestures or narrative threads that have lost their communicative purpose or, more concretely, their capacity to go through the separating space. Then, repetition can become an empty form with the purpose of isolating and protecting against otherness, which is experienced as inaccessible. In this case, both analyst and patient end up sharing a feeling of painful isolation. The space separating them becomes hyper dense, crammed with objects foreign to their function, or turns into a black hole that swallows and thwarts all attempts to make contact.

It was the possibility of focussing on how we used the relational space that allowed me to deal with the feeling of powerlessness with a patient who had, for a long time, used repetition as a defensive shell in her analysis. In particular, thinking in spatial terms opened the way to figurative associations that overlapped fruitfully, as I shall illustrate here.

The reproduction of a pattern is an experience we frequently find in art and is part of the normal creative process of an artwork. For many artists the repetition of the same subject is used to analyze all its potential in terms of form, light, color, or space (see Morandi, 1996, pp. 16–18). From a psychic stance, the reiteration of a subject can lead to a variety of experiences, which range from the predictable repetition of a pattern—as happens overtly in the Greek key design—where one experiences a feeling of safety (to mention the simplest one), to the containment of psychotic parts of the personality.

The idea of looking at repetition in art helped me imagine how a transformation of experience can occur when the patient has an inadequate function of containment and, especially, when he uses repetition in a strictly defensive way. In particular, as I will try to show through my clinical experience, it is possible to explore "artistically" a psychic area of the field where the analyst's mind and analysand's mind can share an archaic sensory form imbued with unthinkable emotions. In this sense, the artistic representation—which becomes such not at an abstract level but in grappling with the matter—can give us some helpful clues.

## The role of repetition between mother and child

In the prenatal stage the child lives the experience of continuity, through the rhythmical repetition of the mother's heartbeat and breathing more than through the discontinuity of the sounds from outside. Only the mother's voice, which is perceived from within and without at the same time, seems to constitute a transitional experience that can teach the child how to put together early forms of continuity and discontinuity.

After birth, what Winnicott describes as the mother's holding capacity can be thought of as an extension of this prenatal situation. The persistence of smells, the identifiability of the style with which the mother holds the baby in her arms, the constancy of her tone of voice—even in the modulation of its intensity—are important elements that enable the child to feel a general predictability of experience, where discontinuity becomes a relatively occasional fact that can be progressively dealt with. Through these caring features and the identical repetition of many interactions, the mother provides the child with an experience that protects him from potentially traumatic experience. In particular, repetitive forms along with those combining repetition and some new elements, offer the baby the possibility of learning how to recognize and to anticipate in his imagination the other-than-himself. So, repetition lays the foundation of trusting the other person and one's own capacity to develop some ability to tolerate loneliness and the anxiety stirred by change.

Bion, like Winnicott, studies the beginnings of the capacity to deal with unpleasant feelings generated by the discontinuity of satisfaction. Winnicott does it from the point of view of environmental and relational continuity; Bion from the point of view of the capacity to master unconscious emotions.

Beginning with the aspects of pre- and post-natal psycho-physical consonance, Bion says that "a state of expectation" (Bion, 1963, p. 23) for an external capacity of containment can give rise in the child to some kind of innate preconception of being contained. This assumption may lead us to think that at first the baby could be inhabited by a phantasy of self-containment. In this regard, Bion postulates in the grid the existence of the "β-element-row" (Bion, 1989, p. 7) that is not connected with the need to expel intolerable sensations or feelings.

This kind of β elements are not the result of the transformative failure of the α-function. They are not expelled from the psyche as the product of an experience that cannot be transformed. Rather, they are a primary unit of an experience that constitutes a proto-symbolic system, an area of the mind where sensory and mental experiences remain indistinct (Bion, 1962a, 1992). They form, in the proto-mental system, some sort of sensory and emotional boundary that emerges from the flow of sensory exchanges between two interacting people, and registers the shape of the objects through the mimetic function (Cartwright, 2010). They could assume a configuration and act as precursors of a real function of containment.

We can speculate that there are two functions that develop parallel to one another at two different levels: a transformative level that, through the α-function, leads the transformation of sensory experience into sense-making forms; and a level where the psyche takes shape through a process of mimesis, a flow of adhesive identification forms in which the primitive phantasy is not to project into the object but to adhere to the object, to its shape, to its spatial density.

Bion assumes that this second kind of β elements can simulate psychic functioning through their capacity to agglomerate and disperse, similarly to ♀/♂—PS<->D, yet remaining in a context where there is not any difference between body and mind (Bion, 1963). If development goes smoothly, the β proto-container continues to work in a silent manner, without creating any obstacle and keeping its function of hosting aspects of the merging experience by moderating its role and keeping ♀/♂ functioning in a subordinate place.[1]

So, we can assume that the form of any psycho-physical interaction is screened by two systems. One system evaluates the sense of inner sensory consistency (consistency among sensing, feeling, and thinking), the other one identifies the interaction in a proto-symbolic register. The latter evaluates its consistency through forms of identity or difference that do not include properly mental aspects, and can be translated into a feeling of merging with the objects or, on the contrary, with a feeling of abysmal distance. In the former case, touching or seeing an object over and over allows the experience of presence to be extracted from it and the mental awareness of the object that remains constant in spite of appearing in different forms to be based on this experience. It is an operation that transforms a multidimensional experience in one form, "common sense", which lays down the ground of a feeling of psycho-somatic integrity and initiates a container-contained (♀/♂) interaction that can foster mental development. In the latter case, if merging does not take place, the reiteration of experience will be in charge of looking for it, though preventing all transformative function.

We can imagine the mental container as a complex and stratified function that can expand in relation to repeated, attuned, sensory and emotional experiences of merging or consonance. Sensory attunement would be dominant in the pre- and perinatal stages of life, whilst emotional attunement would progressively become more important in subsequent stages. These overlapping experiences during early development remain active throughout life, although to different degrees.

Using a biological metaphor, we could compare it to the proto-container of the cartilage areas that allow for an expansion of the skull at the beginning of life. These areas, which are fairly numerous and large before birth, play a fundamental role in ensuring the required plasticity for quite a fast brain growth in the first two years of life. Later, they tend to become considerably and progressively smaller and are replaced with bony tissue that is more capable of bearing traumatisms. At the end of development they remain as thin areas around the cranial sutures.

If the proto-container does not gradually decrease in size, it takes up space in processing the experience and appears in apparently uncommunicative adhesive forms. Sensory data maintain a role in a non-transformed, non-psychic state; the objects do not have any three-dimensionality and exist through a form of repetition that does not get integrated and transformed. The proto-container keeps a form of "knowledge" with the only purpose of marking the presence of the object and of impressing the boundaries in its mind by giving rise to a feeling of flowing together rather than being an interacting subject.

### "What kind of artists we can be?" (Bion, 1980, p. 73)

If the function of containment is transposed to the analytic function, it is reciprocal and recursive. It creates traces of experience that, in turn, affect the subject of analysis and lead to the emergence of new relational configurations and thoughts. I would like to focus on the kind of cooperation that exists at the basis of the function of containment, as it is there that we find the creativity of the analytic pair (Harris Meltzer, 2010; Meltzer, 1967). This paper aims to explore how the function of containment develops, starting from a proto-container that registers the form of the "thing-in-itself" at sensory level. This form, representing a substrate in the normal mental functioning, emerges and becomes a key aspect in the analysis of patients with pockets of autistic withdrawal, where thinking seems to be enclosed in an area of concreteness that can hardly be transformed. The hypertrophic functioning of this kind of proto-containment makes emotional attunement and a creative ♀/♂ relation particularly difficult.

With these patients, the possibility to swing from sharing the image (C3) to sharing a process in which the psyche begins a transformation forgery of the sense-impression as if it was the "thing-in-itself" (C2)—this latter being a more difficult kind of sharing—seems to me an indispensible aspect in restoring the thinking function (Bion, 1962a, p. 26). This backward process is relatively accessible for a mother with her infant, but it is very difficult during the analytic process.

Two aspects, in my opinion, can facilitate it. On the one hand, the analyst trusting in the patient—which implies a decrease in the analyst's inner tension to achieve a symbolic transformation and opens up to the possibility of accessing states of reverie characterized by a specific artistic slant. The patient plays a very important role in leading the analyst to a deep place in his mind where the swarms of β elements, identified in the first column, change aesthetically so that they can be suitable for the subsequent transit (Grotstein, 2007). Being together with the patient, in some processing of the experience mediated by the proto-containment, means surrendering to the experience of the form, the composition of the words and not their content. In this way, the defensive repetition put in place in order to carry the analyst to that archaic place of experience gives in and makes room for a relationship where the image frames the ♀/♂ relation (C3). This enables both analyst and analysand to share the experience through a symbolic code.

With regard to the kind of listening and the particular kind of reverie that the analyst needs in order to leave these difficult situations, the artistic process allows us to intuit some of their specificities. The creation of an artwork implies a deep emotional and sensory involvement and transition through the experience of repetition. By repetition, I mean a formal quest of reproducing the same subject, as well as going through intermediate forms that herald the final one considered by the artist as the form that can express what he wants to formalize.

An aspect of seriality that drew my attention and helped me think was the seriality that Matisse inaugurated in 1945 when he displayed, at the Galerie Maeght, six paintings surrounded by blown-up photographs of previous stages of some of his artworks. For a decade he had kept photographic records of his unfolding work, illustrating his work in progress. In the exhibition of these black and white, repetitive blow-ups, he wanted to show not only how a painting is generated but also how the vision of reality comes into being.[2]

This suggestion led me to consider the exasperating repetition I had been experiencing in the relationship with one of my patients. I regarded it not only as a defensive form, but also as a desperate call to follow her into an area of her mind where the "thing-in-itself" goes through a process of transformation. In this process, the α-function collects some elements of reality and discards others and the dream performs an early aesthetic processing of sensation (Bion, 1962a, p. 7).

## *Communicating pictures*

During a session at an advanced stage of her analysis, a patient—I will call her Elisa—brought a picture to let me know visually how she wished to look physically. It was a framed photograph representing two couples: a newlywed smiling couple and the couple of my patient and her partner as they were going through a deep relational crisis. Elisa just told me that she wished she had the same physical appearance as the bride.

Lately Elisa had started to bring to the session some pictures of herself to show me how ugly she felt she looked or some cut-out pictures from magazines to show me the body shape she wished for herself. She asked me to keep these pictures and I put them in a drawer in my cabinet. Her unusual need to use a photographic representation to make clear to me how ugly she allegedly looked immediately appeared to me as an odd act, since nothing prevented me from looking at her directly. I had to assume that I probably did not see what Elisa was trying to show me, so that the pictures might seem to her to be a helpful tool to open the eye of my mind.

When Elisa brought the framed picture to the session, it was the unusual element of the frame that made me look at the photographs and the magazine clippings in a different way. They had accumulated like some visible trail of her addictive attempt to generate the dreams of a more fruitful pairing.

The content of the framed picture, depicting a happy couple and a deeply troubled one, emphasized the idea that the emotional union at the basis of the container's expansion was an oscillating experience with moments when emotional understanding was missing. In my mind I associated the formal element of the frame and the sequence of layering images in the drawer with an artwork by Grazia Varisco, a contemporary artist whose stylistic key feature implies a destabilization of common sense and involves the onlooker's active participation. In particular an artwork from her series called "Communicating pictures" came to mind (Varisco, 2012).

G. Varisco, Communicating pictures.

It is a set of frames enclosing a portion of space where empty space and color combine in a variety of ways. By observing this work in its wholeness one notices how the pictures run after one another on the wall and create some sort of communication that leaves out all contact, transgressing and, at the same time, recreating its straight order. In this way, the pattern expected by the viewer is in fact unfamiliar and the mind is involved in a necessary creative operation in order to feel a relation with the artwork at another formal level.

These remarks, along with the title "Communicating pictures", drove me to consider this work as a reverie associated with what the analysand and I were experiencing. The element of the frame made me think about the succession of sessions, the continuity linking them, and the need for each of them to be a separate work thanks to the analyst's capacity to experience every session "without memory and desire".

Outside the session I associated the work with Bion's grid. The emotional turbulence that, as Bion showed, is always present at every transition from one row to another, is generated by a new ♀/♂ relation. Moreover, the line crossing each oblong forming the above-mentioned artwork represents well the slash, the mark that registers the labor involved in the transformation of proto-emotions into emotions, in the formation of reality or in the distinction between self and other (Civitarese, 2013; Grotstein, 2007). However, besides referring to a real transformative process, that artwork made me aware of a repetitive form I was experiencing in the relationship with Elisa, which had nothing to do with transformation but rather with the opposite experience of rigid defense.

In transforming the title "Communicating pictures" into "Communicating containers" I forced myself to consider again, from an aesthetic stance, the images and the bodily sensations that Elisa and I had shared, looking for some traces of the function of an effective psychic containment and mutual transformation.

*The impossibility and the possibility to cope with transformation*

The issue that led Elisa to analysis was, so she said, in a sense aesthetic: she perceived her body as disgusting, though to my outsider's eye it was not. The distance between her own image in the mirror and her self-image was the only way this young woman could think about her psychic discomfort. This originated from the sudden and long-lasting loss of a stable enough physical and psychic containment during childhood. This loss had produced a distortion in the relational processes by which the mind settles in the body, a distortion that became visible in the mirror through the perception of a disharmonious body that was seen as being obese in some places and too slim in others. In particular, she described her face as being wide and flat at the same time, her chest huge, her legs thin and slim like the legs of a girl. When she described herself in this way, the visual association that appeared in my mind was always with the deformed faces and bodies of the work of Francis Bacon. It seemed to me that Elisa, like the painter, was trying to fight the catastrophe of chaos through representation. Just like Bacon, my analysand had apparently found out how the slight distance from reality that photography produces in fact references reality more violently, as if photography reveals what the seen, lived, touched reality hides, in short, "the brutality of things".

The missing integration between what Elisa's eyes could see and her body image could be ascribed to the failure in maintaining aesthetic contact in her primary relationship. This was reproduced in the analytic setting and was embodied in the field through sharing certain forms of relatedness and the images that formed in my mind.

The analysand's suffering, located in a very primitive area, could be inferred from a metaphor that she often used: "I am like a pregnant woman whose abdomen keeps on growing, but she does not want it, she continues to imagine herself like before and, only at a given time, she has the strength to look at herself and then she thinks she is horrible." I assumed that something had prevented her from accepting her own development and had made her remain, in some respect, like a very young child incorporated in her mother. Elisa found herself denying her feelings of catastrophic loss, attributing the halt of that early, intimate, and concrete relationship to some deficiency inscribed in her own body. The metaphor also included an indication of her need for tolerating a claustrophobic feeling induced by that early form of merging containment (Neri, 1985), as a condition for differentiation and her need to find, in our current relationship and not in the past, some opportunity to start a mutual transformation.

### *From the frame's bi-dimensionality to the three-dimensional space of the drawer*

The pregnancy metaphor led me to think how the ♀/♂ concept arises from the body, or rather from bodies in an intimate relationship—mouth/nipple, mother/child, vagina/penis—to evolve to more abstract and mental relationships in the dual or group setting. To symbolize the concept of container, Bion uses the female symbol. The difficulty of putting the framed picture in the drawer confronted me concretely with the issues of space, surrender, and the limit. Elisa wished to have with me a relationship of inclusion, not contact.

This hypothesis would explain why, while searching for the words most appropriate to establish an emotional closeness, we had produced a small change in our relationship.

A detail that she often mentioned was the perception of her own face as a flat object, causing it to have disproportionate width. But the three-dimensional space of the drawer where I was trying to put the framed picture helped me notice that detail. In looking at herself in the mirror, Elisa would lose the three-dimensionality of her face, as if something had damaged the internalization of the relational space that begins with the mother and infant playing by touching and gazing at one another (Bonaminio, 2009, 2012; Winnicott, 1967). In her, sight as a sense used to convey distance, seemed to have been excluded from the formation of "common sense"[3].

However, the drawer represented an area of the field where a three-dimensional space had come into being, whereas the function of containment and the accumulation of photographs represented a concrete layering of our looking together.

### *The sensory adhesion as a gate to transformation*

Elisa started her analysis because she saw in the mirror a horrible image of herself and she was completely blind to any relational reality that she experienced as a problem within herself. For a long time I too had offered her something ineffective, as it was exactly specular. With the intention of introducing the other-than-oneself, I had closed my eyes before her "ugliness" and attributed "the ugly" to the experiential precipitate of her intolerable emotions. In this way, I ended up not considering the somatic and sensory aspects that she continuously brought up as a priority.

Only with hindsight can I now understand the deep emotional truth that Elisa was telling me about as she described herself using words in the way a blind person might use her hands, which—she explained to me—touch the other person confusedly and often too much, so that they end up being annoying and embodying an unintentional and bothersome intrusiveness. Elisa wished for the ability to keep silent without using a shell of words to protect herself against the catastrophic sense of silence that she experienced in the relationship. At the same time, she lived every word I said as intrusive, excessive, blind. Alternatively, she used the words or the metaphors in such a repetitive way as to empty them of all relational meaning, as happens with the gestures of autistic children.

Paradoxically, what I was not able to see and use, for a long time, were the pictures. Although I looked at them carefully, I ended up not seeing them in the *form* Elisa wished I would see them. Leaving the emotional "vision" of the relationship was the *sine qua non* to access the generative power of those pictures produced in the field. This enabled me to grasp in them, that is, in the sensible, the first traces of a truth that could be shared.

The pictures manifested themselves in the field by defining an analogic space "between" the two of us. The perception of this space did not correspond to our relating to each other, but emerged with it and manifested itself through it. The drawer where I put the pictures constituted some kind of "non-place" that made room for a field of forces capable of loosening up and relativizing our respective visions of reality.

As Elisa had suggested through the pregnancy metaphor, the mental place in which mother and infant mix together could open up a new perspective and, above all, it could create a contact with a reality that went beyond the sum of our personal visions.

Through the pregnancy metaphor Elisa was also making a specific contribution to our thinking together. With the mutually transformative body of the mother–infant couple she introduced in the field an image that went beyond the issue of being. With the idea of pregnancy she wanted to show the image of becoming in a relationship where mind and body merge together by mutually touching and showing themselves as two sides of a "living body" (Merleau-Ponty, 1945).

Elisa was asking me to practice a thought-in-progress that would relinquish the intention to slip some meaning into the object prematurely. In this perspective, the artistic aspect of psychoanalysis and "the feminine"—where the container becomes a symbol—have a point of contact: they both "hint at" the linguistic expression of the aesthetic data and practice a language prior to speech. Both art and "the feminine" belong to the sensible area, where they end up merging because they both contain and hide in themselves an arcane language that does not culminate in a definite meaning. As a vision, the analytic experience that Elisa brought to me could not be split from the mute *logos* of the living body.

The intersubjective mental container could exist in this stage of analysis as a category of the potential space that expands only through forms of non-verbal communication. We were trying to work through and bring about an experience of contact and, at the same time, of physical and psychic distance so as to generate an experience of containment and intersubjective relationship.

### *Elements of space and composition as psychic functions to build the proto-container*

Elisa was able to depict the pain originating from the difficulty of not having found any containment able to support her development. At the same time, though, she let me have a bodily experience of attunement with her pain.

So, I started to consider the interactions around our exchange with greater interest when Elisa brought some pictures to the session. She would pull out the photographs from her pocket or her purse, as she was lying on the couch, and would give them to me without turning. This often produced a casual and unexpected contact between our hands, as hers was a sightless gesture deprived of all directional awareness. Letting me look at the pictures carried also an unconscious intentionality to create a contact, not only in the abstract sense of the word. We were busy learning about the function of body containment, where the gaze becomes touch and, in the separation, the contact becomes gaze.

The pictures that Elisa handed me were frequently folded several times so that they ended up being small rectangles. The folding had two aesthetic effects. It partly deformed the image, which reminded me of an aspect of processing by which Bacon created his paintings. He used to start from some photographs that he kept in his studio. He let them fall down to the floor and be trampled on, partly erased, stained with color; in other words, he let those pictures be metaphorically brutalized (Sylvester, 1975).

The other effect was that in unfolding the pictures in my hands, they were no longer a flat sheet, but became more sinuous and almost three-dimensional, projecting their plane into the domain of sculpture. In this way, I think that Elisa was unconsciously working artistically to make her flattened container—made thinner by her life's vicissitudes—three-dimensional, but she was also actively contributing to create volume in the field of our interaction. In bringing the pictures to me she seemed to be dealing with an early representational form of her own body and of her inner mother. At the same time, she was showing her difficulty dealing with and symbolizing the pain of a distance that could not yet be defined as such. In fact, it was nameless anxiety.

To go back to the grid's categorization, it was like moving from C1 to C2. In C1 we are blind, that is to say, the β-elements are non-thoughts, bizarre objects, "pitch dark"; in C2 we can open or close our eyes. In closing them we can cut out, cut off, deny the sensory and emotional stimuli, but when we open our eyes we can also take in these stimuli and start to organize them. In this way, some screening of reality takes place. Its purpose is to keep some elements and discard others, so that the α-function can create the contact-barrier between unconscious and consciousness. In C3 we have dream images that we can share through narrative derivatives, visual derivatives, etc.

By associating the opening and closing of the drawer with the rhythmical movement of the eyelid and with the invisibility of the origin embodied in gestation, it seemed to me that Elisa and I were able to start to oscillate between C2 and C3. In this way, we could seize something of the folding (or slash), that is, the invisible pain that it conceals. Our senses, our sight, could start to know and endure pain.

> Now if tears *come to the eyes*, if they *well up in them*, and if they can also veil sight, perhaps they reveal, in the very course of this experience, in this coursing of water, an essence of the eyes, of man's eye, in any case, the eye understood in the anthropo-theological space of the sacred allegory. Deep down, deep down inside; the eye would be destined not to see but to weep. For at the very moment they veil sight, tears would unveil what is proper to the eye. And what they cause to surge up out of forgetfulness, there where the gaze or look looks after it, keeps it in reserve, would be nothing less than *alētheia*, the *truth* of the eyes, whose ultimate destination they would thereby reveal: to have imploration rather vision in sight, to address prayer, love, joy, or sadness rather a look or gaze. [...] The revelatory or apocalyptic blindness that reveals the very truth of eyes, would be the gaze veiled by tears. (Derrida, 1990, p. 126)

### Healing with the photographs or healing from the photographs?

At first, I thought that Elisa had to heal from the photographs that I regarded as concrete objects and as a rigid encrustation along the road to psychic transformation. From this assumption, I felt the need to move away from that level of concreteness that was supposedly preventing her from accessing more evolved thoughts.

But Elisa asked me to go over her experience, inaccessible to consciousness, of developing the function of containment and being held through a process that originated from a regressive experience: a shift from dream forms (C3) to aesthetic and sensory forms of communication (C2). In this sense, she led me through a process commonly experienced by artists. The shift from conceiving a representation to manipulating the matter forces the artist to get in contact with deep processes, in which senses prevail over conception and engage a turbulent relationship with the latter. If the primitive emotions and the senses can find an effective containment, the emerging form will be alive and capable of emotional communication. This process sets the stage for an expansion of the α-function and therefore the transformative capacity of the intrasubjective and intersubjective ♀/♂ relation.

But if a proto-containment process prevails, sensations do not have the chance to combine with painful feelings effectively, and the transformative process to symbolization seems to halt and embrace an ineffective repetitiveness. The repetitiveness of the gesture becomes prevalent and the ensuing form—unable to complete a process of emotional transformation—is uncommunicative and often unsatisfying, even for its creator.

The possibility of grasping some embodied traces of pain in this ineffectiveness is carried by the analyst through a long and difficult process, which the mind resists strongly, as it implies going through experiences that are psychotic and disruptive for the self. In my clinical experience, this difficulty appeared in Elisa's monotonous and extremely concrete verbal exchange, which conveyed a feeling of stifling constraint. It was a situation similar to that when a reiterated gesture—whose communicative meaning we miss—can make us feel a sense of fatigue that soon turns into withdrawal.

The exploration of the reiteration of a subject and the seriality in the artistic field allowed me to tolerate this situation. By giving up on trying to find the *meaning* of the words, and, rather, by looking for the *form* in them, both the analysand and I could go along a road leading to sense-making. In following this process together we found restructuring moments of aesthetic contact and emotional unison.

Bacon, in a long interview about his unique creative process, talks about his admiration for Monet. In particular he is captivated by the series of paintings that the French painter made in order to explore the endless variety of color nuances by which nature and reality reveal themselves to our senses. And, with regard to the shout depicted in some of his paintings, Bacon says that he has always dreamed of painting the mouth in the way that Monet painted the sunset (Sylvester, 1975).

Painting a shouting mouth was the essential act of creating a physical container so as to get in touch with a painful contained. Painting this psychic mouth allowed us to explore the reiteration and how it had to be a mute mouth that could express pain only through the form of anxiety. With Elisa I went through the brutality of the catastrophe inherent in the non-containment but I also experienced the beauty of being able to paint a shout of pain together. This occurred when the mouth turned into a hollow container, through the endless nuances by which our senses gave a *form* to it.

## Notes

1. It is possible that this aspect of the mental function becomes part of the procedural memory-building process.
2. In this exhibition Matisse anticipated an aspect that was later developed by some conceptual artists. See, for example, *On Kawara: 97 Date-paintings consécutives et journaux de 1966 à 1975* (exhibitioncatalogue by P. Hulten). (Paris: Pompidou, 1977).
3. By common sense Bion means the need to define actual or emotional-unconscious aspects only if they are common to more than one sense: "I shall consider an object to be sensible to psycho-analytic scrutiny if, and only if, it fulfils conditions analogous to the conditions that are fulfilled when a physical object's presence is confirmed by the evidence of two or more senses" (Bion, 1963, p. 10).

## References

Bion, W. R. (1962a). A theory of thinking. In: *Second Thoughts: Selected Papers on Psychoanalysis* (pp. 110–119). London: Heinemann, 1967.
Bion, W. R. (1963). *Elements of Psychoanalysis*. London: Karnac.
Bion, W. R. (1980). *Bion in New York and Sào Paolo* (Ed. F. Bion). Strathclyde, Perthshire: Clunie.
Bion, W. R. (1989). *Two papers: "The Grid" and "Caesura"*. London: Karnac.
Bion, W. R. (1992). *Cogitations*. London: Karnac.
Bonaminio, V. (2009). The psyche indwelling in the body: States of integration. The 13th Annual International Frances Tustin Memorial Lectureship. November 7 2009. The New Center for Psychoanalysis, Los Angeles.
Bonaminio, V. (2012). On Winnicott's clinical innovations in the analysis of adults. *International Journal of Psychoanalysis, 93*: 1475–1485.
Cartwright, D. (2010). *Containing States of Mind: Exploring Bion's Container Model in Psychoanalytic Psychotherapy*. London: Routledge.
Civitarese, G. (2013). Bion's Grid and the truth drive. *The Italian Psychoanalytic Annual, 7*: 91–114.
Derrida, J. (1990). *Memoirs of the Blind: The Self-Portrait and Other Ruins*, Chicago: University of Chicago Press, 1993.
Grotstein, J. (2007). *A Beam of Intense Darkness: Wilfred Bion's Legacy to Psychoanalysis*. London: Karnac.
Harris Meltzer, M. (2010). *The Aesthetic Development*. London: Karnac.
Meltzer, D. (1967). *The Psychoanalytical Process*. London: Karnac.
Merleau-Ponty, M. (1945). *Phenomenology of Perception*. London: Routledge.
Morandi, G. (1996). *Oggetti e stati d'animo*. Milano: Skira.
Neri, C. (1985). Contenimento fusionale e oscillazione contenitore <—> contenuto. *Rivista Psicoanalisi, 31*: 316–325.
Oli, D. (1971). *Vocabolario della lingua italiana*. Torino: Le Monnier.
Sylvester, D. (1975). *The Brutality of Fact: Interviews with Francis Bacon*. London: Thames & Hudson.
Varisco, G. (2012). *Se …* Milano: Mazzotta.
Winnicott, D. W. (1967). Mirror-role of the mother and family in child development. In: P. Lomas (Ed.), *The Predicament of the Family: A Psycho-Analytical Symposium* (pp. 26–33). London: Hogarth.

# INDEX

Abel-Hirsch, Nicola 186–187, 251–257
Abella, Adele 447–448, 451–466, 474
achievement, language of 165–168, 349
aesthetics and the aesthetic experience 447–449
    Bion-inspired aesthetic model 464–465
    classical psychoanalytical aesthetic models 447–448, 453–456
    container-contained interaction and 489–500
affect 148, 210, 310
    groups and 393–396
aggression and beauty 455
    *see also* violence
Alexandria (Egypt) and Ungaretti 476–477, 479–480, 483–484
*All My Sins Remembered* 48, 53, 58–59
*All Quiet on the Western Front* 391–392
allergies, Hartke's patient A 126–132
alliances, unconscious 434–435, 440
alpha elements (α-elements) 112, 195–196, 202, 204, 211, 245, 313, 364, 470–473
alpha-function 28, 54, 110, 124–125, 136, 195–197, 204, 207, 210, 245, 251–254, 311, 313, 322–323, 471, 491, 493, 498
    groups and 437–438, 440
Alphonsus de Guimaraens (poet) 110

Alves, Castro, poem 7
Amiens, battle of 30, 47–48, 50–52, 58, 61
a-motion 259, 262
analysis
    before and after Bion 157
    Bion himself with Klein 45
    bulwarks in 136, 330, 357
    coupling 197, 216, 230, 308–309, 324, 331, 473
    dyad/couple/pair 125–126, 136–138, 142, 197, 216, 230, 308–309, 324, 329, 331, 339–340, 393, 473
    evidence in 331, 369–376, 440
    group *see* group therapy
    hidden tsunamis of the encounter in 229–231
    Junqueira de Mattos with Bion 3, 5–21
    literature and 448, 454, 467–487
    mental states and emotional relations in analytic setting 121–139
    supervised *see* supervisions
    trust in 161, 255, 492
    working-through *see* working-through
Andrade, Carlos Drummond de 116
André (Korbicher's analysand) 177–180
animal (human), Bion's notion of 427
Anna (Ferro's analysand) 190

anxiety/anxieties
    Edward's (Brown's analysand) 335–337
    evacuation of 198
    in groups 411–412, 416–417, 423–424, 426–429
    of not-knowing/the unknown 224, 346, 358
    psychotic 410–412, 416
    see also fear; separation anxiety
Anzieu, Didier 25, 416, 432, 439–441
aphasia, expressive 145
applied science 34
arts 447–448, 451–466, 471, 473–474, 492–493
    contemporary 448, 451–466
    practical 34
    repetition in 489–490
    seriality in 448, 493, 499
    the feminine and 397
a-sensuous constant conjunction 349
at-one-ment 309–310
attachment
    infant 161
    to O 163, 168
attention, floating 8, 135, 157
*Attention and Interpretation* 30, 49, 53, 59, 99, 158, 252, 286, 301, 308–310, 379, 381
audience 161
    internal 156–157, 162–164
    receptive 162
autistic phenomena 171–181
    autistic withdrawal 173, 448, 492
autobiography
    Bion's (*The Long Weekend 1897–1919*) 30–31, 42–43, 47–50, 52, 54, 56–58
    Bion's fictionalized see *Memoir of the Future*

babies see infants and babies
Bacon, Francis 347, 495, 497, 499
bad job, Cairo's making the best of a 330, 353–359
bad theory 310
balpha elements 210, 212, 215
basic assumption in groups (theory) 28, 34, 44, 241, 391, 407, 410–411, 422, 426, 436–437
battles 31–32
    of Amiens 30, 47–48, 50–52, 58, 61
    of Cambrai 42, 50, 58
    of Ypres 31, 51, 56, 59
beauty and art 455–456, 459, 479

Beckett, Samuel 41–42
being (sense of being and being human) 207, 476, 479, 484
bell tower, demolished (dream of Ferro's analysand) 194
beta elements 28, 174, 195–197, 205–207, 209, 241, 245–246, 311, 316, 322, 470–471, 473, 491–492, 498
beta screen 174–175, 244–247
*Bhagavad Gita* 160
Bion Talamo, Parthenope 23, 25–27, 48
Bion, Wilfred 39–46
    autobiography (*The Long Weekend 1897–1919*) 30–31, 42–43, 47–50, 52, 54, 56–58
    biographer (Bléandonu) 39–40, 45, 392, 461
    cultural/historical/national background 39–46
    daughter (Parthenope) 23, 25–27, 48
    first wife (Betty), death in childbirth 242
    psychoanalysis before and after 157
    wartime experiences see battles; First World War; Second World War
birth attendants in analytic field 219
birth, Bion's 39
    see also rebirth
Blanchot, Maurice 48, 53, 346
Bléandonu, Gérard (Bion's biographer) 39–40, 45, 392, 461
body
    affect and the 394
    language of the 254–255
body image, Elisa's (Molinari's analysand) 494–495
body–mind (psyche–soma) relationship 186, 223–224, 227–228, 236, 253–256
    dissociation 57, 186–187, 199, 209, 242–243, 341, 394
    vertical 223, 233, 235
Boltanski, Christian 448, 456–461, 463
Bonsey (in *The Long Weekend*) 56
Boston Change Group 329, 339–341
bougainvillea and Hartke's patient A 133–135
brain
    Bion on capacity of 13
    Broca's area lesion 145
    development 13, 492
Braithwaite, R. B. 35–36

breast 112, 175, 202, 242, 364, 371
    good 240
    loss/absence 11–12, 252
brilliant analysand, role of 288
Brito, Gisèle Matos 105, 107–119
Britton, Ronald 3–4, 29–38, 218
Broca's area lesion 145
Bronstein, Catalina 186, 239–249
Broome (soldier in *The Long Weekend*) 50
*Brothers* (*Fratelli*), Ungaretti's 482–483
Brown, Lawrence J. 141, 253, 329, 333–343
Budd, Susan 468–470, 474
bulwarks in analysis 136, 330, 357
    *see also* survival and defense
*Buried Harbor* (*Il porto sepolto*) 448, 474, 483–484

caesura 20–21, 202–204, 330–331, 340, 347, 349, 361–368
*Caesura* 331, 361–368
    quotes 5, 8, 18, 20
Cage, John 448, 457, 459, 461–462, 474
Cairo, Irene 330, 353–359
Cambrai, battle of 42, 50, 58
capability, negative 41, 106, 180, 210–216, 226, 236, 286, 363, 366, 448, 461
Capello, Francesco 448, 467–487
Cartwright, Duncan 185–186, 201–222
Cassorla's commentary on supervision A34 67–68, 73–77
casting of characters 90, 191, 198, 288
Castoriadis-Aulagnier, P. 439
catastrophic change and experiences 296, 308, 365, 382, 417, 438, 440
catastrophic trauma 47–63
    phenomenology 49–53
    theoretical perspectives 53–60
cave paintings 14
CEFFRAP 432, 436
certainty 36–37, 157, 168, 373, 379, 464
    *see also* uncertainty
Change Group (Boston) 329, 339–341
characters
    casting of 90, 191, 198, 288
    patient bringing or not bringing along 190
Chaslin, P. 266
childhood (Bion's) 39

children playing 97
    *see also* infants and babies; mother
Christ, Jesus 27, 159–160, 282
    passion 313, 316
Christianity 29, 34, 40, 167
Churchill, Winston, Sutherland's painting 18
Chuster, Arnaldo 331, 369–376
Civitarese, Guiseppe 295, 297–306, 448, 469
    commentary on supervision D14 89–91
closing one's mind 347–348
cloudy floating thoughts 260–261
*Cogitations* 60, 206, 308, 311
Cohen (soldier in *The Long Weekend*) 58
coherence, Junqueira de Mattos (in analysis) on 13
Colasanti's *Weaver Girl* 108
Coll, S. 395
*Communicating Pictures* 449, 493–494
communication 355
    emotion and 145
    inter-analyst 453
    of genuine affect 393, 397
    verbal *see* language
    *see also* language
composition and the proto-container 497–498
conjunctions and connections 224, 316, 348–349
    constant *see* constant conjunction
connections *see* conjunctions and connections
conscience, Junqueira de Mattos (in analysis) on 19
conscious (the), passion and 318
constant conjunction 224–225, 349–350
    a-sensuous 349
construction(s), Junqueira de Mattos (in analysis) 11–12
contact barrier 180, 195, 204, 244–247, 364
containment/container/contained (theory of) 150, 162, 201–222, 239–240, 327–328, 359, 412–413, 437–438, 449m, 489–500
    autistic mind and 176
    Cartwright's patient 207–219
    flexible containing 413
    groups and 359, 412–413, 437–438
    Hartke's patient 130
    in group therapy 412–413
    Junqueira de Mattos on 6–8
    Korbicher's patients 178–180

Lombardi's patient 233
proto-container 205–207, 209–210, 215, 218–219, 491–492, 497–499
psychosomatic illness and 239–240
continuity, Junqueira de Mattos (in analysis) on 13
conversion 196
convexity and emotional grammar 199
Corrao, Francesco 23–27
Corrêa, Raimundo (poet) 14–15
Cortinas, L. P. 244
cost of analysis, Junqueira de Mattos and 20
countertransference 141–153
    Abel-Hirsch's 255
    evolution of the concept 143–144
    working-through 141–153
couples (twosomes/pairs/dyads)
    analytic 125–126, 136–138, 142, 197, 216, 230, 308–309, 324, 329, 331, 339–340, 393, 473
    Elisa (Molinari's analysand) and 493
    parental 187
    psyche–soma/body–mind 187, 256
creativity 162–163, 196, 346, 362–363, 365, 476
criticism (psychoanalytic) 469, 471, 473–474
Cro-Magnon man 14
crying, Junqueira de Mattos (in analysis) 10
culture
    Bion's cultural background 39–46
    groups and 432, 440–441

D (Migliozzi's analysand) 318–323
Da Vinci 348–349, 373
deadness (psychic) 208–209, 310
death in Bion's autobiographical narrations 48, 51, 53–54, 56–57, 59–61
    *see also* killing
defecation (bowel movement) dreams 129–130, 234–235
defense *see* survival and defense
delusions, similarity to transformations in hallucinosis 112
dependency, feelings of 10–11
depression
    essential 244
    Mr. A (Bronstein's analysand) 243
    Philip's (Resnil's analysand) 266–267

depressive position 149, 159, 218, 245
    Philip (Resnik's analysand) 266–267
Descartes, René 158, 254
desire 225–226, 228, 329, 333–343, 366
    attempting to be without 79, 89, 286, 331, 341, 378, 381, 448, 459, 494
    sexual 100, 234–236, 256, 316, 454
detachment 251–252
Diary (Bion's) 47–48, 55, 58
digestion of facts and experiences 185, 206, 300, 361, 366–367, 472
    *see also* undigested facts and experiences
discordant madness, Chaslin's 266
discursive symbolism 146–147, 149
dissociation (and disassociation) 57, 186–187, 199, 209, 242–243, 341, 394
Distinguished Service Order (DSO) 31–33, 42
dos Anjos, Augusto (poet) 16
dramatic construct 291–292
drawer, Elisa (Molinari's analysand) 449, and the 493, 495–496, 498
dread 286
    nameless 31, 202, 286, 308, 338
dream(s) (and dreaming) 148, 307–314, 467–487
    Abel-Hirsch's analysand (Pm) 256
    Bion's 31
    Brito's analysand (Isaura) 109–111, 116
    Cairo's analysand 356–358
    Cartwright's analysand (Sarah) 213–218
    common and shared dream space 440
    Ferro's analysands 191–196
    Hartke's analysands
        patient A 128–131
        patient Z 132–135
    in *The Long Weekend* 58–59
    language 354, 356–357
    latent content 311–313
    Lombardi's analysands
        Giovanni 230
        Karl 231–235
    meaning and 338
    Migliozzi's analysand (D) 322
    Migliozzi's, D's appearing in 322
    parallelism of analysand's and analyst's 230
    polyphonic organization 440
    symptoms 194–195, 197

transformation in 189, 198, 303–304
undreamt/not dreamed 193, 197, 472
working-through and 337–338
*see also* nightmares; reverie; waking dream thought
*Dream, The* 48, 303
dream-work 214, 308, 311–312, 472
drive and motivation 121
DSO (Distinguished Service Order) 31–33, 42
Duchamp, Marcel 448, 456, 461–462, 464
dyads *see* couples
dynamic systems 210
non-linear 203–205, 217

eczema 246–247
Edward (Brown's analysand) 335–339
ego 157, 228, 242, 254, 381
groups and 411, 421
Einstein, Albert 157–158
*Elements of Psychoanalysis* 206, 251, 295, 298, 300, 307–308, 310
Elisa (Molinari's analysand) 449, 493–499
embryo or fetus, experiences and emotion 241–242, 264, 362–364, 374–375
emotion(s)
art and 451–452, 457
catastrophic trauma and evacuation from/denuding of the mind of 54, 58
evacuation from mind *see* evacuation
grammar and 198–199
in groups 407–419
language and 106, 145
literature and 469, 471
prenatal experiences/feelings and 241–242, 264, 362–364, 374–375
reason and 315
subthalamic *see* subthalamic emotions
turbulent *see* turbulence
*see also* specific emotions
emotional growth 42, 218, 347, 380, 382
emotional reality 203, 301
*see also* O
emotional relations in analytic setting 121–139
emotional terrorism *see* terrorism
empowerment in groups 394–395
*Endgame* (Samuel Beckett) 42

envy 112, 160, 264, 267, 288
Erlich, H. Shmuel 421–430
essences 349–350, 373–374
Establishment 302, 380–382, 441
*Eterno* (*Eternal*—Ungaretti's poem) 474–476, 483–484
ethnicity and conflict 399
evacuation (of emotion from the mind) 54, 57, 196, 241, 246
anxieties 198
projective identification and 215, 242, 355
evidence 331, 369–376, 440
evocation 145–150
existence 55, 60–61, 331
dreaming into 329, 335
tragic dimension of 427
*see also* non-existence
experiences 345–351
learning from *see* learning from experience
of loneliness *see* loneliness
prenatal (embryonic/fetal) emotions and 241–242, 264, 362–364, 374–375
sensuous awareness and 42, 81, 297–300, 379
undigested facts and 59, 178, 206, 210, 219, 253
*Experiences in Groups* 297, 408–410, 431, 436
expression 147–148
evocation and 146
expressive aphasia 145
expressivity 144–147

family (Bion's) 39–40
family group 410–411
fathers and mothers, game of 96
fear, subthalamic 47, 51, 330, 375
*see also* anxiety
feminine, the 497
Ferro, Antonino/Nino 122, 135, 137, 144, 146, 185, 189–200, 210–211, 287, 303, 337, 448, 470, 473, 479–480
fetus or embryo, experiences and emotions 241–242, 264, 362–364, 374–375
field (concept/theory of) 3, 24–25, 90, 101, 185, 189–197, 202–222, 287–288, 303, 308, 448, 496
containment and 202–222
*Fifty Amazing Stories of the Great War* 43

fight-flight response 26, 391, 408–409, 432
First World War (WWI) 30–33, 42–45, 253, 279, 287
    battles *see* battles
    tank 3, 30–32, 42–44, 47, 49–52, 57–58, 60–61, 392
Flaubert, Gustave 468
flexible containing (in group) 413
flight of ideas or thoughts 187, 259–269
floating attention 8, 135, 157
flow and movement 207, 348–350
flying thoughts and flight of ideas 187, 259–269
Font-de-Gaume cave paintings 14
Fornari, Franco 24–27, 469
fragmentation
    in groups 416–417
    of thought 161, 229, 391–392, 437
frames (picture) 449, 493–495
Francesca (Ferro's analysand) 193–194
*Fratelli* (*Brothers*), Ungaretti's 482–483
free association 5, 8, 305, 363, 370–371, 468
freedom, Junqueira de Mattos (in analysis) on 19
Freud, Anna 338
Freud, Sigmund 333–334, 467
    aesthetic model 453–454
    body–mind relationship 227, 334
    dream-work 311
    groups and 421
    loneliness experienced by 253, 256
    mental work 151
    observational model used by 372
    personality and 363
    sublimation and 453–454, 464
    *Totem and Taboo* 410
    working-through 338
frustration, art and the choice between avoiding and modifying 456–457

games *see* playing and games
Genius, the 302
Germans and Israeli Jews, group relations conference 423
Giovani (Lombardi's analysand) 230
God 156, 158, 164, 233, 282, 288, 350
    Godhead vs 159–160
    the God within 160–163

Godhead 156, 159, 164, 227, 229, 378
    vs God 159–160
*Gospel of Judas* 160
grammar, emotional 198–199
grandfather
    Bion as 26
    Bion's paternal 40
grandmother, Ferro's analysand's 191
grandparents, Hartke's analysand A 130
"grid", "the" 29, 32, 123, 192, 346, 412, 463, 491, 498
"Grid", "The" (Bion's paper) 5, 8, 11, 18, 202
Grotstein, J. 62, 74–75, 141, 155–156, 159–160, 162–163, 175, 202, 204, 217, 318, 393–394, 451, 476, 481, 492
group(s) 385–444
    basic assumptions 28, 34, 44, 241, 391, 407, 410–411, 422, 426, 436–437
    dynamics 387, 407–408, 410–411, 417
    early group projects 408–410
    flexible 413
    internal 416, 434, 437
    invariant in 415–417
    large groups (LG) 391–392, 398, 412, 421–430
    linking phenomena 412, 416–417, 434–435, 440
    overview of Bion's theory 390–393
    part-object group 411–412
    primary task 392, 422–423
    primitive emotional states 407–419
    psychic apparatus 433–434, 436–437
    rigid group 414
    small groups (SG) 391, 421–422, 426, 437
    three challenges from Bion's theory of 389–390
    Trotter and 33, 408–409
    work group 28, 362, 391–392, 396, 409, 421, 426
    *see also Experiences in Groups*
group-as-a-whole 392–393, 396, 398, 400–401, 403, 417, 422, 425–426, 433–435, 439
group relations (GR) conferences 397, 422–424
    Tavistock 395, 422
group therapy/psychotherapy (incl. psychoanalytic work) 417, 435–436
    as containing 412–413
    Italian school 23–24
*Guernica*, Picasso's 14

hallucination and hallucinosis 112, 301, 304–305
　　transformations in 112, 172–173, 179–180, 196, 304–305
Hartke, Raul 105, 121–139
hate (H) 143, 149, 316
Heisenberg, W. 36–37, 157
hell, Isaura's (analysand) 113–114
herd instinct 34, 427
　　conflict between individuality and 427
　　*Instincts of the Herd in Peace and War* 33, 45
Hinshelwood, R. D. 407–419, 472
historical background of Bion 39–46
*History of the Royal Tank Regiment* 31
Hokusai, Katsushika 330, 348–349
holding 137, 143
　　maternal 140, 490
Holocaust 423–424, 427
hope and Junqueira de Mattos in analysis 7
human animal, Bion's notion of 427

Idea, The (poem) 16
ideas, flight of thoughts or 187, 259–269
identity, threats to, leading to isolation and violence 395–397
*Il porto sepolto* (*The Buried Harbor*) 448, 474, 483–484
imposter alien baby, Sarah's (Cartwright's patient) 216–217, 219
individuality 55, 303, 369, 427
　　conflict between herd animal and 427
ineffable (the) 45, 216, 227, 331, 380, 452
infants and babies 412
　　attachment 161
　　audience need of 163
　　neurosis 337–338
　　newborn 241, 247, 264, 364
　　repetitions between mother and 490–492
　　Sarah (Cartwright's patient) and 213–219
　　*see also* mother; separation anxiety
*Instincts of the Herd in Peace and War* 33, 45
interdependency in groups 389–390
internal audience 156–157, 162–164
internal groups 416, 434, 437
internal relationship
　　analysand 233
　　analyst 323

International Psychoanalytic Association (IPA) Congress
　　Berlin 424
　　Prague 424–425
interpersonal relationships *see* relationships
interpretations 371–372
　　Junqueira de Mattos in analysis 8–12, 14–15
　　*see also Attention and Interpretation*
intersubjectivity 141–143, 224, 291, 473, 497
　　disorders of 432
　　intersubjective analytic third 122, 126, 473
　　passion and 318
　　primary 206
intuition 147, 318, 331, 348, 363, 366, 373, 415, 440
　　Junqueira de Mattos (in analysis) on 8, 10
　　supervisions and 82, 84, 89–90, 99
invariants (in transformations) 174, 179, 416–417
　　in groups 415–417
　　Junqueira de Mattos (in analysis) 18
Isaura (analysand) 107–119
isolation (in groups), threats to identity leading to 395–397
Israeli Jews and Germans, group relations conference of 423
Italian Psychoanalytic Society (SPI) 3, 23–24
　　first major congress on Bion's work 25
Italian school of group psychotherapy 23–24
Italian seminars (in Rome) 25–27, 219, 366

Jesus *see* Christ
Jews
　　Israeli, group relations conference of Germans and 423
　　supervision A42 and patient of Jewish origin 68, 93–101
　　*see also* Holocaust
Johnson, Samuel (quote from) 383
judging (in supervisions) 80, 84, 89–90
Junqueira de Mattos, José Américo 3, 5–21

K *see* Knowledge
Kaës, René 431–444
Kant, Immanuel 10, 37, 45, 160, 349, 373, 378, 415
Karl (Lombardi's analysand) 231–236
killing 13

babies, Sarah's (Cartwright's patient) statement of 213–214
Klein, Melanie 240, 267, 411
    Bion's analysis by 45
Knowledge (K) 107, 143, 149, 174, 226, 243, 254, 316, 362
    opposite of (not knowing; –K) 157, 174, 316, 331, 346
Korbivcher, Celia Fix 106, 171–181
Krishna 160

language(s) (and verbal communication) 149–150, 156–157, 372, 375, 447, 452, 462, 465, 497
    caesura and 358–359
    dream 354–357
    effects in 149
    function 149–150
        emotive 106, 145
    in supervisions 82–83, 85–86, 89–91
        confusion of 73–75
    see also communication
    of achievement 165–168, 349
    of the body 254–256
    of the mind 254–255
large groups (LG) 391–392, 398, 412, 421–430
latent content of dreams 311–313
learning from experience 33, 210, 366, 461
    emotional growth and 380
    in groups 395
*Learning from Experience* 35, 58, 297–298, 456
Leonardo Da Vinci 348–349, 373
Les Eyzies-de Tayac, prehistoric man 14
*Letture Bioniane* 27
Levi, Primo 54–55
Levine, Howard B. 68, 146, 285–290, 307–314, 377–383
    commentary on supervision A42, 99–101
    on myth 296, 304
    on O 331, 377–383
lies of the mind 28, 136, 165–166, 354, 357, 459–461
linking phenomena in groups 412, 416–417, 434–435, 440
*Lire Bion* 27
listening 286, 370–371, 493
literature, psychoanalytic 448, 454, 467–487
Lombardi, Riccardo 186, 223–237, 299–300, 394

loneliness 251–252, 256, 353, 490
    Bion's experience of 3, 56
    Freud's experience of 253, 256
*Long Weekend 1897–1919, The* (Bion's autobiography) 30–31, 42–43, 47–50, 52, 54, 56–58
*Lost in Translation* (film) 73–74
love, Junqueira de Mattos (in analysis) and capacity to 18–19
Luigi (Ferro's analysand) 194–195

*Madame Bovary* 468
madness and sanity, Isaura's (patient) intense encounter 107–119
Mafia violence 400
*Making the Best of a Bad Job* 330, 353–359
Martha (Bronstein's analysand) 246–247
maternal reverie 163, 241, 244, 251–254, 256, 304, 317, 364, 393, 440
meaning 148–151, 307–314
    dreaming and 338
    passion and 315–316, 322–323
medicine 32, 34, 331, 367
Meltzer, Donald 125, 129–130, 132, 136–137, 151, 196, 198, 205, 315–317, 322, 407
*Memoir of the Future* (fictionalized autobiographies; trilogy) 45, 47–53, 56–57, 60, 159, 190, 251, 303, 416, 453
    *The Dream* 48, 303
    *The Past Presented* 159
memory 225–226, 264, 302, 329, 333–343, 366
    attempting to be without 79, 89, 286, 331, 341, 378, 381, 448, 459, 494
mental functioning/activity (mentation)
    sensation and 228–229
    two principles of 228, 334
    see also mental work
mental states and systems (states of mind) 162
    analytic setting 121–139
    caesura and 162, 362–366
    prenatal 241–242, 264, 362–364, 374–375
    primitive (proto-mental state) 186, 205–207, 229, 239–244, 260, 365–366, 394
    unrepresented 186, 242, 330, 338, 347, 365–366, 377
    see also mentalization

mental work 151
mentalization 105, 121–123, 136, 196–197, 285, 287, 347, 438
mentation *see* mental functioning/activity
metabolization 196–197, 439
metaphor 116
metapsychology 29, 33, 141, 151, 361, 470
    of catastrophic trauma 49, 61
    of countertransference 144
    of interpersonal relations 141
Migliozzi, Anna 296, 315–325
Milton's *Paradise Lost* 6, 10–12, 19, 53, 348
mind(s) (psyche)
    body and *see* body–mind
    caesuras and expanding of the 367
    catastrophic trauma and 48–63
    coupling *see* couples
    evacuation of emotion from *see* evacuation
    expressivity 144–147
    language of the 254, 355
    lies of the 28, 136, 165–166, 354, 357, 459–461
    opening and closing 347–348
    organizers of the combination and adjustment of the 434
    psychotic *see* psychotic phenomena/mind
    states of *see* mental states
    theory of 472
mindfulness 160–162, 166
Mitchell, Frank 43–44
Modell, A. H. 393–394, 397
Molinari, Elena 448–449, 489–500
Monet, Claude 499
mother(s) 412
    breast *see* breast
    container function 202
    D dragging Migliozzi into role of 320
    game of fathers and 96
    holding 140, 490
    repetitions between child and 490–492
    reverie 163, 241, 244, 251–254, 256, 304, 317, 364, 393, 440
    *see also* infant; separation anxiety
motivation and drive 121
mourning 194, 216, 289, 389–390, 394
    in groups 399–403
Moussorgsky's *Pictures at an Exhibition* 21

movement and flow 207, 348–350
Mr. A (Bronstein's analysand) 242–244
music 18–19, 21, 90, 207, 402, 454, 457, 463
mysticism and the mystical 157–159, 302, 318, 382
myth 296, 298–299, 301, 304, 307–314, 374, 410
    extension into the domain of 299

nameless dread 31, 202, 286, 308, 338
narcissism 34, 121, 124, 190, 288, 435, 454, 465
narrative derivatives or genres 196, 217, 304, 448, 479–480, 484, 498
Nastasi, Antoine 275–284, 287–290
national background of Bion 39–46
Nazareth conference (Israeli Jews and Germans) 423
Neanderthal man 14
negative capability 41, 106, 180, 210–216, 226, 236, 286, 363, 366, 448, 461
negative tropism 60
Neri, Claudio 3, 23–28
neurosis (and neurotic mind) 37, 172, 174, 314
    infantile 337–338
    transference 333–334
newborns 241, 247, 264, 364
Newton, Isaac 36–37
nightmares 31
    in analysis 230
    in autobiographical narrations 58–59
Nina (Korbicher's analysand) 176–180
non-analytic influences 29–38
non-existence, state of 54–55, 60, 174, 201, 291, 476
non-linear dynamic systems 203–205, 217
non-symbolic processes 205–206
nothingness 291, 476–477
    undetected 55, 59
not-known/not-yet knowable *see* unknown

O (concept of) 106, 155–168, 186, 223–237, 377–383
    attachment to O 163, 168
    groups and 416
    transformations 310, 348, 365, 438, 461
object
    proper 211, 214–215
    truth 156, 163–164, 168
object relation 121, 124
observational model used by Freud 372

*Odyssey, The*, Penelope in 117
oedipal issues 187, 256, 468
    Cairo's analysand 355–358
    family group and 410
Ogden, Benjamin 469, 473
Ogden, Thomas 196–197, 205, 247, 315, 322, 329, 335, 339, 393, 469, 471–473, 480
Olga (Civitarese's analysand) 304–305
omnipotency 56, 156, 167, 233, 380, 455–456
opening and closing one's mind 347–348
Oxford University 31, 33, 40, 44–45, 53

P (Cairo's analysand) 355–358
paintings 145, 452, 459, 463, 472
    Bacon's 497
    Matisse's 493
    Monet's 499
    Picasso's 10–11, 15, 18, 83, 374
    van Gogh's 145, 260
    Vermeer's 472
    *see also* photography; pictures
pairs *see* couples
*Papillon* (film) 19
*Paradise Lost*, Milton's 6, 10–12, 19, 53, 348
paranoid-schizoid position 159, 240, 245, 396, 437
part-object group 411–412
passion 296–299, 304, 308–310, 313, 315–325
    extension into the domain of 299
past and future, Junqueira de Mattos (in analysis) 13
*Past Presented, The* 159
patience 106, 226, 236, 334, 354
Paton, H. J. 3, 33, 45
Pb (Abel-Hirsch's analysand) 255
*Pellegrinaggio* (*Pilgrimage*), Ungaretti's 477–484
Penelope in *The Odyssey* 117
penetrativity, emotional grammar 198
personal accounts
    Junqueira de Mattos 3, 5–21
    Neri 3, 23–28
personality and caesura 362–367
phantasies 146–147, 240, 242, 246, 364, 367, 391
    D's (Migliozzi's analysand) 320–321
phenomenology
    catastrophic trauma 49–53
    of transference 265–266

Philip (Resnik's patient) 261–267
Philosopher King (Plato's) 329, 336–340
philosophy
    O and 378
    science and 35–37
photography (and photographs)
    Boltanski and 458–460, 463
    Elisa's (Molinari's analysand) 493, 495, 497–499
    Matisse's 493
    *see also* paintings; pictures
phylogenetic fantasy 410
Picasso, Pablo 10–11, 14–15, 19, 83, 374
pictogram 195–197, 224, 264, 470
pictures
    Elisa's (Molinari's analysand) 493–497
    frames 449, 493–495
    *see also* paintings; photography
*Pictures at an Exhibition*, Moussorgsky's 21
*Pilgrimage* (*Pellegrinaggia*), Ungaretti's 477–484
Plato 45, 350, 378, 451, 464
    *Phaedo* 374
    Philosopher King 329, 336–340
    *Republic* 336–337
    Tyrant 329, 336–340
playing and games
    children 97
    origin in our inner world 264
pleasure
    killing animals, Bion's experience 13
    principle of 226, 228–229, 236, 346, 453–454, 481
Pm (Abel-Hirsch's analysand) 255–256
Poincaré, Henri 8, 29, 31, 36, 45
polyphony of the dream 440
Pontalis, J.-B. 431–432, 436, 440
positive tropism 59–60
preconceptions 6, 364–367, 371–372, 437
pregnancy metaphor, Elisa's (Molinari's analysand) 495–496
prehistoric man's cave paintings 14
prenatal (embryonic/fetal) experiences and emotions 241–242, 264, 362–364, 374–375
present, past and future, Junqueira de Mattos (in analysis) 13
presentational symbolism 147

presentification (making present) 150
pre-verbal process and containment 210–211
primary task in groups 392, 422–423
primordial and primitive phenomena 174–175
    emotional states, in groups 407–419
    mental states/proto-mental states 186,
        205–207, 229, 239–244, 260, 365–366, 394
probability 36–37
projection 196
    emotional grammar 198
projective identification 143–146, 148, 175, 197,
        207, 210–211, 239–244, 313, 317, 355, 364,
        411, 414
    communicative 285, 310, 355
    evacuative 215, 242, 355
    pathological 267, 364
    psychosomatic illness and 239–244, 246–247
    transformations in 452
proper object 211, 214–215
proto-container 205–207, 209–210, 215, 218–219,
    491–492, 497–499
proto-mental states (primitive mental states) 186,
    205–207, 229, 239–244, 260, 365–366, 394
psoriasis 242–244
psyche *see* body–mind; mind
psychic apparatus 122, 365–366, 439
    group 433–434, 436–437
psychic deadness 208–209, 310
psychic groupality 434, 437
psychic reality 31, 37, 296, 348, 379, 433, 435,
    437–438, 440
psychoanalysis *see* analysis
*Psychoanalysis in a New Context* 393
psychosis 49, 159, 259, 267–268, 347
    group psychotic experiences 411–412, 416
    *see also* soma-psychosis
psychosomatic illness 239–249
psychotic anxiety 410–412, 416
psychotic phenomena/mind 53, 55, 171–181
    anxiety 411–412, 416, 419

Quakerism, Rickman's 45

reading (act of) 330, 473–474
    Edward's (Brown's analysand) difficulties 336
*Reading Bion* 27

reality (psychic) 31, 37, 296, 348, 379, 433, 435
    D's (Migliozzi analysand) 319–320
    emotional 203, 301
        *see also* O
    principle of 58, 236, 312, 334, 453
    three spaces of 437–438, 440
    ultimate 158–159, 225, 227, 318, 364, 378
    unknown 348
reason 348
    emotion and 315
rebirth, Isaura's (analysand) 114–117
receptive audience 162
receptivity, emotional grammar 198–199
red balloon, Hartke's patient A 131, 136
Regina (Reiner's analysand) 164–168
Reiner, Annie 106, 155–169
relationships (interpersonal) 141, 144
    analysand–analyst (dyad) 125–126, 136–138,
        142, 329, 340, 393
    mother–infant; *see* infant; mother
    *see also* body–mind relationship; couples;
        internal relationship
religion and spirituality 29, 40, 45, 156, 159–160,
    186, 227
    O and 378
    supervision A34 70–71, 76
    supervision A42, 93
    *see also* God
Remarque's *All Quiet on the Western Front* 391–392
Renoir's painting 14
reparation 448, 454, 464
repetitions (and repeating) 306, 334, 364
    art 489–490
    dreams 129
    in working through 333–334
    mother and child 490–492
representation
    of catastrophe 49, 55–63
    symbolic 146–147, 215–216, 218, 241, 449
repression 122, 245, 313, 333, 341, 439, 470
resemblance, Junqueira de Mattos (in analysis) on
    13
Resnik, Salomon 187, 259–269
responsibility in groups 389–390, 394–395, 398–399
responsible being/adult, Junqueira de Mattos (in
    analysis) 17–18

reverie 105–106, 141–151, 197, 210–215, 317, 364, 393–394, 440, 449, 493–494
    groups and 390, 392–397, 400–402
    maternal 163, 241, 244, 251–254, 256, 304, 317, 364, 393, 440
        paradox of 393–394
    *see also* waking dream thought
re-viewing (group theory) 407, 410
Richter, Gerhard 463
Rickman, John 45, 390, 408–409
rifle (dream of Ferro's analysand) 194–195
rigid group 414
Rocha Barroses (Elias and Elizabeth) 105–106, 141–153, 337–340
Rome, Italian seminars in 25–27, 219, 366
Rosenfeld, Herbert 358

Saint Cyprien, Junqueira de Mattos and Bion at 14, 17–19
Saint Sulpice, statue of 292
Salvio, P. 400
Sarah (Cartwright's patient) 207–219
schizophrenia 259
    Resnik's patient 261–267
school, Bion at 40–41
science 35–37, 158, 309–310, 461–462
    applied 34
    philosophy and 35–37
*Second Thoughts* 30, 59, 353
Second World War (WWII) 30, 45, 387
*Secret Evil* (poem of Raimundo Corrêa) 15
Segal, Hanna 209, 243, 454, 464
self, Junqueira de Mattos (in analysis) on 12–13
self-discipline 461
self-harm, D's 320
selflessness in groups 394–395
self-sufficiency (in groups), illusion of 390, 393–394, 397, 399
semantic nests 192
sense 295–296, 308–309
    extension in the domain of 298–299
sense-able, the 300–303, 305
sensible, the 300–303
sensory processes (incl. perception) 230, 265, 302
    mental functioning and 228–229

    non-symbolic 206
    transformations and 496–497
sensuous (awareness and experience) 42, 81, 297–300, 379
sentient intelligence 187, 259
separation anxiety, Edward's (Brown's analysand) 335–337, 339
seriality in art 448, 493, 499
sex 96
    sexual desire 100, 234–236, 256, 316, 454
sexuality 254, 257, 347
Shields, Walker 389–405
skin
    eczema 246–247
    psoriasis 242–244
skull 259–260, 263, 491–492
small groups (SG) 391, 421–422, 426, 437
Soavi, Giulio Cesare 24
*Solitary Reaper* (Wordsworth) 389, 400–403
solitude, feelings of 10–11
soma–psyche relationship *see* body–mind relationship
soma-psychosis 239, 241–242, 374
somatization 196
Sosnik, Rogelio 330–331, 361–368
space and the proto-container 497–498
speech impediment in dream 356–358
Speziale-Bagliacca, Roberto 468
spirituality *see* religion and spirituality
splitting 161, 244–245, 363, 411
    D's (Migliozzi's analysand) 320
    temporal 373
squiggle game, Winnicott's 136, 312, 400
Steinbeck (Steenbeck), the (stream in Bion's dream) 31, 59
stupor 304–305
sublimation 453–454, 464
subthalamic emotions 303, 364
    fear 47, 51, 330, 375
superego 22, 58–59, 156–157, 162–163, 167–168, 170, 246, 256, 319, 357
supervisions 13, 24, 65–91
    A34 67, 69–77
    A42 68, 93–101
    D14 79–91
survival and defense 50

against anxiety of not-knowing/the unknown 346
group 417, 432, 435, 441
mechanisms/structures 53, 56, 59, 121–122, 162–163, 197, 434, 440
*see also* bulwarks
Sutherland's painting of Churchill 18
Sweeting (Bion's runner in *A Memoir of the Future*) 50, 52–53, 56
symbolization and symbolism and symbolic processes 24, 124, 126, 146–148, 150, 215–219, 226, 232, 242, 245, 338, 499
constant 226
containment and 215–219
discursive 146–147, 149
evocation and 146–147
presentational 147
representational (symbolic representation) 146–147, 215–216, 218, 241, 449
*see also* non-symbolic processes
symptoms, dreaming 194–195, 197

*Taming Wild Thoughts* 189
tanks (WWI) 3, 30–32, 42–44, 47, 49–52, 57–58, 60–61, 392
Tavistock Clinic, Bion at 408
Tavistock group relations conferences 395, 422
Tavistock seminars 378, 381–382
Taylor, D. 160–161, 236
temporal splitting 373
terrorism (emotional) 180, 319
in groups 320, 396–398
*see also* violence
thalamic speculations 313
thing-in-itself 97, 225, 309, 318, 378, 415, 492–493
unknowable/not fully knowable 158, 331
thinking 393, 439
apparatus for 439
Bion's theory of 393, 438
fragmentation 161, 229, 391–392, 437
group 407–408, 439
thought(s) 439
capacity to think thoughts 105, 112, 471
cloudy floating 260–261
flying, and flight of ideas 187, 259–269
Resnik's schizophrenic patient 261–267
wild 68, 99, 267, 286, 459
without a thinker 15, 112, 229, 303
"toilet breast" 129, 158
*Totem and Taboo* 410
transference
groups and 25
neurosis 333–334
phenomenology of 265–266
transformations 171–181, 301, 304–305, 437–439
autistic 171–181
impossibility and possibility to cope with 494–495
in dreaming 189, 198, 303–304
in groups 437–439
in hallucinosis 112, 172–173, 179–180, 196, 304–305
in O 310, 348, 365, 438, 461
in projective identification 452
invariants see invariants
Junqueira de Mattos (in analysis) 18
of cloudy floating thoughts 260–261
sensory adhesion as gate to 496–497
*Transformations* 49, 56, 60, 112, 158, 172, 300, 415, 452, 457, 463
transitionality (transitional phenomena) 312–313, 438, 448, 455, 464, 480, 490
transmission of psychic life between generations 439
trauma, catastrophic *see* catastrophic trauma
tree model, Volkan's 399
tropisms (notion of) 174–175, 205
negative 60
positive 59–60
Trotter, Wilfred 32–36, 45, 408–409
groups and 33, 408–409
trust 161, 255, 492
truth 28, 155–169, 378, 381, 383, 459–461
craving 465
Junqueira de Mattos (in analysis) 16–17
truth object 156, 163–164, 168
tsunami (2004), patient experiencing 230
turbulence (emotional) 308, 330–331, 345–350, 373, 494
Isaura's (analysand) 107–119
Turquet, P. 397, 412, 422, 426

twosomes *see* couples
Tyrant (Plato's) 329, 336–340

ultimate reality 158–159, 225, 227, 318, 364, 378
uncertainty 36–37, 106, 157–159
unconscious (the) 195, 313
    groups and 390–393, 397, 403, 434–435, 440
    O and the 378
    passion and 318
    unformulated 146
undigested facts and experiences 59, 178, 206, 210, 219, 253
unformulated unconscious 146
Ungaretti, Giuseppe 448, 467, 474–484
unknown/not-known/unknowable/not-yet knowable 3, 8, 15, 17, 156–160, 187, 224, 323, 345–351, 371, 373, 378, 380, 452, 459–463
    anxiety of 224, 346, 358
    searching for and reaching 459–463
unrepresented mental states 186, 242, 330, 338, 347, 365–366, 377
unsaturated condition characteristic of O 227

van Gogh, Vincent 145, 260
Varisco, Grazia 449, 493
*Veglia* (*Vigil*), Ungaretti's 481–482, 484
verbal language *see* communication
verbal squiggle game 136
Vermeer, Johannes 472
Vermote, Rudy 236, 330, 345–351, 453
vertex (concept of) 126, 137, 227, 300, 303–304, 308, 371
*Vigil* (*Veglia*), Ungaretti's 481–482, 484
violence (incl. feelings/imagination/impulses) 259, 395–400
    D's (Migliozzi's analysand) 320, 322
    in groups, threats to identity leading 395–397
    Karl (Lombardi's analysand) 231–234
    Nina's (Korbivcher's analysand) 178–180
    P's (Cairo's analysand) 355–358
    *see also* aggression; terrorism
visual element in analysis 196
Volkan, Vamik 399–400

waking dream thought 195–196, 209, 212, 214, 218, 303–304, 390, 392, 448
    *see also* reverie
wartime experiences *see* First World War; Second World War
*Weaver Girl* (Colasanti's) 108
wild thoughts 68, 99, 267, 286, 459
Winnicott, Donald 206, 247, 260, 304, 312, 438, 448, 455–456, 490
    squiggle game 136, 312, 400
withdrawal
    autistic 173, 448, 492
    in groups 432
womb, prenatal experiences and emotions 241–242, 264, 362–364, 374–375
Wordsworth's *Solitary Reaper* 389, 400–403
work group 28, 362, 391–392, 396, 409, 421, 426
working-through 121, 229, 232, 236, 333–343
    countertransference 141–153
    Giovani (Lombardi's analysand) 230
    Karl (Lombardi's analysand) 232–233
World War I *see* First World War
World War II (Second World War) 30, 45, 387
*Writing of the Disaster* 48–49

Ypres 31, 51, 56, 59

Zubiri, Xavier 259

Printed in France by Amazon
Brétigny-sur-Orge, FR

20426173R00301